Editor's Fore

The cinema of Ireland is not like that of most other countries. Over the past half century or so, the Irish have created an indigenous film industry that has consistently turned out locally and internationally acclaimed films, some of which depict a place that might seem strange to those familiar with a clichéd, touristy representation of the country. It has also created outward-looking films aimed at an international market and produced by overseas production companies, with the cast, crew, and finances coming from outside Ireland. Therefore, while much of the industry is driven by an artistic, culturally engaged impulse, much also stems from purely commercial concerns. And the Irish government has played a crucial role in creating financial opportunities to incentivize film (and television) production.

This second edition of the *Historical Dictionary of Irish Cinema* contains an introduction, chronology, and dictionary section (double the size of the first edition) filled with entries on significant actors, directors, producers, and organizations as well as short films and feature films, documentaries, and animated movies. Some are typically Irish, and others are more international, and moviegoers will be familiar with many of them.

This almost entirely new edition was written by Roderick Flynn and Tony Tracy but builds on the first edition by Dr. Flynn and Pat Brereton, published in 2007. Dr. Flynn is an associate professor in film and media studies and chair of the Masters in Contemporary Screen Industries at the Dublin City University's School of Communications. He has written and lectured widely on Irish cinema and media, most recently publishing 2017's *Irish Media History* (with John Horgan), which is the standard textbook on the subject. Dr. Tracy is director of the Huston School of Film and Digital Media at NUI Galway, where he teaches classes on film history and theory. He has previously worked as education officer at the Irish Film Institute and coedits (with Dr. Flynn) the *Annual Review of Film and Television* for the journal *Estudios Irlandeses*. Between them, they have produced the largest and most useful reference work on Irish cinema to date.

Jon Woronoff
Series Editor

HISTORICAL DICTIONARY

The historical dictionaries present essential information on a broad range of subjects, including American and world history, art, business, cities, countries, cultures, customs, film, global conflicts, international relations, literature, music, philosophy, religion, sports, and theater. Written by experts, all contain highly informative introductory essays of the topic and detailed chronologies that, in some cases, cover vast historical time periods but still manage to heavily feature more recent events.

Brief A–Z entries describe the main people, events, politics, social issues, institutions, and policies that make the topic unique, and entries are cross-referenced for ease of browsing. Extensive bibliographies are divided into several general subject areas, providing excellent access points for students, researchers, and anyone wanting to know more. Additionally, maps, photographs, and appendixes of supplemental information aid high school and college students doing term papers or introductory research projects. In short, the historical dictionaries are the perfect starting point for anyone looking to research in these fields.

HISTORICAL DICTIONARIES OF
LITERATURE AND THE ARTS

Jon Woronoff, Series Editor

American Radio Soap Operas, by Jim Cox, 2005.
Fantasy Literature, by Brian Stableford, 2005.
Lesbian Literature, by Meredith Miller, 2006.
Scandinavian Literature and Theater, by Jan Sjåvik, 2006.
Hong Kong Cinema, by Lisa Odham Stokes, 2007.
French Cinema, by Dayna Oscherwitz and MaryEllen Higgins, 2007.
Australian Radio and Television, by Albert Moran and Chris Keating, 2007.
Polish Cinema, by Marek Haltof, 2007.
Old Time Radio, by Robert C. Reinehr and Jon D. Swartz, 2008.
Chinese Theater, by Tan Ye, 2008.
Italian Cinema, by Gino Moliterno, 2008.
Postwar German Literature, by William Grange, 2009.
Modern Japanese Literature and Theater, by J. Scott Miller, 2009.
Animation and Cartoons, by Nichola Dobson, 2009.
Modern Chinese Literature, by Li-hua Ying, 2010.
Middle Eastern Cinema, by Terri Ginsberg and Chris Lippard, 2010.
Spanish Cinema, by Alberto Mira, 2010.
Film Noir, by Andrew Spicer, 2010.
French Theater, by Edward Forman, 2010.
Choral Music, by Melvin P. Unger, 2010.
Westerns in Literature, by Paul Varner, 2010.
Surrealism, by Keith Aspley, 2010.
Science Fiction Cinema, by M. Keith Booker, 2010.
Children's Literature, by Emer O'Sullivan, 2010.
Latin American Literature and Theater, by Richard A. Young and Odile Cisneros, 2011.
German Literature to 1945, by William Grange, 2011.
Neoclassical Art and Architecture, by Allison Lee Palmer, 2011.
American Cinema, by M. Keith Booker, 2011.
American Theater: Contemporary, by James Fisher, 2011.
English Music: ca. 1400–1958, by Charles Edward McGuire and Steven E. Plank, 2011.
Rococo Art, by Jennifer D. Milam, 2011.
Japanese Cinema, by Jasper Sharp, 2011.
Modern and Contemporary Classical Music, by Nicole V. Gagné, 2012.
Russian Music, by Daniel Jaffé, 2012.
Music of the Classical Period, by Bertil van Boer, 2012.
Holocaust Cinema, by Robert C. Reimer and Carol J. Reimer, 2012.
Asian American Literature and Theater, by Wenjing Xu, 2012.
Beat Movement, by Paul Varner, 2012.
Jazz, by John S. Davis, 2012.
Crime Films, by Geoff Mayer, 2013.
Scandinavian Cinema, by John Sundholm, Isak Thorsen, Lars Gustaf Andersson, Olof Hedling, Gunnar Iversen, and Birgir Thor Møller, 2013.
Chinese Cinema, by Tan Ye and Yun Zhu, 2013.
Taiwan Cinema, by Daw-Ming Lee, 2013.
Russian Literature, by Jonathan Stone, 2013.
Gothic Literature, by William Hughes, 2013.
French Literature, by John Flower, 2013.

Baroque Music, by Joseph P. Swain, 2013.
Opera, by Scott L. Balthazar, 2013.
British Cinema, by Alan Burton and Steve Chibnall, 2013.
Romantic Music, by John Michael Cooper with Randy Kinnett, 2013.
British Theatre: Early Period, by Darryll Grantley, 2013.
South American Cinema, by Peter H. Rist, 2014.
African American Television, Second Edition, by Kathleen Fearn-Banks and Anne Burford-Johnson, 2014.
Japanese Traditional Theatre, Second Edition, by Samuel L. Leiter, 2014.
Science Fiction in Literature, by M. Keith Booker, 2015.
Romanticism in Literature, by Paul Varner, 2015.
American Theater: Beginnings, by James Fisher, 2016.
African American Cinema, Second Edition, by S. Torriano Berry and Venise Berry, 2015.
British Radio, Second Edition, by Seán Street, 2015.
German Theater, Second Edition, by William Grange, 2015.
Russian Theater, Second Edition, by Laurence Senelick, 2015.
Broadway Musical, Second Edition, by William A. Everett and Paul R. Laird, 2016.
British Spy Fiction, by Alan Burton, 2016.
Russian and Soviet Cinema, Second Edition, by Peter Rollberg, 2016.
Architecture, Second Edition, by Allison Lee Palmer, 2016.
Renaissance Art, Second Edition, by Lilian H. Zirpolo, 2016.
Sacred Music, Second Edition, by Joseph P. Swain, 2016.
U.S. Latino Literature, by Francisco A. Lomelí, Donaldo W. Urioste, and María Joaquina Villaseñor, 2017.
Postmodernist Literature and Theater, Second Edition, by Fran Mason, 2017.
Contemporary Art, by Ann Lee Morgan, 2017.
Popular Music, by Norman Abjorensen, 2017.
American Theater: Modernism, Second Edition, by James Fisher and Felicia Hardison Londré, 2017.
Horror Cinema, Second Edition, by Peter Hutchings, 2018.
Australian and New Zealand Cinema, Second Edition, by Karina Aveyard, Albert Moran, and Errol Vieth, 2018.
Baroque Art and Architecture, Second Edition, by Lilian H. Zirpolo, 2018.
African American Theater, Second Edition, by Anthony D. Hill, 2018.
German Cinema, by Robert C. Reimer and Carol J. Reimer, 2019.
Leonard Bernstein, by Paul R. Laird and Hsun Lin, 2019.
Romantic Art and Architecture, by Allison Lee Palmer, 2019.
Irish Cinema, Second Edition, by Roderick Flynn and Tony Tracy, 2019.
Woody Allen, by William Brigham, 2019.
Modern and Contemporary Classical Music, Second Edition, by Nicole V. Gagné, 2019.

Historical Dictionary of Irish Cinema

Second Edition

Roddy Flynn
Tony Tracy

ROWMAN & LITTLEFIELD
Lanham • Boulder • New York • London

Published by Rowman & Littlefield
An imprint of The Rowman & Littlefield Publishing Group, Inc.
4501 Forbes Boulevard, Suite 200, Lanham, Maryland 20706
www.rowman.com

6 Tinworth Street, London SE11 5AL

British Library Cataloguing in Publication Information Available

Library of Congress Cataloging-in-Publication Data

Names: Flynn, Roddy, author. | Tracy, Tony, author.
Title: Historical dictionary of Irish cinema / Roddy Flynn, Tony Tracy.
Description: Second edition. | Lanham, Maryland : Rowman & Littlefield, [2019] | Includes bibliographical references.
Identifiers: LCCN 2019004603 (print) | LCCN 2019007542 (ebook) | ISBN 9781538119587 (electronic) | ISBN 9781538119570 (hardcover)
Subjects: LCSH: Motion pictures—Ireland—Dictionaries.
Classification: LCC PN1993.5.I85 (ebook) | LCC PN1993.5.I85 F695 2019 (print) | DDC 791.4309415016—dc23
LC record available at https://lccn.loc.gov/2019004603

Contents

Preface

Although technically an update of a book first published in 2007, this second edition of the *Historical Dictionary of Irish Cinema* is effectively a new book. It is twice as long, and virtually all of the original entries have been substantially revised or rewritten. This reflects not only the exponential growth in activity and achievements within the Irish audiovisual sector in the intervening decade but also the utterly transformed informational context within which this edition is published. In the age of Wikipedia and the Internet Movie Database (IMDb), one might reasonably ask why a book like this needs to exist at all. In answer, we would suggest that at one level it remains a work of reference—a go-to text covering the key figures, films, institutions, and policy developments of more than a century of film production in and about Ireland. However, in contrast to resources such as IMDb or even the monumental Irish Film and TV Research Online project led by Kevin Rockett at Trinity College Dublin in the mid-2000s, this book gathers information between two covers in a way databases cannot. Arising from our experience in creating a digital database of Irish cinema produced during two decades of the Irish Film Board (IFB) (1993–2003) under a range of rubrics (themes, directors, gender, etc.), we learned that, when deciding what to include and exclude, the key issue was understanding what individual films mean in the context of a larger definition of cinema. This book, then, is an attempt to build a mosaic of Irish cinema, although it is by necessity partial and imperfect. We repeatedly asked ourselves not just what is intrinsically significant about this entry but also what piece of the larger jigsaw puzzle does it occupy? We have thus sought not only to describe and comment on individual films, actors, behind-the-camera talent, and institutions but also to suggest how they are interconnected. The book should be approached in a spirit of relationality rather than modularity.

We have also proceeded on the assumption that different readers will bring with them varying degrees of knowledge: some will be familiar with canonical or international productions made in and about Ireland, and others might be unfamiliar with indigenous filmmaking and filmmakers, particularly during the industry's prolific growth in recent years.

With these frameworks established, our core criteria in determining what to include and exclude have been influenced by a commonsense definition of a film text: live action, structured by narrative, feature length, and intended for big-screen exhibition. Given that indigenous production did not begin to occur on a regular basis until the 1980s (and even then on a very limited scale), the total output of Irish filmmakers remains relatively modest, perhaps no more than 400 to 500 feature films in total. Nonetheless, this constitutes a significant body of work in absolute terms. In the first edition of this book, we sought to be exhaustive in our coverage of films; in this edition, we have been forced to discriminate between significant works (assessed in terms of their critical impact, public reception, or box office success) and less prominent titles. Recognizing that many readers will associate a number of "foreign" films with Irish cinema, we also discuss American, British, and French films shot in Ireland in an attempt to situate indigenous films within a wider cultural context.

Our stress on fiction film, however, means that documentary film and animation receive less attention. Although most of what little indigenous production that occurred in Ireland before 1970 was nonfiction, the documentary form subsequently migrated largely to television and thus fell outside the scope of the first edition. Against that, the decision by the IFB to more actively support feature-length documentaries from 2005 to 2006 means that nonfiction texts are notably more evident in this edition than in the original. So in addition to the earlier discussions of documentarists such as Robert Flaherty, Louis Marcus, and John T. Davis, more contemporary voices, such as Donald Taylor Black, Pat Collins, Alan Gilsenan, and Paul Duane, occupy a prominent place in this text. Similarly, in the case of feature-length animation, Ireland had produced relatively little work in this area up to 2009 compared to live-action films. But, while this edition retains an overview of attempts at establishing an industrial-scale animation sector in the 1980s, it emphasizes the reemergence and phenomenal success of an indigenous animation sector from the 1990s on, reflected in the high-profile success of companies like Brown Bag and Cartoon Saloon.

We—as many before—have grappled with the question of what specifically constitutes *Irish* film. To begin, we worked within an impossibly zealous definition: anything produced in Ireland by an Irish director with an Irish story. This meant, for example, that we could discuss more or less any film supported by the IFB since the 1980s. However, even that approach presented problems—how would we deal with a film such as *How Harry Became a Tree* (2001), an IFB-supported film directed by a Serb and based on a Chinese folktale (albeit set in Ireland)? Should we include *Room* (2015), a U.S.-set story, with no Irish cast members but produced by an Irish production company from a script by an Irish writer and directed by an Irish director? Clearly, we needed a broader definition to account for films that have helped define how Ireland and the Irish are understood by filmmakers outside Ireland and also by audiences in Ireland and elsewhere. Thus, our broader definition includes mainly American and British pictures that have defined the acceptable limits of how things Irish may be represented not merely for subsequent foreign filmmakers working in Ireland but, arguably, also for Irish directors working in Ireland.

In this volume, film is simultaneously treated as both a form of cultural expression and a commercial artifact. This dual lens of textual analysis and political economy has defined our collaborative research of Irish film over the past decade (see the bibliography) and acknowledges the inescapable truth that few national film industries can exist without state support through either direct funding and/or a range of tax incentives. Thus this volume gives as much consideration to institutions such as the Irish Film Board (renamed Screen Ireland in 2018), the Irish Film Institute, and political figures such as Michael D. Higgins and Síle de Valera as it does to directors such as Neil Jordan and Lenny Abrahamson and producers like Katie Holly and Rachel Lysaght.

Acknowledgments

We should first acknowledge the work undertaken by our colleague Pat Brereton in preparing the first edition of this book, without which this revised and expanded version could not exist at all. We would also like to thank our colleagues Debbie Ging at DCU and Sean Crosson Conn Holohan at the Huston School of Film & Digital Media for their input (knowingly or otherwise) into the reflections that inform the entries. Further afield, we would like to acknowledge how the scholarship of figures such as Luke Gibbons (Maynooth University), Kevin Rockett and Ruth Barton (Trinity College, Dublin), Harvey O'Brien and Diane Negra (University College Dublin), Maeve Connolly and Díóg O'Connell (Institute of Art, Design, and Technology), and Denis Condon (Maynooth University) have cumulatively informed and enriched our understanding of Irish cinema. For their assistance in providing various hard-to-track-down information, let us also thank Niall Murphy of *Scannain* and *CinEireann*, Louise Ryan at the Irish Film Board, Sunniva O'Flynn and the librarians at the Irish Film Institute, Julie Allen (formerly of the Dublin City University Library), the staff of the National Archives, David McLoughlin (formerly of Screen Producers Ireland), and Morgan O'Sullivan of World 2000.

Over the years, our work has been informed by the work undertaken by the students we have encountered, especially at a postgraduate level. We would like to particularly acknowledge a debt to the work of Denis Murphy, Laura Canning, Angela Nagle, Aileen O'Driscoll, Eileen Culotty, Kassandra O'Connell (of the Irish Film Archive), Sinead Gillett, Nicholas Fennell, Niamh McCole, Trevor Curran, and Eimear O'Kane.

Roddy Flynn would also like to acknowledge the financial support made available by the Research Advisory Panel at Dublin City University, which facilitated work on the first edition by providing a fellowship for the year 2005.

Massive thanks, too, to series editor Jon Woronoff, senior production editor Kellie Hagan, and acquisitions editor April Snider for their patience and forbearance.

Finally, we would both like to thank our families, without whom none of this would have been possible or worthwhile. For their infinite tolerance of weeknights and weekends spent poring over hot keyboards, we would like to send all our love and thanks to Ciara, Romy, Ava, Kerry the dog, Claire, Saoirse, Mia, and Fionn.

Acronyms and Abbreviations

ABC	Associated British Cinemas
ABC	American Broadcasting Company (United States)
ACC	Agricultural Credit Corporation
AIDS	Acquired Immune Deficiency Syndrome
AIFM	Association of Independent Filmmakers
AIP	Association of Independent Producers
AMC	American Movie Classics (cable channel)
BAFTA	British Academy Film and Television Arts Awards
BBC	British Broadcasting Corporation
BES	Business Expansion Scheme
BFI	British Film Institute
CBS	Columbia Broadcasting System (television)
CD-ROM	Compact Disk–Read Only Memory
CEO	Chief Executive Officer
CGI	Computer-Generated Images
CIA	Central Intelligence Agency
CRC	Cultural Relations Committee
DCP	Digital Cinema Package
DCU	Dublin City University
DFVC	Derry Film and Video Co-Operative
DIT	Dublin Institute of Technology
DOP	Director of Photography
DVD	Digital Video Disk
DVFC	Derry Film and Video Co-Operative
DSLR	Digital Single Lens Reflex (camera)
EAVE	European Audiovisual Entrepreneurs
EFDO	European Film Distribution Office
EEC	European Economic Community

EFC	Experimental Film Club
EFS	Experimental Film Society
ESB	Electricity Supply Board
EMI	Electric and Musical Industries
ESS	Economic and Social Studies
EU	European Union
EVE	Espace Vidéo Européen
FBI	Federal Bureau of Investigation
FCOI	Film Company of Ireland
FIFS	Federation of Irish Film Societies
FII	Film Institute of Ireland
FMI	Film Makers Ireland
FTC	Fair Trade Commission
GAA	Gaelic Athletic Association
GMIT	Galway-Mayo institute of Technology
GNP	Gross National Product
HBO	Home Box Office (television)
IADT	Institute of Art, Design, and Technology
IBEC	Irish Business and Employers Confederation
ICC	Industrial Credit Corporation
ICTU	Irish Congress of Trade Unions
IDA	Industrial Development Authority
IFA	Irish Film Archive
IFB	Irish Film Board
IFC	Irish Film Centre
IFCB	Irish Film Centre Building Ltd
IFFC	Irish Film Finance Corporation
IFI	Irish Film Institute
IFS	Irish Film Society
IFT	Irish Film Theatre
IFTA	Irish Film and Television Academy
IMMA	Irish Museum of Modern Art

IPP	Irish Parliamentary Party
IPU	Independent Production Unit (RTÉ)
IRA	Irish Republican Army
IRSP	Irish Republican Socialist Party
ITGWU	Irish Transport and General Workers' Union
ITN	Independent Television News
ITV	Independent Television (United Kingdom)
LGBT	Lesbian-Gay-Bisexual-Transgender
MD	Managing Director
MGM	Metro-Goldwyn-Mayer
MoMA	Museum of Modern Art (New York)
MTM	Mary Tyler Moore Productions
NADCorp	National Development Corporation
NAMA	National Asset Management Agency
NBC	National Broadcasting Company
NCAD	National College of Art and Design
NFII	National Film Institute of Ireland
NFSI	National Film Studios of Ireland
NIFTC	Northern Ireland Film and Television Commission
NUI	National University of Ireland
PIRA	Provisional Irish Republican Army
PWC	PriceWaterhouseCoopers
RADA	Royal Academy of Dramatic Arts
RIA	Royal Irish Academy
RIC	Royal Irish Constabulary
RKO	Radio-Keith-Orpheum
RSC	Royal Shakespeare Company
RTÉ	Radio Telefís Éireann (Irish TV broadcaster)
RUC	Royal Ulster Constabulary
SFX	St. Francis Xavier
SPI	Screen Producers Ireland
SXSW	South by Southwest (festival)

TCD	Trinity College Dublin
TD	Teachta Dála (Irish member of parliament)
TG4	Telefís na Gaelige
TVC	Television Cartoons
TVS	Television South (U.K. broadcaster)
UCD	University College Dublin
UCI	United Cinemas International
UGC	Union Generale Cinematographique
UIP	United International Pictures
UPA	United Productions of America
UTV	Ulster Television
UVF	Ulster Volunteer Force
VHS	Video Home System
VOD	Video On Demand
WDF	Westdeutscher Rundfolk Koln (German television)
ZDF	Zweites Deutsches Fernsehen (German television)

Chronology

1896 The first public cinema screening takes place at Dan Lowrey's Star of Erin Ballroom (now the Olympia Theater) on Dublin's Dame Street as an element of a variety performance.

1897 The earliest known moving-picture footage in Ireland is shot by a Lumière cameraman on Dublin's O'Connell Street.

1899 Belfast doctor Robert A. Mitchell becomes the first Irish person to film in Ireland, taking as his subject the Bangor Yacht Race.

1909 One of the first designated cinema spaces in Ireland—the Volta—opens on Mary Street in Dublin with James Joyce as manager.

1909 The Cinematograph Act passes in the British Parliament in London. This act allows local councils across the United Kingdom and Ireland to censor the screening of films in cinemas operating within their jurisdiction.

1910 The New York–based Kalem Company becomes the first American production company to cross the Atlantic for the purpose of shooting on location in Ireland, producing the first Irish fiction film: *The Lad from Old Ireland*. Kalem goes on to make approximately 30 films in Ireland. D. W. Griffith makes *The Fugitive*, from a script by John MacDonagh, brother of 1916 hero Thomas MacDonagh and a future founding director of Film Company of Ireland. Although the film was originally set in Ireland, where unionists and nationalists were at war, Griffith changes it to the American Civil War with a plot that prefigures his notorious *Birth of a Nation*.

1911 The Horgan brothers begin producing Ireland's first animated short films in their native Youghal, featuring the Youghal Town Hall Clock standing on its head and pirouetting in place. The brothers will later open a purpose-built 600-seat cinema, the Horgan Picture Theatre, in the town.

1916 Irish American lawyer and diplomat James Mark Sullivan establishes the Film Company of Ireland in Dublin. Sullivan is briefly arrested during the Easter Rising and uses the opportunity to bring attention to his new venture.

1917 After already screening for a week in Dublin, *Ireland, a Nation*, produced by Waterford-born but Hollywood-resident screenwriter Walter Mac-Namara, is banned by British authorities for its staunchly nationalist content (the 1798 rebellion, the Great Famine, the execution of Robert Emmet, and the Catholic Emancipation). The film was produced in 1914, but the delay in its exhibition was caused by its original print sinking with the *Lusitania* in 1915. Norman Whitten establishes the General Film Supply Company in Dublin, the first regular newsreel supply service. Whitten would later produce a series of comedies with Jimmy O'Dea.

1918 The Film Company of Ireland releases the first Irish-produced feature film, *Knocknagow*, adapted from a best-selling novel by Charles Kickham.

1920 *Willy Reilly and His Colleen Bawn*, the second and final feature produced by the Film Company of Ireland, is released. Irish-born Rex Ingram directs *The Four Horsemen of the Apocalypse*, a masterpiece of Hollywood's silent era that makes Rudolph Valentino an overnight star.

1922 The Irish Free State is established.

1923 Despite the ongoing civil war, Dáil Eireann replaces the existing 1909 Cinematograph Act with a new Film Censorship Act. This places control over film censorship in the hands of a single film censor with responsibility for the entire Irish Free State. The first film censor, James Montgomery, is appointed and remains in the post until 1941.

1926 The state approves the production of *Ireland*, the first government information film. The film (produced by the ad agency McConnell-Hartley) is first screened in 1929. *Irish Destiny*, an amateur film on the Irish War of Independence, written and produced by Dublin pharmacist Dr. Isaac Eppel, is released.

1929 Dublin's Savoy Cinema opens with the premiere of *Ireland*.

1930 The Dublin Amateur Film Society is established.

1932 A Fianna Fáil government led by Eamon De Valera takes power. Sean Lemass is appointed minister for industry and commerce, a position he will hold intermittently until 1958.

1934 *Man of Aran*, shot by Robert Flaherty in the Aran Islands off the west coast of Ireland, is released to widespread acclaim.

1935 John Ford's *The Informer* is the second and best-known adaptation of the novel by Liam O'Flaherty. A forerunner of film noir in style and set in 1920 during the War of Independence, the film would be nominated for four Academy Awards and win two, including Best Director.

1936 The encyclical *Vigilanti Cura* by Pope Pius XI is published, representing the first attempt by the Church to deal with the new media of cinema. The pope encourages the creation of Catholic organizations for the promotion of morally valuable movies. *The Dawn*, the first indigenous sound production made in Ireland, is released after several years of production activity. Shot by garage owner Tom Cooper with the assistance of family and friends in his native Killarney, the War of Independence–set narrative proves a major success with Dublin audiences. The Irish Film Society is established by Liam O'Leary and Eddie Toner, among others.

1937 Father Richard Devane, leader of the 1920s campaign against "evil literature," lobbies Eamon de Valera to establish a state inquiry into the role of cinema in Irish national life.

1938 Minister Sean Lemass establishes the Inter-Departmental Committee on the Film Industry—the first such initiative by the Irish state. The committee's report is finally submitted four years later.

1939 World War II (termed "The Emergency" in Ireland) commences. The Emergency Powers Order permits censors to ban films on the grounds that they might undermine Irish neutrality.

1941 Former Cumann na nGaedhael TD (Irish member of parliament) and medical doctor Richard Hayes replaces James Montgomery as film censor. He will continue in that role until 1954.

1943 The National Film Institute of Ireland is formed under the auspices of Archbishop John Charles McQuaid. Laurence Olivier films elements of *Henry V* in neutral Ireland, as he is unable to do so in the United Kingdom because of wartime conditions. The film results in a reported cost of £100,000 during its two-month shoot in Ireland.

1946 Sean Lemass submits proposals to the cabinet for a national film studio. The cabinet rejects the proposals. *A Nation Once Again*, the first of the films funded by the National Film Institute, is released.

1948 After 16 uninterrupted years in government, Fianna Fáil loses an election to a Fine Gael–led coalition. The Cultural Relations Committee is established under the auspices of the Department of Foreign Affairs. It will support the production of several short films exploring various aspects of Irish culture designed to be screened overseas via Irish embassies and consulates.

1951 *The Quiet Man* is shot on location in Ireland and Hollywood by John Ford. The Arts Council of Ireland is established, but the film is excluded from its remit. The Fianna Fáil party is returned to power.

1953 Gael Linn is established to promote the use of the Irish language in the media, including film. It will sponsor the George Morrison films *Mise Eire* (1959) and *Saoirse* (1961).

1954 Former Fianna Fáil TD and medical doctor Martin Brennan replaces Richard Hayes as film censor. He will remain in the post until his death in 1956.

1955 Douglas Sirk directs *Captain Lightfoot*, a Technicolor picture about 19th-century Irish highwaymen starring Rock Hudson and shot on location in Ireland. Because there are no studio production facilities, one is constructed inside a Dublin badminton court.

1956 The Cork Film Festival (the first of its kind in Ireland) runs for the first time with support from the Irish Tourist Board. Gael Linn launches the first Irish-language newsreel service, "Amharc Eireann" (A View of Ireland). Former Gaiety Theatre manager Liam O'Hora is appointed as the new film censor—in 1958, he famously bans "King Creole" because of star Elvis Presley's "suggestive" dancing.

1957 Release of *The Rising of the Moon*, a compendium of three Irish stories and starring mostly Abbey actors shot on location in Ireland by John Ford and produced by the Four Provinces company.

1958 Sean Lemass formally opens Ireland's first permanent film studio at Ardmore in Bray, County Wicklow.

1959 Release of *Mise Eire* (1959)—the first film ever made in the Irish language. Sponsored by Gael Linn and directed by George Morrison, it will be followed by *Saoirse* (1961), the second of a proposed but never-completed trilogy of films.

1960 March: The Industrial Credit Corporation establishes the Irish Film Finance Corporation to loan money to incoming productions. **July:** Death of Dublin-born Cedric Gibbons, production designer at MGM and the most honored man in Oscar film history with 39 nominations and 11 wins. He also designed the "Oscar" statuettes.

1963 Francis Ford Coppola shoots his debut feature *Dementia 13* for Roger Corman in Ireland, in part at Ardmore Studios.

1964 Dr. Christopher Macken, a psychiatrist, is appointed as the new film censor.

1965 Minister for Justice Brian Lenihan appoints a new Censorship Appeals Board with a specific remit to liberalize the censorship regime.

1967 May: *Rocky Road to Dublin*, a documentary on the influence of the Catholic Church in Ireland, screens at the Cannes Film Festival. The Irish government blocks its screening or broadcast within Ireland—a de facto ban that lasted 30 years. **July:** Taoiseach Jack Lynch visits the set of John Huston's *Sinful Davy* at Ardmore. The government appoints Huston to head an inquiry into the film industry in Ireland.

1968 The *Report of the Film Industry Committee* (the *Huston Report*) is published, recommending establishment of the Irish Film Board to fund indigenous and overseas filmmaking in Ireland.

1969 *Ryan's Daughter*, a wide-screen hymn to the Irish landscape, is directed on the Dingle Peninsula in County Kerry by David Lean.

1970 The Film Bill is introduced to the Dáil based on the findings of a report by the Film Industry Committee. However, the bill is shelved due to a political crisis involving illegal gunrunning, which became known as the "Arms Crisis," substantially delaying the creation of an Irish Film Board.

1972 Dermot Breen, previously a cinema manager and the founder of the Cork Film Festival, becomes the first Irish film censor with a background in cinema.

1973 Radio Telefís Éireann purchases the near-bankrupt Ardmore Studios on instructions from the minister for industry and commerce, Justin Keating. A new Arts Act sees the Arts Council remit extended to include film.

1975 Ardmore is reestablished as the National Film Studios of Ireland. Bob Quinn's first film, *Caoineadh Airt Ui Laoire* (Lament for Art O'Leary), is released.

1976 The Arts Council announces the establishment of a new Film Script Award.

1977 The Restrictive Practices Commission investigates allegations of discrimination in Dublin cinema release patterns. This leads to an informal agreement to quicken the release time for suburban cinemas. The Arts Council sets up the Irish Film Theatre, which begins screenings in the Sugar Company Cinema, Earlsfort Terrace, Dublin. The Federation of Irish Film Societies is established. Joe Comerford's *Down the Corner* is released.

1978 Journalist and broadcaster Frank Hall becomes film censor, remaining in the post until 1986. **May:** London consultancy firm A. D. Little presents a report to Minister for Industry and Commerce Desmond O'Malley on the prospects for turning the National Film Studios of Ireland into a viable going concern. The report concludes that the state should introduce some form of financial incentives to encourage foreign productions to use Ireland (and the studios) as a location.

1979 November: The Irish Film Board Bill 1979, creating the legislative basis for the Irish Film Board, receives it first reading in Dail Eireann. However, it is not substantially debated until the following year in October 1980.

1981 The Film Board Bill becomes law, and the Irish Film Board is finally established. Pat Murphy's first feature, *Maeve*, is released.

1982 June: The state places the Ardmore facility, which had lost money throughout its incarnation as the National Film Studios of Ireland, into receivership for the fourth time in the studio's history. **December:** A new Fine Gael–Labour coalition creates a new junior minister position within the Department of the Taoiseach. Fine Gael TD and ex-broadcaster Ted Nealon is appointed as the first minister of state for arts and culture. He will remain in the position for the lifetime of that administration (until 1987). The move is significant because it signals a move away from adopting a primarily industrial orientation with regard to film policy in Ireland. The first feature film funded by the Irish Film Board, Neil Jordan's debut *Angel*, is released.

1984 The Irish Film Theatre closes due to an economic crisis driven by reduced audiences. Pat O'Connor's first feature, *Cal*, is released.

1986 Sheamus Smith, former chief executive of the National Film Studios of Ireland at Ardmore Studios, becomes film censor, remaining in the post until 2003.

1987 A Fianna Fáil–Progressive Democrat coalition wins the general election. Citing the national economic crisis, the new government suspends operation of the Film Board. Section 35 of the Finance Act is introduced, and the European Union MEDIA project begins its pilot phase. **March:** Josie Mac-Avin wins Oscar for Best Art Direction for *Out of Africa* (1986). *Cinema and Ireland*, by Kevin Rockett, Luke Gibbon, and John Hill, is published by Syracuse University Press and becomes the first comprehensive academic survey of Irish cinema and the Irish on-screen.

1989 Jim Sheridan's first feature, *My Left Foot*, is released in Ireland.

1990 The European Union's MEDIA '95 program begins. Thaddeus O'Sullivan's first feature, *December Bride*, is released.

1991 Daniel Day-Lewis and Brenda Fricker win Best Actor and Best Supporting Actress Oscars for their respective roles in *My Left Foot*. *Far and Away*, starring Tom Cruise and Nicole Kidman, is shot in County Kerry.

1992 June: A report on the indigenous audiovisual production industry (the *Coopers & Lybrand Report*) is published. **September:** The Irish Film Institute's long-cherished desire to find a permanent home is realized when the

Irish Film Centre, incorporating cinemas, a bookshop, and bar/restaurant, opens in Temple Bar. **December:** Ireland joins Eurimages. A report of the special working group on the film production industry is published. The independent television production sector report (the *FMI Report*) is published.

1993 January: A new Fianna Fáil–Labour coalition government comes to power and creates a new Department of Arts, Culture, and the Gaeltacht. Labour TD Michael D. Higgins becomes the new department's first minister. **March:** Neil Jordan wins the Best Original Screenplay Oscar for *The Crying Game*. Within 24 hours, Michael D. Higgins announces the reestablishment of the Film Board. **June:** Section 35 is radically altered by Minister for Finance Bertie Ahern to encourage greater private investment in filmmaking. Sixteen feature films are made in Ireland. **August:** Rod Stoneman is appointed chief executive of the Film Board.

1994 July: *Braveheart* begins shooting at the Curragh in County Kildare and at Ardmore Studios. **October:** Oliver Stone's *Natural Born Killers* is banned by the censor Sheamus Smith, one of the last mainstream films to suffer this fate in Ireland.

1995 February: *The Economic Impact of Film Production in Ireland 1993*, the first IBEC report assessing the impact of state support for film production in Ireland, is published. The report concludes that supporting the Irish Film Board and forgoing tax revenue through Section 35 results in a net gain to the economy.

1996 November: *Michael Collins* is released and breaks box office records in Ireland, helped, in part, by the censor's decision to award it a Parental Guidance certificate (instead of its original 15 Cert) because of the film's historical significance.

1997 June: A Fianna Fáil–Progressive Democrat coalition wins a general election. Síle de Valera (granddaughter of Eamon) is appointed minister for arts, heritage, Gaeltacht, and the Islands.

1998 February: Neil Jordan's adaptation of *The Butcher Boy* is released. **May:** John Boorman wins Best Director at the Cannes Film Festival for *The General*. **September:** Having been announced by Minister Síle de Valera in March, the Irish Screen Commission begins operations.

1999 January: *The Strategic Development of the Irish Film and Television Industry 2000–2010* (the *Kilkenny Report*) is published.

2000 August: Ireland signs the European Convention on Co-Production.

2001 May: After several years of planning, Ireland's first mobile cinema—the Cinemobile—commences operations backed by support from the Irish Film Board, the Arts Council, and the Film Institute of Ireland.

2002 March: Ruairí Robinson's *Fifty Percent Grey* (2001) and Cathal Gaffney's *Give Up Yer Aul Sins* (2001) are nominated in the Animated Short Film category at the Academy Awards. **June:** John O'Donoghue, Fianna Fáil TD for South Kerry, is appointed minister for arts, sport, and tourism. Remaining in the position until June 2007, he becomes the longest-serving minister to date in the role. **December:** Minister for Finance Charlie McCreevy announces the end of the Section 481 tax break. However, after a lobbying campaign from the domestic industry, the decision is reversed.

2003 April: The first Irish Film and Television Awards take place (*Intermission* wins Best Irish Film). The PriceWaterhouseCoopers Review of Section 481 is published. Ex-RTE Controller of Programs and film producer John Kelleher is appointed film censor. He will be the last individual to hold that title after the word "censor" is changed to "classifier" in 2008. **August:** Rod Stoneman steps down as chief executive of the Irish Film Board after 10 years and is replaced by Mark Woods, former head of acquisitions at Showtime Australia.

2004 August: Lenny Abrahamson's first feature, *Adam and Paul*, is released to critical acclaim.

2005 April: After just 18 months on the job, Mark Woods steps down from his role at the Film Board and returns to Australia, where he become chief executive at AusFilm. **November:** Simon Perry is appointed as the new Film Board chief.

2006 March: Martin McDonagh wins Oscar for Best Short Film (Live Action) for *Six Shooter* (2006). **May:** *The Wind That Shakes the Barley* wins the Palm D'Or at the Cannes Film Festival. The Irish Screen Commission opens an office in Los Angeles.

2007 March: John Carney's *Once* is released in Ireland and later wins the Audience Award at the Sundance Film Festival. **May:** Lenny Abrahamson's *Garage* is awarded the C.I.C.A.E. prize at the Cannes Film Festival. **June:** Fianna Fáil TD Seamus Brennan replaces John O'Donoghue as minister for arts, sport, and tourism. He becomes the shortest-serving minister in that role after he is forced to resign due to ill health less than a year later.

2008 March: *Once* wins the Oscar for Best Song. Aged just 12, Saoirse Ronan becomes one of the youngest-ever nominees in the Best Supporting Actress category for her performance in *Atonement*. **May:** *Hunger*, starring Michael Fassbender, wins the prestigious Caméra d'Or award for first-time filmmakers at Cannes. The Irish Film Board's capital funding from the state reaches an all-time peak of €20 million. Following a cabinet reshuffle, Fianna Fáil TD Martin Cullen becomes minister for arts, sports, and tourism. **July:** In a reflection of its changing role in Irish life and its less prescriptive function, the Irish Film Censor's Office is renamed the Irish Film Classification Office.

2009 July: The *Report of the Special Group on Public Service Numbers and Expenditure Programmes* (aka the *McCarthy Report*) proposes shutting down the Irish Film Board to save €20 million and transferring its activities to the economic development body Enterprise Ireland.

November: John Kelleher steps down as head of the Irish Film Classification Office. He is replaced by Deputy Censor Ger Connolly, but because of restrictions on public service promotions and pay in this period, Connolly is not formally appointed as full director of film classification until 2016.

2010 February: *The Secret of Kells* (2009), produced by Cartoon Saloon, is nominated as Best Animated Feature at the Academy Awards. Although it loses to Disney/Pixar's *Up* (2009), it subsequently wins Best European Feature at the April 2010 British Animation Awards. Juanita Wilson's *The Door* is nominated for Best Short Film and Brown Bag's *Granny O'Grimm's Sleeping Beauty* for Best Animated Short. **March:** Fianna Fáil TD Mary Hanafin becomes minister for tourism, culture, and sport, a portfolio that includes responsibility for film policy. **July:** It is announced that Simon Perry will step down as head of the Irish Film Board at the end of the year.

2011 February: James Hickey replaces Simon Perry as head of the Irish Film Board. **March:** Following a general election that returns a Fine Gael–Labour coalition government, Kerry Fine Gael TD Jimmy Deenihan is appointed minister for arts, heritage, and the Gaeltacht. John McDonagh's *The Guard* becomes the most successful independent Irish film at the domestic box office, taking in €4.13 million.

2012 January: Element Pictures launches Volta.ie, an online video-on-demand service, making available a large back catalog of Irish films. **March:** Terry George wins Oscar for Best Short Film (Live Action) for *The Shore*. **April:** A new studio facility (Ashford Studios) opens at Ballyhenry in County Wicklow. Three soundstages initially play host to the History Channel production *Vikings*. Minister for Finance Michael Noonan announces that Section 481 will switch from its investor-led basis to a tax credit–type system starting in 2015.

2014 May: Fine Gael TD Heather Humphries replaces Jimmy Deenihan as minister for arts, heritage, and the Gaeltacht. **July:** *Stars Wars* episode 7 (*The Force Awakens*) begins filming on the remote island of Skellig Michael, a UNESCO World Heritage Site.

2015 January: New Section 481 tax credit system introduced. **March:** Cartoon Saloon's *Song of the Sea* (2014) is nominated in the Best Animated Feature category at the Academy Awards (*Big Hero 6* [2014] wins the award). **August:** Brown Bag, one of Ireland's most successful indigenous animation companies, is sold to 9 Story Media Group, a Toronto-based animation operation. (In April 2016, Brown Bag's managing director, Cathal Gaffey, is appointed chief operating officer at 9 Story.) **October:** Having seen its funding fall every year between 2008 and 2014, the 2015 national budget records a small increase in the Irish Film Board's total financial allocation (though at €14.2 million, it is still far below the 2008 peak figure of €23.2 million). **November:** Ardmore Studios subsidiary Troy Studios signs a lease to use a former Dell factory in Limerick as a new studio production facility.

2016 February: Irish cast and crew are nominated in an unprecedented nine Academy Award categories, including Best Actor (Michael Fassbender), Best Actress (Saoirse Ronan), and Best Picture (*Room*). **October:** Made for a reported production budget of €50,000, *The Young Offenders*, a low-budget Irish comedy, becomes a local hit, taking in more than €1 million at the Irish box office.

2017 February: *The Lobster*, produced by Irish production company Element Pictures (but directed by Greek filmmaker Yorgos Lanthimos), is nominated for Best Screenplay at the Academy Awards and at the Golden Globes. Ruth Negga is also nominated at both ceremonies for her role in *Loving*. Consolata Boyle receives the second of her three Oscar nominations for her work on *Florence Foster Jenkins*. **March:** A new Film Board is announced with five of the seven positions occupied by women. **November:** Fine Gael TD Josepha Madigan replaces Heather Humphries as minister for culture, heritage, and the Gaeltacht.

2018 January: Irish Film Board announces POV scheme alongside existing funding initiatives aimed at achieving 50/50 gender parity in Irish screen industries. **February:** Five Irish nominations for the 90th Academy Awards are announced, including Saoirse Ronan for Best Actress in *Lady Bird* (her third Oscar nomination), Martin McDonagh's *Three Billboards Outside Ebbing, Missouri* for Best Original Screenplay, Cartoon Saloon's *The Breadwinner* for Best Animated Feature, and Consolata Boyle for Best Achievement in Costume Design for *Victoria & Abdul*. **March:** After 32 years in existence, Filmbase announces that it is ceasing operations immediately and enters liquidation. **June:** The Irish Film Board is officially renamed Screen Ireland.

Introduction

Attempting to identify the birth or foundational texts of a particular national film industry is problematic in the best of times, but in the case of Irish cinema, the issue is made even more complex by the fact that when cinema technology emerged in the 1890s, Ireland did not exist—at least not as a recognized independent state but rather as a part of the United Kingdom of Great Britain and Ireland. While official histories in the 20th century would argue that Ireland (i.e., the people and culture) had been in existence for centuries (if not millennia), the political institution of the nation-state did not come into existence until the Westminster Parliament ratified the Anglo-Irish Treaty in December 1921. Official state nomenclature aside, the first known moving pictures of "Ireland"—shots of O'Connell Street in Dublin—were recorded by a Lumière cameraman in 1897, and a year later, Robert A. Mitchell (a Belfast doctor) became the first Irishman to shoot a film within Ireland, capturing documentary footage of a yacht race.

The first public screening took place in 1896 in Dan Lowrey's *Star of Erin* theater on Dublin's Dame Street, and public exhibition developed rapidly throughout the rest of that decade and into the new century. For the most part, screenings were elements of music hall variety shows or took place as part of the performances of itinerant showmen touring towns and villages outside Ireland's main cities. In 1909, what was long considered the first permanent cinema—the Volta—conceived of and managed by an as-yet-unknown James Joyce—opened in Dublin's Mary Street. (Film historian Denis Condon has more recently exploded this attractive "myth," pointing to the prior existence of a cinema in the Queen's Theatre.) Nevertheless, in contrast to many other European nations that developed substantial filmmaking infrastructures during the early 1900s, regular filmmaking activity did not develop in Ireland until the 1910s and even then—as we shall see—was defined by sporadic and largely foreign-backed activity until late in the 20th century. In summarizing more than a century of activity, we now outline three broad phases of Irish film history with distinctive characteristics, institutional structures, and modes of address. Although these are discussed here within a broad paradigm of "national cinema," "Irishness" emerges overall less as a fixed identity position than as a moving signifier at the intersection of industrial, cultural, and political imaginaries and exigencies.

INWARD GAZES: 1910S–1970S

Largely rural and poor, detached from the industrial and cosmopolitan centers of the United Kingdom, and long viewed through a colonial lens as backward, merely picturesque, or both, Ireland was less visible than many Western countries in early cinema. Additionally, moving images of the silent era were largely products of nonresident producers and dominated by historical representations, tendencies that would be repeated for most of the 20th century.

The New York–based Kalem Company was groundbreaking not only in producing the first fiction films (beginning with *The Lad from Old Ireland* [1910]) but also in its rejection of earlier stage-Irish stereotypes and their engagement with anticolonial historical themes that caught the mood of the nation in the run-up to the 1916 Easter Rising. Led by director/actor Sidney Olcott and screenwriter/actress Gene Gauntier, the "O'Kalems" arrived in Killarney, County Kerry, in 1910 and eventually produced a filmography of approximately 30 titles over five summers. Initially made for a diasporic audience in the United States, their varied narratives (usually adaptations from existing literary sources) and photographic quality ensured broader appeal, and Kalem's promotional materials emphasized how the Irish stories were filmed in the "actual" locations depicted. The success of these films in the United States encouraged Irish-born filmmakers who had emigrated to the United States to return home. Inspired by Kalem's interest in history, the Waterford-born screenwriter and producer Walter MacNamara returned to shoot *Ireland, a Nation*, which recounted political events in Ireland from Grattan's Parliament in 1780 to Robert Emmet's 1803 rebellion. (Ironically, the first print of the film sank with the *Lusitania* in May 1915, a key event in a world war that would indirectly contribute to Ireland's becoming a nation.) In 1916, James Mark Sullivan, an Irish American lawyer and U.S. ambassador to the Dominican Republic—perhaps also inspired by Kalem's pictures of his native Killarney—returned to establish the Film Company of Ireland along with several figures connected with cultural nationalism. This was the first professional indigenous production company and produced several short and feature films before the end of the decade, notably *Knocknagow* (1918) and *Willy Reilly and His Colleen Bawn* (1920).

Through a combination of personal and professional circumstances (including the death of his wife and infant), Sullivan returned to the United States in 1920, and thus there was no indigenous production company by the time the Irish Free State was established in 1922. The absence of such a company indirectly contributed to the atmosphere in which the new state debated and passed its first piece of cinema-related legislation. Given that indigenous film production seemed impossible in this period, censorship equipped the nascent state with a (rather blunt) tool to shape the "official" culture of Ireland by strictly determining the range of representations available to the Irish cinema-going public. In July 1923, while a civil war raged, the de facto government of Ireland found time to pass the Censorship of Films Act, the only piece of legislation directly related to film passed in Ireland until the 1970s. That highly conservative instrument was informed by a Catholic ethos and led to the banning or cutting of some 11,000 films by 1960.

A few films were made in the 1920s but sporadically and without the momentum necessary to develop an industry. Norman Whitten (1881–1969), an English-born newsreel producer, made three Irish-set comedies in 1922, of all which featured variety hall legend Jimmy O'Dea (later King Brian in Disney's *Darby O'Gill and the Little People*). Isaac Eppel, a Dublin Jewish doctor, wrote and produced the stirring *Irish Destiny* in 1926, banned in Britain for depictions of the War of Independence. Neither Whitten nor Eppel persisted due to the financial challenges posed by the small scale of the Irish market, and both subsequently emigrated to England. The 1930s saw a similar pattern: playwright Denis Johnston directed a silent adaptation of a Frank O'Connor short story, *Guests of the Nation* (1935), and in 1936, a Killarney (again!) garage owner, Tom Cooper, premiered the result of two years of work in the form of *The Dawn*, an accomplished amateur drama about the War of Independence. In 1938, Jimmy O'Dea starred in and produced the comedy *Blarney*, but again none of these individuals remained involved in cinema production in the long term.

In the meantime, some of the most popular representations of Ireland were produced in Hollywood or by British producers. In 1935, John Ford made the first of his Irish-themed talkies, adapting Liam O'Flaherty's novel *The Informer*. (The novel had previously been adapted in 1929 by German director Arthur Robison.) Although Ford's atmospheric film proved a commercial and critical success (nominated for six Academy Awards, it won four, including Best Director), it was eclipsed in cultural terms by *Man of Aran*, a British-produced documentary made two years earlier by Robert Flaherty. The mythic tone of the film and its stress on a frugal, self-sufficient way of living echoed the mythology of the Irish cultural revival and chimed with the political vision of then Taoiseach Eamon de Valera (arguably much more so than the one government-sponsored film made up that point: *Ireland* [1929]). *Man of Aran* was also enthusiastically received overseas and had a decisive and lasting influence on subsequent representations of Ireland and the Irish, emphasizing a premodern culture as well as relationships between people and landscape.

The late 1930s also saw the beginnings of a debate about the role of cinema in Irish life, reflected in the establishment in 1936 of the Irish Film Society, which sought to make available images other than those of Hollywood productions. In 1937, a Jesuit priest, Father Richard Devane, called on Eamon de Valera to establish a public inquiry into how cinema might be actively used to promote national ideals rather than simply being treated as a threat to the moral fabric of the country. However, then Minister for Industry and Commerce Sean Lemass hijacked the resulting inquiry, which concerned itself mainly with questions of how to go about establishing a commercially viable film industry in Ireland, a question to which it concluded that there was no convincing answer. The inquiry did, however, indirectly lead the state to partially fund the operations of the National Film Institute of Ireland, established under the auspices of the Catholic Church in 1943 and the closest thing to a state film body until the 1980s.

Until the 1990s, film was regarded by the Irish state as an industrial undertaking rather than a cultural one, and policy was formulated accordingly. Postwar film policy was more focused on attracting large-scale overseas productions to film in Ireland than it was concerned with the development of an indigenous production sector. Thus, although politicians acknowledged that the representation of Ireland as a primitive backwater in films such as *The Quiet Man* (1951) was regrettable, such imagery was to be tolerated if the film had a positive economic impact through increasing tourist numbers, casual employment, or Irish whiskey sales. This thinking was brought to its logical conclusion in the establishment of Ardmore Studios outside of Dublin in 1957, funded mostly by the Department of Industry and Commerce. (Minister Sean Lemass had submitted plans for a state-funded studio as early as 1946 but was thwarted by the Department of Finance.) Although it was officially understood that financing the establishment of Ardmore would gradually facilitate the development of an indigenous production sector, in fact, the studios failed spectacularly to accomplish this goal. A policy designed to ensure that productions filmed at Ardmore had access to British government funding for film production ensured that Irish personnel were largely excluded from working on productions in the 1960s and 1970s. While Ardmore's existence did encourage more filmmakers from overseas to create movies in Ireland than had been the case before, the studios found it difficult to secure a constant supply of clients and spent much of the 1960s and 1970s on the brink of financial collapse.

In 1967, the noted Hollywood director John Huston convinced then Taoiseach Jack Lynch of the potential to create the conditions not only for more filmmaking in Ireland but also for an indigenous film industry. Lynch appointed Huston to head a 24-member committee to study the question; it published its report (the *Huston Report*) in 1968. Unusually, the committee argued that the development of an indigenous production sector was of such cultural importance that the state should fund small-scale domestic production through the establishment of an Irish Film Board. Even more unusually, Minister for Industry and Commerce George Colley accepted these recommendations and arranged for the drawing up of a bill to put them into effect. Unfortunately, a political scandal brought an end to this possibility, and while film production continued, it relied almost exclusively on overseas productions that used Ardmore as a location.

Throughout the 1970s, Irish state policy focused almost obsessively on Ardmore because of both its constantly perilous financial situation and the belief that a native industry required, more than anything, a studio infrastructure. In 1973, Radio Telefís Éireann acquired the nearly bankrupt facility, and two years later, the National Film Studios of Ireland at Ardmore was established by Minister for Industry and Commerce Justin Keating under the chairmanship of director John Boorman, himself a major client of the studios. Ardmore thus became a state-run film studio, and substantial sums were invested in upgrading its facilities. Despite this, Ardmore continued to be affected by a failure to secure regular clients. The state's insistence on making support of Ardmore the main element of national film policy increasingly became a source of tension with the emerging independent film sector, which argued that the money put into Ardmore could be better utilized by funding an Irish Film Board. Matters came to a head in the late 1970s after another minister for industry and commerce, Des O'Malley, appointed a private consultancy to investigate the running of the studios. The resulting report concluded that, when set alongside similar institutions in other countries, Ardmore was disadvantaged by the absence of any measures incentivizing international producers to film in Ireland. It thus proposed establishing a state-funded Film Board to offer financial aid to such producers. O'Malley accepted this but, mindful of the views of the independent filmmaking sector, proposed augmenting the putative board's resources with funding that would be exclusively available to indigenous producers. In practice, when finally published in 1979, the Film Board Bill avoided precise stipulations as to how that institution should divide its funds. Despite pressure from independent Irish filmmakers to require that the board dedicate 80 percent of its expenditure to indigenous projects, the final text of the 1980 Film Board Act stated only that the board should consider the need to reflect national culture in allotting its funds.

THE FIRST WAVE: 1970S–1980S

Even in the absence of a Film Board, the mid-1970s had witnessed the beginnings of semiregular indigenous production capacity. From the early 1970s, an increasing number of television commercials were shot in Ireland, and regular work for film crews began to emerge. The 1973 Arts Act extended the remit of the Arts Council to include film, and in 1977, director

Bob Quinn completed his first feature, *Poitín*, with the proceeds of the first Arts Council Film Script award. Other recipients of Arts Council funding in this period included Kieran Hickey, Joe Comerford, Cathal Black, and Pat Murphy, a group who would form the basis of the "first wave" of indigenous Irish filmmakers in the late 1970s and early 1980s.

The formal establishment of the Irish Film Board in 1981 brought the greatest opportunity for the nurturing of local filmmakers and stories in almost a century of the medium, and during its first six years of operation, it conspicuously concentrated on domestic projects, partially funding 10 feature films between 1981 and 1987 along with a range of shorts, documentaries, and experimental works. The first-wave films were characterized by local casts, crews, and themes, and most were also antimainstream in form, emerging as they did from a leftist, avant-garde, and post-1968 perspective and frequently honed from visual arts rather than commercial film perspectives. Films such as *Maeve* (Pat Murphy/John Davies, 1981), *On a Paving Stone Mounted* (Thaddeus O'Sullivan, 1978) *Down the Corner* (Joe Comerford, 1976), and *Our Boys* (Cathal Black, 1980) were critically well received and generated a substantial academic literature concerned with their foundational significance in the long-awaited development of a national cinema. For the most part, however, they were not commercially successful, a point that would prove critical in the economically depressed days of the mid-1980s. In 1987, when 50,000 Irish people were emigrating each year and with unemployment rates reaching 20 percent, a newly elected government introduced major cuts in public expenditures. When the Irish Film Board was established in 1980, it had been optimistically assumed that returns from film investments would obviate the need to fund the board on an ongoing basis. In practice, this never happened, and the new government decided to suspend the operations of the board rather than—as they saw it—continue to throw good money after bad. To mitigate this decision, the government emphasized the introduction of a new scheme under the 1987 Finance Act—known as Section 35—which allowed companies to write off investments in film production for tax purposes. Taken together with a new EU program—called simply MEDIA—to develop the European audiovisual sector, the government argued that these initiatives would more than compensate for the loss of the Film Board.

THE SECOND WAVE—IRISH FILM BOARD: 1993–2005

There was some truth in this, but MEDIA was prohibited from funding production, whereas Section 35 was generally considered too complex to attract many investors. As a result, production levels gradually declined significantly between 1987 and 1993, when the Irish Film Board was in a hiatus. Nonetheless, it was during this period that two of the most significant works in Irish film history were made. In 1989, Jim Sheridan directed *My Left Foot*, which, in contrast to the films produced under the first Film Board, was a classic populist text in the Hollywood mold. The film was well received in Ireland but initially enjoyed only modest box office success. In the United States, however, it was nominated for five Oscars, including Best Director and Best Film, a remarkable achievement for a first-time director. After Daniel Day-Lewis, who played Christy, and Brenda Fricker, who played his mother, won the Best Actor and Best Supporting Actress categories, respectively, the film took in $14 million in the United States and was rereleased in Ireland, becoming a massive hit. This unprecedented critical and commercial success had a profound and lasting influence on the idea of what an Irish film should be and do. *My Left Foot* created a template that second-wave producers in the 1990s and the early 21st century would attempt to emulate: the local story crafted within universal (American) generic conventions. Four years later, director Neil Jordan's *The Crying Game* was nominated for six Oscars, and Jordan himself won in the Best Screenplay category. On the face of it, this came from a different mold: *The Crying Game* explored national and gender politics through a motif of border crossing that was intellectual and literary. However, it did so within a thriller format, complete with a stunning twist that was compelling for audiences entirely unfamiliar with the film's political and historical nuances. Unsurprisingly, both filmmakers quickly found themselves working within a Hollywood context, although Sheridan initially used the opportunity to tell exclusively Irish stories, while Jordan mixed fare such as *Interview with the Vampire* and *In Dreams* with *Michael Collins* and *The Butcher Boy*. Nonetheless, their career paths arguably suggested that the ultimate objective for the Irish industry might be to operate as an offshoot of Hollywood.

In the background of these Oscar successes, moves were under way to address the gap left by the suspension of the Irish Film Board. In the summer of 1992, two major reports stressed the economic importance of developing the film industry, particularly as it affected employment. An election in November 1992 produced an unusual coalition of the populist Fianna Fáil party together with the social democratic Labour party. One of the representatives of the latter, Michael D. Higgins, became minister at the new Department of Arts, Culture, and the Gaeltacht (Gaeltacht refers to the Irish-speaking regions of Ireland). As a sociologist and poet, Higgins was a highly unusual politician (and later president of Ireland), but he proved highly effective, exploiting the wave of euphoria following Neil Jordan's Oscar success to reestablish the Irish Film Board in March 1993 and later encourage the expansion of the Section 35 tax incentive.

The impact of these developments is difficult to overstate. While the first Irish Film Board supported 10 features over six years, the second board funded the development of more than 500 ideas and the production of approximately 250 features between 1993 and 2003. During the same period, more than €640 million was raised for film production via the Section 35 tax break (redesignated as Section 481 after 1997). In the space of just five years, Ireland went from having no film industry to speak of to being the fastest-growing audiovisual production center in the European Union. Furthermore, the fact that Section 35/481 was available to any production using Ireland as a location drew in a number of big-budget overseas productions, starting with *Braveheart* in 1994 and later including *Saving Private Ryan*, *Reign of Fire*, and the most recent big-screen version of *King Arthur*.

The increase in the levels of indigenous production did not necessarily translate into popular success. The initial focus of the reincarnated Film Board was on one-off projects, with considerations of company development, distribution, and marketing considered secondary. By the end of the 1990s, a series of reports on the industry increasingly emphasized the need to develop stronger indigenous production companies characterized by greater scale, capitalization, business acumen, and editorial expertise that could successfully compete in the international market. In parallel with this, by the start of the 21st century, film policy formation was increasingly influenced by the need to maintain the position that Ireland had established within a new international division of cultural labor. When, in December 2002, Minister for Finance Charlie McCreevy announced his intention to remove the film tax incentive on the grounds that a film industry had now been established, the ensuing industry-led campaign successfully argued that such incentives were crucial weapons in Ireland's fight to secure foreign productions. If this was suggestive of how elements of the indigenous sector had come to regard the main objective of film policy (i.e., maintaining a flow of incoming productions), subsequent events would prove how vulnerable such ambitions were to exogenous factors. In early 2004, however, the United Kingdom's incentive schemes were radically restructured, and incoming projects could no longer "double-dip" into Irish and U.K. tax incentives. Furthermore, as the dollar weakened after 9/11, it suddenly became more expensive for Hollywood companies to shoot in Ireland. The total value of audiovisual activity fell to its lowest level in nearly a decade, while employment fell to 1,053, a huge decline from the 1,700 peak recorded five years earlier in 2000.

A THIRD WAVE—FROM NATIONAL TO TRANSNATIONAL

The Irish state's response to the crisis of 2003–2005 confirmed the overseas orientation of the industry. The tax incentive was tweaked to allow individual productions to access larger sums, while the Irish Film Board, which had previously focused on indigenous production, was now directed to consider international production as well. The overall value of the Irish audiovisual sector did pick up after 2005, but this was driven largely by a shift toward large-scale television production and a significant expansion of activity within the Irish animation sector.

Indeed, the audiovisual sector was almost unique in bucking the trend of the rest of the economy. As the rest of the economy went into a free fall after 2008, the audiovisual sector, buoyed by international production, continued to post relatively healthy results. Nonetheless, the crash did affect the Irish Film Board and the tax regime. The board saw its capital funding nearly halved between 2008 and 2015: perhaps driven by a desire to access alternate sources of funding, the late 2000s saw the board invest small sums in a large number of European coproductions originating outside Ireland. This gave a distinctly cosmopolitan look to the board's output: a multitude of films with scant or no textual connection to Ireland were added to the roster of board-supported output. As for the tax incentive, the fact that the benefit of the scheme was disproportionately realized by high-net-worth private investors rather than Irish film producers became politically untenable in an era of austerity. Thus, as part of the 2013 budget measures, Minister for Finance Michael Noonan announced that, though extending the film tax relief scheme to 2020, it would move to a tax credit model in 2016. Despite initial protest from Irish producers, the transition to the new tax system went relatively smoothly, and there was little evidence of production lost as a consequence of the new system.

CONCLUSION

As this brief history suggests, the question of what kind of cinema Irish screen policy has encouraged and, by extension, what kind of texts, institutions, and individuals should appear in this book is not straightforward. Indeed, defining and demarcating an "Irish cinema" in particular poses a problem unique among Western nations because an indigenous Irish film *industry* (as opposed to more sporadic production structures) did not appear until the 1980s (and arguably not until the 1990s). A strict definition of an Irish film would doubtless demand that an Irish film be shot and set in Ireland with an Irish cast, that it be made by an Irish crew, and that it be funded with Irish money. (Purists might mischievously add that the language should be Irish rather than English.) Were such criteria to be enforced, this would indeed be a slim volume: it might perhaps include Tom Cooper's *The Dawn*, those films commissioned by the various state bodies over the decades, and the early work of Bob Quinn, Cathal Black, and Joe Comerford but little else. The sheer cost of making films has meant that overseas money has long played a key role in funding production in Ireland, with all the implications (e.g., story and cast) that come with "foreign" money. Furthermore, definitions of what "foreign" means have long been blurred in Ireland by Ireland's de facto status as an Anglophone country with a long history of emigration (and thus a population dispersed to the four corners of the earth). It has long been the case that filmed stories about the Irish and Ireland have emerged from a variety of national film cultures and, in particular, from the United States.

This latter point influenced Irish film historian Kevin Rockett's theoretical move in his 1996 *Irish Filmography* of recuperating as Irish films that were shot in Ireland or that feature Irish themes or characters even if they are notionally "foreign" productions. Although this has provoked controversy and disagreement in some quarters, we follow Rockett's lead here in including entries on the Kalem company and films such as *The Purple Taxi* (1977) and *The Quiet Man* (1952). To simply confine such texts to the status of "foreign" is not only to miss their cultural legacy and role in shaping subsequent constructions of Ireland (in indigenous and international filmmaking) but also to overlook how they fit into the political economy and (painfully slow) the emergence of Irish government policy. It would also needlessly overlook the role that such films played in giving experience—albeit sporadic—to Irish actors and craftspeople. By the same token, we have not included every overseas film that mentions Ireland or that features Irish cast and crew, as doing so would include a multitude of works the individual influence of which on shaping local and international understandings of Ireland has been very limited. Similarly, in a country long characterized by outward migration, though literally hundreds of Irish talents have worked in Hollywood since the 1910s, they have often worked on films that are textually unconnected with Ireland.

If we acknowledge the role of international representations of Ireland and the Irish, this book concentrates on indigenous work. The formal instigation of the Irish Film Board in July 1981 not only represents the beginning of an indigenous screen industry in Ireland but also transformed the context for academic work on the idea of an Irish cinema. Notwithstanding the stop-and-start nature of the board's early existence and the ongoing (indeed ultimately significantly enhanced) role of international production in Ireland, the board inaugurated the regular production of indigenous works from Irish cast and crew built around narratives filmed and set in Ireland for the first time. For the current authors, it is possible to identify three broad "waves" of indigenous Irish cinema emerging as a consequence between the late 1970s and the second decade of the 21st century. The first wave—covering the period up to 1993—might be summarized as an artist/director-led cinema with roots in postcolonial, feminist, and avant-garde practices and ideas, characterized by formal experimentation and a desire to challenge hegemonic modes of representation.

A second wave, commencing in 1993 with a reincarnated Film Board (see below), was markedly less experimental in nature, distinguished by its focus on reflecting a contemporary, urban Ireland via conventional dramatic narratives. Although often characterized as a more overtly commercial cinema, the limited funding resources in this period often meant faltering career progression for behind-the-camera talent, a situation reflected in the uneven quality of the films made in this period. That the second wave coincided with a period of economic prosperity in Ireland raised the suggestion that the more cosmopolitan, universal scope of indigenous second-wave films were cinematic symptoms of the homogenizing tendencies of economic and cultural globalization.

This body of work has in turn been gradually superseded since 2003 by a third wave that we regard as a transnational cinema. Although it can be argued that Irish cinema has been characterized by transnational production modes from its inception (insofar as it was dominated by international productions shot in Ireland), it might also be argued that the increasingly market-driven nature of the Irish Film Board has seen it increasingly support works characterized by transnational modes of *narration*: although drama remains the primary genre, there has been a remarkable growth in the number of Irish horror films since 2003, and the Film Board has increasingly supported works that entirely eschew signifiers of Ireland or Irishness.

Yet, lest this be interpreted as a blanket dismissal, it should also be acknowledged that third-wave cinema is also characterized by a massive growth in confidence, technical skill, and a greater plurality of approaches and voices. *Adam and Paul* (2004) exemplifies this as a film that works in two directions at once—a culturally and geographically accurate depiction of a setting (the city of Dublin) that eschews a historically and socially determined sense of place. The film works toward abstraction in rejecting a sociopolitical critique of contemporary Ireland in favor of focusing on how its twin protagonists are trapped within their social and existential circumstances. In taking this approach, *Adam and Paul*'s director, Lenny Abrahamson, and screenwriter and lead actor Mark O'Halloran opened up a portal for a new generation of Irish filmmakers to produce narratives less obsessively fixated on the condition and importance of being Irish. John Carney's *Once* is another film critical to the transition between the second and third waves in part because, despite a minuscule budget, it went on to win an Academy

Award for Best Song, rake up a healthy box office, and spawn a lucrative and award-winning stage musical. However, it also paved the way for a transnational Irish cinema to reach a much wider audience via key North American film festivals, such as Toronto, Sundance, Telluride, and South by Southwest.

Indeed, so powerful has this outward-looking impulse become that some more recent works that *are* Irish at a production level are not extensively considered in this text precisely because they bear little in the way of Irish textual markers. Paddy Breathnach's *Viva* (2015) (written by Mark O'Hallorhan) is set in Cuba and shot in Spanish. Lenny Abrahamson's *Room* (2014) is set in the United States with a U.S. cast. Even Abrahamson's previous film *Frank* (2014), though starring two Irish actors—Michael Fassbender and Domhnall Gleeson—cast them as American and British, respectively. In sum, then, though this book concentrates on work for the cinema, the modern transnational Irish screen audiovisual sector is constituted by a plurality of approaches: art house feature films that circulate via prestige festivals and channels, long-form television drama production produced in Ireland for an international small-screen market, short films that seek and very frequently receive international screenings and awards, and a thriving animation sector. To the extent possible within the confines of a finite text, this book seeks to reflect this extraordinary variety.

A

ABBEY THEATRE. The Abbey has been strongly associated with all the great literary figures of the Gaelic revival at the start of the 20th century, particularly W. B. Yeats and J. M. Synge, who actively sought inspiration from the West and was regarded as the purest embodiment of Irish identity and individuality. Yeats helped found the Irish Literary Theatre and the Abbey Theatre with Lady Gregory (1899), and the resultant literary renaissance produced plays like *The Countess Cathleen* (1899), *Diarmuid and Grainne* (1901), and *Cathleen Ni Houlihan* (1902), mythologizing a feminized form of Irish nationalism. Synge's plays, especially *Riders to the Sea* (1902) and *The Playboy of the Western World* (1907), also helped mark a new independent Irish identity. While this provoked much controversy, it also endorsed a heightened romantic sensibility that has been carried over into classic films like **Man of Aran** and **The Quiet Man**. A Dublin working-class sensibility was brilliantly captured by the plays of Brendan Behan, such as *The Borstal Boy* (1967), *The Plough and the Stars* (1926), and *Juno and the Paycock* (1924), which were translated into film by **John Ford** and Peter Sheridan.

Furthermore, the central importance of Abbey actors can be seen in the large number moving to work in newer media industries. Their theatrical skills and unique style have marked many Irish American films over time. As early as 1916, the **Film Company of Ireland**'s productions drew heavily on the Abbey's resources: both J. M. Kerrigan (later a Hollywood character actor) and Fred O'Donovan made their film debuts in the company's *O'Neil of the Glen*, which Kerrigan also directed. Subsequently well-known actors like **Noel Purcell**, **Jimmy O'Dea**, and **Cyril Cusack** built long careers in film together with their theatrical work, alongside more contemporary figures like **Niall Toibin**, **Donal McCann**, and **Colm Meaney**, who honed their craft in the Abbey and in Dublin theater generally during their formative acting years.

Given the absence of any sustained indigenous production activity until the 1980s, the Abbey was also long identified as a potential basis for a domestic film industry. In 1937, the Abbey Theatre submitted a memo to the

Department of Finance seeking IR£20,000 from the state via the Trade Loan Guarantee Act, with a view to obtaining a matching IR£20,000, which was offered by the Milton Shubert Organization, then one of the biggest theatrical groups in New York. This money was to be used to equip a studio in Dublin for film productions, to be made under the artistic control of the Abbey Theatre, which would also provide the subjects and actors. The American group would advise on apparatus and technical services. Although the department's refusal to countenance such a loan meant that nothing came of the 1937 proposal, a very similar idea would later underpin the establishment of **Ardmore Studios**. In 1957, **Louis Elliman** produced a 55-minute made-for-TV version of George Shiel's Abbey play *Professor Tim*. The film, which was directed by **Emmet Dalton**, was produced under the auspices of Dublin Film and Television Productions Ltd, of which Elliman and Dalton were directors. Crucially, however, the two were joined on the board of a sister company—Dublin Film Productions Management Ltd—by Ernest Blythe, then chairman of the Abbey.

The relationship between these two companies (and Blythe's presence on the board of the latter) was explained by the fact that *Tim* was designed to test the potential of the American market. If the film took off in the United States, then the two companies would collaborate to produce film versions of other Abbey plays. Dublin Film Productions Management Ltd would deal with the question of rights for the Abbey plays, and Dublin Films and TV Productions Ltd would actually shoot them.

Tim led to a deal with RKO Teleradio in New York to produce a series of Abbey plays as made-for-TV movies, and this apparent guarantee of work was the basis for Ardmore's construction. Although the RKO deal apparently fell through within a few years, Abbey stage productions constituted a sizable number of the films made at Ardmore in its first five years of operation, including the first film shot at Ardmore, an adaptation of Walter Macken's *Home Is the Hero* (1958); another George Shiel play, *The New Gossoon*, released as *Sally's Irish Rogue* (1958); and Hugh Leonard's *The Big Birthday*, released in the United Kingdom as *Broth of a Boy* (1959).

***ABOUT ADAM* (1999).** This breezy Celtic Tiger rom-com, written and directed by **Gerry Stembridge**, centers on a charismatic young man (played by **Stuart Townsend**) who is capable of casting a spell over any woman (or indeed man) he encounters. Having become engaged to Lucy Owens (Kate Hudson), he then proceeds to bed most of her family, a rake's progress that the film presents as a series of comic interludes. Along with this unprecedented attitude of openness and the casting of bright and beautiful young actors (notably Hollywood star Hudson), what is most striking about *About Adam* is its entirely original portrayal of Dublin. Stembridge goes out of his way to avoid the seedy, grime- and crime-filled portrayal of the city that dominated crime films of the period, opting instead to represent it as a modern and cosmopolitan European capital peopled by middle-class characters inhabiting a tasteful and stress-free milieu of classic cars and chic urban apartments.

About Adam is a rare but key example of Celtic Tiger cinema. This means that it was criticized for its alleged "non-Irishness," lack of identifiable place marks, and open attitude to sexuality both at home and abroad. The light tone and casting helped the film receive wide international distribution from its producer, Miramax. However, although the film performed well in Ireland, taking in IR£660,000, it disappointed elsewhere. In the United States, for example, it was limited to an 11-print release, which ended after three weeks with just $160,000 earned.

ABRAHAMSON, LENNY (1966–). Lenny Abrahamson is arguably Ireland's most highly regarded contemporary director, with an intelligence and creative ambition that places him at the forefront of a new generation of filmmakers. His feature film debut, *Adam and Paul*, written in collaboration with actor/writer Mark O'Halloran, was voted Irish Film of the Decade (Dublin Film Critics Circle) and can retrospectively be seen as heralding the emergence of a "'third wave'" of Irish cinema, initiating a shift from narratives imagined solely in terms of "Irishness" toward films characterized by a transnational art house and auteurist sensibility. Key to this shift has been Abrahamson's influence in privileging individual experience and existential themes—a cinematic sensibility closer to a postwar European outlook than the nationalist/postcolonial outlook that dominated earlier Irish cinema. Abrahamson can also be contrasted with predecessors such as **Jim Sheridan** and **Neil Jordan** in the degree of control he has retained over his projects and career trajectory. While both moved from low-budget Irish material to American stories and studio relationships in order to develop their career prospects, Abrahamson's embrace of U.S. and British settings has been done within the context of an Irish production company (**Element Pictures**) and key collaborators. This has clearly been a deliberate choice, affording him a degree of choice and control over projects that has not always been available to his predecessors while also reflecting the changed realities of the cinematic marketplace.

A descendant of Jewish émigrés on both sides, Abrahamson's paternal grandfather and namesake Leonard Eliezer Abrahamson was professor of pharmacology at the Royal College of Surgeons in Ireland, having emigrated from Belarus with his family as a small child. His maternal grandfather, Mendel Walzman, was from Poland and served in the Polish army during World War II before eventually fleeing to Ireland. Their grandson's Jewish identity has been more secular—indeed, publicly so in his commitment to liberal causes—but it is not hard to find this background of relevance in both direct and indirect ways. His first film was a filmed interview with Mendel recalling his background and experiences, while Abrahamson's body of work to date shows a deep empathy with a variety of outsiders and misfits and the fragility of identity within shifting social contexts.

Abrahamson attended Trinity College Dublin as an undergraduate student of philosophy and while there developed an interest in film and made friendships that would guide and shape his future career, notably producer **Ed Guiney** and composer **Stephen Rennicks** (who has scored all his films). In college, he made two films: the previously mentioned *Mendel Walzman* and a short comedy called *3 Joes* (1991) featuring Dominic West (*The Wire*'s Jimmy McNulty), comedian Gary Cooke, and actor Mikel Murfi. However, this did not lead directly to a career in film, and for a time, Abrahamson pursued academia, commencing a PhD at Stanford University before abandoning it to return to Dublin and screenwriting.

These efforts, inspired more by European auteurs than by commercial ambition, met with little success. A sideways shift into directing commercials with the Speers Company offered a lifeline. He quickly developed a reputation for well-resourced, glossy, yet witty work, including a memorable sequence of Carlsberg ads in the 2000s. While commercials have traditionally been viewed as a compromised endeavor in artistic terms, Abrahamson not only found the work fulfilling for a time but also realized that he had a real talent for it. This "detour" proved a boon to his creative development, providing a stimulating and collaborative work environment, regular on-set experience, and access to higher budgets than many first-time Irish directors have.

Abrahamson would reteam with one of the stars of a famous World Cup ad he directed for Carlsberg, Tom Jordan Murphy, in *Adam and Paul*. Developed with actor/writer Mark O'Halloran (Murphy's partner of the time), the film retained the wit of his short-film and commercial work within a more somber thematic trajectory. Set in contemporary Dublin, *Adam and Paul* was built around a pair of hapless, incoherent junkies (Murphy and O'Halloran) as they trace their own meandering journey through the darker corners of the city in a quest for another hit. Coincidentally, it takes place exactly a century after **James Joyce**'s *Ulysses*, but where Joyce's text was hailed for its encyclopedic documenting of the urban space as Leopold Bloom and Stephen Dedalus move around it, Adam and Paul experience Dublin as a disjointed, alien, and often hostile setting. Far less intimate than Joyce's city, Celtic Tiger–era Dublin is rendered as a space in disorienting transition from the local to the global, emphasized through a subtext of misrecognition (e.g., the search for "Clank" and an encounter with an eastern European immigrant).

Adam and Paul was a huge critical success, being nominated for eight IFTAs (winning Best Director) and winning further awards for screenplay, acting, and best film in the United Kingdom, Spain, and Romania. Such acclaim helped with the development of subsequent projects, although they were some time in coming. But as with buses, having waited two years for a successor, two arrived at the same time.

In the autumn of 2007, **Radio Telefís Éireann** (RTÉ) broadcast Abrahamson's only TV drama to date (also written in collaboration with Mark O'Halloran), the ironically titled *Prosperity*—four stand-alone episodes centering on individual characters excluded from the seemingly ubiquitous excess of Celtic Tiger Ireland. A single mother, a stuttering child from a deprived background, an unemployed part-time father, and a recent immigrant from Nigeria separated from her son formed a quadriptych of stories that sought to remind Irish audiences that the rising tide did not lift all boats. Although acclaimed, Abrahamson has subsequently spoken of his dissatisfaction with the project, believing it to be underdeveloped as well as undermined by its producers, who scheduled the opening episode opposite a controversial documentary on RTÉ's other channel.

A week after the final episode of *Prosperity* was broadcast, Abrahamson's second feature, *Garage*, was released. Although it can be viewed as something of a companion piece to his debut—focusing on another example of marginalized Irish masculinity, this time in a rural setting—it was less jaunty in tone and darker in its conclusions. **Pat Shortt** as Josie is one of the most inspired pieces of casting in Irish cinema, brilliantly flipping his long association with a string of Irish comic "culchies" to reveal a deep and widely unacknowledged pain in Irish masculinity, a theme given topical emphasis through a plotline dealing with property development and accusations of sexual abuse. The film ends on a similarly bleak note to *Adam and Paul*, revealing a cruel and contemptuous rural Ireland infected with late-phase commodity capitalism (real estate) that leaves its central character with literally no home to go to.

Abrahamson's third film was without O'Halloran as writer but can nevertheless be read as the third part of a loose trilogy of works dealing with contemporary Irish masculinities. *What Richard Did* was loosely based on Kevin Power's *Bad Day in Blackrock*, a quasi-fictionalized account of the violent assault and death of an Irish teenager outside a Dublin nightclub in 2000 at the hands of a group of middle-class schoolboys. Young, confident, handsome, and popular, Richard (**Jack Reynor**) is unlike Adam, Paul, or Josie in almost every respect. Here, Abrahamson's concern is less with the rejection than with the acceptance of his central male character and the social mechanisms that permit and perpetuate such privileged belonging. While *What Richard Did* is highly accomplished and offers an acute portrait of an influential and underrepresented section of Irish society, it is harder to like than the preceding films, its setting of privilege offering limited opportunity for an audience to empathize with its protagonist's dilemma.

Frank marked an unexpected and decisive departure in themes, tone, and career ambitions. Set almost entirely outside of Ireland, the film was also categorized as a "loose adaptation" of a real-life figure: the oddball 1980s English pop star Frank Sidebottom, created by Manchester musician Chris Sievey. Scripted by British journalist turned writer Jon Ronson (who had interviewed Sievey in the 1990s), *Frank* tracked the story of a wannabe musician (**Domhnall Gleeson**) who meets Frank and his merry band of misfits and conspires to provide direction and management to the group. This journey brings them from England to recording an album in Ireland and then to the famed SXSW (South by Southwest) music festival in Austin, Texas. While tonally exaggerated to the point of absurdity—not least because **Michael Fassbender** plays the title role almost entirely in a large papier-mâché mask—the film has a surprisingly engaging emotional core centering on questions of authenticity, acceptance, and success. (It also boasts a terrific sound track of pop pastiche by Stephen Rennicks, including 'I Love You All' with lyrics by Abrahamson and Rennicks which rivals the pop pastiche "Riddle of the Model" from **John Carney**'s *Sing Street*). *Frank* represented an odd but successful path forward, markedly different from Abrahamson's previous work except perhaps in its concern with an central male figure who finds himself literally outside the group (of oddball musicians) and who is once again left to face the world alone.

Room continued this trajectory: a massive and unexpected breakout success that placed Abrahamson at the forefront of "independent" Anglophone cinema, garnering four **Academy Award** nominations—Best Director, Best Picture, Best Actress, and Best Adapted Screenplay—and winning one (Best Actress). Emma O'Donoghue's 2010 novel *Room* (winner of the Man Booker Prize [2010]) captivated Abrahamson on first reading, and he wrote an impassioned five-page letter to the Irish-born, Canadian-resident writer explaining why and how he would like to bring it to the screen. Collaborating closely once again with a writer, the film offered a powerful and moving story centering on a mother and her young son who are held captive at the mercy of the boy's father as well as exploring their subsequent freedom, acculturation, and changed relationship. Inspired by the infamous Josef Fritzl case, *Room* explored love and abuse in the most extreme of circumstances, evocative, it might be said, of the concentration camps half a century earlier and the haunted experience of survival that followed for the fortunate few.

The Little Stranger (2017) offered another departure: a period film set in 1950s England and a world away from the settings of *Adam and Paul* and *Garage* although again concerned with an isolated male protagonist who is not at home in the world in both literal and figurative senses. Adapted from the 2009 best-selling novel by Sarah Waters (by Abrahamson and British screenwriter Lucinda Coxon), the story is a sophisticated variation on the haunted house genre with subtle and engaging results. It centers on the figure of Dr. Faraday (Domhnall Gleeson), a recently qualified doctor from a working-class background who journeys to Hundreds Hall, the stately but now dilapidated home of the Ayers family he knew from his childhood, where he encounters the last two members of the near exhausted family line: Roderick (Will Poulter) disfigured by the war and his sister Caroline Ayers (Ruth Wilson), with whom Faraday strives and partly succeeds in striking up a romantic relationship. Although derived from a long British tradition of old house horror, *The Little Stranger*, as one would expect from Abrahamson, is a more complex film than merely genre variation. In unexpected ways, it can be related to his previous work, notably *Frank*, in which Gleeson played a comparably aspirational interloper, at once sensitive and enabling to a marginal group of individuals and at the same time covetous of their distinctive sociocultural attributes and identity (not to mention property). The horror here is less supernatural than psychological and intimately social, an eruption of trauma that Faraday serves to bring to the surface in the interregnum between the horrors of World War II and the usurpation of hereditary privilege by the swinging 1960s (Lennon and McCartney were, after all, children of Irish immigrants).

Following the success of *Room*, *The Little Stranger* was eagerly awaited but disappointed at the box office despite positive if less-than-ecstatic reviews and strong central performances from Wilson and Gleeson. This may have been because it was marketed, mistakenly, as a period/horror film in order to increase its American audience when it would have been better approached as another strong auteurial effort from Abrahamson. Similarly, its British setting and themes were unlikely to ever set the Irish box office alight.

Although a late and, indeed, slow starter, Abrahamson has established himself at the forefront of Irish film. While we have suggested recurring themes and motifs, his work is defined more by an uncommon level of emotional intelligence and rigor than by specific tropes, qualities to the fore in his public discourse. Chiming with an all-but post-Catholic Ireland, his secularism, deep empathy for the weak, and perhaps nontraditional Irishness are key elements central to Abrahamson's popularity and influence within Irish film and culture.

ACADEMY AWARDS. Given the lack of continuity of production until the 1980s and the still small size of the indigenous industry, Irish success in the Academy Awards has been limited, with notable exceptions in recent years. It is somewhat ironic therefore that the "Oscar" statuette was designed by Dublin-born art director Cedric Gibbons. As head of MGM's illustrious art department between 1924 and 1956, Gibbons was himself nominated 38 times for Art Direction/Production Design on films as diverse as *The Wizard of Oz* (1939) and *The Bad and the Beautiful* (1952), winning on 11 occasions.

Other notable Irish successes included Belfast-born actress Greer Garson, who won Best Actress for *Mrs. Miniver* in 1942, and **Barry Fitzgerald**'s Best Actor award for *Going My Way* in 1944. Set designer **Josie MacAvin** won an Oscar for her work on *Out of Africa* (1985) (her third nomination), and Irish-born makeup artist Michelle Burke won on two separate occasions for her work on *Quest for Fire* (1981) and *Bram Stoker's Dracula* (1992). Two Irish films have won the Oscar for Best Short Film (Live Action): *Six Shooter* (Martin McDonagh, 2006) and *The Shore* (**Terry George**, 2012). In 2002, the Academy awarded **Peter O'Toole** an honorary Oscar for providing "cinema history with some of its most memorable characters," while **Maureen O'Hara** received a Lifetime Achievement award in 2015. That same year, "Falling Slowly" from the **John Carney** film *Once* won best original song, while **Lenny Abrahamson** was nominated for Best Director for *Room* (Brie Larson won Best Actress for her performance in the film) and **Saoirse Ronan** for several performances, including *Atonement* (2008), *Brooklyn* (2016), and *Lady Bird* (2018).

Although the Oscars take place in a geographic and cultural space far removed from Ireland's small audiovisual sector, they have made an important impact on Irish film policy and ambition. From the 1950s to the 1970s, the nominations for short films and documentaries by talents as diverse as Hilton Edwards (for *Return to Glennascaul*), **Patrick Carey**, and **Louis Marcus** consistently demonstrated what Irish directors could achieve even in the absence of a proper infrastructure for filmmaking. The successes of Daniel Day-Lewis and **Brenda Fricker** in the Best Actor and Best Supporting Actress categories at the 1990 Academy Awards for performances in **Jim Sheridan**'s *My Left Foot* led to renewed calls for the revival of the recently disbanded **Irish Film Board** (IFB). When then Taoiseach Charles Haughey (who had closed the IFB in 1987) praised the makers of this "Irish film," it was pointed out that the film had been funded largely by a British television company.

However, it was another Irish success that would have the single greatest impact. **Neil Jordan**'s *The Crying Game* was nominated for six Oscars in 1993. As the night proceeded, it appeared that the film was destined to win nothing, losing in its first five categories. However, in the last (Best Original Screenplay), it won. Within 24 hours, Minister for Arts, Culture, and the Gaeltacht **Michael D. Higgins** announced the reinstatement of the IFB with immediate effect. Furthermore, several months later, the **Section 35** tax incentive was radically altered, leading to a huge increase in the level of funding available for films made in Ireland.

Since 1993, Irish nominations/wins at the Oscars, the Cannes Film Festival (where *The General* won Best Director for **John Boorman** in 1998 and *The Wind That Shakes the Barley* won the Palme D'Or in 2006), and increasingly at North American "indie" festivals, such as Toronto, Sundance, and Telluride, have functioned not only to recognize talent but also to reinforce the importance of ongoing state support for film production in Ireland and have been championed as such by the IFB/Screen Ireland, which now rely heavily on festival success as a marketing tool at home and abroad.

In this regard, 2015 proved a bumper year, when the IFB's promotional literature celebrated as diverse a range of "Irish cinema" as imaginable. *The Lobster*, directed by Yorgos Lanthimos and featuring **Colin Farrell**, won the Jury Prize at the 2015 Cannes Festival, while Irish films and actors were nominated in nine categories at the 2016 Academy Awards with Lenny Abrahamson's *Room* and John Crowley's *Brooklyn* accounting for seven nominations between them. This might be seen as something of a turning point in the IFB's understanding of itself and its role—a shifting away from the notion of Irish cinema as an indigenous cultural endeavor toward a transnational cultural industry.

Given that the nature of Irish production makes it unlikely that indigenous productions will achieve blockbuster financial status, the critical approval associated with awards has come to play a central role in framing appeals for the retention and, indeed, increase of state support, such as from the IFB/Screen Ireland and **Section 481**, and in the branding of Ireland as a creative (i.e., postindustrial) and outward-looking modern economy.

ACCELERATOR **(1999).** Director Vinny Murphy's feature debut follows Johnny T. (Stuart Sinclair Blyth) on the run from paramilitary vigilantes because of his "antisocial" behavior. In Dublin, he meets Whacker (Gavin Kelty), who challenges him to a car race from Belfast to Dublin for a £1,200 prize, aided and abetted by contributions from other gang members who also want to get in on the action. The resulting road movie involves a number of young gang members as they pair off and journey up north to steal cars in Belfast before racing them home.

This younger generation are less cognizant of the politics of the north, but as their convoy of stolen cars drives toward the border, they meet army checkpoints with dramatic consequences. Although made for a relatively low budget, the high-octane pace of the film chimed with working-class male audiences, especially in Dublin, and the film became a minor local hit.

ACCESS CINEMAS. *See* IRISH FILM SOCIETY.

ADAM AND PAUL **(2004). Lenny Abrahamson**'s feature debut immediately marked him as a key figure in Irish cinema. Structured around a day in the life of the two eponymous heroin addicts constantly teetering on the edge of oblivion, the film makes much of the language of the doped-up junkie and in turn is pathetic and blackly comic (not to say reminiscent of Samuel

Beckett's *Waiting for Godot*). This is augmented by the filmmakers' visual humor, which perversely echoes the classic comic film duo Laurel and Hardy. Yet, at the same time, the status of the pair as social detritus is not made light of, and audience sympathy for them is underwritten by the core performances of Mark O'Halloran (who also wrote the screenplay) and the late Tom Jordan Murphy. Of the two, O'Halloran's Adam is the more grounded, older, and better resourced than his naive, spaced-out, and hopelessly accident-prone sidekick Paul.

The narrative follows the two "flaneurs" across Dublin, capturing their colloquial syntax and portraying their bleak existence while maintaining a tight balance between alienating voyeurism and sentimental identification. (Such is the sympathy generated for the characters—their strained communications notwithstanding—that the viewer is delighted when the pair score a bag of heroin.) This strategy is reinforced by regular use of wide shots, filmed by lighting cameraman James Mather, situating the duo as tiny figures in an urban landscape. On separate occasions, the two antiheroes are dwarfed by the Poolbeg electricity station chimneys, the (since-demolished) Ballymun flats, and statues on O'Connell Street. Although echoing the dislocation of the characters, these landmarks are not in themselves valorized as identifiable markers of the city. As their story follows various engaging comic and other gags and incidental meetings, their journey's pain and ecstasy ends as it began.

The film performed extremely well on the European festival circuit. Belatedly following Abrahamson's short and critically acclaimed silent calling card *3 Joes* (1991), after his extensive work in the advertising industry, the film marked the beginning of a loose trilogy of films exploring aspects of contemporary Irish society and masculinities.

AGNES BROWNE **(1999).** Based on Brendan Carroll's 1994 comic novel *The Mammy*, the film offers a humorous but warm portrayal of a large inner-city Dublin family during the 1960s. Angelica Huston (daughter of **John Huston**) optioned the property as an opportunity to act in and direct an Irish-themed story to follow her directorial debut *Bastard Out of Carolina* (Jim Sheridan worked uncredited as director on additional scenes). She stars as the eponymous heroine: a street trader and widow with seven children who finds romance in the unlikely shape of a French baker, Pierre (Arno Chevrier). Extensive reference is made to the comic patter of Dublin's famous Moore Street traders, cultural touchstones of urban working-class values who have since largely disappeared from the city. Although the film was only mildly successful, the character of Mrs. Brown would prove a massive and unexpected hit with U.K. and Irish television audiences 12 years later when Brendan O'Carroll revived it in the BBC/**Radio Telefís Éireann** sitcom *Mrs. Brown's Boys* (2011–) and its various spin-offs.

AILSA **(1994).** Adapted from a short story by writer Joe O'Connor, *Ailsa* is the feature debut of director **Paddy Breathnach**. Starring Brendan Coyle and Andrea Irvine, the film charts the descent of its protagonist Miles into voyeuristic obsession with his neighbor Sara. Miles uses the skills acquired in his day job—writing genealogies for Irish Americans and tracing their identities—to gradually build up a picture of Sara's existence. His growing obsession is expressed through voice-over illustrating the slow disintegration of a man unable or unwilling to find meaning in his own life. Miles's disconnection from reality is reflected in the style of the film, which self-consciously espouses the look and themes of European art house cinema (along with the influence of Alfred Hitchcock). Careful set design evokes the claustrophobia of the living quarters, while Cian de Buitlear's cinematography renders Miles's world in glacial blue and gray tones. *Ailsa* won the Euskal Media Prize at the 1994 San Sebastian Film Festival for Best First Film, and the prize money was used by director Breathnach and producer **Ed Guiney** to partially fund the development of their respective next efforts: *I Went Down* and *Guiltrip*.

ALARM **(2008).** Despite its topicality, *Alarm* made little impact on its release and has been largely forgotten. To a degree, this is to be expected—its tone, themes, and execution were unlikely to attract widespread enthusiasm—but perhaps also unfortunate. For despite its downbeat execution and an ultimately unsatisfactory denouement, the film might usefully be included within considerations of an obsession with property/home during the Celtic Tiger period.

Written and directed by **Gerry Stembridge**, *Alarm* offers a radically different vision to his breezy *About Adam* in a narrative centered on Molly (**Ruth Bradley**), a young professional woman who has just purchased her first house in a newly developed housing estate. A succession of disturbing occurrences gradually corrode her sense of domestic security to the point of paranoia and terror. There are clearly strong shades of Roman Polanski's "apartment trilogy" in the plot, but Stembridge's interest is more social than psychological as he explores the consequences of Ireland's obsession with "getting on the property ladder." Primary among these is a collapse in community and trust in the opportunistic, nonserviced housing developments that mushroomed all over Ireland during the boom when young people, often 30-something single professionals, found themselves living farther out on the commuter belt in places they had little or no relationship with. This separation between place (as history) and space (as commodity) is expressed in the film as a sense of the uncanny as Molly grows progressively more terrified of her own home and cannot locate any neighbors with whom she can establish a sense of community. In the end, she finds a kind of respite and release, but Stembridge's theme, while not subtle, marks a decisive departure for representations of the Irish home: transforming them from refuges into spaces of dread and insecurity, thus undoing that most fundamental of Irish proverbs: *Níl aon tinteán mar do thinteán féin* (There's no hearth like your own hearth).

ALBERT NOBBS **(2012).** A long-cherished project for its star, co-screen-writer, and producer Glenn Close, *Albert Nobbs* was shot on location and in studio in Dublin/Ardmore during 2011. Close first played the titular charac-ter in a 1982 New York stage production and spent 15 years trying to turn it into a film. Directed by Rodrigo Garcia and adapted for the screen by John Banville (who had also been involved with the project for many years) from the eponymous 1918 novella by Irish novelist George Moore (1852–1933), the film centers on a woman passing as a man in order to work and survive in 19th-century Dublin. The prestige of Close attracted a high-caliber cast, in-cluding Mia Wasikowska, **Jonathan Rhys Meyers**, **Brendan Gleeson**, Janet McTeer, Pauline Collins, and **Brenda Fricker**. Despite a modest budget and its period setting, the film was critically well received, earning three **Acade-my Award** nominations—Best Actress (Glenn Close) and Best Actress in a Supporting Role (Janet McTeer) and Best Makeup—along with similar nom-inations in the Golden Globes and the Independent Spirit Awards. Brian Byrne's work on the score and song "Lay Your Head Down" (cowritten by Byrne and Close) likewise received a number of nominations and awards.

ALL SOULS' DAY **(1997).** Loosely inspired by Oscar Wilde's *Ballad of Reading Gaol*, **Alan Gilsenan**'s experimental feature film explores themes of love and subjectivity, particularly with regard to how we construct mean-ing through stories and the reliability of narrative in such a process. In a twist on the trope that structures the likes of *Citizen Kane* (1941) and *Rashomon* (1950), *All Souls' Day* suggests that the story recounted by a narrator is not necessarily the same story heard by an audience. The film explores this idea in an elliptical and dreamlike fashion through the use of a variety of formats, including video, Super 8, and 16 mm. An aesthetically ambitious and intel-lectual deviation from the dominant tendencies in 1990s Irish cinema, *All Souls' Day* is an unclassifiable outlier that nonetheless both foreshadows Gilsenan's documentary work on Irish institutional spaces and provides a link between the first-wave experimental films of **Joe Comerford** and others and more recent essay/artist films by the likes of **Pat Collins**/Tadgh O'Sullivan, Dean Kavanagh, and Anja Mahler.

AMERICAN WOMAN (THE CLOSER YOU GET) **(2000).** Bored and un-able to find suitable partners among the women in their small town, a group of rural Donegal males decide to pool their resources and put an advertisement in the *Miami Herald* inviting American women to their local town dance. The heroine of the film is Siobhan (Cathleen Bradley), who will stand for no nonsense from Kieran (Ian Hart), ringleader of this crazy plan.

Imagined by producer Umberto Pasolini (who scored an enormous international success with *The Full Monty* [1997]), one assumes, as a cross between **The Quiet Man** and the 1998 crossover hit **Waking Ned**, Aileen Richie's film featured a strong cast that included Ian Hart, **Sean McGinley**, Cathleen Bradley, Niamh Cusack, and **Ruth McCabe**. Despite their performances, its charming tone, and its lush cinematography, its central conceit was judged unacceptably contrived by both critics and audiences and performed badly at the box office, a particularly derivative and unconvincing entry in the Irish American genre of romantic comedy.

ANGELA MOONEY DIES AGAIN (1996). **Tommy McArdle**'s film stars Mia Farrow (daughter of **Maureen O'Sullivan**) and **Brendan Gleeson** alongside Irish comics **Pat Shortt**, Jon Kenny, and Tommy Tiernan in a black comedy centered on the theme of modernization in rural Ireland.

Gleeson plays a bespectacled husband attempting to placate his "mad" wife, Angela (Mia Farrow), and prevent her highly public suicide attempts, which are apparently designed to wake up the natives, whom she considers sheeplike in their acceptance of religion and global capitalism (the latter exemplified by the buyout of the local creamery by a big American corporation).

Flashbacks reveal Angela's passionate love affair with outsider John Malone. In an undercooked narrative, the rejection of their relationship by the community and her family apparently explains her psychological imbalance. The film nevertheless provides an interesting portrait of mental illness—albeit tinged with romantic excess and spectacle—within a small-minded rural Irish environment where boredom is frequently alleviated by outbursts of bacchanalian indulgence.

As the celebrations to commemorate the takeover of the creamery reach a climax, its new American owner (**Patrick Bergin**) is revealed as Angela's former lover, who has nevertheless forgotten those events of his youth. As he flies away, he remarks to his pilot how strange the Irish are. Meanwhile, Angela is being carted off to the hospital again in an ambulance. In a strangely downbeat conclusion to otherwise comic proceedings, it appears that this time she has succeeded in performing her "final act."

ANGELA'S ASHES **(2000).** "Worse than the ordinary miserable childhood is the miserable Irish Catholic childhood," a narrator claims at the outset of Alan Parker's film adaptation of Frank McCourt's hugely successful memoir recounting his youth growing up in the slums of 1930s Limerick. The following two hours set about envisioning that assertion.

Three actors play the young Frank as the narrative traces his time in Ireland from early childhood through his late teens. Frank's father Malachy (Scottish actor Robert Carlyle) is an unemployable alcoholic who compounds this by spending the family's social welfare payment on drink. Presented as a pathetic (and often absent) figure, he is drawn in stark contrast with Frank's angelic mother Angela (Emily Watson), a physically slight but emotionally strong figure. Reminiscent of *My Left Foot*'s depiction of the Irish maternal figure, it is Angela who maintains the family in the face of grinding poverty, lack of education, and, in Frank's case, a bout of typhoid. Confronted with the indifference of the state and ecclesiastical authorities, the film is nonetheless characterized by a triumph-against-adversity plot structure. Figures such as his inspirational teacher Mr. O'Hallorhan (Brendan Cauldwell) recognize Frank's intellect and offer temporary respite from his wretched existence through emphasizing the life of the mind.

As a project supported by Hollywood (Paramount Pictures) with a distinctly unimpoverished $50 million budget, director Parker was never likely to deliver Ken Loach–like realism: shards of real and metaphorical light repeatedly shine through its relentlessly cloudy skies and downbeat narrative. Ultimately, as is so often the case in historical Irish narratives (e.g., the work of the **Kalem Company**), deliverance is promised in the form of immigration to the United States, the goal to which the teenage Frank devotes all his energies.

ANIMATION. Animation is a singular success story in Ireland's audiovisual industry: a production category in which Ireland not only punches above its weight but also is recognized as a key player in a highly competitive and internationalized sector. While Irish film production has waxed and waned over the past 30 years, attempting to find its place in an unpredictable and changing cinematic landscape, the trajectory of Irish animation has been uniquely upward. To understand how this happened, it is necessary to trace the key figures and initiatives that fostered the industry as we know it.

In 1964, Gunther Wolf left his native Germany to set up a studio producing animated TV commercials, becoming Ireland's first animation studio. He was followed in the early 1970s by Harry Hess, a former UPA animator who had worked on classics such as *Mister Magoo*, and then by Jimmy Murakami, who arrived in Ireland in 1970 to work as art director on **Roger Corman**'s *The Red Baron* (1971). Hess established his own studio and in 1973 became a lecturer at the National College of Art and Design (NCAD), where he oversaw the production (with **Radio Telefís Éireann [RTÉ]**) of an award-winning short animation, *Pinpoint*. Murakami also set up a studio, Murakami Films, to produce live-action and animated commercials, although he punctuated this by occasional feature work, including working as director on Corman's classic *Battle Beyond the Stars* (1981).

Inevitably, this confluence of production/education activity contributed to the emergence of indigenous talent. Aidan Hickey (1942–) trained at NCAD before completing a postgraduate film course in London. On returning to Ireland in the early 1970s, he made his first film for RTÉ, *An Saol ag Dul Thart*, and subsequently produced a series called *The Magic Piano*, which was sold to 16 countries. Other Irish animators from the 1970s and early 1980s included Steve Woods, who trained under Harry Hess, and Tim Booth, who began his career in London in the early 1970s before returning to Ireland and working with Murakami Films.

For the most part, however, prior to 1985, the animation sector in Ireland was little more than a cottage industry. In that year, the Industrial Development ment Authority (IDA), recognizing that animation was a labor-intensive growth industry, created an attractive package of incentives (grant aid along with a special 10 percent corporate tax rate) to international animation studios. The impact was immediate, leading to the establishment of two major companies, Sullivan Bluth and Emerald City, and subsequently Murakami Wolf.

Born in 1939, Don Bluth had worked as an apprentice at Walt Disney Studios from 1955, returning there as a full-fledged animator in 1971. He worked on a series of Disney animations, such as *Robin Hood*, *Winnie the Pooh*, and *The Rescuers*, before leaving Disney again in 1979 with two colleagues to set up an independent animation studio. This company produced only one feature—*The Secret of NIMH* (1982)—but it attracted the attention of Steven Spielberg, who secured funding from Universal for Bluth to produce his next picture, *An American Tail* (1986).

Don Bluth also partnered with Morris Sullivan, a millionaire and former financial consultant, who recognized that for Bluth to compete in the global market, he needed to locate outside the United States, where labor costs were lower. This coincided with IDA policy, and in 1985, Sullivan Bluth was established, first in North County, Dublin, then at a fully equipped studio near Phoenix Park.

Emerald City was a subsidiary of the New York–based D. L. Taffner company, which, in contrast to Sullivan Bluth, produced hour-long versions of classic stories, such as *Oliver Twist* and *Phantom of the Opera*, for American television. In 1989, Jimmy Murakami established a Dublin subsidiary of the Los Angeles firm he had established with Fred Wolf. Murakami had spent the early 1980s working in the United Kingdom with animation company TVC London on adaptations of Raymond Briggs's *The Snowman*

(1982) and *When the Wind Blows* (1986). Murakami Wolf concentrated on television production, securing the contract for the highly successful *Teenage Mutant Ninja Turtles* series.

At its peak, the 1980s animation sector was the jewel in the IDA's crown. From virtually nothing, the sector grew to employ more than 500 people (one-third of all persons working in the Irish audiovisual industry at that time) by 1991. A by-product of the development of the animation industry was the development of training courses at Ballyfermot College, Dublin, initially set up in conjunction with Sullivan Bluth. It became a Hollywood-style conveyor-belt animation course that left room for the development of a more art-based course at the Dún Laoghaire Institute of Art, Design, and Technology, with both feeding directly into this burgeoning area of media production.

An American Tail was a massive box office hit, and Sullivan Bluth followed it with the high-profile *Land Before Time* (1988) and *All Dogs Go to Heaven* (1989). By 1991, indigenous companies, such as Animedia Teo (where Steve Woods worked), Quin Films, Tim Furnee's Moving Still Animated, and Aidan Hickey's Grafliks, provided an indigenous continuity of production.

However, 1991 also marked a dramatic turning point. Emerald City shut down with the loss of 50 jobs, while Murakami Wolf cut the number of employees from 130 to 30 after it failed to secure consistent follow-up work on completion of the *Turtles* series. Eventually, Murakami and Wolf went their separate ways, although both continued to work in Ireland. Fred Wolf Films continued to employ more than 30 people to produce the cartoon series *Budgie, the Little Helicopter*, based on children's books written by former Duchess of York Sarah Ferguson. In 2000, the firm finally shut down.

Sullivan Bluth lasted longer than most, although the company went through several incarnations (including a 1992 liquidation) before emerging in 1993 as Don Bluth Ltd. However, in April 1994, Don Bluth returned to the United States (taking many of the creative staff he originally brought over from the United States with him) when he was offered the chance to head up the new 20th Century Fox animation division. Although several companies (among them **Merlin Films**, which held a 10 percent stake in the company) expressed an interest in acquiring the Irish studios, they finally closed with the loss of 300 jobs in 1995. Animedia Teo also shut down in this period.

Although animation had initially appealed to the IDA because it appeared to offer—in contrast to live-action work—the promise of full-time, permanent employment, it proved as transient as the rest of the audiovisual sector. Projects appeared irregularly, and workers were sourced on a per-project basis; thus, much of the industry worldwide was freelance. Geographically, Ireland was peripheral to the core of an industry located in California. Finally, and probably most important, the animation process had a counterintuitive logic of production. While the creative part of the process (writing scripts, recording sound tracks, designing the characters, and producing detailed storyboards) could be done in Ireland, the more mechanical and time-consuming inking and painting was often subcontracted. While the IDA envisaged the labor-intensive part locally for the first two years of its operation, it proved too expensive, leading to much of it being completed in countries like the Philippines, Korea, Singapore, and Taiwan. By 1997, an industry that a few years earlier had a turnover of £12 million was reduced to sales of just £100,000.

However, the burst bubble left behind a skilled and determined workforce that constituted the basis for the modern Irish animation sector. In December 1992, Steve Woods and Ballyfermot graduate Cathal Gaffney (later cofounder of **Brown Bag Films**) launched Anamu, a lobby group and resource center for the emerging domestic sector. When the **Irish Film Board** (IFB) was reestablished in 1993, animation was not initially included in its remit, but persistent lobbying from Anamu and its members saw this altered. In July 1995, the IFB, in conjunction with RTÉ, the **Arts Council**, and the **Northern Ireland Film Council**, inaugurated the Frameworks scheme to support short animation productions from both emerging and establishment directors. Although Frameworks initially concentrated on supporting avant-garde works produced by artisan-scale outfits, by the turn of the 21st century, larger-scale companies like Brown Bag, Kavaleer, and **Cartoon Saloon** accounted for greater shares of the funding made available.

To an extent, these new domestic companies filled the vacuum left by the U.S.-based companies. Gerard O'Rourke, for example was employed as an accountant with Sullivan Bluth (by then trading under the name Screen Animation Ireland) until the firm shut down in 1995. When Screen Animation Ireland's overseas clients inquired as to whether there were other firms in Ireland that could take over that work, O'Rourke promptly acquired some of his former employer's equipment and set up Monster Productions to help service commercials, pop videos, and feature films, such as *Space Jam* (1996) and *Anastasia* (1997). Terraglyph, set up in Dublin in 1995, employed up to 45 employees at the peak of production. Their first feature, *Carnivale* (1999), was released internationally, winning a number of awards. Subsequent features include *Help! I'm a Fish* (2001) and *Duck Ugly* (2002). And a year before Bluth Studios closed, German producer Ralph Christians established Magma Films in Galway, which, although doing live-action work, worked primarily on animation series, such as *Loggerheads* and *Norman Normal*, for the European market.

These new companies had to devise new business models to remain viable. In the 1970s and 1980s, the smaller-scale indigenous players had just about managed to eke out an existence based on producing short (five-minute duration) series for RTÉ. By the start of the 1990s, broadcasters were looking to fill 30-minute slots, a scale of production beyond many of the older, indigenous animation producers. Furthermore, the high cost of supporting Irish animation as compared with the ready availability of much cheaper content produced overseas saw RTÉ increasingly invest in acquisitions of foreign material rather than commission Irish content. Thus, while Brown Bag films had been established in 1994 to produce the series *Peig*, a comedic adaptation of the stories of Blasket Islands *seanachaí* (storyteller) Peig Sayers, founders Cathal Gaffney and Darragh O'Conel understood that the viability of the company would rely on establishing a much broader clientele.

That market was further augmented by the expansion of the Irish economy as the Celtic Tiger boom matured in the late 1990s and early 2000s. One side effect of the economy's apparently rude health was a massive upsurge in expenditures on television commercials, a market that firms like Brown Bag and Cartoon Saloon (established in 2000) increasingly looked to in order to increase the cash flow for their businesses while more ambitious projects were being developed. However, from the early 2000s, Irish animation companies were increasingly involved in serial production for television, whether working on projects initiated overseas, as coproduction partners with other international producers, or developing and producing their own homegrown series.

Having being nominated for an Oscar for their 2001 short **Give Up Your Aul Sins** (which animated recordings of actual 1960s Dublin schoolchildren recounting interpretations of Bible stories), Brown Bag would subsequently expand the concept into a full series for RTÉ. By 2007, Brown Bag was producing adaptations of the children's book characters *Olivia* for Nickelodeon and *Noddy in Toyland* for Channel 5 in the United Kingdom. (Indeed, so successful was the TV production element of the company's work that it moved out of the production of commercials entirely in 2009.) In 2011, the company commenced work on *Henry Hugglemonster*—an in-house project based on a character created by Irish author and illustrator Niamh Sharkey aimed primarily at the international market via Disney Junior.

To varying degrees, other leading companies in the Irish animation industry, such as Monster, JAM Media, Kavaleer, Telegael, and Cartoon Saloon, adopted similar strategies involving a mix of original productions, coproduction work, and acting as facilities for hire. Such players have proven remarkably successful at accessing international markets, which now constitute the primary home for Irish television animation. Although Irish broadcasters may well acquire Irish-made animation, especially for children's schedules, today virtually nothing is produced exclusively for Irish television. As a consequence, an industry that was worth €12.2 million in 1996 was worth more than four times that a decade later (€51.4 million in 2006). By the mid-2000s, the turnover of the Irish animation sector was comfortably in excess of the value of feature film production in Ireland with IFB figures suggesting that the total value of Irish animation projects with **Section 481** funding attached had reached a massive €81.6 million by 2016.

The inevitable consequence of such internationalization is a noticeable softening of the Irish accent of such material. Although **Chris O'Dowd** may voice Cartoon Saloon's *Puffin Rock* for Anglophone markets, for the most part, material originated in Ireland is localized to suit the specific needs of overseas markets, and there is little in the visual texture of such texts that might mark them as Irish for viewers in those markets.

Nonetheless, it is clear that those works that have made a virtue of the local specificity of their works are the ones most likely to be singled out for critical acclaim. Brown Bag's two nominations for Best Animated Short at the **Academy Awards** were for texts centered on manifestly Irish characters (*Give Up Your Aul Sins* in 2001 and *Granny O'Grimm's Sleeping Beauty* in 2009). Notwithstanding the complex nature of international animation coproduction, the same is true of the feature output of Kilkenny-based Cartoon Saloon, which has seen three of its feature films nominated for Best Feature Animation at the Oscars. Although the third of these—the Nora Twomey–directed *The Breadwinner* (2017)—is set in Afghanistan, the first and second (directed by Tomm Moore), ***The Secret of Kells*** (2009) and *Song of the Sea* (2014), are unmistakably Irish in setting, narrative, cast, and creative talent.

ANNE DEVLIN **(1984).** Directed by **Pat Murphy**, this historical drama deals with the iconic Irish rebel Robert Emmet (Bosco Hogan) as he plots the rising of 1803. However, rather than focusing on the action of the rebellion and Emmet's heroic role in it, the film foregrounds Emmett's housekeeper Anne Devlin, herself a fervent nationalist, and her struggles to support his political activities. In effect, the film portrays the military struggle for Irish freedom as paralleled by a struggle for female emancipation, most overtly in the scenes in which a British army officer interrogates Anne about Emmet. The film is built around a tour de force central performance by **Brid Brennan**, who appears in almost every scene and about whom the cultural critic Luke Gibbons has described as being silent, passive, and enduring in the face of torture as a calculated act of resistance. Murphy's compelling mixture of melodrama and Republican revisionism thus unearths a hitherto unacknowledged female agency in a period often regarded as profoundly patriarchal.

ARDMORE STUDIOS. For more than half a century, Ardmore Studios was the only for-hire facility in Ireland capable of accommodating full-scale feature film production. However, although the Bray, County Wicklow, studio complex enjoyed some of its financially most successful years in the early 2000s, it also faced increasing competition from newer studio facilities better geared to the demands of 21st-century filmmaking.

Established as a private company by impresario **Louis Elliman** and producer **Emmet Dalton** in 1958, the studios were in fact underwritten by the state from their inception as a means of drawing filmmaking activity to Ireland. From the outset, Ardmore found it difficult to attract a steady throughput of work and, despite support mechanisms like the **Irish Film Finance Corporation**, were in financial difficulties throughout the 1960s. Sold into private ownership by the Industrial Credit Corporation (a state bank) in 1964, the studio went into receivership three times between 1958 and 1972. In 1973, faced with the prospects that the land might be redeveloped for housing, then Minister for Industry and Commerce Justin Keating instructed **Radio Telefís Éireann** to purchase Ardmore (at a cost of £500,000) on behalf of the state as an essential element of the national filmmaking infrastructure.

Used for two years as a base to service productions of commercials and filmed documentaries, in 1975, the Department of Industry and Commerce established a state-sponsored body—the National Film Studios of Ireland (NFSI)—to run Ardmore Studios. Chaired by director **John Boorman** and run by Sheamus Smith (later film censor), the NFSI invested substantial sums of money in upgrading the studios as well as marketing them to overseas producers. To facilitate this, between 1975 and 1982, the state advanced grants of £1.5 million to the company. Despite this, the NFSI failed to secure a steady supply of work. This fact, together with the lack of a proper capital structure, which resulted in heavy interest payments, saw the studios incur losses of around £500,000 per annum before grants. In its final year of operation (1981–1982), the board of the NFSI projected losses of approximately £780,000: this was on top of debts to commercial banks of some £2 million. Thus, in May 1982, the minister for industry and commerce, Albert Reynolds, announced the closure of the studios.

The Dáil resolution closing the studios required that the purchaser use them exclusively for the purpose of film studios for at least three years following the close of sale. Such a stipulation made them difficult to sell. Eventually, Pakistani financier Mahmud Sipra acquired the studios in July 1984 but went bankrupt before the studios could be reopened. Then in 1986, Mary Tyler Moore Productions, together with Morgan O'Sullivan's Tara Productions and NADCorp (the state-owned venture capital company), took control. After an investment of £1.2 million to refurbish and build a fourth soundstage, the complex reopened as MTM Ardmore. MTM used the studios to shoot several episodes of their detective series *Remington Steele* starring **Pierce Brosnan**. In 1988, MTM was taken over by Television South (TVS), an independent British broadcaster. Then in 1990, the promoters, who included rock band U2's manager Paul McGuinness and accountant Ossie Kilkenny, acquired the Tara and TVS stakes, leaving NADCorp with a 32 percent share in the studio.

This ownership change coincided with the most successful period in the studio's history. Following the upturn in filmmaking activity in 1993, Ardmore's books were consistently in the black, as the studio played host to indigenous productions and such large-scale undertakings as *Braveheart*, *Reign of Fire* (2002), and *King Arthur*. However, after 2003, the level of large-scale overseas feature film activity in Ireland declined. In 2003, 70 percent of audiovisual production in Ireland was accounted for by feature film production. By 2007, however, feature production's share of output had fallen to less than 10 percent. In its stead, independent television production came to the fore, accounting for 62 percent of all production activity by 2010.

Ardmore's viability between 2006 and 2009 was based on hosting four seasons of the **Morgan O'Sullivan**–produced *The Tudors* for the U.S. Showtime cable channel. That series was immediately followed by *Camelot* (another Morgan O'Sullivan production for the Starz network). However, the increased level of television production created its own difficulties: Ardmore could accommodate only one major film or television production at a time, creating an opportunity for Irish entrepreneur Joe O'Connell to construct a competing set of studios in Ballyhenry near Ashford, County Wicklow.

Ballyhenry's three soundstages addressed a key difficulty faced by Ardmore: scale. The significance of this consideration has been emphasized by the particular nature of the television dramas shot in Ireland since 2006: all have been set in period or fantasy contexts that require extensive use of Green Screen technology to create the settings for the productions. This necessitated access to larger-scale (in excess of 12,000 square feet) studio spaces. Ardmore, a facility originally constructed in a very different filmmaking era, had one such soundstage compared with the three on the Ballyhenry lot.

Thus, when in June 2011 the Starz network declined to renew *Camelot*, Ardmore lost a production that had spent €32 million in the previous year. That loss was compounded by the news that another major series—the History Channel's *Vikings*—would instead be shot at the Ballyhenry facility. As a result, Ardmore had no major projects on-site through 2011, and in March 2012, it was reported that the studios faced closure.

In June 2012, it was announced that the veteran managing director at Ardmore, Kevin Moriarty (who had been with the studios in one capacity or another since the 1970s), would be succeeded by a new chief executive, Siún Ní Raghallaigh, the former director of marketing at the Irish-language television station TG4. Ní Raghallaigh immediately introduced spending cuts, cutting the full-time staff complement from 15 to four and establishing a cost base on which to rebuild the studios. A key element in this process was securing *Penny Dreadful* (2014–2016), a Showtime series that, eschewing computer-generated imagery, fully exploited Ardmore's five sets and back lots and spent more than €30 million in Ireland.

By 2014, Ardmore and Ballyhenry were providing 110,000 square feet of studio space in Ireland. However, Ní Raghallaigh argued that Ireland was still missing out on larger-scale productions. Together with Ardmore director Ossie Kilkenny and producer John Kelleher, she began to explore the possibility of repurposing a former Dell Computer factory in Limerick as a studio facility. In May 2015, it was announced that the Limerick City Council had purchased the factory site for €6 million and were in negotiations with Ardmore to develop it as a 350,000-square-foot film and television production facility. In 2017, the factory reopened as Troy Studios, the largest production facility in Ireland, and quickly secured a major long-term client: an NBC Universal adaptation of George R. R. Martin's 1980 novella *Nightflyers* to be screened on the Syfy cable channel and Netflix.

In late 2016, the announcement that Ardmore itself was to put up for sale raised concerns that the facility might be redeveloped for residential housing. However, in January 2017, it was confirmed that the studios were to be sold as a going concern, and in March 2018, Olcott Entertainment (whose major shareholder Joe Devine also holds a substantial stake in Troy Studios) acquired the entire complex, stressing their intention to retain the existing employees and to continue servicing films.

ARTS COUNCIL. Established by the Arts Act of 1951, the Arts Council initially had little impact on film culture in Ireland mainly because of the decision to define the arts as referring exclusively to "painting, sculpture, architecture, music, the drama, literature, design in industry and the fine arts and applied arts generally." Some indication as to why film was excluded can be gleaned from then Taoiseach John A. Costello's introduction to the Arts Bill, which contrasted "real art" with "the shoddy meretricious products of modern entertainment industry" (among which he specifically included film).

However, a second Arts Act in 1973 broadened the council's responsibilities to include film. The council did not immediately make film awards (although, ironically, it did make a drama award of £1,000 to a young **Jim Sheridan** in 1973) but first consulted with the **National Film Studios of Ireland**, the **National Film Institute**, the **Irish Film Society**, and the organizers of the Cork Film Festival with a view to identifying gaps in film support. The result of these discussions was a decision to initially support low-budget production and the use of film in education. In 1975, **Cathal Black**, **Joe Comerford**, and **Bob Quinn** all received small (less than £1,000) awards to allow them to develop scripts. Education was dealt with through an initially small grant to the National Film Institute. In 1976, the council's literature and film officer, **David Collins**, organized two weeks of European films, the success of which led to the establishment of the **Irish Film Theatre** as a subsidiary of the Arts Council and implicitly added exhibition support to the council's responsibilities. Similarly, when the **Federation of Irish Film Societies** was established in 1977, the council offered sufficient funding to allow the federation to employ full-time staff to cope with the rapid growth in membership. Finally, in 1980, the council took over the funding of the Cork Film Festival from Bord Fáilte (Irish Tourist Board) and subsequently provided funding to the Dublin and Galway festivals as well.

In 1977, the council instituted a script award worth £6,000, which was supplemented with £5,000 from **Radio Telefís Éireann** (RTÉ) and the promise of technical and equipment assistance from the National Film Studios of Ireland. Early recipients included Bob Quinn for *Poitín*, **Kieran Hickey** for *Exposure*, and Joe Comerford for *Travellers*. However, in 1982, RTÉ, citing financial difficulties, announced that it could no longer support the awards (by now worth £55,000). Although a one-off deal between the council, RTÉ, and the **Irish Film Board** ensured that that year's recipient (**Pat Murphy** for *Anne Devlin*) eventually received her full award, the council conceded that future awards would be significantly smaller.

The arrival of the Irish Film Board in 1981 had in any case raised questions about the council's future role with regard to film. Following a review of its cinema policy, the council's 1983 annual report declared its ongoing commitment to supporting exhibition, access to equipment, the encouragement of educational services, and "the maintenance of the status of artist for the film-maker." To support production, the council broadened the scope of its awards to more experimental work emphasizing film as a visual art. Typical of this was the 1985 award to Bob Quinn for a feature-length silent film scored by avant-garde composer Roger Doyle. (The project, then titled *End as a Gander*, would eventually emerge as *Budawanny*.)

With the suspension of the Film Board in 1987, the council was again forced to reconsider film policy. Initially, the council sought an increase in grant-in-aid from the state to allow it to increase its script award funding in lieu of the Film Board's activities. In fact, however, the overall council budget was cut in 1987, and this was reflected in a decline in expenditure on film. Nonetheless, the Arts Council continued to support feature development and short-film production throughout the hiatus in the Film Board's activities, and the more prominent role of the council in supporting film was reflected in the appointment in 1989 of the council's first dedicated film officer.

As a latecomer to the Arts Council's remit, it was perhaps unsurprising that for much of the 1970s and 1980s, film received only a tiny portion of the total council budget. In 1975, the total value of film grants was £2,900, just over 2 percent of the council's total grant budget. Although the £104,000 granted to film a decade later was a vast increase in numerical terms, it actually constituted a slight proportional decrease relative to the overall Arts Council budget. This changed somewhat in the wake of the mid-1980s announcement by the **Irish Film Institute** (IFI) of its intention to pursue the establishment of an **Irish Film Centre**.

The council had supported the IFI since 1975 but substantially increased the level of funding to that organization after its dramatic reinvention in 1979. By 1994, the grant of £330,000 to the IFI was the third-largest grant made by the council to a single organization.

Despite this, the council came in for criticism from filmmakers in the 1990s for the lack of clarity in its film role, especially after the reestablishment of the Film Board in 1993. In 1997, the council commissioned Erika King Associates to ascertain the views of the film community and to outline future avenues for the council. The recommendations of that report (and the *Developing Cultural Cinema in Ireland* report that followed it in 2001) found their practical expression in the council's 2004 action plan, which prioritized three areas for support: the production of experimental and innovative work of high artistic ambition, improving access to international platforms for Irish filmmakers and their work, and in general terms improving the environment for exhibiting cultural cinema in Ireland through supporting the development of a regional network of art house cinemas, enhancing the film work of regional arts centers, and developing audiences through film education initiatives.

These objectives have been reflected in the council's subsequent activities, which emphasize support for film institutions (especially those focused on exhibition) and the production of experimental/arts-themed work. The council played a major role (along with the Irish Film Board) in the establishment of the Cultural Cinema Consortium in 2001. Initially making relatively small grants to existing venues (from €10,000 to the Caherdaniel Film Club to €150,000 to the Letterkenny Arts Centre) playing art house material in order to allow them to upgrade their facilities, the main focus of the consortium was funneling funds to support the development of new art house cinemas in Dublin (the **Light House**, which opened in 2008) and Galway (the Pálás, which opened in 2018).

More ambitious supports for film and film culture were curtailed by the post-2008 economic crash, which saw the Arts Council's budget cut by more than a quarter from €83 million in 2007 to €56.7 million in 2014. Spending under the heading of cultural cinema (directly supporting exhibition venues), which had totaled €1.2 million in 2008, was entirely cut. The single-largest film-related recipient of Arts Council Funding, the IFI saw its grant fall from €936,000 in 2008 to €750,000 in 2015 (though this still accounted for approximately 20 percent of the IFI's total income). Funding for the three largest film festivals fell from €551,000 to €400,000 in the same period, while funding for some smaller festivals was entirely withdrawn. Even more severe cuts hit funding to **Filmbase** and the Galway and Cork Film Centers, which saw aggregate funding of €630,000 in 2008 fall to €300,000 by 2015. Direct production funding programs, such as "Splanc!" (in conjunction with RTÉ) and the Reel Art program, have continued to run but often with reduced resources. Thus, although the Reel Art program (run in conjunction with Filmbase and the Dublin International Film Festival) continued to offer up to €80,000 to support documentaries, taking some aspect of the arts as their subject, the number of such awards fell by three in 2008 and by two in 2015. Furthermore, with the close of Filmbase in 2018, the future of even that scheme was in doubt.

AS IF I AM NOT THERE (2010). *As If I Am Not There* is a drama film written and directed by Juanita Wilson. Adapted from Slavenka Drakulić's 1999 novel of the same name, the film is set during the Balkan wars of the 1990s and offers a harrowing portrait of rape and sexual exploitation based on a true story. Shot in the Serbo-Croat language, the film was selected as the Irish entry for the Best Foreign Language Film at the 84th **Academy Awards**, but it did not make the final short list.

The film features Macedonian actress Nataša Petrović (who had to learn Serbo-Croat for the role) as Samira: a young middle-class woman from Sarajevo who has taken a job as a teacher in a rural village, even though she has been told it places her personal safety in danger because of its proximity to the Bosnian civil war. Not long after she has settled, she and the other women of the town are rounded up by Bosnian troops while all the men are shot. Soon after, Samira is gang-raped by soldiers in the prison camp where they are held while the other women are likewise made sex slaves. Samira is confronted by stark and morally complex choices in order to survive.

Following her Oscar-nominated short film *The Door* (2008), Wilson set about bringing Drakulić's highly personal novel to the screen as her debut feature, having optioned it some years earlier. Emboldened by her success in directing *The Door* in Russian—and stepping outside the bounds of what has been traditionally understood as "Irish" cinema—she decided to direct the feature herself with more than €600,000 of development and production finance assistance from the **Irish Film Board**.

A compelling central performance from Petrović and sensitive direction and strong visuals from Irish cinematographer Tim Fleming combine to produce a compelling and moving portrait of the vicissitudes of war in contemporary Europe. The film makes an important if deeply disturbing contribution to representations of the 1990s Balkan wars and enlarges conceptions of the function and focus of national cinema in a European context.

ASSOCIATION OF INDEPENDENT PRODUCERS. *See* SCREEN PRODUCERS IRELAND.

ATTRACTA **(1983).** Based on William Trevor's short story of the same name and adapted by the author, this film is considered a high point of director **Kieran Hickey**'s career, following his equally accomplished *A Child's Voice* (1978). The veteran stage and screen actress Wendy Hiller, who won an Oscar for her performance in *Separate Tables*, was cast in the central role of the Protestant spinster teacher who visits the grave of a Belfast victim of violence, evoking memories of her own. The strong supporting cast includes Kate Thompson, **John Kavanagh**, and Deirdre Donnelly. This is an unusual and quietly powerful meditation on the Troubles told from a unique point of view.

B

THE BARGAIN SHOP **(1982).** The film tells the story of Billy (**Garrett Keogh**), who embraces the new commercialized Dublin by trashing his antique shop in favor of a franchised bargain-basement enterprise. The story, directed by **Johnny Gogan**, could be read as an allegory around the nascent Irish film industry and its need to craft its unique voice rather than nakedly pursuing commercial goals. This is expressed by several characters in the film who fight a rearguard action against the inevitability of "regeneration and progress," which have no meaning or real worth beyond promoting the sale of cheap, mass-produced imports.

The specifics of the somewhat underdeveloped narrative include a conspiracy to siphon money to a corrupt planning official to allow extensive rezoning for a massive and lucrative high-rise project orchestrated by Jim (**Brendan Gleeson**), the well-dressed golf-playing businessman who pulls the strings from his rooftop office. The attempt to save the bargain shop and the neighborhood is complicated by a growing romantic attachment between Billy's new assistant, Maria (**Emer McCourt**), and Packy (Stuart Graham), who pontificates on the Troubles. This subplot appears at odds with the main narrative. Nevertheless, the ending of the film, as the shop front is pulled down, remains enticingly enigmatic.

BARRETT, GERARD (1987–). Gerard Barrett's first two feature films—*Pilgrim Hill* (2013) and *Glassland* (2014)—propelled the young writer/director to the forefront of the "millennial generation" of Irish filmmakers. A native of rural County Kerry, Barrett demonstrated clear potential with his debut, *The Valley of Knockanure*, an assured 35-minute film based on a popular ballad detailing the assassination of three Irish Republican Army Volunteers in his native district during the Irish Civil War. Made for just €1,500, the film's tiny budget belied strong performances by the male leads (Gerard Kearney, David Coakley, and Liam Burke), a strong sense of time and place, and an oblique cinematic style that avoided the clichés associated with Irish historical subjects. These elements were also central to Barrett's widely celebrated debut feature, *Pilgrim Hill*, which centered on an unmarried and socially isolated middle-aged farmer, Jimmy Walsh (Joe Mullins), whose life consists of looking after his aging father and the family farm. The film's episodic structure follows Jimmy's banal daily routines and a series of crises that threaten to overwhelm him. Inspired by Barrett's bachelor farmer neighbors and shot in his native northern Kerry, the film was also self-funded and made for an astonishingly low budget of €4,500. While several commentators bemoaned *Pilgrim Hill*'s perceived lack of story, its documentary-like attention to character and setting, and its portrait of widely acknowledged but rarely represented rural social issues, the film garnered widespread media attention and praise in Ireland. In fact, the film's lack of a clear narrative arc was key to its originality, formally reflecting the inertia of its protagonist's condition. It is tempting also to read the film in light of the period of austerity and national self-doubt that arose from the collapse of the Celtic Tiger: its setting in rural Ireland being both a return to traditional settings and themes and an entirely contemporary image of (masculine) emotional and economic fragility.

Eager to stretch himself beyond familiar themes and settings (and following **Lenny Abrahamson**'s lead in flipping the traditional rural–urban binary in his first two features), Barrett's second feature, *Glassland* (2014), was set in suburban Dublin and offered a grim portrayal of working-class lives on the edge. Clearly ambitious to reach beyond the boundaries of Irish cinema and audiences, Barrett cast (Australian) Toni Collette and (British) Will Poulter as well as rising Irish star **Jack Reynor** in this harrowing and tightly focused story of alcohol addiction and filial love. With a narrative again pared back to the borders of coherence, *Glassland* reconfigured *Pilgrim Hill*'s dramatic structure in an urban setting in which a son (Reynor) looks after his chronically alcoholic and emotionally crippled mother while making ends meet by means of an underdeveloped criminal subplot. In contrast to the preceding film, the child is here imagined as a more confident and capable figure who moves between public and private spaces with stoic endurance. While the film's conclusion again largely failed to satisfy, it impresses overall on the level of commitment to its central characters, recalling the highly wrought cinema exemplified by John Cassavettes's early work.

For his third feature, Barrett adapted American writer Susannah Cahalan's memoir *Brain on Fire* (2016), dealing with a rare autoimmune disease, with a starry international cast that included Chloë Grace Moretz, Richard Armitage, and Carrie-Anne Moss. Despite its ambition, however, the film failed to gain traction among critics or audiences. Perhaps because of this, he returned to local themes with the highly topical though underdeveloped *Limbo* (2017), dealing with a single mother and daughter who find themselves homeless and living in temporary accommodations. After a single, late-night screening at the Galway Film Fleadh (Festival), the film disappeared (and is absent from the director's Internet Movie Database profile), although its themes were subsequently taken up by the Roddy Doyle–scripted **Rosie** (2018). *Smalltown*, a three-part miniseries for **Radio Telefís Éireann**, was more successful. Revisiting the themes of his first two features, it again centers on the burden of filial duty: the personal cost of responsibility to one's parent and the isolation this engenders. Once again, this is a story of a son, Conor (Charlie Kelly), who is initially urged to leave his rural home by his father (**Pat Shortt**) and mother (Pauline O'Driscoll) to head to London but is then forced to return when his mother gets sick. It follows his struggle to readapt to his hometown and the changes that have taken place while he's been away. Chaneling aspects of Eugene O'Brien's landmark *Pure Mule* (2005), *Smalltown* may not have been the quantum career leap that Barrett aspired to, but it reinforced his talent as a storyteller of deep empathy. While his best work centers on a single, reconfigured theme—the self-sacrificing son looking after the incapacitated father/mother—he has handled it thus far with empathy and formal ambition. Clearly ambitious to move to a bigger stage, it remains to be seen how he can extend his undoubted talent for character, casting, and mood to the international settings he craves.

BARRY LYNDON (1975). This stylish, picaresque, historical costume drama is based on the novel by William Makepeace Thackeray and is heavily influenced by 18th-century painting whose careful use of light in representing both interiors and exteriors is echoed by the dreamy cinematography of John Ascott. (The film's attention to visual detail was rewarded with three **Academy Awards**: Cinematography, Costumes, and Production Design.) The blurb for the narrative teases, "How does an Irish lad without prospects become part of the 18th-century English nobility?" Although many find Ryan O'Neal's imitation of an Irish accent somewhat flawed, O'Neal, in the title role of Redmond Barry, is surrounded by a strong cast of Irish and British actors as the story moves from Ireland to Europe and the Seven Years' War. Barry is an Irish rogue who falls in love with Nora, already matched with an English officer. Fearful of losing a "good match" for their daughter, however, her family tricks Barry into fleeing his home, inadvertently sending him on a series of adventures that help him ascend socially to eventually become, for a period at least, an established member of the French aristocracy.

Film lore has it that the shoot in the Waterford area was a very secret affair, with cult director Stanley Kubrick overseeing every aspect of the production. He is said to have rewritten his screenplay constantly, often while shooting took place, and take after take was made of various scenes. Consequently, however, the viewer is treated to the beauty of several exterior battle scenes that are choreographed using natural light that put many contemporary special effects–driven epic battle films to shame. The film's leisurely pace, coupled with a length of more than three hours and a requirement that the viewer carefully follow the narrative's many twists and turns, contributed to its box office failure. Nevertheless, the film remains one of Kubrick's lesser-known cinematic treasures.

BECKETT, SAMUEL (1906–1989). Widely celebrated Irish playwright and novelist, Beckett won the Nobel Prize for Literature in 1969 and spoke often of his admiration of silent/slapstick film comedy, eventually working with Buster Keaton in the production of *Film* (1965). Directed by Alan Schneider, Keaton starred as "O" (after Charlie Chaplin declined the role), a character who seeks to evade the gaze of "E" (the camera) and thus to dissolve his selfhood. Described by Beckett himself as an "interesting failure," the experimental, dialogue-free work received wildly mixed reviews: while philosopher Giles Deleuze regarded it as among the greatest films made, others regarded it as incomprehensible.

In 1999 and 2000, Michael Colgan of Dublin's Gate Theatre coordinated a major project initiated by **Radio Telefís Éireann** and **Channel 4** to film all 19 of Beckett's plays. Although some purists described this as a sacrilege, the producers sought to broaden their appeal of the plays beyond the more rarefied highbrow theatrical experience, using advantages of film, such as the close-up and more natural speech patterns, that are more difficult to reproduce for audiences in large auditoriums. More than 11 hours of drama were filmed in a year, at a cost of around €5 million, by an impressive cast of international filmmakers. Adaptations by local heroes **Neil Jordan** and **Damien O'Donnell** of "Not I" and "What Were" were interspersed with work from Anthony Minghella (*Play*), Patricia Rozema (*Happy Days*), Atom Egoyan (*Krapp's Last Tape*), David Mamet (*Catastrophe*), Karel Reisz (*Act with Words*), and even conceptual artist Damien Hirst's 45-second take on *Breathe*. Yet despite this array of filmic talent, what emerges most strikingly from any assessment of the adaptations in aggregate is the manner in which the original texts impose themselves on and, to an extent, defy the filmic form, remaining ineluctably identifiable as works of theater.

Less literally, Beckett's influence can be clearly felt in **Lenny Abrahamson**'s blackly comic *Adam and Paul* (2004), in which, after *Waiting for Godot*, two heroin addicts wander around Dublin waiting for their fix to show up (which it does, with fatal consequences).

BERGIN, PATRICK (1951–). Bergin was born in Dublin, the middle child in a family of five (older brother Emmet was a noted television actor). His father was a member of the Labour Party and was a senator during the 1950s. He studied English and drama at the university and for a brief period worked as a teacher in London. While in London, he established his own theater company, initially working offstage but increasingly as an actor. His appearance in a short produced under the auspices of the National Film and Television School in England led him into screen acting. This in turn led to roles in *The Courier*, opposite **Gabriel Byrne**, and in television miniseries *Act of Betrayal* (1988) and *Taffin* (1988), opposite **Pierce Brosnan**.

By the early 1990s, he was rapidly becoming Ireland's best-known international actor. Following a lead role as Victorian explorer Richard Burton opposite **Fiona Shaw** in Bob Rafelson's *Mountains of the Moon* (1990), he appeared opposite Julia Roberts in the stylish thriller *Sleeping with the Enemy* (1991), playing her psychotic husband. The film was a major hit and remains his best-known role. A series of lead roles in film and television productions followed: *Robin Hood* (1991), *Patriot Games* (1992), *and Map of the Human Heart* (1993).

Since then, his star power has waned. He found a niche playing Victorian characters, such as Victor Frankenstein in *Frankenstein* (1992), a police inspector hunting Jack the Ripper in *The Ripper* (1997), and the lead role in an adaptation of Arthur Conan Doyle's *The Lost World* (1998). He returned to Irish film with *Angela Mooney Dies Again* in 1996 and played the key detective role in *When the Sky Falls* (2000) and an Irish Republican Army member in *Silent Grace* (2001). While occasionally playing in theater (playing the role of Edward Carson opposite **Adrian Dunbar**'s Oscar Wilde in a revival of Ulick O'Connor's *A Trinity of Two* in 2007), Bergin's later career has been confined to lower-budget U.S. and U.K. genre work, such as *Cage* (2016), *We Still Steal the Old Way* (2017), and Michael Flatley's vanity project *Blackbird* (2018), and television, such as the BBC soap *East Enders* (2017–2018), **TV3**'s *Red Rock*, and the TG4 drama *Fir Bolg*.

BEST (2000). A rare Irish sports-themed feature film, Best was cowritten by director **Mary McGuckian** and her partner **John Lynch**, who is possibly miscast in the lead role of George Best, arguably the greatest soccer player Ireland ever produced. The film traces Best's rise but also his failure to fulfill his early promise and his decline into alcoholism (which contributed to his death in December 2005). However, it offers little insight into Best's struggles with drink, the failure of those around him to intervene, or the aftermath of his high-flying career with Manchester United. Despite its miscasting and underrealized screenplay, Best himself was apparently quite happy with how the film portrayed him both on and off the field.

BINCHY, MAEVE (1939–2012). During a long and prolific writing career, Maeve Binchy became Ireland's best-selling novelist nationally and internationally and arguably did more than anyone to influence a generation of popular writers and foster a now well-established Irish "chick-lit" publishing industry. While she sold around 40 million books, surprisingly few of her 16 best-selling novels or 11 short-story collections have been adapted for cinema, and only *Circle of Friends* (1995) has made any box office impact. The sprawling scope and inherent "chattiness" of her novels perhaps mitigates against more frequent adaptation, but as *Tara Road* (2005) and *How About You* (2007) demonstrate, Binchy's plots possess an imaginative and generous interest in human foibles that makes for pleasurable (if often conventional) storytelling. While there have been a few adaptations for Irish TV, her general absence seems an oversight and one that would not occur in countries with a stronger commitment to drama on the part of national broadcasters.

BIRTHISTLE, EVA (1974–). Birthistle is unusual among Irish actresses in that most of her experience is on-screen rather than onstage, where previously she has made only a handful of appearances. A native of Bray, County Wicklow, she moved at age 14 with her family to Derry, where, though raised a Catholic, she attended a mainly Protestant school. From there, she went on to study at the Gaiety School of Acting in Dublin. On graduating, she took on a number of film roles before achieving domestic stardom through a stint in the rural soap *Glenroe*. She left the security of the soap after less than two years, a decision justified by her subsequent success.

Birthistle secured a variety of leading roles from the outset of her career. Her debut in **Alan Gilsenan**'s *All Souls' Day* (1997) as a mentally disturbed young woman with an even more psychotic boyfriend was a minor tour de force. This was followed by major roles in *Drinking Crude* (1997), *Saltwater* (2000), *Timbuktu* (2005, again with Gilsenan), and **Neil Jordan**'s *Breakfast on Pluto* (2005).

Having moved to the United Kingdom in her 20s, she began to appear in a range of one-off roles in mainstream British television dramas, including *Silent Witness*, *Holby City*, and both retellings of the Bloody Sunday story (*Sunday* and *Bloody Sunday*). In 2004, she was awarded an Irish Film and Television award for her role in Ken Loach's *Ae Fond Kiss* and was named a Shooting Star by the European Film Academy.

Although still occasionally appearing in Irish films—*Wake Wood* (2009), *Life's a Breeze* (2013), *Noble* (2014), and *Brooklyn* (2015) (in the role of Georgina)—she is now seen mainly in leading roles in British TV drama, such as the police procedural *Waking the Dead* (2000) and the somewhat gung-ho actioner *Strike Back* (2010) and, more recently (2015–2017), as Hild in the Saxon/Viking era-set *The Last Kingdom* for the BBC. These roles share a certain steely character: physically petite, Birthistle projects a ruthless determination that, though hinting at psychological frailty, reflects the driven nature of her roles. This was perhaps less evident in the role for which Irish audiences will know her best: the mother of a missing child in **Radio Telefís Éireann**'s controversial 2014 drama *Amber*.

THE BISHOP'S STORY (1993). The relationship between *The Bishop's Story* and **Bob Quinn**'s earlier film ***Budawanny*** (1987) is difficult to explain. *Budawanny* (literally "priest's penis") relates the tale of a parish priest (**Donal McCann**) on the western seaboard who has a relationship with a woman (Maggie Fegan) he may or may not have known previously in London. She becomes pregnant, and the priest confesses his impending fatherhood to his flock ("Soon you will have another reason to call me father") but seeks to stay on as parish priest. The woman, unwilling to be cast in the role of a Magdalene on the island, departs suddenly for the mainland, leaving the priest to confront his loss of faith.

The Bishop's Story (which Quinn has described as the finished version of the story) retells this story, using most of the footage from *Budawanny* but adding new material: the priest, now promoted to an atheistic bishop (McCann, reprising his earlier role behind a thick beard), offers his own retrospective and highly cynical narration of the tale to a younger priest. This effectively replaces the commentary from *Budawanny* delivered by the priest's bishop (Peadar Lamb), an interior monologue that is interspersed with the narrative of the film. However, both narration and commentary in the two films serve the same purpose, expressing a conviction that the Church's real function is social rather than spiritual, the theocracy acting more as a bureaucracy.

There are other changes besides different narrators, however. *Budawanny* was shot in black and white without sound: in effect, a silent movie with only very occasional recourse to intertitles. These strictures, although prompted by a limited budget rather than deliberate intent, suited some of the themes of *Budawanny* admirably; the backdrop against which the story unfolds—Irish rural culture and the economic problems faced by the Gaeltacht areas—occasionally comes to the foreground over the central narrative. In fact, the grainy feel of the footage recalls nothing as much as Robert Flaherty's ***Man of Aran***, which shares these thematic concerns. This served to give *Budawanny* a uniquely Gaelic appearance: the frugality of the people and the barren quality of the landscape were reflected by the absence of Hollywood-style sweeping camera shots and special effects. It also made it a fascinating experiment in moviemaking. Denied the facility of sound to recount the tale, Quinn risked reliance on older cinematic codes, including music, montage, and so on, and succeeded in communicating some extraordinarily complex ideas and sentiments. *The Bishop's Story* takes the *Budawanny* footage and sepia-tints it, emphasizing its status as a memory. It also partly revoices it: ghostly disembodied voices emerge from an aural gloom when characters speak, the echoes again emphasizing the operation of memory.

Indeed, sound plays a crucial role in both films through the dominance of Roger Doyle's largely electronic score. Music was one of the driving forces of *Budawanny*, a virtually silent film, directing the audiences' attention as efficiently as a pointing hand: moods were created, conflicts expressed via sweeping soundscapes and clashing melodies. In *The Bishop's Story*, the same sound track is used to similar effect, although the failure to update the score's electronic instrumentation simply serves to date the film.

BLACK, CATHAL (1952–). Cathal Black grew up in Phibsboro, on Dublin's north side, where as a child he encountered a local myth of a man with a movie camera setting off explosions up by the Royal Canal for a war movie he was making. Intrigued, Black began to explore filmmaking and even before leaving school at age 16 was experimenting with Standard 8 film. This led to his joining **Radio Telefís Éireann** (RTÉ), where he was employed as a cameraman. Finding this too restricting, he left after 16 months, at which point he met **Joe Comerford**, with whom he collaborated on *Withdrawal*, a stark look at the culture of heroin use in Dublin.

One of the earliest recipients of **Arts Council** funding, Black made his solo debut in 1976 with *Wheels*, a 20-minute adaptation of a somber John McGahern short story, "Nightlines." The story follows a boy who returns to his parents' small farm only to escape again to the city to flee their suffocating expectations. In interviews, Black has described the film as similar to his own relationship with his father, who disapproved of Black's decision to leave a safe job at RTÉ for the insecurities of working in film.

His first widely seen short, *Our Boys* (1981), is a powerful examination of the abuse of students by the Christian Brothers. It uses archival footage of the 1932 Eucharistic Congress in Dublin and was made shortly after Pope John Paul II's 1979 visit to Ireland. Because of its controversial subject matter, it was not aired by the national broadcaster (RTÉ) until 1994. The film was considered ahead of its time in Ireland for its use of the drama-documentary format, mixing footage of interviews with former Christian Brother pupils with dramatizations of the treatment meted out to them.

Pigs (1984) was Black's first feature-length film and offered a powerful evocation of 1980s Dublin poverty and a portrait of a motley crew of (mostly male) squatters in a large decaying Georgian house. As an early and atypical example of social realism in Irish film, the representation was a long way from the usual romantic evocation of rural Ireland.

With the closure of the **Irish Film Board** in 1987, Black found himself unable to secure sufficient funding to allow him to continue directing, and he became a lecturer on film production at the College of Commerce (later the Dublin Institute of Technology) in Rathmines. In an interview, he has stated that the enforced sabbatical from filming shaped the way he would subsequently approach film, making him more patient and allowing him to imbue his work with a hitherto unavailable sensitivity.

With the revival of the Film Board in 1993, Black might reasonably have anticipated that he could rely on support for new features, and initially this was the case. Black directed two Film Board–funded features in 1995 and 1998. The first, **Korea** (again based on a short story by John McGahern), was well received, winning both the Jury Prize at the Amiens Film Festival and the Asta Nielsen Award at the Copenhagen Film Festival. This paved the way for the more ambitious *Love and Rage* (1998), a sumptuously photographed gothic tale starring Greta Scacchi as a wealthy liberal Scottish woman living on Achill Island at the end of the 19th century who begins an affair with her newly employed manager, James (a pre–James Bond Daniel Craig). Growing suspicious of his motives, she has him fired, and a tale of violence and revenge ensues. The narrative had a storied pedigree: it was based on *The Playboy and the Yellow Lady* (1986) by James Carney, itself based on events that took place at Valley House, Achill Island, in 1894 that were also the inspiration behind J. M. Synge's *The Playboy of the Western World.*

Remarkably, though Black has sought to remain active in fiction features since then and has developed a number of projects, his output as a director has been limited to documentary and short fiction films. Notable are *Learning Gravity* (2008), a glorious but largely unseen documentary about the Irish American poet Thomas Lynch, who combines his artistic pursuits with a career as a mortician, and the short film *Butterfly* (2014), which explores the damaged youth of Teri (Antonia Campbell-Hughes), a graphic designer convicted of theft.

Black's work is character driven, focused on psychologically damaged individuals who personify the impact of a wider social violence: the lead male roles in **Korea**, directly and indirectly twisted by the long reach of the Irish Civil War, exemplify this. He is now a member of **Aosdána**, an elite group of artists recognized by the **Arts Council** of Ireland as having made an outstanding contribution to the Irish creative arts.

BLACK, DONALD TAYLOR (1951–). Black's position as creative director of the National Film School (2001–2016) saw him directly influence the work of a generation of young Irish filmmakers. However, he preceded and interspersed his career in film education with the production of one of the largest bodies of documentary work of any Irish filmmaker.

After graduating from Trinity College (where he was involved with the University Players), Black won an **Arts Council** bursary to train as a director at the **Abbey Theatre**. He would subsequently direct more than half a dozen theater productions by writers as diverse as Pat Ingoldsby and Leland Bardwell at the Abbey and at the Focus and Project Arts Centre in the late 1970s. He then moved to work as programmer at the Cork Film Festival and, in 1982, on the Celtic Film Festival.

While working on the last of these, he came into contact with John Rane-lagh, the recently appointed commissioning editor for Ireland at **Channel 4**. When Black began to devise his debut film (a profile of **Liam O'Leary**), he contacted Ranelagh, who offered a presale (with the proviso that an experi-enced executive producer, **Kieran Hickey**, be attached to the project) that, along with funds from the British Film Institute, **Radio Telefís Éireann** (RTÉ), and the **Irish Film Board**, completed the budget.

The resulting film, *At the Cinema Palace: Liam O'Leary* (1983), marked the beginning of a sequence of works in the mid-1980s focusing on cultural figures from Ireland's past: actor/comedian Jimmy O'Dea, author/doctor (and inspiration for Buck Mulligan in James Joyce's *Ulysses*) Oliver St. John Gogarty, and Sam Thompson, the leftist Protestant shipyard worker and play-wright. A concern with arts and culture would continue to mark his later works: *From Ballybeg to Broadway* (1993) traces the life cycle of the Brian Friel play *Wonderful Tennessee* as it transferred from the Abbey Stage to Broadway. *Dear Boy—The Story of Michael MacLiammoir* (1999) would trace the career of the cofounder of the Gate Theatre and his reinvention of himself as a scion of the Irish arts world.

Faced with the challenge of summarizing 100 years of filmmaking activity for the 1996 Centenary of Cinema celebrations in *Irish Cinema: Ourselves Alone?*, he and **Kevin Rockett** constructed a text that was as focused on the lengthy political failure to support an indigenous film industry as it was on the texts actually produced in Ireland. That political engagement is more overt in his later works: *Hearts and Souls* (1995) gained remarkable access to the antidivorce campaign in the lead-up to the 1995 Marriage Referendum, while *Skin in the Game* (2012) traces the response of Irish artists to the social and economic fallout from the post-2008 financial crash. Even his 1997 four-part series for RTÉ, *The Joy*, went beyond a straightforward exploration of the day-to-day workings of Mountjoy Prison in Dublin to offer a much broader critique of the Irish penal system.

Black has adopted an eclectic range of approaches to these subjects. Al-though his earlier works lean to the expository mode with their combination of talking heads and archival footage, the move to an observational approach in *Down for the Match* (the film focuses on the 36 hours of preparations for the All-Ireland Senior Football Championship by supporters rather than the game itself) presaged later explorations of that form. The often comedic effect of *Hearts and Souls* is amplified by a cinema verité approach with Black's camera dispassionately observing the antidivorce campaign as their best-laid plans go awry. By contrast, *The Joy* blurred the boundaries between the observational and interactive modes, combining a neutral gaze within the prison with direct interviews with both inmates and prison wardens offering personal insights into the tensions created by negotiating the literally and figuratively cramped penal confines.

Along with the late Kieran Hickey, Black was responsible for establishing a producers' training course under the auspices of the Irish Film Board in 1983, acted as chair of DOCUMENTARY, a MEDIA '92 program to channel EU funding into creative documentary production, and in 2014 was appointed vice chair of GEECT, the European Grouping of Film and Television Schools.

***BLACK ICE* (2013).** Having focused on disaffected youth in 1970s Dublin, director **Johnny Gogan** turns his attention to their contemporary equivalents in the border counties of Donegal. A complex narrative structure sees Alice (Jane McGrath) return to her hometown to attend the funeral of her brother before flashbacks recount how he came to pass away. Alice, from a well-to-do local family but bored of the limited scope for entertainment offered by her locale, falls in with the boy-racer set. She is particularly drawn to Jimmy (Killian Scott), a Skyline-driving bad boy with professional rally ambitions who, when he isn't showing off his drifting skills at a local quarry, moonlights as a "sweeper" for a local cross-border fuel-smuggling operation, checking that roads are clear of police presence before the merchandise is moved. Jane finds herself increasingly drawn into his clandestine activities with ultimately tragic consequences.

Compared to the nine-figure budgets underwriting obvious Hollywood antecedents such as the *Fast and Furious* franchise, *Black Ice* is somewhat underpowered. The early racing sequences are delivered with verve but can hardly match the visceral impact of better-resourced counterparts. Director Gogan seeks to compensate by emphasizing plotlines about police investigations and corrupt businessmen from the middle of the second act, but this distracts from the arguably more interesting Alice–Jimmy relationship. That there remains an interesting film to be made about the mainly masculine speed culture of the Irish Midlands, perhaps one that precisely reflects on the cultural influence of Hollywood, is suggested by the fact that *Black Ice* is at its most interesting when it emphasizes the locally specific aspects of the street-racing genre. Nevertheless, this is an ambitious effort to give representation to a marginal and otherwise unrepresented subculture and place—a borderland in both senses.

BLINDER FILMS. Director Kieron J. Walsh (***When Brendan Met Trudy*** [2000]) initially established Blinder Limited in 2005 as a vehicle for his commercial production work. However, within a year, he partnered with Katie Holly, former head of production at **Treasure Films**, to establish Blinder Films to develop drama and documentary projects. Together, they quickly established a diversified production slate, working on television comedy, indigenous feature production, and international coproductions along with high-profile theatrical documentaries. The company produced Conor Horgan's postapocalyptic *One Hundred Mornings* (2009) via the **Irish Film Board**'s Catalyst scheme and **Tom Hall**'s *Sensation* (2010) with **Domhnall Gleeson**. These were followed by increasing success with coproduction partnerships, commencing with the ultra-low-budget *Come on Eileen* (2010), Whit Stillman's Jane Austen adaptation *Love and Friendship* (2016), and the Chanya Button–directed *Vita and Virginia* (2018) starring Gemma Arterton and Elizabeth Debecki as the titular Vita Sackville-West and Virginia Woolf.

Although Walsh continued to work on projects outside the Blinder banner (notably television dramas *Raw* [2007] for **Radio Telefís Éireann** [RTÉ] and *Vexed* [2012] for the BBC), he has increasingly used the company as a vehicle for his own directorial endeavors. These include an adaptation of Lisa McGee's Derry-set *Jump* (2012), the RTÉ Web series *Rapt* (2015), and several series of David McSavage's controversial RTÉ sketch comedy *The Savage Eye* (2009–2014), which he also cocreated. Blinder also simultaneously produced RTÉ's acclaimed revival of the *Irish Pictorial Weekly* (2012–2016) sketch comedy.

In the field of feature documentary, Holly and Walsh repartnered with Conor Horgan for his critically and commercially successful bio-doc of Irish drag queen Pantibliss, *The Queen of Ireland*, the release of which coincided with Ireland's introduction of marriage equality, allowing same-sex couples to marry, in 2015. The company has also developed an ongoing relationship with director Sophie Fiennes, who has directed *The Pervert's Guide to Cinema* (2006), made in collaboration with philosopher Slavoj Žižek, and its successor, *The Pervert's Guide to Ideology* (2012), along with the bio-doc *Grace Jones: Bloodlight and Bami* (2016).

Blinder has avoided reliance on any one source of finance by carefully assembling a wide portfolio of work that includes two series of the RTÉ prime-time drama *Striking Out* (2017–) starring **Amy Huberman**. Walsh remains a very active and award-winning director of commercials, while Holly has augmented her producer duties with the chairmanship of Filmbase; with her active involvement with the Women in Film and TV group, which seeks gender equity within the industry; and as a board member of the **Irish Film Board**/Screen Ireland.

BLOODY SUNDAY **(2002).** Produced for the 30th anniversary of the awful events of 1972 that were a major turn for the worse in the Troubles, writer/director Paul Greengrass's film attempts to capture the "fly on the wall" reality of a pivotal day in the life of the Northern Ireland when the British army shot 13 people during a march protesting internment without trial.

Viceral, narratively sophisticated, and powerfully acted, the film won the Golden Bear award at the Berlin Film Festival and the World Cinema award at the Sundance Film Festival.

The drama-documentary used ex-soldiers, even paratroopers, who knew how to perform their role, alongside some of the actual families who were affected by the original atrocity. Filmed at a cost of $5 million, it was shot in Dublin's Ballymun high-rise estate, which accurately replicated the original location. The movie cuts rapidly between scenes involving a number of major characters, most particularly Protestant Member of Parliament Ivan Cooper (**James Nesbitt**), who is leading the march. Other characters include a 17-year-old Gerry Donaghy (Declan Duddy), who was previously arrested for rioting, and Major General Ford (Tim Pigott-Smith), who tells Brigadier MacLellan (Nicholas Farrell) what to do on the day. It is from their various perspectives that we see the events of the day unfold. Although the film is careful to avoid slavish subscription to any one of the various theories about who was ultimately responsible for the killings, the filmmakers leave no doubt as to the culpability of the soldiers and their commanders.

Bloody Sunday marked a watershed in the civil rights organization in Northern Ireland, influenced by Martin Luther King Jr. in the United States and the peaceful revolution headed by Mahatma Gandhi in India. Made in the aftermath of the Good Friday Agreement, the film seeks to remember the origins of the conflict before the "men of violence" on all sides took center stage.

BLOOM (2003). Starring **Stephen Rea** as Leopold Bloom, Angeline Ball as his wife Mollie, and **Hugh O'Conor** as Stephen Dedalus, Sean Walsh's film adapts **James Joyce**'s *Ulysses* and steers the viewer through many of the key episodes to make it more accessible while retaining some of its cross-references and nonlinear appeal. In a highly personal project more than 10 years in development (Walsh wrote, produced, and directed the film), Walsh went through hundreds of drafts attempting to distill the essence of Joyce's novel and, in particular, to bring to life its three central characters. Thus, the film begins and ends with Molly Bloom's stream of consciousness and, in a departure from Joyce, intercuts the stories of the two central male figures from the outset. Although lacking the finesse of **John Huston**'s *The Dead*, this is an intelligent, entertaining, and all-too-infrequent adaptation of Joyce and of the novel described by Eisenstein as "the bible of the new cinema," following the only other attempt, by **Joseph Strick** in 1967.

BOGWOMAN (1997). This poignant tale follows the experiences of Maureen (Rachel Dowling), a young unmarried mother from an island off Donegal who moves to Derry at the close of the 1950s to marry her boyfriend

Barry (Peter Mullan). Written and directed by Tom Collins, the film uses Maureen's perspective—that of a Catholic living in Derry—to trace the emergence of the Troubles as they developed during the 1960s. The title is an allusion to the Catholic Bogside area of Derry, where Maureen and her family live, as well as, perhaps, to Seamus Heaney's series of bog-body poems about the conflict, inspired by the Iron Age sacrificial corpses discovered in Irish bogs in which Heaney found "symbols and images adequate to our predicament."

BOLGER, SARAH (1991–). Accompanying her younger sister to open-call auditions for **Jim Sheridan**'s *In America*, Sarah Bolger found herself cast (age 10) as the wise-beyond-her-years daughter Christy, delivering a sensitive and mature performance that grounded an often abstract and impressionistic film. While her cute-as-a-button sister Emma grabbed all the media attention on that occasion, Sarah would slowly but surely build a steady reputation among casting agents for her photogenic and commanding performances in front of the camera. Deciding to finish her studies before pursuing acting, Bolger's career has so far been a slow burn (particularly in comparison to her near contemporary **Saoirse Ronan**), but along with a number of notable performances in feature films such *Tara Road* (2005), *Stormbreaker* (2006), and *The Spiderwick Chronicles* (2008), the Showtime series *The Tudors* offered her a chance to extend her range and profile, and she delivered a memorable Princess Mary Tudor over 23 episodes.

Her career highlights since have mixed young adult–oriented films and quality U.S. TV, with *The Moth Diaries* (2011) and *As Cool As I Am* (2013) being notable examples of the former, while the ABC fairy-tale drama *Once upon a Time* (2012–2015) has ensured both mainstream public recognition and subsequent roles in shows such as *Mayans M.C.* and *Counterpart* (both 2018).

BOORMAN, JOHN (1933–). Born in London, Boorman lived through the Blitz (an experience that would later inform his 1987 film *Hope and Glory*). He joined Independent Television News in 1955 and became an editor before moving to a commercial station, Southern Television, in 1957 as an editor/director. In 1961, he moved to work with the BBC, producing and directing a series of well-received documentaries that gathered good ratings and the ambitious one-off drama *The Quarry*, a thinly veiled first outing for Boorman's King Arthur obsession. This led to an offer to direct a film featuring the popular band the Dave Clark Five. The resulting *Catch Us If You Can* (1965) launched Boorman's feature career, although it wasn't until the release of the nihilistic *Point Blank* (1967) that his star really began to rise. He has subsequently remained one of Britain's most interesting directors, working on a diverse range of material, from *Deliverance* (1972) and *Zardoz* (1973) to *Hope and Glory* (1985), and finally achieving a lifetime ambition to film the Arthur legend *Excalibur* (1981).

Apart from such achievements, Boorman has been a key figure in the Irish film industry for several decades. While editing *Leo the Last* (1969) at **Ardmore Studios**, he and his wife fell in love with the Wicklow countryside and decided to buy a vacation cottage. The former rectory that they purchased in Annamoe, County Wicklow, became their home. Although Boorman's marriage subsequently ended, he has continued to live in Annamoe ever since, and its surroundings were the setting for his 1991 television meditation *I Dreamt I Woke Up*. He has subsequently shot many of his films in Ireland, regardless of their nominal location, and over the past three decades, he has been the most consistent customer of **Ardmore Studios**. *Deliverance* was edited at Ardmore, *Zardoz* was shot there (and on location in the Wicklow Mountains), and the studios were used for model shots and the editing of *Exorcist II: The Heretic* (1976).

Boorman was thus the obvious choice as chairman when the studios reopened as the **National Film Studios of Ireland** in 1975. However, although he was not involved with the day-to-day operation of the studios, his association with them did not endear him to independent Irish filmmakers. Ever since **Louis Marcus**'s seminal 1967 articles on the irrelevance of Ardmore to a putative indigenous industry, Irish filmmakers tended to regard the studios as part of the problem of a misguided state film policy rather than an element of the solution.

This simmering resentment came to the surface as a result of Boorman's mentoring of **Neil Jordan**. Boorman encountered Jordan via the latter's 1976 short-story collection *Nights in Tunisia*. Noting the visual quality of Jordan's writing, Boorman invited him to collaborate on a never-filmed screenplay, *Broken Dream*. Boorman subsequently gave Jordan his first directorial experience, a documentary on the making of Boorman's 1981 production of *Excalibur*.

Excalibur was notable in itself in part because it was the largest production shot in Ireland since ***Ryan's Daughter*** but also because of the opportunity it afforded a whole generation of Irish actors: **Gabriel Byrne**, **Liam Neeson**, and **Ciará n Hinds** all made their feature debuts in the film. With *Excalibur* complete, Boorman was immediately appointed to the newly formed **Irish Film Board** and began working as executive producer on Jordan's first feature, ***Angel***, a condition of **Channel 4**'s agreement to finance the film. However, when the Film Board was still only partially appointed and it awarded a substantial proportion of its initial budget to *Angel*, Boorman was accused by the **Association of Independent Producers** (AIP) of having abused his position on the board. For his part, Boorman argued that he hadn't been present when the decision was made, though he also asserted that, in his view, Angel did deserve Film Board support. The AIP conceded that even a full board might have made the same decision but argued that the optics of the decision-making process remained problematic.

The lasting bitterness engendered by the *Angel* controversy clearly altered Boorman's level of engagement with domestic film politics. The National Film Studios of Ireland were disbanded in April 1982, and Boorman resigned from the Film Board in the same month. Perhaps coincidentally, his use of Ardmore also declined in the 1980s. Both *The Emerald Forest* (1985) and *Hope and Glory* (1987) were shot outside Ireland.

However, at the start of the 1990s, Boorman appeared to reengage with Ireland. He cofounded **Merlin Films** in 1989 and in 1998 made a triumphant return to form with *The General*, a film that won him the Best Director award at the Cannes Film Festival (a year after the Irish Film Institute had presented him with a Lifetime Achievement award). Remarkably, this was his first fiction film explicitly set in Ireland but one that clearly reflected his three decades of living within Irish society. As he entered his 70s, he continued to work on large-scale production with, where possible, Irish technicians and locations. A glance down the crew list of *The Tailor of Panama* (2001), starring **Pierce Brosnan**, reveals myriad Irish names in senior crew positions, and though the film is set in South America, parts of it were shot in Ireland. Similarly, though *Country of My Skull* (2004) was shot in South Africa, the cinematographer was **Seamus Deasy**, by now Boorman's cameraman of choice. In 2006, he completed a second Ireland-set fiction feature, *The Tiger's Tale*, featuring **Brendan Gleeson** in the dual roles of a Celtic Tiger property developer and his doppelgänger twin opposite Kim Cattrall as the businessman's wife. A somewhat clumsy attempt to explore the underbelly of the Celtic Tiger (which would spectacularly implode two years later), the film appeared to represent Boorman's swan song. Despite this, after an eight-year hiatus, he reappeared in 2014 with *Queen and Country*, a sequel to *Hope and Glory*. In 2012, his daughter Katrine directed the bio-doc *Me and Me Dad*, a sensitive portrait that concentrates on communing with the river that runs through his home in Wicklow.

BORSTAL BOY **(2000).** A screen adaptation of Brendan Behan's famous stage play, directed by Peter Sheridan (brother of **Jim Sheridan**), who harbored a long-held but never realized ambition for a biopic on the Dublin playwright. The film follows 16-year-old Behan's (played by Shawn Hatosy) experiences in a British jail after he was arrested for Republican (Irish Republican Army) political activities in Liverpool during World War II. While in prison, he reconsiders his Republican beliefs—or at least the methods he has hitherto assumed were necessary to achieve Republican goals.

THE BOXER **(1997).** Having previously offered one political reading of the Northern Ireland Troubles with his drama on British injustice, *In the Name of the Father*, **Jim Sheridan** here tries to demonstrate the need for creating an alternative to political violence. Danny Flynn (Daniel Day-Lewis) emerges from prison after serving 14 years for carrying out a Provisional Irish Republican Army (PIRA) operation where he came to recognize the limits of political violence. He seeks to create a new family and community based on tolerance and reconciliation using the sport of boxing as a way to unify sectarian communities. Fighting by the (British) Queensbury rules is signaled as the only road to creating a new nonsectarian community. In contrast to this ethical stance, his old IRA commander, Harry (**Gerard McSorley**), wants him to continue with them.

Issues are further complicated by the still-smoldering fires of romance between Danny and Maggie (Emily Watson), daughter of the IRA chief of staff (played with aplomb by Brian Cox). Maggie is a prisoner's wife: though estranged from her IRA-member husband, the rules of Republican community make it impossible for her to be seen to be involved with another man. The issue comes to a head when Maggie's son, furious at the prospect of his mother being taken away from him, burns down the boxing gym that Danny has established with his old coach (Ken Stott). A police murder follows, and the support of official authorities for the nonsectarian boxing club sparks riots—the political grassroots community is not yet ready to support an impartial police force following years of division. Eventually, narrative resolution is achieved as the newly created family can eventually "come home."

BOY EATS GIRL **(2005). Stephen Bradley**'s second feature is a zombie horror-comedy, an apparently odd direction for a director who had aspired to more recognizably art house fare with his debut *Sweety Barrett* (1998). Yet *Boy Eats Girl* is illustrative of a decisive shift in Irish film during the first decade of the new millennium as a number of filmmakers sought to move beyond the themes and tone of 1990s production, the better to reach wider markets and audiences. The eruption of horror as a popular genre can be seen as a relaxing of the concept of "national cinema" at the level of both product and audience.

While the relatively sudden emergence of horror is relatively easy to explain at an industrial level, its textual and cultural meanings have yet to be fully explored. Within such readings, *Boy Eats Girl* has a central place. Drawing on tropes and the anticapitalist subtext of George Romero's seminal zombie movies (*Night of the Living Dead* [1968]), the success of Edgar Wright's *Shaun of the Dead* (2004), and story elements of the black romantic comedy *My Boyfriend's Back* (1993), Bradley's film resituates the genre to the Celtic Tiger suburbs, where local and global are united through mindless consumerism. Scripted by **Derek Landy**, the film's complex plot unfolds with the revival from death of Nathan (David Leon) effected by his mother (Deirdre O'Kane) after he committed suicide following the discovery that the object of his affections (Samantha Mumba) had been on a date with another guy. Once revived, however, he discovers he's a zombie but is determined not to be a force of contagion. As the film's clichéd high school cast succumb to the "invasion," David and Jessica (Mumba) work to overcome the flesh-eating teens and restore normality. One of the film's most memorable scenes is Jessica driving a tractor across open fields, sending body parts flying as she runs down zombies. The image not only is germane to the requirements of the genre but also offers an ironic comment on the restoration of tradition-al Irish (rural) values: ironic because it is a young, biracial woman who is literally and symbolically at the steering wheel.

Ambitions for international audience were fulfilled when, after an initial delay in release due to an Irish censorship ban on the film (quashed on appeal), the film was sold to several territories, including the United States.

***THE BOY FROM MERCURY* (1996).** Harry, an eight-year-old boy grow-ing up in the suburbs of 1960s Dublin, copes with the death of his father by submersing himself in a fantasy world informed by his love for Flash Gordon movie serials in his local cinema. Watched over by his mother (Rita Tushing-ham) and eccentric uncle (Tom Courtenay), Harry slowly comes to terms with the absence of his father, convincing himself that he actually comes from Mercury, whence his true parents will one day return to bring him home. Like many classic children's narratives, the story follows conventional Hollywood rules of emotional identification and development, effectively deploying magic realist techniques to reflect Harry's alienation, a state final-ly relieved when his big brother takes him under his wing and protects him from bullies, doubling as an alternative father figure. Despite a warm critical reception, the film performed poorly at the Irish box office. By contrast, demonstrating the interest of Irish audiences in tales made for children, when it was screened on Irish television, more than 468,000 people (45 percent of the audience share) watched director **Martin Duffy**'s children's parable, which points to both the nature of audiences' strategic decisions about at-tending Irish films at the cinema and the limited marketing resources avail-able to indigenous Irish cinema.

BRADLEY, RUTH (1987–). Bradley was born to Irish parents in New-foundland, Canada, where her father worked as a general practitioner. Her mother, Charlotte Bradley, is also an actress and appeared in a recurrent role in the Irish soap *Fair City* in the mid-1990s as well as in a series of smaller roles in films such as *The Van*, *About Adam*, and *Veronica Guerin*. At the age of five, she and her mother returned to Ireland. While at the Irish-language secondary school Scoil Naofa, she began appearing in professional stage productions (touring the country in a production of John B. Keane's *Sive*). However, as Irish television drama production experienced a post-2000 upsurge in activity, Bradley's stage career was set aside, as she was cast in recurring roles in *The Clinic* (2003), *Love Is the Drug* (2004), and *Showbands* (2005). (Her next theater role, in an Abbey production of *The Playboy of the Western World*, would not come until 2008.)

After beginning a degree in German at Trinity College in 2005, Bradley dropped out and moved to London, where for a time she roomed with **Amy Huberman**. A period of auditioning followed, eventually leading to recurring roles in the BBC's *The Innocence Project* (2006) and Channel 4's *Plus One* (2009) comedy series. When ITV's sci-fi series *Primeval* (2007–2011) moved to film in Ireland for its fourth series in 2010, Bradley joined the cast of that too.

Her fluency in Irish helped her secure a role in TG4's 2007 drama *The Running Mate*, and when *Love/Hate*, a hit series by **Radio Telefís Éireann** (RTÉ) set in Dublin's criminal underworld, launched in 2010, she was among the high-profile talent used by the show (others included **Aiden Gillen**, **Ruth Negga**, and **Robert Sheehan**), appearing as Mary (sister to Robert Sheehan's Darren), one of the few characters not actively engaged in crime. Despite her prominence, she abruptly departed at the end of series 2, having secured a leading part in ABC Television's *Beauty and the Beast* pilot in Los Angeles. This appeared to presage a Hollywood career, but the series was not commissioned. However, it did result in a talent-holding deal with ABC Studios, and as a result, Bradley has continued to participate in U.S. "pilot seasons" (including the lead role in *Big Thunder* in 2013, a 19th-century–set supernatural western based on a Disneyland theme park ride.) Subsequent roles saw her return to U.K. and Irish television work: the **Channel 4** sci-fi hit *Humans* (2015–2018) and as one of three female leads in RTÉ's major drama around the centenary of the 1916 Easter Rising, *Rebellion* (2016).

Although it would be overstating things to suggest that Irish television drama constitutes a progressive arena in terms of representing women, it does at least offer a range of female roles. This poses the question as to why Bradley has not enjoyed quite the same level of exposure in Irish cinema. **Gerry Stembridge** singled her out for praise as the lead in his (sub)urban psychological drama *Alarm* (2008). Her portrayal of a psychotic Australian teen in *In Her Skin* (2009) led to a Best Actress award at the Milan International Film Festival, and her casting in the comedy-horror *Grabbers* (2012) reflected the degree of audience recognition she brought to the project. For whatever reasons—and it is not outlandish to speculate that the paucity of strong female roles in Irish film is a central one—momentum has not been built in terms of big-screen roles, although she finds herself in steady employment in U.K.-based TV dramas and series, such as the Channel 5 TV film *Agatha and the Truth of Murder* (2018), in which she played the title role.

BRADLEY, STEPHEN (1967–). Bradley is an Irish-born writer/director/producer whose professional career began when he established Temple Films with **Ed Guiney** in 1992. While Guiney initially drove the company's development slate, Bradley set about writing and directing a feature debut that he achieved with the offbeat *Sweety Barrett* (1998) starring **Brendan Gleeson** as a simpleminded circus performer who finds himself caught up in crime in small-town Ireland.

While continuing to direct short films and documentaries (*Deirdre O'Kane Live at the Olympia* [2002] and *Chasing the Lions* [2005]), Bradley made his second feature, the horror-comedy *Boy Eats Girl* (2005), which met with moderate success in Ireland and the United Kingdom.

After a long interval and a move to London, Bradley reemerged with the biopic *Noble* (2014) starring his wife Deirdre O'Kane as the Irish children's rights activist and humanitarian Christina Noble. A well-produced and inspirational tale, the film won several awards on the international film festival circuit, received widespread theatrical and video-on-demand distribution, and scored well at the national and international box offices, notably in New Zealand.

BRADY, ORLA (1961–). Raised on Dame Street in Dublin, where her family owned a successful public house, Brady moved to Paris in the mid-1980s to study acting at L'Ecole Philippe Gaulier. On returning to Dublin, she secured the role of Adela in the *House of Bernarda Alba* at the Gate Theatre. Her early career was almost exclusively onstage, and she built a strong reputation in repertory work from playwrights as diverse as Anton Chekhov and J. M. Synge. In 1993, Brady moved to London and found herself in constant demand in British television drama, often cast in roles as strong-willed, intelligent, and not necessarily Irish women. Typical of these was her Cathy in the London Weekend Television adaptation of *Wuthering Heights*.

Her screen debut was in **Mary McGuckian**'s *Words upon the Window Pane* (1994), in which she played the strongly independent Hester van Homrigh, mistress to writer Jonathan Swift. This was followed four years later by her commanding lead role in *A Love Divided* as a Protestant wife (again based on a real-life figure) married to a Catholic man who refused to bow to the social convention of 1950s Ireland that the children of such mixed marriages should be raised as Catholics. The role won enthusiastic reviews and secured her the Best Actress award at the Monte Carlo International Television Festival. She then appeared in an adaptation of Nabokov's *The Luzhin Defence* (2000) and the little-seen Czech film *Fogbound* (2002). Back in Ireland, she played a Republican prisoner in Maeve Murphy's unjustly overlooked **Silent Grace** (2001), a film with an intriguing premise (about female Irish Republican Army [IRA] hunger strikers) but unfortunately released at a point when the IRA cease-fire made such stories difficult to sell at the box office. The film had a small cinema release and had to wait until 2017 for its Irish TV premiere.

Although she played the lead role character of Maureen Boland in the hit drama *Proof* by **Radio Telefís Éireann** from 2004 to 2005, the bulk of her roles have been in U.K. productions, including *Mistresses* (2008–2010), *Eternal Law* (2012), and *Banished* (2015). Her 2003 marriage to Los Angeles–based photographer Nick Brandt brought further breath to her career with recurring roles in Fox's *Fringe* (2008–2013) and NBC's *American Odyssey* (2015). This has had unexpected consequences: she was cast as Lydia in AMC's martial arts fantasy *Into the Badlands* (2015–2017), and the show switched to Ireland as a shooting location after its first series.

Brady still makes occasional forays into Irish cinema. A small role in Marian Quinn's *32A* (2007) and a more much substantial one in the Maeve Binchy short-story adaptation *How About You* (2008) were followed by the lead in **Mary McGuckian**'s *The Price of Desire* (2015), a visually impressive but awkwardly constructed biopic of the brilliant Irish designer Eileen Gray.

BRAVEHEART (1995). Considering that the narrative of Mel Gibson's multi-Oscar–winning epic traces the life and death of a 13th-century Scottish folk hero, *Braveheart* is not an obvious candidate for inclusion in this book. However, from a political economy perspective, it occupies a significant symbolic place in the development of the Irish film industry since the 1990s.

The $70 million film was jointly financed by 20th Century Fox and Paramount and was to have been shot over 16 weeks on location in Scotland. However, the filmmakers faced the logistical difficulty of securing sufficient extras in Scotland for the massive battle scenes that constitute the dramatic high point of the film. The executive producer of *Braveheart*, Steve McEveety, contacted Irish producer **Morgan O'Sullivan** to ask if Ireland would be a more flexible location. O'Sullivan in turn went to the Department of Arts, Culture, and the Gaeltacht, which was sufficiently enthused by the project to send an assistant principal officer to O'Sullivan's next meeting with the producers in London. At that meeting, it was apparent that the producers were promised access not only to **Section 35** funding but also to 1,600 reservist soldiers as extras (reportedly for a nominal cost). These were to be housed in the Curragh army base, which was adjacent to a potential location for shooting the battle scenes.

As a consequence, the film's Scottish shoot was shortened to five weeks with the remaining 11 shifting to Ireland, six at **Ardmore Studios**, and five on various Irish locations. In Great Britain, opposition politicians lamented the loss of the film, criticizing the Conservative government for failing to match Ireland's filmmaking incentives. In Ireland, however, the arrival of the film, coming just a year after the reestablishment of the **Irish Film Board** and the radical changes to Section 35, appeared to suggest that a Hollywood-scale industry was a real possibility.

However, the major significance of the shift was the clear demonstration of the lengths to which the Irish state was willing to go to attract large-scale audiovisual productions to Ireland. Mel Gibson reported that the decision to move to Ireland was based purely on creative factors, but in addition to literally having a small army placed at its disposal, the production was able to raise $10 million via Section 35, then the most substantial use of that tax break in a single film. The message was not lost on overseas producers, who, in the wake of the *Braveheart* production, lined up to use Ireland as a location.

BREAKFAST ON PLUTO (2005). Neil Jordan's second adaptation of a Patrick McCabe novel following *The Butcher Boy* offers a roll call of well-known Irish actors caricaturing Irish stereotypes, in many cases with great humorous effect. **Liam Neeson**—revising his seminal role as priest in *Lamb*—plays the "father" in both the biological and the spiritual senses to a colorful transvestite son, Patrick (Kitten) (**Cillian Murphy**), and has to deal with the consequences after the mother leaves the baby at his door before departing for England.

The story follows Kitten's journey to find his mother (and himself) and his encounters with various larger-than-life characters along the way. These include Billy Rock (Gavin Friday) and his Mohawks band (which he briefly joins to the consternation of the confused band members); Silky String (Bryan Ferry), a homicidal seducer; Bertie (**Stephen Rea**), an eccentric magician; and John-Joe (**Brendan Gleeson**), an Irish immigrant dressed up in a "Wombles" costume at a children's fairground. The setting of the story—in a border town—ensures that the Troubles remain a constant presence, but Jordan has been at pains to stress that this is not a film about politics but rather addresses the question of how an individual can preserve his or her own identity when powerful competing ideologies seek to win followers. Kitten does this by remaining an eternal optimist in the tradition of Voltaire's *Candide*. Thus, although Republican sympathies are called on, Kitten remains aloof from it all. When he is implicated in an Irish Republican Army attack in London, his optimism renders his interrogation strangely comic and ensures that the narrative remains at a surreal level.

Eventually, Kitten and his father are reconciled, and the priest "does the right thing" by supporting his transvestite son and an unwed but pregnant friend in spite of violent local opposition.

The story is carried by Murphy's deft central performance and is characterized by judicious use of 1970s music and pop songs that reflect Kitten's rose-tinted perspective on the world and ensure that nostalgia for the period is maintained at all times.

BREATHNACH, PADDY (1964–). Having begun his career working with the likes of Eamon de Buitlear, **Joe Comerford**, and **Bob Quinn** and in the Gunther Wulff **animation** studio, Paddy Breathnach's work as a film director has been more noticeably mainstream and populist than such mentors, with a preference for transnational genre work and comedy in particular. Since his feature debut, *Ailsa* (1994), he has also demonstrated himself to be one of the most versatile of the (second-wave) generation of filmmakers who collectively benefited from the reestablishment of the **Irish Film Board** in 1993, forging a career in fiction, documentary, and TV formats.

A native of Bray, Co. Wicklow, Breathnach studied at University College Dublin, where he ran the satirical magazine *60/84* with a group that included the writer Joe O'Connor. He made an immediate impact with his first short film, *A Stone in the Heart* (1991), a gentle drama built around a family bereavement observed through the eyes of a young child, winning the Best Irish Short award at the 1991 Cork Film Festival. In 1992, Breathnach established **Treasure Films** (later Treasure Entertainment) with producer Robert Walpole but produced his debut feature, *Ailsa*, through **Ed Guiney**'s fledging Temple Films as an Irish–French–German coproduction. A self-consciously arty adaptation of a Joe O'Connor short story dealing with an obsessive young man (shades of early Roman Polanski), *Ailsa* won the Euskal Prize at the San Sebastian Film Festival in 1994. Breathnach subsequently invested his share of the £250,000 prize into *I Went Down* (1997), while Guiney put his into *Guiltrip* (1995).

Ailsa's award success notwithstanding, Breathnach professed himself uninterested in the confines of art house cinema and pursued a very different path with his follow-up *I Went Down*. With a career-defining turn from **Brendan Gleeson** as loquacious criminal Bunny Kelly, **Conor McPherson**'s sharply funny screenplay transposed tropes of American gangster and road movies onto the Irish Midlands to comic and hugely popular effect. Picked up for distribution in Ireland by the Walt Disney Company, the film went on to become the most successful indigenous Irish film up to that point (a record subsequent shattered by *The Guard*, a film clearly in debt to *I Went Down* in terms of casting and reworking of American crime genres in rural Irish contexts).

Four years were to separate *I Went Down* from **Blow Dry** (2001), a British comedy set in the world of competitive hairdressing starring Alan Rickman, Natasha Richardson, and Josh Harnett. Although produced by Miramax and working in comparable territory as crossover Britflick hits like *The Full Monty* (1997), *Blow Dry* received a lukewarm critical/commercial reception. Breathnach returned to Ireland for his next feature, **Man About Dog** (2004). Also a broad comedy set in a working-class subculture—this time the world of greyhound racing—the film was a surprise local hit, grossing more than €2 million at the box office and becoming the 10th most successful film released in Ireland that year. Although dismissed by many local critics, Breathnach clearly aimed the film at a very specific demographic—the young adult male—who flocked to it in droves.

His next film, **Shrooms** (2007), is one of the early texts of the Irish horror wave initiated by **Dead Meat** (2004) and **Boy Eats Girl** (2005), which attempted to meld local settings and inflections with well-established genre tropes in a bid to increase international appeal (while also leaving room for sociocultural analysis). The film is built around a youthful, largely American cast led by Jake (played by **John Huston**'s grandson Jack) on a mushroom-induced hallucinogenic trip through a forest and a derelict former industrial school in the Irish Midlands. Convinced that they are being followed by the spirit of a deranged cleric, the young characters meet a series of grisly deaths. In spite of a mixed critical reception, the film secured widespread international distribution and attention (aided by its generic status), and Breathnach immediately followed it with another, less successful teen horror: the largely forgettable *Freak Dog* (2008), this time set in the United States. By the late 2000s, it wasn't clear if Breathnach still considered himself part of the indigenous industry at all, and he seemed intent on moving into the American marketplace, spending extended periods in Los Angeles. Between 2008 and 2015, he made just one Irish film, *An oíche a gineadh m'athair* (2012), a 45-minute documentary following his father's efforts to unearth details about his own father's life and death.

Breathnach's next feature, *Viva* (2015), could therefore hardly have been more surprising: a Spanish-language drama, set and filmed in Cuba, about a transvestite's struggle to be accepted by his homophobic family and wider community. The genesis of this unusual project film went back to a 1998 trip by Breathnach and Robert Walpole to Havana and their experience of drag culture there. Drafting in **Adam and Paul** (2004) actor/screenwriter Mark O'Halloran to write a script (first in English, then in Spanish), they secured Irish Film Board funding for the project and shot it on location in Havana. *Viva*'s sympathetic portrayal of its central character made it a critical hit and, uniquely, saw it long-listed as Ireland's official entry for the Best Foreign Language **Academy Award** in 2016.

Ever eclectic in his interests and style, Breathnach subsequently returned to Ireland to direct *Rosie* (2018), a topical and socially engaged narrative scripted by Roddy Doyle (his first since **When Brendan Met Trudy** [2000]). Based around Ireland's post–Celtic Tiger housing crisis, *Rosie* explores how a mother (played by Sarah Greene) attempts to negotiate her family's homelessness and marks Breathnach's most locally engaged fiction in 14 years.

BRENNAN, BRID (1955–). A *New York Times* article from 1992 musing on who was likely to win that year's Tony for Best Feature Actress noted that although three actresses had been nominated from Brian Friel's *Dancing at Lughnasa*, Brid Brennan, who played "the sister with the sad face who did the knitting," had the best chance. Brennan duly went on to win the award and won an Irish Film and Television Academy Award for Best Actress when she reprised the role of Agnes in **Pat O'Connor**'s film version of *Lughnasa* (having previously appeared in O'Connor's *Ballroom of Romance* a decade and a half earlier).

Originally from Belfast, Brennan made a brief debut in **Excalibur** before securing the more eye-catching role of Roisin in **Pat Murphy**'s feminist experiment **Maeve** (1981). Between 1982 and 1984, she appeared in Graham Reid's *Billy* trilogy on the BBC opposite the young Kenneth Branagh, touchingly attempting to hold her family together after her mother's death from cancer. This was immediately followed by what remains her outstanding screen role as the eponymous protagonist in **Anne Devlin** (1984). Appearing in virtually every frame, her riveting performance embodied a character who was far more than just "'the faithful servant' of Robert Emmet," as her headstone in Glasnevin has it.

She has subsequently established herself as a versatile player on the film screen and has become a familiar face to British audiences through a series of memorable one-off roles in television crime dramas, such as *Cracker: Brotherly Love* (1995) and *Doctor Who* (2010). Having appeared in a variety of Irish films in the 1990s—**Words upon a Window Pane** (1994), **Trojan Eddie** (1995), and **Felicia's Journey** (1999)—her big-screen appearances in the 21st century have tended to be in more minor roles (e.g., in *Brooklyn* [2015] as "Nettles" Kelly). A key exception to this was her role as the matriarch of a Republican family in **Shadow Dancer** (2012). Cast by director James Marsh in part because she had grown up in West Belfast during the Troubles and thus had lived experience of the political violence that the film depicts, Brennan's "Ma" silently expresses the turmoil of at once trying to protect her children while asserting a nationalist outlook in the midst of conflict. The role won Brennan two awards: one at the IFTAs and one at the Edinburgh International Film Festival.

BROADCASTING AUTHORITY OF IRELAND. Initially established as the Independent Radio and Television Commission (IRTC) in 1988 as Ireland made provision for legal private commercial broadcasting, the institution initially operated primarily to license radio and television franchises in Ireland and to ensure that licensees complied with the content requirements of the 1988 Radio and Television Act. Over the succeeding decades, however, the responsibilities of the IRTC (and its successors, the Broadcasting Commission of Ireland [2001–2009] and the Broadcasting Authority of Ireland [BAI] [2009–present]) expanded to include the operation of the Broadcasting Complaints apparatus in Ireland; the development of content codes for all Irish broadcasters, including **Radio Telefís Éireann** (RTÉ); and, since 2014, a key role in advising on Irish media mergers regardless of whether they involve broadcasters or not.

However, the body has also become a significant source of feature film funding as a consequence of its operation of the Sound and Vision scheme since 2003. Introduced by the 2003 Broadcasting (Funding) Act, the scheme cut first 5 percent (2003–2009) and then 7 percent (from 2009 on) of the monies raised via the Ireland television license scheme. Until that point, 100 percent of that money had gone to RTÉ. However, the Sound and Vision scheme created a contestable fund that any broadcaster—public or private—operating on the island of Ireland (including Northern Ireland) could apply for to support the production of high-quality public service–oriented radio or television programming. Between 2005 (when the scheme first began dispensing funds) and 2017, the BAI disbursed more than €166 million in Sound and Vision funds. Although these were initially concentrated on documentary productions, the scheme gradually widened its purview and from 2007 on began offering support to feature film production, such as *Garage* and *Kings* (both 2007). By 2017, the scheme had made available more than €9 million in funding to nearly 40 Irish feature film projects. The levels of funding vary from as little as €65,000 for a film like *The Front Line* (2006) up to €650,000 for **Conor McPherson**'s *The Eclipse* (2013).

In 2011, the **Creative Capital Report** recommended that control of the fund be shifted away from the BAI and given instead to the **Irish Film Board** on the grounds that the granting of funds was incompatible with the BAI's regulatory function but also because the board had established expertise in assessing projects for development. To date, however, the fund has remained within the BAI.

BROKEN HARVEST **(1994).** Structurally similar to *This Is My Father* (both frame stories from 1950s Ireland with a contemporary American setting), *Broken Harvest*, from director Maurice O'Callaghan, traces the impact on family and community of a feud between Art O'Leary (Colin Lane) and Josie Lane (Niall Buggy), two farmers who had taken opposite sides in the

Irish Civil War and who had also fought for the love of Catherine (now Art's wife, played by Marian Quinn). The film was a labor of love for director/producer/writer Maurice O'Callaghan, who spent the best part of a decade making the picture and raising the £1.25 million budget.

BROOKLYN (2015). Produced in the aftermath of the post–Celtic Tiger crash *Brooklyn* represents a return to traditional tropes of Irish cinema: a period setting, the frustrations of small-town life, immigration to the United States, and a longing for home. Its critical and commercial success, particularly in the United States, suggests that these are themes that continue to have cinematic currency more than a century since they were established in the first transatlantic Irish American story, *The Lad from Old Ireland* (1910). Adapted from Colm Tóibín's best-selling 2009 novel, *Brooklyn* was clearly aimed at the international mainstream marketplace (particularly the United States), but it rises above many immigration/period films in its unusual treatment of the familiar "Golden Door" theme and the sophistication of **Saoirse Ronan**'s central performance.

Ronan plays Eilis Lacey, a young Irish immigrant navigating her way through 1950s Brooklyn, where she embarks on a familiar American Dream progression of opportunity and romance. However, just as she begins to settle into her new life, she is called back to Ireland by family circumstances and quickly becomes enmeshed in the nets of the small-town relationships and outlook. The film uses this return to complicate the traditional emigrant longing for home, pondering questions of agency and opportunity that go beyond an emigration narrative to universal themes of personal choice. In its conclusion, the film suggests that we are products of both circumstance and choice and that our success in life lies in recognizing and responding to this tension.

Brooklyn marked a significant career advance for its director and leading actor. John Crowley had shown himself a capable director of actors and smart scripts with his earlier efforts *Boy A* (2007) and ***Intermission*** (2003) as well as his work in theater (particularly with Martin McDonagh). While already well known and widely admired, the film also provided its star, Ronan, with the opportunity to cross over into more adult roles after a distinguished series of child and young adult characters as well as the critical and commercial success that had strangely eluded her since her breakthrough in *Atonement* (2000) despite the quality of the projects she engaged in.

BROSNAN, PIERCE (1953–). Although born in Navan, County Meath, he and his mother moved to Putney, London, in 1964 after his father abandoned the family. He quickly adopted a cockney accent to fit in at school, a fact that subsequently allowed him to play Irish and English roles with equal facility.

Although initially working as a commercial artist (Brosnan still paints in his spare time), he would spend his evenings at the Arts Lab in London's Oval Theatre. Exposed to experimental theater, he was sufficiently bitten by the acting bug to resign his day job and commit to theater. He enrolled in a drama school in 1973 and did several years of experimental theater before appearing in several West End productions. In 1979, he moved to screen acting, securing lead billing in his first role in *Murphy's Stroke* for Thames Television. He made an eye-catching if brief appearance as an Irish Republican Army (IRA) member in the classic gangster film *The Long Good Friday* (1980) before securing another lead in an American television miniseries, *The Mannions of America*, which followed a family of 19th-century Irish immigrants to the United States. He followed this with the key role in the long-running television series *Remington Steele* in 1982, which indelibly established his suave star persona.

Brosnan was courted by 007 producer Albert Broccoli for the role of James Bond when Roger Moore retired after *A View to a Kill* (1985), but Mary Tyler Moore Productions refused to allow him to break his Steele contract. Brosnan was bitterly disappointed, particularly after *Remington Steele* was canceled the following year (1987).

For a period, Brosnan seemed condemned to spend the rest of his career in B movies and television series. (He later returned to Ireland in 1988 to make the poorly received *Taffin*, costarring former Bond girl Alison Doody.) In 1991, his wife died of cancer, leaving him to look after her two children from her first marriage and the son they had together. However, in the early 1990s, his career began to pick up with *The Lawnmower Man* (1992), loosely based on a Stephen King short story. This was an unexpected hit, and he demonstrated a gift for self-deprecating comedy in *Mrs. Doubtfire* (1993). However, his career was transformed in 1995 when he received a second shot at the role of Bond after Timothy Dalton's two 007 films had underperformed. In *GoldenEye* (1995), Brosnan reinvigorated the role and the coffers of Metro-Goldwyn-Mayer (MGM) that financed it. Three further Bond outings followed, each more successful than the last: *Tomorrow Never Dies* (1997), *The World Is Not Enough* (1999), and *Die Another Day* (2002).

Mindful of the fate of previous former Bonds, he interspersed his secret agent outings with roles in a variety of genres—eccentric scientist in the postmodern comedy *Mars Attacks* (1997), geologist hero in eco-thriller *Dante's Peak* (1997), and fur trapper turned conservationist in Richard Attenborough's *Grey Owl* (1999). His most successful non-Bond outings during this period—*The Thomas Crown Affair* (1999) and the **John Boorman**-directed *The Tailor of Panama* (2001)—suggested that the public was most at home with him in the Bond persona.

He went one stage further in ensuring the longevity of his career by turning producer and establishing the production company **Irish Dreamtime** in 1996 with producing partner Beau St. Clair (who sadly passed away in 2016). As a direct consequence, he turned in an increasing number of Irish roles: although *The Nephew* (alongside a final role for **Donal McCann**) was not a terrific fit for his talents and looks, his performance in *Evelyn*, as a father in 1950s Ireland attempting to reclaim his children from the care of the state, suggested a thespian potential rarely displayed in previous work. He lost the Bond role in 2005, apparently due to disputes with the producers over money, but, if anything, the period since has been his busiest yet.

More recent roles tend to resolve into a number of categories. Inevitably, his star persona—and casting—still reflects his stint as Bond: even in his 60s, he continue to essay action-adventure roles (*The November Man* [2014], *Survivor* [2015], and *No Escape* [2015]). However, developing the knack for self-deprecating humor (often directed at his sex symbol status) evident in *Remington Steele* and *Mrs. Doubtfire* (1993), he has also increasingly moved into comedy (*Salvation Boulevard* [2011] and *The Love Punch* [2013]) and can still plausibly play a leading romantic role in romantic comedies, such as the megahit *Mamma Mia!* (2008) and *Mamma Mia! Here We Go Again* (2018). On occasion, the Bond/comedy roles merge, as in his Golden Globe–nominated performance as a washed-up hit man in *The Matador* (2005).

With age, too, has come gravitas, and the suspicion that Brosnan traded on his looks rather than his acting chops in his early decades has diminished. He has become a credible casting for more serious roles, appearing as the patriarch in a family recovering from the violent death of their son in *The Greatest* (2009), a similar role opposite Robert Pattison in *Remember Me* (2009), and, perhaps most impressively, as a Tony Blair–style former British prime minister facing accusations of war crimes in the Roman Polanski adaptation *The Ghost Writer* (2010).

Notwithstanding the ongoing operation of Irish Dreamtime, however, his overtly Irish roles have been few and far between in recent decades, effectively limited to channeling another politician, this time Sinn Féin leader Gerry Adams as an ex-IRA man turned politician, in the Netflix-distributed *The Foreigner* (2017) directed by Martin Campbell, with whom he had earlier collaborated in his Bond debut, *GoldenEye* (1995)—an odd and unexpected closing of his career circle.

BROWN BAG FILMS. Despite two **Academy Award** nominations in 2001 and 2009 for short films, Brown Bag has not engaged in for-theatrical-release feature production activity and remains tightly focused on and highly successful as a producer of small screen and multiplatform content.

Formed in 1994 by two Ballyfermot College of Further Education students, Cathal Gaffney and Darragh O'Connell, the company was launched on the back of a £2,000 loan. Although winning an early commission from **Radio Telefís Éireann** (RTÉ) to produce a satirical take on the Irish-language autobiography *Peig* (previously the bane of a generation of Irish secondary students), Brown Bag's early work consisted mainly of service animation, commercials production, and, increasingly, Web-based design. The company was an innovator with computer technology, pioneering the use of digital workstations in Ireland from the late 1990s to grow production for television and commercials.

That technology was also brought to bear on more creatively driven short-film productions, such as the award-winning *The Last Elk* (1998) directed by Alan Shannon (featuring additional animation from Nora Twomey, later of **Cartoon Saloon**). One of those projects provided a major breakthrough for the company: based on tapes of 1960s Dublin schoolchildren recounting idiosyncratic versions of Bible tales, *Give Up Yer Aul Sins* (2001) proved a major hit with Irish audiences when screened on television and secured the company's first Oscar nomination. Brown Bag would subsequently expand the short into a series for RTÉ that in turn became a major DVD sell-through hit, shifting more than 70,000 copies.

Although securing short-series commissions from RTÉ in the late 1990s, including the children's series *Why?*, which sold widely in international markets, the stop-start commitment of the national broadcaster encouraged the company to seek out direct international commissions through assiduous cultivation of contacts in markets such as MIP-TV. As the company developed, Gaffney moved more into a business development role while O'Connell remained in charge of production. International work duly followed: *The Boy Who Had No Story* and *Tales Wot I Know* for ITV, the latter essentially transposing the *Give Up Yer Aul Sins* approach to the U.K. market. In 2006, Brown Bag sold *Wobblyland* to Henson International Television (HIT), a *Mr. Men*–style series based on a 2003 short by Catherine Little that Brown Bag had optioned.

The company would increasingly shift toward 3-D animation from the late 2000s. A major breakthrough came with a 2007 commission from New York–based Chorion Pictures to produce a 52-episode 3-D series adapting Ian Falconer's popular *Olivia* books (based around a charismatic pig). Quickly sold to more than 20 countries, the success of the series led to subsequent commissions on a revamp of Enid Blyton's *Noddy* (2009–), *The Octonauts* (2011), and Disney's long-running *Doc McStuffins* (2012–) (the last a reflection of the company's decision to open a Los Angeles office in 2009). *Olivia* also saw Brown Bag invest €2 million in a new purpose-built high-definition animation facility in Dublin's Smithfield. Already one of Europe's largest animation producers by volume, by 2009, the company was employing nearly 60 staff on a full-time basis and, notwithstanding its lucrative nature, decided to withdraw from commercial production to focus on long-form television work. The same year saw it named European Producer of the Year at the annual Cartoon Forum event and complete the Nicky Phelan–directed *Granny O'Grimm's Sleeping Beauty*, which secured a second Oscar nomination for the firm.

Despite a mooted move into feature-length production in 2010, the company remained focused primarily on television with a mix of in-house–originated material, such as *Henry Hugglemonster* (2011), and another Chorion-commissioned revamp, this time for Beatrix Potter's *Peter Rabbit* (2012), a series that secured an armful of Emmy awards from 2014 on. Indeed, such was the scale of Brown Bag's output that further expansion became critical: in addition to opening a third premises in 2013, in 2014, the company opened a new production facility in Manchester. In 2016, the company unveiled another 30,000-square-foot studio on the Smithfield site in Dublin.

In 2015, Toronto-based 9 Story Media, one of North America's largest 2-D animation studios, acquired Brown Bag for an undisclosed sum. Not only did the deal leave Brown Bag's management and 300 staff in place, but Cathal Gaffney was appointed 9 Story's chief operating officer. In a reflection of Brown Bag's industry recognition, 9 Story's entire animation division was rebranded under the "Brown Bag" label in 2017 with Dublin becoming the group's animation headquarters. Brown Bag could reasonably claim to have the largest audience reach of any Irish-based production studio, maintaining a dozen ongoing productions, screened in more than 100 countries, and produced by more than 300 animators from more than 30 different countries.

BUDAWANNY (1986). Director **Bob Quinn**'s take on Irish Catholicism is unusual in that, in contrast to films such as *The Magdalene Sisters* and *Song for a Raggy Boy*, it offers a sympathetic discussion of religion in Ireland from the perspective of a priest rather than from that of the victim of Church authority. The film opens with the bishop (Peadar Lamb) trying to dictate a letter to his ex-priest (**Donal McCann**), and the narrative is framed around flashbacks of the actual story, which is told from the bishop's point of view. Interspersed with the black-and-white and subtitled flashbacks are the bishop's comments on the need for religion and his job to make it "work"—a long way from the more authoritarian monologue of a bishop in charge of his flock. Luke Gibbons (Rockett et al. 1988) affirms that there are two narrative styles at work: the "realist" sections attempt to act as a framing "master" narrative that controls the stylistic excesses of the melodramatic silent sequences. This stylistic conflict exemplifies a struggle between the bureaucratic modern Church and the more popular—albeit pagan—religion of the islanders.

The core narrative follows the development of a relationship between the priest, then serving an island parish off the west coast (filmed on Clare Island, County Mayo), and a young woman, Marian, who comes to work as his housekeeper. The relationship becomes a romance and takes on a sexual dimension. In a sermon to his conservative flock, the priest informs that soon they will have another reason to call him father. *See also THE BISHOP'S STORY* (1993).

BUSINESS EXPANSION SCHEME. In 1984, the Fine Gael–Labour government introduced a scheme to encourage private capital to invest in small-scale business enterprises. Investors were allowed to subtract from taxable income any investment (up to a maximum of £25,000 per annum) in a manufacturing business (this included a number of service industries, such as filmmaking) on condition that they maintained the investment for at least five years. An individual was not permitted to make more than £75,000 in Business Expansion scheme (BES) investments in his or her lifetime. Although not explicitly targeted at film, at least two film production companies used the scheme between 1984 and 1990. The most notable example of this was **Strongbow Films**, which was originally set up purely to take advantage of the scheme and which raised £900,000 for *Eat the Peach* from BES investors in 1986 alone.

The scheme was not used more often by film companies because of the limit of £25,000 per annum. At a time when even a low-budget feature cost around £500,000, raising funds based on this scheme alone required a substantial selling effort on the part of producers. Furthermore, given that film projects—which were considered inherently high risk by investors—were competing with other, less risky areas for BES investment, film producers found it difficult to find willing BES investors. This was particularly true after *Eat the Peach* recorded an official loss of £750,000 for its 273 BES shareholders despite having performed well in local markets. Thus, the *Coopers & Lybrand Report* found that between 1987 and 1991, 10 projects had raised just £1.18 million between them through the BES. In the longer term, the BES was significant because it paved the way for the introduction of the **Section 35** incentive, which even in its original 1987 form was regarded as a dramatic improvement on the BES with all of its strictures.

THE BUTCHER BOY (1998). Neil Jordan's acclaimed masterpiece from the novel of the same name by Pat McCabe became a major critical success, with much academic analysis given over to the film. The story focuses on

Francie Brady (Eamonn Owens), a boy who we soon begin to suspect is a paranoid schizophrenic, living in an extremely dysfunctional family. The film oscillates between mystical nostalgia for a rural past and a futuristic vision of American mass culture. The story is framed against the geopolitics of the Cold War and the pervasive fear of nuclear catastrophe. Francie takes his cue from the media, which in itself offers a critique of the various moral panics of the time, especially with the impact of mass media and religious spectacle on morality and cultural identity. At one stage, Francie imagines that he is Richard Kimble from the long-running television series *The Fugitive*, and at another, he has a vision of the Virgin Mary. Jordan's casting of controversial iconic Irish singer **Sinead O'Connor** as the Mother of God serves to question conventional religious worship while exploring its psychic potency. Some critics have even pointed out how the image of Mary playing a harp outside Francie's model Irish cottage represents an attack on Eamon de Valera, the political leader and architect of the 1937 Irish Constitution, who was a strong believer in maintaining close ties between Irish politics and Catholicism and promulgated the idealized patriarchal notion of a "comely Irish maiden" needing protection from the vagaries of sexual promiscuity and modernity generally.

While the film enjoyed a good critical reception, placing it as one of the great Irish and even European films, it has not been as commercially successful as it perhaps ought to have been, possibly because of its difficult subject matter.

BYRNE, GABRIEL (1950–). One of six children born into what Byrne describes as a "solid working-class family" from Crumlin in Dublin, he was educated by the Christian Brothers. Although attending a seminary in England from age 12 to 17 to become a priest, he left before being ordained and trained instead as a teacher. He joined the Dublin Shakespearian Society in 1974 and from there came to work at the Project Theatre (where he encountered **Jim Sheridan**, **Liam Neeson**, **Neil Jordan**, **Ciarán Hinds**, and **Stephen Rea**). Early film roles included those in **Thaddeus O'Sullivan**'s *On a Paving Stone Mounted* (1978) and *The Outsider* (1979) before being brought to a wider audience via **John Boorman**'s decision to cast him in the key role of Uther Pendragon in *Excalibur* in 1980. A winning turn in the gothic soap *Bracken* by **Radio Telefís Éireann** (RTÉ) as the titular dark, brooding dairy farmer was followed by appearances in European art house work (*Reflection* [1983] and *Hannah K* [1983]) before his breakthrough as the journalist who knows too much in the superbly taut 1985 thriller *Defence of the Realm*. Then followed roles in Ken Russell's *Gothic* (1986) as well as nonmainstream film roles in *Julia and Julia* (1987), *Siesta* (1987), and *A Soldier's Tale* (1988).

He moved to the United States in 1988 and made a major impact in the Coen Brothers' 1990 film *Miller's Crossing*. He married Ellen Barkin, and they had two children before their marriage ended in 1999. In the decades following *Miller's Crossing*, he has appeared in more than 40 feature films in the United States. However, he also remained closely allied to the Irish film industry both as an actor and more unusually as a producer via his own company, Plurabelle Films. He lent star power to *The Courier* in 1988, acted in and coproduced *Into the West* (costarring his then wife Ellen Barkin) in 1992, and then appeared in at least one Irish film per year between 1994 and 1998: *All Things Bright and Beautiful* (1994), *Frankie Starlight* (1995), *The Last of the High Kings* (1996), *Draíocht* (Magic) (1996), *This Is the Sea* (1997), and *The Brylcreem Boys* (1998). Indeed, he even wrote the screenplay for *Draoicht*, an Irish-language drama (directed by his former partner Áine O'Connor) and had a hand in the script for *The Last of the High Kings*. That list might have been longer still: he was scheduled to play an Irish Republican Army prison leader in *In the Name of the Father* (1993) but fell out with Jim Sheridan, although he retained a credit for executive producer on the film. He also sat on the **Irish Film Board** for a number of years in the 1990s. Given this, it is perhaps surprising that he hasn't appeared in an Irish feature film since 1998 (though he lent his vocal talents as narrator on *Perrier's Bounty* [2009]).

Nevertheless, Byrne has consistently played Irish-inflected characters: Tom Reagan in *Miller's Crossing*; cop-turned-criminal Dean Keaton in *The Usual Suspects* (1995); Benjamin Madigan in the short-lived sitcom *Madigan Men* (2000); Stewart Kane in *Jindabyne* (2006), an Australia adaptation of Raymond Carver's short story "So Much Water So Close to Home"; and psychiatrist Paul Weston in the HBO series *In Treatment* (2008–2010). All of these roles were played as Irish (or at least Irish American) despite the fact that the roles were not obviously written as such. Indeed, in the case of *Miller's Crossing*, the character that became Tom Reagan was originally Jewish, while the role of Paul Weston is based on a character created by Israeli actor Assi Dayan.

That these characters "became" Irish was explicitly due to Byrne's intervention. And in at least some of these cases (*Miller's Crossing* and *In Treatment*), Byrne argued for the foregrounding of this ethnicity. It may not appear surprising that an actor would seek to remain within his or her own ethnicity if the opportunity presented itself. However, Byrne's decision to remain "visibly" Irish in the roles he has chosen stands in stark contrast to contemporaries like Liam Neeson or **Pierce Brosnan**, for whom adopting an American accent was a passport to roles in big-budget, high-concept blockbusters. Byrne has consistently avoided that path. Indeed, far from choosing roles characterized by their physical agency, unlike Brosnan as Bond or Neeson in any number of tough-guy roles post-*Taken* (2008), it is striking that most of the roles Byrne has opted to play as Irish share a performance of masculinity that firmly rejects the deeply ingrained stereotype of physical violence. To be sure, violence is very much a part of *Miller's Crossing*, *The Usual Suspects*, and *Jindabyne*. There is violence as well in *In Treatment* albeit more psychic than physical in nature. However, Byrne's characters are consistently reluctant to resort to violence themselves. This is reflected in Byrne's public persona: interviewers stress his thoughtfulness and intellectual curiosity. And this is reflected in how casting directors deploy him: *In Treatment*'s Paul Weston needed a star whose persona fitted with a dialogue-heavy show where the main character's role is to listen rather than talk.

Indeed, Byrne is on the record as explicitly disavowing violence, not least that stemming from the physical and sexual abuse he experienced at the hands of the Christian Brothers as a child (an experience he first publicly acknowledged in 2011). Violence is also repeatedly visited on Byrne's Irish characters. Virtually every character in *Miller's Crossing* assaults Tom at some stage in the film. In *The Usual Suspects*, he is beaten up during police questioning, while in *Jindabyne*, his best friend breaks his nose. And in *In Treatment*, Paul Weston must endure constant verbal assaults from patients unwilling to confront their own frailties. Even in later roles, such as the father in *Louder Than Bombs* (2014) seeking to keep his family together after his wife's suicide, he is the rock on which the pain of others crashes. Crucially, his characters rarely respond in kind but stoically accept their punishment. In *Miller's Crossing*, Tom Reagan's response to a beating suggests a character that masochistically accepts violence as an inherent aspect of his existence. He accepts it not as a product of his ethnic heritage but rather of how things are in the world. Crucially, in a reversal of stereotype, he calmly and deliberately refuses to be drawn into it.

In so doing, Byrne has repeatedly played against the stereotypes of Irish screen masculinity. It might be further argued that he has sought to overtly construct Irishness as an identity on which violence is visited in a more politically balanced reflection of Irish history than has heretofore been made available in Anglo-American representations.

In between these roles, Byrne in the 1990s and 2000s had a hit-and-miss relationship with Hollywood. There were plenty of leading roles in big-budget movies: as mentor to a trainee agent in *Point of No Return* (1993), D'Artagnan in *The Man in the Iron Mask* (1998), Satan taking on Arnold Schwarzenegger in *End of Days* (2000), and a corrupt police captain in the remake of *Assault on Precinct 13* (2005). However, the quality of the films has remained variable: *The Usual Suspects* (1995), Jim Jarmusch's *Dead Man* (1995), and David Cronenberg's *Spider* (2002) were all well received. Most of the rest had a poor reception.

For a period, he seemed more at home onstage, receiving a Tony nomination for his performance in the 2000 Broadway revival of Eugene O'Neill's *A Moon for the Misbegotten* and later (2005) essaying the playwright's *Touch of the Poet* in the role of the monstrous father Cornelius Melody (again on Broadway). His three-year stint as Paul Weston on *In Treatment* seemed to suggest a renewed interest in screen work. The camera's close scrutiny of Byrne's visage as the psychiatrist perfectly suited an actor skilled at communicating profound inner turmoil with the most subtle of facial expressions.

Since 2010, he has embarked on a difficult-to-codify range of roles across film and television. There's a clear preference for shoots in his native New York: as the grieving husband opposite Isabelle Huppert in Joachim Trier's critically acclaimed *Louder Than Bombs* (2015), as an on-his-uppers actor in the comedy *No Pay, Nudity* (2016), and again as the father struggling to parent a precocious daughter in the comedy-drama *Carrie Pilby* (2016). These are interspersed with character roles in work as diverse as 2015's *Endless Night* (where he plays an Arctic explorer in the 1900s) and a standout turn as an on-the-spectrum aging resident at controversial psychologist R. D. Laing's "asylum" in *Mad to Be Normal* (2016). For the most part, then, he continues to focus on character-driven material, eschewing genre work (although arguably his most commercially successful film in the 2010s, *Hereditary* [2018], is firmly a horror film, albeit one that evades the visual clichés of other contemporary chillers).

He returned to Ireland in 2013 to film the History Channel's hit drama *Vikings* (playing respected Viking chieftain Earl Haraldson), then again as the lead in *Quirke* (2014), a BBC/RTÉ coproduction based on the character created by Irish novelist John Banville under the pseudonym Benjamin Black.

C

CAL **(1984).** Adapted from his own novel by Bernard McLaverty (who also wrote *Lamb* [1986]), the film explores the trauma experienced by a young Irish Republican Army man, Cal (**John Lynch**), in the aftermath of the cold-blooded murder of a policeman he has participated in. Formed by the daily sectarianism visited on his Catholic household with his father Shamie (**Donal McCann**) on a Protestant estate, Cal can hardly evade being drawn into the armed struggle yet remains a reluctant "solider." In an effort to exculpate his guilt, Cal, who is symbolically employed in a slaughterhouse at the outset, seeks work on the farm of the RUC man he has killed but soon becomes attracted to his widow Marcella (Helen Mirren). As Cal seeks to distance himself from his military comrades and he and Marcella become lovers, he remains tormented by his memories of her husband's death. The film thus sought, during the height of the Troubles, to communicate the human cost of sectarian violence.

Produced by David Puttnam's Enigma Films and featuring a terse score by Dire Straits front man Mark Knopfler, *Cal* was shot in the Republic of Ireland and marked **Pat O'Connor's** graduation to directing feature films. While films supported by the fledging **Irish Film Board** struggled to attract international attention at the time, *Cal*'s success at the 1984 Cannes Film Festival (Helen Mirren won Best Actress and O'Connor was nominated for the Palme d'Or, a remarkable feat for a debut) was widely interpreted as heralding the emergence of an indigenous Irish industry capable of international recognition. Yet the film was also criticized for the manner in which it privileged the personal over the political, failing to confront the political complexities of Northern Ireland during the 1980s. Cal aside, the film presents Republicans as fanatical ideologues driven to violence by atavistic urges. Furthermore, those who oppose such impulses are represented as having little agency, suggesting that they are doomed to remain trapped between the opposing forces of nationalism and the British state.

CALVARY **(2013). John Michael McDonagh**'s second feature film (following his hugely successful debut *The Guard* [2011]), *Calvary* takes as its subject a rural Irish priest whose life is threatened in the opening sequence by an unseen parishioner in the confessional box. Structured by this seven-day ticking threat, the film's protagonist, Father James (**Brendan Gleeson**), sets about identifying who among his motley flock might have it in for him. This blackly humorous and often surreal investigation is given depth and a degree of complexity by the visit of his daughter (Kelly Reilly, the result of his pre-priesthood marriage), who has recently attempted suicide, as well as his own reflections on his vocation and moral outlook. For a film defined, as was *The Guard*, by a strongly provincial theme and tone, Gleeson's presence and performance as the troubled cleric was among the finest of his career and guaranteed the film wide praise in and beyond Ireland. In casting the locals, McDonagh assembled a strong and internationally recognized supporting cast, including **Aiden Gillen**, **Chris O'Dowd**, Dylan Moran, and **Pat Shortt**, who cope well with the task of interpreting a script that alternates wildly between a measure of naturalism and Flann O'Brien–esque flights of caricature. Comparisons with the cult TV series *Father Ted* (1995–1998) were inevitable, and indeed much of the film's Sligo setting recalls the shenanigans of Craggy Island albeit with less humor. Others have also recognized the film's debt to Bernano's *Diary of a Country Priest* and for all the indulgent extravagance of the locals; the seriousness of Gleeson's performance and dilemma gives the film weight and cultural significance. Beyond the incongruities of its narrative universe, *Calvary* clearly functions on an allegorical level as one of the most reflective and sympathetic meditations on the "death" of Irish Catholicism to have yet emerged.

THE CANAL **(2014).** Although reaching a far wider audience of industry figures and film spectators than in the past, *The Canal* is in many respects a logical progression from director Ivan Kavanangh's earlier works applying the horror genre–inflected approach of *Tin Can Man* (2007) with the intense focus on the dysfunctional families of *Our Wonderful Home* (2008) and *The Fading Light* (2009).

Cracks begin to emerge in the hitherto untroubled existence of film archivist David (U.K. actor Rupert Evans), his Dutch wife Alice (Hannah Hoekstra), and their five-year-old son Billy (Calum Heath). These coincide with David's discovery of archival footage—brought to his attention by colleague Claire (Antonia Campbell-Hughes)—identifying their period home as the site of a macabre mass murder a century earlier. Believing that Alice is having an affair with a colleague, David follows her after she leaves work and finds his suspicions apparently confirmed. Distraught, he returns to their sleeping son to find that Alice has not returned home. He reports her disappearance to a skeptical police officer, McNamara (Steve Oram), who leads a search that finds Alice's body in the canal near their home. David becomes convinced that malevolent forces from the past have killed her and are now pursuing him and Billy.

Judged as a straightforward genre piece, *The Canal* is a minor triumph. Careful visual construction sees a shift away from naturalistic lighting to an increasingly garish color scheme as the film progresses. Careful editing limits David's (and the audience's) glimpses of dark figures to peripheral sightings, while the profoundly affecting sound design gradually ratchets up the tension. Although it wears its influences on its sleeve—Nic Roeg's *Don't Look Now* (1973) and Hideo Nakata's *Ringu* (The Ring) (1998) loom large in this respect—such overt nods to horror history are legitimated by David's status as a film buff. Given the carefully cultivated ambiguity as to whether he is experiencing psychosis rather than an actual supernatural assault, it makes sense that his imagination might be shaped by previously watched films.

However, although viscerally effective, there remains a question of filmmaker intent. While shot in Dublin, the dominant role of the U.K. and Dutch cast, plus the complete absence of recognizable landmarks, cloaks any local specificity. The setting is thus not Ireland but rather one conjured by David's imagination, a decision that doubtless left the film a more open text for overseas audiences. Furthermore, by simply rehearsing well-established horror tropes, it is ultimately far less resonant than some of Kavanagh's early works, constituting instead an impressive calling card. If that was the intent, the film succeeded in spades, bringing him to the attention of a far wider industry audience (especially in the United States) than in the past.

CAOINEADH AIRT UÍ LAOIRE (1975). Although at 56 minutes not strictly a feature-length film, **Bob Quinn**'s independently produced adaptation of Eibhlín Dubh Ní Chonaill's celebrated 18th-century poem (composed on the subject of the death of her husband in 1773) represents a key moment in the filmmaker's development toward longer-form narratives.

The multilayered work sees an English director (John Arden) take on a stage version of the narrative of Art Ó Laoghaire, an 18th-century Catholic persecuted and ultimately killed under the Penal Laws. Tensions quickly develop between the director and the Irish-speaking cast led by Sean Ban Breathnach (who in turn plays the role of Uí Laoire). In the play, Uí Laoire is pursued by the sheriff of Cork, Abraham Morris, who, as the anti-Catholic Penal Laws permitted, demands that Uí Laoire sell his prize horse for £5 (the highest price a Catholic could demand). When the director decides to intersperse the stage narrative with filmed inserts, the contemporary action of the film begins to blend with sequences from the 18th century, and the director/cast tension is transposed to that between Breathnach's Uí Laoire and Morris (John Arden again, mirroring his role as the director). As the preparations for the performance continue, the cast increasingly questions the director's interpretation of the source material and the manner in which he has transposed the original Irish text into English. Although the historical figure of Uí Laoire was ultimately shot and killed on Morris's orders, the parallel modern confrontation sees the Uí Laoire figure emerge triumphant and the entire cast (including the defeated director) celebrate with a final *ceilidh* (festive gathering).

That *Caoineadh Airt Uí Laoire* should be regarded as a political text is obvious: less obvious perhaps is the scope of those politics. Its critique of the history of British colonialism in Ireland, symbolized by two centuries of sectarian Penal Laws, is overt, but the decision to gradually merge the time lines of the story of Airt, and the staging of the play about him strongly suggests that imperialism remained an oppressive force in late 20th-century Ireland. That the film was largely financed largely by Official Sinn Féin is more than suggestive in this regard. By the mid-1970s, Official Sinn Féin had effectively renounced the use of military means to achieve a 32-county Irish republic (the military wing of the party, the "Official" Irish Republican Army, went on permanent cease-fire in 1972) and were far more focused on pursuing a class-based Marxist politics: if the party could succeed in convincing Catholic and Protestant workers alike that their interests were fundamentally aligned, the sectarianism that divided the country would cease and a 32-county socialist republic inevitably emerge. Thus, in funding Bob Quinn's film, Sinn Féin was keen that it should emphasize how modern imperialism (signified by the English director) continued to rob Ireland of its natural resources—its people, its land and oil, and its minerals and gas. As such, *Caoineadh Airt Uí Laoire* was not merely a history lesson but also an exercise in consciousness raising for a contemporary audience.

Yet the film's politics operated at a third level. Produced by Bob Quinn's Cinegael and exclusively drawing on human capital from the Connemara region (even John Arden was a playwright who also ran the Corrandulla Arts Centre in East Galway), the very fact of the film's existence demonstrated, as Quinn expressly intended it to, the possibility of creating filmed work beyond the confines of the metropolis.

CARDBOARD GANGSTERS (2016). Director **Mark O'Connor**'s visceral, fourth feature reunites him with regular collaborator actor/screenwriter John Connors for a Dublin-set take on material more commonly associated with U.S. director John Singleton's exploration of Los Angeles gang culture. Entirely set within the deprived Dublin suburb of Darndale (where Connors grew up), the narrative centers on Jason (Connors), an unemployed small-time drug dealer hoping to make it as a deejay. When his social welfare check is canceled because the local office believes him to be making a full-time living from music, Jason, with an eye to his pregnant girlfriend, determines to secure a bigger slice of the local heroin market along with his crew. This brings him into violent confrontation with Derra (Jimmy Smallhorne), the long-established local kingpin, and increasingly onto the radar of the local police.

Made for a €430,000 budget (funded largely by the Broadcasting Authority of Ireland), *Cardboard Gangsters* became a significant box office hit on its Irish release, its €550,000 take second only to the performance of *Maze* in 2017. Its success owes much to its embrace of generic tropes in its depiction of the hypermasculine criminal underworld and its compelling visual texture, which owes much to the cinematography of Michael Lavelle's fluid photography (characterized by a mix of handheld shots with the use of Steadicam to facilitate long sequences) and Tony Kearn's energetic editing. (O'Connor peppers the narrative with montage sequences depicting daily existence: kids on bikes or galloping over the green on horseback, backed by pulsing music from local hip-hop artists.)

As Jason, Connors makes for a compelling lead (rewarded by an **Irish Film and Television Academy** award in 2018), whether rising through the local heroin-dealer ranks, seducing Derra's moll (Kierston Wareing), or ultimately breaking down in the arms of his mother as the impossible pressures associated with his ascent accumulate. Yet with Connors's charisma also serves to suture over the film's more problematic aspects: Jason's casual misogyny and his unproblematic recourse to extreme brutality. The film implicitly suggests that such behavior stems from precisely the setting Jason seeks to transcend through drug dealing. However, the decision to exclusively locate the film within the immediate setting of Darndale obviates the possibility of connecting such behavior with the larger social violence long visited on derived areas of Dublin by, at best, state indifference.

CAREY, PATRICK (1916–1994). Although largely unacknowledged at the time of his death in 1994, in the 1960s and 1970s, Patrick Carey's short-film works were considered among the high points of Irish cultural life. The son of a Gate actress and cofounder of the **Irish Film Society**, Carey emigrated in the 1940s to England, where he trained as a cameraman and discovered a gift for nature photography. He then went to Canada, where he worked for that country's National Film Board. In the early 1960s, he returned to Ireland, and in 1965, he was commissioned by the **Cultural Relations Committee** (CRC) to make a documentary to celebrate the centenary of W. B. Yeats's birth. *Yeats Country* went on to win the Golden Bear award at Berlin, an **Academy Award** nomination, and other international prizes.

Further commissions from the CRC, **Radio Telefís Éireann** (RTÉ), Bord Fáilte, the Department of Lands, and Roinn na Gaeltachta led Carey to direct and shoot a series of well-received shorts, including *Errigal*, *Waves*, and *Oisín* (for which he received a second Oscar nomination in 1970). **Louis**

Marcus has written of Carey's work in this period that it demonstrated a unique chemistry between his personal sensibility and the Irish countryside. For Marcus, Carey presented Ireland as a land of clouds and mist, of threatening woods, of looming mountains and dark fields occasionally caressed by a passing band of sunlight. This was in stark contrast to the representation offered by **John Ford** in *The Quiet Man*.

By the mid-1960s, Carey was also frequently employed by international directors—including Fred Zinneman on *A Man for All Seasons* (1966)—seeking to exploit his ability to convey this atmospheric sense of the countryside. Indeed, by the end of that decade, his stature at home was such that he was invited to become a member of the **Huston Committee**. However, when the Film Board Bill that emerged from that committee's report was sidelined in the early 1970s, Carey returned to Canada, where he worked and lived until his death.

It might also be argued that the kind of films Patrick Carey made were falling out of favor by the end of the 1960s. With the disappearance of the supporting short in cinema programs and—until Michael Moore's more recent polemical work—the shift of the documentary form to television, Carey's lyrical shorts found it harder and harder to find a home on-screen.

CARNEY, JOHN (1972–), AND TOM HALL. Although known in Ireland primarily for their hit comedy-drama series *Bachelor's Walk*, which ran for three years from 2001 (and which was also directed by Kieran Carney, brother of John), the pair have also been behind some of the most interesting low-budget work produced in Ireland in the past decade.

Neither Carney nor Hall had much training in film before embarking on their first film, a road movie titled *The Edge of the World*. Tom Hall had studied at the National Film School in Dun Laoire for just six months before leaving. Carney, by contrast, spent the early 1990s in The Frames, a popular local band (whose lead singer, Glen Hansard, had been a member of *The Commitments* cast). The Frames experience proved educational, however: it was Carney's exposure to shooting on video while making promos for the band that encouraged him to link up with Hall in 1995 to make their own films.

Although *The Edge of the World* was never completed, the experience of shooting it (on Super VHS) proved vital for subsequent work. Their actual feature debut—*November Afternoon*—premiered at the 1996 Cork Film Festival, where it created something of a sensation. Made with a crew of two (Carney and Hall) and a cast of four, the film cost virtually nothing to produce beyond the cost of studio space. Beautifully shot on video in black and white, the finished film—with its jazz-inflected score composed by Carney—was reminiscent of a John Cassavettes film. Much of the polished appearance was due to the postproduction on the film, which the **Irish Film Board** funded after Carney and Hall showed them a trailer of the completed shoot and which allowed them to screen the film on 35-mm film.

However, the low-budget approach was not simply an aesthetic choice: as their later work would show, it allowed them a freedom to explore territory—incest in the case of *November Afternoon*—in a manner that might have been difficult to finance using traditional funding models. Their next production, *Just in Time*, a 50-minute one-off drama made as part of **Radio Telefís Éireann**'s short-lived *Real Time* drama slot, was equally warmly received, with a subject matter—middle-class, middle-aged angst—that was more palatable to prime-time audiences. Once again, it was characterized by sumptuous lighting and a script that realistically captured the natural rhythms of contemporary speech.

If Carney and Hall had followed the normal career trajectory for most Irish filmmakers after *Just in Time*, they would have proceeded to make a mid-budget feature. Instead, they returned to the low-budget approach of *November Afternoon* to make *Park*, which they shot on digital video for a few thousand Irish pounds. Again using minimal crew and cast, in *Park*, they dealt with another taboo subject—the sexual abuse of minors. The result was less visually dramatic than their debut, but the budgetary freedom afforded by the format allowed the filmmakers to concentrate on the two lead performances, creating an unsettling tale of the encounter between a park keeper and a girl apparently skipping school.

Carney worked alone on his next film, *On the Edge*, starring **Cillian Murphy** and produced (under the title *The Smiling Suicide Club*) by **Hell's Kitchen** with finance from Universal Pictures. Perhaps predictably, it is more conventional than the films the pair made, although the decision to examine yet another Irish taboo—young male suicide—set it apart. Carney himself was on record as being unhappy with the final cut of the film, feeling that Universal's vision of the film (they wanted a teen movie, and Carney wanted an adult movie about young people) did not coincide with his. The result did not satisfy either party, and the film was not widely released.

Afterward, Carney and Hall worked mainly in television on the previously mentioned *Bachelor's Walk* and *The Last Furlong*. The pair also shot another unreleased film in 2003 titled *Zonad*, starring Cillian Murphy as an alien who arrives in an Irish village intent on drinking and hitting it off with the local women. Its production—it was also shot on digital video—suggested that Carney and Hall were not in a hurry to return to the strictures of large budgets.

A remake of *Zonad*, which was finally released to a muted response in 2009, would prove to be the last Carney–Hall collaboration to date. Tom Hall would direct two further features, neither of which quite hit the mark either at the box office or with critics. *Wide Open Spaces* (2009) reunited the *Father*

Ted (1995–1998) sitcom writer Arthur Matthews with Ardal O'Hanlon, who had played the hapless Father Dougal in said series. *Wide Open Spaces* saw Hanlon's character Myles and Ewan Bremner's Austin in a surreal tale—part Beckett, part satire—of an attempt to create a Famine-based theme park in a Midlands quarry. Although the premise of the comedic *Sensation* (2010), which featured **Domhnall Gleeson** as a young farmer who attempts to set up a brothel in rural Ireland, attracted more attention, not all of this was positive, as the film's gender politics in particular were singled out as problematic.

For his part, exemplifying the low-budget ethos, John Carney's next film was a solo-directed project made for a reported €125,000 (with Carney apparently deferring his own fee to ensure that the cast received more than a token payment). Although a curiously old-fashioned tale (struggling musician meets winsome immigrant who acts as both a muse and a co-songwriter), *Once* (2007) arguably best exemplified **Rod Stoneman**'s faith in the policy of "radical pluralism" (i.e., if one keeps supporting a wide variety of work, some of it will make a connection with audiences). Picked up by Fox Searchlight in the United States, the film became an indie hit, its $20 million global revenues making it stunningly profitable relative to its budget. In this, it was aided by **Academy Award** success with lead actors (but also songwriters) Glen Hansard (lead singer of Carney's old group The Frames) and Marketa Irlgova winning the Best Song category at the March 2008 Oscars. (In 2011, the film was relaunched as a stage musical with a book written by *Disco Pigs* screenwriter Enda Walsh: after transferring to Broadway in 2012, the show was nominated for 11 [and won eight] Tony Awards).

Once relaunched Carney's career. Although his next release was a poorly received, low-budget Irish horror (*The Rafters* [2012]), this was followed by a full-on Hollywood production. *Begin Again* (2013) followed a somewhat similar structure to *Once* with Kiera Knightley and Mark Ruffalo partially reprising the Hansard/Irlgova roles. Carney's description of making the film suggests that it was a mixed experience for him: though he would later apologize for the remarks, he spoke of his reluctance to work with "supermodels" (a thinly veiled reference to Knightley) again. Although shot on a tiny (by Hollywood standards) budget of $8 million sourced largely from the Weinstein Company, the film's disappointing U.S. box office ($16 million) was eclipsed by the $47 million earned in other territories, the respectable cumulative take sufficient to maintain relations with the U.S. mini-major. Reviews too, though mixed (*Variety* and the *Hollywood Reporter* loved it, but the *Guardian* and *Time Out* were less enthused), were sufficiently enthusiastic to maintain Carney's status.

Thus, when Carney proposed to return to his roots for his next project, *Sing Street*, a 1980s-set tale of a Dublin schoolboy setting up a band to win the heart of the unattainable cool girl, Weinstein weighed in with a similar budget to *Begin Again*. Although hardly setting the box office alight, *Sing*

Street was a festival hit and enthusiastically reviewed: nominated for a Best Comedy/Musical award at the 2017 Golden Globes, it had the misfortune to be in the same category as the all-conquering *La La Land* (2017), thus denying it the bounce that *Once* had previously benefited from.

Carney now has an international reputation and choices available to few Irish directors of his generation. He has stayed close to his roots, however, and sought to feed the success of *Once* back into the Irish creative sector, in 2009 setting up (along with **Kirsten Sheridan** and **Lance Daly**) The Factory, a collective of screen artists housed in a former warehouse in Dublin's Docklands. This has since become "Bow Street," a popular creative hub for young actors and filmmakers that is home to the Actors Studio, the Young Screen Actors Academy, and Spotlight Ireland. In 2017, he became an adjunct professor of film at the Huston School of Film and Digital Media.

CARTOON SALOON. Founded in 1999 by Tomm Moore, Paul Young, and Nora Twomey, Cartoon Saloon is unquestionably Ireland's most successful producer of indigenous animated feature films. Remarkably, each of the company's first three features—***The Secret of Kells*** (2009), ***Song of the Sea*** (2014), and *The Breadwinner* (2017)—has received **Academy Award** nominations, a stunning record for, by Disney and Pixar standards, a relatively small-scale operation based in the Midland town of Kilkenny.

Tomm Moore and Paul Young studied **animation** at Ballyfermot Further College of Education in the 1990s at a point when the Irish industry was dominated by U.S. firms, such as Sullivan Bluth and Emerald Bluth, which operated out of Dublin but produced content primarily for the U.S. market. By the time they graduated, that foreign direct investment–based animation model had collapsed. Determined not to take the same path as many of their contemporaries—immigrating to the United States to work in the animation industry there—Moore and Young contemplated establishing an indigenous operation instead, having already commenced freelance illustration and animation work while still at Ballyfermot. (Indeed, some of that work ended up being assessed as part of their respective qualifications.)

Nora Twomey came to Ballyfermot at age 22, having previously dropped out of secondary school. Recognizing that a career working on an assembly line wasn't for her, she initially began a fine arts qualification before moving to animation, where she encountered Moore and Young. Although initially working for **Brown Bag** after graduation, she moved to Kilkenny when Moore and Young began discussing their own stand-alone operation.

Having secured grant aid from Young Irish Film Makers in Kilkenny, a small-scale film school established by Mike Kelly in the 1990s, Moore relocated to his native town and with a dozen collaborators spent the summer of 1999 working on a trailer for what would become their first feature, *The Secret of Kells*. In the interim, however, the company focused on commercials and corporate work to survive, including website design and CD-ROM production, with Moore taking on animation and Young focused on illustration.

The company scaled up significantly, bringing in 75 staff to work on their first major international television hit, *Skunk Fu*. Directed by then staffer Aidan Harte and based on a concept originally developed in 2002, the series was an immediate success when pitched to international buyers at the 2003 Cartoon Forum in Varese, Italy. Quickly picked up by both the BBC and TG4, the series initially aired in 2007 and by 2008 was available in 120 countries.

Although starting on a small scale, the company's obvious ambition attracted early support from the **Irish Film Board**. *The Secret of Kells* received development funds as early as 2001, but the company as a whole also benefited from the board's Company Development scheme in 2003 and received multiple-project funding from the same source in 2006. Although *Skunk Fu* was the main breadwinner during the mid-2000s, a number of Film Board–funded animated short productions began to build Cartoon Saloon's critical reputation. *From Darkness* (2002) and *Cuilin Dualach (Backwards Boy)* (2005), both directed by Nora Twomey, were garlanded with local and international awards, and the company continues to produce such works often with international directors working at the company (e.g., Adrien Merigeau's *Old Fangs* [2009] and Julien Regnard's *Somewhere Down the Line* [2015]).

The Secret of Kells established the company on the international scene. Assembling the $10 million budget commenced in 2001 when French producer Didier Brunner came on board as an early investor after an encounter at the Cartoon Movie festival in Berlin. However, it took another six years to complete the complex funding jigsaw puzzle made up of 18 separate institutions, including the Film Board, the Broadcasting Authority of Ireland, the MEDIA program, and Canal+. The resulting French–Belgian–Irish coproduction demanded remarkable coordination, bringing together contributions from, in addition to Cartoon Saloon itself, animation companies in Belgium (Walking the Dog), France (Blue Spirit), Hungary (Kecskemet), Brazil (Lightstar Studios), and France (sound designers Piste Rouge).

Despite this, the resulting film was unmistakably Irish in setting and appearance, taking Irish traditional arts as an inspiration for a 2-D animated tale opening in an eighth-century Irish monastery, defending knowledge against the shadow of the Dark Ages. Mindful of his funders, Moore worked with Fabrice Ziolkowski, a French American screenwriter, to ensure that the story was comprehensible to an international audience, and Moore has overtly cited Joseph Campbell's work as shaping the film's hero-journey structure.

The international reception of the film was remarkable. It won Best Feature Film at the 13th Seoul International Cartoon and Animation Festival, the Audience Award for Best Feature Film at the 33rd Annecy Animation Festival in France, and the Edinburgh Film Festival's Standard Life Audience Award. Championed in Ireland by Disney, Moore was selected for the Screen Directors Guild of Ireland's Directors Finders Series, allowing him to showcase the film at the Directors Guild of America Theatre in Los Angeles, bringing it to a much wider market. After acquiring the U.S. rights, distributor GKIDS released *Kells* in a limited run in December 2009 and, despite high-profile competition from U.S.-based studios, succeeded in securing an Oscar nomination.

The transformation in the company's profile (Cartoon Saloon won Producer of the Year at the Cartoon Movie Tributes ceremony in 2010, and Moore was invited to join the Academy of Motion Picture Arts and Sciences in 2011) radically altered the company's prospects. More television work arrived, including the animation sequences for **Chris O'Dowd**'s hit comedy *Moone Boy* and partnering with O'Dowd again as lead voice talent on a children's animated series *Puffin Rock* (coproduced with Derry-based company Dog Ears), which began production in September 2013 and debuted on air in 2014.

But it was the feature animation context where the most obvious changes appeared. In addition to working on international productions, such as the adaptation of illustrator Tomi Ungerer's *Moon Man* (2012) or the 2014 anthology project *The Prophet*, the success of *The Secret of Kells* oiled the wheels for later in-house productions. Fund-raising for the follow-up film—the fairy-themed but contemporary-set *Song of the Sea* (2014)—took just two years with Cartoon Saloon in the unusual position, for a nonstudio animation company, of being able to attract international presales. Distribution in the United Kingdom and Ireland was secured (via Optimum Releasing) in 2011, three years before *Song of the Sea*'s completion, and it was selected for the influential Toronto International Film Festival (TIFF) in September 2014 and again nominated in the Best Feature Animation category at the Oscars.

This in turn led to the company's first feature set outside Ireland: an adaptation of Deborah Ellis's acclaimed 2000 novel *The Breadwinner*, set in Taliban-era Afghanistan. Canadian producers Aircraft Pictures held the adaptation rights and approached Paul Young and Cartoon Saloon's managing director Gerry Shirren at an animation market event to discuss a coproduction. Nora Twomey took on directorial duties on the Irish–Canadian–Luxembourg coproduction, which commenced work in 2016. The film received a profile boost when Angelina Jolie came on board as an executive producer via her Jolie Pas Productions. Premiering at TIFF, the film demonstrated the company's capacity to work outside an Irish visual repertoire and almost inevitably secured, among other awards, a third Oscar nomination and an invitation for Twomey to join Moore in the Academy of Motion Picture Arts and Sciences.

Cartoon Saloon is now an established player within the global animation industry with a slate of projects in development, including Tomm Moore's *Wolf Walkers*, set in 17th-century Kilkenny. Confirmation of that status came with the February 2017 announcement of the creation of Light House Studios, a Kilkenny-based 2-D animation operation established in partnership with Mercury Filmworks, a Canadian independent animation house. Potentially adding 140 jobs to those already created by Cartoon Saloon, Light House promises to identify Kilkenny as an animation hub, attracting talent by making permanent work for animators a realistic prospect.

CASSIDY, ELAINE (1980–). Cassidy grew up in Kilcoole, County Wicklow, near the set of now defunct Irish soap *Glenroe*, a fact that encouraged her to consider acting as a career, and first appeared in Geraldine Creed's **short film** *The Stranger Within Me*. Two years later, Creed cast her again opposite Angie Dickinson and Gina Moxley in *The Sun, the Moon and the Stars*. In 1998, she was offered both a recurring role in *Glenroe* and the eponymous lead in Atom Egoyan's film adaptation of William Trevor's short story *Felicia's Journey*. She proved a revelation as Felicia, the pregnant teenager abandoned by her boyfriend (**Peter McDonald**), who falls prey to the sinister schemes of Bob Hoskins's psychopath.

A run of film roles followed that drew on her youthful innocence. Cassidy was mute but eye-catching in the international horror hit *The Others* (2001) and managed to be simultaneously otherworldly and natural as Runt in Kirsten Sheridan's *Disco Pigs*, where she more than held her own opposite **Cillian Murphy**. She again played an innocent (Hitler's niece) in *Uncle Adolf* and also played Maud, the only apparently innocent character in Irish director **Aisling Walsh**'s adaptation of Sarah Waters's novel *Fingersmith*.

Cassidy relocated relatively early in her career to London, where she has made occasional forays into theater, including Brian Friel's *Fathers and Sons* in the Donmar and *Les Liaisons Dangereuses* in the National Theatre. And, although she appeared in Shimmy Marcus's 2007 short comedy *Hannah Cohen's Holy Communion* and the little-seen *Property of the State* (2016) (based on the story of the sister of serial murderer Brendan O'Donnell), like many other Irish actors of her generation (notably female ones), she has become far better known for her prominent, ongoing roles in British (and other) prime-time television dramas. These include the aristocratic Katherine Glendinning in the BBC's period drama *The Paradise* (2012–2013) and a sequence of appearances in crime dramas, including the central role of Dinah, a Mancunian/Polish policewoman in Paul Abbot's **Channel 4** drama *No Offence*. She also made a brief return to Irish screens as the lead in RTE's legal drama *Acceptable Risk*. These latter productions have seen the innocence of earlier characters jettisoned in favor of more complex and grittier screen personas: an undercover cop in Channel 4's *The Ghost Squad* (2005), a suspected murderer in CBS's *Harper's Island* (2009), and a bereaved wife of a murdered business executive delving into the murky connections of her husband's employer in *Acceptable Risk*.

CENSORSHIP. It has long been a source of wry amusement that in July 1923, amid the smoke of civil war, Dáil Éireann found time to pass the Censorship of Films Act, which until the introduction of the **Irish Film Board** Act at the close of the 1970s had the unique distinction of being the only piece of Irish legislation directly related to film. The introduction of the legislation was all the more surprising given that the new state had inherited the British Cinematograph Act of 1909, which already permitted local councils to act as censors over material screened within their jurisdictions.

Arguably, however, the civil war created an atmosphere in which the act became inevitable. Kevin O'Higgins, the minister who introduced the act, while conceding that cinema could not be blamed for "*all* our present troubles," could not help mischievously speculating whether Eamon de Valera was "addicted to frequenting cinemas when he was young." Arguably, the act was also designed to equip the nascent state with another tool for determining the "official" view of Ireland. That view—which would prevail until the 1960s—was captured in one of the contributions to the parliamentary debate on the 1923 act from Professor William Magennis, who would subsequently become the first chairman of the Films Appeal Board:

> Purity of mind and sanity of outlook upon life were long ago regarded as characteristic of our people. The loose views and the vile lowering of values that belong to other races and other peoples were being forced upon our people through the popularity of the cinematograph.

This highly conservative Catholic ethos actively informed the framing of the act. O'Higgins had been prompted to bring it forward after receiving a deputation made up of the Irish Vigilance Association, the Priests' Social Guild, and representatives from the Catholic, Episcopalian, and Presbyterian churches. Consequently, the act laid down guidelines for the censor requiring that films should be banned if they were "indecent, obscene or blasphemous." Furthermore, the membership of the Appeals Board provided for by the act included senior members of both the Catholic and the Protestant clergy for the first 40 years of the act's operation.

Thus, from 1924 to 1965, films dealing with (or even mentioning) illegitimacy, divorce, abortion, contraception, and, in the postwar years, rape and homosexuality were excluded from Irish cinemas: 11,000 films were cut or banned by 1980. Furthermore, despite the specific provision in the 1923 act for a limited certificate allowing some films to be screened in "the presence of certain classes of persons," by 1945, no censor had exercised it. Both the censors and the Appeals Board felt that the labeling of a film with a limited certificate "would arouse unhealthy curiosity."

Thus, every film that passed received a universal certificate (equivalent to the U, or General, certificate). Even after "limited certs" were first introduced, they were used sparingly. Furthermore, while it may have appeared that cutting was better than banning because it allowed the film to be shown, this did not always hold true. Otto Preminger's 1959 film *Anatomy of a Murder* is a courtroom drama dealing with an alleged rape and features a key scene presenting forensic evidence. However, when presented by its distributor for certification in Ireland, the censor cut all references to the rape and forensic evidence, rendering the film meaningless: the character on trial was clearly accused of something, but what?

The only screenings exempt from these controls were those undertaken by the **Irish Film Society** from 1936. From its inception, the society argued that since its screenings were for members only, they were effectively private and thus fell outside the purview of the act. In effect, then, the society established a precedent whereby films screened in club conditions did not require prior certification by the Irish censor. (Various film **festivals** and more permanent art house venues that emerged from the 1950s would subsequently use this precedent.) That the Department of Justice permitted the precedent arguably reflected a class prejudice that was exhibited in a tolerance of viewings of uncensored films by those members of society equipped with sufficient cultural capital to inoculate them against the "vile values" referred to by Professor Magennis.

However, the close of the 1950s saw massive change sweep through the country. Traditional restrictions, imposed by the introspective economic and moral protectionism operating in Irish society, loosened, fueled by the economic crisis of the 1950s and the obvious failure of social and economic policies of the previous decades. At the same time, a new generation of journalists, born after independence and equipped with a more international outlook, came to the fore. Events such as the lifting of the *Lady Chatterley* ban in Britain in 1960 led to a questioning of traditional precepts and to wider social debate on this side of the Irish Sea.

Simultaneously, Irish distributors and exhibitors began to apply pressure to relax censorship: the availability of product was now restricted by both censorship and the decline in the output of American studios. This coincided with the appointment of Brian Lenihan as minister for justice in October 1964. Sympathetic to the distributors and exhibitors (and facing a press barrage over the banning of Henry Hathaway's *Of Human Bondage*, which had been made in Ireland, and by the demand to cut Stanley Kubrick's *Dr.*

Strangelove), Lenihan in January 1965 appointed an entirely new Appeals Board (the previous chairman, J. T. O'Farrell, had been a member for more than 40 years). The new board had a specific brief: start issuing limited certificates (i.e., certificates limiting entry to specified age-groups). Until this time, the Censorship of Publications Appeals Board had largely rubber-stamped the censors' decisions. After 1965, the incumbent censor, Dr. Christy Macken, continued to issue bans, but increasingly the board began to overturn them: 29 of the 42 films banned by Macken in 1965 were subsequently passed by the board albeit with cuts and limited certificates. After 18 months, Macken began to issue a greater number of limited certificates, although he continued banning a substantial numbers of films. The board for its part continued overturning the majority of these bans. Finally, in 1972, Macken was replaced by Dermot Breen, director of the Cork Film Festival, whose appointment was regarded as completing the liberalizing process. The first film censor who actually had a background in film, Breen consolidated the Appeal Boards policy: although he also banned films, he did so at a greatly reduced rate so that the Appeals Board had less and less work to do. Indeed, Breen was regarded as so liberal—at least in relation to his predecessor—that it was argued that the Appeals Board would now have to "catch up" with *him*.

Breen remained censor until 1978, when former **Radio Telefís Éireann** (RTÉ) host Frank Hall replaced him and largely maintained Breen's approach. However, when Hall retired in 1986, his replacement became the first overtly liberal (as opposed to *relatively* liberal) holder of the post. Like Dermot Breen, Sheamus Smith also had a background in film, having acted as chief executive of the National Film Studios of Ireland at **Ardmore Studios**. Between 1986 and 2003, Smith would ban outright only 10 films released to theaters, although these included *Showgirls* (1995), *From Dusk Till Dawn* (1995), and *Natural Born Killers* (1994). The last of these caused a minor furor, however, when, in the wake of Smith's refusal to certify it, the **Irish Film Centre** (IFC) announced plans to screen the film on an open-ended run. The IFC assumed that since the screenings were limited to members, they would be covered under the club screenings "rule." However, the unusually open-ended nature of the run left the **Irish Film Institute** (IFI), which operated the cinemas, open to Smith's criticism that the screenings were prompted more by commercial than cultural considerations. Smith drew the attention of the Department of Justice to the screenings, which in turn threatened to issue an injunction against the IFI if the film were screened. Faced with the threat of time in prison, the IFI board met three hours before the first scheduled screening of *Natural Born Killers* and decided to pull the film. The incident was significant in that it indicated that the same paternalistic rationale that had informed the "gentleman's agreement" permitting limited access to uncertified material in the 1930s was still in place 60 years later.

For the most part, however, Smith brought a new degree of sensitivity to the post, especially with regard to the traditionally complex field of certifying art house material. The passing of Peter Greenaway's brilliant but grotesque *The Cook, the Thief, His Wife and Her Lover* (1989) without any cuts represented something of a breakthrough, a recognition that it was aimed at a particular audience segment (a fact made explicit by its exhibition at Dublin's **Light House Cinema**).

Smith retired in 2003, to be replaced by John Kelleher, a former RTÉ and feature film producer (including *Eat the Peach*). As the first actual filmmaker appointed to the position, Kelleher went of his way to be more responsive to public opinion. This has led to the (unprecedented) publication of censorship decisions and an enunciation of the general principles informing the work of the censor and his staff, among which is the view that adults should be free, within the law, to choose what they wish to view. In effect, then, Kelleher has begun to redefine the role of the office, acting less as a censor and more as a classifier of material. This was reflected in the change of the official title of the institution from the Irish Film Censor's Office to the Irish Film Classification Office in 2008. In 2009, Kelleher stepped down to be replaced by Deputy Censor Ger Connolly. However, because of a then operational ban on public sector pay increases, though Connolly de facto took on the role of censor, he was not officially confirmed in that role until 2016.

CHANNEL 4. Channel 4 began broadcasting in the United Kingdom in 1982, having been set up as an indirect result of the recommendations of a government-commissioned report on the allocation of a fourth channel. The *Annan Report* concluded that rather than simply handing the channel over to the existing British broadcasters, the fourth channel should be run independently with an explicit remit to address niche audiences hitherto ignored by the other terrestrial broadcasters, the BBC and ITV. In practice, Channel 4 came under the financial umbrella of ITV (which funded the channel in return for the right to sell advertising around Channel 4's programs) but retained editorial independence. Channel 4 adopted a publisher/broadcaster organizational model whereby it commissioned a substantial proportion of its programs from independent producers. As part of its remit, the new channel was to address the programming needs of ethnic minorities within Great Britain. Although this was not immediately obvious at the time, this would prove a massive boon to filmmakers and television personnel within Ireland.

By the early 1980s, there were approximately 1.5 million people of Irish extraction living in the United Kingdom, nearly 2 percent of the population. In effect, the Irish constituted an ethnic minority. In addition, Jeremy Isaacs, the channel's chief executive from 1982 until 1989, had a previously demonstrated interest in Ireland, having already produced *Ireland: A Television History*. In March 1982 (eight months before Channel 4's first broadcast),

Isaacs informed an audience at the Third Celtic Film and Television Festival in Wexford that he planned to include Irish sports and politics as part of the channel's weekly schedule. In practice, those particular nonfiction programs failed to materialize, although in June 1986, the channel did commission eight documentaries on contemporary Ireland under the collective title of *The Irish Reel*. From its inception, however, the channel was a major cofunder, with **Radio Telefís Éireann** (RTÉ), of Irish-themed television drama, partially financing series such as *The Year of the French*, the **Little Bird**–produced *The Irish RM*, *Caught in a Free State*, and **Strongbow**'s *When Reason Sleeps*.

The channel was also a key source of funds for feature films. Often credited with single-handedly reviving the British film industry in the 1980s (indeed, for a period it *was* the British film industry), the channel's Film on Four Strand would prove a crucial source of funding for Irish film. The first Irish filmmaker to benefit from Channel 4's largesse was **Neil Jordan**, whose debut feature, ***Angel***, was funded (to the tune of £800,000) largely by Channel 4. (The Jordan association would continue with the director's subsequent *The Company of Wolves*, **The Miracle**, and **The Crying Game**, the last of which was one of its most successful at the box office, taking $62 million in the United States.) The remainder of *Angel's* budget—£100,000—came from the **Irish Film Board**, and this funding partnership continued throughout the existence of the first Film Board: **The Outcasts**, *The Country Girls*, **Eat the Peach**, **Budawanny**, **Reefer and the Model**, and **The Courier** were all cofunded by Channel 4 and the board. Indeed, given the complaint by the Film Board's first chairman, **John Boorman**, that the money given to the board (around £500,000 per annum) was insufficient to make "half of one decent film," it is arguable that very few of the board projects would have come to fruition in the absence of Channel 4 Films.

However, Channel 4's support of Irish cinema during this period was not limited to Film Board projects. Under a policy of supporting workshop production in the regions, Channel 4 funded both the **Derry Film and Video Co-Operative** (and the collective's only feature production, ***Hush-a-Bye Baby***) and Belfast Independent Video.

In 1988, however, Isaacs stepped down as chief executive and was replaced by former BBC director of programs Michael Grade. Perceived as more commercially minded than his predecessor, Grade's tenure saw Irish television drama and documentary commissions dry up. However, Channel 4 Films continued to invest in Irish features through the 1990s; these included ***Trojan Eddie***, ***Dancing at Lughnasa***, and ***Southpaw***. In 1998, Channel 4 Films was rebranded FilmFour and continued as a production and distribution entity. However, in 2000 and 2001, the company posted losses of £3 million and £5.4 million, respectively. Although these were not in themselves unsustainable losses, they highlighted a structural weakness in the company—namely, the absence of a long-term relationship with one of the major U.S. studios, which had allowed other, smaller operators, such as Miramax and Working Title, to sustain occasional losses. In July 2002, then, FilmFour was effectively closed and reintegrated into Channel 4's drama department. However, in 2006 Channel 4 reintroduced "FilmFour Productions" to coincide with the launch of their stand-alone Film4 dedicated film channel. The new entitty has continued to fund Irish-themed projects, especially those led by UK-based directors such as Steve McQueen (*Hunger* [2008]), Martin McDonagh (*In Bruges* [2008]), **Ken Loach** (*Jimmy's Hall* [2014]), and Yann Demange (*'71* [2014]). The company has also established an ongoing relationship with **Element Pictures**, which has seen it invest in **Lenny Abrahamson**'s most recent films—*Frank* (2014), *Room* (2015), and *The Little Stranger* (2018)—and those of Yorgos Lanthimos: *The Lobster* (2015), *The Killing of a Sacred Deer* (2017), and *The Favourite* (2018).

CHAOS/DEATHGAMES (2001). Geraldine Creed's sci-fi fiction is a dystopian vision of Ireland set in 2020 where individuals have lost many rights, such as those to education and work. Killer (Jason Barry) rebels against this and joins Alf's (Tommy O'Neill) "Chaos Circus," a touring metal circus incorporating motorcycles and chainsaws. Alf's daughter Grace (Lindsey Harris) falls in love with Killer, and in a grotesque effort to permanently secure their relationship as well as his services for the carnival, Alf has his putative son-in-law kidnapped. He then amputates one of his arms and legs, which are then replaced by artificial limbs constructed by Grace, and the mutant Killer becomes a star act.

Creed's second feature marked a radical tonal and thematic departure from her debut coming-of-age comedy *The Sun, the Moon and the Stars* (1996) and a rare foray for Irish film into science fiction, although one might consider it alongside the Belfast-set *Sunset Heights* (1999) and Kevin Barry's 2011 novel *City of Bohane*. *Chaos* eschews sci-fi's usually relentlessly urban sheen in favor of a deliberately lo-fi visual aesthetic. Although this ultimately undermines its efforts to transcend realism, it marks an attempt to broaden the scope of Irish film away from the dominance of naturalist drama and might best be viewed as an early effort to broaden the parameters of indigenous visual storytelling via transnational generic means. In this regard, Creed's film anticipates the emergence and ongoing cycle of Irish **horror** films initiated soon afterward by **Conor McMahon**'s *Dead Meat* (2004). It is surely more than coincidental that *Chaos* was produced by Brendan McCarthy, who, as head of production and development at the **Irish Film Board**, would green-light McMahon's film and go on to write/produce many more genre films (through his company **Fantastic Films**), including the sci-fi *The Last Days on Mars* (2013) and the horrors *Wake Wood* (2011), *Stitches* (2012), and *Nails* (2017). Although widely overlooked in Ireland, *Chaos* won the Audience Award at the Luxembourg Fantasy Fest 2001.

CHARLIE CASANOVA **(2011).** Having watched a number of his scripts secure development funding only to go into "turnaround" (i.e., not get produced) and enter development hell, actor/writer/director Terry McMahon (a longtime contributor to **Radio Telefís Éireann**'s flagship soap *Fair City*) was determined to make a film using his own resources. Mobilizing his contacts on Facebook, he sought assistance and rapidly secured cast and crew. An intense 11-day shoot followed, and, with the talent effectively working for free, *Charlie Casanova* was completed for a reported budget of less than €1,000.

McMahon's script is a raging piece of class warfare, placing Ireland's social elite firmly within its crosshairs. Charlie Barnum (aka Casanova [Emmett J. Scanlon]) is an obnoxious middle-class businessman renting out flats to immigrants, snorting coke, and carrying on an affair with his best friend's wife, Una (Leigh Arnold). Bringing his friends and their wives to a hotel for the weekend, Charlie unveils his philosophy: to escape the confines of social mores (which he clearly feels his exalted class status exempts him from anyway) and live a life determined instead by chance and opportunity. Charlie soon gets the opportunity to embrace this outlook. On a quest for coke, he knocks down a working-class girl, flees the scene, burns his car, and moves to proceed as if without consequence. The police, with apparently irrefutable evidence of his guilt, arrest him, but during his witness interview, Barnum turns the tables, humiliates the guards, and walks out to continue his odyssey.

Composed largely of dialogue-heavy sequences tightly focused on his actors (making a virtue of the absence of sets), Charlie stands as a deliberate caricature of the macho excesses of the Celtic Tiger. Infinitely confident of his inherent superiority, he repeatedly pours scorn on the working class and bleeding-heart liberals. Testing the limits of what his class status will allow him to get away with (almost literally murder), even he seems occasionally surprised by how far he can go.

It is tempting to describe critical reaction to McMahon's film as "divided," but in truth, most reviewers hated it, citing Charlie's relentlessly unsympathetic character and the chaotic narrative structure. Charlie's wordy rants (name-dropping cultural philosophers) punctuate every scene in a manner that is wearyingly repetitive.

Unsurprisingly, McMahon vigorously defended his film's characterization and narrative structure. As the representative for an infinitely entitled elite class, Charlie is not meant to be sympathetic in any way: he is the enemy, convicted by his own words. Additionally, this character is intended to defy the parameters of traditional narrative precisely because his experience of life (and that of his social cohort) is consequence free. Having committed a hit-and-run, moral and legal norms demand that Charlie experience some form of punishment. However, McMahon structures the film so that this simply never arrives, confounding audience expectations. For many viewers, this rendered the film a difficult experience. Nonetheless, it did find champions in influential quarters, not least the South by Southwest festival, which offered the film a platform for its world premiere, permitting it to be subsequently picked up by Studio Canal and bringing it to a far wider audience than its paltry budget initially appeared to promise. In some senses at least, McMahon's maverick choices would appear to have been vindicated.

CHERRYBOMB (2009). The allusion to explosives in its title notwithstanding, *Cherrybomb* is very much a post-Troubles film, reflected in its setting amid the symbol of Belfast's renewal, the Titanic Quarter. If there is conflict in this film, it is intergenerational strife. The nihilistic views of adulthood by Luke (**Robert Sheehan**) and Malachy (Rupert Grint) are interrupted by the arrival of Michelle (Kimberley Nixon), daughter of Malachy's boss. Both boys are attracted to her and begin to compete for her attention.

The three-way relationship is complicated by difficulties that all three experience in their parental relationships. Malachy chafes at his parents' interference in his life, while Kimberley is caught between her separated father and mother. Luke's is the most extreme: an entirely absent mother, an addict father, and a corrupt businessman older brother. These conflicts spiral out of control, leading to a violent conclusion.

While the casting of *Cherrybomb* is interesting—it confirmed Sheehan's cocky bad-boy screen image and put light-years between actor Rupert Grint and the character Ron Weasley (Harry Potter's best friend)—the film is hindered by a woefully underdeveloped screenplay. Characterization is thin, and the attraction between the leads is unconvincing, as, indeed, is much of the character motivation. In spite of convincing Northern Irish accents, Grint's and Nixon's performances are low-key to the point of anonymity. As a consequence, the film's explosive ending seems contrived rather than earned.

Cherrybomb demonstrates a nascent post-Troubles Northern Irish cinema. Ironically perhaps, the directors of the film, Lisa Barros D'Sa and Glenn Leyburn, would achieve greater success when they returned to the 1970s in **Good Vibrations**, a far richer film that explores the struggle for a normal existence in a conflict zone. While *Cherrybomb* showcases a certain visual flair, at times, the narrative gaps are papered over by extensive reliance on a pop video aesthetic.

CIRCLE OF FRIENDS **(1995).** Based on a best-selling Maeve Binchy novel, the film opens in a small village in 1950s Ireland. Three friends—Benny (Minnie Driver), Nan (Saffron Burrows), and Eve (Geraldine O'Dawe)—are confirmed together and pledge everlasting friendship, but shortly afterward, Nan and her family move away. Half a decade later, however, the three are reunited in college in Dublin. Nan's years living in Dublin have given her a veneer of sophistication compared to her friends—Eve is an orphan being raised by nuns, and Benny must return home to her village every night.

In college, Benny meets Jack (Chris O'Donnell), a medical student and college rugby star. At a party hosted by Eve, Benny and Jack begin a frustratingly chaste relationship. Benny's parents, however, are determined that she will marry the repulsive Sean (Alan Cumming), who works in her father's business. When her father suddenly dies, Benny is forced to leave college and work in the shop with Sean, whose advances she attempts to ward off. Meanwhile, Nan meets the local Protestant landlord Simon Westward (Colin Firth) for illicit assignations in Eve's cottage. However, when she becomes pregnant, Westward dumps her. Desperate, Nan seduces Benny's boyfriend Jack, who is drunk, and then informs him that he is the father of her baby. Unhappily, he agrees to stand by her, and they become engaged, thus breaking Benny's heart.

From this opening synopsis, it is not hard to see why *Circle of Friends* was easily the most successful film funded by the Irish Film Board in the early 1990s. Its adherence to a familiar narrative structure and its soft, primitive depiction of Ireland doubtless contributed to its $24 million performance at the U.S. box office and the $4.5 million it took in the United Kingdom. However, given filmmaker **Pat O'Connor**'s pedigree, it was an enormous disappointment. Most depressing are the film's Victorian values: Nan, who sleeps with the local landlord, becomes the "bad girl" willing to betray her best friend to get a husband. Meanwhile, Benny, who retains her chastity for most of the film, is rewarded for her (as it turns out) temporary virtue. Nan is last seen leaving for a boat to England and is never heard of again, while Benny not only gets her man but also turns out to be a successful writer.

Disappointing too is the film's John Hinde postcard–style representation of Ireland of the 1950s. Although the film stops short of showing flame-haired children with turf-carrying donkeys, virtually every shot looks like it received Tourist Board (**Bord Fáilte**) approval: glistening streams, neat villages arranged around a picturesque green, and so on. Occasionally, this is technically impressive: the film's signature establishing shot for University College Dublin (ironically, actually Trinity College shot from the Dublin Castle end of Dame Street) looks like contemporary footage. But for the most part, it serves only to underline the good-girls-go-to-heaven, bad-girls-don't fantasy element of the narrative itself. The Michael Kamen score, drenched in saccharine Irish-style melodies, does nothing to counter the effect of the visuals.

The saving grace of the film lies in some of the performances, especially that of Minnie Driver, who lent the character intelligence not evident in Andrew Davies's script. This role as the outwardly tough but inwardly vulnerable Benny proved a career breakthrough for her. Inevitably, however, given the absence of Irish actors in lead roles, audiences were subjected to cringe-worthy attempts at local accents, some so bad as to obscure the dialogue. Chief among the culprits was Chris O'Donnell, clearly chosen to give the film international appeal but always looking more like an American high school jock than what in the 1950s would have been a rare creature in Ireland—a university student.

***CITADEL* (2011).** As an 18-year-old, writer/director Ciaran Foy was violently set on by a gang of teenagers, leaving him traumatized and afraid to go out in public. That experience informs the premise of his feature debut. Tommy (Aneurin Barnard) lives with his pregnant wife in a wintry and menacing social housing complex (set in an uncertain space between Dublin and Glasgow). As she goes into labor, they leave for the hospital, but she is assaulted by a group of feral children. Before she dies, she gives birth to their daughter. Plagued by chronic agoraphobia, Tommy retreats into his apartment, his solitude compounded by his inability to bond with his child. While nurse Marie (Wunmi Mosaku) encourages him to try to reintegrate into society and forgive the actions of those who killed his wife, a renegade priest (Scottish actor James Cosmo) insists that he must confront the still-at-large group of monstrous hoodie-wearing children. Tommy thus commences a journey to overcome his trauma while reconnecting with his daughter.

With a €1.2 million budget funded jointly by Creative Scotland and the **Irish Film Board**, Foy's horror eschews blood and gore in place of a relentless sense of psychological dread that is both postapocalyptic and rooted in recognizable social circumstances. It is also unusual and of interest in placing this terror within the psyche of its male protagonist. It emerges that the malevolent teenagers can sense fear: recurring shots focus tightly on Tommy's face, capturing every facial twitch as he responds to real or imagined threats. The film's decision to delay confirming the true nature of the children—are they merely products of an atomized society or supernatural creations?—adds the further possibility that Tommy is suffering from paranoid delusions.

Foy's film was received to much acclaim at the prestigious SXSW (South by Southwest) festival in Austin, Texas, in March 2012, winning the Audience Award and setting off a bidding war among distributors: a remarkable achievement for a debut low-budget film shot in just 23 days. The film's eventual U.S. release unintentionally coincided with the controversy over the murder of Trayvon Martin, a hoodie-wearing black youth, at the hands of a neighborhood watch member. Viewed in that light, *Citadel* might be read as a less-than-liberal revenge fantasy. Nonetheless, it brought Foy to the attention of Hollywood writer/director Scott Derrickson, who pegged him to direct the sequel to his 2012 psycho-horror *Sinister*. That film went on to gross $52 million worldwide in 2015, leading to additional U.S. offers and opportunities in the horror genre, including *Eli* (2018), which again centers on male fear—a boy suffering from an autoimmune disorder discovers that the house he is living in isn't as safe as he thought.

CLASH OF THE ASH (1987). Scripted and directed by Fergus Tighe, who later scripted *2by4*, the drama incorporates an effective rite-of-passage debut that ties in with a series of Irish films that can loosely be described as "Leaving Certificate" films. Starring Vinny Murphy, Alan Devlin, and **Gina Moxley**, the story focuses on a young man who has to decide what he wants to do with his life in a small rural Cork environment, where most of the excitement is played out on the hurling pitch. Railing against parental pressures (and their mapped-out plans for his future), he craves the excitement of distant shores (represented by Moxley's Mary, who has already moved to London). Yet he is simultaneously frightened of the unknown quantities associated with all forms of **emigration**. This gentle story captures the social reality of the period and regional place, remaining a memorable first outing for Tighe.

COLLINS, DAVID. *See* IRISH FILM THEATRE; SAMSON FILMS; STRONGBOW FILMS.

COLLINS, PAT. Pat Collins occupies a unique position in Irish film, having established a critically acclaimed reputation and a body of work that has eschewed fictional narratives in favor of creative documentary. In the process, he has created something approaching his own genre in which, taken together, his films offer a poetic and often wistful analysis of the Irish place and condition during a period of dramatic social transformation.

A native of West Cork (where he continues to live), Collins began his career in Galway, where he edited *Film West* and programmed the Galway Film Fleadh (Festival). He moved into film production with a series of evocative portraits of Irish writers—*Michael Hartnett: Necklace of Wrens* (1999), *John McGahern: A Private World*, and *Frank O'Connor—The Lonely Voice* (2003)—each of which foregrounded an appreciation of Ireland as a fundamentally rural place that both produces and is produced by acts of the imagination. In a filmography funded largely by Irish TV broadcasters and more recently the **Arts Council**, Collins is drawn to creative individuals who exemplify in some sense a "fifth province" where nation and imagination intersect and has produced documentaries about a diverse range of Irish artists, including the actor **Gabriel Byrne** (*Gabriel Byrne: Stories from Home* [2008]), writer/cartographer Tim Robinson (*Tim Robinson: Connemara and Pilgrim* [2011]), Irish-language poet Nuala Ní Dhomhnaill (*Nuala Ní Dhomhnaill: Taibhsí I mBéal na Gaoithe* [2009]), and comedian Tommy Tiernan (*Tommy: To Tell You the Truth* [2014]). His film on Robinson can be seen as a key text in his progression as a filmmaker, combining as it does a portrait of a significant (if sometimes overlooked) Irish cultural figure (Robinson is British but has lived in the west of Ireland for more than 40 years) with an evocation of landscape and place that artfully deploys the distinctive sound and visual properties of the essay film. In this regard, Collins's collaboration with sound/picture editor Tadgh O'Sullivan (who is developing a reputation in his own right since his debut *The Great Wall* [2015]) has been central to the evolution of his creative practice.

Tracing the ley lines of the Irish identity has been a constant feature of Collins's work, particularly visible in the baggy, poetic film essays *What We Leave in Our Wake* (2010) and *Living in a Coded Land* (2014). Clearly inspired by Robinson's lifelong dedication to "mapping" the west of Ireland, Collins set about making **Silence**, one of only two "fiction" features to date. This widely praised drama-documentary hybrid (whose plot displays similarities to Wim Wenders's *Lisbon Story,* 1994) deals with an Irish immigrant (Eoin Mac Giolla Bhríde) who returns to Ireland on a work assignment from Berlin to record "silence" but finds his task continually interrupted by man-made sounds and encounters with real individuals (including Tim Robinson) who alert him to the stories of the places he passes through. While highly original in conception and execution and offering visual representation to places that have heretofore been ignored by both indigenous and non-Irish filmmakers alike, *Silence* might nevertheless be accused of a kind of solipsism in its obsession with an "Atlantic Ireland" on the verge of disappearance to the exclusion of a multicultural, globalized reality. In a similar vein, *Song of Granite* (2017), Collins's austerely beautiful mixed fiction/nonfiction biography of famed *sean-nós* singer Joe Heaney, is an attempt to capture not simply an individual voice but also a physical and cultural place that fostered an entire musical tradition and is increasingly facing extinction. Documentary pioneer Robert Flaherty was accused of restaging reality in his efforts to salvage on film evidence of disappearing cultures, whether they were in northern Canada or the South Pacific. Collins seeks to evade that critique in *Song of Granite* by explicitly fictionalizing episodes of Heaney's life (using three actors to play him as a boy, as middle aged, and as elderly) while intercutting archive footage of the real Heaney in performance.

Collins's work is defined by a vision of Ireland in which place shapes culture (rather than the other way around) and in his more traditional documentaries demonstrates an affection for artistic voices who defy the homogenizing effects of capitalism and modernity. His prolific output to date can be read as a richly evocative if also fundamentally narrow and conservative assertion of Irish identity.

COMERFORD, JOE (1949–). Having studied at Dublin's National College of Art and Design (NCAD) in the 1960s, it was perhaps unsurprising that Comerford would become one of the leading lights of the radical tendency that briefly flourished within Irish cinema of the 1970s and 1980s, becoming a founding member of the **Association of Independent Producers** alongside contemporaries **Bob Quinn**, **Cathal Black**, and **Pat Murphy**. From his first public work, *Emtigon* (1971), he was clearly interested in subverting the cinematic form, seeking to combine narrative with an almost painterly visual abstraction. Comerford first made an impact with a series of short experimental films, including *Withdrawal* (1974/1982), a traumatic film set in a psychiatric ward. His first short feature (60 minutes), ***Down the Corner*** (1977), made with the assistance of the British Film Institute and Dublin's Ballyfermot Community Workshop, examined working-class poverty. It became a highly influential text in "first-wave" Irish cinema, frequently cited by subsequent Irish filmmakers as inspiring their early work. Notably, it is less experimental in form than his previous works. His next feature, the realist *Traveller* (1981), dealt with Ireland's indigenous "others," the Traveller community, and though adopting an improvised approach to filming incorporating real events as they befell the key protagonists (a newlywed Traveller couple smuggling goods across the Irish border), it was based on script developed with **Neil Jordan**. He turned again to abstraction with *Waterbag*, an **Arts Council/Irish Film Board** (IFB)–funded project recalling the work of Len Lye in its use of direct painting on film before turning to concentrate on feature production. Comerford was one of the last recipients of funding from the first IFB, which partially financed his next feature, ***Reefer and the Model*** (1988). This much later film dealt with smugglers in Connemara, County Galway, who get mixed up with the Irish Republican Army. His most recent film, ***High Boot Benny*** (1993), is situated in the north as the peace process begins to take off, but for some critics, the film remains overly confusing and insubstantial.

Indeed, it might generally be argued that watching Joe Comerford's work is rarely an easy task. It is often deliberately antirealist, and concern for a linear narrative is absent (when his films are synopsized, the story must frequently be inferred). In fact, to try to understand Comerford's work by looking at the story is almost to miss the point. His films often proceed as a series of vignettes where scenes bear scant relation to those immediately following or preceding them. Ironically, his films suggest a filmmaker who mistrusts the power of image and narrative. For example, in *Reefer and the Model*, the lead female protagonist refuses to have her photograph taken on the grounds that in her honeymoon photos, "I looked happy in them and I wasn't." The antirealism is often evident too in the characters themselves, frequently larger than life with a romantic past; they are given to cryptic dialogue delivered in a deliberately over-the-top manner.

A cynic might suggest that Comerford simply does not understand the medium. It is also possible to believe the obverse: that Comerford understands cinema so well that he is attempting to make it do something totally new, to invent a new cinema language. In that regard, it is disappointing that Comerford has apparently been unable to secure regular support for his craft. Although a boxed set covering his entire output was released in 2016, it included only one film from the 21st century, the prison suicide–themed *Roadside* (2008).

***THE COMMITMENTS* (1991).** Based on the best-selling book by **Roddy Doyle**, the film version directed by **Alan Parker** includes a cast of young unknown actors in the story of the rise and fall of a working-class Dublin blues band. The narrative structure conforms to classic Hollywood preoccupations with the dream of success, and the characters themselves are also preoccupied by American cultural influences. Jimmy Rabbitte (Robert Arkins) has a vision to bring soul music to Dublin and assembles a potentially successful young band mentored by an aging guru saxophonist, Joey the Lips (Johnny Murphy).

Parker, a northern British film director (who also directed *Angela's Ashes*), has been criticized for taking on local indigenous stories and over-universalizing them so that they will appeal to mass audiences. The often repeated tagline in the film—"They had nothing, but they were willing to risk it all"—legitimates the band's domestication of black American blues by styling working-class youths from the north side of Dublin as "blacks of Ireland." As the critic Lance Pettitt perceptively notices, the deep schism between Dublin's working class and the huge hinterland and rural community, dramatized in Doyle's novel, is carefully avoided to maintain a universal audience (Pettitt 2000, 126–27). The film ultimately became a moderately successful feel-good movie about the struggle against adversity. The strong sense of local identity owes much to its previously unknown cast of locals, which, together with Doyle's effective use of the vernacular (though the film was scripted for screen by veteran British comedy writers Ian La Frenais and Dick Clement), put a contemporary Irish working-class characterization on the world map.

CONAMARA **(2000).** A little-seen curiosity, *Conamara* is a German–Irish coproduction, crewed largely by German technicians. Its importance is more industrial than textual. Other than festival screenings, the film went unreleased in Ireland and does not appear to have been theatrically screened anywhere except Germany. It marked an early dalliance on the part of the **Irish Film Board** (IFB) with supporting projects initiated outside Ireland, something that would become standard practice following **Simon Perry**'s stint as the IFB's chief executive (2006–2011).

The narrative follows Maria (Ellen Ten Damme), a German woman who has lived in Galway for more than a decade with local boatbuilder Antaine and their daughter (Darragh Kelly). Their rural life together is disturbed when Axel (Adreas Schmidt), Maria's former boyfriend, makes an unexpected visit and old flames are rekindled.

CONCORDE ANOIS TEORANTA. *See* CORMAN, ROGER (1926–).

CONDON, KERRY (1983–). In the opening scene of one of her earliest films (*Intermission* [2003]), Kerry Condon's shop assistant character is suddenly assaulted by **Colin Farrell**'s charming but vicious thug. The shot of the reeling girl lying on the floor, hand to her bloodied nose, remains one of the most arresting images in recent Irish cinema. And, though her career is increasingly concentrated in the United States, Condon has continued to feature prominently in indigenous productions including, most recently, Niall Heery's *Gold* (2014).

Raised in Thurles, County Offaly, Condon determined to become an actress at the age of 11 but had little professional experience before attending an open casting call for Alan Parker's adaptation of *Angela's Ashes* (1999). That she won out over hundreds of competitors to secure the role of Theresa, the sexually experienced consumptive who relieves the lead protagonist of his virginity, suggests a certain drive. Subsequent choices seem to confirm a remarkable self-possession and confidence in her choices. She began working on a drama degree at Trinity College but decided to abandon it after a few days to take on the role of Marietta, daughter of a Dublin deliveryman who find himself transformed into a rodent in *Rat* (2000). Pressured by her U.S. agent to audition for *Agent Cody Banks 2* (2004), she point-blank refused, unwilling to participate in a trashy teenage spy franchise just to secure a Screen Actors Guild card. That patience paid off in a career trajectory that has seen her become a staple of U.S. quality television drama, an integral part of the ever-expanding Marvel Cinematic Universe (as the voice of Tony Stark's F.R.I.D.A.Y. artificial intelligence) while still appearing in her choice of Irish film roles.

Perhaps influenced by the template of her role in *Angela's Ashes*, her roles had in common a curious mix of the somehow knowing sexual ingenue. As Eileen, the newly married wife seduced by her employer in **How Harry Became a Tree** (2001), it is unclear as to how unwelcome her character regards these illicit advances. Certainly, it is suggested that she exploits her newfound sexual experience to become far more self-assertive, ultimately both rejecting her seducer but also convincing her timid husband to turn away from his revenge-obsessed father.

Having moved to London in 2001 at only age 18, she found herself cast opposite Heath Ledger and Orlando Bloom in *Ned Kelly* (2003), from a screenplay adaptation (by John Michael McDonagh) of Robert Drewe's novel about the legendary Irish Australian outlaw. Cast as Ned's sister, Kate, it is her refusal of a local policeman's advances that initially sets into motion Ned's confrontation with the law. Yet while protesting her dislike of Constable Fitzpatrick, the film clearly suggests that she has in some fashion encouraged his interest. Similarly, as Octavia in *Rome* (2005–2007), the mammoth HBO/BBC series that brought her to the wider attention of U.K. and U.S. audiences, her character is both pawn and player, integrated by others in their nefarious schemes but equally capable of devising her own— and deploying her sexuality (even to the extent of seducing her brother) for strategic purposes.

Condon's move to London also brought some high-profile stage work. Still only 18, she originated the key role of Mairead, a 16-year-old crack-shot Republican besotted with an INLA member in *The Lieutenant of Inishmore* for the Royal Shakespeare Society by Martin McDonagh (brother to John Michaek), simultaneously essaying Ophelia for the same company's 2001 production of *Hamlet*. Condon would spend nearly a third of the following decade playing in McDonagh's work on stages in London and New York and subsequently features in his Oscar-winning feature *Three Billboards Outside Ebbing, Missouri* (2017).

Still only 22, *Rome* transformed Condon's career. J. J. Abrams cast her in the lead of his medical drama *Anatomy of Hope* (2009), and though that show did not proceed beyond a pilot, plenty of others did: recurring roles followed in HBO's *Luck* (2011–2012), AMC's *The Walking Dead*, Alfonso Cuaron's sci-fantasy *Believe* (2014), and the key role of Stacey Ehrmantraut in Netflix's *Breaking Bad* prequel *Better Call Saul* (2015–). Her characters in these shows share a common, fundamental decency in spite of often morally compromised contexts: her Clara in *The Walking Dead* willingly becomes a zombie to stay with her husband, while Dr. Zoe Boyle, her *Believe* research scientist, turns on her former employers when she can no longer tolerate their exploitation of a telepathic child. As daughter-in-law to Mike Ehrmantraut, ex-cop turned drug gang fixer in *Better Call Saul*, Condon's Stacey and her daughter constitute the main motivation for Mike's turn to the dark side.

Although her *Walking Dead* character is played as Irish, Condon generally plays American in these shows. Indeed, it is striking how often she plays American in *Irish* work. Although both *The Shore* and Paolo Sorrentino's **This Must Be the Place** (2011) are partially set in Ireland, she plays, respectively, the U.S.-raised daughter of **Ciarán Hinds** and a U.S. Army war widow. More recently, in the U.S.-set *Bad Samaritan* (2018), though **Robert Sheehan**'s lead is clearly coded as Irish, Condon is cast as American.

Regardless of their nationality, more recent roles have seen her repeatedly cast as a lone parent left to raise children alone, a status that, coincidentally or otherwise, reflects Condon's own upbringing. Although her Alice has remarried in **Gold** (2014), in **This Must Be the Place**, *Better Call Saul*, and **The Runway** (2010), her casting as a single mother plays on her capacity to simultaneously embody a certain vulnerability while retaining the agency to address her circumstances.

CONROY, JACK. Conroy originally entered the film industry in the early 1970s working as a gaffer (electrical supervisor) on a number of **Ardmore**-based projects, including Robert Altman's *Images* (1972) and John Boorman's *Zardoz* (1974). In 1984, however, he made the switch to camera operator, initially working on adaptations of Frederick Forsyth novels. The international and Oscar success of **My Left Foot**, on which he worked as a cinematographer, brought his work to the attention of the wider world, and although he has worked on Irish projects, such as **The Field**, **The Playboys**, and **Gold in the Streets**, since the mid-1990s, he has increasingly worked in the United States. Much of this work has been on made-for-television projects, such as **Terry George**'s adaptation of Neil Sheehan's book on Vietnam, *A Bright Shining Lie* (1998), and Dennis Quaid's 1998 directorial debut *Everything That Rises* as well as the Pamela Anderson vehicle *VIP* in 1998. While maintaining a link with lower-budget U.S. productions in the 21st century, he has also worked on a sequence of Bollywood productions (including *The Gold Bracelet* [2006] and *Sonne Da Karra* [2016]) and in 2016 made his debut as director on the ultra-low-budget Irish production *The Gaelic Curse* (on which he was also director of production).

CONROY, RÚAIDHRÍ (1979–). Rúaidhrí made his acting debut at the age of eight in an **Abbey Theatre** production of **The Field** in which his father—Brendan Conroy—was also appearing. When in 1996 he appeared in **The Van** as Kevin, the role of his sister, Diane, was played by Neilí Conroy, Rúaidhrí's real-life sister. (However, the entire family dynasty has yet to appear together in a single screen production.)

Rúaidhrí made his film debut in 1990 in **Pat O'Connor**'s *Fools of Fortune* before appearing in *Hear My Song* the following year. He followed that with what remains his best-known role, that of Tito in *Into the West*, in which his portrayal displayed streetwise savvy and affecting vulnerability in equal parts. On the strength of this, he was offered what is arguably his most accomplished screen role, that of the bruised but sensitive Conrad, a student at a special needs school, in the British film *Clockwork Mice* (1995). He followed this with another warmly received lead role in *Moondance*, offering a skilled depiction of the turmoil of adolescent sexuality.

Since then, much of his work has been onstage rather than on-screen, although in addition to Irish films such as *Nothing Personal* (1995) and *When the Sky Falls* (2000), he appeared in the British supernatural thriller *Deathwatch* (2002) with **Hugh O'Conor** and the Hollywood wartime legal drama *Hart's War* (2002), which also featured **Colin Farrell**. On the stage, however, he has received critical plaudits, especially for Martin McDonagh's *The Cripple of Inishmaan*, which is set on the Aran Islands during the filming of Robert Flaherty's *Man of Aran* (1934). When the original London production of the play moved to New York, only Conroy, who played the lead role, remained with the show. He subsequently collaborated on McDonagh's first foray into film, the short *Six Shooter* (2004), which, in addition to winning awards at the Foyle, Cork, and British Independent film festivals, secured the **Academy Award** for Best Short Film in 2006. Although playing opposite the much higher profile **Brendan Gleeson**, Conroy's is the eye-catching performance as an unhinged youth tormenting train passengers unable to escape his attentions until they reach their destination.

Despite such early promise and high-profile work, Conroy subsequently withdrew somewhat from acting, retraining as a teacher. Although continuing to make occasional forays into small-screen works in particular (such as **Radio Telefís Éireann**'s *Raw* [2008] and Sky Television's Ireland-shot adaptation of *Treasure Island* [2012]), he has been relatively absent from feature work with the marked exception of his role as a medieval monk, Brother Rua, in **Brendan Muldowney**'s low-budget actioner *Pilgrimage* (2017).

COOPER, TOM. *See THE DAWN* (1936); HIBERNIA FILMS, 1933.

COOPERS & LYBRAND REPORT. In 1991, the Industrial Development Authority (IDA), together with Temple Bar Properties, the state agency charged with developing the capital's Temple Bar area into a Left Bank for Dublin, asked the Irish Film Centre Building Ltd (IFCB), the body created by the **Arts Council** to oversee the redevelopment of what would become the **Irish Film Centre**, to produce a report on the Irish film industry with a view to identifying opportunities for creating film-related jobs in the Temple Bar area and Ireland in general. The IFCB in turn commissioned the international accounting firm Coopers & Lybrand to develop an Irish strategy focused on job creation and to recommend specific initiatives to put that strategy into effect. The bulk of the research was carried out by independent producer (and later **TV3** commissioning editor) Jane Gogan.

When the resulting report (officially titled the *Report on Indigenous Audiovisual Production Industry* but colloquially referred to as the *Coopers & Lybrand Report*) was published in June 1992, it was immediately identified as marking a sea change in Irish film lobbying in that it granted equal emphasis to audiovisual production as an artistic and industrial (read "job-creating") undertaking. It would subsequently become an influential point of reference for the dramatic changes in Irish film policy inaugurated by **Michael D. Higgins** in 1993.

Given its length (the summary, conclusions, and recommendation chapter alone runs to 29 pages), no summary could possibly do justice to its content. However, the report considered every conceivable aspect of audiovisual production, ranging from feature films to corporate video to **animation**. It argued that the demand for audiovisual content within the European market was likely to substantially increase in the coming decade, presenting lucrative windows of opportunity for those countries positioned to avail of them.

In this respect, however, the report criticized previous Irish approaches to developing and positioning the industry. The comments made about the **Irish Film Board**'s activities from 1981 to 1987 are indicative of this critique. Although it praised the training and development that came about as a result of the board's activities, the report noted that the board's decision to focus on low-budget production with indigenous casts meant that the resulting films lacked international appeal. By definition, then, the report concluded that the board's funding decisions were not driven by commercial considerations. The report went on to argue that this difficulty was exacerbated by an absence of understanding and contacts for the distribution and sales of film in the international marketplace.

Not surprisingly, therefore, the report's core observation was the need for the sector to become much more market driven, and to this end, it made a series of recommendations relating to training, marketing, and finance. With regard to training, it recommended greater communication between the audiovisual sector and third-level institutions with a view to better relating curricula to real-world employment opportunities. The report also noted that a focus on achieving production had meant that Irish producers were underemphasizing the marketing of their pictures and suggested that the Irish Trade Board might adopt a greater role in that respect. However, it was the section on finance that perhaps reveals the most about the philosophy underlying the report. Rather than focusing primarily on how to fund individual films, the report consistently referred to the need to aid the development of production companies capable of securing funding in the international marketplace. Thus, the report identified the IDA as the key body in driving the future development of the sector rather than—as might have been expected—pushing for the reestablishment of the Film Board. In stressing the need to actively promote Ireland as a location for offshore production, the report also referred to the IDA.

Where the report did directly address making production finance available, it concentrated on the role of the Arts Council and fiscal incentives. It praised the Arts Council's role in supporting short films and low budgets, which it considered important from a cultural, educational, and training perspective. However, in discussing mainstream film production, it pointed to the limitations of the **Business Expansion Scheme** (especially for individual as opposed to corporate investors) and recommended adjusting **Section 35** to compensate for these.

It concluded by stressing the need for "joined-up" policymaking, a reference to the approach used up to that time to spread policymaking across a range of state bodies. Crucially, however, the arguments throughout the report for film industry support were couched—the status of film as a cultural undertaking notwithstanding—in hard-nosed financial language. The report clearly suggested that the increased state investment in the sector would be more than compensated for by increases in the return to the exchequer from income and other forms of taxation. Taken together with the approaches discussed in the *Independent Television Production Sector Report* and the *Report of the Taoiseach's Special Working Group on the Film Industry*, which were published in the same period, the commercial approach implicit in the *Coopers & Lybrand Report* would inform film policymaking through the 1990s.

CORMAN, ROGER (1926–). A renowned schlock-horror B-movie maker, Corman was involved with filmmaking in Ireland for more than five decades. In 1963, he allowed his then apprentice Francis Ford Coppola to leave the set of Corman's *The Young Racers* in England to go to Ireland, where Coppola shot his debut picture, *Dementia 13* (1963), on a budget of less than $50,000. Seven years later, Corman himself followed Coppola to Ireland to direct his take on the Red Baron story, *Von Richthofen and Brown* (aka *The Red Baron* [1971]).

However, Corman's place in Irish cinema history is cemented by his setting up in 1995 of Concorde Anois Teoranta, a small-scale studio facility in Tully, County Galway (now occupied by Telegael), as an offshoot to his famed New Horizon Pictures. Corman cited a belief that protectionist measures emanating from the European Union (presumably the 1989 "Television Without Frontiers" directive, which enjoined European broadcasters to reserve at least 51 percent of broadcast time for European content) would make it harder for his films to access the European market. However, by establishing a base within the European Union, such restrictions might be circumvented. Although attracted partly by the potential availability of **Section 35** funding, Corman was also actively courted by Udarás na Gaeltachta, the state authority with responsibility for developing industry in the Gaeltacht (Irish-speaking) regions of Ireland. Udarás would eventually provide around £1 million to help establish the Corman operation. This wooing of Corman fit with **Michael D. Higgins**'s general "western strategy," which attempted to decentralize audiovisual production from its east coast (and mainly) Dublin orientation. Thus, the negotiations were facilitated on the part of the state by the active intervention of both Higgins and then Minister for Enterprise and Employment Ruairí Quinn. Irish producer **Kieran Corrigan** acted as an intermediary for Corman and subsequently became a director of the film production company associated with the studio.

Inevitably, the venture raised concerns about its possible linguistic impact in one of the strongest remaining Irish-speaking areas, but these were apparently allayed by assurances that the highest number possible of people employed at the studios would be Udarás-trained Irish speakers.

In cultural terms, the contribution of the studios to Irish cinema was negligible. Although Corman did expresses an interest in producing a version of Joyce's *Portrait of the Artist as a Young Man* and in developing a film on the life of Charles Stewart Parnell, the only nod to the local was the—to put it generously—somewhat amateurish *A Very Unlucky Leprechaun*. The half dozen pictures produced each year were typically exploitation films intended for the straight-to-video market, as suggested by titles like *Criminal Affairs*, *Detonator*, and *Bloodfist VIII: Trained to Kill*.

Two years after the studios arrived, the local Galway Film Fleadh (Festival) decided to screen the first Irish-directed feature completed by Concorde, *Criminal Affairs*, prompting a minor furor. Questions were raised about the wisdom of allowing Udarás and Section 35 funding to support the production of films featuring rape, murder, and what were generally regarded as some pretty tacky sex scenes. Udarás responded by pointing out that they had funded some 20 film and television companies in the previous decade but did not feel they had a role in making editorial decisions about the kinds of films the companies they supported should make.

Given this, the real contribution of the studios to Irish cinema was industrial. Corman promised to employ 60 to 70 people once the studios were in full swing, 90 percent of whom would be local. Although in practice those who have worked at the studios expressed dissatisfaction over low wages, long hours, and poor training opportunities, as the 2012 documentary *It Came from Connemara* recounted, the Corman facility nonetheless provided otherwise unimaginable opportunities for young Irish filmmakers to experience filmmaking firsthand. Furthermore, the studios arguably created a partial alternative to Dublin/Ardmore–centered filmmaking, which sees the vast bulk of films shot within a 40-mile radius of **Ardmore Studios** in Bray, County Wicklow.

However, Corman himself rarely attended the studios, acting mainly as executive producer on projects in the 1990s. Furthermore, production activity fell off significantly in the 21st century. (Indeed, it may be that *Moving Target* [2000] was the last full-scale production completed at the studios.) Corman cited changing international distribution practices as reducing the market for low-budget content while also noting that, in practice, restrictions on U.S. access to the European market were not as problematic as he initially feared. However, it was also apparent that Concorde was at least indirectly associated with legal difficulties surrounding projects whereby the Irish Revenue Commissioners refused to approve the issuance of tax clearance certificates necessary for film investors to write off their investments via the **Section 481** tax break. Although the main issue lay with Kieran Corrigan's **Merlin Films**, which had a joint venture with Corman (the Merlin Concorde Film Fund), a 2009 court judgment found that monies secured by Merlin for the production of a specified set of Section 481–funded projects had in part been spent on other projects and that a substantial amount of the monies was paid to Concorde Anois. Furthermore, some of the Concorde Anois money appeared to have been transferred out of Ireland entirely, ending up in a Philippines-based company, Transpacific Corporation. As a consequence, the court held that the Revenue Commissioners were correct in withdrawing Section 481 clearance from investors in those films.

CORRIGAN, KIERAN. *See* MERLIN FILMS.

COUNTRY **(2000).** Like Kevin Liddy's previous short film *Horse*, the story revolves around a young child and the secrets of his family. Twelve-year-old Jack Murphy (Dean Pritchard) lives with his widowed father, Frank (Des Cave), and his brother, Con (Gary Lydon), in the rural Ireland of the 1970s. Frank, an ex-alcoholic, may or not have been responsible for the death of his wife, Bridget, and consequently lives a broken life laced with regret. When Jack's Uncle Jimmy (Peter Dix) dies of a heart attack, his Aunt Miriam (Lisa Harrow) returns for the funeral and stays on indefinitely, acting as a catalyst for the healing of emotional familial wounds. She advises Con and his girlfriend Sarah (Marcella Plunkett) to make positive changes in their lives and lightens Jack's existence by opening him up to possibilities outside his limited patriarchal world. However, a vicious rape results in the girl having to emigrate as local Travellers are scapegoated for the crime.

While the story has been criticized for a stereotypical evocation of rural stultification, internecine conflict, and miscommunication, this does not detract from the elemental truth of the narrative, which is beautifully visualized through **Donal Gilligan**'s lingering shots of the evocative landscape of the west of Ireland.

THE COURIER **(1988).** *The Courier* represented an early attempt, supported by the first **Irish Film Board** and Palace Pictures, to make a homegrown genre thriller with international appeal. Scripted by Frank Deasy, who codirected with Joe Lee, the plot follows motorcycle courier Mark (Padraig O'Loinsigh), who discovers that his employer, Val (**Gabriel Byrne**), uses his courier business as a front for a drug ring and that he (Mark) has unwittingly been delivering heroin around Dublin. Having come into film via community-based video production in the early 1980s (formalized in the creation of the City Vision production company in 1984), Deasy and Lee had previous exposure to the Dublin drug scene and completed community videos drawing attention to the risks of addiction faced by residents of the St. Theresa's Gardens local authority housing scheme in Dublin's deprived inner city. A subsequent City Vision production—*Sometime City* (1986)—had signaled a desire to produce longer-form narrative work. Nonetheless, *The Courier* still represented a quantum leap forward in ambition. As packaged by Deasy and Lee (along with producer Hilary McLoughlin), the IR£820,000 budget film was carefully designed to sell to both Irish and international audiences. A recognizable generic plot was overlaid on a gritty representation of Dublin's seamier side, internationally recognizable actors were cast in key roles (Byrne then becoming established as a Hollywood star and veteran British actor Ian Bannen in the role of a Dublin detective), and, in a previously unheard-of move for an Irish film, the release was trailered by the prior launch of a sound track album populated by then high-profile Irish acts (including U2). As a consequence, the film was notionally in profit even before its release, bolstered by advance international sales. Yet, in practice, hampered by an inconclusive ending, it received lukewarm reviews (even in Ireland), failing to set the box office alight. Frank Deasy would go on to become a noted screenwriter for British television before his untimely death in 2009, but *The Courier* marked the end of City Vision's international ambitions.

COWBOYS AND ANGELS **(2003).** Director David Gleeson's feature debut introduces Shane (Michael Legge), a lonely and deeply untrendy 20-year-old civil servant from the country, as he moves to Limerick and finds himself sharing a flat with Vincent (Allan Legge), a gay (indeed impossibly camp) fashion student with dreams of immigrating to the United States. Witnessing and increasingly sharing elements of Vincent's lifestyle rapidly broadens Shane's perspectives, a process accelerated by the latter's friendship with an older civil servant, Jerry (Frank Kelly), who expresses his regret at lacking the nerve to leave his safe civil service job when he was a younger man. Increasingly frustrated by his quotidian existence, especially after encountering the exotic Gemma, Shane begins to dream of another life.

Although hampered by a plot built on an increasingly unlikely set of plot contrivances and a distracting drug-smuggling subplot, *Cowboys and Angels* was notable among Irish films for its relatively early depiction of an unabashedly gay character entirely at peace with his sexuality. Indeed, Vincent is characterized as significantly happier than the more "normal" straight-laced Shane precisely because he can call on the support structure offered by the local gay community, a resource that Shame lacks. In an inversion of older narratives, it is Vincent who helps Shane "come out" not as homosexual (Shane is firmly established as straight) but rather as something more than a repressed civil servant (the film ends with Shane giving up his job to enter art school). The film was novel, too, in its depiction of Limerick city: eschewing the common images of the city as a deprived crime capital with gang feuds and stabbings (see, e.g., *Angela's Ashes* [1999]), Limerick emerges instead as a far more cosmopolitan locale, not least in the manner in which the film depicts its thriving gay scene.

CREATIVE CAPITAL REPORT. The publication of the Creative Capital Report in July 2011 represented the conclusion of a two-year-long exploration of Irish audiovisual policy initiated by then Minister for Arts, Sports, and Tourism Martin Cullen in 2009. Like most previous reports in this area, it constituted a policy blueprint for the following half decade, arguing that, if followed, the report's recommendations could double the turnover of the industry from €500 million to €1 billion and the number employed in it from 5,000 to 10,000.

Broadly speaking, the report made a series of recommendations aimed at achieving the following ends:

- Developing the capacity of native production companies
- Encouraging the export of indigenous audiovisual productions (an area that the industry had not distinguished itself in hitherto)
- Ensuring that industry skill sets met national and international standards
- Developing a demand for Irish audiovisual content in the domestic market

All of the above would occur in the context of much greater cooperation between institutions such as the **Irish Film Board** and state-run industrial development institutions such as Enterprise Ireland and the Industrial Development Authority. Specific recommendations included the creation of an international television coproduction fund to incentivize overseas productions to shoot in Ireland; the development of a sales and marketing plan for audiovisual exports on the part of Enterprise Ireland, the Irish Film Board, **Culture Ireland**, and the **Irish Film Institute**; and the need to address a perceived "match/mismatch" between Irish third-level curricula and the needs of the audiovisual industry. Perhaps most significantly, the report proposed a wholesale reorientation of the Irish Film Board as an industry development body. Identifying the board as focused primarily on the development of the indigenous industry, the report suggested that it be reoriented in a more industrial development direction "to enable the organisation to act as a *specialist development agency for the entire audiovisual industry* alongside its current remit of developing the industry for the making of Irish film and television."

Creative Capital was remarkable mainly for the almost complete absence of any reference to the cultural importance/significance of audiovisual content. The discourse throughout was industrial in its orientation, emphasizing the importance of developing the industry (better access to funding, scaling up of operations, and better research and development and market gathering to facilitate more success in export markets).

Film and television (and putatively game) texts were not only primarily but also almost exclusively conceived of as commodities (rather than as containers of nationally specific, locally engaged meaning). Policymakers were exhorted to "foster a 'make-to-sell' culture," encouraging a proactive engagement with market partners and audiences as early as possible in the development of project. Even when audiovisual texts were overtly referred to within a cultural discourse, there remained a sense that such texts were not significant in themselves but rather existed instrumentally to serve other means: films were described as providing "a valuable showcase for differing Irish forms of culture" and "significant economic and social spin-off effects for Ireland," most notably through encouraging inward tourism.

In practice, the report had little meaningful impact. In this regard, it may have been hindered by its insistence that the sought-after outcomes could be achieved only if all the recommendations were implemented. However, in some respects, it offered little that was new: the recommendation that an Irish film channel be established had been embodied in law (if not in reality) since the 2009 Broadcasting Act. The proposal to create a fund targeted at encouraging international productions to locate in Ireland simply codified a practice the Irish Film Board had introduced in 2005 when it first set aside funds for just that purpose. The one concrete proposal that could have been implemented—the suggestion that the Film Board take over the operation of the Broadcasting Authority of Ireland's Sound and Vision Fund—was not actively endorsed by television producers or by the Broadcasting Authority of Ireland, though it was warmly welcomed by the Film Board.

CREATIVE EUROPE. Scheduled to run from 2014 to 2020 and armed with a €1.57 billion budget, the Creative Europe program is an EU initiative that subsumes two older projects—the Culture programs and the MEDIA program—under a single administration. Of these, the MEDIA element, to which €900 million has been assigned up to 2020, is most directly associated with the film industry.

First begun on a pilot basis in 1987 before becoming a full-fledged program in 1990, the MEDIA program of the European Union represents a concerted attempt to slow the steady decline of the European film industry. In fact, there have been four MEDIA programs running in succession since 1987: MEDIA '95, MEDIA II, MEDIA Plus, and MEDIA 2007, which ran until 2013. All of the programs have been informed by the same cultural and economic considerations. Culturally, the dominance of the American audiovisual product has been seen (particularly in France) as undermining the very fabric of European society through cultural imperialism. At the same time, American domination of European cinema and television screens has had a damaging economic influence on the U.S.–European balance of trade: in 1993, there was a UK£3.7 billion deficit in terms of European audiovisual trade with the United States.

Rather than directly fund European production—this was felt to be the province of national film boards, and, in any case, **Eurimages** was already funding pan-European production—the programs sought to address the structural factors underpinning the perceived weakness of the European audiovisual sector. Although the MEDIA '95 program split its €200 million budget across 19 separate projects in areas as diverse as encouraging multilingualism in television programs and support of the **animation** sector, subsequent programs concentrated their efforts in three areas: supporting development, **distribution**, and training.

Given the condition of the Irish audiovisual industry in 1989–1990, when MEDIA '95 was established (most notably the "retirement" of the **Irish Film Board** in 1987), the program was embraced by both Irish producers and successive Irish governments as—**Channel 4** aside—the most promising source of finance for Irish producers (albeit upstream and downstream of actual production funding). The Irish government reacted enthusiastically to the MEDIA program initially because it displaced responsibility for the domestic audiovisual industry onto the shoulders of the then European Community.

From the outset, Irish films and companies punched above their weight in terms of receipts from the program (Ireland accounted for 1 percent of the EU population in 1990, but the €6 million secured from MEDIA '95 was equivalent to 2 to 3 percent of the program's total budget). Early Irish beneficiaries included *Reefer and the Model*, *The Miracle*, and *Hush-a-Bye Baby*, which cumulatively received 600,000 ECU (European Currency Units—a pre-euro currency) from the theatrical distribution support agency EFDO. However, for Irish producers, the MEDIA program was beneficial in ways difficult to capture in monetary terms. For example, the EAVE program (aimed at enhancing the skills of European producers) allowed Irish producers to meet and work with producers from other European countries, thus giving them access to a network of pan-European contacts and facilitating subsequent coproductions. Thus, while direct funding to Irish production from the MEDIA program amounted to £0.6 million in 1993, much of the £0.8 million that went into Irish production from other EU sources results from the network of contacts established by MEDIA for Irish producers.

The MEDIA '95 program officially came to a close on 31 December 1995 but was immediately followed by MEDIA II, a program with more money (€310 million) that concentrated on training, development, and distribution. The changes were a response to the complaint from many European producers that MEDIA '95 funding had been spread too thinly over too many projects. Similarly, the decision to concentrate some 60 percent of the total MEDIA II budget on distribution acknowledged the limitations of EFDO and EVE (the two MEDIA '95 bodies responsible for distribution) given the size of their budgets.

In addition, although MEDIA II followed the same basic remit as its predecessor, there was markedly greater emphasis on the influence of market forces and more concentration of activity with money targeted on significantly fewer projects. Administrative and budgetary power was also concentrated: whereas in MEDIA '95 each EU member state (apart from Greece) had at least one MEDIA project situated in its territory with the power to decide its own spending priorities, the new projects were to be financially administered from Brussels.

This tripartite division introduced by MEDIA II was largely retained by the MEDIA Plus program, which commenced in 2001 with an operational budget of €400 million. MEDIA Distribution continued to swallow up the bulk of this finance to fund its support for distribution of European works across theatrical, broadcast, and domestic (i.e., video and DVD) markets. To support cinema distribution, the project operates a combination of what are termed automatic and selective schemes. Automatic schemes are post hoc in that they "automatically" reward distributors and sales agents who successfully distribute European works across European borders by offering them funds—the precise amount is based on the box office performance of previous European films—to support further distribution of European works. In selective schemes, by contrast, funds are awarded in advance of release to facilitate the subsequent pan-European distribution of European works. Both automatic and selective schemes are designed to encourage the emergence of pan-European distribution networks capable of competing with the operations of the U.S. majors in Europe. MEDIA Development not only supports the development of individual projects but also, through the provision of slate funding (i.e., supporting a range of projects associated with one company), encourages the development of production companies with a long-term strategic outlook. Finally, the MEDIA Training Program encourages the establishment of pan-European training initiatives to allow filmmakers to develop their competence and their competitiveness on the international market—in 2003, a fourth strand, European Film Promotion, was added to support access of European productions to international markets and festivals.

That broad division—distribution, development and training—has remained characteristic of the MEDIA program in its subsequent iterations notwithstanding the fact that the overall impact of the MEDIA project is difficult to assess objectively. Judged by the trend in European audience figures for European films since the inception of the program in 1990, it would be difficult to regard the project as an unqualified success. European attendance at European films actually declined in the 1990s, and by the early 2000s, European films were routinely accounting for less than a quarter of all cinema tickets sold across the European Union. Although this would pick up subsequently—between 2012 and 2017, European films enjoyed market shares of between one-quarter and one-third of the EU box office—the United States remains the dominant force in that market. Against this, it might be argued that only the existence of the MEDIA program has prevented the situation from being much worse. Certainly, the European Commission has consistently expressed confidence in the scheme. Although MEDIA Plus was closed in 2006, the commission had already published proposals for a "MEDIA 2007" program in 2004. Subsequently renamed MEDIA Plus, the scheme ran from 1 January 2007 until the end of 2013 on a budget of €755 million (though this was less than the €1 billion originally envisaged in 2004).

Over the course of the first four iterations of the scheme, the Irish film industry secured a total of €34.3 million from the various elements of the program. Notwithstanding the notional emphasis on distribution within the Creative Europe project as a whole, distribution support appears to have constituted a relatively small proportion of the Irish funding. This remains the case with the post-2013 incorporation of the program into the larger Creative Europe infrastructure. Between 2013 and the end of 2017, Irish projects and production companies benefited from more than €6.8 million from Creative Europe support schemes. The largest single element of this,

€3.3 million, was accounted for by development slate funding, that is, supporting companies with three or more projects in development, followed by single-project development funds of €1.3 million. By contrast, just €75,000 was granted to Irish distribution companies. Thus, the MEDIA program has certainly been directed to the financial viability of a series of relatively healthy indigenous production companies. However, it is also the case that the intranational emphasis of the various schemes offered under the training element of the program—EAVE and ACE in particular—has contributed to the outward orientation of the Irish production, arguably an essential prerequisite for securing ongoing finance in the context of a relatively small available pot of domestic funding.

CRUSHPROOF **(1997). British director** Paul Tickell's background in television documentary and serial drama gave little inkling of the nature of his feature debut. Characterized by handheld camera, jump-cut editing, frequent (by Irish standards) recourse to sex scenes, and a pulsing technoindustrial sound track, *Crushproof* follows 18-year-old Neal (Darren Healy) as he returns to his deprived housing estate home after a spell in prison for drug dealing. Few are glad to see him: his ex-girlfriend refuses to grant him access to their child, his mother (now in a lesbian relationship) makes it clear that she's not interested in him, while his alcoholic father cannot even remember his son's name. Instead, Neal rejoins his former gang of "ponykids," who steal back their horses (previously impounded by the police) and make for the mountains. (Even this is not straightforward, as Neal inadvertently kills one of the gang members who he believes testified to the police about his drug dealing.)

Crushproof owes little to Irish cinematic antecedents; unconcerned with recurring debates about national identity common to other Irish texts, it seems less focused on the depiction of Ireland in particular than on creating a mythical land of adolescent fantasies and male bonding that knows no national boundaries. The initial urban setting is anonymous: an opening montage offers classic images of decay, including continuous low-angle shots of a high concrete wall and children dwarfed by the concrete structure of the pillar in Phoenix Park. The affinity of the youths with their horses—an early wide shot shows a string of horses crossing a bridge over a highway— suggests a connection with a more primal, premodern sense of identity, but the film in no way suggests a harking back to some prelapsarian time. Not just amoral but almost asocial, Neal and his cohort are relentlessly (irredeemably?) violent: for them, there really is no such thing as society, their norms (and even, to some extent, their language) being self-created.

THE CRYING GAME **(1992). Neil Jordan**'s films are frequently preoccupied with the crossing and blurring of boundaries between countries, for example, Ireland and Britain in *Angel* and *Michael Collins*. *The Crying Game*, by contrast, was critically and commercially acclaimed for its blurring of gender politics. Jody, a black British army soldier serving in Northern Ireland, is lured into a kidnapping by the Irish Republican Army (IRA). He befriends one of his captors, Fergus, an IRA man increasingly disillusioned with the "armed struggle," and shows him pictures of his black girlfriend. The relationship is suddenly terminated by a British army assault on the IRA hideout during which Jody is accidentally killed. Fergus escapes to London, where, under an assumed name, he finds Dil, Jody's girlfriend, and they strike up first a friendship, then a romance. However, when Fergus sees Dil naked for the first time, the camera pans down "her" body to rest briefly on male genitalia. Shocked, Fergus lashes out, fleeing Dil's apartment. Nevertheless, Fergus gradually comes to terms with Dil's gender identity, and reconciliation is effected. However, Fergus's former IRA colleagues come back into his life, insisting that Fergus participate in an assassination.

Given the background of its lead character, *The Crying Game* could hardly avoid being a political film, but it goes far beyond the narrow confines of the politics of nationhood. The decision to set the opening scenes in the north foregrounds such politics, but ultimately, Irish partition comes to represent far more fundamental divisions and differences in gender, race, and sexual preference.

The film constructs these divisions along an oppressor–oppressed axis. Jody initially represents the oppressor—both a British army soldier, regarded by the IRA as an invader, and a heterosexual male who is in a position to be kidnapped only because he attempts to ravish a female member of the IRA cell. Yet the film tacitly argues not merely that such roles are quite fluid but also that they are artificially constructed. Jody the oppressor, for example, is simultaneously the oppressed: a black man sent to "the only place in the world where they still call you nigger to your face." The fluidity and artificiality of such roles is even more evident in the relationship between Fergus and Dil. Initially, Fergus, a white, apparently heterosexual male, relates to Dil as a black, heterosexual female. Although little physically changes about Dil during the film, in the wake of the revelation about Dil's sexuality, Fergus's perception of him/her immediately shifts to that of a homosexual male (an earlier comment from Jody about his own sexual organs—"It's only a piece of meat"—takes on a new resonance in this scene). Jordan has been criticized for his "rabbit-out-of-the-box" approach to this scene, but given that viewers may well have brought the same prejudices and preconceptions to the film as those demonstrated by the characters, the surprise is arguably essential not merely to shock people out of their passive consumption of the narrative but also simply to draw attention to the ongoing process we all engage in of making unconscious assumptions and readings in understanding the people we meet.

The oppressive forces in the film are represented by the British army and the IRA. Thus, oppression itself is identified as institutional in origin. Jody argues with Fergus that it's not in the nature of terrorists (and, by extension, the Irish) to release hostages, but, crucially, he excepts Fergus from this generalization, conceding the primacy of individual humanity over the demands of the organization. Yet at a wider level, the film identifies society at large as an oppressive force, imposing norms in relation to gender roles, sexuality, and race. There is even an indirect commentary on the role of Hollywood—as part of society at large—in reinforcing norms. Director Jordan draws attention to and subverts the "male gaze" of Hollywood's representation of women that renders them as objects for the (implicitly male) spectator to watch. Dil, first seen in a photograph, immediately becomes an object not only for the cinema audience but also for the characters within the diegesis of the film. However, after the narrative bombshell that she is a he, the filmic representation of Dil changes: voyeuristic, lingering full-body shots are dropped in favor of close-ups.

Given the construction of society as the oppressive force, Fergus, existing outside society (both society at large and the smaller IRA infrastructure) and unconstrained by the dogmatic pursuit of ideology that dictates the actions of his IRA colleagues, is increasingly motivated by his essential humanity and compassion. Jody and Dil are similarly situated; their color and sexuality in a frequently racist and conformist society position them in society but not of it. Acceptance of one's essential humanity, overcoming the barriers of the artificial constraints imposed by society, represents the goal for the lead characters in *The Crying Game*. Jody and Dil ("I can't help what I am") have already achieved this before the narrative starts. Thus, the story of the film is Fergus's journey to that goal, a journey prompted by his internal struggle with the contrasting directions of IRA orders and his own compassion and ending with his acceptance of his feelings for Dil.

In the end, Jordan seems to be saying that love can conquer all divisions, be they along lines of race, gender, nationality, or sexual preference. This may appear overly simplistic: clearly, the differences at the heart of *The Crying Game*—genitalia, skin color, and so on—are real and cannot be reasoned out of existence. The point that *The Crying Game* makes, however, is that the effect of these differences on how we relate to one another is socially constructed and artificial and ultimately can be overcome.

CULTURAL RELATIONS COMMITTEE. In January 1949, Clann Na Poblachta Minister for External (Foreign) Affairs Sean MacBride established an advisory Cultural Relations Committee (CRC) to carry out, or give financial support to, Irish cultural projects of a high artistic standard with a view to enhancing Ireland's image and reputation overseas. The committee would assess applications for funding on their artistic and cultural merits and consider the views of Irish embassy staff in the country for which an event was proposed before making recommendations. Although this was not overtly stated at first, in deciding on the activities to be assisted, the committee would also assess their potential to promote tourism and foreign direct investment. In contrast to most governmental committees, for the most part, the CRC was made up not of civil servants but rather of influential figures within the indigenous arts sector.

In its first year of existence, the committee received £2,600 to defray the cost of a wide range of cultural activities. In his first Dáil speech on the committee, in August 1949, MacBride referred to a long-term scheme to build up a library of short documentary films on Irish life and activity. That scheme bore its first fruit with the CRC-commissioned *W. B. Yeats: A Tribute*, produced by the **National Film Institute of Ireland**. The committee continued to commission documentaries through the 1950s and 1960s, perhaps most notably with **Patrick Carey**'s *Yeats Country*, which was nominated for an **Academy Award** in 1966. However, not all of these documentaries immediately saw the light of day. In 1951, the committee commissioned **Liam O'Leary** (himself a committee member) to make *Portrait of Dublin*. However, by the time the film was completed, a new Fianna Fáil administration was in power and effectively quashed the film.

By the 1970s, the committee had effectively ceased commissioning new film work, although it did occasionally fund activities that might indirectly lead to filmmaking activity, such as travel to and from Ireland. For the most part, however, from the 1970s on, its film activities were limited to assisting screenings of Irish films at overseas festivals. This was somewhat formalized in 1993 when then Minister for Foreign Affairs Dick Spring announced that the committee was engaged in an ongoing program, in cooperation with the **Irish Film Institute**, to purchase outright prints of Irish films with a view to making them available for screening at festivals abroad.

Indeed, as the 1990s progressed, increasing doubts were raised about the wisdom of placing responsibility for promoting Irish culture overseas in the hands of Department of Foreign Affairs, especially given the obvious potential for overlap with the activities of the **Arts Council**. In 2003, therefore, that year's Arts Act placed responsibility for the CRC in the hands of the Department of Arts (although continuity with the Department of Foreign Affairs was maintained through the ongoing presence of a senior civil servant from that department on the committee). This was followed in 2005 by the decision to replace the committee with Culture Ireland, a new national agency charged with establishing a strategic plan for the international promotion of Irish art and culture. It was anticipated that it would spend its initial €2 million budget on grants to Irish artists and arts organizations for overseas activity and for the funding and facilitation of Irish participation at international arts events.

Considering that the **Irish Film Archive**'s festival work ("Green Screen") had been financially supported by the CRC for several years, it was appropriate that the Irish Film Institute's director, Mark Mulqueen, was among the first set of members. One of the first decisions undertaken by the agency was to support the archive's *Reel Ireland* package of Irish film that was to be made available to noncommercial exhibitors throughout 2005 and 2006.

As with virtually every other aspect of public expenditure in Ireland after 2008, the impact of the post–Celtic Tiger economic crash saw Culture Ireland's budget nearly halved from a peak of €4.7 million in 2008 to €2.5 million by 2014 (although it did climb to €3.5 million in 2017). Monies granted under the film heading typically support exhibition of Irish films at international film festivals. Reflecting the expectation that audiences overseas will typically access such Irish content through commercial cinema, the finance granted to film projects from Culture Ireland constitute a relatively low proportion of total disbursements from the fund each year. Thus, in 2016, and notwithstanding the membership of the Irish Film Board's chief executive officer, James Hickey, on Culture Ireland's board, film accounted for €60,000 all monies spent as opposed to, for example, the €595,000 granted to touring theater projects.

CUNNINGHAM, LIAM (1962–). The fame associated with Liam Cunningham's role as smuggler-turned-knight Davos Seaworth in global television behemoth *Game of Thrones* since 2012 obscures the fact that he had already been working on-screen for nearly two decades.

Born in the North Wall area of Dublin, he trained as an electrician and worked for several years with the Electricity Supply Board. After a three-year stint working on rural electrification schemes in Zimbabwe, he returned to Dublin in 1987 looking for a change of career. He joined an acting school, and his professional stage debut quickly followed with the lead role in a production of Dermot Bolger's *Lament for Arthur Cleary*. (He would later reprise the role in a television version of the play.) From there, he went to work with the Passion Machine theater group at the same time as **Brendan Gleeson**, although the two never appeared in a production together. He then moved to London, working first at the Royal Court and then with the Royal Shakespeare Company for 18 months.

This brought him to the attention of British television. He received a Best Actor nomination from the Royal Television Academy in 1995 for a one-off role in the psychological drama *Cracker*, and he has continued to alternate between television and film work ever since. In 1994, he appeared in *War of the Buttons*, a Warner Bros. film shot in Ireland, which won him another leading role in a 1995 feature adaptation of Frances Hodgson Burnett's *A Little Princess* and brought him to the attention of American audiences. Roles in Jerry Zucker's *First Knight* (1995) and *RKO 281* (1999), in which he played famed Hollywood cinematographer Gregg Toland, followed.

In the late 1990s, he enjoyed an unusual degree of exposure in Ireland. In addition to leading roles in the critically acclaimed **Sweety Barrett** (1999) and *A Love Divided* (1999), he also starred in the **Radio Telefís Éireann/** BBC coproduction *Falling for a Dancer* (1998), set on the Beara peninsula in Cork. By 2000, Cunningham had a well-established presence in Ireland and Britain, and, though based in Dublin, he effortlessly shifted back and forth across the Irish Sea, appearing in a number of British television series (especially detective shows, such as *Messiah* and *Prime Suspect*) and a number films shot in Ireland, including *The Abduction Club* (2002) and **Breakfast on Pluto**, and in a key role as Dan, the committed Republican socialist in Ken Loach's **The Wind That Shakes the Barley** (2005).

Appearances in major-budget films in small but critical roles became increasingly the norm for Cunningham in the late 2000s, appearing as Brick (opposite **Michael Fassbender**) in *Centurion* (2010), Solon in *Clash of the Titans* (2010), and an army doctor in Steven Spielberg's adaptation of *War Horse* (2011). To an extent, he was similarly deployed in Irish cinema, offering comic relief as gangster "The Mull" in **Perrier's Bounty** (2009) and the even more violent but oddly reflective gangster Francis Sheehy-Skeffington (not to be confused with the Irish peace activist murdered in 1916) in **The Guard** (2011). However, the standout role in this regard came in 2008 when he played Father Moran opposite Michael Fassbender's Bobby Sands in **Hunger**. In Steve McQueen's otherwise dialogue-free mediation, the protracted disputation between Moran and Sands constituted the intellectual core of the film, a debate about the moral efficacy of hunger strikes as a political weapon. Although unsuccessful in his attempt to deter Sands from embarking on a path of self-destruction, Cunningham's Moran displays sympathy, wit, and integrity.

Of course, these are precisely the characteristics of Davos Seaworth in *Game of Thrones*. Happily for Cunningham (and unusually for the series), Seaworth has survived the infinite machinations visited on the characters, conferring on him a global recognition. To an extent, this has afforded Cunningham access to higher-profile roles (the central role of "Six" in *Let Us Prey* [2014] and the father in *The Childhood of a Leader* [2015]), but it has also placed him in a position to deploy his fame to wider effect. Endowed with a working-class sensibility and manner, which effectively merges his star persona and major roles, Cunningham has publicly railed against social injustice. This is most evident in his role as an ambassador for World Vision, the child-centered international aid agency on whose behalf he has both traveled to centers for refugees fleeing from the Syrian Civil War and called on the Irish government to significantly increase their intake of said migrants.

CUSACK, CYRIL (1910–1993). One of a handful of Irish actors with an international reputation in the 1960s, Cusack was also famed for his ability to underplay his roles (and, indeed, to steal scenes). He was born in Kenya, where his father, James Cusack, was a police sergeant. His mother was a vaudeville actress, and when his parents separated while he was still a young child, Cusack's mother brought him back to England, where she worked in theater. Soon afterward, she and her new partner, Breffni O'Rourke, moved to Ireland to join O'Brien and Ireland Players, a touring company. So when he was just seven, Cusack made his stage and film debuts in the play *East Lynne* and the film ***Knocknagow***.

Cusack continued to appear onstage while attending Dominican College in Newbridge and University College Dublin (UCD), where he considered becoming a barrister before leaving without a degree to join the **Abbey Theatre** in 1932. He was an almost constant presence on the Abbey's boards until 1945, although he also made occasional appearances at the Gate Theatre and on the London stage, including a performance as Christy Mahon in J. M. Synge's *The Playboy of the Western World*.

He made a number of appearances in British films from 1935, including a key role in Carol Reed's ***Odd Man Out***. From the late 1940s in particular, he became a staple in British films made and set in Ireland, including *Jacqueline* (1956), *The Rising of the Moon* (1957), ***Shake Hands with the Devil***, and *A Terrible Beauty* (1960). He used the income from this work to establish his own touring theater company, and between 1947 and 1960, he brought plays by George Bernard Shaw, Shakespeare, and Franz Kafka to stages in Dublin, Paris, and New York.

By the mid-1960s, he was an increasingly recognizable character actor in international cinema, with roles in Martin Ritt's *The Spy Who Came In from the Cold* (which used Dublin as a double for East Berlin in 1966), Francois Truffaut's *Fahrenheit 451* (1966), and Fred Zinneman's *The Day of the Jackal* (1973). These roles were interspersed with appearances in less memorable films, including a sequence of Italian productions between 1971 and 1976 with lurid titles, such as *Hired to Kill* (1972), *Run, Run Joe* (1974), and *Street War* (1976).

Throughout this period, he remained keenly engaged with theater work. In addition to his own company, he briefly managed the Gaiety Theatre after the war and in 1956 brought a highly controversial production of Sean O'Casey's *The Bishop's Bonfire* to the same theater. He also returned to the Abbey both as a shareholder and, from 1965, as one of the directors. And, of course, he continued acting onstage, drawing critical acclaim for performances in works by Anton Chekov, Brian Friel, Sean O'Casey, and William Shakespeare.

Cusack was at the cutting edge of the nascent film industry in the late 1970s, taking the lead role in Bob Quinn's *Poitín*, his first in an indigenous film since *Knocknagow* in 1917. The role perfectly captured Cusack's most commonly utilized on-screen persona: a vague, almost fey exterior that masked a ruthless cunning and steely determination to secure his objectives. When his character of the poitín maker is threatened by the louts played by **Donal McCann** and **Niall Toibin**, he exacts a cold, merciless revenge.

Despite his age, his screen work did not tail off in the 1980s. He made three more appearances in Irish features: in *The Outcasts* (1982), a cameo in **Jim Sheridan**'s *My Left Foot*, and in *Far and Away*, his penultimate performance. He also reached a new domestic audience through television in **Radio Telefís Éireann** (RTÉ) major drama series *Strumpet City* (1980) and **Pat O'Connor**'s *The Ballroom of Romance* (1982) and in a recurring role in RTÉ's rural soap *Glenroe*. His stage work also seemed unabated: he gave a memorable performance in a 1987 production of Oscar Wilde's *John Bull's Other Island* and in a 1990 production of Chekhov's *Three Sisters*, in which three of his daughters—Sinead, Niamh, and Sorcha—played the three sisters. (In 1989, he appeared on-screen with his son-in-law, Jeremy Irons—husband of Sinead—and his grandson, Samuel Irons, in a television version of Roald Dahl's *Danny, the Champion of the World*.)

Cusack passed away in October 1993; he had suffered from motor neuron disease but never retired. Although not a member of a political party, he was avowedly Republican in his leanings and was a champion of the Irish language. He was also a writer of some note—he was a published poet, adapted Kafka's *The Trial* for the stage, and wrote his own play, *Tar Éis an Aifreann* (After the Mass). Finally, although he never completed his studies at UCD, in 1977, the National University of Ireland (of which UCD is a component college) awarded him an honorary doctorate, as did Trinity College Dublin in 1980.

D

THE DAISY CHAIN* (2008).** Noted mainly for her (highly acclaimed) television work, director **Aisling Walsh** makes a rare foray into a theatrical release based on a horror genre script by Irish television screenwriter Lauren Mackenzie. In a trope familiar to Irish horror films (see also ***Wake Wood), grieving couple Tomas and Martha Conroy (Steven Macintosh and Samantha Morton) move to a remote Irish village after the death of their infant daughter. There, they encounter Daisy, a young girl who appears to be autistic but is treated as far more malevolent by the locals. It emerges that they believe her to be a changeling, a fairy child swapped at birth with her human counterpart. Initially dismissing this as superstition, the couple—now pregnant again—become increasingly cautious as Daisy is repeatedly associated with a series of unexplained (supernatural?) and increasingly violent episodes.

For most of its duration, the film deliberately avoids a definitive answer to the question of Daisy's provenance. Daisy's autism so "others" her (in terms of both how she relates to other people and how "normal" people perceive her) that, for a time, the question of whether she has a disorder or is full-on evil seems moot. Ultimately, however, the narrative resolves in a manner demanded by horror's narrative conventions without ever fully exploring the potentially more interesting issues raised along the way.

DALTON, EMMETT (1898–1978). Although of interest in this book primarily for his later career as a film producer, Emmet Dalton's early experiences offer ample material for any screenwriter looking to recount a "boy's own"–style story. (Indeed, it is arguable that he at least partially inspired two screen roles, in **Neil Jordan**'s ***Michael Collins*** and, as discussed below, in ***This Other Eden***.) Born in Massachusetts but raised in Ireland, Dalton joined the British army in 1915, went to the front in France, won a Military Cross for bravery, and was promoted to major while still in his teens.

When the first (preindependence) Dáil was established in 1919, Dalton returned to Ireland and joined the Irish Volunteers, the force that would become the Irish army after 1922. He was a high-ranking officer during the War of Independence and became a close aide and friend to Michael Collins.

Among his escapades in this period was an extraordinary attempt to free Volunteer General Sean MacEoin from Mountjoy Jail: Dalton led a team of volunteers, wearing their old British army uniforms, to the prison in a stolen army vehicle and presented the governor with fake papers for MacEoin's transfer. The ruse worked until the governor rang Dublin Castle, the seat of British authority in Ireland, for confirmation of the release, at which point Dalton and his men had to fight their way out of the prison.

After the treaty establishing the Irish Free State was signed, Dalton sided with the pro-treaty forces and was promoted to general of the Free State army with particular responsibility for prosecuting the anti-Republic campaign in the Cork region. Consequently, he was with Michael Collins when the latter was assassinated in an ambush at Béal na Bláth, and Collins literally died in his arms.

However, although most historians agree that had Collins's driver heeded Dalton's instruction to burst through the roadblock that set up the ambush Collins would have lived, Dalton came under suspicion for having assassinated Collins himself (largely because the bullet that killed Collins struck the back of his head—a fact generally ascribed to a ricochet bullet). In November 1922, apparently devastated by Collins's death, he resigned his commission and for a short while acted as clerk of the Senate. However, he also left this post and emigrated from Ireland with his wife.

His return to Ireland came through an entirely different path. In 1942, he entered the film business, working first with Paramount and then the Samuel Goldwyn Company before becoming an independent producer in 1955 and establishing Emmet Dalton Productions. At this point, Dalton began to negotiate with the **Abbey Theatre**'s chairman, Ernest Blythe (with whom Dalton had a long relationship dating from Blythe's position in the Free State's first cabinet), with a view to producing filmed adaptations of Abbey plays. At approximately the same time, Dalton contacted **Louis Elliman**, and all three men became directors of Dublin Theatre and Television Productions, which produced the first of the projected Abbey adaptations, *Professor Tim*, for American television. When the distributors of *Tim*, RKO, offered Dalton a deal to produce 12 pictures in a single year, Dalton and Elliman decided to proceed with plans to build **Ardmore Studios**.

Once the studios were built, Emmet Dalton Productions became a key early client. Between 1958 and 1962, the company would make seven films there. These included four Abbey adaptations—*Sally's Irish Rogue*, *Home Is the Hero*, *The Big Birthday*, and *This Other Eden*—and three further pictures financed by the **Irish Film Finance Corporation** (IFFC): *The Devil's Agent*, *Middle of Nowhere*, and *Lies My Father Told Me*. (It should be noted that Dalton had been instrumental in convincing the Industrial Credit Corporation to establish the IFFC.)

Of all these pictures, *This Other Eden* is perhaps the most interesting both intrinsically and in terms of how it related to Dalton's past. Based on a 1953 play from Louis D'Alton, the prologue sequence set during the War of Independence clearly paralleled Dalton's Civil War experiences. The sequence depicts a senior Irish Republican Army officer driving to meet a British agent to discuss peace terms. When the officer is shot (by Black and Tans), the friend who accompanied him, Devereux, is suspected of his betrayal. The film then moves forward to the 1950s, when Devereux—now living an obscure existence as the editor of a local newspaper—has adopted an ambiguous attitude toward the treatment of the past "glories" of the War of Independence and the manner in which his erstwhile comrade is commemorated. While it is not clear that Louis D'Alton was explicitly basing his play on Dalton's life, the similarities may have accounted for Dalton's decision to film the play.

By the time Ardmore went into receivership in 1963, Dalton was 65, and his involvement with production appears to have come to a close. Yet the attendance at his funeral in 1975 suggested that Civil War rivalries were not entirely a thing of the past: despite his former senior military status, not one member of the Fianna Fáil cabinet attended his interment.

DALY, LANCE (1970–). From modest beginnings, Daly's output has been incremental in both its quality and its success, but this ambitious and talented Irish filmmaker has never quite achieved the international breakout (though he has come close) that would give him the status and recognition he clearly aspires to. Daly emerged with his debut feature, *Last Days in Dublin* (2004), a "no-budget" picaresque centering on Monster (Grattan Smith), a young Dubliner who has decided to leave the city for far-off fields. His last days are narrated by a self-aware and ironic voice-over that describes the difficulties he encounters in the style of an explorer's journal, all the while failing to move beyond Dublin's inner city and suburbs. Channeling Joyce's *Ulysses* by way of *Moby-Dick*, Monster's odyssey consists of encounters with a motley crew of "natives," "merchants," "mysterious strangers," and "sea captains," contrasting the real and surreal in an appealingly daft and at times very funny series of vignettes.

Also set in inner-city Dublin, his second feature was ***The Halo Effect*** (2004), a dark comedy based on personal experiences of working in a fish-and-chips shop. Strong ensemble casting and a good relationship with actors have consistently been strength of Daly's films, and here the reliably hang-dog **Stephen Rea** plays Fatso, chip-shop owner and compulsive gambler. Along with his gambling addiction, Fatso's natural inclination to help every loser down on their luck (including staff members) means that he is in constant financial difficulty and suffers regular intimidation from loan sharks (who include the traditional bogeymen of Irish cinema **Gerard McSorley** and **John Kavanagh**). While likable and featuring a strong central performance from Rea, *The Halo Effect* is nevertheless underdeveloped and ultimately fails to engage.

Daly followed up with *Kisses* (2008), a modest but far better odyssey narrative centering on two preadolescents (played by nonprofessional rascals Shane Curry [age 11] and Kelly O'Neill [age 12]) who temporarily escape the hardships and tedium of their deprived north-side Dublin suburb. While the film can be linked to Daly's earlier features in its clear love of Dublin and its working-class citizens, it represented a clear advance in every way from the coherence of its characterization and narrative progression to its imaginative style, gradually transitioning from black and white to color as the children experience the delights of the city and then back once they return home. The film was notable too for its sound track, which features a number of well-placed Bob Dylan tracks. Well received on the film festival circuit and gaining a small U.S. release, *Kisses* significantly enhanced Daly's reputation and career prospects.

With *The Good Doctor* (2011), a psychological thriller featuring Orlando Bloom fresh from his success with *Lord of the Rings*, Daly achieved his ambition of moving to an international level. But as **Neil Jordan** discovered with *We're No Angels* (1989), **John Carney** with *On the Edge* (2001), or **Jim Sheridan** with *Dream House* (2011), when it comes to Hollywood, you have to be careful what you wish for. There were rumors of differences of opinion between Daly and his producers on the film's final cut (he did not write the script), and the film fared poorly with critics and audiences. While there was talk of future U.S. projects, Daly returned to more familiar, Dublin-based settings and characters for his next film, which he again wrote and directed.

Life's a Breeze (2013) was a broad "recession comedy" concerning the search for a lost mattress and the life savings stuffed inside it, and it represented Daly's career highlight to date. While somewhat old-fashioned (if topical) in its premise and structure (one critic compared it to an Ealing comedy), the writing is sharp and funny, the cast a seasoned and highly talented ensemble (headed by **Fionnula Flanagan** and **Pat Shortt**), and the direction lively. Indeed, the gusto with which the film unfolds suggests that Daly was pleased to be once again in a familiar cultural space (both behind and in front of the camera) and that the disappointment of the Hollywood experience could be mitigated by writing and directing an uncomplicated script driven by clear character types and situations.

That, as John Carney discovered with *Once*, you can go home again and triumph was confirmed by the welcome accorded to the 2018 release of the Daly's long-gestating *Black '47*, a western-style thriller set during Ireland's Great Famine, an ambitious undertaking starring Jim Broadbent and Hugo

Weaving alongside Stephen Rea, Sarah Greene, and Moe Dunford that recouped almost $2,000,000 in the UK and Ireland (but bombed at the U.S. box office).

Alongside his activities as writer/director, Daly is cofounder of Fastnet Films and, along with Kirsten Sheridan and **John Carney**, of The Factory (subsequently Bow Street), an innovative screen-acting school situated in Dublin's city center.

DALY, REBECCA (**1980–**). After reading theater and English literature at Trinity College Dublin, Daly completed an MA in film at the Dublin Institute of Technology. Her first feature film, *The Other Side of Sleep*, was selected for the Cannes Cinéfondation Residency and premiered in the Directors' Fortnight at the Cannes Film Festival. Her second feature, the well-received *Mammal* starring Rachel Griffiths and **Barry Keoghan**, premiered at the Sundance Film Festival (2016), while her third, *Good Favour*, premiered at the Toronto International Film Festival (2017).

To date, Daly's films have been distinguished by themes of trauma and emotional distance and an accompanying narrative opacity that is often accompanied by a nonspecific sense of place and character identities. For some this is a meeting of style and meaning and for others a lack of clear narrative goals. While it is difficult to situate Daly's films within traditional conceptualizations of national or Irish cinema in terms of local themes or setting, their eschewing of such markers echo, paradoxically, tropes in contemporaneous Irish films, such as **Glassland**, *Room*, *Killing of a Sacred Deer*, and others (although such films might be linked through themes of dysfunctional parent–child relations). Whether this can be read as a desire to escape the obsessional preoccupation with Irishness by earlier filmmakers, a reflection of transnational tendencies within millennial Irish cinema, or simply undercooked screen writing is open to debate.

DANCING AT LUGHNASA (**1998**). Pat O'Connor's screen adaptation of Brian Friel's famous play features an all-star cast, including Meryl Streep as the eldest of the Mundy sisters, a schoolteacher who can barely afford to feed her siblings (played by Kathy Burke, Catherine McCormack, Kathy Bates, Sophie Thompson, and **Brid Brennan**, reprising her Tony Award–winning role on Broadway). **Michael Gambon** also appears as their brother Jack, a priest who returns from Uganda after 25 years having assimilated pagan rituals and apparently renouncing his Catholic faith. Various economic and other hardships befall the sisters as they try to find love and manage their frugal existence. However, when a radio is installed, bringing music into their home, the sisters find it possible to express passions denied any other outlet by the stultifyingly conservative society in which they live. At the pre-Christian midsummer festival of Lughnasa, the sisters are unified in a spontaneous dance of unrestrained joy.

That dance was very much the high point of the highly successful stage version. On-screen, it fails to make the same impact, especially in the narrator's brief but glum account of the fates that subsequently befell the sisters. In no small part as a consequence, reviews of the film were muted in their praise, describing it as an efficient transposition of the source material but little more.

DARBY O'GILL AND THE LITTLE PEOPLE (1959). Often derided as the apogee of "screen Oirishess," *Darby O'Gill* is, in fact, one of the more interesting of Hollywood-Irish narratives in terms of both backstory and choice of material. Adapted from a 1903 short-story collection by Anglo-Irish writer Hermione Templeton Kavanagh (*Darby O'Gill and the Good People*), the film was the culmination of a decade-long process of development by the Disney company as it sought to move into live-action feature films after World War II.

The film seen by audiences in 1959 had been in development since 1946, when Walt Disney visited Ireland in search of a folkloric material that might be adapted to the big screen. It seems certain that Disney's imagination had been stirred by the recent success of *Finian's Rainbow* on Broadway, a production that starred Belfast-born Albert Sharpe in the leading role, later taken by Fred Astaire in Francis Ford Coppola's 1968 screen adaptation. Sharpe, long since retired, would later be tracked down for the role of Darby after first choice Barry Fitzgerald proved unavailable due to age and illness.

When Disney came to Dublin, he met with Seamus Delargy, energetic director of the Irish Folklore Archive at University College Dublin who for the next several years would communicate with Disney researchers and writers about the many stories available to them from Ireland's vibrant and underappreciated folklore tradition. Despite consistent and repeated efforts to steer Disney away from leprechauns, it wasn't until the studio optioned Templeton Kavanagh's collection that the project moved forward.

Although basically a simple, romantic story, *Darby* contains darker elements that distinguish it from *Finian's Rainbow* (really a socially conscious satire of race in the United States that just happens to invoke leprechauns) and link it to its underlying folk elements. Darby, a laborer with a fondness for drink, regales his drinking partners of his (unsuccessful) attempts to capture the king of the Leprechauns, King Brian (**Jimmy O'Dea**). Darby's employer determines to replace him with Dublin laborer Michael (Sean Connery) but softens the blow by providing a rent-free cottage for Darby and his daughter Katie (Janet Munro). That night, Darby is kidnapped by the leprechauns to forestall the need to reveal to his daughter that he has lost his job.

Although grateful, Darby secures his freedom through a war of wits with King Brian, gaining three wishes into the bargain. Meanwhile, Michael and Katie become romantically entwined, but when she learns of her father's deception, she runs to Knocknasheega, a magic mountain where she is fatally injured by a banshee. Darby must use his final wish to save Katie from a trip to the Land of the Dead.

In many respects, *Darby O'Gill* is a whimsical piece of wish fulfillment that seeks to depict Ireland not as it is (or ever has been) but as a tourist (or, in Disney's case, as a third-generation Irish American) might want to see it. As a fantasy, it is effective, conjuring a Ruritanian Ireland out of Hollywood studio sets as well as clever and often terrifying special effects, not least when the Death Coach comes for Katie. Conversely, it also invokes a range of negative stereotypes of Irishness: superstition, alcoholism, atavistic violence, and a general representation of Ireland as trapped in a temporally unspecific state of primitivism.

However, what *Darby* does especially well—and what has often been missed by such literal-minded criticisms is bringing Irish folklore to the screen as no other film before or, arguably, after—was done with conviction. The source stories were written in Ireland at the turn of the century when their underlying superstitions was still vibrant and credible to many. Templeton Kavanagh's world may be quaint, particularly in the construction of Darby, but it is based on her experiences among the rural Irish and offers a counterdiscourse to that of the contemporaneous Celtic Twilight. The film's folklore is surprisingly accurate, and in the unexpected introduction of the banshee, it also draws on the darker, feminine, and less well known aspects of the tradition. Finally, the film functions as folklore should: as a cautionary tale. In this, it grasps the central function of the leprechaun as a metaphor for greed and the loss of true values that may accrue from the blind pursuit of money.

The film had its world premiere at the Savoy Cinema in 1959 in the presence of Walt Disney, Sean Lemass, and President Éamon de Valera. In many respects, this was highly apt: the film marked a nodual point between Ireland's folkloric, premodern past and industrial future. Conspicuously, Delargy could not attend.

***A DATE FOR MAD MARY* (2016).** "Mad" Mary McArdle (Seana Kerslake) returns home from prison to find out that she's the maid of honor in her best friend Charlene's (Charleigh Bailey) wedding. When Charlene refuses her a "plus one" invitation on the grounds that, with her reputation, she couldn't find a date, Mary sets out to prove her wrong with funny and surprising consequences.

A Date for Mad Mary began its life as the stage show *10 Dates with Mad Mary*, a monologue about a young woman's struggles after leaving prison, written and performed by Irish Pakistani actor Yasmine Akram. Directed by Darren Thornton, it was performed at Project Arts Centre in Ireland in 2010 and later at the prestigious Edinburgh Theatre Festival. Following positive audience reaction to the central character, a film adaptation was then pursued with a screenplay written by Thornton and his brother Colin, and with substantial funding from the Irish Film Board, the film went into production in 2014.

A key aspect of the adaptation shifted the axis from Mary's experiences on the dating circuit to her growing apart from her best friend, enlarging its focus and placing it more squarely within a tradition of quirky, female-centered romance comedies (e.g., *Muriel's Wedding* and *Bridesmaids*). Furthermore, Thornton's screenplay and direction are characterized by a cosmopolitanism: a sense that its themes were contemporary and experienced beyond its setting (Ireland). The film's relative indifference to place and specificity evoked largely positive reviews in Ireland. This cosmopolitanism is further augmented through the film's central romance, where after a number of false starts, Mary falls for a young woman called Jess (Tara Lee), prompting shock and rejection among her peers. Their tentative and unconventional relationship brilliantly injects freshness into an otherwise familiar story held together through a brilliant performance from Kerslake, who renders Mary as a mercurial combination of vulnerability and unpredictability.

A Date for Mad Mary might be placed alongside Irish films from the first decade of the 2000s, such as ***Mammal*** (2016), ***Glassland*** (2014), and others, which, often drawing on the influence of contemporary European and British independent cinema, focus on the emotional struggles of isolated individuals in urban settings of anomie. Such narratives are frequently left ambiguous or open ended and can be said to emerge from both a desire to reach cosmopolitan (rather than simply local) audiences and a weakening of the national myth, effected on both stylistic and narrative levels. They might thus be categorized as postnationalist though not postnation, their placelessness belying an underlying concern with the lives of young, isolated characters struggling to connect outside of traditional structures of community.

The film premiered at the Karlovy Vary International Film Festival in July 2016 and soon after won Best Irish Feature Film at the Galway Film Fleadh (Festival) (2016).

DAVIS, JOHN T. (1947–). "Remember nights in Amarillo, Silver spurs and silver bullets," lyrics from the 2016 country-and-western album *Last Western Cowboy*, do not necessarily immediately suggest that their author might be a noted Irish filmmaker, but documentary maker John T. Davis's late career shift to music absolutely reflects many of the concerns of his screen work.

Davis was born in Belfast, studied in the College of Art, works out of his own studio, and has become one of the most innovative documentary film-makers in Ireland today. Inheriting an 8-mm camera from his Uncle Jack (John McBride Neill, a noted cinema architect and subject of Davis's 1996 documentary *The Uncle Jack*) in 1974, he immediately moved to produce experimental work, such *Transfer* (1975), before committing to a career as a documentary maker in 1977. He jointly directed the experimental feminist fictional **Maeve** (1982) along with **Pat Murphy**. Drawing on his love of music, he initiated his documentary career with *Shell Shock Rock* (1979), which dealt with Northern Ireland's punk music scene. (A 1980 film, *Self Conscious over You*, recorded a concert organized by Good Vibrations Records that would later be reproduced in **Good Vibrations** [2012].) In addi-tion to music, his work is infused by a fascination with Americana. *Route 66* (1985) explores how forgotten communities situated along the road linking the East and West coasts of the United States fared after being bypassed by highways. For *Hobo* (1991), Davis effectively lived a Woody Guthrie exis-tence, smuggling his camera onto freight trains and living out of dumpsters as he followed the existence of a late 20th-century drifter, "Beargrease."

In *Power in the Blood* (1989), broadcast in the BBC's *Arena* arts slot, Davis displays his visual storytelling powers aided by the stunning cinema-tography of Se Merry Doyle. In the opening scenes, we meet evangelical country-and-western singer Vernon Oxford, who travels from his native Ten-nessee to try to save the souls of the people of Northern Ireland. The docu-mentary journey includes a highly charged treatise on the power of religion to affect people's lives.

Davis was unable to film one scene near the end inside the Long Kesh prison, where Vernon's Loyalist friend is imprisoned. So Vernon performs a concert for the prison wardens, who are members of a country-and-western fan club. In a scene outside the clubhouse, some of the members (in full cowboy costume) let off steam by displaying their shooting skills. Given that these individuals are agents of a state that ostensibly maintained the "repres-sive state apparatus" of the troubled Northern Irish state, the scene ranks as one of the most incongruous representations of the Protestant community in this period.

Davis's insider point of view and frequently poetic examination of the potency of the Bible Belt as extended to Northern Ireland continues in *Dust on the Bible* (1989). After a fallow period, he made *Uncle Jack* (1996), a nostalgic portrait of his uncle, who designed many of Ulster's most spectacu-lar cinemas. The director's poetic stylization and lyrical valorization of the local Northern Irish as part of a wider global identity has helped ensure that his documentaries have universal appeal. Unfortunately, a disastrous 1999 fire at his home threatened his filmmaking career, as his archive and film-making equipment were destroyed. However, he bounced back with *Travel-*

lers (2000), which he codirected with photographer Alen MacWeeney. The film follows MacWeeney as he revisits the subjects of a photo-essay he completed in the mid-1960s: Ireland's Traveller community. Since 2001, although he has acted as a cinematographer for other documentary makers (including Tom Collins and **Paul Duane**), his output as a director has been limited to *A House Divided* (2003), a film portrait of the members of the Northern Irish Assembly, and *Tailwind* (2008), a poignant account of Northern Ireland's wartime role in the air campaign against the Axis built around interviews with surviving airmen and airwomen.

THE DAWN (1936). Produced by **Hibernia Films**, *The Dawn* is a key historical artifact in Irish cinema history. Its significance lies not in narrative or technical qualities but simply in the fact that it was made at all. Between 1933 and 1936, Killarney garage owner Tom Cooper and 250 locals—none of whom had any previous experience in filmmaking—assembled an ambitious feature-length film set during the Irish War of Independence. All filming was done on a single camera with a fixed focal length, while much of the equipment used—studio, microphone booms, editing facilities, and so on—was built from scratch. A local pharmacy acted as a film laboratory.

The story commences in 1866, when Brian Malone, a member of the Fenian Brotherhood (a nationalist underground group), is wrongly accused of betraying his comrades to the British. Flash forward to 1919, when his grandson (also called Brian Malone) is a member of the local Irish Republican Army (IRA) fighting column. His brother Billy, however, refuses to participate in these activities, bringing disgrace to the family.

With the onset of the War of Independence against the British, members of the column raise doubts about Brian's trustworthiness, citing his grandfather's apparent disloyalty, and they vote to exclude him from their activities. Furious, Brian changes sides and joins the British-run police force in Ireland, the Royal Irish Constabulary (RIC). Inevitably, he is ostracized by his family and his girlfriend, Eileen.

As the War of Independence grows more savage, the British introduce a new paramilitary force—the Black and Tans—to quell the Irish insurgency. As an RIC officer, Brian finds himself part of a Black and Tan raid on Eileen's home, increasing her enmity toward him. Meanwhile, the IRA column (led by Eileen's father, Dan) uses information from its mysterious intelligence officer to unmask a British spy in their midst. Turning the leak to their advantage, they send a false report to British intelligence to lure the Black and Tans into an ambush.

Unaware of the trap but disgusted by the methods of the Black and Tans, Brian deserts just before the ambush. In the aftermath, however, Brian's brother Billy Malone is shot dead by the local RIC. Brian and Billy's father accuse the IRA of the murder, but it emerges that Billy was the column's intelligence officer, responsible for its success up to this time. John Malone is comforted by the news that his son died for Ireland.

Given the level of amateur participation, *The Dawn* is a remarkably accomplished piece of work. Despite a lack of formal training, director Cooper had clearly internalized the rules of cinema language. Indeed, the use of montage implies an awareness and understanding of the formalism of 1920s Soviet cinema. Only the occasional clumsy edit or sound dubbing undermines the otherwise seamless production quality. Where amateurism does show, however, is in the acting, which clearly owes much to a theatrical rather than cinematic tradition. Nonetheless, *The Dawn* is never less than entertaining—Cooper was not above throwing the odd song or comedic interlude into the mix to keep the action going. This doubtless contributed to the warm reception the film received from contemporary Irish audiences and critics who (prematurely) hailed the film as releasing Irish cinemagoers from the bondage of Hollywood.

The film's representation of the War of Independence was very much influenced by the prevailing Irish political orthodoxy of the period in which it was made. The portrayal of IRA activities is, to say the least, romanticized: IRA members are depicted as overgrown boy scouts lounging in fields while awaiting orders for the next attack. They are to a man "good sorts"—captured prisoners face not a beating but, rather, civilized treatment. The Black and Tans, by contrast, are caricatures, their commanding officer rarely without a drink in his hand, laughing gleefully when IRA prisoners are shot without trial.

The film also appears to criticize the political settlement of 1922: the IRA is clearly established as seeking not simply an independent Ireland but also a republic. One of the IRA characters argues that they want only to be left alone and not to have anything to do with Britain. When Billy Malone dies, his father, John, stresses that the fight must go on—to the implied ultimate goal of an Irish republic. While implicitly criticizing the treaty of 1922 and legitimating the Civil War that followed it, the film sidesteps an explicit consideration of such issues by confining the narrative to 1919. Given this, *The Dawn* is indicative of the ambiguous attitude toward the whole 1916–1923 period that prevailed in the Ireland of the 1930s, just as **Neil Jordan**'s *Michael Collins* displayed the more conciliatory attitude of the 1990s.

***THE DAWNING* (1988).** Set in southern Ireland against the backdrop of the Irish War of Independence, the Jennifer Johnson novel *The Old Jest* (winner of the 1979 Whitbread Award) is brought to the screen by a classy cast of British thesps. The story centers around 18-year-old Protestant orphan Nancy Gulliver (Rebecca Pidgeon), who lives with her once wealthy Aunt Mary

(Jean Simmons in her first role in a decade) and ailing grandfather (Trevor Howard in his final film, which is dedicated to him) in a fading "Big House" by the sea. On one of her daily walks by the beach, she encounters "Cassius" (Anthony Hopkins) hiding in her private hut. Initially believing that he may be her long-lost father, she continues to visit him. It emerges that he is an ex–British army soldier, Major Angus Barry, who, having returned from World War I, has thrown in his lot with the Irish Republican Army and is now on the run. Nancy agrees to bring a message on his behalf to a contact in Dublin. The next day, she suddenly realizes the significance of her action when 12 British officers are shot at a race meeting. Although horrified, Nancy remains loyal to Cassius, but as the net closes in on him, she is ultimately unable to keep him safe.

Made during the height of Northern Ireland's Troubles and shot on location on the Cork–Waterford border, *The Dawning* marked a rare foray for a British production into the origins of the conflict and is all the more remarkable for its sympathetic portrait of the Republican characters as they fought the British Empire. The focus on an Anglo-Irish family offered an accessible perspective for U.K. cinemagoers (clearly the main intended audience), not least through the quintessentially British casting (Hopkins, Howard, Simmons, and, as a potential love interest for Nancy, Hugh Grant). Nevertheless, the film is ultimately largely unconcerned with politics, operating in the main as a female coming-of-age story. Nancy's allegiance is less to any abstract political conviction that it is to the quasi-paternal character of Cassius himself.

THE DEAD (1987). Closely adapted from **James Joyce**'s final short story from *Dubliners*, *The Dead* is a fitting swan song for a major Hollywood director and Irish citizen, **John Huston**, as well as the greatest screen performance of beloved Irish actor **Donal McCann**. Drawing from the years that Huston spent with his family in Galway, it stars his daughter Anjelica in the role of Gretta Conroy (an alter ego of Joyce's Galway-born wife Nora) and was scripted by his son Tony. The story recounts a dinner party celebrated on the Feast of the Epiphany in Dublin 1904 (6 January, also known as Nollaig na mBan, or Women's Christmas) by two spinster sisters, Aunt Julia and Kate, and their niece Mary Jane, as they welcome middle-class guests into their Liffey-side home. Chief among the attendees is their sophisticated nephew, Gabriel Conroy (McCann), and his wife Gretta (Huston) along with other locals of various ages and outlooks. Conroy feels superior to the others, preferring European culture and ideas, for example, to the more primitive, as he sees it, west of Ireland, which he associates with backward nationalist values.

During the evening, his wife becomes listless as the well-known ballad "The Lass of Aughrim" is sung by Bartell D'Arcy (played by renowned Irish tenor Frank Patterson). Later, back in their Gresham hotel room, she tells Gabriel that it reminded her of a young man whom she loved years earlier in Galway. He was very ill but came out to see her in the rain to display his love for her. Later, she heard how he died soon afterward, and she wonders if he died for her. As she falls asleep, Gabriel realizes that he has never loved like this and in a moment of epiphany feels a sense of solidarity with all the living and the dead and decides that it is time for him "to go westward."

The particularly literary nature of Joyce's work has consistently posed a challenge for those who seek to transpose it to the big screen. *The Dead* is perhaps the most successful Joycean adaptation to date, born of Huston's deep sympathy with the material and a brilliant ensemble cast of actors. This is all the more remarkable since it was filmed largely on sets built in a California warehouse, with just a few exteriors shot on location by a second unit, its aging director too ill to travel back to Ireland.

DEAD BODIES (2003). Genre thriller from first-time screenwriter Derek Landy and director Robert Quinn (also his first feature). Likable protagonist Tommy (**Andrew Scott**) is looking for an easy life but is constantly plagued by his mouthy, high-maintenance ex, Jean (Katy Jones). During one of their more vociferous arguments, Jean accidentally slips, bangs her head, and dies. Convinced that the authorities will hold him responsible, Tommy enlists his friend Noel (Darren Healy) to help "disappear" her by burying her body in the Dublin mountains. However, while digging a makeshift grave, Tommy and Noel happen on another discarded corpse. Matters are further complicated by Tommy's efforts to hide the fact of Jean's death from his new love, Viv (Kelly Reilly), all while being pursued by the local police (led by **Sean McGinley**) and a corrupt politician (**Gerard McSorley**).

As fashioned by Landy and Quinn, *Dead Bodies* was clearly aimed at the kind of audiences that had flocked to see Danny Boyle's thematically similar breakout hit *Shallow Grave* (1994) a decade earlier. The deployment of a young and attractive cast, a hip sound track, and a macabre plot overcame a limited (€1 million) budget, some awkward plot contrivances, and a faint whiff of misogyny to create a comedic psycho-thriller with potential international appeal.

DEASY, SEAMUS (1947–). Seamus Deasy made his first short film—*The Island*—in 1966 when he was still only 19, and he has subsequently worked in a wide range of genres and types of films. He initially worked in Bill Stapleton's private radio studio assisting in the production of sponsored programs for **Radio Telefís Éireann** (RTÉ). When Stapleton expanded the operation to film work, Deasy found himself part of the first external camera crew supplied to RTÉ on a "for-hire" basis. During the 1970s and 1980s, as the indigenous film industry began to emerge, he was **Bob Quinn**'s cameraman of choice, working on *Poitín* (1977) and *Budawanny* (1986) (and the revamp of *Budawanny*, *The Bishop's Story* [1993], and *Atlantean* [1983]). (Deasy had earlier worked with Quinn in the late 1960s for elements of RTÉ's *Horizons*.) He also collaborated twice with **Bill Miskelly**: on *The Schooner* and *The End of the World Man*.

Deasy's most critically acclaimed output has come about as a result of his work with **John Boorman**, with whom he has worked on six occasions. Having shot *Two Nudes Bathing* for Boorman in 1995, Deasy was the logical choice to shoot Boorman's biopic *The General*, about Dublin criminal Martin Cahill. The film was nominated for a series of awards, and Boorman won Best Director at Cannes in 1998. However, virtually every review of the film also singled out Deasy's luscious black-and-white cinematography. *The Observer*'s veteran critic Philip French even compared Deasy's high-contrast images to the work of photographer Bill Brandt. This was ironic since the film was actually shot on color stock and color desaturated in postproduction.

However, the film cemented Deasy's reputation, and in 2003, Boorman used him as director of photography on *In My Country*. Although poorly received, the film was significant because it was shot not in Ireland but in South Africa. Boorman could have chosen any cinematographer but selected Deasy. Similarly, when Karel Reisz and Michael Lindsay-Hogg came to Ireland to shoot *Act Without Words* and *Waiting for Godot*, respectively (both 2000), as part of the series of Samuel Beckett adaptations undertaken by Parallel Productions and the Gate Theatre, both chose Deasy as director of photography. So too did Barry Levinson when he shot *An Everlasting Piece* in the same year.

Although he continues to occasionally work overseas (*Neverland* [2011] and *Thirteen Steps Down* [2012] and with Boorman again on the latter's 2014 feature *Queen and Country*), his work's center of gravity has shifted back to Ireland: between 2008 and 2009, he lensed **Martin Duffy**'s *Summer of the Flying Saucer* (2008); two back-to-back **Ian Fitzgibbon** films, the blackly comic *A Film with Me In It* (2008) and *Perrier's Bounty* (2008); as well as Danis Tanovic's *Triage*, featuring **Colin Farrell** as a Dublin-based war photographer.

DEATH OF A SUPERHERO (2011). Oscar-nominated screenwriter Anthony McCarten (*Theory of Everything* [2014] and *Darkest Hour* [2017]) originally planned to adapt and direct his third novel, the young adult *Death of a Superhero*, in his native New Zealand. However, when his European financier Bavaria Pictures found a coproducer in **Grand Pictures** (with the support of the **Irish Film Board**), the story was transposed to an Irish setting with comedy director **Ian Fitzgibbon** moving to helm the production.

Donald (English actor Thomas Brodie-Sangster) is a 15-year-old middle-class Dublin schoolkid who has been diagnosed with terminal cancer. Faced with his imminent demise, he seeks refuge in art, creating a fantasy world in which he is a strong but silent superhero battling a sadistic villain, "The Glove," an analogue for cancer. In his day-to-day existence, he superficially appears to be coping with his diagnosis—certainly better than most of the people around him—but his occasional lapses into bouts of fury lead his parents (**Michael McElhatton** and Sharon Horgan) to call in death therapist (or "thanatologist") Adrian (Andy Serkis). This becomes one of two key relationships for Donald, the other being with Shelly (Aisling Loftus), a self-confident classmate whose interest in Donald is undiminished by his illness. Refreshingly, the film is not interested in "solving" the problems Donald faces; rather, it explores how these relationships facilitate his coping with his situation. Adrian never pretends to offer pithy insights or sound bites that might alleviate Donald's condition but rather behaves as a calm sounding board. Shelly suggests not that love can conquer death but rather that it can recuperate what life there is to be lived.

Director Fitzgibbon reverses his earlier comedy work to produce this much more somber piece. Faced with a profoundly delicate subject, the script (transposed to Ireland by Fitzgibbon and writer/actor Mark Doherty) is consistently unsentimental yet often moving as it traces Donald's navigation of his situation. Brodie-Sangster's outstanding central performance soft-pedals histrionics to emphasize how Donald is more than simply a product of his condition and remains a regular adolescent experiencing the same confusion, curiosity, and desires as his contemporaries.

The mere fact that *Death of a Superhero* focuses primarily on and is addressed to young adult characters makes it a rarity among Irish films. But it is also unusually visually ambitious: live-action scenes filmed in Dublin (gorgeously photographed by German cinematographer Tom Fahrmann) are interspersed with animated sequences (courtesy of German company Trixter Film) that bring Donald's drawings to life. Rather than express his inner turmoil through shouty scenes of high drama, the animations work to reflect the manner in which his primary preoccupations—sexual fantasies, his own mortality, and how to protect both himself and those he loves from the fallout of his personal catastrophe—become intertwined, ultimately permitting some transcendence of his impossible circumstances.

DECEMBER BRIDE (1989). Thaddeus O'Sullivan's first "straight" fiction feature (having deliberately rejected a narrative approach for his 1978 film *On a Paving Stone Mounted*) was adapted from an acclaimed 1951 novel by

Ulster Scots writer and broadcaster Sam Hanna Bell. Set in the milieu of a Presbyterian community living around Strangford Lough, County Down, at the beginning of the 20th century, the story follows the developing relationship between Sarah (Saskia Reeves), a domestic servant, and the two brothers she works for, Hamilton and Frank Echlin (**Donal McCann** and **Ciarán Hinds**). To the horror of their conservative brethren, Sarah begins a relationship first with Frank and later with Hamilton. Unrepentantly living as a trio, they are shunned by the rest of the community (including Sarah's mother, Martha), especially after Sarah becomes pregnant and refuses to identify which of the brothers is the father. The local minister (Patrick Malahide) insists that one of the brothers marry her but is informed by Hamilton that Sarah has steadfastly refused to contemplate this. A generation later, Sarah's daughter, also named Martha (Dervla Kirwan), now seeking to be married herself, pleads with Sarah to enter wedlock so that she might have a father to walk her down the aisle. Sarah makes that sacrifice, her belated marriage to Hamilton (with Frank as best man) making her a "December bride."

Made during interregnum between the first and second incarnation of the **Irish Film Board** (and thus funded largely by **Channel 4**), O'Sullivan's painterly reconstruction of an isolated corner of Ireland a century before invokes the European art house tradition of a Karl Dreyer, Robert Bresson, or Theo Angelopoulos. That visual sumptuousness cannot conceal the text's political radicalism. Restrained performances from the principal leads may reflect the stoic nature of the community from which their characters stem but also point to hidden reserves of assertive individualism in the face of pressures to socially conform. Given the still-taken-for-granted nature of gender roles in late 1980s Ireland (north and south), Sarah's sustained assertion of female autonomy in the face of patriarchal pressure was in its own way as significant as the similar stances adopted in **Pat Murphy**'s *Maeve* or *Anne Devlin*. Even more remarkable was the manner in which the film challenged prevailing stereotypes, especially in the Republic of Ireland, regarding the intransigence of Ulster Protestantism. At a point when the Protestant community seemed exclusively associated with negation (reflected in the phrase "Ulster Says No" in the face of any suggested change to the political arrangements in the north), *December Bride* challenged such essentialist characterization by highlighting the capacity for tolerance of new social arrangements within even the most conservative contexts.

DERRY FILM AND VIDEO CO-OPERATIVE. The Derry Film and Video Co-Operative was established in 1984 as the first independent film and video workshop in the northwest of Ireland. From its inception, the workshop received annually reviewed grants from **Channel 4** as part of its policy of supporting workshop production in regional areas of the United Kingdom. The establishment of the group was driven by a desire to allow the people of Derry to make programs that reflected their own perceptions of the reality of Derry life as a means of countering the often sensational and inaccurate representations offered by visiting film crews.

The group's first project was Derry Video News, followed by a series of documentaries on strip-searching and British army involvement in urban planning. These projects reflected the group's nationalist perspective. They were followed by the co-op's most ambitious documentary, *Mother Ireland*, in which director Anne Crilly explored a range of female images that had historically been used to represent Ireland with a view to understanding how they emerged and their ideological impact. In the course of the documentary, Crilly interviewed several women from a Republican background, including then active Irish Republican Army (IRA) member Mairead Farrell.

This led to the documentary being banned in the Republic of Ireland under Section 31 of the Broadcasting Act, which allowed the minister for communications to prohibit any program carrying interviews with members of "subversive" organizations. Furthermore, despite having funded the production in the first place, Channel 4 also refused to screen the film, as it became the first production to fall foul of the 1988 decision by the British government to use the Prevention of Terrorism Act to require broadcasters to refrain from carrying direct statements by members of proscribed organizations (including the IRA).

After producing *Mother Ireland*, the group shifted to a subject informed by a different kind of politics that grew out of a drama workshop on sex and sexuality organized for Derry teenagers. The result was **Hush-a-Bye Baby**, directed by *Mother Ireland*'s producer, Margo Harkin.

Although the co-op ceased to exist in the 1990s, a report commissioned by the group and published in February 1988 had a lasting impact on the environment for filmmaking in Northern Ireland. The *Fast Forward Report*, written by Sara Mackie, offered a detailed assessment of the critical state of audiovisual funding in the north. Given that between the British Film Institute, the Arts Council of Northern Ireland, the European Union, and Channel 4 only the last had made any kind of significant funding available for independent filmmakers, the report recommended the establishment of a Media Council for the North, which would have responsibility for scripting, production, postproduction, education, research, and training. This recommendation was taken up a year later in the establishment of the **Northern Ireland Film Council**, initially as a body of volunteers and later with funding from the Northern Ireland Arts Council.

DESPERATE OPTIMISTS. Desperate Optimists is a creative partnership between the Dublin-born, London-based writer/directors **Christine Molloy** and **Joe Lawlor**. Moving from an initial interest in theater during the 1990s, Molloy and Lawlor directed a number of episodic, interactive works for the

Internet and large-scale community video projects for galleries between 2000 and 2003. Between 2003 and 2010, Molloy and Lawlor produced, wrote, and directed 10 acclaimed 35-mm short films under the collective title *Civic Life*, which toured international festivals.

In 2008, they wrote and directed their critically acclaimed feature debut, *Helen*, developing methodologies from previous films (particularly the nine-minute *Joy* [2008]) in a narrative centering on the fragile title character: an 18-year-old girl as she leaves home and finds herself in the wider world for the first time. The filmmakers worked closely with communities across Dublin, Liverpool, Newcastle, Gateshead, and Birmingham to create the finished film.

Similar themes were taken up in their second feature, ***Mister John*** (2013), starring **Aiden Gillen**, an atmospheric, largely wordless drama in which Gerry Devine (Gillen) goes to Singapore in the wake of his brother's death and—in the course of coming to know the life he lived there—the distinctions between their mutual identities gradually begin to dissolve.

Liminal in both form and themes and growing organically from an extended period of artistic development outside of the feature film format, Desperate Optimists offer a singular case in relation to Irish film practice. While they trace their origins to Ireland, have received (partial) support from Irish state agencies, and might be read in relation to themes of (postcolonial) identity, they largely eschew traditional aspirations and the critical framework of national cinema, a framework that they might justifiably reject.

DICK, VIVIENNE (1950–). As an avant-garde filmmaker, Dick's work is unfamiliar and until relatively recently all but inaccessible to all but a small coterie of Irish audiences. While much Irish cinema might be regarded as "art house" (especially when consumed outside Ireland), there is a sense that Irish full-on avant-garde cinema and its practitioners have long been marginalized. Thus, while Dick was increasingly the subject of scholarly discussion in art journals from the early 1980s on, it was not until the early 2000s that her work was subject to sustained scrutiny within Ireland, perhaps most notably in the work of Maeve Connolly.

Born in County Donegal, Dick notes that growing up, she had a limited engagement with screen or visual media: uninterested in the mainly American commercial fare at the local cinema, she also largely shunned Irish television. Only when she later moved to live in France, Germany, and India did she begin to actively engage with film as a medium of self-expression. While studying archaeology and French at University College Dublin in the early 1970s, she was exposed to the ideas of second-wave feminism and in 1975 was encouraged to move to New York, believing that it offered a more progressive space for women.

Having received some initial training in stills photography, she advanced to explore the possibilities of Super 8 film after joining the Millennium Film Co-Operative on New York's Lower East Side. Encountering like-minded individuals—"No Wave" filmmakers Beth and Scott B., Eric Mitchell, and James Nares—via the Colab (Collaborative Projects) group, she began to produce no- and low-budget short films both as a solo artist and in conjunction with others, screening them between punk bands at music venues or at the New Cinema: a "storefront theater" in the center of New York's East Village. (No Wave musician Lydia Lunch would star in several of Dick's early films, while Dick briefly performed keyboards in one of Lunch's bands, Beirut Slump.)

It is difficult to do justice to the variety of Dick's early output. Work such as *Staten Island* (1978; Museum of Modern Art [MoMA]), *Beauty Becomes the Beast* (1979; **Irish Film Archive** [IFA], MoMA), and *Liberty's Booty* (1980; IFA, MoMA) employ a mix of modes, borrowing techniques from home movies, narrative cinema, and even animation to offer sometimes ironic, sometimes confessional critiques of consumerism, patriarchy, and sexual exploitation. Such works rarely reference Ireland directly (though *Liberty's Booty* included footage of Pope John II's 1979 visit to Ireland and a reference to a strike by workers at the McDonald's franchise in Dublin), but Maeve Connolly has suggested that Dick's work reflects the hold of American pop culture, accessed via cinema and television, over the imagination of those growing up in Ireland from the 1960s on.

Her 1981 film *Visibility Moderate* (18 minutes) marked a shift both in her exhibition strategies and in her content. The film was no longer screened in the same punk venues as her earlier work but was included in the 1983 Whitney biennial, a highly influential survey of contemporary American art. *Visibility Moderate* also directly engaged with Ireland, negotiating the difficulty of representing the nation by following an Irish American tourist's voyage through a sequence of picture postcard locations. That sequence is immediately followed (and undercut) by an interview with former national political prisoner Maureen Gibson as she recounts the ritual humiliations of life during the 1980–1981 Armagh Prison Dirty Protest.

Dick's textual reengagement with Ireland may have been encouraged by encounters with **Bob Quinn** and **Thaddeus O'Sullivan** when they screened films in New York in 1978 and 1979. On Quinn's recommendation, she made contact with the Project Arts Centre in Dublin and helped curate screenings of contemporary Irish film output, including her own work. She returned to live in Ireland in 1982, exhibiting at small venues such as the Ha'Penny Film Club and, along with **Lelia Doolan**, helping to run the first film production course at the College of Commerce, Rathmines (now part of the Dublin Institute of Technology). However, although she would complete one significant work in this period (*Like Dawn to Dust* [1983]), she found it hard to find funding to continue working in Ireland, particularly given the reluctance of the newly established **Irish Film Board** to recognize Super 8 as a legitimate format. She then moved to London in 1984 and became a member and director of the London Filmmakers' Co-operative. There, she continued to explore the representation of Ireland and its landscape in works such as *Trailer* (1986) and *Images/Ireland* (1988). In *Rothach* (1985), her camera slowly pans over the western landscape, treating it as a palimpsest text on which a series of narratives are written and compete for supremacy.

While living outside Ireland, Dick's work increasingly came to be recognized as significant if often overlooked elements of the Irish film/visual art canon. Indeed, she reflects on her own status as an artist/exile in works shot in 16 mm, including *London Suite* (1990) and *New York Conversation* (1991), the latter a notably more traditional work of documentary consciously intended by Dick to be more accessible to a mainstream audience than previous work.

In the mid-1990s, she moved to the west of Ireland, where she raised her family and taught at the Galway-Mayo Institute of Technology. (That domesticity is reflected in works such as *To Be Two* [1999], a four-minute piece watching her young son as he sleeps, and *Felis Catus* [2016], which uses Dick's housecat to comment on the predatory behavior of human beings.) Her 1994 film *A Skinny Little Man Attacked Daddy* (the title drawn from a dream) sees Dick back in Donegal among her family. An intensely personal reflection on how Dick's identity was shaped by her childhood (but also how her previously exilic status afforded her the distance to reflect on those influences), the film features footage of Dick's terminally ill sister and recalls the death a decade and a half earlier of her mother.

By the start of the 21st century, Dick's work was increasingly found in the context of the art gallery rather than the cinema. *Excluded by the Nature of Things* (2002) is a three-screen installation using six speakers to create an arrangement of acoustic and visual space wherein Dick explores the tension between Catholicism and older, pagan forms through recurring images of two figures, a man and a woman, drifting across the creens interspersed with footage of a pilgrimage on Croagh Patrick.

Later works in the first decade of the 2000s tended to be shorter and focused on place: against the aural background of German electronica artist Arovane, *Saccade* (2004) moves from day to night, tracing the shoreline at Salthill in Galway, concluding amidst the sound and lights of the nearby fairground. *Molecular Spaces* (2005), shot midwinter in New York City, tracks a man entering his apartment and then listens to him talk while the camera focuses on random scenes: a sunlit carpet, a close-up of a coffee cup, Manhattan viewed through the window, and so on. Like much of Dick's work, it feels like a series of chance moments stumbled on through happenstance but assembled to create a vibrant warmth (despite the cold exterior).

Dick's later work might be broadly summarized as informed by a more global—perhaps ecological?—outlook. As its title suggests, the Arts Council–supported 2013 text *The Irreducible Difference of the Other* explores the history of colonialism, referencing inter alia marches against the Iraq War, the Arab Spring, and antiausterity protests in its search for a means of relating to difference that does not relay on dominating the "othered." While celebrating the carnivalesque through dance, performance, and the spoken word, *Red Moon Rising* (2015) seems to invoke James Lovelock's Gaia hypothesis proposing a renewed relationship between humanity and the planet at a time of looming ecological catastrophe. *Augenblick* (2017) takes this one step further in its mesmerizing imagining of a posthuman world. This last work was included in "93% Stardust," the 2017 survey of Dick's work at the Irish Museum of Modern Art. The exhibition finally reflected her status as an internationally recognized Irish artist along with similar retrospectives at the Tate Modern, London; the Seville European Film Festival; and the Berlin Film Festival. Dick's work is now part of the permanent collections at the Anthology Film Archives, MoMA, New York, and since the late 1990s the Irish Film Archive.

THE DISAPPEARANCE OF FINBAR (1995). Adapted from Carl Lombard's 1992 novel *The Disappearance of Rory Brophy* by its English director Sue Clayton and Irish novelist Dermot Bolger, the film is mostly significant as an early example of a pan-European "Irish" film (facilitated by a complex Irish–U.K.–Swedish coproduction structure pulled together by **Samson Films**). In his first leading role, **Jonathan Rhys Meyers** plays Finbar Flynn, a promising schoolboy soccer player seeking to escape his working-class upbringing through a career in professional soccer. Scorned by his father when this fails to transpire, Finbar climbs to the edge of an uncompleted highway off-ramp, jumps off the edge, and completely disappears. Left behind are his best friend, Danny (Luke Griffin), and a bewildered community. As the years pass with no sign of Finbar, a cult emerges around his mysterious absence, prompting the penning of a hit song. As the song becomes a European phenomenon, Danny receives an out-of-the-blue call from Finbar, who has been living in Scandinavia. Seeking to track him down and solve the mystery of his disappearance, Danny travels first to Sweden, then to a tiny village on the northernmost tip of Finland. There, he encounters a quirky community of locals and undesirables, the enticing Abbi (Fanny Risberg), and ultimately Finbar.

Director Clayton's first feature (after two decades working in documentary) is very much a film of two halves. The first is characterized by a gritty, urban realism set within an anonymous working-class Dublin housing estate. However, when the film shifts to the snowy landscapes of Sweden, the tone shifts to a lighter, comedic, quasi-magical realism. These tonal shifts reflect a confused and confusing story built around an accumulation of narrative strands few of which reach resolution. Danny's journey to the Arctic inaugurates a potentially interesting discussion of what it means to be Irish in an increasingly globalized world, but the central conundrum—what happened to Finbar?—is insufficient to hold audience interest not least because Finbar vanishes before the screenplay has an opportunity to establish him as a character of any interest or depth.

DISCO PIGS **(2002).** First performed onstage in 1996, **Enda Walsh**'s second play would prove the making of him as a playwright, its two leads (**Cillian Murphy** and Eileen Walsh) as professional actors, and Corcadorca, which first staged it, as a theater company. Five years later, after the stage version completed an international tour, Walsh revisited the work with a screen adaptation (directed by **Jim Sheridan**'s daughter Kirsten) that expanded the temporal span of the story from two nights to 17 years. The narrative opens with the simultaneous births of two children, Darren and Sinead, in the same Cork City hospital. Placed onto adjacent cots, they commence a lifelong bond that becomes increasingly intense as they grow older. Living in neighboring homes (the film depicts them constructing a hole through their shared bedroom wall, through which they hold hands as they fall asleep), the pair communicate through a secret language constructing a fantastical world in which, under their adopted personas "Pig" and "Runt," they reign as King and Queen of Pork City (Cork). However, as adulthood beckons, the norms of mainstream society begin to impinge on their imagined realm. Pig is increasingly sexually drawn to Runt: when she meets another boy, Pig is unable to restrain his jealously and beats the rival to death. Although still bonded to her playmate, the conclusion sees Runt recognize that Pig will never be able to integrate into a normal life and take definitive action to separate them forever.

Enda Walsh's provocative reworking of his play saw Cillian Murphy reprise his stage role as Pig with **Elaine Cassidy** taking on the role of Runt. Although comparisons are invidious, the success of the stage play owned much to the manner in which Walsh's dialogue, expressed through a *Clockwork Orange*-style argot, successfully conjured Pig and Runt's surreal world into existence on an otherwise bare stage. On-screen, the interface between reality and their surreal imagination is simply shown to the audience with the result that characterization comes to the fore. Although both leads are impressive—Murphy's trademark intensity in full flow while Cassidy deftly sutures over the transition from childhood innocence to the stirrings of adulthood—the script's reluctance to "explain" the nature of the characters, especially as they take on more violent personas, becomes increasingly problematic. Rather than being a fully rounded exploration of a problem society, the film sketches a psychological study of two enigmatic and flawed individuals, but, lacking a context for those flaws, it becomes harder to maintain empathy with either character. To her credit, Sheridan works to invoke binary discourses—urban/rural, masculine/feminine—that hint at such explanations. The rural is identified as a space of escape from an urban psychosis, not least when Runt's parents seek to break the increasingly dangerous bond between the pair by sending her to school in Donegal. Pig seems unable to evade an atavistic masculinity, while Runt's potential for socialization seems rooted in her feminine capacity for empathy. Nonetheless, the links between these discourses and the nature of the characters remain oblique, and while the final result marks a visually interesting foray into magical realism for Irish cinema, it never quite engages the emotional identification of the viewer.

DISTRIBUTION. This has been long identified as a key problem for Irish and most non-Hollywood production since without distribution, films cannot find an audience. As early as 1937, when a coherent policy on encouraging production in Ireland began to emerge, it was pointed out that the small scale of the Irish market meant that any hypothetical industry would ultimately have to look to the export market to become viable. The difficulty lay with the fact that in the 1930s (as today), Hollywood-based companies dominated global distribution. Since the 1930s, these companies have also been production companies and are vertically integrated, and there was little hope that they would willingly distribute films made by outside production concerns based in Ireland. This stark reality was a key factor in the realignment of film policy in the postwar period that began to examine ways to attract overseas (especially American and British) production companies to work in Ireland rather than creating an indigenous industry

In a somewhat different fashion, distribution remains a key problem for the modern Irish film industry. Few "Irish" films receive a theatrical release outside Ireland, although recent developments in streaming and online distribution have ameliorated this somewhat. Indeed, many makers of Irish films find it difficult to access cinema screens *within* Ireland. This is because the Irish distribution market remains dominated by the local offices of the American majors—Universal, Paramount, 20th Century Fox, Sony, Warner Bros., and Buena Vista (Disney). (Universal and Paramount distributed through a jointly owned company, United International Pictures [UIP], in Ireland—and other territories outside North America—from the 1980s until 2007, when they established separate distribution entities. The move was in part motivated by European Commission concerns regarding UIP's dominance of the European distribution market.) In theory, these U.S.-based companies could acquire the Irish distribution rights for Irish films. In practice, this has tended not to occur largely because, historically, the Irish market has been treated as a subsidiary element of the U.K. market. Consequently, the

Irish offices of the majors—with one exception—have had relatively little independence in relation to their London-based head offices. (The one exception to the rule is Buena Vista, which on occasion has acquired rights for the more commercial Irish films, such as *I Went Down*, which received a 50-print release, comparing favorably with many Hollywood blockbusters.)

There have been several indigenous distribution companies, but until the 21st century, only two operated on a consistent basis. One of these was Abbey Films, part of the **Ward Anderson** empire in Ireland. For the most part, however, Abbey acted as an agent for smaller U.S. distributors rather than acquiring rights in the true sense of a distributor. The other significant company was Eclipse Pictures. Originally formed as Clarence Pictures, the company was established in 1993 by the Irish production company **Little Bird** to handle distribution for its films in Ireland. In addition to acting as an agent for three U.S. production companies—Icon Film Distribution, UGC Films, and Verve Pictures—Eclipse was for a time the first port of call for Irish producers seeking to release their films in Ireland.

However, in the past two decades, the changing nature of distribution as a whole has seen new local players enter the Irish industry. The shift to digital exhibition has significantly reduced the logistical issues associated with physically transporting five or six reels of celluloid. Films are now typically transported in the form of much smaller (and cheaper) hard disks known as Digital Cinema Packages. In theory, the physical distribution element of cinema could be entirely dispensed with and films transmitted directly to cinemas, but security concerns have deterred the major distributors from actively exploiting this possibility. However, the digital turn in distribution has also blurred the lines between theatrical distribution and home entertainment, leading to a shorter theatrical release window and direct distribution of content to homes via either streaming services, such as Netflix, or direct downloads. Thus, although theatrical **exhibition** remains relatively healthy in Ireland, video-on-demand (VOD) is an increasingly important conduit for audiovisual content in Ireland: as of 2017, it is estimated that a fifth of Irish homes have subscribed to Netflix. This flexibility has been exploited by **Element Pictures**, which formally added a distribution portfolio to its operations in 2007, and by the more recently established Wildcard Distribution, set up in 2013 by the former **Irish Film Board** head of distribution Patrick O'Neill with Suzanne Murray.

Given the scale of Element's production output, the logic of setting up a distribution arm to push the company's own titles in Ireland was obvious, although the company also distributes on behalf of other entities, such as Studio Canal and the Royal Opera House in London (screening live performances in selected screens across Ireland, including the Element-owned **Light House Cinema** in Dublin). However, in 2012, Element also established the largest Irish-owned direct-download service for films in Ireland,

Volta.ie, which houses the largest collection of on-demand Irish productions in addition to a growing catalog of international art house content. In the same year, Element signed a multiyear licensing agreement with Netflix to make available 20 Irish films via that platform.

For its part, Wildcard's catalog, though smaller than that of Element, is more reliant on Irish content, with a particular emphasis on feature documentaries. Like Element, Wildcard has, in addition to its more traditional theatrical distribution activities, sought to exploit the disruptive potential of online distribution to broaden the reach of Irish cinema. In 2014, the company made two documentaries—*Hill Street* (2012), about the Irish skateboarding scene, and *Barbaric Genius* (2011), **Paul Duane**'s study of writer John Healy—more or less globally available via a combination of territory-specific VOD deals and sites offering the films via direct download. In the same year, the company organized the live presentation of *The Guarantee*, streaming the film and a postscreening panel debate to 18 cinemas across Ireland via satellite, a first for an Irish production. Wildcard has also signed deals with Netflix, which has seen recent hits, such as *The Young Offenders* (2016) and *Handsome Devil* (2016), appear on the streaming service.

***DIVORCING JACK* (1997).** If, as Karl Marx, observed history repeats itself, "first as tragedy, then as farce," there is little doubt where Colin Bateman's screen adaptation of his own novel *Divorcing Jack* is situated. Directed by David Caffrey (later better known for his work on *Love/Hate* by **Radio Telefís Éireann**) and featuring a mainly U.K. cast in Northern Irish roles (David Thewlis, Jason Isaacs, and Robert Lindsay along with Aussie Rachel Griffiths), the film is set in a near-future, post-cease-fire Northern Ireland, now reconstituted as an independent state. With the Troubles now consigned to history (though paramilitary gangs still play a criminal role), Dan Starkey (Thewlis) is a hard-drinking Belfast journalist covering an upcoming election where Troubles-era explosion survivor Michael Brinn (Lindsay) looks certain to become prime minister. Left by his wife after he sleeps with college student Margaret, Starkey's life is turned upside down after he finds Margaret dying, having been viciously assaulted by—or so he believes—her former boyfriend, paramilitary thug "Cow Pat" Keegan (Isaacs). It emerges, however, that Margaret had incriminating evidence about Michael Brinn's past, captured on a cassette tape that Starkey must track down to discover why Margaret was murdered.

Filmed as the Northern Ireland peace process was gathering pace (after the Irish Republican Army cease-fire but before the signing of the Good Friday Agreement in 1998), *Divorcing Jack* is an early attempt at imagining what a "normal" Northern Irish society, one not strictly demarcated by the Loyalist–Nationalist schism, might look like. Largely unconcerned with politics, the film is driven by a breakneck chase-thriller structured narrative, laced with the blackest of Northern Irish humor and peopled by a cast of eccentrics (not least of which is Thewlis's Parker but also Rachel Griffiths's nurse-by-day, stripper-by-night Lee). The result is a funny, gripping (if often uncomfortable) watch but one that inadvertently suggests that the psychic impact of three decades of political violence might not fade away overnight.

DOCUMENTARY. The long-delayed commencement of regular and routine filmmaking activity in Ireland meant not only that few fictional films were produced previous to the 1970s but also that there was a dearth of documentary output. Nonetheless, in the first half of the 20th century, nonfiction films—broadly defined to include early actualities, government-sponsored information films, and expository documentaries—significantly outnumbered the production of fiction works.

While the earliest known actual footage of Ireland has long been identified as a 52-second shot of Dublin's O'Connell Street taken by a visiting **Lumière** cameraman in 1897, a fortuitous discovery of 800 rolls of nitrate film in Blackburn in 1994 added substantially to the Irish-themed filmography of early cinema, with 26 (one-reel) films taken in Irish cities between 1901 and 1902 by the U.K. company of Mitchell and Kenyon. Along with footage from Belfast, Derry, Dublin, and Wexford, the bulk of the surviving Irish films were shot in Cork, which, its famed Republican sympathies notwithstanding, is depicted as an imperial city, its citizens cheering representatives of the British army and Royal Irish Constabulary against an urban streetscape adorned with Union Jacks.

By the early 1910s, the filming of "topicalities" (newsworthy current events) was well established in Ireland. J. T. Jameson's Irish Animated Picture Company (whose cameraman Louis de Clerq made what is often cited as the first Irish documentary in 1904, *Life on the Great Southern and Western Railway*) commonly captured events for screening in the three Dublin cinemas owned by Jameson. In 1910, the French company Gaumont also filmed topical Irish material and established an office on Dublin's Lord Edward Street. Pathé also began to work regularly in Ireland, as did the English-born cameraman Norman Whitten, who advertised his services shooting topicalities in Dublin from 1913. Thus, there were a number of companies and individuals present to capture key moments of political turmoil in the tumultuous period around World War I, such as the 1913 Dublin Lockout, the 1916 Easter Rising, and the War of Independence. This increasing culture of visualization of Irish life led Whitten to produce, via his "General Film Supply" company, the first regular newsreel program, *Irish Events*, between 1917 and 1921.

It might be expected that the government of the newly formed nation would have sponsored factual films to mark its independence from the British Empire. Yet, although there is evidence that within the Department of

External Affairs in particular there was concern with how Ireland was perceived internationally, in practice, the Irish state was reluctant to invest in filmmaking. *Ireland* (1928), a now lost travelogue-style film designed for distribution primarily via consulates and embassies and commissioned by the Department of Industry and Commerce, constituted the sole long-form state-sponsored nonfiction film prior to World War II.

As with fiction film, it was left to overseas filmmakers to create the majority of documentary shot in Ireland in the interwar period. The outstanding example of this outsider gaze is Robert Flaherty's **Man of Aran** (1934). Although lauded by then Taoiseach Eamon de Valera, Flaherty's "ethno-salvage" approach occasionally resorted to staging long-dead customs and cultural practices and presenting them as contemporary rather than mirroring the actual political and social realities of life on Ireland's offshore islands.

The **National Film Institute of Ireland** was established in 1943 (with some state funding) and provided rudimentary infrastructure for supporting the production of informational films. Although the institute lacked the expertise to produce films itself, it acted as a kind of clearinghouse for commissions from government departments and other state entities, overseeing the production of nonfiction work by third parties. The first such production saw the Department of Education commission the institute to produce a work celebrating the centenary of the death of Irish writer and political activist Thomas Davis. The institute in turn approached director Brendan Stafford and novelist John D. Sheridan to produce *A Nation Once Again* (1946), which mixed expository documentary modes with dramatic reconstructions to bring Davis's ideas to life. There followed a sequence of official information film commissions from the Departments of Tourism, Local Government Health, and (partially funded by Marshall Aid) External Affairs on subjects as diverse as hotel management, cycling safety, dental hygiene, and rural electrification. Local production companies, including **Hibernia Films**, the First National Film Corporation, and the Colm O'Laoghaire/Kevin O'Kelly–owned Comhar Cino, sprung up to service such projects.

In a similar vein, mindful of Ireland's postwar isolation from the international community because of its having adopted a neutral stance during World War II, the 1949 establishment of the **Cultural Relations Committee** saw some investment in more reflective documentary work intended to present Ireland in both an artistic and a touristic light. The first of these was *W. B. Yeats—A Tribute* (1950), codirected by **George Fleischmann** and John D. Sheridan, which combined poetry recited by **Cyril Cusack** and Michael MacLiammoir over images of pastoral settings associated with Yeats's life and work.

Regular indigenous newsreel production picked up again from 1956 with the inauguration of **Gael Linn**'s ambitious and pioneering *Amharc Eireann* series, which offered first monthly (1956–1959) and then weekly

(1959–1964) snapshots of Irish life narrated through Irish until 1964, when the presence of **Radio Telefís Éireann** (RTÉ) had largely obviated the rationale of the newsreel. Indeed, for some decades, the Irish documentary largely migrated to the small screen. Key among such television work was the prolific output of Radharc between 1962 and 1996. Produced by a film unit initially funded by John Charles McQuaid, the Catholic archbishop of Dublin, and exclusively staffed by Catholic priests, Radharc would, over the course of more than 400 films, trace the work of the Irish Catholic Church overseas and offer an extraordinarily diverse depiction of day-to-day life in the global south to Irish television audiences. Other notable projects supported by RTÉ though the 1970s and 1980s included David Shaw-Smith's remarkable *Hands*, a 37-part series recording traditional handcrafts at a point when they were disappearing, and the monumental RTÉ/BBC coproduction *Ireland: A Television History* (1980–1981), a 13-part series in the vein of comparable efforts by its producer, Jeremy Isaacs (e.g., *The World at War*), written and presented by English historian/broadcaster Robert Kee, that traced the development of the country from the pre-Christian era to the present.

Given the lack of alternative funding sources, the dominance of state or semistate players tended to blunt the critical edge of documentary production. Overtly political content was almost entirely eschewed in favor of an overwhelming focus on Irish art and culture. Figures like **Patrick Carey** and **Louis Marcus** were critically acclaimed for such work: Carey's *Yeats Country* and Marcus's *Flea Ceoil* won, respectively, the Golden and Silver Bear awards at the 1966 and 1967 Berlin Film Festivals, while Marcus was also nominated for an **Academy Award** in 1973 and 1975 for *Paisti Ag Obair* and *Conquest of Light*. Nonetheless, such subject matter was unlikely to ruffle feathers. Against this, Gael Linn did support the first two parts of **George Morrison**'s ideologically charged creative documentaries on the foundation of the state: *Mise Éire* (1959) and *Saoirse* (1961). Formally innovative in its creative repurposing of found (newsreel) footage, *Mise Éire* won popular acclaim for its rousing depiction of the struggle for independence up to Sinn Féin's success in the 1918 general election. However, *Saoirse*, covering the period from 1918 to 1922, was much more somber and thus less popular, so much so that a projected third film in the trilogy exploring post–Civil War social divisions was shelved indefinitely. There remained a keen public appetite for politically divisive work, but it was left to the few externally funded filmmakers—most notably Peter Lennon on *The Rocky Road to Dublin* (1968)—to conjure such material. Even then, such critical work was difficult to see within Ireland. *Rocky Road*'s thesis that the independent Ireland had essentially replaced one authoritarian institution (the British Empire) with another (the Catholic Church) saw it limited to a single festival screening at Cork and to a run in one cinema: Dublin's International Film Theatre.

Although figures like Carey and Marcus would remain active in documentary production through the 1970s (and, in the case of Marcus, well into the 21st century), as an indigenous film sector began to emerge in the 1970s, the bulk of the work emerging from that early cohort tended to focus on fiction. **Kieran Hickey**'s production vehicle BAC Films was initially established in the 1960s to produce a series of mainly industry-funded short documentaries, including *Faithful Departed* (1968) and *The Light of Other Days* (1972), both studies of early 20th-century Ireland as represented in contemporary photos (the latter's sponsorship by Esso reflected in the emphasis on the arrival of motor vehicles). However, after the **Arts Council** began supporting film work after 1973, BAC would increasingly focus on fiction work, commencing with *Exposure* in 1978. Although **Thaddeus O'Sullivan, Joe Comerford**, and **Cathal Black** would engage with the documentary form, this was limited largely to docudramas, including O'Sullivan's emigration-themed *A Pint of Plain* (1975) and *On a Paving Stone Mounted* (1978), Comerford's institutional study *Withdrawal* (1982), and Black's examination of the role of the Christian Brothers in Irish society, *Our Boys* (1981). While also making notable contributions to narrative fiction production, **Bob Quinn** distinguished himself in his ongoing commitment to the documentary form through the 1970s and 1980s. His study of the art of stone carving, *Cloch* (1975), was one of the first films to receive Arts Council support and was followed by a series of short documentaries examining aspects of life—music, boatbuilding, and even the work of a rural dentist—in the west of Ireland. In 1979, Quinn directed *A Film Board for Ireland*, exploring the possibilities of such an institution. When the first **Irish Film Board** actually came into being in 1981, Quinn's *Atlantean*, a three-part series tracing the long history of connections between the west of Ireland and North Africa, was again among the first recipients of funding.

The establishment of the Irish Film Board raised the possibility of producing documentary work outside the traditional confines of government department, corporate, or RTÉ funding. Yet although the board quickly demonstrated a willingness to include documentary in its bailiwick, funding established figures like wildlife documentarist Eamon de Buitlear and emerging talent like **Donald Taylor Black**, this typically occurred in conjunction with broadcasters such as RTÉ and, as the 1980s went on, **Channel 4** in the United Kingdom. In consequence, the documentary form remained wedded to the strictures of television, and the notion of the feature-length documentary designed primarily for theatrical consumption was scarcely considered in this period.

Nonetheless, the arrival of Channel 4, bringing as it did funding external to Ireland, created scope for more critical work. In 1988, the channel commissioned six directors to reflect on contemporary Ireland under their "Irish Reel" strand, supporting work from figures as diverse as **Donald Taylor**

Black (on sports) and **Bill Miskelly** (on religion). However, the work with the greatest impact was unquestionably **Alan Gilsenan**'s critical state-of-the-nation film *The Road to God Knows Where* (1988), a work uncomfortably received by Irish social elites and one that, given the sensitivities of RTÉ's relationship with its main shareholder, the Irish state, the national public service broadcaster might have been reluctant to support. The station's reluctance to upset the status quo had already resulted in censorship of documentaries such as *Rocky Road to Dublin* (finally shown on RTÉ in 2006, 38 years after its initial release), Cathal Black's *Our Boys* (1979) (commissioned but not screened until 1991 because of its negative depiction of the Christian Brothers), and even Bob Quinn's *The Family* (1979), about an alternative community (colloquially referred to as the "Burtonport Screamers") based in Donegal, which was finally given a single screening in 1992. As late as 1994, RTÉ would effectively censor *50,000 Secret Journeys* by Hilary Dully and Fintan Connolly, a documentary it had commissioned about women forced to travel to the United Kingdom for abortions.

British funding did not guarantee that the hand of the censor would be stayed. Television in the United Kingdom *was* critical in supporting the output of Belfast-based filmmaker **John T. Davis**, whose explorations of religion and Americana across works like *Route 66* (1985), *Dust on the Bible* (1989), and *Hobo* (1990) relied on funding from ITV, Channel 4, and the BBC. However, though concerned with Northern Ireland, Davis's works rarely strayed into overt politics. By contrast, those filmmakers who did quickly fell afoul of state censorship. In 1985, Margaret Thatcher's government instructed the governors of the BBC to block the station's transmission of *At the Edge of the Union*, a documentary exploring the day-to-day lives of those engaged in sometimes profoundly violent political struggle. In 1988, the U.K. government invoked the Prevention of Terrorism Act to block the transmission of voices associated with paramilitary organizations on U.K. television. One of the indirect victims of this was the **Derry Film and Video Co-Operative**'s *Mother Ireland* (1988). Directed by Anne Crilly, the documentary examined the manner in which Ireland had historically been personified in the form of a woman and included an interview with Mairead Farrell, an Irish Republican Army member who had spent a decade in jail for offenses related to the use of explosives. When an unarmed Farrell was shot and killed by a British army SAS unit weeks after the filming was completed, Channel 4 suspended the screening of the film (although an edited version did appear three years later in 1991).

With the revival of the Irish Film Board in 1993 and its sustained existence over the following decades, documentary work found a new support framework. Between 1993 and 2017, the board offered production funding to more than 250 documentaries, hugely expanding both the range of subjects covered and the resources available to filmmakers. These supports would be augmented by the establishment of Teilifís na Gaeilge (later TG4) in 1996, an Irish-language publisher/broadcaster with a particular emphasis on commissioned documentary and the inauguration of the **Broadcasting Authority of Ireland**'s Sound and Vision scheme in 2001, which used television license fee revenue to directly fund high-quality broadcast content and in particular documentary work.

Summarizing such a wide variety of content is almost impossible, but, in addition to an ongoing commitment to a significant number of bio-docs on figures from the Irish arts from directors like **Pat Collins** (*Michael Hartnett: Necklace of Wrens* [1999], *John McGahern: A Private World* [2005], and *Nuala ni Dhomhnaill: Taibhsí i mBéal na Gaoithe* [2006]) and **Alan Gilsenan** (on Tom Murphy in *Sing on Forever* [2003] and *The Legend of Liam Clancy* [2006]), Irish documentary from 1993 engaged with subject matter rarely examined hitherto. This was in part a reflection of the rapid pace of social change exemplified by the election of Mary Robinson as Ireland's first female head of state in 1990, the decriminalization of homosexuality in 1993, and the introduction of divorce in 1996.

A sequence of works reclaimed from historical obscurity a variety of women's voices and experiences. Trish McAdams's three-part *Hoodwinked* (1998) set the scene by looking at the place of women in Irish society since the 1920s, while Steve Woods's *Estella* (2000) and Geraldine Creed's *Guns and Chiffon* (2003) recuperated and celebrated female political activism in Ireland. Although Niall Byrne's literally titled *My Great Grandmother Was a Boxer* pointed to an early 20th-century example of a woman challenging gender norms, Adrian McCarthy's *Fairy Wife: The Burning of Bridget Cleary* (2006) looked back further to a 19th-century rural society where female behavior judged aberrant by the patriarchy could legitimate murder.

Donald Taylor Black's *Dear Boy—The Story of Michael MacLiammoir* traced how the cofounder of the Gate Theatre negotiated his identity as a gay man in mid-century Ireland. Vitorria Colonna's *Identities* (2009) looked at the transgender community in Ireland, Maurice Linnane's *Stand Up: My Best Friend* (2010) is a study of platonic relationships between straight and LGBT individuals, and Anna Rodger's short *Hold on Tight* (2011) contributed to the more progressive context that facilitated the passage of Ireland's marriage equality referendum in 2015.

As Northern Ireland entered an era of reconciliation after 1994, documentary makers sought to capture the sense of change. Tom Collins's *More Than a Sacrifice* (1995) looked at how four Republicans adjusted to a post-ceasefire way of life, while Adrian McCarthy's *Living the Revolution* (2002) followed Sinn Féin's Martin Ferris and Gerry Adams as the party moved into mainstream politics in the Republic of Ireland. Louis Marcus's *No Rootless Colonists* (2003) examined the history of Protestant settlers in Ireland and unearthed surprising revelations about their role in promoting Irish language and culture, while Margo Harkins's *Eamon, Banty and the Paratrooper* (2006) explored contrasting accounts of the violence of Bloody Sunday in 1972. More recently, Sinead O'Shea's *A Mother Brings Her Son to Be Shot* (2017), a chilling five-year-long exploration of the persistence of extrajudicial violence in some Northern Irish communities, pointed to the unfinished business of the peace process.

The 1990s would also inaugurate a reexamination of darker aspects of Official Ireland's past and in particular the church–state nexus that effectively controlled the country for much of the 20th century. Over three episodes, Louis Lentin's *Stolen Lives* (1999) delineated the horrific abuse meted out to children committed to Ireland's industrial schools throughout the 20th century. Some sense of that history had already begun through the belated screening of Cathal Black's *Our Boys* by RTÉ in 1991 and Johnathan White's 1996 film *The Moon on My Back* (1996), based on Pat Tierney's account of his horrific childhood in orphanages, Christian Brothers schools, and detention centers. By far the most impactful of these was Louis Lentin's *Dear Daughter* (1996), detailing the nightmarish childhood of Christine Buckley, a mixed-race woman raised in Goldenbridge, a Dublin industrial school operated by the Sisters of Mercy. Along with a subsequent 1999 RTÉ series from producer Mary Raftery, *States of Fear*, Lentin's film was instrumental in prompting the establishment of a commission of inquiry into the operation of the industrial schools and subsequently a redress board to compensate their victims.

While the state might mount the "the past is another country" defense in relation to industrial schools, a number of documentaries examined how Ireland was negotiating ongoing changes to patterns of ethnicity driven by the increasing immigration into the country from the 1990s on. Alan Grossman and Aine O'Brien's *Here to Stay* (2006) and *Promise and Unrest* (2010) adopted a quasi-observational approach to their study of the uncertain status of (Filipino) migrant labor in Ireland. In their work *Seaview* (2007), Paul Rowley and Nicky Gogan drew attention to the still more precarious context for those recent immigrants caught in the limbo status of Ireland's "direct provision" system. In a more nostalgic mode, Nino Tropiano's *Chippers* (2008) offered an account of a century of Italian-run fish-and-chips shops across Ireland. John T. Davis's *Traveller* followed photographer Alen Mac-Weeney as he revisited the subjects of his 1965 photo-essay on the Irish Traveller community and found that culture much diminished in the intervening decades.

Following the reverse trajectory of the long history of Irish emigration has provided a varied and ongoing attraction for Irish documentary filmmakers. Geraldine Creed's *Exile Files* (2006) unearthed a forgotten history of Irish mass immigration to France in the 17th and 18th centuries, while Des Bell's *Hard Road to the Klondike* (1999) adapted Mici Mac Cabhann's autobiographical tale of emigration from Donegal to the United States in the late 19th century and his participation in the 1898 gold rush. Louis Lentin's *Ar Dover Fein* (1999) investigated the remarkable tale of how 10 men from Achill Island emigrated to Glasgow in 1937 looking for work but died (or perhaps were murdered) by carbon monoxide poisoning on the night of their arrival. Both Barrie Dowdall and Brendan Culleton's *An Bothar Fada* (2000) and Enda Hughes's *Men of Arlington* (2011) looked at the disappearance into obscurity of the generation that emigrated to the United Kingdom in the 1950s.

Works raising difficult questions about the relationship between the state and external institutions have not confined their scrutiny to the Catholic Church or even the past. Risteard O'Domhnaill's *The Pipe* (2010) exposed the manner in which the Irish state facilitated Royal Dutch Shell's exploitation of the Corrib gas field off the coast of Mayo and forcibly overrode local objections to the building of an onshore gas pipeline. O'Domhnaill's subsequent film, *Atlantic* (2016), sustained this critique while expanding it to the state's poor management of the country's fisheries. Feargal Ward's mesmeric *The Lonely Battle of Thomas Reid* (2017) blended observational film with courtroom reconstructions to recount a bachelor farmer's struggle to retain his family farm against the combined forces of Intel Corporation and the state's Industrial Development Authority. In a similar vein, Pat Collins's *What We Leave in Our Wake* (2010) asked "quo vadis" for a post–Celtic Tiger Ireland cast on the unpredictable currents of global financial recession.

While a healthy skepticism or downright anger at internal state institutions has marked much valuable documentary output, it would remiss to fail to acknowledge the increasingly outward-looking gaze of recent work. The Irish Film Board has funded or cofunded documentaries exploring contempo rary life in locations as far flung as Iran (John Murray's *Bezad's Last Journey* [2006]), India (**Pat Murphy**'s *Tana Bana* [2015]), Romania (Irina Maldea's *Wonderland* [2010] and Dieter Auner's *Off the Beaten Track* [2011]), and the Himalayas (Donagh Coleman's *Stone Pastures* [2009]). Perhaps the most extreme example of this was **Emer Reynolds**'s awe-inspiring yet also deeply human *The Farthest* (2017), tracing the 10-billion-kilometer journey of the Voyager probes launched into deep space in the 1970s.

If the contemporary Irish documentary demonstrates a wide variety of subject matter, there is a consistent level of political engagement, usually leftist in sympathies. *Chiapas* (1997), codirected by David Rane (codirector of the Guth Gafa Documentary Festival), follows Deirdre Ní Arragáin and Eamonn Ó Dochartaigh from Dublin's suburbs to living with Mayan Indians on land ("Chiapas") occupied by the Zapatista rebels following their uprising against the Mexican government in 1994. Five years later, Irish filmmakers Kim Bartley and Donnacha O'Briain were in Venezuela making a documentary about left-wing president Hugo Chávez when an army coup sought to topple him. Caught up in events, their resulting widely acclaimed documentary *Inside the Coup: The Revolution Will Not Be Televised* (2004) demonstrated the murky role of the U.S. government and the collusion of Venezuelan private media with the leaders of the ultimately unsuccessful coup. The film was widely screened both on the international festival circuit and across global television markets.

Finally, reflecting the maturation of the audiovisual sector, Irish filmmakers have increasingly begun to reflect on their own history, prompting a flowering of documentary work on Irish cinema itself, starting with the first documentary funded by the second Irish Film Board, Donald Taylor Black's *Irish Cinema: Ourselves Alone?* (1994), which traced repeated attempts to jump-start an indigenous screen sector from the foundation of the state. This was followed by a series of films reflecting on the production and reception of key Irish filmic texts: **Paul Duane**'s *The Making of the Rocky Road to Dublin* (2006), Se Merry Doyle's *Dreaming the Quiet Man* (2010), Peter Flynn's *Blazing the Trail* (about the Kalem film company's pioneering films in Ireland), and Mac Dara O'Curraidhin's *A Boatload of Wild Irishmen* (2010), which looked at **Robert Flaherty**'s production of *Man of Aran* (1934) (a worthy successor to George Stoney's *How the Myth Was Made* [1979]). Robert Quinn's *Cinegael Paradiso* (2004) fondly recalled his father Bob Quinn's Sisyphean struggle to almost single-handedly sustain a screen production presence in 1970s Connemara, while Ciarin Scott's *Waiting for the Light* (2008) considered the legacy of *Mise Éire* director George Morrison's contribution to early Irish indigenous filmmaking.

Although most of the works discussed above were funded by the Irish Film Board, they were nonetheless destined to be seen primarily on the small screen, reflecting cofunding with Irish (and overseas) broadcasters. However, the past two decades have also witnessed the reemergence and growth of the feature documentary, commencing with *Southpaw* (1999), which followed the life story of Francie Barrett, the first man from the Irish Traveller community to represent Ireland at the Olympic games. While director **Liam McGrath**'s earlier studies of marginal Irish masculinities *Boys for Rent* (1994) and *Male Rape* (1996) had won festival plaudits, *Southpaw* secured theatrical releases on both sides of the Atlantic and paved the way for subsequent films. In the 2000s, in the wake of the success of Michael Moore and others, the Irish Film Board reconfigured documentary funding to specifically support feature-length films with high production values, capable of appealing to an international audience. The result was to reinvigorate the form and, on occasion, to achieve remarkable box office returns. Given the global popularity of its subject, it is hardly surprising that Gavin FitzGerald's biodoc of UFC fighter Conor McGregor, *Notorious* (2017), became the most successful locally produced documentary in Irish cinema history, a record that previously belonged to the very different *His and Hers* (2010). **Ken**

Wardrop's feature debut traced the relationships of generations of Irish women with the men in their lives and took in more than €300,000 in a three-month run, more than three times its production budget. Indeed, it is evident that the more local and idiosyncratically Irish the tale is, the more likely a documentary is to succeed in Irish cinemas. Maya Derrington's *Pyjama Girls* (2010), a fly-on-the-wall piece tracking the relationship between two young working-class women permanently clad in sleepwear, used a successful Irish Film Institute run to access bigger cinema chains across Ireland. Frank Berry's account of a children's choir emerging triumphantly from the most deprived area of Dublin, *Ballymun Lullaby* (2011), charmed local audiences, while both Alex Fegan's *Older Than Ireland* (2015), based on interviews with Irish centenarians, and Conor Horgan's *The Queen of Ireland* (2015), which offered a portrait of drag artist Panti Bliss against the backdrop of the marriage equality referendum, surpassed €100,000 at the Irish box office.

For all its popular success, Irish documentary has only recently begun to experiment with formal innovation. With TV funding long the norm and commissioning editors keen to increase audiences as much as possible, the classic expository and observational modes have long dominated with cameras either dispassionately observing the documentary subject or stitching together a sequence of talking heads. However, thanks in part to the funding provided by the Arts Council Reel Art strand, this has begun to shift. Pat Collins's interweaving of image and sound (with the frequent collaboration of editor Tadgh O'Sullivan, whose own *The Great Wall* is a haunting essay film on migration in Europe), Fergus Daly's philosophically oriented *Experimental Conversations* (2006) and (with codirector Katherine Waugh) *The Art of Time* (2014), and Donal Foreman's *The Image That You Missed* (2017), along with Sophie Fienne's collaborations with Slavoj Žižek (*The Pervert's Guide to Cinema* [2006] and *The Pervert's Guide to Ideology* [2012]), point to new orientations and possibilities. That Conor Horgan's *The Queen of Ireland* could use Panti Bliss as its subject while deploying her as both the film's narrator and intratextual commentator points to a growing awareness of the potential for a more reflexive approach to the form.

DOOLAN, LELIA (1935–). The career arc of Lelia Doolan mirrors and, to a considerable extent, shapes Irish cultural life—particularly in areas of activism, theater, film, and television—since the mid-1960s.

Born in Cork, she was educated in a Dublin convent before studying languages at University College Dublin (UCD), where she won the Browne Gold Medal for French and German. Her active involvement in Dramsoc and the Music Society at UCD led to postgraduate work in Berlin (on Berthold Brecht), where she also moved into theater and journalism. These talents were combined when she joined **Radio Telefís Éireann** (RTÉ). Initially appearing as an actress in one of RTÉ's earliest dramas, *Down at Flannerys*

(1963), she became a full-time producer/director working across both news and drama. Critically, she established the long-running *Riordans* series and founded the seminal current affairs program *Seven Days*.

In 1969, when she was only 34, she became head of light entertainment at RTÉ, but her appointment was short lived. Complaining about RTÉ programming policy, which she described as "trivial, emasculated and contrary to the national cultural spirit," she resigned her post (later outlining her reasons for doing so in the book *Sit Down and Be Counted*, which she coauthored with colleagues Jack Dowling and **Bob Quinn**).

In 1971, Doolan was appointed artistic director of the **Abbey Theatre** but again departed under controversial circumstances after two years. Moving to Belfast, she worked in community video and adult education and gained a PhD in social anthropology from Queen's University Belfast. A committed educationalist, from 1979, she taught media and communications (the first courses of their kind in Ireland) at the College of Commerce, Rathmines, in Dublin.

In the 1980s, Doolan moved to Galway, where she founded the Galway Film Fleadh (Festival), studied homeopathy, and worked as an executive producer for the **Irish Film Board** on Fergus Tighe's *Clash of the Ash*. From 1984 to 1987, she worked to raise £1.4 million to produce **Joe Comerford**'s *Reefer and the Model*. The story of how that money was raised amply demonstrates Doolan's energy and dynamism. Having raised half the budget from RTÉ, **Channel 4**, and the Irish Film Board, she secured the rest from **Strongbow** and British/American producer Hemdale. However, both Strongbow and Hemdale subsequently withdrew their funding just before the film was due to go into production in April 1987. Undeterred, Doolan flew to Hemdale's Los Angeles office, where she met company head John Daly, armed with Irish sausages and rashers. At the end of the meeting, Daly agreed not merely to honor Hemdale's original commitment but also to fund the completion bond for the picture. Another £25,000 resulted from persistent calls to Irish financier Tony O'Reilly, allowing the picture to go ahead.

By the start of the 1990s, Doolan was a director of the Galway Film Resource Centre and the **Irish Film Centre** and a manager of the European Script Fund. Then, in April 1993, **Michael D. Higgins** appointed Doolan chair of the revived Irish Film Board, a decision that was warmly welcomed by the Irish filmmaking community because she brought a mix of cultural sensitivity and financial pragmatism to the position. Doolan was regarded as an active chair, continually lobbying government for increased funding for the board. When the British *Evening Standard* film critic Alexander Walker accused the board of funding nationalist propaganda (citing **Thaddeus O'Sullivan**'s *Nothing Personal* [1995] in particular), Doolan personally entered the fray, noting that the board judged projects by their artistic quality and authenticity rather than by political criteria.

In 1996, she initiated a project to acquire a touring cinema—the Cinemo-bile—to bring nonmainstream film to smaller towns lacking their own cine-mas. In May 2001, the project came to fruition, and Doolan chaired the Galway-based body that ran the Cinemobile. Meanwhile, in November of that year, she used her introduction to the Film Board's annual report to call for the establishment of a levy on cinema seats to provide a secure fund for Irish film production. In December that year, Doolan announced that she was resigning as Film Board chair, citing a desire to pursue other interests.

Among these was a return to directing for the first time since the 1960s. Her 2011 documentary on the remarkable Bernadette McAliskey, a leading Northern Irish Republican politician, was the culmination of a decade of work, combining archival footage of McAliskey's vigorous political activity in the 1960s and 1970s with scenes (shot by Joe Comerford) of the more contemplative figure of the 21st century. Prompted by Doolan's puzzlement at the absence of references to McAliskey during the Northern Ireland peace process, *Bernadette: Notes on a Political Journey* (2011) demonstrated that Doolan retained her capacity to assemble compelling work, securing her an IFTA in 2012 for Best Feature Documentary.

She remains a vibrant and active figure in contemporary Irish cultural life and politics. She is still a member of the Council of the **Irish Film Institute** and was the central figure in the establishment of the Picture Palace (aka Pálás), a dedicated art house cinema in Galway.

DOWN THE CORNER (1977). If, as Robert Warshaw has famously as-serted, the gangster genre is "the 'no' to that great American 'yes,'" then *Down the Corner* is the original "no" to picture postcard representations of Ireland. Directed by **Joe Comerford** and produced in conjunction with the Ballyfermot Community Arts Workshop (with additional support from Dub-lin City Council, **Radio Telefís Éireann**, and the British Film Institute), *Down the Corner* focuses on a gang of working-class youths living in a bleak Dublin suburb. While not quite an antinarrative film (especially in compari-son with Comerford's more avant-garde work), the film cannot be reduced to its story. Instead, *Down the Corner*'s lasting significance and influence de-rives from its (then) radical choice of subjects and form. That it is not better known is a great shame, although its influence can be directly felt in Frank Berry's films *I Used to Live Here* and *Michael Inside*, which emerge from similar practices of working with communities.

Up until Comerford's film, working-class Dublin youths simply hadn't appeared on the big screen in the manner depicted here. Collaborating with his subjects to determine the shape and content of the final film, the director deploys a skeleton narrative to build a remarkably intimate portrait of the Ballyfermot community, one that crucially foregrounds the perspective of the locals rather than that of the filmmaker. We see the kids as rascally (an extended sequence follows the gang as they rob an orchard) but also as family centered (another sequence connects the two kids to their grandparents' generation as she recalls a disturbing memory from the War of Independence) as well as wise and empathetic beyond their years. After a minor altercation with local drunk Mr. Lynch, some of the kids excuse his behavior by explaining how he has been driven to drink after losing his job in the local foundry.

These sequences are mediated to the audience in a quasi-observational style. Indeed, at times, the film is indistinguishable from documentary: Comerford actively includes spontaneous events caught on camera into the loose narrative story. The realist aesthetic is further accentuated by naturalistic lighting and sound design, which makes frequent recourse to overlapping dialogue. Representations of the Dublin working class before and since often soften vocal inflections to render them comprehensible to overseas audiences, but *Down the Corner* makes no such concessions.

At only 48 minutes long, *Down the Corner* was not quite a feature-length film but nonetheless demonstrated the radical potential of Irish cinema. Remarkably, it did so long before the routinized production activity that followed the establishment of the **Irish Film Board**. Thus, *Down The Corner* could not even be said to be an expression of frustration at a more conservative mainstream cinema; rather, it emerged sui generis from Comerford's impulse to allow a subaltern community to express itself in as unmediated a manner as possible.

DOWNEY, COLIN (1975–). Colin Downey can be situated within the millennial generation of Irish filmmakers who emerged at the turn of the millennium with microbudget, largely self-funded features shot on digital. To date, Downey has written and directed nine feature films as well as a number of shorts and has worked as a cinematographer on several more.

A graduate of the National College of Art and Design, Dublin, Downey made his feature debut with the self-funded *Paranoia* (2005), the first installment in his self-described "Dreams Trilogy," which continued with *King for a Day* (2006) and *Dream Diary* (2007).

Favoring stories broadly described as fantasy, Downey achieved a number of awards on the international film festival circuit, leading to **Irish Film Board** funding for his subsequent feature films *The Looking Glass* (2011) and *The Shadows* (2013), the latter of which was adapted from a George MacDonald fairy tale and shot for a meager €100,000.

In 2015, his screenplay for *The Brave Tin Soldier* (based on the Hans Christian Andersen story) won first place at the Los Angeles Screenplay Competition, while the feature film *Daria* (2016) won awards at a number of international film festivals.

Despite such awards and a prodigious amount of work, Downey's profile remains stubbornly low, though he has also experienced success as a cinematographer, collaborating with director **Ivan Kavanagh** on his films *Tin Can Man* (2007) and ***The Fading Light*** (2010).

DOYLE, RODDY (1958–). Internationally successful novelist and author of film scripts and several plays, Doyle was raised in Kilbarrack in Dublin and taught English and geography at the secondary level for 14 years after getting his degree from University College Dublin. He continued to teach even after achieving success at his writing, and it wasn't until the publication of his fourth novel, *Paddy Clarke Ha Ha Ha*, which won the Booker Prize in 1993, that he left teaching for his current career in full-time writing.

Doyle first came to public attention in 1987 for his work for the Passion Machine Theatre Company. The first production of his play *Brownbread*, a comic tale of three kids who kidnap a bishop simply to kill their boredom, brought contemporary Irish voices (and, in particular, Dublin vernacular) to the stage. (*Brownbread*'s initial run also featured the then unknown **Brendan Gleeson** among its cast: he would also appear in Doyle's subsequent play *War* [also for Passion Machine] in 1989.) That emphasis on speech was also characteristic of Doyle's novels (and, in particular, his earlier works): the "Barrytown Trilogy" (*The Commitments* [1987], *The Snapper* [1990], and *The Van* [1991]), which focused on various members of the Rabbitte family, is constituted almost entirely by dialogue. Since the original novels were, for all intents and purposes, scripts, it was perhaps less than surprising that they were adapted as screenplays. More surprising, however, was that ***The Commitments*** (1991), his originally self-published debut, was picked up by Hollywood and directed by veteran director Alan Parker. Its success in Ireland and the United States immediately saw the sequels, ***The Snapper*** (1993) and ***The Van*** (1996), picked up and produced for BBC Films. Doyle also moved into television drama in 1994 with *Family*, a searing **Radio Telefís Éireann/** BBC–produced portrayal of a working-class Dublin family terrorized by **Sean McGinley**'s alternately violent and charismatic patriarch Charlo. (His subsequent novel, *The Woman Who Walked into Doors* [1996], filled in the backstory of Charlo's wife Paula.) The critical reception afforded to his first original film script, ***When Brendan Met Trudy*** (2000), suggested that Doyle's center of gravity might remain in screen production. However, despite subsequent reports that he was working on an adaptation of Liam O'Flaherty's 1937 novel *Famine*, Doyle's 21st-century output has been concentrated largely in the literary sphere, his screen output limited to writing the source material short story for Steph Green's short film *New Boy* (2007), about an African immigrant joining an Irish primary school, and, more recently, *Rosie* (2018), an urgent, angry film centering on an ordinary family suddenly cast into homelessness by the vicissitudes of Ireland's property market.

DOYLE, TONY (1942–2000). Doyle grew up in County Roscommon and graduated from University College Dublin in the 1960s and spent most of his acting career working in Great Britain, cutting his teeth in many of the famous "Play for Today" anthology television dramas in the 1960s. From his base in Britain, he went on to star in many television series, including *Bally-kissangel*, *Between the Lines*, and the Irish rural soap *The Riordans*. In 1997, he negotiated the almost impossible feat of making audiences sympathize with a tyrannical patriarch in a television adaptation of John McGahern's novel *Amongst Women* (1997). In Irish film, he was cast in smaller but often key roles in films, including *Eat the Peach*, *Circle of Friends*, and *A Love Divided*; he also performed as a veteran gangster in *I Went Down*. Before his untimely death, Doyle was the epitome of the ambiguous Irish father figure, a central trope within Irish screen narratives.

DRIFTWOOD (1996). Directed by **Ronan O'Leary** and coscripted with Richard Wearing, *Driftwood*'s narrative is remarkably similar to that of Rob Reiner's earlier classic adaptation of the Stephen King novel *Misery* (1990). Sarah (Anne Brochet) finds The Man (James Spader) washed up on a beach. She brings him back to her lonely home on the shore. When he awakes, he is suffering from total memory loss, unable to recall even his name. However, it emerges that Sarah herself also suffers from mental ill health. Away from The Man, she talks to her deceased mother (Anna Massey), who, though conjured by Sarah's imagination, berates her daughter for her inability to maintain a relationship. The film is a study of obsession, with Sarah telling The Man that he has washed up on an island that is visited only once a year by a supply vessel. It later emerges that this is a ruse designed to bind him to her. Sarah's house is in fact on the mainland just a few miles from the nearest village.

Shot at **Ardmore Studios** and on location in the Aran Islands, the film suffered from the inevitable comparisons with *Misery*. Critics also pointed to its overly slow pacing and occasional farcical dialogue. Consequently, it received a very limited and brief release in Ireland and France (as *La geôlière*) before receiving an equally limited video release.

DRINKING CRUDE (1997). Kerryman Owen McPolin is now recognized mainly for his extensive work as a cinematographer on U.K. and Irish film and television *Drinking Crude* marked his first (and, to date, only) work as a feature film director. Another addition to the small canon of Irish films set against the background of the Leaving Certificate (the final secondary school assessment), the film follows Paul (**Andrew Scott**) as he decamps from his small hometown for London, having apparently failed his exams. Quickly finding himself homeless and penniless, he is taken under the wing of the roguish Al (James Quarton), a Scottish laborer who offers him work cleaning oil tankers. The pair are soon joined by abused mother Karen (**Eva Birthistle**) and her baby, the four forming an unlikely family unit.

Beautifully lit and fluently edited, the look of *Drinking Crude* belies the miniscule budget (£100,000) painstakingly assembled by McPolin (after receiving development funding from the **Irish Film Board**). While the script (also written by McPolin with Eamonn Maguire) at times lacks narrative drive, the film works primarily as a character-driven piece, well served by its youthful leads in this regard.

***THE DRUMMER AND THE KEEPER* (2017).** Gabriel (Dermot Murphy) is a laconic drummer in a three-piece Dublin band starting to attract record company (and groupie) interest. Something of a tortured soul, he has been diagnosed with bipolar disorder "with psychotic and delusional episodes" and is self-medicating with a cocktail of booze, drugs, and late nights. After his sister Alice (Aoibhinn McGinnity) and bandmates Pearse and Toss (Charlie Kelly and Peter Coonan) stage an intervention, he agrees to meet psychotherapist Dr. Flahavan (Annie Ryan), who prescribes therapy in the form of a weekly soccer training session with the patients of a developmental disorder care center run by Eric (Adrian Hudson). On the field of play, Gabriel encounters goalkeeper Christopher (Jacob McCarthy), who is on the autism spectrum. After a rocky start, the two strike the beginnings of a friendship, based initially on mutual convenience: Christopher needs someone to practice penalties with, and Gabriel (or, rather, his band) needs a roadie (something Christopher's eye for detail makes him preternaturally gifted at).

Although representations of mental health have been a recurring trope in Irish cinema, explorations of the specific categories of intellectual disability and/or developmental disorders have been less common in Irish work (*Sanctuary* [2016] aside). Writer/director Nick Kelly is better equipped than most to explore this area given that his own son has Asperger's.

While the text sets up overt parallels between Gabriel and Christopher—one orphaned, the other de facto abandoned by both parents (both institutionalized)—their respective conditions place them in very different situations. Delusional episodes aside, Gabriel can usually "pass" as normal. Christopher doesn't have this luxury. Although high functioning, he finds it difficult to cope with novel social interactions for which his learned-by-rote behavioral routines are inappropriate. Through its two leads, the film discreetly invokes two contrasting discourses relating to people with disabling conditions. The medical discourse, embodied in the pivotal figure of Dr. Flahavan, identifies conditions such as Gabriel's bipolar disorder as immanent to the individual and treats them accordingly. By contrast, Christopher's character permits some exploration of the social model of disability. Commonly applied to discuss physical disability, the social model suggests that individuals do not "have" a disability but rather "are disabled by" a built environment designed primarily for the mainstream of society.

The film offers a complex negotiation of these discourses. Having dutifully taken his meds and gone straight as demanded, Gabriel's bandmates complain that he no longer plays like he used to and move to replace him with another drummer. This creates an impossible bind for Gabriel, his wish to be identified as a drummer dependent on precisely the identity he wishes to suppress. Christopher's main life goal might be summarized as "belonging," symbolized by his wish to move back in with his mother, and his efforts to internalize behaviors acceptable in mainstream society represent steps on this path. However, in another nuancing of the social discourse, it is suggested that, even while mimicking normal behaviors, Christopher also embraces Asperger's as a key component of his identity.

It is not always clear as to where the film situates itself in relation to these discourses around mental health. That the medical discourse is expressed mainly by the glacial Dr. Flahavan seems calculated to damn that discourse by association. Yet the film also depicts the catastrophic consequences of entirely rejecting her pharmaceutical solution. The film does *seem* to endorse the social discourse even while acknowledging that it will demand a sea change in social attitudes to become operative.

The film also draws attention to how aberrant behavior is just as common among the notionally "normal" characters: bandmates Pearse and Toss are portrayed as self-interested, a groupie with whom Christopher has his first sexual experience turns out to be exploiting him in order to get back with Gabriel, and Christopher's stepfather is a reactionary brute, while Dr. Flahavan's robotic adherence to her professional guidelines is not obviously distinguishable from Christopher's coping strategies. Indeed, ironically, it is Christopher who ultimately emerges as the most sympathetic character in the film. He persistently forgives those who trespass again him, going out of his way to be helpful to Gabriel and, after Gabriel's second-act implosion, emerging as the figure who ultimately resolves both his own and Gabriel's problems with a left-field but internally logical proposal that makes a virtue of combining his and Gabriel's disorders. The film leaves Gabriel and Christopher as an inverted reincarnation of the Odd Couple: though both are intrinsically odd as individuals, as a unit, they are depicted as amounting to more than the sum of their parts. Ultimately, the film concludes that one's mental status is less important than whether one is a fundamentally decent person.

DUANE, PAUL (1969–). Paul Duane's **short film** *Ink* (1988) (his graduation project from the Institute of Art, Design, and Technology) marked an auspicious debut and became the first student film to be acquired and screened by **Radio Telefís Éireann** (RTÉ). Nonetheless, it would take another two decades before Duane could again exercise a similar level of creative control. Since 2011, however, he has become both a prolific director (of documentaries) and a producer via Screenworks, the company he cofounded in 2008 with Rob Cawley.

A native of Cashel in County Tipperary, Duane worked in a variety of positions in the Irish audiovisual sector before securing RTÉ/BBC Northern Ireland support for his professional debut, a perplexing time-travel short based on a Seamus Mac Annaidh script, *Misteach Baile Atha Cliath* (1994). Work on children's television for the new Irish-language channel TG4 followed, but Duane's horizons were significantly broadened by the response to his next short film, *My Dinner with Oswald* (1997), supported by RTÉ/**Irish Film Board** funding. The film is one of the great Irish shorts, a visually striking, witty trip through the psyche of a Kennedy assassination–obsessed conspiracy theorist that attracted both international sales and an agent who brought Duane to the attention of BBC Northern Ireland, then crewing *Ballykissangel* (1996–2001), a prime-time drama about an English priest in rural Wicklow. Working with substantial budgets and large crews for the time, Duane had to adapt to the discipline of directing a television hour every two weeks. He would transfer those skills to other U.K. television, including hospital dramas *Casualty* (2001) and *The Royal* (2003).

Duane has spoken of how reading famed Hollywood producer Robert Evans's 1994 biography *The Kid Stays in the Picture* taught him the importance of developing his own project and retaining the intellectual property therein. Lacking the resources to option a novel, he instead focused on a new medium, acquiring the TV rights to *Diary of a London Call Girl*, the 2003 **Guardian** blog of the year. Working in conjunction with Tiger Aspect, a major U.K. independent television production company, Duane and producer Avril MacRory eventually sold the project to ITV in September 2007, and it became an international hit with buyers, including U.S. cable network Showtime and remakes in several other territories. Having retained a cocreator credit and a stake in the financial performance of the show, Duane started, with Rob Cawley, Screenworks, which has, among other things, coproduced the four-part drama series *Amber* (2014) for RTÉ and the feature *In a House That Ceased to Be* (2014) as well as Duane's prodigious output as a documentary director.

Between 2011 and 2018, he directed five feature documentaries, and while his choice of subjects has been eclectic, these films have been characterized by at least two common features: a focus on individuals with difficult life histories and an apparent reluctance to work with Irish subjects. *Barbaric*

Genius (2011) tracks down John Healy, whose classic 1992 memoir *The Grass Arena* recalled his difficult upbringing in the London Irish community and his descent into alcoholism and crime before reemerging from prison as, of all things, a chess genius. Although Healy's memoir had brought him a level of public recognition in the early 1990s, by the early 21st century, he had disappeared into obscurity again. Duane found him eking out a lonely existence in a small flat supported only by a state pension. The shoot proved protracted due in part to intermittent finance (Duane self-financed the initial shoot) but also because, though a warm, charming individual in private, Healy clammed up on camera. Duane spent five years cultivating his subject's trust before getting usable material.

That kind of intimacy with his subject is also evident in his second feature, *Very Extremely Dangerous* (2012). Duane had long been intrigued by the extraordinary story of outlaw musician Jerry McGill. An initially promising musical career (including a single with Sun Records in 1959) went off the rails, as McGill was repeatedly incarcerated for a spectacular sequence of criminal offenses, including attempted murder. Learning that McGill was to make his first album since 1959 after being diagnosed with terminal cancer, Duane traveled to the United States to document the recordings. However, the anticipated narrative of redemption was blown apart by the ongoing train wreck that was McGill's existence. Acting as his own cameraman, Duane's film captures McGill shooting up, imbibing dog tranquilizers, and physically abusing his partner. After three months, Duane concluded that his own life would be in danger if he continued filming. The resulting film, combining elements of the observational with the interactive (at one point, Duane witnesses McGill's verbal last will and testament), is a stunning portrait of an individual comprehensively blowing every chance offered to him.

Natan (2013) marked a stylistic departure. Where *Barbaric Genius* was straight documentary (a mix of archive footage and talking heads) and *Very Extremely Dangerous* adopted a gonzo handheld approach, Duane employed a more poetic mix of modes to explore the lives of the extraordinary story of the largely forgotten Bernard Natan, the man who both saved the French film industry and then was accused of bringing it into disrepute. Duane's film recuperates Natan and comprehensively disproves the slanderous charges leveled against him.

In 2013, *Variety* named Duane one of 10 directors to watch, securing him a U.S. agent. Both his subsequent films were largely filmed in the United States. *While You Live, Shine* (2018) explores musicologist Chris King's belief that early music has played a crucial healing role in communities by traveling to Epirius in northern Greece, where an isolated community plays music dating back to the pre-Christian era. Although Bill Drummond, the subject of his subsequent work, *Best Before Death*, is Scottish, the film returns to the United States as the maverick musician commences a "world tour" of Memphis in 2016.

Duane has acknowledged that his personal preference for subjects with troubled pasts hasn't always made for commercial fare and frequently meant that he has had to self-fund projects. Nonetheless, his recuperative impulse to seek out and retrieve figures from relative obscurity has created a coherent body of work. He remains striking also for his assertion that being an Irish documentary filmmaker doesn't necessarily equate with mining Irish subjects.

DUFFNER, J. PATRICK. Duffner is a long-established film editor who was involved with **Kieran Hickey** and Sean Corcoran in B.A.C. Films from the mid-1970s. As a result, he was editor on virtually all of Hickey's work, from shorts such as *A Child's Voice* (1978), the long-form breakthrough *Exposure* (1978), and later films such as *Criminal Conversation* and *Attracta*. Hickey passed away in 1993, but by that point, Duffner had already broadened his range of collaborators. He was editor on both **Neil Jordan**'s debut, *Angel* (1982), and **Jim Sheridan**'s first film, *My Left Foot* (1987). He would subsequently work with both again on *Michael Collins* and *The Field*. He also edited **Thaddeus O'Sullivan**'s eye-catching debut, *The Woman Who Married Clark Gable*. In the 21st century, he has tended to work on smaller but no less significant projects: these include the mammoth **Radio Telefís Éireann** history of the Irish state *Seven Ages* (2000), **Lance Daly**'s *Kisses* (2008), and **Donald Taylor Black**'s *Skin in the Game* (2012), a critical examination of how Irish artists have responded to the post-2008 economic recession.

DUFFY, MARTIN (1952–). Outside animation, there has been a limited amount of production of Irish film work aimed at younger audiences. The nearest thing to an inheritor of **Bill Miskelly**'s mantle is arguably Martin Duffy, whose four features to date as a director focus on youthful protagonists.

Born in Dublin, Duffy initially worked as a postman who began writing (unpublished) novels in the mid-1970s to stave off the boredom of his day job. In 1978, he sold the play *Your Favorite Funny Man* to **Radio Telefís Éireann** (RTÉ), which produced it as a television drama. Immediately thereafter, he joined RTÉ as a trainee editor, working through the grades until, by the mid-1980s, he was cutting large-scale (by RTÉ standards) dramas, including *Caught in a Free State* (1984) and *The Price* (1985). He thereafter embarked on a freelance career that saw him move into editing features for Margo Harkin (*Hush-a-Bye Baby* [1991]) and **Bob Quinn** (*The Bishop's*

Story [1994]). In 1995, he swapped the cutting desk for the director's chair, debuting with the self-penned *The Boy from Mercury* (1995), a warmly received nostalgic tale about a boy growing up in 1960s Ireland who believes himself to have been abandoned by his Mercurian parents. He returned to themes of childhood and loss in *The Bumblebee Flies Anyway* (1999), an adaptation of Robert Cormier's dystopian 1983 novel that starred a pre–*Lord of the Rings* Elijah Wood and Rachel Leigh Cook. Although again critically well received and nominated for the Grand Special Prize at the Deauville Film Festival, the film was not widely distributed. Duffy immediately followed this with *The Testimony of Taliesin Jones*, a film that, though based on a 1996 novel, *Rhidian Brook*, structurally recalled *The Boy from Mercury*: Taliesin is a young boy growing up in rural Wales who seeks solace in the belief that he can heal people after his parents split. Nominated for prizes at a host of festivals (and securing the Best Feature at the 2001 Berlin International Film Festival), *Talieson Jones* should have boosted Duffy to greater things. And yet, perhaps in a reflection of the inferior status accorded to children's cinema, he struggled to complete another feature afterward. In 2003, he moved to Berlin, where he continued to write across a variety of media: novels, nonfiction, children's animated television, and developing scripts for screenplays. He has also worked in radio documentary, producing material for both German radio and RTÉ. In 2008, he directed his last feature to date, the **Irish Film Board**–supported *Summer of the Flying Saucer*, another whimsical story following Danny (**Robert Sheehan**), who revels in his outsider status as a hippie in 1960s rural Ireland but who encounters even more unfathomable beings in the shape of stranded aliens. Let down by weak special effects (where *The Boy from Mercury* could legitimately embrace 1920s-style sci-fi effects, *Summer of the Flying Saucer* needed something beyond the standard of low-budget television drama), the film again made little impact. Duffy has continued to seek to produce new feature work, contemplating crowdfunding as a possible way forward.

DUNBAR, ADRIAN (1958–). The eldest of seven children born into an Enniskillen, County Fermanagh, family, Adrian Dunbar attended the local Catholic school—Saint Joseph's—before taking his first job in the local Unipork factory, where his job entailed chopping pigs' heads in half. From this inauspicious beginning, he moved to become a jobbing musician, got involved in amateur dramatics, and finally ended up at the London Guildhall School of Music and Drama. Although he made his screen debut in 1984, the vast majority of his work during the 1980s was onstage, although he did appear—well down the cast—in two Irish-themed films during this period: *The Dawning* (1988) and **Jim Sheridan**'s *My Left Foot* (1987). His first major screen role was in the BBC's Northern Ireland one-off drama *The Englishman's Wife* (1990), but it was Peter Chelsom's light comedy *Hear*

My Song the following year that properly established Dunbar as a leading man. The film established key elements of his screen persona: charming but often untrustworthy or even menacing. Like many Irish actors, he is best known in the United Kingdom for his television work, where he is frequently cast in psychological thrillers, typically playing husbands who are not all they seem (cf. *Suspicion* [2003]).

His big-screen work has been concentrated largely in Irish films. Although he appeared in two back-to-back British gangster films in 2002 (*Shooters* and *Triggermen*), he has appeared in seven Irish feature films since *Hear My Song*. For the most part, however, he is carefully cast in supporting roles. Dunbar played the depressed farmer in **The Playboys** (1992), the amorous son in **Widows' Peak** (1994), and Martin Cahill's first in command in **The General** (1998). He played an ideologically motivated IRA man in **The Crying Game** (1992), his character acting in stark contrast to **Stephen Rea**'s reluctant protagonist and Miranda Richardson's near psychotic temptress. He was also well cast in **How Harry Became a Tree** (2001) as **Colm Meaney**'s nemesis, in which he managed the near impossible feat of remaining at least semisympathetic as he ravished the young heroine.

In 1999, George Lucas cast him in the role of Bail Organa in the first of the *Star Wars* prequels, *The Phantom Menace* (1999). Although he was limited to five or six lines in the movie, his role as stepfather to the character of Princess Leia meant that he would have played a larger role in the subsequent prequels. However, after filming Dunbar's part, Lucas cut Dunbar entirely from the film for plot reasons, and American actor Jimmy Smits ended up playing the role in the subsequent films of the trilogy, *Attack of the Clones* (2002) and *Revenge of the Sith* (2005). In interviews, Dunbar has been philosophical about the missed opportunity, and he has taken on more stage work than would have been the case had the *Star Wars* role led to more Hollywood work. His limited appearances on the big screen since have seen him return to his Northern Ireland roots, playing a Catholic father opposite **Ciarán Hinds**'s Protestant father in **Mickybo and Me** (2005), then portraying Ulster Unionist Party leader David Trimble opposite Juliet Walter's Mo Mowlam in *Mo* (2010) before appearing in D'Sa and Leyburn's rambunctious **Good Vibrations** (2012).

Yet his extensive stage work as an actor and sometimes director (often of Brendan Behan's work) aside, television remains where he is most commonly found: as Martin Summers in the second series of the cross-dimensional police show *Ashes to Ashes* (2008), as Ralph Nickleby in *The Life and Adventures of Nick Nickelby* (2012), and in the lead role of the moralistic Superintendent Ted Hastings in Jed Mercurios's hit drama *Line of Duty* (2012–2019), a role that plays on Dunbar's ethnicity. (Accused of racism in the opening series, Hastings recalls his early career as a Catholic police office in Northern Ireland, concluding, "There's no-one blacker than me, son.") In a neat career symmetry, given that his first television role was in writer Jimmy McGovern's *Cracker* (1995), a recent TV appearance was as Father Peter Flaherty, confessor to the Sean Bean priest protagonist in McGovern's most recent critical success for the BBC, *Broken* (2017).

E

***EARTHBOUND* (2012).** Reluctant (at last partly for budgetary reasons) to embrace the kind of full-on visual effects–driven approach exemplified by Ruairi Robinson's *Last Days on Mars* (2013), Irish sci-fi has generally adopted a unique work-around. In films such as *Zonad*, *The Boy from Mercury*, or *Summer of the Flying Saucer*, scripts have tended to skew toward 1950s B-movie pastiche, introducing alien characters only to doubt their authenticity within the incongruous banalities of everyday Irish life. *Earthbound* continues this tradition.

Joe (Rafe Spall) leads a quiet life working in a Dublin comic book store. Unbeknownst to his colleagues, he is the last survivor of the planet Zalaxon, a secret revealed to him as a child by his dying father (David Morrissey), whose holographic form Joe sporadically consults via a device disguised as 16-mm projector. (Indeed, Joe maintains a small arsenal of seemingly innocent devices with hidden capabilities.) His home planet destroyed by aliens, Joe must keep his true identity secret while seeking a compatible mate with whom he can begin to rebuild his species. That mate appears in the form of Maria (Jenn Murray), but when Joe reveals his true identity, she immediately calls for a psychiatrist (Stephen Hogan), who, harboring his own designs for Maria, begins to systematically undermine Joe's alien identity, positing instead a severe case of psychosis.

On his first feature, writer/director Alan Brennan fills out the central "is he/isn't he" conundrum with enough pop culture sci-fi references to keep geeks happy while the sometimes somewhat crude visual effects enhance the uncertainty surrounding Joe's ontological status. Likably played by leads Spall and Murray and an excellent supporting cast, *Earthbound* steers a careful path between comedy and psychological study. As an adult man/alien still trapped in a childlike state (as, to an extent, is Maria, whom he first encounters as she tries to offload some still-treasured childhood dolls), Joe must grow to maturity regardless of his true nature. And even if the film is fundamentally ridiculous, Spall's endearing characterization of Joe contributes to the overall plausibility of the enterprise, as our identification with his quiet, sweet nature leaves the audience clinging to the hope that he's not human after all.

EAT THE PEACH (1986). Perhaps the most overtly commercial film to be funded by the first **Irish Film Board**, *Eat the Peach*, directed by Peter Ormrod, is a tragicomedy based on fact. It follows two men—Vinnie (Stephen Brennan) and Arthur (**Eamon Morrissey**)—who respond to the oppressiveness of their Midlands existence by building a motorcycle "wall of death" (inspired by the Elvis Presley movie *Roustabout*) in the middle of a bog. For Vinnie, riding the wall offers a brief escape from the everyday obligations to family and community and his humdrum existence. Like that of Icarus, however, his escape proves all too short, and—although the film ends on an optimistic note—he crashes back to Earth.

Despite its commercial ambitions, the film eschews the kind of classic Hollywood narrative that follows clearly drawn characters driven by explicit motivations. Stephen Brennan's performance is so low-key as to be invisible. Vinnie's motives are explained less by overt dialogue and more by shots sticking him in the middle of a flat landscape that stretches to the horizon. The film is not necessarily about individual characters but rather captures a rural Ireland frequently sidelined in cinematic representations. Some critics have even suggested that the constructed precarious spectacle of the "wall of death" the characters create echoes the nascent filmmaking experience in Ireland as artists try to create and live out their dreams. It also works as a historical document capturing a pre–Celtic Tiger Ireland where Japanese semiconductor factories, venal politicians, smugglers, and country-and-western bars exist side by side.

The fact that the film presents an Ireland that a home audience could actually recognize may have contributed to its massive domestic success. Equally, its refusal to countenance a *Quiet Man/Ryan's Daughter* style of representation probably sealed its fate outside Ireland, where it failed to make an impact.

THE ECLIPSE(2009). A made-for-TV supernatural drama film written and directed by **Conor McPherson**, starring **Ciarán Hinds**, Iben Hjejle, and **Aidan Quinn**. Michael Farr (Hinds) is a widower who teaches in the small seaside town of Cobh, County Cork, where he lives with his two children. He begins to experience strange, possibly supernatural occurrences connected to his elderly father-in-law, who is close to death in a local nursing home. When Michael volunteers at the town's annual literary festival, he is assigned to look after visiting writer Lena Morelle (Iben Hjejle). Lena is known for her ghost stories, and Michael shares his recent experiences with her. While

Michael and Lena grow closer, another author, Nicholas Holden (Aidan Quinn), arrives in town for the festival, hoping to rekindle an affair he had with Lena. As Michael and Nicholas clash over her, Michael's supernatural visions grow stronger and more disturbing.

Adapted by McPherson and Billy Roche from a short story by Roche, *The Eclipse* is handled with skill and panache both in front of and behind the camera. (McPherson and Hinds had previously worked together on the stage with *The Seafarer*.) Alternating long, subdued passages with eruptions of supernatural horror, the film blends traditional and contemporary ghost story elements with a touching and unusual midlife romance. That it doesn't quite know which of these genre elements to side with somewhat weakens the film's overall effect, but it is carried by strong performances from all three leads, particularly Hinds, whose palpable sense of grief provides the basis of the film's haunting.

ELEMENT PICTURES. Arguably the most ambitious Irish production company of the past 30 years and the one that most skillfully blends the commercial and artistic ambitions of Irish screen policy. Producer **Ed Guiney** and former head of business affairs at the **Irish Film Board** (IFB) Andrew Lowe established Element Pictures in June 2001, taking advantage of the new IFB company development initiative (2001) to develop a wide slate of productions and coproductions.

In 1993, Guiney established **Temple Films** with Stephen Bradley, initially as a television production company making factual programs for **Radio Telefís Éireann** (RTÉ), UTV, and **Channel 4**. In 1994, Temple produced its first feature, *Ailsa*, directed by **Paddy Breathnach**, which won the Euskal Media Award at that year's San Sebastian Film Festival. From that point, Guiney arguably became the most consistent producer of domestically originated cinema, including *Guiltrip* (**Gerard Stembridge**, 1995), *Sweety Barrett* (Stephen Bradley, 1998), *On the Edge* (**John Carney**, 2000), and *Disco Pigs* (Kirsten Sheridan, 2001).

The decision to transform Temple into Element was driven by an express desire to combine existing strengths in the production of new Irish work with an added focus on larger-scale European-originated material. This in turn led to the relationship with Guiney's partner at Element, Andrew Lowe. A chartered accountant by trade, Lowe's duties at the IFB included negotiating and monitoring a wide range of feature films cofinanced with international partners. This led to the signing of a first-look deal between Element and Kuhn and Co. (run by Michael Kuhn, former head of Polygram Films) at the Cannes Film Festival in May 2002.

Element subsequently acted as Irish coproducer on the Irish-themed *Magdalene Sisters* and *Omagh* (both of which won multiple awards) in addition to the most recent remake of *Lassie*. However, the company continued to produce more "local" fare, such as the comedy-horror *Boy Eats Girl* and *Adam and Paul* (with the Speers Company).

Through a previous joint venture with **Hell's Kitchen**, Element also acted as Irish coproducer on projects originating in North America. A second joint venture with **Samson Films**—Accomplice Television—produced several drama series for RTÉ, such as the **John Carney**/**Tom Hall**–directed comedy-drama *Bachelor's Walk* (2001–2006) and the highly acclaimed *Pure Mule* (2005). When commercial channel **TV3** sought to create a homegrown soap in 2015, Element won the contract. The resulting *Red Rock*, set around a suburban police station, proved a hit not only in Ireland but also overseas, where it sold to, among others, the BBC in the United Kingdom and Amazon Prime in the United States. Element has also acted as coproducer on the BBC/Amazon show *Ripper Street* (2012–2017), which, though set in Victorian London, is shot in Dublin.

However, the company's greatest successes relate to its increasingly varied and adventurous filmic output. A central relationship is with **Lenny Abrahamson**, beginning with *Garage* (2007) and *What Richard Did* (2012) before moving beyond Irish story sources and settings. While *Frank* (2014), an adaptation of Jon Ronson's book about eccentric musician Frank Sidebottom, featured two Irish actors—**Michael Fassbender** and **Domhnall Gleeson**—in lead roles, neither played them as Irish. Similarly, though Irish set, the budget and casting of both *The Guard* (2012) (featuring **Brendan Gleeson** opposite Don Cheadle) and *Shadow Dancer* (2012) (featuring Clive Owen, Andrea Riseborough, and Gillian Anderson) suggested a more international ambition than might typically characterize indigenous productions. This was confirmed by the company's role in two films with veteran Polish director Jerzy Skolimowski (*Essential Killing* [2010] and *11 Minutes* [2015]) and their ongoing relationship with cult Greek director Yorgos Lanthimos, which has thus far seen Element produce *The Lobster* (2015), *The Killing of a Sacred Deer* (2017) (featuring **Colin Farrell** and Nicole Kidman), and *The Favourite* (2018), featuring Emma Stone and Rachel Weisz. Meanwhile, Abrahamson's next film, *Room*, was set in an unspecified North American setting, while *The Little Stranger* (2018) was set in 1940s England.

The first of the Lanthimos collaborations, *The Lobster*, combined with *Room*, represented Element's most successful year to date. *The Lobster* was nominated for a multiplicity of awards, including the Oscars and the Golden Globes, and won the Jury Prize at Cannes. *Room* also received nominations: four at the **Academy Awards**, along with Brie Larsen winning Best Actress, as well as at the Golden Globes, the Screen Actors Guild Awards, and the BAFTAs. Element subsequently produced the Lanthimos films *The Killing* *of a Sacred Deer* (2016) and *The Favourite* (2018)—arguably the most successful "Irish" film ever with box-office revenues of approximately $100 million.

At the same time, Element continued to produce more locally engaged but also critically acclaimed low-budget films, such as **Gerard Barrett**'s *Glassland* (2014) and Darren Thorton's *A Date for Mad Mary* (2016).

In 2007, Element established a **distribution** subsidiary to handle its own productions, an increasing number of Irish films, and selected international art house titles (often in cooperation with Pathé). This operation is complemented by **Volta.ie**, launched in 2012, an online digital platform serving the Irish market. This venture came within a week of Element's takeover of the **Light House** in Smithfield, Dublin, a specialized art house cinema that has proven a resounding commercial success. In 2016, Element made another foray into exhibition, controversially acquiring the completion and subsequent operation of a long-delayed Galway art house cinema, the Pálás. Putting all these factors together makes Element, which reportedly employs around 50 full-time staff, by far the most (vertically) integrated film and television company in Irish history.

ELLIMAN, LOUIS (1906–1965). Louis Elliman could reasonably be described as the greatest Irish theatrical impresario of the first half of the 20th century, but he was also a key figure in Irish cinema. One of 12 children born into a Dublin Jewish family, his father, Maurice, arrived in Dublin in 1900 after fleeing tsarist persecution in Latvia. Although Maurice started out as a grocer, he became involved in the cinema trade, initially by establishing a cinema-seating business on Dublin's Camden Street and later by opening his own cinema—the Theatre De Luxe—on the same street.

Louis attended the National University of Ireland and was subsequently apprenticed by his father to a pharmacist on South Richard Street. However, he left that position after a few years and moved to London, where he became the agent for First National Films, thus launching his entertainment career. In 1936, Maurice Elliman moved from cinema into theater, when, advised by Louis, he purchased the Gaiety Theatre (which remained in Louis's control until his death in 1965). "Mr. Louis," as he became known, introduced a number of innovations to the Gaiety: he instituted the still-extant Christmas pantomimes, which were initially produced by **Jimmy O'Dea**'s O'D productions; established annual seasons of performances by the Dublin Grand Opera Society; and for several years invited Hilton Edwards and Micheál MacLíammóir, founders of Dublin's Gate Theatre Productions, to give spring and autumn seasons of plays.

In 1936, Louis Elliman also acquired the recently (and lavishly) rebuilt Theatre Royal on Dublin's Hatch Street, the largest theater ever built in Ireland. Acquisitions continued through the 1930s, and by the start of the

1940s, the Elliman Group owned cinemas—through Amalgamated Cinemas and Irish Cinema Ltd—in most major Irish cities and in Dublin's southern suburbs.

In 1945, however, the Rank Organization acquired a majority interest in the Elliman Group's cinema holdings, reorganizing them under the Odeon (Ireland) Ltd brand. Elliman continued to act as managing director of the cinema chain (a position he maintained until 1963) and took a central role in the running of the flagship Theatre Royal. However, as the heyday of the theaters began to wane, Elliman's interest moved toward film production. In 1951, he executive-produced the Hilton Edwards Oscar-nominated short *Return to Glennascaul* and subsequently acted as its distributor in the United Kingdom and Ireland.

However, Elliman's ambitions went far beyond short film production. In January 1957, the *Sunday Independent* carried an interview with him in which he discussed plans to produce a 55-minute made-for-TV version of George Shiel's **Abbey Theatre** play *Professor Tim*. *Tim* was directed by **Emmet Dalton** and produced under the auspices of Dublin Film and Television Productions Ltd, of which Elliman and Dalton were directors. The two were joined by Ernest Blythe, chairman of the Abbey, on the board of a sister company: Dublin Film Productions Management Ltd.

The relationship between these two companies (and Blythe's presence on the board of the latter) was based on the use of *Tim* as a pilot to test the potential of the American market. If *Tim* took off in the United States, then the two companies would collaborate to produce film versions of 26 to 39 more Abbey plays. Dublin Film Productions Management Ltd would deal with the question of rights for the Abbey plays, and Dublin Films and TV Productions Ltd would actually shoot them.

Tim appears to have led to a deal with RKO Teleradio in New York to produce Abbey adaptations, and on the basis of this apparently guaranteed work, Elliman became convinced that there was a sound financial case for building a studio in Ireland. In August 1957, Elliman announced the acquisition of a site for a studio at Ardmore Place, Herbert Road, in Bray, County Dublin. At a press launch for the studios, Elliman stated that their films would all have an Irish background—either the story content or the writer would be Irish. He even suggested that Ardmore would become a miniature Hollywood. A month later, **Ardmore Studios** (Ireland) Ltd was registered with the Companies Office and included among its principal objects the business of motion picture production.

With a budgeted construction cost of £161,000 Ardmore was a substantial financial undertaking. Although initial reports suggested that Elliman funded the studios privately, it subsequently emerged that the studios were funded largely by the Department of Industry and Commerce via the Industrial Development Authority and the Industrial Credit Corporation. Fittingly, then, it was **Sean Lemass**, the minister for industry and commerce, who conducted the official opening ceremony in May 1958.

However, the studios were not a success and ran into a series of funding and union-related difficulties. By 1963, they were placed into receivership, and any involvement Elliman might have had with them came to an abrupt conclusion. In any case, ill health forced him to retire the same year. He died the following year at only age 59, but his standing in Irish society was evinced by the attendance at his funeral, which included representatives of then President Eamon De Valera, then Taoiseach Sean Lemass, and members of various theatrical and cinema organizations, such as the Irish Cinemas Association, the **Irish Film Society**, and the Cork Film Festival.

EURIMAGES. Designed to complement the support schemes offered under the European Union's **MEDIA** program, the Council of Europe established Eurimages as a pan-European film support fund in 1988. The (as of 2017) 38 Eurimages member countries finance the fund, the precise sum donated by an individual country based on a formula relating gross national product (GNP) and population. In contrast to the MEDIA program, Eurimages seeks to encourage European coproduction by offering interest-free production loans. To qualify for support, a coproduction must involve at least three independent producers from the fund's member countries. In addition, Eurimages supports **distribution** of films in and from those member states outside the European Union, which are thus unable to avail of distribution support from the MEDIA program. Support for **exhibition** is available under similar conditions.

Ireland became a member in 1992, a decision that coincided with the publication of the *Coopers & Lybrand Report*, which strongly recommended Irish membership. Irish involvement—initially costed at £110,000 per annum—was originally funded jointly by the Department of the Taoiseach and **Radio Telefís Éireann** (RTÉ). Subsequently, the **Irish Film Board** paid the Irish subscription from its own resources. Irish membership was considered particularly advantageous in 1992 given the fund's stated bias toward small countries with a low audiovisual output and the fact that the refusal of the British government to join made Ireland the first English-speaking country to do so. (The United Kingdom did join in 1993 but pulled out again in 1997.)

Although only a handful of Irish films have received distribution support under Eurimages, the coproduction-funding element of the scheme has been a major boon for Irish producers. In the initial period of Irish membership, between 1992 and 2005, projects with an Irish involvement received €9.2 million in return for a contribution of approximately €2 million. Furthermore, although the list of films with Irish producers attached includes titles like *Messaggi Quasi Segreti*, the majority of the projects supported in the initial period were recognizably Irish (i.e., characterized by an Irish setting, cast, and story). Several Irish producers have used the scheme on a number of films: James Flynn of **Metropolitan Films** has partially funded three films (including *Nora* [2000], which received more than €600,000) via the scheme; **Ed Guiney**'s **Temple Pictures** used it for *Guiltrip* [1995] and *Sweety Barrett* [1996]; and **Little Bird** availed of it for both feature and documentary support. The scheme was also very effectively used by Irish **animation** companies: Terraglyph raised more than €1.3 million for two feature-length animations (*Help, I'm a Fish* and *Moby Dick—The Legend Returns*), while Magma succeeded in drawing down €550,000 for their *Ugly Duckling and Me* coproduction.

Although Irish production companies have benefited from Eurimage coproduction funding worth nearly €14 million on another 40 productions (as against a contribution of just over €3.1 million to the fund) between 2005 and 2017, the nature of the productions supported has markedly "internationalized" (i.e., become less obviously textually connected to Ireland). Just seven of the films (including **Martin Duffy**'s *Summer of the Flying Saucer* [2008] and **Cartoon Saloon**'s *Song of the Sea* [2014]) featured Irish directors, and nearly half are set entirely outside Ireland. This shift coincided with a stated policy on the part of the Irish Film Board under the tenure of **Simon Perry** to encourage Irish participation in international coproduction.

EVELYN **(2002).** Loosely based on the true story of Desmond Doyle, an Irish carpenter who took on the Irish state in the mid-1950s to regain custody of his children, *Evelyn* was something of a pet project for its star and producer, **Pierce Brosnan**. Overseen by director for hire Bruce Beresford, the narrative is triggered when Doyle, a barely functioning alcoholic, and his children are abandoned by his wife. As per the legal norms of the day regarding children in broken marriages, Doyle's three children (including the titular Evelyn) are placed into the dubious care of a Church-run orphanage. Confounding prevailing social norms, Doyle determines to win back his children through a legal battle, struggling to remain sober and earn a living sufficient to demonstrate his capacity to provide for his family. Along the way, he is aided by other examples of star power: Bernadette, a local barmaid (played by U.S. actress Julianna Margulies); her solicitor brother, Michael (**Stephen Rea**); a generous American benefactor (**Aidan Quinn**); and Doyle's barrister, **Thomas Connolly** (Alan Bates). Profoundly sentimental throughout (not least in its reliance on a spiritual deus ex machina intervention at its conclusion) and hugely overstating the long-term significance of the real case taken by Doyle (which, contrary to the epilogue's suggestion, did not definitively establish the parental rights of fathers under Irish law), the film nevertheless retains an affecting quality, based largely on the warm glow of the core performances, not least the young Sophie Vavasseur as Evelyn and—counter to his then prominent Bond persona—Brosnan's surprisingly convincing turn as a down-at-the-heels if compassionate alcoholic.

AN EVERLASTING PIECE **(2000).** A comedy about two barbers living in Belfast in 1980s who join up to try to design the ultimate toupee (referred to in local argot as a "piece") in the hope of making it big in the Irish market. The film portrays clashing religious beliefs and various other difficulties, and the business deal produces some humorous episodes. The film was written by and stars Barry McEvoy, who developed it from stories told to him by his father, and features a strong supporting cast of character actors, including Brian F. O'Byrne, Anna Friel, Billy Connolly, and **Colm Meaney**. When McEvoy staged a reading of his screenplay in New York in the 1990s, it came to the attention of celebrated casting agent Louis DiGiamo, who in turn brought it to director Barry Levinson and producer Stephen Spielberg. Despite such a wealth of talent, however, the film fails to ignite any dramatic fire, offering nothing more than a series of well-polished anecdotes coated in Hollywood sentimentality.

EXCALIBUR **(1981).** Although at a textual level only tangentially connected to Ireland, the industrial impact of the filming of **John Boorman**'s long-gestated, operatic take on Thomas Malory's *Morte D'Arthur* was highly significant at a point when the **Irish Film Board** was still very much in its infancy. Even though it was not quite resourced with a blockbuster budget (Boorman reportedly secured $11 million from backers Orion Pictures), *Excalibur* was arguably the highest-profile film shot in Ireland since David Lean's *Ryan's Daughter* Set in a mythic ancient Britain, the film was, however, entirely filmed in Irish locations, mostly in the environs of Boorman's home in Wicklow (a climatic fight sequence between Arthur and Lancelot was filmed on the Powerscourt Estate) but also at Cahir Castle in Tipperary and the Kerry Coast as Arthur sails to Avalon. Although roles as heads of department among the crew were staffed largely by U.K. technicians, the film provided an extended stepping-stone for Irish below-the-line crew at less senior levels and saw Boorman employ the then unknown **Neil Jordan** to document on film the making of the film. However, Irish involvement is most obvious at the casting level with a small army of then unknown Irish actors—including **Gabriel Byrne** as Uther Pendragon, **Liam Neeson** as Gawain, and **Ciarán Hinds** as Lot—featuring in key roles.

Although receiving mixed reviews (some felt that the core narrative was overshadowed by Boorman's insistence on constructing mythic archetypes), the film's stunning cinematography and production won universal plaudits, and the film became a touristic showcase for Ireland's natural beauty. The film not only evinced Boorman's ongoing commitment to his adopted home but also demonstrated to international filmmakers that Ireland was a plausible venue for high-profile, high-cost production activity.

EXHIBITION. The key figure in early cinema exhibition in Ireland was unquestionably impresario Dan Lowrey, who gave the first public presentation of moving pictures in Ireland at his Star of Erin Music Hall (now the Olympia Theatre) on Dublin's Dame Street in April 1896. Although initial audiences were reportedly not overly enthusiastic about the screening, Lowrey persisted, bringing Lumière films to his Empire Variety Theatre in Belfast later the same year and Professor Jolly's "cinematographe" to his Palace Variety Theatre in Cork in 1897. Meanwhile, Edison films were screened at the Rotunda Hall in Dublin from November 1901. Irish cinema exhibition grew rapidly, with films being screened in music halls, fairgrounds, towns, and village halls or indeed anywhere with enough room for a traveling projectionist to set up the apparatus.

In the early decades of film, all classes of Irish society enjoyed going to the cinema but not necessarily to the same venues. **Liam O'Leary** has noted that a working-class theater such as the Dame Street Picture House could be refused permission to run films on a Sunday morning lest its patrons mix with the socially "superior" classes emerging from the nearby Quaker Meeting House in Eustace Street (which would later become the **Irish Film Centre**). Meanwhile, the entourage of the king's representative in Ireland might patronize James T. Jameson's screenings at the Rotunda Round Room.

Jameson would go on to become a prosperous exhibitor, operating three of the nine permanent Dublin venues by 1913: the Rotunda, the Theatre De Luxe, and the Volta Picture Theatre. The last shared its name with what was long—but erroneously—regarded as the first cinema built for that purpose in Ireland, the Volta, which opened on Dublin's Mary Street in December 1909. The cinema was initially managed and programmed by **James Joyce**, who had encouraged four Italian businessmen to put up the capital for the venture. However, after Joyce returned to his family in Italy, leaving the cinema in the hands of one of the Italian partners, audiences declined, and the cinemas were sold at a loss to an English firm, the Provincial Theatre Company.

In fact, the Volta had been preceded by a number of specialist cinema venues across Ireland. Denis Condon has pointed to the operation of Hales's Tours from 1907 off Dublin's Grafton Street, using projected images to simulate exotic railway journeys in a cinema resembling the interior of a railcar. Two cinemas opened in Belfast in mid-1908, while the People's Popular Picture Palace at the Queens Theatres on Dublin's Pearse Street opened in March 1908, some 21 months before the Volta.

The number of permanent venues expanded rapidly in the 1910s and 1920s, from 150 in 1916 to 190 by 1935 and again to 220 by 1939. Not surprisingly, Dublin accounted for a disproportionate number of these: by 1939, nearly a quarter of all cinemas and a third of total national seating capacity were based in Dublin and its environs (the seating capacity reflected the prevalence of auditoriums of more than 1,000 seats in the capital). However, by the 1930s, virtually every town of any size had a cinema: 80 of 190 permanent establishments extant in 1935 were located in towns with a population of less than 4,000. In effect, then, cinema acquired a status parallel to that of the Church in Ireland: omnipresent and frequently attended. The 1942 *Report of the **Inter-Departmental Committee on the Film Industry*** estimated that those cinemas had recorded 28 million admissions in 1939, equivalent to 10 visits per annum per person.

Indeed, the same report considered complaints from Dublin exhibitors that the number of cinemas in the capital had reached the saturation point and that further openings would inevitably cause existing theaters to close. Yet, although the committee did not believe that the exhibition business should be an exception to the operation of the free market, it did express a concern with growing tendencies toward oligopoly in the market. These concerns were prompted by the fact that in the 1930s, ownership of cinemas in the larger towns of Dublin, Cork, Waterford, and Galway was dominated largely by overseas groups and in particular Associated British Cinemas, the flagship cinema of which—the Savoy on Dublin's O'Connell Street—had opened in 1929. However, in 1946, a duopoly structure emerged as another British Chain—Rank—took a majority interest in the Amalgamated Cinemas and Irish Cinemas Ltd, which had previously been owned by the **Elliman** family. Thus, Rank came to own some of the largest cinemas in the capital, including the Metropole, the Capitol, and the largest theater in Ireland, the Theatre Royal. Indeed, Rank continued to expand throughout the 1940s, controlling 19 cinemas by 1950 (and acquiring four cinemas in 1949 alone).

Little came of the 1942 report's concerns, although a decade later, Rank's growing influence in particular prompted the Department of Industry and Commence to propose a new investigation of the extent to which foreign chains dominated the exhibition sector. The department was particularly concerned about the possibility that independently owned Irish exhibitors might be crowded out of the market. Once again, however, little of practical value came of the investigation.

In any case, by the end of the 1950s, the first signs of decline in cinema going began to emerge. In the United States, cinema attendance peaked in the immediate postwar era and declined consistently until the mid-1970s. In Ireland, a similar decline was noted, but it began a decade later. Cinemagoing in Ireland peaked in 1954, when 54 million admissions were recorded in the 327 cinemas operating within the republic. However, within a decade

(1966), this figure had fallen dramatically to 22 million as alternative leisure activities emerged. Inevitably, this led to a rash of closures: between 1962 and 1977, around 160 to 190 cinemas closed; by 1975, there were just 184 screens operating. The number of cinemas was smaller still because those that stayed in business usually did so by subdividing their single auditoriums into multiple smaller theaters. Thus, in 1969, Odeon's flagship cinema in Dublin, the Savoy, changed from a single-screen venue of more than 2,000 seats into a two-theater cinema and then in 1975 into a three-screen cinema. (By the 1990s, further subdivision had increased the number of theaters within the Savoy complex to six.) Other large-scale cinemas either followed suit or, as with the 4,000-seat Theatre Royal, simply closed down. The decline in audiences continued throughout the 1970s, reaching its lowest point in 1985, when 4.5 million admissions were recorded to the 135 screens still operating in the Republic of Ireland. The effect of this decline was disproportionately felt in smaller towns—between 1962 and 1977, 47 towns saw their only cinema close.

The decline in audiences brought with it dramatic shifts in the ownership structure of Irish exhibition. In 1969, the British EMI Group bought out Associated British Cinemas, thus acquiring the two-cinema Adelphi-Carlton group in Dublin. (Although numerically small, the Adelphi and Carlton were economically significant, both being based in Dublin's city center and accounting for 4,304 seats between them.) Meanwhile, through the 1950s and 1960s, the Irish-owned **Ward Anderson** group had taken advantage of the declining value of cinemas to gradually acquire substantial holdings, first outside Dublin, then within the Dublin market, beginning with the acquisition of the Green Cinema on St. Stephen's Green in 1968. Thus, by the start of the 1970s, Ward Anderson was the dominant force outside Dublin and by 1983, after acquiring Rank's remaining Dublin cinemas, was the dominant force everywhere.

So dominant was Ward Anderson that in the early 1970s, a series of accusations were leveled at the group that it (along with Adelphi-Carlton Ltd and Rank) was colluding with distributors to prevent independent cinema owners in the provinces and Dublin suburbs from accessing major releases. Eventually, in 1976, the Restrictive Practices Commission investigated the structure of the industry, but although it found that provincial cinemas were indeed experiencing difficulties in accessing titles, it concluded that this was due to commercial considerations aimed at maximizing revenues from individual titles. The commission specifically stated that it found no evidence of any kind of secret agreement between Ward Anderson and film distributors operating in Ireland aimed at conferring a monopoly on the group. Nonetheless, the commission did recommend that the industry as a whole adopt a disputes resolution procedure for dealing with future problems in the **distribution** of films to cinemas across the country.

In effect, then, as of the mid-1980s, the Irish cinema market was split between Ward Anderson, the Adelphi-Carlton group, and independent cinema owners based outside Dublin's city center. From the mid-1980s, however, attendance began to increase again from the 1985 low point of 4.5 million to 7 million by the end of the decade. This trend continued throughout the 1990s as Ireland recorded the highest per capita rates of cinema attendance in Europe. Much of the renaissance was due to the arrival of multiplex cinemas in 1990 (although multiplexes cannot account for the upturn prior to this date). The arrival of the multiplexes transformed the industry. Generally located in suburban locales, they offered free parking, prebooking of seats, and—with a minimum of 10 screens—greater choice than any Irish cinema had previously made available. They also introduced a new cinema business model, laying as much stress on the revenues from sales of soft drinks and snacks as from ticket sales.

The first Irish multiplex was opened in Tallaght, South County Dublin, by United Cinemas International (UCI—a joint venture of Universal and Paramount), which quickly opened a second site a year later in the northern suburb of Coolock. (A third UCI opened in the western suburb of Blanchardstown in 1996.) By the mid-1990s, the Tallaght and Coolock UCIs alone accounted for 20 percent of all cinema admissions in the Republic of Ireland. Rather than competing head-on with the newcomers, Ward Anderson sought to develop greenfield sites for its own multiplexes in the Dublin suburbs of Santry and Dún Laoghaire and to consolidate its provincial dominance by closing older cinemas in provincial towns and building new "miniplexes" instead.

However, the obvious attraction of the multiplex model had a devastating effect on smaller independently owned cinemas. As of 1992, there were 79 cinemas in Ireland with 189 screens. Of those, 31 were single screen, and only three cinemas had 10 or more screens. By 2000, however, only 10 single-screen cinemas remained, and virtually every major town in the country had at least a four-screen cinema. Furthermore, as of 2005, there were only 66 cinemas in Ireland but 329 screens. Cinema closures in this period were concentrated in towns with populations of less than 10,000 situated in the less economically successful border, Midlands, and western counties, many of which have only one cinema. (Indeed, County Roscommon had no cinema at all.) Thus, although single-screen cinemas in smaller towns still exist, they are often economically marginal and family run. Those independent cinema owners with a long-term interest in the business have themselves followed the multiplex route.

Despite the ongoing decline in cinema numbers, it is irrefutable that the arrival of the multiplexes boosted overall attendance. In 2003, 17.3 million admissions were recorded in the Republic of Ireland, nearly 4.4 per person and twice the average European attendance. The seemingly infinite potential in the market attracted a range of new players through the 1990s albeit largely to the Dublin market. In 1993, the Adelphi-Carlton group (then owned by MGM) built a city-center multiplex. This passed through several hands (including Virgin and UGC) before being bought out by a British venture capital company, the Blackstone Group, in December 2004, by which point the cinema had been expanded to encompass 17 screens. Prior to that, the largest cinema had been a 14-screen west Dublin multiplex, owned by the South African chain Star Century. This too was sold—to a British firm, Vue Entertainment—in May 2005. And in August of the same year, another venture capital firm, Terra Firma, bought the UCI's three Dublin cinemas.

Faced with such competition, smaller cinema owners complained that they find it difficult to access prints of films while they are still fresh. For their part, distributors were reluctant to bear the cost of striking additional prints for what might prove to be small audiences. However, an initiative announced in April 2005 appeared to offer some hope for the future. Avica Technologies, a U.S. digital exhibition equipment firm, drew up plans through its Thurles-based subsidiary, Digital Cinema Limited, to install 515 digital projectors in 105 Irish cinemas (i.e., effectively every cinema in the republic and Northern Ireland) by April 2006. Although attracting worldwide press attention, Avica's plans took significantly longer to come to fruition, and by early 2008, only 13 cinemas had been equipped with digital projectors. Nonetheless, in the following half decade, there was a gradual transition to digital projection, which, while demanding an initial capital investment in the new technology, meant that the cost of making additional prints—now stored in digital form on hard disks—dropped from around €1,000 per print to less than €50 (and later still less). By the start of the summer of 2008, the Spurling Cinema Group's four-screen Dungarvan cinema had become the first all-digital cinema in Ireland, followed months later by the opening of the first purpose-built exclusively digital cinema—the Ward Anderson–owned Wexford Omniplex—in July 2008. When it became clear by late 2007 to early 2008 that the Avica business model would not suit smaller or specialized venues, the Cultural Cinema Consortium, a joint **Irish Film Board**/Arts Council initiative commissioned the "Digital Cinema in Ireland" report looking at the implications of the digital turn for art house exhibition in Ireland. Published in April 2008, the report led to the creation of a "Cinema Digitisation Grant Scheme" targeting venues such as the then newly reopened **Light House Cinema** for support to convert to digital projection; €750,000 was awarded to seven such venues in the initial round of grants in January 2009.

The shift to digital projection had a marked impact on the nature of theatrical content. In June 2009, Ward Anderson announced plans to upgrade their digital systems to allow 3-D screenings, as that format experienced a renewed popularity. Digital projectors also permitted live screencasts of theatrical events: increasingly, cinema audiences across Ireland could take for granted access to live performances from the New York Metropolitan Opera, productions from the United Kingdom's National Theatre, and ballet from the Royal Ballet in London.

These innovations arrived at a point when the industry as a whole was struggling. The impact of the post-2008 recession depressed cinema attendance audiences, which, having peaked at 18.4 million in 2007, fell by more than 20 percent to 14.4 million in 2014. This had a concomitant impact on revenues, which fell from their 2009 peak of €124 million to just under €100 million in 2014.

Some more marginal cinemas fell by the wayside. In 2009, the Kino in Cork City, the only permanent art house venue outside Dublin, shut its doors, unable to maintain its viability. Such events encouraged other players to reduce their engagement with the industry. In 2008, Storm, a five-cinema regional chain owned by businessman Patrick O'Sullivan, was acquired by Entertainment Enterprises. (O'Sullivan would retain an interest in two other cinemas in Limerick and Ashbourne.) At the time, Entertainment contracted with UCI-Odeon to operate the Storm cinemas on their behalf. This relationship was further cemented in 2010 when Entertainment acquired the three Dublin-based UCI cinemas from the UCI-Odeon chain, although, as per the Storm cinemas, UCI-Odeon continued to operate the cinemas on a day-to-day basis. This was further complicated in June 2011 when Entertainment announced that they were selling not merely the three UCI cinemas but also a temporarily closed cinema in the Dublin suburbs and the five former Storm cinemas to UCI-Odeon. In 2012, the UCI brand disappeared entirely, and "Odeon" became the public face of Terra Firma's operations in Ireland with the company operating 11 cinemas around the country by 2016. (In the same year, the Chinese-owned but U.S.-based AMC Entertainment acquired the entire Odeon group from Terra Firma.) Yet the narrative of Odeon's emergence as a key player also demonstrated that the exhibition market remained an attractive investment, promising long-term returns. This appeared to be confirmed in June 2013, when Doughty Hanson sold the entire Vue chain, including their Irish site, to two Canadian-based pension funds (Omers Private Equity and Alberta Investment Management).

The sale of the Vue chain was preceded by a seismic shift in the structure of the industry when, in January 2013, after more than half a century in existence, the Ward Anderson chain split in two, following a falling-out between the descendants of the original founders, Leo Ward and Kevin Anderson. Two new groups emerged from Ward Anderson's ashes: the 15-strong IMC Group headed by Paul Ward and the Omniplex Group with 13 cinemas overseen by Paul Anderson. Between them, the 39 cinemas owned by the Odeon, IMC, and Omniplex groups accounted for more than half of the 74 full-time cinemas operating in the Republic of Ireland by mid-2018.

Another 15 lay in the hands of single-cinema independent operators, while the rest lay with smaller groups, typically accounting for two or three cinemas each (although the Spurling family's acquisition of two Dublin multiplexes in January 2018 brought their chain up to four cinemas in all).

Furthermore, despite the impact of the recession, the overall health of the Irish exhibition sector began to recover after 2014. Admissions grew to 16.1 million by 2017, while revenues reached €114 million in the same year. This reflected the apparently sustained appetite for cinema-going among Irish audiences: 3.38 attendances per capita were recorded in 2017, well above the EU average of 2.10. Indeed, Iceland was the only European country to record a higher rate of cinema attendance (at 4.06 visits per capita) than Ireland. Buoyed by these figures, new forms of cinema exhibition began to emerge. Having been shut for a decade, the Stella Cinema in the Dublin suburb of Rathmines reopened in November 2017 as an upmarket cinema/dining experience. After a decade-long gestation, the first art house cinema outside Dublin since the closure of the Kino saw the light of day when the Pálás Cinema in Galway opened in February 2018 under the management of **Element Pictures**. Mainstream cinemas, too, appeared to be relatively healthy. In May 2015, the Omniplex Group purchased the two-cinema Gaiety Chain for €8 million and embarked on a major refurbishment of the rest of its chain, while, as of 2017, IMC recorded €1.3 million in annual profits and accumulated profits of just over €9 million. Even Cineworld declared their confidence in the Irish market, adding a 4DX "augmented" screen experience to their site in Dublin's city center, complete with moving seats, environmental effects (smoke, smells, rain, and so on) in early 2018. Perhaps less encouraging, however, was the apparent failure of Irish films to connect with their domestic audience via these local cinemas. Even as overall attendance figures grew, the share of the Irish box office accounted for by Irish films remained dispiritingly low at just 2.4 percent in 2017.

EXPERIMENTAL FILM. The history of an Irish experimental cinema is both sporadic and surprisingly contemporary for a mode most closely identified with the modernism of the 1920s and avant-garde art movements of the 1960s and 1970s. It is during this second phase that the origins of both an indigenous and an Irish experimental cinema (commonly referred to today as "artist cinema") can be traced, a coincidence that echoes, in perhaps underexplored ways, Tom Gunning's observations about the heterogeneity of early cinema and the subsuming of the avant-garde to the hegemony of narrative. In 1977, the founding members of the **Association of Independent Producers** included **Bob Quinn**, **Cathal Black**, **Pat Murphy**, **Joe Comerford**, and **Thaddeus O'Sullivan**, and each, in different ways, engaged with the medium of film in nontraditional and experimental means—some formally, others in thematic or representational ways. Notable titles from this intense and unprecedented period of Irish moving-image production include Quinn's *Caoineadh Airt Ui Laoire* (1975); Pat Murphy and John T. Davies's *Maeve* (1982), Comerford's *Down the Corner* (1977) and *Waterbag* (1984), O'Sullivan's *On a Paving Stone Mounted* (1978), and Black's *Our Boys* (1981). However, despite occasional excursions into artist/avant-garde practices (and recent developments to which we shall refer in a moment), Irish film has been dominated since the reconstitution of the **Irish Film Board** in the early 1990s by modes of naturalism and narrative.

Parallel to these early efforts, Donegal-born filmmaker **Vivienne Dick** was working in New York (where she lived from 1977 to 1982) within and without the heterogeneous and short-lived No Wave movement. After many years spent living in London (where she was a member of the the London Film-Makers' Co-op), Dick returned to Ireland in the late 1990s and has in recent years been recuperated by Irish filmmakers and culture as a key figure of Irish experimental film through a series of writings and events—including retrospectives at Crawford Gallery, Cork, and LUX (2009); the Tate Modern (2010); and IMMA (2017)—that have made her feminist-inspired work more widely shown and celebrated. Key titles from her New York period are *Guérillère Talks* (1978), *She Had Her Gun All Ready* (1978), *Staten Island* (1978), *Liberty's Booty* (1980), and *Visibility Moderate* (1981), while more recent work includes *The Irreducible Difference of the Other* (2013).

In tandem with the recognition of Dick's work has been an upsurge in interest in both the history and the contemporary potential of experimental film in Ireland. Although this has been largely an organic development, we might identify several, often intersecting underpinnings. First, there has been a steady growth in the numbers of and international recognition for Irish visual artists working in moving-image media. Key figures in this trend include the late Paddy Jolley (1964–2012) (and frequent collaborator Reynold Reynolds), Claire Langan, Gerard Byrne, Grace Weir, and others. Inevitable by-products of the growing profile of such artists have been a critical literature and curated events that have sought to position their work within wider histories of Irish and international artistic expression.

A second, key development has been the activity of a small, intertwined, and highly committed group of researchers, practitioners, and curators working at the margins of naturalist/narrative Irish film, increasingly defined by transnational modes of address and success. Responding to what was perceived as a lack of opportunities to view and consider avant-garde cinema, the Experimental Film Club (EFC) was initiated in 2008 by young Dublin-based filmmakers and researchers Aoife Desmond, Esperanza Collado, Donal Foreman, and Alan Lambert. Later joined by Daniel Fitzpatrick and Alice Butler, the EFC established a monthly screening event that ran at the **Irish Film Institute** from 2010 to 2015.

In 2016, Fitzpatrick and Butler established the organization *aemi* as a successor to the EFC's curatorial role, proposing "a creative platform dedicated to supporting and exhibiting artists & experimental moving image" (http://aemi.ie). Together, they curate a range of events and screenings, including the biannual PLASTIK Festival of Artists' Moving Image.

These activities led the Irish Film Institute International (supported by **Culture Ireland**) to commission a curated traveling program from the **Experimental Film Club**—the first of its kind—titled "Absences and (Im)possibilities: A Selection of Films from 1897 to 2013, Chosen for Their Relation to the Possibility of an Irish Experimental Cinema."

Somewhat confusingly, the Experimental Film Society (EFS) (www.experimentalfilmsociety.com) is a primarily production-focused entity whose emergence and activities coincided and frequently overlapped with those of the EFC. The EFS was established by Iranian filmmaker Rouzbeh Rashidi in his native Tehran in 2000 before transposing it to Dublin when he moved there in 2004. Four of Ireland's most prolific filmmakers—Rashidi, Dean Kavanagh, Maximillian Le Cain, and Michael Higgins—have worked under the umbrella of the EFS, with other members having come and gone. Rashidi brought a cosmopolitan and internationalist outlook to the group as well as a prodigious energy and sense of purpose. Under his energetic direction, EFS has produced hundreds of titles, established a video-on-demand platform, published a collection of essays (*Luminous Void: Experimental Film Society Documents*), and become a limited company to facilitate the increasingly ambitious and professionally funded projects it now focuses on.

Of this core group, some brief comments are necessary. Max Le Cain is a writer and filmmaker who works out of Cork, where he continues to produce and screen films under the EFC banner, with a filmography in excess of 100 films. He also founded and edited the high-quality online film journal *Experimental Conversations* (www.experimentalconversations.com) between 2008 and 2014 and continues to publish on a range of film practices, including those of fellow EFS members. Le Cain collaborates frequently with Vicky Langan on installations as well as films. Michael Higgins is an editor, photographer, and filmmaker who has produced more than a dozen feature films, beginning with the "Road Movie Trilogy": *Roadside Picnic* (2010), *You Have Been Killed* (2011), and *Birds on a Wire* (2011). Higgins's films often mix scripted and "found" elements. *Smolt* (2013) offered an avant-garde portrayal of two 12-year-old Irish boys left to fend for themselves in Dublin City. *At One Fell Swoop* was photographed on expired 16-mm black-and-white film and offered an oneiric portrait of a stone carver and his metamorphic wanderings through rural Ireland. Dean Kavanagh has produced approximately 65 experimental short films and five experimental feature films to date, including *Animal Kingdom* (2017), funded by the **Arts Council of Ireland**.

A final and important indication of the belated interest, appreciation, and indeed activity in artist filmmaking is the MExIndex, established in 2015 by artist Fifi Smith, a kind of extension and corrective to the **Irish Filmography** project. The MExIndex is an online database with access to "key information and writing on experimental and visual arts-based moving image works by Irish artists . . . on subject-matter relating to Irish history, politics, culture and society." More than just a database, the website has a curatorial dimension, featuring a rotating exhibition of work (www.mexindex.ie).

EXPOSURE **(1978).** Directed by **Kieran Hickey** and produced by Hickey's B.A.C. Films with funding from the **Arts Council**, **Radio Telefís Éireann**, and the **National Film Studios of Ireland**, the film follows a three-man ordnance survey team from Dublin—Dan, the leader (**T. P. McKenna**); Eugene (Niall O'Brien); and Oliver (Bosco Hogan)—as they arrive at a hotel on the west coast of Ireland, where they will spend a week mapping the area. They quickly encounter the hotel's only other guest, Caroline, a German photographer. Stuck in a remote location, the four quickly establish a rapport over drinks in the bar. Both Dan and Eugene are in unhappy marriages, so it is left to bachelor Oliver to strike up a relationship with Caroline, which becomes a source of tension among the men.

The dearth of dramatic filmic material in Ireland of the 1970s renders any picture from the period fascinating. This would be the case with *Exposure* regardless of when it was made. Its ambition belies its short running time (52 minutes) and relatively small budget, and its success owes much to the screenplay. At a time when more mainstream subjects might have claimed the attention of Irish filmmakers, director Hickey with his co-screenwriter, Philip Davison, offered an incisive study of the nature of Irish masculinity and Ireland's relationship to modernity.

The political rhetoric prevalent in the 1970s insisted that Ireland had become a modern nation, pointing to EU membership, rapid industrialization, and increasing wealth, reflected in the widespread acquisition of consumer goods. *Exposure*'s ordnance survey team embodies this rather narrow definition of modernity: urban, relatively sophisticated, and equipped with high-tech mapping equipment.

However, the persistence of stifling premodern social mores in 1970s Ireland is also evident in the film. The society portrayed in *Exposure* remains openly patriarchal, demanding appropriate behavior not only from women but also from men. The men are unable to discuss anything but the least sensitive subjects among themselves: Dan and Eugene's discussions of their marriages are confined to furtive conversations with their wives in the hotel's phone booth. Eugene is portrayed as craving some declaration of affection from his wife, while she—apparently conditioned to believe that men do not need such reassurance—is unable or unwilling to do so.

These norms are implicitly challenged by the figure of Catherine, who represents the social consequences of pursuing precisely the kind of modernity that Ireland already identified itself with; she is cosmopolitan, sexually liberated, and independent of men. By identifying such characteristics with Catherine, however, Hickey associates them with "the other." Catherine thus unwittingly represents a test of Ireland's claim to modernity: the response of other characters to her acts as a marker of the actual extent to which they accept the full logic of modernity. Mrs. Sinnott, owner of the hotel, is immediately identified as part of the "old order": rural, elderly, and actively applauding the men's heavy drinking. It is therefore not surprising when she fails the test through making her disapproval of Oliver and Caroline's relationship quite clear.

However, the real test comes with the response of the men to Caroline. Unable to verbally express their frustration with their own marriages and their envy of Oliver's relationship with Caroline, Dan and Eugene can find an outlet only in their drunken rampage through Caroline's room. However, even Oliver, when faced with the choice of sticking to the safety of Irish society or abandoning it for the exotica represented by Caroline, automatically—if shamefacedly—takes the safe option. Ultimately, then, it is ironic that Caroline's photographic assignment is to capture images of Ireland: it is precisely only images that she succeeds in capturing. The drama's closing shot is of Catherine, exposing a photograph of the men before it has time to fix on the paper: as their image is exposed, the three men fade from view.

F

THE FADING LIGHT (2009). **Ivan Kavanagh**'s fourth feature-length drama in three years shares the claustrophobic atmosphere of his earlier films *The Solution* (2007) and *Tin Can Man* (2007). Successful businesswoman Yvonne (Valene Kane) and her struggling actress sister Cathy (Emma Eliza Regan) return to their family home to care for their terminally ill mother (Bibi Larrson). There, they are confronted with decisions regarding the future care of their intellectually challenged brother Peter (Patrick O'Donnell) once their mother has passed. As they struggle to cope with their mother's physical and mental decline (as her faculties desert her, she unleashes a torrent of abuse directed at her daughters), their return to their childhood environment recalls earlier traumas surrounding the death of their father.

Once again working on a small budget (though substantially greater than the five-figure sums available for his first features), Kavanagh delivers a grueling emotional experience. Indeed, it is precisely this low level of funding that makes the film's singular nature possible: it is hard to imagine a mainstream financier willing to take the risk associated with supporting such a difficult piece. *The Fading Light* is absolutely unflinching in its depiction of both the immediate consequences of the mother's condition and its impact on the autistic Peter. Initially believing his mother to be merely ill, the sequence in which his sisters reveal the truth of her condition is beyond harrowing, O'Donnell offering an almost unbearably raw portrayal of fear, confusion, and despair.

Shot by frequent collaborator **Colin Downey**, *The Fading Light* recalls the intensity of Ingmar Bergman and John Cassavettes in its dissection of family life, with parents and siblings depicted as sources of both comfort and pain.

FANTASTIC FILMS. Formed in 2000 by John McDonnell, who was joined by Brendan McCarthy after the latter completed his tenure as head of production and development at the **Irish Film Board** (IFB) (2001–2005), Fantastic Films occupies a niche in the Irish audiovisual sector through its interest in primarily developing and producing genre-based film, notably horror. McCarthy had shown a penchant for genre before the IFB—when he produced Geraldine Creed's dystopian *Chaos* (2001)—and during—when he supported **Conor McMahon**'s low-budget gore-horror *Dead Meat* (2004), going decidedly against the grain of the dominant IFB ethos that had sought to create an "Irish cinema" largely through art house drama and local comedy. McCarthy's support of *Dead Meat* represented an unlikely—and largely unacknowledged—landmark insofar as it extended the parameters of the kinds of films the IFB might support, acknowledging in the process that a national cinema industry could also encompass the lowbrow, nontheatrical, and transnational marketplace. (Much horror is reviewed and distributed via fan networks.) More concretely, it opened the door to the slow but steady emergence of a body of Irish screen horror films, many of which have been produced by Fantastic Films, including David Keating's *Cherry Tree* (2015) and *Wakewood* (2011), Conor McMahon's *Stitches* (2012), *I Am Not a Serial Killer* (Billy O'Brien, 2016), *The Hallow* (Colin Hardy, 2015), *Let Us Prey* (2014), and *Outcast* (2010). Fantastic recently extended its reach and ambitions beyond Ireland with *Nails* (2017), directed by Los Angeles–based screenwriter Denis Bartok (longtime programmer of the American Cinematheque and head of art house distribution company Cinelicious), and the Spanish horror *Muse* (2017), directed by the widely recognized Jaume Balagueró, responsible for the widely acclaimed and highly profitable *REC* series. Other notable credits include the ambitious sci-fi films *The Last Days on Mars* (2012) and *Vivarium* (2019).

FAR AND AWAY (1992). Shot on 65 mm and directed by Ron Howard, the film was conceived as a vehicle for then husband and wife Tom Cruise and Nicole Kidman. Apparently inspired by the plays of 18th-century dramatist Dion Boucicault, screenwriter Bob Dolman, along with the director, created a whimsical romantic historical comedy that opens in 1890s Kerry. Although from opposite ends of the social spectrum, tenant farmer Joseph Connelly (Cruise) and aristocratic Shannon Christie (Kidman) emigrate on the same boat to the United States after Joseph's father is killed by unscrupulous landowners. Once there, they fall in love, and in the film's closing set piece, they participate in the spectacular Oklahoma land rush.

Boucicault aside, the story also clearly takes *The Quiet Man* (1952) as a reference point. This is evident in the portrayal of Kerry villagers as disheveled but charming inebriates, the tourist board landscapes, and, in particular, Kidman's portrayal of Shannon as a staunchly independent woman who overtly recalls **Maureen O'Hara**'s Mary Kate from the earlier film. Both films also share a romantic tone: the representation of the voyage to the United States is at some remove from the actuality of 19th-century emigrant "coffin ships." That said, in placing a tenant laborer and a landlord's agent

(Thomas Gibson) at the center of the narrative, *Far and Away* at least hints at political, social, and cultural divisions entirely absent from *The Quiet Man*'s ecumenist vision of Irish life.

Shot in western Kerry (in many of the same locations used for *Ryan's Daughter*) and Dublin (which doubled for 19th-century Boston), *Far and Away* was the biggest picture shot in Ireland since *Ryan's Daughter* in 1969. Although the £40 million spent by the production was welcomed by the state, it placed the sum spent on indigenous films the same year—£3.5 million—in stark relief and demonstrated the extent to which the Irish audiovisual sector depended on overseas projects.

FARRELL, COLIN (1976–). Colin Farrell's career to date splits fairly neatly in two: the first period spans his flurry of high-profile work often in "actioners" bookended by his breakthrough turn in Joel Schumacher's *Tigerland* (2000) and in Michael Mann's 2006 reboot of *Miami Vice*. Then there's the second era, characterized by a shift away from blockbuster productions to more intimate, character-centered work in both Irish-themed and full-on art house material. Although he retains considerable star power (as evinced by his casting in the expanded *Harry Potter* universe emerging from the *Fantastic Beasts* [2016] sequence), he seems increasingly drawn to character rather than star roles, where he subsumes himself into the character (rather than the other way around).

Farrell grew up in the middle-class suburb of Castleknock attending the local private school but leaving before completing his final exams. It is tempting to construct the young Farrell as a tortured artist, frustrated by the cultural vacuum of his suburban setting. Popular press interviews have certainly done so, citing early dalliances with substance abuse as proof of his yearning for "something more." Early ambitions to become a professional soccer player (like his father and uncle before him) self-destructed but were replaced by an interest in acting encouraged by a stint at the Gaiety School of Acting. His screen debut came in Owen McPolin's *Drinking Crude* (1997), followed by a key role in the **Radio Telefís Éireann**/BBC coproduction *Falling for a Dancer* (1998). While still at the Gaiety, he was cast in a recurring role in the BBC's hit Ireland-set series *Ballykissangel* (1998–1999) before Kevin Spacey spotted him in a play at the Donmar in London and cast him in his take on the Martin Cahill story *Ordinary Decent Criminal* (2000). This in turn brought him onto Hollywood's radar and saw him cast by Joel Schumacher in *Tigerland* (2000). The role of Vietnam-era U.S. soldier Private Roland Bozz was a less cynical take on Richard Gere's character from *An Officer and a Gentleman* (1982) and set something of a screen template for Farrell thereafter: brash, charming, but emotionally vulnerable. Catapulted to A-list status, he suddenly found himself working with Steven Spielberg (*Minority Report* [2002]), Oliver Stone (in the titular role of *Alexander*

[2004]), and Terence Malick (*The New World* [2005]) and sharing equal billing with Bruce Willis (*Hart's War* [2002]), Ben Affleck (*Daredevil* [2003]), and Al Pacino (*The Recruit* [2004]).

Farrell's private life in this period earned him nearly as much attention as his screen roles: high-profile romances, a sex tape, and alcohol and substance addiction. In press interviews, Farrell remained disarmingly open about his appetites and somehow avoiding being pigeonholed with the irredeemable "bad boy" tag. However, the poor reception of Stone's take on *Alexander* was followed by a more headlong pursuit of excess that peaked during the filming of *Miami Vice*. Forced to recognize that not only his career but also possibly his life was on the brink, he entered rehab and emerged sober, a status he has reportedly maintained since.

The nature of subsequent roles changed too: whether by his own choice or not (both *Alexander* and *Miami Vice* proved box office disappointments, though the latter was critically well received), he moved away from lead roles in blockbusters (aside from his 2012 outing in a remake of *Total Recall*, another financial disappointment). Instead, he combined unlikely cameos (a country music star in *Crazy Heart* [2009] and a comedic turn as a scene-stealing, foulmouthed, balding manager in *Horrible Bosses* [2011]) with work in slower-paced Irish-related work, such as **Neil Jordan**'s *Ondine* and Danis Tanovic's *Triage* (both 2009). However, his appearance as a suicidal hit man haunted by visions of a child he has inadvertently murdered in Martin McDonagh's *In Bruges* (2008) offered the best signpost to future possibilities. Holding his own opposite **Brendan Gleeson**, he proved surprising adept at delivering McDonagh's whip-smart dialogue with its blend of the tragic and the absurd. Alternately sexy and infinitively sad, Farrell also demonstrated an untried knack for comedy, earning him a Golden Globe award in 2009.

Farrell would pair with McDonagh again for *Seven Psychopaths* (2012): his performance as an overtly Irish-coded Hollywood screenwriter arguably made more compelling by his decision to eschew the working-class persona adopted in earlier Irish roles in *Intermission* (2003) and *In Bruges*. Notwithstanding their surface unpleasantness—child-killing hit man and seemingly self-obsessed Hollywood scribe—the success of both McDonagh roles are built around exploiting Farrell's embodiment of a fundamental innocence. When called on to embody straightforward malevolence, however, as in Peter Weir's *The Way Back* (2010) (where he plays opposite **Saoirse Ronan** as a criminal condemned to the Russian gulag), the depiction feels much cruder and more one-note. This is not to suggest that such roles are beyond him—gifted with much richer characterization in the second series of HBO's *True Detective*, he successfully embodies the violence and corruption of detective Ray Velcoro—but he is clearly more at home with kinder, gentler roles. This is particularly evident in his casting as the doomed Travers Goff in *Saving Mr. Banks* (2013), the real-life inspiration for the patriarch in *Mary Poppins*. It's certainly the case with regard to what remains his most left-field role to date, that of David in Yorgos Lanthimos's absurdist dystopian vision *The Lobster* (2015). Cast against type, Farrell plays David as a diffident, paunchy middle-aged man who must find love or, bizarrely, submit to being transformed into an animal of his choice (hence the title of the film). Lanthimos's approach demands dispassionate—indeed detached—performances from his cast. Nonetheless, Farrell deftly evokes the quiet desperation of his character he yields to the increasingly farcical logic of his situation. *The Lobster* cast him in a new light for audiences and opened new avenues for Farrell's career. Conversely, Farrell's status drew entirely new audiences to Lanthimos's offbeat, absurdist work and raised the film's profile at award ceremonies (securing Golden Globe and **Academy Award** nominations for Farrell and Lanthimos, respectively, and winning the Jury Prize at the 2015 Cannes Film Festival). The pair subsequently reunited to similar effect for the creepy *The Killing of a Sacred Deer* (2017). Subsequent roles—in Steve McQueen's *Widows* (2018) and Disney's live-action version of *Dumbo* (2019)—suggest that Farrell will continue to move between art house roles and more mainstream material, making him one of the most interesting actors working in film today.

FASSBENDER, MICHAEL (1977–). The performance that introduced Irish audiences to Michael Fassbender immediately established aspects of his screen persona: intense, handsome, and rivetingly charming. That performance arrived not in a television or screen drama but in a 2004 advertisement for Guinness depicting Fassbender swimming across the Atlantic to convey an apology to a friend in New York. It would be several more years before audiences came to identify him with longer-form screen performance, but his rise, when it came after 2008, was so meteoric and placed him in such demand that he immediately became one of the highest-profile and more omnipresent screen actors to emerge from Ireland in the 21st century.

Born in Heidelberg, Germany, in 1977 to a German father and Irish mother, Fassbender grew up in Killarney, County Kerry, after his parents moved there in 1979. (Fassbender spent summers in Germany and remains a fluent German speaker.) Having attended primary school in Killarney, it was while at secondary school that he became involved in the local theater group. After school, he moved first to Cork and then in 1996 to study at the Drama Centre London. He dropped out before completing his studies, however, to tour a version of Chekov's *Three Sisters*.

There followed some lean years, filled with small-scale theater and interspersed with some U.K.-based television work, including a recurring role in *Band of Brothers* (2001) (a series that was something of a spawning ground for up-and-coming actors, featuring as it did in minor roles **Andrew Scott**,

Simon Pegg, and James McAvoy). In 2005, he played the recurring role of Caz Miller opposite **James Nesbitt**, who played the eponymous Murphy in *Murphy's Law*. The same year saw him play the demon Azazeal in Sky Television's short-lived sub-Buffy romp *Hex*.

However, two films in 2007 and 2008 transformed his career: Zack Snyder's computer-generated imagery–heavy adaptation of Frank Miller's graphic novel *300* (as Stelios, one of Leonidas's troops) and Turner Prize–winning artist Steve McQueen's remarkable film debut ***Hunger***, set during the H-Block hunger strikes of 1981 and in which Fassbender played Bobby Sands. Fassbender's intense performance is the core of the film and includes a bravura 17-minute dialogue shot in one take between Sands and a priest (**Liam Cunningham**) (in a film otherwise characterized by the complete absence of speech). To play Sands in the later part of his hunger strike, Fassbender lost one-fifth of his body weight, dropping to 58 kilograms. So extreme was the experience that Fassbender reportedly took a month to recover. The film was acclaimed on its release, and both McQueen and Fassbender were showered with award nominations.

Thereafter, the offers poured in. Between 2009 and 2011, Fassbender appeared in 10 feature films (in addition to a couple of shorts and voicing a video game). These ranged from small-scale art house material like Andrea Arnold's *Fish Tank* (2009) to working with Quentin Tarantino on *Inglourious Basterds* in 2009 (a role that put Fassbender's fluency in German to good effect) but also full-on blockbuster fare like the *X-Men: First Class* prequel (2011), where Fassbender embodied the role of Magneto originated by Ian McKellern (Fassbender has since reprised the role three times, including in *X-Men: Dark Phoenix* [2018]).

Fassbender's screen persona is complex. In screen interviews, he projects an antsy physical presence, humming with energy: this physicality is obvious in films like *300*, *Centurion* (2010), and, albeit in a different context, *Shame* (2011). Yet he is also capable of embodying stillness: the philosophical Bobby Sands in *Hunger*, Archie Hicox's steely calm under pressure in *Inglourious Basterds*, and the controlled reserve of the android David in Ridley Scott's *Prometheus* (2012) and *Alien: Covenant* (2017). Physically attractive (Fassbender quickly came to feature on "Sexiest 100" lists), he is almost casually seductive in films like *Shame* and *The Counselor* (2013). Yet this outward appearance often disguises internal trauma hinted at through personas that are not merely untrustworthy but that also carry a latent threat of violence.

David Cronenberg clearly spotted this potential when he cast Fassbender as Carl Jung (opposite Viggo Mortensen's Freud) in *A Dangerous Method* (2011), as did Cary Fukunaga, who cast him as Rochester opposite Mia Wasikowska's *Jane Eyre* (2011), and Justin Kurzel, who cast him as the eponymous *Macbeth* (2015). It is even present in his Oscar-nominated turn as Steve Jobs in Danny Boyle's 2016 biopic, where Fassbender exposes the capacity for casual cruelty of the revered entrepreneur. However, it is his collaborations with Steve McQueen that cumulatively constitute his most interesting work to date. After *Hunger*, he played Brandon in *Shame*, an attractive and charming but psychically damaged man completely unable to form relationships who seeks to annihilate his interior world (childhood memories?) by obsessive reveling in the physical act of sex. The performance made for uncomfortable viewing—almost too raw, too exposed (which may account for why, despite expectations, it did not result in award nominations).

As Edwin Epps, a white plantation owner, in *12 Years a Slave* (2013), Fassbender once again found himself playing a damaged character. Although notionally at the top of the social hierarchy, Fassbender's performance demonstrates how the institution of slavery perverts all associated with it: his Epps is psychotic and randomly and spectacularly violent. Yet despite his loudly proclaimed assertions of his rights over his human "property," Fassbender's portrayal hints at the character's subconscious awareness of the perversity of the institution of slavery.

Although primarily appearing in U.S. and U.K. roles, his roles are often coded as Irish (Bobby Sands, Connor in *Fish Tank*, Paul in Steven Soderberg's *Haywire*, and even briefly channeling **Peter O'Toole** in *Prometheus*). Despite this, his direct involvement with the Irish film industry has been very limited. And, ironically, his most recent appearance in a "proper" Irish film saw him play an American. As the eponymous ***Frank*** (2014) in **Lenny Abrahamson**'s collaboration with English writer Jon Ronson, Fassbender came the closest he has yet to playing a comedy role: as an eccentric singer in an impossibly obscure band. Yet even here, there is hidden damage and hidden pain (literally hidden given that Fassbender wears a papier-mâché head for virtually the entire film), first hinted at, then overtly demonstrated.

FASTNET FILMS. Originally established by producer and former film censor John Kelleher in the wake of **Strongbow Film**'s post–*Eat the Peach* (1986) demise, Fastnet Films acted as an on-again, off-again production vehicle for Kelleher in between his numerous other activities. However, in 2003, Kelleher ceded day-to-day control of the company to his son Macdara, along with producer Morgan Bushe and director **Lance Daly**. Since then, Fastnet has quietly become one of the most prolific Irish film production companies, behind only **Samson Films** and **Element Pictures** in terms of completed projects. (Indeed, in 2012, the **Irish Film Institute** was able to run a minifestival derived entirely from Fastnet's back catalog.)

Prior to Fastnet, Bushe and Kelleher worked as first assistant director and camera operator, respectively, on Daly's first feature, *Last Days in Dublin* (2001). Kelleher graduated to producer for Daly's follow-up *The Halo Ef-*

fect (2004) and has produced all of Daly's subsequent features through Fastnet up to and including *Black '47* (2018). Fastnet is far more than a production vehicle for Daly, however. In addition to producing **Rebecca Daly**'s first two features, the company has specialized in a combination of low-budget indigenous works (such as Ian Power's *The Runway* [2010] and Brendan Grant's *Get Up and Go* [2014]) while acting as Irish coproducer on a sequence of international productions, including the Swedish-originated *Princessa* (2009), the Australian *Strangerland* (2015) starring Nicole Kidman, and the U.S. coproduction *The Professor and the Madman* (2017) featuring Mel Gibson. Although the division of labor is not strict, Macdara Kelleher works mainly on fiction features, while Bushe concentrates on documentary production, including Ross McDonnell's *Colony* (2009), Klaartje Quirjin's *Anton Corbijn: Inside Out* (2012), and a sequence of sports and history television documentaries with director Andrew Gallimore. (Bushe has also used Fastnet as a vehicle for his own directorial output, including his feature debut, *The Belly of the Whale* [2018] starring **Pat Shortt**.)

Fastnet's integration into European coproduction networks owes something to the European Film Promotion's Producers on the Move scheme. Kelleher received the Irish nomination for the scheme in 2008, followed by Bushe in 2012. Kelleher paired with the 2008 Dutch nominee Reinier Selen's Rinken Films to produce *Nothing Personal* (2009) and subsequently *The Other Side of Sleep* (2011) and **Brendan Muldowney**'s *Love Eternal* (2013). Muldowney's producer, Conor Barry, who also received the Producers on the Move award in 2013, has also produced with Fastnet, working on **Rebecca Daly**'s *Mammal* (2016) and producing her follow-up *Good Favour* (2017) through his own production company SP Films.

Like **Element Pictures**, Fastnet has also moved to engage in a degree of vertical integration. When former **Irish Film Board** executive Patrick O'Neill established a new distribution company, Wildcard Films, in 2013, Fastnet backed the venture and has subsequently used it to distribute the bulk of its fiction feature and theatrical documentary output. (Wildcard also sub-distributes for U.K. and U.S. companies and has picked up Irish rights for films such as *The Young Offenders* [2016] and **Cardboard Gangsters** [2016]).

In a neat symmetry, Macdara Kelleher's move into large-budget television production with an adaptation of George R. R. Martin's *Nightflyers* (2017–) for the U.S. cable channel Syfy has reinforced his professional contact with his father, John Kelleher (who also coproduced *The Other Side of Sleep* and is a non–executive director of Wildcard). The scale of the sci-fi–horror drama made Limerick's Troy Studios, whose board of directors include the elder Kelleher, a perfect fit for international television production.

FEDERATION OF IRISH FILM SOCIETIES. *See* IRISH FILM SOCI-ETY.

FELICIA'S JOURNEY (1999). It speaks volumes about the extent to which the post-1993 explosion in filmmaking activity conjured an allure around the idea of filming in Ireland that a sequence of North American directors temporarily decamped across the Atlantic to film (often unlikely) narratives (John Sayles's **The Secret of Roan Inish** [1994], a tale based around the myth of the "selkie" [seal people] being perhaps the most left-field example). However, given the prominence of damaged young women, dangerous men, and the lasting influence of childhood trauma in his previous works, Atom Egoyan's decision to adapt William Trevor's 1994 novel is perhaps less surprising.

   Elaine Cassidy (in a revelatory performance) is the titular Felicia, an innocent abroad. The slowly executed thriller follows the pregnant young Irish girl across the Irish Sea to Birmingham as—disowned by her own father—she searches for the unborn child's father (**Peter McDonald**), who has abandoned her. In Birmingham, she encounters the middle-aged Quincy (Bob Hoskins), the lonely yet somewhat sinister catering manager of a big factory who offers to help her find her former boyfriend. Both are wounded though in different ways. Felicia's father (**Gerard McSorley**) insists on her unconditional acceptance of his rules. His nationalist background cannot tolerate the idea of his daughter consorting with a boy who does not want to stay at home and, worse, who entertains the idea of joining the British army. Quincy's pathology stems from a smothering maternal influence 40 years earlier from which he has never progressed (a status emphasized by the 1950s decor of his house and his car, a vintage Morris Minor). And, as the film progresses, we are offered murky hints of the fate of other young women whom Quincy has previously encountered.

   The conclusion, though basically consistent with that of the source material, reliant as it is on the fortuitous intervention of the evangelical Miss Calligary (Claire Benedict), might have stretched credibility in another director's hands. In Egoyan's often antinaturalistic work, however, such coincidences are not only tolerated but also a critical element of the director's toying with audience expectations, resulting in a film that, though partially set *in* Ireland, rarely feels *of* Ireland.

FERNDALE FILMS. *See* PEARSON, NOEL.

FESTIVALS. Film festivals began in Ireland in 1956 with the establishment of the Cork International Film Festival, which has run ever since. The Cork Festival was driven largely by the initiative of Dermot Breen, a former manager of the Palace Theatre in Cork, the city's first public relations manager and in the mid-1970s the official Irish film censor. Breen sold the festival as a means of drumming up tourist trade and convinced **Bord Fáilte** (Irish Tourist Board) to financially support the festival as an element of the annual An Toastál arts festival. Bord Fáilte would remain the sponsor until the 1980s, expending generous sums of money to bring over international guests, especially journalists from British newspapers, thus ensuring international coverage for the event. Unusually, Breen initiated a short-film competition as part of the festival, a move his successors continued after Breen's death in 1978.

From 1986 to 2013, the Cork Festival was closely identified with programmer and (from 2009) chief executive officer Mick Hannigan, who had previously founded Cork's Triskel Film Club in the 1980s. Hannigan combined his festival work with working as the first programmer at the **Irish Film Centre** and running Cork's art house Kino Cinema between 1996 and 2009. However in 2013, the board of the festival controversially dismissed both Hannigan and then programmer Una Seely, citing an unsustainable management structure in the wake of losses recorded that year. (Hannigan and Seely took an unfair dismissal case against the festival, which was settled privately in 2015.) Although the Cork Festival subsequently continued operating, it found itself in competition with IndieCork, a cooperatively organized festival established by Hannigan and Seely.

Cork remained the only ongoing annual festival in Ireland until the 1980s. However, with the closure of the **Irish Film Theatre** in 1985, Dublin was left without a venue for 35-mm screenings of nonmainstream material. To at least partially address the gap, journalists Michael Dwyer and Myles Dungan established the Dublin Film Festival the same year. Despite being regarded initially—even by its founders—as a stopgap measure, the first Dublin festival was extremely successful with audiences, even recording a financial surplus at the end of the first year. Consequently, even when new permanent art house venues, such as the **Light House**, opened in Dublin in 1988, the festival not only survived but actually thrived, arguably enjoying its most successful year in 1992 not simply in terms of audiences but also in terms of the range of guests who attended the festival. These included Oliver Stone, Krzysztof Kieślowski, Theo Angelopoulos, cinematographer Freddie Francis, documentarist Errol Morris, and composer Michael Nyman, whose band performed during the festival.

By the end of the 1990s, however, the Dublin Festival was beset by financial and staffing difficulties. The figures behind its early successes, Dwyer and Dungan, together with programmers like Martin Mahon (of Yellow Asylum) and administrators like David McLoughlin, had all amicably ended their involvement by the mid-1990s. In 1998, the festival lost its major sponsor (ACC Bank) and its main venue, the **Ward Anderson**–owned Screen

Cinema. In 2001, the **Arts Council** commissioned a report on the difficulties at the festival that identified the absence of a coherent programming policy and an unworkable management structure. The report's analysis came too late to save the festival, which last ran in 2001.

However, in 2003, a new organization, the Dublin International Film Festival, picked up where the previous one had left off. Indeed, there were striking personnel overlaps between the two organizations: the new festival was programmed by Michael Dwyer and chaired by David McLoughlin, who had become a film producer (for *Dead Bodies*, among other films) in the interim. For all intents and purposes, the new festival was a relaunch of the original, even down to the retention of the Surprise Film feature, which had proved an unexpected hit with audiences of the original festival. That said, with the appointment of Grainne Humphreys, former head of the Junior Dublin Film Festival and an education officer with the **Irish Film Institute**, as full director of the festival in 2007, a new lease on life was injected into the capital's celebration of cinema. Two high-profile sponsorships—the first with Jameson Whiskey and the second with Audi—coincided with a much more aggressive marketing of the festival, establishing it as a key staging post in Dublin's calendar of cultural events. In addition to the core functions of screening films (roughly 1,500 between 2003 and 2017, of which nearly 300 were Irish features) and hosting guests (the festival has brought in more than 500 cast and crew since 2003), the festival has engaged in active year-long outreach activities, including branded premieres for new works.

The last long-established festival operating in Ireland is the Galway Film Fleadh (Festival), which first ran in 1988, using the Claddagh Palace cinema as a venue. Founded by **Lelia Doolan** and Miriam Allen, the fleadh operated on a smaller scale than either the Dublin or the Cork Festival, but nonetheless the fleadh found a niche in the annual festival calendar. Widely regarded as the most intimate and laid back of the major festivals, it also introduced a quasi-professional element from its inception, running master classes and seminars on various aspects of film production and policy from its inception. The annual Film Forum offers an opportunity for the domestic industry to reflect on the state of play within the sector, while the Marketplace slot effects introductions between selected producers and sales agents, distributors, television companies, and so on. It has also been a competitive festival since its inception, initially offering prizes for best short and later offering awards for best Irish and international features.

The fleadh's status was indirectly enhanced from 1993, when the reformed **Irish Film Board** established its headquarters in Galway and in particular when organizer Lelia Doolan became chair of the Film Board. This created an added incentive for Irish film professionals to make the journey to the west coast. In 1995, the fleadh lost its core venue when the Claddagh Palace was bulldozed to make way for apartments, but the fleadh has subsequently thrived in Galway's Town Hall cinemas and in the mobile Cinemobile facility. Under programmer Gar O'Brien, who took over the reins in 2010, the existing emphasis on short-film work has been augmented by the swelling number of lower-budget indigenous works that have seen the fleadh act as a launching pad for local hits, such as *A Date for Mad Mary* and *The Young Offenders* (both 2016).

In addition to these, there are now an increasing number of newer festivals around the country. Dublin alone hosts festivals for gay and lesbian (GAZE), French, German, Spanish, documentary (Stranger Than Fiction, with the Guth Gafa festival run 65 kilometers away in Kells, County Meath), and digital (Darklight and Digital Biscuit) cinema. Virtually every major town (Limerick, Waterford, and Derry) now host annual festivals, and even less populous locales, such as Clones in County Monaghan and, incredibly, Tory Island (population 144) off the Donegal Coast, run events. All Irish film festivals are usually financed by a mixture of sponsorship, box office income, and Arts Council funding. The last of these is particularly critical for the smaller festivals. Until 1980, Bord Fáilte had financed the only festival then in place—the Cork Festival—but from that year, responsibility for such funding was transferred to the Arts Council, which awarded the Cork Festival £42,500 in its first year alone. As of 2015, the council directly grant-aided eight film festivals to the tune of €490,000 and indirectly financed several others through funding for arts festivals with film components.

THE FIELD (1990). In adapting John B. Keane's classic stage play to the screen, director/screenwriter **Jim Sheridan** transposes the setting from County Kerry of the early 1960s to Connemara of the 1930s, shifting readings of the text away from its original sociocultural context (the play was inspired by an actual murder over land in rural Kerry) into protomythical meanings. Other alterations were undertaken in part for commercial reasons (the key character of a returned emigrant, originally from England, becomes American [Tom Berenger]) and in part for tragic ones: **Ray McAnally** played Bull McCabe in the original 1965 stage production and was set to reprise the role when he died suddenly and was replaced by *Richard Harris*.

An opening credit sequence establishes the film's central characters and preoccupations. We see two figures in silhouette pushing a cart over a mountainous landscape and unceremoniously dropping the carcass of a donkey into the sea below. In the first of several intertextual references to classic films set in Ireland by nonindigenous filmmakers, Sheridan references Robert Flaherty's *Man of Aran* as they gather seaweed and carry it in baskets up the mountains to fertilize and regenerate the precious soil of the eponymous field. Revealing the driving force of his life as well as his monumental ego, Bull McCabe (Richard Harris) proclaims, "God made the world," but "seaweed made the field."

The field is not owned by McCabe but rather is rented from a widow (Francis Tomelty) who does not wish to sell it (echoes of the Widow Tillane in *The Quiet Man*). Bull's dull and cruel son Tadgh (Sean Bean) has grown up under his father's obsessive attitude to the field and secretly torments the widow by means of cruel pranks. His willing accomplice is Bird Flanagan (John Hurt) in a performance that reprises the village idiot played by John Mills in *Ryan's Daughter*.

As with the earlier screen representations of Irish rural life referenced by these scenes, the local community functions as passive recipients of fate, waiting for things to happen, with no apparent work ethic or ambition. Reminiscent of a Greek chorus, they also serve to affirm the prevailing attitudes and values of the society, endorsing the atavistic attitudes associated with "the law of land" over and above any common law. When Bull confronts the publican about the impending sale of the field (the widow having finally decided to sell it), he is warned that "outsiders" might bid for the prize possession. This activates a reaffirmation of anticolonial and national solidarity, evoking victimhood and a common enemy "who drove us to the coffin ships." Nonetheless, rousing the passion of the pub crowd and citing an unspecified earlier struggle (the War of Independence?), Bull asserts that "I drove them out" and that "no outsider will bid for the field." However, just such an outsider materializes in the form of Tom Bergenger's slick Irish American who has returned to buy a piece of the home country (another reference to *The Quiet Man*). In a theatrical denouement, echoing both Shakespeare's *King Lear* and the myth of "Cuchulain's Fight with the Sea," Bull descends into madness, driving his cattle to the edge of the cliff and walking into the sea, trying to control its power.

The film was well received in the United States, earning Harris his first **Academy Award** nomination since 1964 and initiating a late-career revival. This success owed much to Sheridan's adjustments to plot, setting, and characters, designed to appeal to a transatlantic audience as well as seek to find ways of reenergizing the narrative potential of Irish myth for cinema. In subsequent interviews, Sheridan expressed dissatisfaction with Harris's interpretation, saying it had wandered too far from Keane's character and ultimately overshadowed the local dimensions of the story.

THE FIFTH PROVINCE **(1997). Frank Stapleton**'s remarkable debut and only feature is perhaps the most self-reflexive Irish film ever made. Timmy (Brian F. O'Byrne) runs the Innisfree guesthouse (a deliberate nod at *The Quiet Man*) but has ambitions to be a scriptwriter. However, he is advised by script editor Diane (Lia Williams) that traditional Irish stories are out of fashion ("No more stories about Irish mothers, priests, sexual repression and the miseries of rural life") and that only contemporary stories in cosmopolitan settings have any chance of securing funding. Reluctant to abandon one set of conventions only to replace them with another, Timmy attempts to imagine an alternative zone: the eponymous (and long-lost) fifth province. As the narrative progresses, the script takes on Escher-like levels of complexity: it emerges that Diane may (or may not) be a character in a script Timmy has written. When Timmy encounters his mother (Joan O'Hara) in the act of drowning Diane (who has previously tried to seduce Timmy), thereby invoking the Oedipal myth, they turn the tables by tossing his mother into the waters of Glendalough.

Cowritten with Pat Sheeran and Nina Witoszek (Nina Fitzpatrick), *The Fifth Province* is a persistently playful and often surreal exploration of attempts to invent an Irish national cinema in the 1980s and 1990s. Attracted by its startling originality, British Screen (then headed by **Simon Perry**) first offered funding to the project, with the **Irish Film Board** subsequently contributing to its production. Evocatively shot by celebrated French cinematographer Bruno de Keyzer (who contributed a European sensibility to the film's quirky tone), the film is a worthy cinematic successor to the surrealistic perspective of that liminal zone inaugurated by Flann O'Brien.

FILMBASE. Filmbase emerged from an attempt in the mid-1980s by **Channel 4**, in conjunction with the Irish state training agency FAS, to encourage the development of a regional filmmaking cooperative. Although that initial effort proved unsuccessful, it became a springboard for Filmbase, established in 1986. The organization provided a not-for-profit, independent resource facility driven by a philosophy of extending membership to anyone willing to pay the low membership fee. It offered practical courses in scripting, directing, and editing and facilitated the discounted hire of a wide range of advanced audiovisual production and postproduction equipment. Within a year of its establishment, its facilities had been used to produce Fergus Tighe's *Clash of the Ash* (1987), among others, one of only a handful of screen works produced in late 1980s Ireland.

By 2006, Filmbase had reached almost 1,000 members, a quadrupling the 1990 membership. Originally based on Dublin's Dame Street, it was then located in the Irish Film Centre for more than a decade before finally relocating in 2004 to an impressive three-story, glass-fronted building in Temple Bar just around the corner from its old home. It operated here until its closure after 32 years in March 2018.

From its inception, Filmbase was also a de facto lobbying group on behalf of not only the low-budget film sector but also, at times—and in particular after the closure of the **Irish Film Board** in 1987—the entire industry. Until the reestablishment of the Film Board in 1993, the Filmbase Action Committee consistently argued for the establishment of a single state body with responsibility for all aspects of Irish film policy, and its founding members—

including Jane and **Johnny Gogan**, Anne Crilly, Liam O'Neill, and **Tiernan MacBride**—made significant contributions to the influential *Coopers & Lybrand Report*.

In 1987, Filmbase established a bimonthly newsletter, *Filmbase News*, initially to keep members informed about the organization's activities. However, it quickly became a full-fledged magazine devoted to the politics of film support and film culture in Ireland. Its pages were as likely to feature cultural critics like **Kevin Rockett** and Luke Gibbons debating the merits of **Joe Comerford**'s work as it was **Tiernan MacBride** and Film Makers Ireland debating the lack of state support for cinema. In 1992, the magazine was retitled *Film Ireland* to reflect the broader scope of the journal.

In 1987, Filmbase launched an award scheme to fund the production of short films: initially, £3,500 was made available for one project each year, though this expanded after **Radio Telefís Éireann** (RTÉ) became involved as a funding partner in 1992. The Short Shots scheme ran in conjunction with RTÉ and offered €10,000 in cash per project plus access to production and postproduction equipment. A similar value supported the Reel Art scheme run in conjunction with the **Arts Council**. Other awards were also established, including Irish-language channel TG4 awards, and in 2004, two new **documentary** awards were introduced. As the price of digital technology dropped, the organization broadened its ambitions: in 2007, in conjunction with the Irish Film Board, it launched the Catalyst scheme, which offered up to €350,000 in funding (plus access to industry experts) to emerging filmmakers to fund the production of low-budget features. The scheme supported the production of films like *Rewind*, *One Hundred Mornings*, and *Eamon*.

Training and equipment hire remained the core of the Filmbase mission, and it was a member of Screen Talent Europe, a Nordic Culture Fund–supported imitative to encourage cooperation between emerging filmmakers in northern Europe. This included delivering 50 to 60 sponsored workshops each year on aspects of filmmaking, including securing developing finance, acting, and postproduction effects. Access to such workshops augmented Filmbase's delivery of production and postproduction courses and one-off workshops and master classes organized in conjunction with Screen Training Ireland.

Although in its early incarnation Filmbase's equipment was resolutely (and necessarily) analog in nature (including traditional flatbed film editing setups), the early years of the 21st century saw it embrace digital production, ranging from relatively simple digital single-lens reflex cameras to full 4K professional setups. This was mirrored at a postproduction level: by 2017, Filmbase was renting out two digital editing suites based around industry-standard (Final Cut Pro) software.

However, in March 2018, documentary maker **Paul Duane** was informed that his Reel Arts funding would not be available on schedule, and he immediately brought this to attention of the Arts Council of Ireland. The council quickly appointed independent auditors who identified that Filmbase had, over the previous years, amassed an unsustainable debt burden. On 14 March, Filmbase announced that it would immediately enter liquidation with the loss of 13 staff positions. Its loss threw into sharp relief the critical role it had played in sustaining an ecosphere for nascent directors and the many Irish filmmakers compelled to work within a no- or low-budget working environment.

FILM COMPANY OF IRELAND. As James Mark Sullivan, U.S. ambassador to the Dominican Republic, prepared to board a transatlantic liner in New York in July 1915, dockside reporters sought clarification on his status and plans. What they didn't realize was that the Irish-born Sullivan, better known to his Tammany Hall peers as "Big Jim," was accompanying the elderly Mary Jane O'Donovan Rossa to the funeral of her late husband, the much-revered Fenian Jeremiah O'Donovan Rossa, a catalytic event that would change the course of Irish history. In Dublin, Sullivan found himself at the center of the elaborate funeral arrangements organized by Tom Clarke, Patrick Pearse, and James Connolly and activist members of the **Abbey Theatre**, such as John and Thomas McDonagh. Excited by this intersection of politics and culture, Sullivan quickly conceived of a project to establish Ireland's first film production company, the Film Company of Ireland (FCOI). Sullivan quickly raised $5,000 for the venture, and between 1916 and 1920, the FCOI produced some 25 short films and two feature films, including Ireland's first, *Knock-na-Gow* (1918).

The FCOI was registered in Dublin in March 1916 in the names of Sullivan and Henry Fitzgibbon—a local businessman and son of prominent Gaelic Leaguer John Fitzgibbon—who ran a shoe shop on Henry Street behind the General Post Office. (The earliest films of the FCOI were stored in this shop and, ironically, destroyed by fire during the 1916 Easter Rising.) Full of the energy and networking skills that had brought him such success in the United States, the FCOI quickly produced nine short films shot on location in Wicklow and Kerry with J. M. Kerrigan (later a well-resected character actor in Hollywood) as director. The first FCOI film, *O'Neill of the Glen*, premiered with great fanfare and a reception in the Gresham hotel, where Sullivan addressed journalists about the exciting new venture.

While the short films were increasingly well received by critics, Sullivan's ambitions were bigger, and he quickly set in motion plans to produce a feature film, less for profit motives than for Ireland to take its place among the established centers of feature film making, such as the United States and the United Kingdom. In the autumn of 1917, production began on the shooting of *Knock-na-Gow*, an adaptation of Charles Kickham's popular novel, widely considered the most widely read in 19th-century Ireland. It premiered to great fanfare in Dublin on 13 April 1918, and while elements of the British press suggested that the film was "tinged with dangerous political elements," it was mostly well received in its many public performances across Ireland over the following year. Jim Sullivan and his wife Nell then set sail for the United States to tap the lucrative U.S. market for the FCOI films and initially found distribution in the Irish American neighborhoods, schools, and churches on the East Coast. Tragedy, however, struck soon when, having returned to Ireland to rejoin their children, Nell and their infant son contracted tuberculosis and died. Sullivan, a close associate of Michael Collins, then returned to United States in 1919 as representative from the Provisional Government of the Irish Free State.

Still hoping to deliver on his earlier ambitions for an Irish film industry, Sullivan made one more effort to produce a wholly indigenous effort. John McDonagh (brother of the executed Thomas) directed an adaptation of William Carleton's widely known novel **Willy Reilly and His Colleen Bawn** (1920), previously adapted by playwright Dion Boucicault (for stage) and the Kalem film company (for screen). (While shooting the film in Pearse's St. Enda's School, the company also produced a "Republican loan" newsreel featuring Michael Collins and others.) However, it was to be the last FCOI film, and the company was disbanded soon afterward.

With the relative failure of the Easter Rising and a fractious civil war raging and in need of an income to support his surviving daughters, Sullivan left Ireland in 1920 to resume work as a lawyer in New York. A decade later, her retired to Florida, where he died in 1936. His body was subsequently returned to Ireland, and he is buried next to his wife and among the celebrated Irish political figures of 1916 in Glasnevin cemetery. While his contributions to the establishment of a native Irish film industry remain largely overlooked within a wider "failed revolution," his fundamental ambitions and rhetoric continued to echo down the decades and would eventually find fruition with the first wave of Irish filmmakers in the mid-1970s.

FILM EDUCATION. Film and media studies emerged as a degree subject in the late 1970s at the University of Ulster in Coleraine in Northern Ireland and in the republic in the early 1980s at Dublin City University, although colleges such as the National College of Art and Design in Dublin also offered film studies courses from the late 1970s. Most notably, **Lelia Doolan** started a seminal production course in the College of Commerce, Rathmines, which was later co-opted as part of the Dublin Institute of Technology. Film studies as an academic specialty was not established until 1991, when Dublin City University introduced a master's in film (and television), followed a year later by University College Dublin. In 2003, Trinity College Dublin established the first undergraduate degree program in film studies in the Republic of Ireland. Additionally, many of the colleges that developed as institutes of technology—in particular, the National Film School at the Institute of Art, Technology, and Design in Dún Laoghaire—offer specialist undergraduate filmmaking degree courses. As of 2018, virtually every third-level institution in Ireland offers some form of film and media training.

At the secondary level, media and film studies as discrete subjects did not exist at all until recently, and Ireland has been behind most other European countries in developing separate curricula. Efforts to mainstream media literacy as part of the primary- and secondary-level education curricula go back to the 1980s in Ireland. However, it is only quite recently that the state has adopted media literacy as an overt policy objective. In 2011, the Department of Education and Skills published a new National Literacy and Numeracy Strategy, which, for the first time, emphasized media literacy as being among key literacy skills: "the capacity to read, understand and critically appreciate various forms of communications including spoken language, printed text, broadcast media and digital media." In a similar vein, the Broadcasting Authority of Ireland has a media literacy remit under the 2009 Broadcasting Act and has supported several conferences on the subject since 2011. In December 2016, it published a Media Literacy Policy outlining five key media literacy objectives and offered definitions of core competencies for media literacy.

The most coherent and consistent implementation of mandatory media literacy training in Ireland occurs at the primary level as an element of the Social, Personal, and Health Education curriculum, which includes media education as a stand-alone strand. This encourages children to become more discerning in their use of the media and to learn about the techniques and strategies used in advertising and in the media in general. However, media education does not receive extensive attention beyond the primary level.

Although this engagement may be extended at the secondary level, it is not a core element of the curriculum, and students, supported by teachers, must actively choose to study media texts. Furthermore, the approach to media literacy at the secondary level remains focused on training students to critically consume texts rather than producing their own. Although the Junior Cert curriculum for arts, crafts, and design (addressed to 13- to 15-year-old students) includes animation and filmmaking as optional subjects, few Irish secondary schools have the resources to facilitate such education.

The **Irish Film Institute**'s educational outreach work in primary and secondary schools, along with the operation of the "FIS" program (encouraging primary school teachers to oversee student production of audiovisual work), points to an emerging film literacy strategy. However, although the institute reaches some 20,000 students each year through this work, there are more than 900,000 primary and secondary students in Ireland. Similarly, although the FIS program is well established (having been set up in 2000), its annual festival receives 100 entries from primary schools. This is impressive in absolute terms, but those 100 entries represent less than 3 percent of the total number of primary schools in Ireland (3,250 as of 2016–2017).

FILM IRELAND. A film magazine published by **Filmbase**, Dublin. The idea of the magazine began with the 1987 annual general meeting of Filmbase, the then new "low-budget" filmmakers' organization. As *Film Base News*, the journal served as a newsletter for the membership promoting Filmbase's services but also as a space in which to debate and develop responses to Irish screen policy. It also provided an opportunity for critical discussion of the then limited output of Irish filmmakers. These functions came to overshadow its role as a conduit for information about Filmbase, and in 1994, the decision was taken to reflect this broader focus by renaming the publication *Film Ireland*. Its successive editors and contributors offered a critical alternative to the often breathless cheerleading of the industry in the mainstream media. Those editors included **Johnny Gogan** (who subsequently became a filmmaker), Hugh Linehan (now culture editor of *The Irish Times*), and Ted Sheehy (former Irish correspondent for *Screen International*).

Notwithstanding a concerted effort to present Irish cinema as relevant to contemporary Irish audiences (often a thankless task given the difficulty most Irish films found in accessing theatrical distribution), which, by the 21st century, was packaged in well-designed, indeed glossy, packages, *Film Ireland* persistently faced financial pressures and never escaped its reliance on a subsidy from Filmbase itself. By 2013, a cut to Filmbase's funding from the **Arts Council** made it impossible to sustain the publication in print form. Despite this, the publication has continued to operate as an online-only publication (http://filmireland.net) and has continued—albeit in uncertain terms since Filmbase's abrupt closure in March 2018—to be a point of reference for those with an interest in the Irish audiovisual sector.

FILM MAKERS IRELAND REPORT. *See INDEPENDENT TELEVISION PRODUCTION SECTOR REPORT* (FMI REPORT).

THE FILM PRODUCTION INDUSTRY IN IRELAND (REPORT OF THE SPECIAL WORKING GROUP ON THE FILM PRODUCTION INDUSTRY). Taoiseach Albert Reynolds announced the establishment of the Special Working Group on 23 September 1992 at the official opening of the **Irish Film Centre**, adding that he expected a completed report within two and a half months. This short time reflected the fact that the group was not expected to conduct new research but rather to consider the conclusions of the two major reports published in the summer of 1992—the *Coopers & Lybrand Report* and the *Independent Television Production Sector Report*—and to make specific policy recommendations based on those considerations. The group was constituted in such a way as to include persons from virtually every state agency in any way connected with film as well as a smattering of actual filmmakers. The 32-member group thus included civil servants from the Departments of the Taoiseach, Industry and Commerce, Finance, and Tourism, as well as (among others) representatives of the Industrial Development Authority (IDA), **Radio Telefís Éireann** (RTÉ), the **Arts Council**, the **Irish Film Institute**, Film Makers Ireland, and the Irish Film Centre.

The group submitted the report on 24 December 1992, although it would be the new year before its conclusions were made public. The group rehearsed the conclusions of the Coopers & Lybrand and Film Makers Ireland reports for building an argument for state support for the development of employment and economic potential in the audiovisual sector. However, the report also recorded some concerns from the Departments of Industry and Commerce and Finance. Industry and Commerce pointed to the high risk associated with film production and the need, at a time when the state's finances were being tightly squeezed, to ensure that resources were concentrated on those projects with the best chance of yielding *sustainable* employment. The use of "sustainable" clearly expressed Industry and Commerce's doubts about the freelance nature of the industry and may have been influenced in part by the contemporaneous difficulties being experienced in the **animation** sector.

For its part, the Department of Finance's contribution was at pains to stress that the film industry should not receive preferential treatment from the state "because of ill-defined cultural or artistic characteristics."

Despite these caveats, the report argued that the international success enjoyed by Irish and Irish-themed films shot between 1986 and 1991 (i.e., non–Irish Film Board projects) had created a "window of opportunity" for Irish producers and directors. However, since a clear decline in the momentum of activity within the industry had occurred in 1992, there was a risk that the opportunity to exploit the goodwill enjoyed by Irish filmmaking in previous years was fast disappearing and that there was a need for state intervention to ensure that this did not happen.

Specifically, then, the report made five groups of recommendations relating to the role of the IDA, **Bord Fáilte**, the Irish Trade Board, RTÉ, and the State Training Agency; the need to amend the 1990 Broadcasting Act and to establish an Irish-language television channel; the need to amend **Section 35**; the provision of state subventions for developing and producing audiovisual productions; and a set of miscellaneous recommendations relating to European funding and coproduction agreements. Of these, the discussions of tax breaks and state subvention were most significant. On taxes, the group restated the need to extend Section 35 to individuals and to increase the amount of film investment allowed for tax relief. The report stated that a majority of the group favored some kind of annual state subvention to be administered by a specialized agency funded by the Oireachtas. As for which agency, the group considered the Arts Council, the **Irish Film Board**, or a third agency. Although it could see merit in both the Arts Council and the Film Board options, the group recommended establishing a new agency. A new agency could be customized to the conditions relating to film and television production in the 1990s rather than relying on an institution created by legislation drawn up largely in the 1970s. The report also acknowledged that perceptions about the board's past failures might make it politically difficult to revive.

The report went on to make specific recommendations about the level of finance to be made available to the new agency and to suggest that it be subject to periodic review such that, if after five years it was not considered to have been a success from a creative and economic perspective, the agency should be discontinued.

The report's arrival at the Department of the Taoiseach preceded by mere weeks the appointment of **Michael D. Higgins** as the state's first minister for arts and culture. Such was the speed with which Higgins moved to introduce change, however, that by the time the report was ready for general publication, a number of its recommendations were either already in place or had been superseded. Thus, Higgins's introduction to the published version of the report noted the inclusion in the 1993 Finance Bill of changes to Section 35, the introduction of a Broadcasting Authority (Amendment) Bill requiring RTÉ to commission more independent work, and—most significantly—the reestablishment of the Film Board. The last decision, in particular, clearly clashed with the report's recommendation on establishing a new body, suggesting that, for Higgins at least, there were no "perception" difficulties relating to the old Film Board. Nonetheless, the report's stress on reviewing the new board's activities within five years must have created an interesting working environment within that institution.

A FILM WITH ME IN IT **(2011).** A larky Irish crime-comedy of the kind that seems less common than it once did—pace *I Went Down*, *Perrier's Bounty*, *Intermission*, and *Saltwater*. Directed by **Ian Fitzgibbon** and written by Mark Doherty, the film's absurdist plot centers on an accumulation of corpses in the basement flat of failing, boozy writer, Pierce (Dylan Moran), and an equally unsuccessful actor, Mark (Mark Doherty). Reveling in the slacker, politically incorrect persona familiar from his stand-up routine and TV shows, Moran charismatically anchors the incremental mayhem while **Amy Huberman** brings a welcome feminine presence and logic to the proceedings—albeit to limited effect. Combining elements of *Fawlty Towers* and *Withnail and I*, the overall effect is frantic and often very funny without being especially memorable.

FITZGERALD, BARRY (1888–1961). Born to a working-class Dublin Protestant family, brothers William and Arthur Shields (the latter a veteran of the 1916 rising and a screen/stage actor of considerable accomplishment in his own right) are among the most interesting and significant screen actors to emerge in the postindependence era.

Both joined the **Abbey Theatre** on a part-time basis in the mid-1910s. William, then still a full-time civil servant, adopted the stage name Barry Fitzgerald so as not to attract the attention of his employers. While Arthur was often a laconic romantic lead, Barry's comic persona derived and developed from a long tradition of impish characters imagined by Irish dramatists but especially Sean O'Casey, in whose plays he was a defining presence. He played key roles in the stage premieres of O'Casey's *Juno and the Paycock* (1924) and *The Plough and the Stars* (1926) while still only a part-time actor, turning professional at the age of 41, when he made his screen debut in Alfred Hitchcock's 1930 screen adaptation of *Juno*.

Critical success, paired with its financial distress, forced the Abbey to organize several "greatest hits" tours of the United States during the 1930s. On the 1935 tour, Fitzgerald's landmark performance as Fluther in *The Plough* earned him further plaudits, and, to the consternation of the Abbey management, he stayed on to participate in John Ford's 1936 adaptation of the play and to try his luck in Hollywood. After a small role in Howard Hughes's *Bringing Up Baby* (1938), he would star in four more Ford productions: *Four Men and a Prayer* (1938), *The Long Voyage Home* (1940), *How Green Was My Valley* (1941), and *The Quiet Man* (1952). His greatest success, however, came in the Bing Crosby vehicle *Going My Way* (1944), for which he won the Academy Award for Best Supporting Actor and was simultaneously nominated for the **Academy Award** for Best Actor. In this evergreen and hugely popular film, Fitzgerald played Father Fitzgibbon, the elderly immigrant parish priest of St. Dominic's parish who must make way for the reconstruction and social changes of postwar America embodied by the laid-back crooner wisdom of Bing.

Although *Going My Way* was the only occasion when Fitzgerald would play a cleric, there was something priestly about all his roles, whether as the all-knowing matchmaker Michaeleen Og Flynn in *The Quiet Man* or the paternal but cold-eyed Irish detective in Jules Dassin's *Naked City* (1946) and *Union Station* (1950)—unexpected but very successful castings against type. This reflected something inherent in his character: Fitzgerald remained a bachelor all his life, living in Beverly Hills until Parkinson's disease forced him to return to Dublin in the late 1950s. He shared this home with Gus

Tallon, who, the *New York Times* noted, "acts as stand-in, companion and general right-hand man." His last appearance on film was a poignant one: a meeting between himself and Sean O'Casey in 1959 for *Cradle of Genius: Salute to the Abbey Theatre*. It was 35 years since O'Casey had first gifted the actor his great stage roles, and the playwright was shocked by the visible deterioration in Fitzgerald's health. When the actor died in January 1961, O'Casey discovered to his astonishment that he had not forgotten his beginnings and left the fervently socialist playwright, who castigated his "selling out" to Hollywood, $15,000 in his will.

FITZGIBBON, IAN (1962–). A BAFTA-nominated writer/director, most often of distinctively dry, contemporary, and male-centered comedy with notable credits in cinema and TV. Fitzgibbon was born in Dublin and, after spending his childhood in Belgium, graduated from Trinity College Dublin with a degree in languages before training at the Royal Academy of Dramatic Arts, London. This led to an initial career as an actor, principally on English television, with credits including *Prime Suspect* and *Father Ted*.

After directing the short film *Between Dreams*, Fitzgibbon's reputation as a writer/director of contemporary Irish satirical comedy was cemented with the short-lived but widely celebrated mockumentary *Paths to Freedom* (**Radio Telefís Éireann** [RTÉ], 2000), followed by the sitcom *Fergus's Wedding* (RTÉ, 2002) and a spin-off feature film, ***Spin the Bottle*** (2003). Cocreated with actor **Michael McElhatton** (who played the inimitable "Rats" Doyle in the first and last) and produced by **Grand Pictures** for RTÉ, this trilogy of projects turned a cold eye on the excesses of Celtic Tiger Ireland through richly funny portraits of contemporary character types at opposing ends of the social spectrum. And, in spite of its highly specific setting and themes, *Paths to Freedom* was subsequently optioned by Lisa Kudrow, of *Friends* fame, to be adapted for American audiences (no doubt hoping to follow the success of Ricky Gervais's *The Office*). Unfortunately, this unlikely transplanting never came to fruition.

Fitzgibbon's next project was the blackly comic, cruel, and clever feature ***A Film with Me in It*** (2008), starring Dylan Moran, **Amy Huberman**, and Mark Doherty, who also wrote the misanthropic screenplay under the influence of British films such as *Withnail & I*. The film attracted widespread popular and critical praise (including six IFTA nominations) and cleared the way for ***Perrier's Bounty*** (2009), another dark comedy set in a criminal underworld starring **Brendan Gleeson**, **Cillian Murphy**, and Jim Broadbent and also produced by **Parallel Films** from a script by Mark O'Rowe (***Intermission*** [2003] and *The Delinquent Season* [2018]).

Fitzgibbon's third feature represented a change of tone and maturing of his cinematic voice. ***Death of a Superhero*** (2011) was a bittersweet drama about 15-year-old Donald (Thomas Brodie-Sangster), who has been diagnosed with leukemia. Based on the best-selling book of the same name by Anthony McCarten, the story was originally written and set in New Zealand. When Grand Pictures acquired and offered the project to Fitzgibbon, he reteamed with writer Mark Doherty and relocated the film to Dublin. Focusing on the relationship between Donald and his therapist, Dr. King (Andy Serkis), the film interspersed animation with live-action footage to communicate the complex psychological struggles of a male teenage psyche (the "superhero") as he confronts his mortal enemy. Unsentimental and highly creative in its approach to a tragic topic, the film was awarded the Jury and Audience prizes at Les Arcs European Film Festival and subsequently won Best Film and Best Director at the Irish Film and Television Awards along with more than 20 international awards at European film festivals.

Despite this recognition, Fitzgibbon has apparently largely abandoned feature films and returned to (British-funded) TV for subsequent projects. It might be argued, however, that in addition to offering more regular work, episodic TV is more suited to his sensibilities and skill set than the protracted and risky proposition of feature film production. While some of these projects are Irish in focus, it is his talent with comedy and quirky characters that has resulted in a prolific and well-regarded body of work. An extensive résumé includes two seasons of *Threesome* and *Moone Boy: Series 2*, a sitcom about a boy with an imaginary friend written and starring **Chris O'Dowd** for which he won an IFTA as Best Television Director. *The Awkward Age* reunited him with writer/actor Dylan Moran for Sky's *Little Cracker* series, and he has directed two series of *Raised by Wolves* (Big Talk/ **Channel 4**), written by the brilliantly acerbic Caitlin and Caroline Moran.

***FIVE MINUTES OF HEAVEN* (2008).** With the signing of the Good Friday Agreement in 1998 and the subsequent peace process, it seemed inevitable that the cinema of the Troubles would eventually come to include some discussion of how to live in a postconflict society. Yet a decade passed before *Five Minutes of Heaven*, the first major exploration of post-Troubles Northern Ireland, was produced. And, perhaps tellingly, the key behind-the-camera roles were filled by outsiders: an English screenwriter (Guy Hibbert, who also wrote *Omagh* [2004]) and German director Oliver Hirschbiegel (*Downfall* [2004]).

The film is based on two real-life individuals: former Ulster Volunteer Force member Alastair Little (played by **Liam Neeson**) and Joe Griffen (**James Nesbitt**). In 1975, Little shot and killed Griffen's older brother in a sectarian turf war. In 2006, Little, who after 13 years in prison took a new path working in conflict resolution, took part in a BBC documentary about reconciliation called *Facing the Truth*. Little was invited to take part but declined. When the BBC offered Guy Hibbert an opportunity to write a

Troubles-themed drama, Hibbert took inspiration from the documentary and spent several years meeting and interviewing both Little and Griffen to understand the events of 1975 and their impact on their lives afterward.

The first 30 minutes of the film reconstructs the 1975 killing. The final hour, however, is a fictional imagining of what might happen were the two men to meet, using the device of a television documentary as a context for their encounter. An opening sequence cuts between both men en route to their meeting. Little is a professional reformee, well versed in the discourse of trauma and reconciliation. Griffen, by contrast, is nervy, constantly smoking, and clearly damaged by the events three decade earlier (there are repeated flashbacks to his mother blaming him for failing to prevent his brother's death). Yet behind his external facade, Griffen is also damaged: unable to escape the guilt over his actions for even an hour.

As a film on the Troubles, *Five Minutes of Heaven* is unsuccessful in probing the political context for three decades of violence. Although notionally prompted by sectarian politics, Little acknowledges that his willingness to carry out the killing was primarily about achieving status within his community. But explaining the origins of violence is not the primary concern of the film; rather, it is the exploration of the possibility of forgiveness and reconciliation in a community where Loyalists and Republicans, with blood on their hands, live cheek by jowl. The film offers no pat answers or false emotional catharsis: closure is achieved not through reconciliation but through the pragmatic search for coping strategies. And in that respect, at least, the film acts as a kind of critique of those representations of the Troubles that conclude with spurious resolutions of the conflict.

FLANAGAN, FIONNULA (1941–). Born in Dublin and trained at the Abbey Theatre, Flanagan has resided in the United States since 1968 and made her U.S. television debut on *Bonanza* in 1972, the first of more than 40 guest appearances in U.S. television dramas. These included recurrent casting in shows as diverse as *Murder, She Wrote* and three *Star Trek* spin-offs: *Deep Space Nine*, *The Next Generation*, and *Enterprise*. More recently, she has played the domineering mother of an Irish American crime family in *Brotherhood* (2006–2008) and recurring roles in the sci-fi series *Lost* (2007–2010) and *Defiance* (2013) before featuring in the 2017 adaptation of Neil Gaiman's *American Gods* for the Starz network. She won an Emmy in 1976 for a supporting role in *Rich Man, Poor Man* and was nominated again for the television version of *How the West Was Won* in 1978.

Although she won a Jacob's Award for her performance in the screen adaptation of *An Triail* (**Radio Telefís Éireann** [RTÉ]) as far back as 1965, she has rarely featured on Irish television. In 2007, she played the ghost of Peig Sayers in the Irish-language comedy for TG4 and more recently starred in *Redwater* (2017), an RTÉ/BBC coproduction spun off from the popular

U.K. soap *Eastenders*. Onstage, she is regarded as the definitive interpreter of **James Joyce** and received a Tony nomination in 1974 for her performance in *Ulysses in Nighttown*. She cemented her Joycean credentials with her landmark one-person theater show, in which she plays a series of characters—real and fictional—from Joyce's life and works. Flanagan produced a screen version of this performance in 1985 under the title *James Joyce's Women* (she had appeared some 18 years earlier in **Joseph Strick**'s adaptation of *Ulysses*).

Ulysses aside, her big-screen roles were few and far between until the mid-1990s. From that point, she began to appear in a variety of character roles in films such as *The Others*, *Transamerica*, and *The Invention of Lying*. As the Irish film production sector took off in the 1990s, she crossed the Atlantic to appear in a series of comedies (*Man About Dog*, *Waking Ned*, *The Guard*, and *Life's a Breeze*) and to add credibility to Irish-themed international productions, such as *With or Without You* and *Kill the Irishman*. By far her most compelling role during this period came in **Terry George**'s *Some Mother's Son* (1996), in which, reflecting her long advocacy of nationalist politics (a vocal supporter of Sinn Féin), she was well cast as an Irish Republican Army prisoner's mother. As Annie Higgins, she watches her son pursue the hunger strikes of the early 1980s to the bitter end, her performance finely pitched between nationalist militancy and maternal anguish.

FLEISCHMANN, GEORGE (1912–1995). Born in Austria, Fleischmann became interested in film when he worked in a Siemens subsidiary converting silent cinemas to sound. In the early 1930s, he studied as the Berlin Film Academy before joining Universum Film AG, the largest German film production company. He later worked as a cameraman on Leni Reifenstahl's film on the Munich Olympics (*Olympiad* [1936]) and in 1939 won a Gold Medal at the Venice Film Festival for his documentary *Styria*. When the war broke out the same year, he was conscripted and joined the Luftwaffe as an air reconnaissance cameraman. During a sortie over the Bristol channel in April 1941, his Heinkel was damaged by Royal Air Force fighters and crash-landed in a field in Bonmahon, Waterford. Although technically an internee until the conclusion of the war, Fleischmann (like other German internees) was permitted to sign himself out of his camp on condition he promised to return. Thus, he was able to periodically access his camera (retrieved from the wreckage of his plane) to maintain it in working order and to mingle with figures like architect Michael Scott and solicitor Roger Green. When the war ended, rather than return to Germany, Fleishmann stayed on and, with Scott and Green, formed Hibernia Pictures. In that capacity, he worked as a director of photography or a cameraman on a series of government information films, often commissioned by the **National Film Institute of Ireland**. In 1949, he left Hibernia to work on his own, directing newsreel material about

Ireland for Movietone News while continuing to take indigenous work. Indeed, it can reasonably be said that Fleischmann was involved in virtually every significant nonfiction short produced in Ireland from 1948 through the mid-1950s. When the **Cultural Relations Committee** began to commission promotional films about Ireland for overseas distribution, Fleischmann was chosen to direct the first in the series, the elegiac *W. B. Yeats—A Tribute* (1950). He would also act as director of photography on Hilton Edwards's **Academy Award**–nominated short *Return to Glennascaul* (1951). Fleischmann remained a member of Ireland's high-culture milieu through the 1950s, acting as Heinrich Böll's guide during the latter's sojourn on Achill Island (which later resulted in Böll's 1957 *Irish Journal*) and doing second-unit work with **John Huston** on his 1954 production of *Moby Dick*. He appears to have left Ireland in the latter part of the 1950s but returned in the 1960s and picked up where he left off, producing work for Aer Lingus, Bord Fáilte, and the Irish Gas Board. Notable among these was a film commissioned in 1970 by the Department of Foreign Affairs at a point when Ireland was seeking entry to the European Economic Community. *The Saints Went Marching Out* (1970) traced the history of Irish connections with the continent, from medieval missionaries to figures like Francis Taaffe, born in 17th-century Sligo, who founded a dynasty that remained a scion in Austrian politics through the 18th and 19th centuries. By the mid-1970s, Fleischmann was regarded as sufficiently embedded in Irish society to be chosen by 20th Century Fox to direct a 40-minute reflection on the career of former Taoiseach President Eamon de Valera: *Eamon de Valera: Portrait of a Statesman* (1974).

Fleischmann remained in Ireland until the late 1980s, having married Margret McCann, the German-born widow of an Irish doctor with whom he lived for decades in the Killiney House he had designed. He spent his last years in Ontario, Canada (where the couple moved to be close to Margret's son), and he passed away there in early 1995 following a tragic accident.

FORD, JOHN (1894–1973). Among the greatest of American film directors, Ford is also recognized as the quintessential Irish American in Hollywood thanks to frequent treatment of Irish subjects and characters, a carefully maintained "Irish" persona, and a well-publicized fondness for alcohol— both personally and thematically. His Irishness combined ornery "no-bullshit" directness with a romantic, not to say sentimental, worldview that in turn reimagined an essentially colonial doctrine of Manifest Destiny (a term coined by another Irishman, John L. O'Sullivan) in terms of an immigrant yearning for home. These American values found further definition through Ford's unequivocal patriotism before and especially after World War II, sending him and his cameras into the war and inspiring films such as *The Battle of Midway* (for which he won an Oscar), *The Long Voyage Home*, *They Were Expendable*, *Mister Roberts*, and *The Wings of Eagles*.

In 1872, Ford's father, Sean O'Fearna, emigrated from a cottage overlooking Galway Bay and made his way first to Boston and then to Portland, Maine, where he met and married Barbara "Abbey" Curran, a young Irishwoman also from Spiddal (though born on the Aran Islands). Drawing on this collective folklore of migration and new beginnings, their son, Sean "Jack" Feeney (b. 1894), would become a central figure in Hollywood's invention of America's foundation myth: the western. The story goes that Jack was inspired to pursue a career in movies after he saw his older brother Francis on-screen in a local cinema. He promptly abandoned the saloon managed by his father (a setting that would subsequently feature in many of his films), and making use of his brother's contacts and adopted surname Ford, Jack got a job as a bit-part actor before quickly moving to the still-fluid role of director.

Ford's career spans the entire history of Hollywood's studio system: his earliest credit as director was in 1917 (*The Tornado*) and his last in 1966 (*7 Women*). In between, he directed around 130 feature films and won six **Academy Awards**: four for Best Director as well as two more for documentary. Although most of his more than 60 silent films are lost, his first major success is not. *The Iron Horse* (1924) is a spectacular and hugely ambitious two-hour epic saga of the building of the Transcontinental Railroad and an early example of Ford's unmatched feeling for the myth of the West as well as a conception of the United States as a unique environment combining the unmatched "can-do" ambition of the Pilgrim classes with immigrant sweat. It is also notable for the centrality it accords Irish characters, even if here, as throughout his oeuvre, Ford perpetuates stereotypes of the comic and frequently inebriated "Paddy" albeit in a good-natured way.

Although Irish characters were common enough during the 1920s, Ford made a number of explicitly Irish-themed films in the run-up to sound, including *The Prince of Avenue A* (1920), *The Shamrock Handicap* (1926), *Mother Machree* (1928), *Riley the Cop* (1928), and the gothic *Hangman's House* (1928). This last—adapted from a novel by Donn Byrne—showed the strong influence of German expressionism on the director's imagination and artistic development, an influence fomented through his contact with fellow Fox director F. W. Murnau, director of *Nosferatu* (1921) and *Sunrise* (1927). Had the silent cinema endured longer in the United States than it did in Europe, Ford might have developed this style further and perhaps have beaten Arthur Robison to adapting Liam O'Flaherty's novel **The Informer** (1925), which the German director did in a U.K. production in 1929. Ford was nevertheless enthusiastic to bring a sound version of this proto-noir story to the American screen (not least because O'Flaherty was also from Galway/ Aran Islands) and spent several years trying to get it financed. With the help of another Irishman—Joseph Kennedy (father of John F. Kennedy)—RKO reluctantly agreed to put this odd Irish story of political revolution into production on a miniscule budget of $250,000. The effort was worth it, winning four Oscars, including Ford's first as director, and conferring on him the artistic legitimacy he craved. It also commenced his lifelong friendship and collaboration with producer Merian C. Cooper.

The 1930s represented a significant professional deepening of Ford's already profound interest in Irish politics through his relationship with O'Flaherty and his encounter with the touring **Abbey Theatre** production of Sean O'Casey's *The Plough and the Stars*, which he immediately optioned and adapted for the screen in 1936. Although he would be forced to cast Barbara Stanwyck and Preston Foster in the lead roles, Ford developed friendships with several of the Abbey's actors, including **Barry Fitzgerald**, his brother Arthur Shields, Sarah Algood, and Eileen Crowe, all of whom would subsequently pursue film careers. Fitzgerald was retained in the key comic role of Fluther Good, beginning a highly successful career that would lead to an Academy Award for his poignant, scene-stealing portrait of an elderly Irish priest opposite Bing Crosby in *Going My Way* (1945). Arthur Shields would also find success in a number of Irish-themed Ford films, including his adaptation of Eugene O'Neill's *The Long Voyage Home* (1940) and *The Quiet Man* (1952).

In 1957, Ford would enlist many of these players in his first Four Provinces' production *The Rising of the Moon*, a patchy and rather clichéd compendium of three literary adaptations shot mostly on location in Ireland. As the Irish became fully integrated into the hegemonic structures of postwar American society (climaxing in the election of JFK), he also produced a loose trilogy of Irish American–themed stories: the venerated and much-discussed *The Quiet Man*, *The Long Gray Line* (1957), and *The Last Hurrah* (1958). Although very different in themes, setting, and style, these films were unified by a sense of nostalgia and loss located in their respective male protagonists. *The Quiet Man* has been widely discussed and needs little further gloss except to note that while it has often been seen as an immigrant fantasy, it has also been read as a postwar trauma text that prefigures the radically different *The Searchers* (1956). *The Long Gray Line* teamed Tyrone Power and **Maureen O'Hara** for a film based on the true story of Marty Meagher, an Irish immigrant who won the love and admiration of generations of West Point graduates as a physical education instructor. In the film, Ford is again keen to stress how the immigrant Irish balanced and enriched the puritanical instincts of Protestant America, bringing a Catholic tolerance and humanity to Puritan discipline and regimen. *The Last Hurrah* was similarly melancholic, as it marked the passing of the baton from the war-era politics of its protagonist, Frank Skeffington (Spencer Tracy), to a younger generation. Released on the eve of the 1960 U.S. presidential campaign, the film's insight into the new importance of TV in political campaigning was prescient in anticipating the appeal of JFK, whose campaign Ford supported.

Ford would return to Ireland and Irish subjects throughout his life, making his last visit to Dublin in 1965 to shoot *Young Cassidy*, a film based on the life of his longtime correspondent and contemporary (if not actual friend) Sean O'Casey. Unfortunately, he could not complete this opportunity to revisit the controversies around the original staging of *The Plough and the Stars* (which forms a key part of the action), as he had to withdraw after just two weeks of shooting due to ill health and cede directorial duties to Jack Cardiff.

While Ford's visual artistry, gift for casting, and contribution to the western genre have long been celebrated as a foundational elements of Hollywood's iconography, his attitudes to race and women have provoked more negative comment, particularly in recent years. Although many defend his "Irish" sensibility in these areas (meaning that although he may be patriarchal in his attitudes, he is usually so with a wink and a sense of exception), others have been less indulgent. Although we do not directly encounter the racism of D. W. Griffith, it is certainly true that Ford saw his Irishness as offering a "pass" in such matters. Quentin Tarantino, himself no stranger to accusations of racism, put it more directly: "One of my American Western heroes is not John Ford, obviously. To say the least, I hate him. Forget about faceless Indians he killed like zombies. It really is people like that that kept alive this idea of Anglo-Saxon humanity compared to everybody else's humanity."

FOUR PROVINCES LTD. Production company formed in 1954 by Lord **Killanin**, Tyrone Power, **John Ford**, Irish architect Michael Scott, and Irish-born director **Brian Desmond Hurst**. The company was formed to make Irish films and expressed the intention of establishing an Irish studio (pre-**Ardmore**) to be designed by Scott. For a brief period in the mid-1950s, the company promised to form the basis of an Irish film industry, having apparently secured U.S. distribution guarantees (via an arrangement with *The Quiet Man* distributor Republic Pictures) for its work. In addition, since its output would qualify as British quota films (thus securing distribution in the United Kingdom), it appeared that the development of a native film industry might result from the company's endeavors. However, although the company did produce two features—a triptych of shorts directed by John Ford, *The Rising of the Moon* (1957), and a 1964 adaptation of J. M. Synge's *The Playboy of the Western World*—it never engaged in regular production. (As an interesting footnote, the company is still in existence as a production vehicle for Redmond Morris, Killanin's son and sometime **Neil Jordan** producer.)

FRAGMENTS OF ISABELLA (1989). **Ronan O'Leary**'s second feature was based on a stage play, adapted by actress Gabrielle Reidy from the Pulitzer-nominated book by Holocaust survivor Isabella Leitner. Another low-budget shoot for O'Leary, the 80-minute film was completed in a six-day, £150,000 shoot at **Ardmore Studios**. The resulting work is a stark piece that does not seek to disguise its stage origins. The camera focuses on Reidy throughout, who, sitting against a black backdrop, delivers a monologue recounting Isabella's wartime experience from being forced to leave her home in Hungary to being brought to Auschwitz, where she witnesses her mother's death, to her eventual escape while marching to Bergen-Belsen. The resulting sensitively directly film is arguably O'Leary's best-realized work: the beautifully lit (by veteran cinematographer Walter Lassally) monologue sequences operate in stark contrast with grueling documentary footage of the concentration camps.

FRANK (2014). Having attained a high degree of domestic success with his first three Irish-themed feature films, Lenny Abrahamson decided to broaden his narrative canvas and critical reach with his fourth: a musical road movie featuring a number of international stars that begins in the United Kingdom, before moving to Ireland and the United States. Such a description, however, fails to capture the sheer strangeness and originality of *Frank*, a film that centers on a character who spends the majority of the film in a papier-mâché head, played by one of the most physical and in-demand actors in contemporary cinema (**Michael Fassbender**). The perversity of this conceit is entirely in keeping—both thematically and tonally—with the film's questioning of the relationship between creativity and fame, resulting in a film that is intelligently entertaining and subversive. On another level, the film might also be read as both a committed and an ironic bid for wider critical/commercial success on the part of Abrahamson himself.

Frank is a fictional story inspired mostly by Frank Sidebottom, the comic persona of Chris Sievey, and developed by British journalist Jon Ronson from an article he wrote recalling his time in Sidebottom's band. It deals with the (almost accidental) recruitment of an ambitious but talentless keyboard player Jon (played by **Domhnall Gleeson**) into Frank's band (which includes Clara, played by Maggie Gyllenhaal), the subsequent move to Ireland to record an album of songs and the tensions of that process, and the band's journey to the celebrated SXSW (South by Southwest) music festival in Austin, Texas, in search of recognition and success but instead suffering humiliation. Frank eventually runs away but is found by Jon, who recognizes that his ambitions for fame have shattered the fragile, creative dynamic of the band and its members.

FRANKIE STARLIGHT (1995). Based on American writer Chet Raymo's novel *The Dork of Cork*, the film version directed by Michael Lindsay-Hogg stars Matt Dillon, **Gabriel Byrne**, and Anne Parillaud. Set during World War II, it follows Bernadette, an 18-year-old French girl who escapes her war-torn homeland and has a brief liaison with an American GI, resulting in her becoming pregnant before ending up in Ireland. There, she falls under the paternalistic wing of married customs officer Jack Kelly (Gabriel Byrne), who looks after her until the birth of her son—a dwarf—whom he teaches about the stars and nicknames Frankie Starlight. Later, Bernadette falls in love with Terry (Dillon), who brings her and Frankie to the United States. Unable to fit in there, however, Bernadette and Frankie return to Ireland, where Frankie matures into a successful writer.

FRICKER, BRENDA (1945–). As the first (and, to date, only) Irish actress to win an **Academy Award**, Brenda Fricker occupies a critical role in Irish cinema history. Her career spans seven decades, from early appearances in **Radio Telefís Éireann** (RTÉ) dramas to her recurring role in the 2013 Canadian drama *Forgive Me*. Raised in Dublin by her journalist father (Desmond Fricker, who wrote for the *Irish Times*) and a secondary school teacher mother, Bina, both she and her older sister Grainne attended drama lessons at the renowned Ena Mary Burke school on Dublin's Kildare Street. It was Grainne who first won roles on radio, but when she was dispatched to boarding school in Mayo, Brenda was put forward as a replacement. Despite this, the teenage Fricker did not pursue the idea of acting as a career, not least because much of her childhood was spent in hospitals (for kidney failure at seven years old, recovering from a bicycle accident at 14, and contracting tuberculosis at 16). She instead followed her father into journalism, but while she was working at the *Irish Times*, RTÉ director Jim FitzGerald contacted her to offer her a role on the station's first soap opera, *Tolka Row*. That initial tentative foray quickly became permanent as she combined her television work with stage work with the influential Gemini Productions company in Dublin. A move to London theater followed, where she worked first with the Royal Court and later with the National. By the early 1970s, a remarkable run of appearances in British television drama had commenced with roles in *Coronation Street*, *Z Cars*, and *Quatermass*.

The 1980s saw her cast in what arguably remain her three defining roles: as Bridie in the RTÉ/BBC adaptation of William Trevor's *The Ballroom of Romance*, as nurse Megan Roach in the BBC's long-running *Casualty*, and as Bridget Brown in **Jim Sheridan**'s *My Left Foot* (1987), the role that won her the Oscar. These roles reflect the template in which she is often cast: stoic, long-suffering, yet self-assertive characters often in caring/maternal roles: nurses, mothers, and nuns. It is tempting to relate these roles to Fricker's own life experience. As if her recurrent childhood hospitalizations were not enough, she has described her mother as a domineering and sometimes violent presence (though this was countered by the gentle nature of her father). Her marriage to director Barry Davies ended in the late 1980s with Fricker unwilling to tolerate his alcoholism: he would die in 1990 after a fall while she was working in Australia. She has spoken openly of grappling with depression and recurrent suicide attempts.

Although often cast as Irish in U.K. dramas, *The Ballroom of Romance* was her first appearance in an Irish-made drama since *Tolka Row*. Fricker brought dignity and intelligence to the central role of Bridie, a middle-aged woman in 1950s rural Ireland, doomed by social circumstances to either a lonely spinsterhood or making a match with one of the less-than-inspiring remnants of local masculinity. More television work followed, increasingly in recurring roles before, in 1986, she was cast as the Irish nurse Megan Roach in the opening series of *Casualty*, a program that—three decades later—remains at the core of the BBC's drama schedule. Alternately cynical, weary, yet utterly committed to her vocation and in Fricker's hands, Megan became the emotional core of the series until her departure in 1991. (She would return for a poignant one-off finale in 2010.) The decision to leave the series may have been influenced by her Oscar win for the 1989 role of Christy Brown's mother in *My Left Foot*. Fricker's casting was crucial for the relationship between Daniel Day-Lewis's Christy and his mother, which is the core of the film. Eschewing histrionics, the mother–son connection is as much sketched out in sequences of silence as overt declarations and stands in stark contrast with how Christy's father (**Ray McAnally**) relates to his son. (A year later, she would present a defiant presence in the face of unbridled masculinity as Maggie McCabe, the wife of **Richard Harris**'s "Bull" in Jim Sheridan's adaptation of John B. Keane's play *The Field*). Like Bridie in *Ballroom*, Bridget is trapped: this time by poverty, dependence on an alcoholic husband, and her near permanent state of pregnancy. Yet in Fricker's depiction, she remains unbowed: she alone recognizes Christy's fierce intelligence, and it is she who cultivates it.

For a period, the Oscar win brought roles in mainstream U.S. cinema. However, in a town where women are often pigeonholed in mother roles as soon as they hit 30 years of age (Fricker was 45 when she won the Oscar), it was quickly apparent that Hollywood didn't quite know what to do with her. Casting directors defaulted to offering more maternal roles. She played a bag lady dispensing wisdom to Macaulay Culkin in *Home Alone 2* (1992), Mike Myers's tabloid-obsessed Scottish mother in *So, I Married an Axe Murderer* (1993), and a foster mother to Joseph Gordon-Levitt in *Angels in the Outfield* (1994). Occasionally, roles, such as her turn as Mississippi legal secretary in the 1996 adaptation of John Grisham's *A Time to Kill*, hinted at more interesting possibilities: Fricker's calm but compelling dignity threw the film's otherwise often histrionic performances into stark relief.

At home, her newfound stardom also came as something of a gift to casting directors working in the Irish film industry as it emerged in the early 1990s: her now familiar (to Irish and international audiences) face would grace *A Man of No Importance*, *Moll Flanders* (shot in Ireland in 1995), *Resurrection Man*, and *Pete's Meteor* (again opposite Mike Myers in the last). However, she was arguably best deployed in Irish television dramas, heading the cast in RTÉ's *Relative Strangers* (1999) and *No Tears* (2002). Tellingly, in both *No Tears* and the subsequent *Omagh* (2004), she was cast in roles based on real-life characters. *No Tears'* Grainne McFadden was based on Brigid McCole, who died after contracting hepatitis C from blood products provided by the Irish state's blood bank. In *Omagh*, she was imperious as Nuala O'Loan, the real-life Northern Ireland police ombudswoman who criticized the Royal Ulster Constabulary's failure to prevent a horrific Irish Republican Army bombing in 1998. Depicting recent controversies with huge political, social, and personal fallout offered a multitude of hostages to fortune to those unhappy at how those events were presented. Casting Fricker, by then synonymous with integrity, not only immediately deflected the potential for such critique but also contributed to the critical acclaim accorded to both productions.

Fricker retired from acting in 2013, her last major big-screen role as a wife abandoned for a younger woman in *A Long Way from Home*. She lives a modest existence in her home in the heart of Dublin's Liberties. Her Oscar, apparently long used as a doorstop, is now restored to a more dignified setting in her home.

THE FRONT LINE* (2006).** Having combined zeitgeist sexual politics with a drug dealer plot in his well-received debut ***Cowboys and Angels, David Gleeson sought to again combine genre and social topicality in his second feature, *The Front Line*. A German–Irish coproduction the film centers on an African immigrant bank security guard Joe Yumba (Eriq Ebouaney), who turns the tables on some violent Dublin criminals when they force him to be the "inside man" on a bank robbery. The film was among the first (and few) to foreground an asylum-seeking protagonist in an Irish context, and its deeply sympathetic treatment Joe and the criminal exploitation of his vulnerability marked it out as distinctive and relevant. Thematically, *The Front Line* might be compared to Stephen Frears's *Dirty Pretty Things* (2002), which also dealt with the exploitation of an educated and articulate male African trying to survive in a western city (London) and the compromises necessary. While there are fine performances from the film's leads, the screenplay (also by Gleeson) is somewhat underdeveloped and generic, sacrificing character for action in a bid for international audiences. This is a pity since the narrative's focus and themes remain resonant and underexplored.

***A FURTHER GESTURE (THE BREAK)* (1997).** *A Further Gesture* can be read as an interesting albeit ambivalent attempt to imagine a post-Troubles Northern Irish cinema by its coauthors **Stephen Rea** (long a stalwart of the nationalist Field Day cultural project and the source of the story idea) and screenwriter/novelist Ronan Bennett. In a bravura opening sequence, Irish Republican Army (IRA) prisoner Dowd (Rea) and his associate Richard (**Brendan Gleeson**) escape a Belfast prison (a literal if also symbolic gesture) and flee to New York. Dowd takes a job as a hotel dishwasher, but when he is stabbed by a junkie, he is unwilling to see a doctor for fear of being deported and is aided by another hotel employee, Tulio (Alfred Molina), from Guatemala. While recovering, Dowd meets Tulio's sister Monica (Rosanna Pastor), to whom he is attracted, and friend Paco (Jorge Sanz). Dowd learns that the trio plan to assassinate Ramon, a former Guatemalan dictator who killed Monica and Tulio's father. Quickly establishing their unfamiliarity with violence, Sean Dowd agrees to help them avenge their father's death.

Directed by Austrian director Robert Dornhelm (and cofunded by German TV with the **Irish Film Board**), *A Further Gesture* trades on Rea's well-established hangdog persona (familiar to global audiences from his earlier portrayal of another IRA man in ***The Crying Game***). However, although Sean engages in debates concerning the legitimacy of violence, the film is relatively disinterested in politics (either in Northern Ireland or in Guatemala), using the Troubles as the backdrop for a thriller driven by personal rather than political motivation. Its fatalistic conclusion appears to suggest that once an individual has resorted to violence, it is impossible to live outside of it. While on the one hand this might be read as a gloomy commentary on the broader contemporary context of the Northern Ireland peace process, it also contains elements of the familiar redemption-through-violence theme central to revolutionary movements of the 20th century.

G

GAEL LINN. Gael Linn was founded in 1953 by Comhdáil Náisúnta na Gaeilge (National Gaelic Congress). The congress had been founded in the early 1940s to coordinate the promotion of the **Irish language** and culture. Gael Linn was given the remit to use modern media to expand the use of Irish. It commenced film production in 1956 with the production of the *Amharc Eireann* newsreel series. The initial 36 reels (34 of which were directed by Colm O'Laoghaire with **George Morrison** accounting for the remaining two) were produced on a monthly basis, focusing on one topic per film. Thereafter (from 1959), the series moved to a weekly production schedule. Typically running to four minutes in length, each weekly "issue" had to convey news but—with a view to maintaining the interest of a broad-based cinema audience and rejuvenating the Irish language—also had to be entertaining. Thus, an individual issue might cover fashion, church ceremonies, or sporting fixtures alongside politics.

The Irish-language newsreels continued for seven years until 1964, by which time the arrival of **Radio Telefís Éireann** and its news service made them superfluous. Nonetheless, the significance of the newsreels went beyond their purely informational content. *Amharc Eireann* allowed Irish audiences to witness their own way of life through native eyes for the first time since the 1910s. In the longer term, the *Amharc Eireann* material has come to constitute a visual archive of a period of massive change in Irish society and remains the most heavily used source of material from that period for contemporary **documentary** makers.

Gael Linn also sought to financially assist established and emerging Irish filmmakers. To this end, it produced three major documentary films: *Mise Éire*; its 1961 sequel *Saoirse?*, which covered the period from 1917 to 1922; and, in 1966, a special commemorative film on 1916, *An Tine Bheo*.

Louis Marcus, who acted as an assistant editor on *Mise Éire*, subsequently made a series of documentaries for Gael Linn, culminating in his 1973 short *Paistí ag Obair*, which won the Critics' Award at the Cork Film Festival, was screened at the London Film Festival, and finally received an Oscar nomination. Unfortunately, this high point coincided with the end of Gael Linn film production when Roinn na Gaeltachta withdrew the organization's annual filmmaking grant.

GALLAGHER, BRONAGH (1972–). While not the highest-profile film she has ever appeared in, Bronagh Gallagher's feature debut in *The Commitments* (1990) arguably remains her defining role. As Bernie McLoughlin, one of the backing singers in the eponymous band, whose foulmouthed exterior disguised a vulnerable core, Gallagher embodied a defiant, working-class sensibility that she would revisit across a career that has covered film, television, theater, and a high-profile singing career.

Raised in Derry in Northern Ireland, Gallagher developed an interest in drama and music in secondary school, St. Mary's College in Creggan, joining the local Oakgrove Theatre Company before moving to professional work in the **Abbey Theatre**. She was still at school when, at age 17, she auditioned for the role of Bernie, having previously appeared in *Dear Sarah* (1990), **Radio Telefís Éireann**'s take on the Conlon family saga (also the basis for **Jim Sheridan**'s *In the Name of the Father* [1994]). The instant success of *The Commitments* catapulted her and the rest of the cast into public prominence, and a sequence of roles in British drama ensued, leading her to relocate to London for work. It also brought her to the attention of Hollywood, resulting in small but distinctive appearances in massive international hits, playing ingenue addict Trudi in Quentin Tarantino's *Pulp Fiction* (1994) and an ill-fated starship captain in *Star Wars: Episode 1—The Phantom Menace* (1999). (Gallagher briefly lived in Los Angeles but professed not to enjoy the experience.) For the most part, then, though working consistently (with 63 screen appearances between 1989 and 2017), she has generally played smaller character roles, as friend, colleague, or sister (and more recently mother) to the lead character. Although professing a preference for straight roles, she was often used as light relief in dramas or directly cast in feature comedies or sitcoms (*Spin the Bottle* and *The Most Fertile Man in Ireland*). Indeed, though her distinctive facial and vocal presence continues to pepper mainstream international productions (as a colleague to Emma Thompson in *Last Chance Harvey* [2008], a suitable gothic fortune-teller in the Robert Downey Jr. take on *Sherlock Holmes* [2009], and the voice of an elf in *Arthur Christmas* [2011]), her most prominent roles have tended to be in comedy dramas, taking on the recurring role of a 37-year-old grandmother over three seasons of the BBC's *Pramface* (2012–2014), Agent Larsson in the apocalypse comedy *You, Me and the Apocalypse* (2015), and Birdie, a homeless woman seeking companionship in the second series of Graham Linehan's *Count Arthur Strong* (2017).

As one of the highest-profiles actors from the region, she has been a staple of Northern Ireland set work. She shrugged off the Dublin working-class accent acquired for *The Commitments* to reclaim her northern voice as a juvenile delinquent in the Troubles-era *You, Me and Marley* (1992), played the lead role in the BBC's docudrama *Holy Cross* (2003) as a Catholic mother trying to protect her young daughter from sectarian violence, and was a mother again, watching her young son thrill to Northern Ireland's World Cup exploits, in *Shooting for Socrates* (2014).

She's a recurring figure too—again in small but eye-catching roles—in **Irish Film Board**–supported work: girlfriend to **Michael McElhatton**'s Rats in *Spin the Bottle* (2004); Polly in the Maeve Binchy adaptation *Tara Road* (2005); the key role of Cathlemme, the femme half of a 19th-century lesbian couple in *Albert Nobbs* (2011); and landlady Una Maher, facing monsters from outer space in *Grabbers* (2012).

If that volume of work points to a huge work ethic, it's not confined to screen roles. She has been a significant presence in 21st-century theater in Dublin and London and (in David Hare's *Complicit*) on Broadway, book-ended by appearances in Conor McPherson's *Dublin Carol* at London's Royal Court in 2000 and, with **Ciarán Hinds**, the playwright's acclaimed 2017 work *The Girl from the North Country*, based on the songs of Bob Dylan. Growing up in a music-loving family, Gallagher's ambitions in that regard have extended well beyond her role in *The Commitments*. Using downtime between roles to write, she has developed a soul music–based singing career, touring extensively (occasionally appearing with that other *Commitments* alum Glen Hansard) and releasing three well-received albums, including *Precious Soul* (2014) and *Gather Your Greatness* (2016).

GAMBON, MICHAEL (1940–). Gambon appears to be such a quintessentially English actor (he was awarded a CBE by the queen in 1992) that it may come as a surprise to find that he was actually born in the working-class suburb of Cabra in Dublin. Such Irish roots have eased his passage into recent Irish cinema. His parents—an engineer and a seamstress—moved to London at the end of World War II and settled in the suburb of Camden, where he attended a Catholic school. He left at age 15 without qualifications but became an apprentice toolmaker before qualifying as an engineer at age 21. His earliest acting experiences were in an amateur theater run by the local Communist Party office, but he turned professional in 1962, working first at the Gate Theatre in Dublin before joining the English National Theatre under the stewardship of Laurence Olivier in 1963. Until the 1980s, he was known primarily as a stage actor, winning plaudits for his turns in Alan Ayckbourn's *The Norman Conquests* (1974), Peter Hall's production of Pinter's *The Betrayal*, and the critically acclaimed staging of Brecht's *The Life of Galileo* (1980). He was particularly noted for the almost operatic quality of his voice, one capable of filling even large auditoriums, such as the Olivier auditorium at London's National Theatre. However, he had already begun to secure one-off appearances in television dramas by the late 1960s, especially police shows, such as *Softly, Softly* and the BBC's *Play for the Day* series. (He was even considered for the role of James Bond after Sean Connery's [first] retirement from the role but lost out to George Lazenby.) This in turn led to a series of smaller roles in several early 1970s British horror films before playing Irish dramatist Oscar Wilde in the 1976 film *Forbidden Passion*, his first leading role in a feature. More stage and television work followed, and it was not until the mid-1980s that he developed a substantial body of feature film work.

Nonetheless, his stage and television work in this period won him great critical praise, and he won Laurence Olivier Awards in 1986 and 1988 for his roles in the stage productions of *A Chorus of Disapproval* and Arthur Miller's *A View from the Bridge*, respectively, and has been nominated for the same award on four other occasions. In 1986, he also starred in the critically acclaimed BBC production of Dennis Potter's *The Singing Detective*, for which he won Best Actor awards from the British Film and Television Academy and the Royal Television Society.

His breakthrough film role came in 1989 with his performance as the vulgar thief in Peter Greenaway's visually sumptuous *The Cook, the Thief, His Wife and Her Lover* (1989). This brought him to the attention of Hollywood, first in Barry Levinson's *Toys* (1992) and thereafter as a recognizable character actor in films like Tim Burton's *Sleepy Hollow* (1999), Michael Mann's *The Insider* (1999), and Wes Anderson's *The Life Aquatic with Steve Zissou* (2004). Confirmation of his Hollywood star status came when he was chosen to succeed the late **Richard Harris** in the role of Dumbledore in the *Harry Potter* series.

Yet if he is a character actor on-screen, it is hard to identify the character with whom he is consistently identified. Despite his working-class background, aristocratic roles loom large: he has literally played lords in *The Last September* (1999), *Gosford Park* (2001), *Amazing Grace* (2006), *Brideshead Revisited* (2008), and *Victoria and Abdul* (2017). (He also played both Edward VII in *The Lost Prince* [2003] and his son George V in *The King's Speech* [2010].)

Yet the nature of those characters varies—from benign eccentrics in *The Life Aquatic, Quartet* (2012) and the big-screen remake of *Dad's Army* (2016) to much darker characters in *The Insider* and *The Book of Eli*. (In *Gosford Park*, he manages the neat trick of combining both aspects as the apparently harmless yet actually rapacious William McCordle.) These extremes arguably draw on his ethnic roots: as Dumbledore in the last six *Harry Potter* movies, he presented a more aggressive figure than the twinkly-eyed characterization that Richard Harris previously offered. Yet he retained a mischievous tone, noting of his interpretation, "Essentially, I play myself. A little Irish, a little scary."

His first appearance in an Irish film came in 1994, when he appeared opposite Albert Finney's Oscar Wilde–obsessed character in *A Man of No Importance*. This was followed by the role of Leonard, coolly vicious leader of a Loyalist terror gang, in **Thaddeus O'Sullivan**'s *Nothing Personal* and then two quite different roles in **Pat O'Connor**'s *Dancing at Lughnasa* as the amiable Father Jack Mundy and as the scion of an Anglo-Irish family in Deborah Warner's adaptation of Elizabeth Bowen's novel *The Last September*. He returned to the role of gangster—albeit a less menacing one—as Barreler in **Conor McPherson**'s *The Actors*. He had previously worked with McPherson on the latter's version of **Samuel Beckett**'s *Endgame* (2000), which was produced as part of the larger Beckett on Film project that saw all of the playwright's stage works filmed for the big screen. Yet, although he consciously played Dumbledore from 2004 through 2011 with an Irish accent (again in contrast to Harris), his only significant appearance after 2004 in an Irish role came as the patrician Judge Garret Griffin, adoptive father to **Gabriel Byrne**'s pathologist in the eponymously titled BBC/**Radio Telefís Éireann** production *Quirke* (2014). Gambon's description of that character's duplicity perhaps reveals something of the difficulty in pinning down the roles he has chosen: "I like that quality in people: if you look in their faces and you can't quite tell if they're telling the truth or lying to you. That's quite exciting, makes life worth living. So I try to be like that myself."

In 2015, he announced his retirement from the stage due to increasing issues with his short-term memory that made it difficult to recall his lines. He has suggested that he regards himself primarily as a stage actor who takes on screen roles mainly for the accompanying salary. This may simply be another example of his mischievous nature: though his unique personal life sees him supporting two partners, Gambon achieved financial security long ago. Despite this, his screen output, if anything, increased after he turned 70 in 2010. He has taken on recurring roles in six major television series since 2012, including Sky's *Fortitude* (2015) and the BBC's 2018 adaptation of *Little Women*. The rich tones of his voice remain in particular demand, seeing him act as the voice of Uncle Pastuzo in the *Paddington* films (2014 and 2017) and as narrator in the Coen Brothers' *Hail Caesar* (2016) and in *The Death and Life of John F. Donovan* (2018).

GARAGE **(2007).** A full three years separated **Lenny Abrahamson**/Mark O'Halloran's debut *Adam and Paul* from this follow-up feature—testimony to the patience and care that went into its development as well as, perhaps, to their preoccupation with a simultaneous project, the four-part **Radio Telefís Éireann** drama *Prosperity* (2007). Both of these, in different ways, exhibited sensitivity to stories of social marginality in the midst of the Celtic Tiger (that bubble would not burst for a year or so), although *Garage* adopted a more lyrical and, ultimately, enduring approach to its material. Thematically, at least, *Garage* can be viewed as a companion piece to that earlier film focusing this time on rural Irish manhood. In this tale of the single and socially inept Josie, the black humor and philosophical subtext of *Adam and Paul* gives way to a socially aware portrait of the cruelty of small-town life, and homelessness takes on an urgently political resonance.

Pat Shortt plays Josie in a brilliant piece of casting against type that flips this popular performer's long association with a string of Irish "culchies" to reveal a profound pain within rural Irish masculinity. Physically disabled and intellectually slow, Josie tends a gas station for owner Mr. Gallagher, living on the premises in deprived and dilapidated conditions that reflect his wider status. The butt of jokes at the local pub, Josie nonetheless persists with small improvements to the business—notably a preoccupation with engine oils and opening hours—to the indifference and bemusement of the owner. Meanwhile, Gallagher's nephew is given a summer job alongside Josie, who clumsily tries to bond with the younger man by sharing cans of beer and a pornographic video. This brings a complaint to the local police and a caution. Although deeply embarrassing for a sensitive soul like Josie, this is the least of his worries, as Gallagher subsequently tells him that the garage will soon be closing to make way for redevelopment. *Garage* ends on a similarly bleak note to its predecessor, evoking a cruel and contemptuous Ireland that also leaves its central character with nowhere to go at its conclusion. It thus finds a commonality with many Irish films of the early 2000s (while taking inspiration from the earlier writings of McGahern, Murphy, John B. Keane, and others) that attempt to make sense of post–Celtic Tiger Ireland through male protagonists and their relationship to spaces of home (*Parked*, *Pilgrim Hill*, and *Out of Here*). Josie is a man out of time and place, superfluous to a shift from industrial to postindustrial modes of capitalism.

THE GENERAL (1998). **John Boorman** directed **Brendan Gleeson** in a sympathetic portrayal of the real-life figure of Martin Cahill (aka "The General"), a leading Dublin criminal who was murdered in the mid-1990s. Working from the biography by Dublin crime journalist Paul Williams, Boorman is at pains to put Cahill's criminality into a social context, portraying the young Cahill as the product of extreme poverty. This is tacitly recognized by Cahill's lifelong antagonist, Inspector Ned Kenny (Jon Voight), who maintains a grudging respect for the criminal even while trying to catch him.

However, in contrast to **Thaddeus O'Sullivan**'s more Hollywood-style take on the same person (*Ordinary Decent Criminal*), there is no attempt to sanitize Cahill's character: his willingness to resort to brutal methods, for example, is vividly depicted. Furthermore, although the film celebrates Cahill's single-minded determination to live his life according to his own precepts (Cahill maintained simultaneous relationships with two women [both of whom lived with him] and the children by the respective relationships), he is not depicted in a heroic mode: the film's grisly conclusion amply demonstrates how badly he has underestimated the lengths to which the state and paramilitary organizations are willing to go to "remove" him.

Having shot the film in color, Boorman decided to desaturate the film in postproduction, rendering the finished picture black and white. The effect is to afford the story a deeper sense of social realism and avoid what Boorman termed the prettification and romanticization of poverty. He was also at pains to distance the story from conventional gangster tropes: "We're not fucking Eye-talians," exclaims Cahill when one of his henchmen attempts to embrace him.

The film was critically regarded as a return to form for Boorman after the disappointing performance of films like *Where the Heart Is* (1990) and *Beyond Rangoon* (1995). *The General* earned him Best Director nominations in a number of festival and critic awards, and he won Best Director at the 1998 Cannes Film Festival. Surprisingly, this was the director's first film with an overtly Irish setting, although he had lived in the country for more than three decades.

THE GENTLE GUNMAN (1952). Scripted by Roger McDougall from his play and produced at Ealing Studios by Michael Balcon Productions, the film features a stellar cast of John Mills, Dirk Bogarde, Elizabeth Sellers, and Gilbert Harding. Directed by Basil Dearden, it tells the story of Terry, who, after working undercover in wartime London, reconsiders his support for the Irish Republican Army (IRA) and questions the need for violence to achieve independence. However, by adapting a position of peaceful persuasion, he is soon branded a traitor by his brother and more hard-line IRA colleagues.

GEORGE, TERRY (1952–). Terry George's coming of age in Northern Ireland as the Troubles erupted at the end of the 1960s clearly influenced his decision to concentrate his filmic output in politically turbulent conflict zones ranging from the Vietnam War to genocides in Rwanda and Armenia. Born and raised in Belfast, he began work as a civil service draftsman. In 1971, he was arrested without trial and held for eight weeks. Four years later, having become involved with the Irish Republican Socialist Party (IRSP), the political wing of the paramilitary Irish National Liberation Army, he was again arrested for sharing a vehicle with armed members of the IRSP. Sentenced to six years in prison, he ended up in the Long Kesh (alongside future Sinn Féin leader Gerry Adams) but was released for good behavior in 1978. After completing a degree at Queen's University Belfast, he moved to the

United States with his family to become a journalist and writer. He became involved in New York's Irish Arts Center (along with **Jim Sheridan**) and in 1985 saw his first play, *The Tunnel*, produced, based around an attempt to escape the Long Kesh.

That early experience was clearly pivotal for George: as he has noted in an interview, it brought a particular insight to his understanding of political conflict, one that emphasizes the perspective of the victim rather than re-hearsing the official—often state-sanctioned—version of history. This was immediately obvious in his first feature screenplay. The Sheridan connection led to an offer to adapt the autobiography of Gerry Conlon, one of four people falsely convicted of carrying out a pub bombing in Guilford in 1974. The resulting *In the Name of the Father* (1994), directed by Sheridan, was the first of three Troubles-set dramas for George. He subsequently directed his own screenplay for *Some Mother's Son* (1996), depicting the early 1980s hunger strikes in the Maze prison as Republican prisoners sought to gain political status. Although condemned as Irish Republican Army (IRA) propaganda by some U.K. critics, the film was—given George's personal history—remarkably evenhanded in its account of the politics of the strikes. Although the British government clearly emerges as the main villain of the piece, the film also pointedly emphasizes the how Republican politicians sought to exploit the deaths of the hunger strikers for political gain. Two years later, his screenplay for another Jim Sheridan–directed work, *The Boxer* (1997), depicted the challenges of seeking to navigate a neutral path through the politics of Northern Ireland. Inspired by the story of Northern Irish boxer Barry McGuigan, George built the film around the character of Danny Flynn (Daniel Day-Lewis), a former IRA man seeking to escape the political violence of his past through a career in the ring.

The Boxer proved to be George's last feature-length engagement with Ireland on-screen to date. He followed it with an adaptation (which he also directed) of Neil Sheehan's best-selling *A Bright Shining Lie*, about the experiences of U.S. Army Colonel John Paul Vann during the Vietnam War. He then moved to a different war zone—Washington, D.C., then the city with highest crime rate in the United States—for *The District* (2000–2004), a police series he cocreated with Jack Maple for CBS. Maple was a former New York City police commissioner whose experience grappling with the bureaucracy and politics of policing underpinned the dramatic concerns of the series. George wrote only six of the 81 episodes, allowing him time to work on parallel projects, such as the screenplay for the **Colin Farrell** World War II drama *Hart's War* (2002).

George's later work arguably returned him to the thematic concerns of his works on Northern Ireland: the study of state violence and repression as visited on subaltern populations. *Hotel Rwanda* (2004), arguably his most critically and commercially successful film as a director, was set within the turbulent violence of Rwanda following the assassination of President Habyarimana in 1994, which sparked ethnic majority Hutu extremists to begin a systematic genocide of nearly a million Tutsis and moderate Hutus. Although the film features Nick Nolte, Joaquim Phoenix, and Jeno Reno in prominent roles, it is notable for the manner in which it avoided the all-too-common resort of foregrounding a U.S. or European protagonist to make a "foreign" film relevant for Western audiences. George tells the story through the perspective of the African characters (albeit played by U.S. and U.K. actors Don Cheadle and Sophie Okonedo), focusing on the real-life character of Paul Rusesabagina (Don Cheadle), who turns the hotel he manages into a sanctuary for those seeking to escape the slaughter.

George would return to genocide in 2016 for his account of the slaughter of 1.5 million Armenians from 1915 on at the hands of the Turkish state. In embarking on *The Promise* (featuring Oscar Isaac, Charlotte Le Bon, and Christian Bale), George again demonstrated his commitment to revealing hidden histories: the events of the genocide are not widely known in the West, not least because successive Turkish governments have consistently denied they ever occurred. Major studios proved reluctant to embrace the controversial subject matter, and it took the involvement of veteran Hollywood player Kirk Kerkorian, former owner of MGM and himself of Armenian descent, to finance the picture.

George's work has been consistently recognized within the Hollywood community: among other ceremonies, he has been nominated three times for an **Academy Award**, including as screenwriter on *In the Name of the Father* and *Hotel Rwanda*. Ironically, however, it was for his perhaps most straightforward work, *The Shore* (2011), that he actually won the Best Short Film Oscar in 2012. A comedy-drama about the prodigal return of Jim (**Ciarán Hinds**) to the small Northern Irish fishing village that he departed three decades earlier during the Troubles, *The Shore* is a likable if slight work and stands in stark contrast to the turmoil of most of George's feature-length output.

GILLEN, AIDAN (1968–). In an interview, Aidan Gillen has described the trajectory of his acting career as more "pinball" than "linear." This reflects a list of credits that in recent years has seen him intersperse high-profile roles in HBO's *Game of Thrones* and the BBC's *Peaky Blinders* with work in ultra-low-budget Irish features and shorts. His international work—most prominently as Petyr Baelish in *Game of Thrones*—has established an on-screen persona as sly and untrustworthy though, almost in spite of himself, occasionally driven to undeclared adherence to moral codes. However, his filmography includes a whole swath of roles in experimental (and often low-budget) work that are harder to pigeonhole, suggesting that his potential in mainstream screen appearances has not yet been fully exploited.

The youngest member of a family of six from Drumcondra, Aidan Gillen was born Aidan Murphy but later changed his name to avoid confusion with an established actor of the same name. He started acting as a child with the Dublin Youth Theatre, which used the Project Arts Centre for many of their performances. Consequently, he was exposed to productions by other companies using the same theater, such as the early work of the Rough Magic and Passion Machine companies. His film debut came at age 18 with a bit part in Jack Clayton's *The Lonely Passion of Judith Hearne*, which he followed with another small part in **The Courier** (1988).

Having moved to London, his breakthrough role involved a return to the stage in 1988, when he secured a part in a production of Wexford playwright Billy Roche's *A Handful of Stars* at the Bush Theatre. After he reprised the role for a television version, British director Antonia Bird cast him in a lead role in her homelessness drama *Safe* (1993). This was followed by a series of roles in Ireland, including **Circle of Friends** (1995) and **Gold in the Streets** (1997), and the key role of a hunger striker in **Some Mother's Son** (1996).

For some time, he was best known in the United Kingdom for his portrayal of Stuart, the abrasively charming, hedonistic gay man at the center of **Channel 4**'s *Queer as Folk* (1998–), a role he embraced with relish. His then domicile in North London with his family saw *Folk* followed by a number of low-budget independent pictures.

The 21st century saw him increasingly work in the United States. Following a made-for-TV movie, *The Darkling* (2000), he has worked on Broadway, earning a Tony nomination for his role in a production of Harold Pinter's *The Caretaker*. A turn in the Jackie Chan vehicle *Shanghai Knights* (2003) was followed by his then highest-profile U.S. role: Baltimore city council member (and later mayor) Tommy Carcetti in the last three series of the hit HBO series *The Wire*. Although this was interspersed with some appearances in Irish film—most notably in the well-received *Burning the Bed* (2004) and Fintan Connolly's second feature, **Trouble with Sex** (2005)—he was absent from Irish material between 2005 and **Wake Wood** (2009).

Gillen's Carcetti in *The Wire* is far from being a straightforward villain of the piece. He starts out as ambitious yet idealistic, and it is the realpolitik of Baltimore government that sees him make one deal after another with the devil in a bid for personal advancement. By contrast, his other mainstream roles depict him as malevolent, from his early turn as "Baby," a narcissistic psychopath in *Mojo* (1997); his corrupt cop Puttnam in *My Kingdom* (2002) opposite **Richard Harris**; and the sneering aristocrat Rathbone in *Shanghai Knights* (2003). Even when playing notionally "good guy" roles, as with his Central Intelligence Agency (CIA) operative in *The Dark Knight Rises* (2012), he is rarely sympathetic: the audience virtually cheers as Tom Hardy's Bane consigns the CIA agent and his crew to a fiery death.

Physically slight, the malignancy of Gillen's characters is expressed less through violent action and more through psychological subterfuge and cruelty. There is an almost feline quality to his roles as Littlefinger in *Game of Thrones*, the duplicitous Janson in the *Maze Runner* films (2014–), and the gypsy Aberama Gold opposite Cillian Murphy in the final series of *Peaky Blinders* (2014–2017).

To an extent, that smirking, sinister persona appears to have influenced his casting in higher-profile Irish roles since 2010. These include crime boss John Boy Power in **Radio TeIefís Éireann**'s hit series *Love/Hate* (2010–2013) and his turn as the corrupt real-life former Irish Taoiseach Charlie Haughey in the same channel's *Charlie* miniseries (2015). Arguably, they are present too in his appearances in *Calvary* (2013) as the cynical surgeon who tortures **Brendan Gleeson**'s priest with tales of botched operations on children and even as the egocentric father in **John Carney**'s *Sing Street* (2015).

Yet while moving from one iconic television show to another, Gillen has found time to take on less showy roles in lower-profile productions. And, arguably, these are his most interesting. His three collaborations with director Jamie Thraves—*The Low Down* (2000), *Treacle Jr.* (2010), and *Pickups* (2017)—point to if not quite a more lighthearted persona, then certainly one willing to poke fun at himself. In *The Low Down*, he plays an actor called Aidan Gillen, who other characters consistently recognize as "that fella off the telly" before changing their minds on the grounds that he looks too old. In *Treacle Jr.* (2010), arguably his most off-kilter but also most affecting performance role, he plays the intellectually challenged man Aidan Murphy (his real name), who strikes up a brief acquaintance with Tom (Tom Fisher), a man trying to escape the constraints of his humdrum existence. This far more sympathetic screen persona is evident too in his roles in Irish works, such as **Mister John** (2013) and **You're Ugly Too** (2015). In the former, he leaves his family in London to attend the funeral of his brother in Singapore. (Loss—of a daughter and wife, respectively—is also visited on his characters in *Wake Wood* and *Mayday* [2013].) Escaping the obligations of daily life, he commences an aimless odyssey through the seamier sides of Singapore, ultimately confessing to his brother's widow that "he doesn't know what he's doing anymore." The same is broadly true of Will in *You're Ugly Too*, where he tentatively—and belatedly—seeks to become a paternal figure to his orphaned niece. Although his machinations as Littlefinger render him a compelling figure in the *Game of Thrones* universe, it is these latter roles that point to a far wider range than hinted at by his appearances in better-funded productions.

GILLIGAN, DONAL (1964–2010). Besides its inherent importance on personal and professional levels, Gilligan's career is illustrative of the tensions and trajectory of the post-1993 upsurge in Irish filmmaking activity. Beginning as a clapper loader on *Hear My Song* (1991), he made an immediate and memorable impact with three films, beginning with Stephen Bourke's awarding-winning short film *After '68* (1994), set during the civil rights movement in Northern Ireland. His careful and sensitive lighting work on Kevin Liddy's short film *Horse* (1994) the following year won plaudits for the manner it bathed the screen in rustic tones that perfectly served its brutal yet nostalgic story. During the same period, he contributed a strongly cinematic feel to what is arguably **Joe Comerford**'s best film, *High Boot Benny* (1993).

While he subsequently secured work on that portion of Steven Spielberg's *Saving Private Ryan* (1998) that was shot in Wexford, he was now an assistant camera operator, a demotion that was common among Irish technicians of the time working on foreign films made in Ireland. Then, as his career moved into the 21st century, he became one of the most in-demand of Irish cinematographers, his growing experience and confidence reflecting that of the wider industry. In the decade between 2000 and his untimely death in 2010 aged just 46, he clocked up 27 credits, spanning shorts, documentaries (perhaps most notably with **Pat Collins**, with whom he collaborated on three occasions), and an increasing number of high-profile Irish television drama productions, including **Radio Telefís Éireann**'s *Raw* and *Love/Hate*. He was also noted for his feature work, collaborating with a rising tide of new directors: **Conor McPherson** (*Endgame* [2000]), Robert Quinn (*Dead Bodies* [2003]), Tom Collins (*The Boys of St. Columbs* [2009]), and Kieron J. Walsh on four occasions between the Beckett adaptation *Rough for Theatre I* (2000) and *Kitchen* (2007). He was nominated on three occasions for an Irish Film and Television Best Cinematography award, including posthumously for *Love/Hate* in 2010. Gilligan was not only talented but immensely liked in the tight-knit local industry and his passing shocked and deeply saddened also those he had worked with in a career spanning barely two decades.

GILSENAN, ALAN (1962–). Gilsenan's work as a documentary and fiction feature writer and director is so wide ranging (he has directed around 30 screen works alongside extensive theater work) as to be almost impossible to summarize. But, if pressed, one might point to a consistent reluctance to pronounce judgment on his subjects—fictional or otherwise. The eye of his camera adopts a compassionate gaze on individuals who are often in extremis, somehow rendering the most painful moments of life and death more tolerable, encouraging the viewer to engage with experiences we might otherwise prefer to look away from.

Initially raised in a semirural setting in Crossakeel, County Meath, Gilsenan's family moved to Raglan Road when he was a child after his father took up a job with the Turf Club (the Irish horse-racing regulatory body). He attended St. Conleth's, a private school in Ballsbridge and one too small, as Gilsenan has pointed out, to support cliques. Although not particularly a film buff, he instinctively understood from his teenage years that he wanted to write and direct, and he did so, producing his own amateur productions. An academically gifted student, he graduated with a first-class honors degree in English and sociology from Trinity College Dublin and in 1984 won the inaugural A. J. Leventhal Scholarship funding travel to Europe. While still in college, he directed two shorts: *Shelia* (from his own script) and a version of Samuel Beckett's 1966 short play for television *Eh Joe*. Keen to create a vehicle that would permit him creative independence, in 1986, he and producer Martin Mahon established a production company, Yellow Asylum, a moniker with resonances for his later work.

His first major breakthrough came in 1988 when **Channel 4** sought submissions from Irish filmmakers for their "Irish Reel" documentary series, undertaken as part of the channel's commitment to addressing the interests of ethnic minorities in the United Kingdom. Yellow Asylum proposed a state-of-the-nation film, composed largely of talking heads from across the spectrum of Irish society, juxtaposing the "official-speak" of representatives from political parties and industrial development bodies with the marginalized and those dependent on social welfare for survival. Made at a point of economic and social crisis, *The Road to God Knows Where* managed both to reflect the bleak reality of contemporary Ireland and to highlight how the nation's potential creative energy was desperately seeking an outlet. However, what set the film apart was its distinct visual look: the interviews were interspersed with shots of urban desolation carefully lit to evoke a postapocalyptic landscape. Gilsenan's conjuring of a deliberately nonnaturalistic vision of Ireland seemed to suggest that the "real" truth about the country could not be found in any one interview or even the combination of a multitude.

Unusually well resourced (Channel 4 offered a UK£150,000 budget), *The Road to God Knows Where* was critically acclaimed, winning its director both a European Film Award and a Jacobs Award in Ireland. It also won him a—probably undeserved—reputation as something of an angry young man. In person, Gilsenan is, though physically imposing, thoughtful and soft-spoken. He is also far from a knee-jerk radical: though work like *Prophet Songs* (tackling the issue of disenchanted priests who left the Church) may critique institutions such as the Catholic Church, he has argued for an acknowledgment of the role played by Catholicism and nationalism in the making of modern Ireland, suggesting that these broader identities cannot simply be casually discarded in the headlong pursuit of modernity. (The sense that he is unlikely to throw the toys out of the pram is also reflected in a sequence of appointments to influential roles: he has, at various times, sat on the **Irish Film Board** and the **Radio Telefís Éireann** (RTÉ) Authority and was chair of the **Irish Film Institute** in the early 2000s.)

His screen works have been mainly documentaries. Beyond his subsequent forays into state-of-the-nation documentaries (*Road II* [2001] and *The Importance of Being Irish* [2008]), these are marked a persistent concern with biography, as attested to by a sequence of bio-docs on both prominent and less-well-known figures from Ireland's past and present, including Tom Murphy (*Sing On Forever* [2003]), Paul Durkan (*The Dark School* [2007]), Liam Clancy (*The Yellow Bittern* [2009], and Eliza Lynch (*Queen of Paraguay* [2013]). These biographies are paralleled by a second thematic thread running through his work: a focus on the marginalized and the forgotten. *Stories from the Silence* (1990) was the first major exploration of the reality of HIV/AIDS in Ireland, his award-winning short *Zulu 9* (2001) looked at Ireland's attitude toward immigrants, while *The Home* (2010) and *The Hospice* (2007) offered, respectively (and respectfully), fly-on-the-wall perspectives on the experience of being old and on preparing for death in Ireland. (Gilsenan has spoken of how his choice of subject is often inspired by his direct life experience: in this regard, *The Hospice* followed Gilsenan's experience of watching his own mother's last days in a similar institution.)

Within that second thread, a survey of Gilsenan's oeuvre points to a recurring subtheme: mental health and mental illness. *The Hospice* and *The Home* formed a kind of institutional trilogy with *The Asylum* (2005), his groundbreaking and compassionate study of St. Ita's Psychiatric Hospital Mental in North Dublin. This was followed in 2009 by *I See a Darkness*, a three-part series for RTÉ on suicide and the feast for the eyes that is his Festschrift for maverick psychiatrist Ivor Browne in *Meetings with Ivor* (2017). Strikingly, three of his four fiction feature works released to date—*All Souls' Day* (1997), *Timbuktu* (2004), and the 2016 Canadian production *Unless* (2016)—are also centered around characters with some form of mental illness.

That institutional trilogy exemplifies both Gilsenan's sympathy with and his capacity to win the trust of his subjects, gaining him access to some of the most intimate moments ever presented on Irish screens. In *The Hospice*, one of his terminally ill subjects, a young woman, discusses with him how he should film her after her death. Even more remarkably, after her passing, her family invited Gilsenan to film her body in private (without their presence) to complete her narrative.

Visually adventurous, his works are often characterized by the juxtaposition of different formats—Super 8, 16 mm, and digital video—in a manner that both suggests simultaneous multiple perspectives on his stories and emphasizes how memory—indeed, how competing remembered accounts of the same events—informs his narratives.

This is particularly evident in Gilsenan's first fiction feature, *All Souls' Day*, a low-budget (IR£60,000) work indirectly influenced by Oscar Wilde's *Ballad of Reading Gaol* (and, in particular, the line "Each man kills the thing he loves"). A formally experimental work, with an elliptical narrative, the film follows Maddie (Jayne Snow) as she travels to a prison to visit Jim (Declan Conlon), the man accused of murdering her daughter (and his girl-friend) Nicole (**Eva Birthistle**) in an attempt to understand his actions. He begins telling the story of their relationship, and as he does so, the film stock becomes grainier, placing a temporal distance between the characters and the narrated events. His explanation for his action, however, is obtuse and vague, although it ultimately implicates the mother in his actions. She comes to the prison seeking clarification, a straightforward explanation for her loss; instead, the very narrative of the film itself denies such a neat closure, hinting at the ephemerality and contingency of events.

Similar themes are present in Gilsenan's second feature, *Timbuktu*. Although reminiscent in ways of his 1999 documentary *Julie's Journey*, which traces the story of a modern Irish woman who traveled to Japan to become a Buddhist, *Timbuktu* is based on a screenplay by screenwriter Paul Freaney. Set in Algeria (although shot in Morocco), the oblique narrative explores the contemporary global issues within Irish identity using a very broad geographical and experimental canvas. Three childhood friends, all victims of an unspeakable childhood trauma, embark on voyages to rediscover their own identities, transforming the film into a kind of road movie albeit one where it is never clear if the final destination has been reached.

To date, Gilsenan has almost exclusively worked within Ireland, at least partly because the country continues to throw up subjects that drawn his attention. In 1994, **Channel 4** offered him the chance to make a series about another culture: America. The result, *God Bless America* (1994), was a six-part series looking at American cities through the eyes of writers like Gore Vidal, Garrison Keillor, and Patricia Cornwell. Although a success, it did not encourage him to remain overseas. Even after he began a relationship with one of his subjects—Marsha Hunt—it was she who followed Gilsenan back to his home in Wicklow rather than his staying in her native Philadelphia. Although now married to dancer Catherine Nunes and ensconced in Enniskerry with their family, Gilsenan is clearly increasingly open to overseas projects. Although his most recent feature—*The Meeting* (2018), based around the real-life encounter between a victim of sexual assault and her attacker after he is released from prison—was shot in Ireland, he spent several years developing an adaptation of Carol Shields's Toronto-set novel *Unless*, which he finally filmed there in March 2016. Its location aside, *Unless* continues Gilsenan's career-long exploration of liminality and uncertainty.

GIVE UP YER AUL SINS (2001). The making of one of Ireland's first **Academy Award**–nominated animations almost deserves a documentary of its own. In 1961, Peig Cunningham, a teacher at Rutland Street Primary, a Dublin inner-city school, acquired a reel-to-reel tape recorder and encouraged her pupils to recount their versions of tales from the Bible. The often muddled accounts, declaimed in strong working-class Dublin accents, offered a unique perspective, one that captured and revealed more about the youthful tellers of the tale than the characters they described. Yet the tapes lay largely forgotten until happened across by the media-savvy priest Father Brian D'Arcy in his Booterstown parish office in the mid-1970s. D'Arcy tracked down Cunningham, and over the course of the following decade, excerpts from the tapes were played on Irish radio to mostly comic but also nostalgic effect. In 1990, EMI acquired the rights to the full sequence of recordings, releasing them on cassette and later CD. Cathal Gaffney of **Brown Bag** animation encountered the recordings in the same way most Irish people did: via a radio broadcast. Spotting the potential for an animation adaptation, he negotiated rights with EMI and acquired funding from the **Irish Film Board** via its Frameworks scheme.

Selecting a recording voiced by the then eight-year-old Carmel Bride as she offers her version of the story of John the Baptist, Gaffney produced a four-minute short that uses a simple sepia-tinted 2-D animation style to depict not only Bride's story but also the setting (1960s Dublin and Carmel's classroom) in which the story is told. Screened at the Cork Film Festival and the Galway Film Fleadh (Festival), the film's earnestly told but inadvertently hilarious narration proved an immediate hit and led to an Oscar nomination for Best Animated Short.

Although Pixar's *For the Birds* (2001) actually won the category, the film had a mixed impact on Brown Bag. Cathal Gaffney noted how, for a period, Irish advertising companies (then the main clients for Brown Bag) seemed reluctant to approach the company, apparently believing that their Oscar experience would be reflected in higher rates. However, the nomination also led to an approach from **Radio Telefís Éireann** to expand the concept into a full-length series (subsequently released on VHS and DVD), and in the longer term, given that serial production for (mainly U.S.) television would become the core of Brown Bag's activities, *Give Up Yer Aul Sins*'s initial success helped place the company on the radar of key commissioners of work, such as the Walt Disney Company.

GLASSLAND (2015). Although a significant step up in in terms of budget (to a still ultra-low €250,000) and cast from director **Gerard Barrett**'s debut *Pilgrim Hill* (2013), *Glassland* shares with that film a concern for the socially marginalized albeit this time in an urban setting.

John (**Jack Reynor**) is a taxi driver in his early 20s living with his mother Jean (Australian actress Toni Collette) on a council estate in a deprived Dublin suburb. Jean is a mess: abandoned by her husband 18 years previously after their second son, Kit (Harry Nagle), was born with Down syndrome, she has become a full-tilt alcoholic, literally drinking herself to death. In an early scene, John returns home from a shift to find her passed out in a pool of her own vomit. With revealingly practiced ease, he gets her to the hospital, where he is told that she will probably die without a liver transplant. On their return home, a less-than-grateful Jean goes into a furious rage when she can find no alcohol in the house. Still devoted to her, John finds a private recovery program but must raise €8,000 to pay for it. An oblique Faustian pact ensues that sees him secure the money without fully understanding the nature or depth of the debt he has taken on.

The exploration of the child–parent bond is at the core of *Glassland*, even if in the case of John and Jean those roles are reversed: she is the childlike figure dependent on him for emotional (and financial) support. John's only relief from his domestic obligations is his friendship with Shane (Will Poulter), himself a young father, unwillingly estranged from his former girlfriend and their toddler son. Although such bonds are not inviolable—witness the absence of John's father and Jean's reluctance to acknowledge Kit—John remains compassionately committed to his mother in the face of her verbal violence and self-destructive streak. She is the key figure in his life, and Reynor and Collette (both superb) create a compelling mutually dependent relationship: Barrett is careful to include quiet moments of warmth and connection between the pair and even includes a sequence where John drinks with his mother, not as an enabler but in a recognition both that alcohol offers a temporary respite for her and that a drunken connection is better than none. Indeed, the film also works as a provocative study of addiction and the impossible choices it poses for those orbiting around the addict.

For the most part, Barrett's low-key shooting style—a static camera distantly observing the John–Jean interactions—works to show rather than explain the core relationships. At times, however (and, in particular, toward the conclusion), this dispassionate recounting of narrative events complicates viewer comprehension, and the audience must actively join the dots to make sense of the final denouement. Nevertheless, the overall work stands as a powerful study of lives lived in a quiet, desperate extremis.

GLEESON, BRENDAN (1955–). Although American audiences may not necessarily be able to immediately name him, they will almost certainly recognize Brendan Gleeson. He has never enjoyed the kind of star billing in Hollywood productions of contemporaries such as **Pierce Brosnan** or **Liam Neeson,** but a wide range of character roles opposite the likes of Leonardo DiCaprio (*Gangs of New York* [2002]), Matt Damon (*Green Zone* [2010]), and Tom Cruise (twice: *Mission Impossible II* [2000] and *Edge of Tomorrow* [2014]) have made Gleeson's distinctive face a familiar sight. Rivaled only perhaps by **Colm Meaney**, he is *the* leading man of indigenous cinema, not least for his memorable performances in *The General* (1998), *In Bruges* (2008), and John Michael McDonagh's *The Guard* (2011) and *Calvary* (2014), among others. For a younger generation, of course, he is best known for Alastor "Mad-Eye" Moody in the *Harry Potter* franchise and as **Domhnall Gleeson**'s dad.

Born in Artane on Dublin's north side, Gleeson expressed an interest in acting from childhood, and on leaving school, he and several ex-classmates started an acting group. While attending the university, he met Paul Mercier, later a key collaborator onstage and on-screen before becoming a teacher of English and Irish. Teaching afforded him time to indulge his theatrical passion, becoming a key figure in Passion Machine, the theater group established by Mercier in 1984 to produce works reflecting contemporary Ireland. Passion Machine's work was deliberately populist and included material by Mercier himself (most of which Gleeson appeared in), **Roddy Doyle**, and **Gerry Stembridge**. Gleeson himself wrote and directed three plays for the company, including *Breaking Up* and *The Birdtable*.

In 1989, at the age of 34, Gleeson quit teaching to pursue a professional acting career. His first major role came in an **Abbey Theatre** production of Eugene McCabe's *King of the Castle*. He secured a recurring role on the **Radio Telefís Éireann** (RTÉ) soap *Glenroe* and began to build up a range of smaller roles in Irish films of the early 1990s, including *Into the West* (1989). His most prominent early screen role was in the television drama *The Treaty* (1990), in which he played Michael Collins. (He would later appear in **Neil Jordan**'s 1996 biopic of Collins but not in the lead role.)

Mel Gibson's *Braveheart* (1995) brought him to the attention of an American audience for the first time when he was cast in the role of William Wallace's boyhood friend Hamish Campbell. Although he followed this with a series of fourth- and fifth-billed appearances in *Trojan Eddie*, *Spaghetti Slow*, *The Butcher Boy*, and *A Further Gesture*, among others, he attained his breakthrough with two films in the late 1990s: *I Went Down* (1997) and *The General* (1998). Although he played a professional criminal in both, Bunny Kelly (*I Went Down*) and real-life gangster Martin Cahill were strikingly different characterizations, alternately sympathetic and sinister. The influential Boston Society of Film Critics recognized this when they gave him the Best Actor award in 1998 for—unusually—both performances.

The General, in particular, led to a series of calls from Hollywood, first in horror-thriller *Lake Placid* (1999), then in *Mission Impossible II* (2000), Steven Spielberg's *Artificial Intelligence* (2001), and Martin Scorsese's *Gangs of New York* (2002). By the middle of the first decade of the 2000s, he was an established presence in both U.S. and U.K. cinema, a position cemented by his role in *28 Days Later* (2002), *Cold Mountain* (2003), *Troy* (2004), and the previously mentioned "Mad Eye" Moody in the *Harry Potter* franchise.

At one level, Gleeson's casting in international work has played on the stereotype of the Irish male as unpredictable and given to violence, even if he only occasionally plays explicitly Irish roles. He was homicidal as biotech entrepreneur McCloy in *Mission Impossible II*, played a South African torturer in **John Boorman**'s *In My Country* (2004), and was perfectly cast as the given-to-sudden-outbursts-of-fury Alastor Moody. Despite such casting, his most prominent character roles in U.S. work retain a recognizable moral integrity. Although clearly unsympathetic as the ringleader of an android-destroying circus in *Artificial Intelligence* (2001), his character is more quasi-religious zealot than bile-spewing bigot. Introduced with a club in his hand in Martin Scorsese's *Gangs of New York* (2002), Gleeson's "Monk" is, however, one of the few characters to maintain consistent loyalty to his kinfolk. Even when his Colonel Brigham condemns Tom Cruise to almost certain death on the front line of a war against aliens in *Edge of Tomorrow*, he does so because he is offended at the slippery evasiveness of Cruise's military public relations officer.

Certainly, a fundamental decency emerges as a central characteristic in his key Irish roles. Although repeatedly cast as a gangster, his criminals frequently evoke more than a degree of flawed humanity and audience sympathy. When Kevin Spacey essayed the role of Martin Cahill in ***Ordinary Decent Criminal*** (2001), he evaded the more brutal real-life episodes in Cahill's past. By contrast, these events are foregrounded in Gleeson's take on the role in *The General*, including a horrific scene where he oversees the crucifixion of one of his own gang members. Nonetheless, Gleeson's Cahill emerges at least in part as a not entirely culpable product of social circumstances, grinding poverty, and the conservative mores of Irish society.

As his profile has risen in Anglophone productions, it has become increasingly possible to consider Gleeson in lead roles. The Canadian 2013 production *The Grand Seduction* is built and marketed around Gleeson's portrayal of the ebullient Murray French as he attempts to convince a big-city doctor to take up residence in a tiny Newfoundland fishing village. In Vincent Perez's 2016 adaptation of Hans Fallada's wartime novel *Alone in Berlin*, Gleeson stars (opposite Emma Thompson) as the doomed Otto Quangel as he seeks to wage semantic guerrilla warfare against the Nazi regime. He has also headed the cast of David E. Kelley's critically acclaimed U.S. television adaptation of Stephen King's *Mr. Mercedes*. If the impact of these big-screen productions was somewhat underwhelming, it didn't stem the flow of high-profile character roles that include the narrator of the true story that inspired *Moby*

Dick in Ron Howard's *In the Heart of the Sea* (2014), a prohibition-era Irish cop in Ben Affleck's *Live by Night* (2016), and a winning comedic turn as prison chef Knuckles McGinty in *Paddington 2* (2017).

In Ireland, Gleeson has used his public profile to rail against social injustice: passionately criticizing the Irish health care system on RTÉ's *The Late, Late Show* in 2006, lambasting the Irish state's on/off commitment to arts funding in 2016, and so concerned about the waste of Ireland's natural resources that he lent his narration to the 2016 documentary *Atlantic* (**Risteard O'Domhnaill**) on that subject. This public persona has informed the reception of his most prominent Irish roles since 2011. Having appeared in Martin McDonagh's **Academy Award**–winning short *Six Shooter* (2004) and *In Bruges*, Gleeson went onto to work with his brother John Michael in 2011 and again in 2014. In *The Guard*, he played Sergeant Boyle, an iconoclastic rural Gardaí (police) officer who teams up with Don Cheadle's Federal Bureau of Investigation agent to take on drug smugglers. *The Guard* is a problematic text not least because Sergeant Boyle is, at best, politically incorrect and at worst inherently racist and misogynistic. That Irish audiences at least were willing to overlook this (the film became the most successful independent Irish release ever in Ireland) owed much to the affection in which Gleeson is held as well as his nuanced portrayal of what could so easily be a one-dimensional and pretty unpleasant character. The more ambitious *Calvary* saw him take on the role of Father James Lavelle, a priest from the west of Ireland who is informed by an anonymous caller in the film's opening that he will be murdered in one week. Structured as an investigation into who the potential killer might be, the film is informed by the assumption that in contemporary Ireland, nearly everyone in the village is a potential suspect. Yet the casting of Gleeson problematizes their critiques. His Father Lavelle is a priest who refuses to simplistically accept Catholic doctrine, angry at the ingrained corruption of all Irish institutions (the Church included) and compassionate toward those who have fallen afoul of them. He acknowledges critiques of the Church's historically damaging role in Irish society but also seeks to reassert the moral value of Christian virtues at a time when society has lost touch with any sense of fixed ethical principles. The task of representing a priest as quasi-heroic in 2014 Ireland was ambitious and unorthodox, but casting Gleeson was half the battle and gave the film far more depth and complexity than almost any other actor—even Colm Meaney—might have achieved.

GOGAN, JOHNNY (1963–). Born in Sussex, England, he obtained a degree in politics and history at University College Dublin. He was a founding member (with his sister Jane Gogan and Trish McAdam) of the Ha'penny Film Club in 1985, after which he traveled to Latin America, sending home articles on politics there for publication in the *Irish Times*. On return to

Ireland in 1987, he became very active in **Film Base**, establishing and editing *Film Ireland* for three years. Thereafter, having availed himself of Filmbase training, he moved into film production, making his first short, *Stephen* (a fantasy inspired by Irish cyclist Stephen Roche's victory in the 1987 Tour de France), in 1990.

After his sister Jane (herself a producer and later head of drama first at TV3 and then for **Radio Telefís Éireann**) completed a **MEDIA** project training course in 1990, she suggested he contact German television to seek support for his next works. Having struck up a relationship with ZDF/Arte and WDF, his next three productions were all part-German financed.

The first of these, *The Bargain Shop* (1992), was a television drama exploring contentious issues around inner-city redevelopment, the pressures of commercialism, and political corruption. For his first feature-length film, Gogan harked back to Ireland's 1970s flirtation with punk. Produced in the 1990s as Ireland underwent a rapid period of liberalization of sexuality and gender relations, *The Last Bus Home* (1997) overtly reminded audiences that the struggle for social change had its roots in earlier decades, ending with a flash forward to the 1993 decriminalization of homosexuality.

Gogan then left Dublin, relocating to County Leitrim in the northwest of Ireland, apparently in response to the increasingly solipsistic values he encountered in early Celtic Tiger Ireland. He brought with him a script, *Mapmaker*, about a cartographer who encounters a long-buried body while mapping beauty spots on the north–south border. Released in 2002, the film, was shot by cinematographer Owen McPolin and dwells on the local landscape, echoing the central character's exploration of its mysteries.

Thereafter, Gogan became an active member of the northwest film community, establishing the Film Adaptation Festival in 2005 and joining the board of the Leitrim Cinemobile (a touring cinema) in 2004. Gogan has long advocated for the regionalization of Irish screen policy to move away from the east coast production focus. He was appointed to the **Irish Film Board** in 2009 and in 2011 established Studio North West, a forum to push that policy shift. He has remained committed to the region in his screen work ever since, making *Homeland*, about immigration and emigration in Leitrim for TG4 in 2012 and another fiction feature, *Black Ice*, in 2013. Shot on a low budget, the latter explored the world of boy racers, combining crowd-pleasing, high-speed driving sequences with a more psychologically motivated exploration of the motives driving young males in particularly disadvantaged regions of the country to risk their lives behind the wheel.

Since 2013, Gogan has concentrated on feature documentaries, including *Generate the State* (2015), about the building of the Ardnacrusha Hydro-Electric scheme in the 1920s, and *Hubert Butler: Witness to the Future*

(2016), a study of the Irish essayist's experiences in 1930s Soviet Russia and prewar Vienna and his exposure of the massacre of Orthodox Serbs in Croatia during World War II at the hands of the quasi-Nazi regime.

***GOLD* (2014).** Nearly a decade after from his well-received debut, *Small Engine Repair* (2006), writer/director Niall Heery strikes an uncertain tone with his second tale of modern family life. Elements from that earlier film can be found again here: an interest in damaged, fragile Irish masculinities set against a backdrop of nonspecific, Americana settings. On the one hand, *Gold* invokes the quirky world of an auteur, such as Wes Anderson, replete with oddball characters, an unspecified suburban setting, self-conscious tracking shots, and eccentric costuming. On the other, it plows darker depths with themes of emotional dysfunction and male suicide, resulting in an ultimately unsuccessful—though not uninteresting—film that is at once highly mannered and deeply serious.

Twelve years after attempting to take his life, Ray (**David Wilmot**) returns to visit former girlfriend Alice (**Kerry Condon**) and their now teenage daughter Abbie (Maisie Williams, *Game of Thrones*). They now live with the manically uptight Frank (**James Nesbitt**)—once Ray's physical education teacher "Mr. McGunn"—who has sporting ambitions for Abbie (as a long-distance athlete) as well as for his self-devised approach to running, which he believes can become "digital gold" if only he can find a way to market it.

Taking pity on her emotionally vulnerable and homeless ex, Alice takes in Ray to the justifiable discomfort of Frank and general indifference of Abbie, for whom her "father" is a stranger. A complex story line ensues with Ray accidentally causing Frank to fall into a coma, allowing the former family unit to briefly bond before Frank reawakens and dampens any possibility of a lasting reunion.

Although saved from total caricature by James Nesbitt's relatively sympathetic rendering, Frank would fit comfortably into one of the Coen Brothers' more absurdist comedies, and the actor appears to channel George Clooney's more outré screen performances for the role. By contrast, Wilmot's Ray is a fragile, damaged figure played in a realist mode whose emotional history and motivations—beyond making a connection with Alice and Abbie—remain ultimately unclear.

Despite these reservations, *Gold* emerges as an involving proposition. Beyond its likable cast and a reluctance to settle for a textbook ending, there are other compensations, not least its highly original mise-en-scène within which Heery and cinematographer Tim Fleming conjure an entirely novel and unexpected depiction of Dublin, combining mountain backdrops and empty, modernist urban locales to eerie and often beautiful effect.

GOLD IN THE STREET (1996). Directed by Elizabeth Gill and starring Karl Geary, Ian Hart, **Lorraine Pilkington**, and **Aidan Gillen**, the film focuses on the theme of **emigration**. Liam (Geary), a young Irish man, arrives in a New York bar to find that his only contact in the city has left suddenly for fear of being caught as an illegal immigrant. Mario (James Belushi), the well-connected barman, saves the day by introducing him to another native, Des (Hart), who immediately invites him to stay in his apartment along with his friend Paddy (Gillen) and another cousin. Liam quickly fits into the lifestyle of working illegally by day and living it up at night. Over time, however, this nomadic existence takes its toll, most markedly at Christmas, when some of the gang go back home to Ireland, while the others—unsure if they will be able to reenter the United States if they leave—remain in New York, homesick and unsure of their future. This engaging character story thus explores the psychological consequences of being trapped far from home albeit in a context peopled by others in a similar bind.

GOLDFISH MEMORY (2004). Structurally reminiscent of Arthur Schnitzler's often filmed play *Reigen*, which scrutinized the sexual mores of fin de siècle Vienna, Liz Gill's update offers a sophisticated comedy of manners characterized by sharp dialogue examining a complicated set of gay/straight/bi encounters and relationships against the backdrop of a cosmopolitan Dublin.

University lecturer Tom's (Sean Campion) relationship with Ciara (Fiona O'Shaughnessy) ends abruptly when she finds him seducing Isolde (Fiona Glascott), another student. Ciara takes up with Angie (**Flora Montgomery**), a television producer. Angie's friend Red (Keith McErlean) in turn seduces the hitherto straight David (Peter Gaynor), who ends his current, unhappy relationship. Dropped in turn by Isolde, Tom meets Renee (Jean Butler), an American academic visiting Dublin. When she discovers that Ciara has been sleeping with a man, Angie ends their relationship but almost immediately hooks up with Kate (Justine Mitchell), while Ciara brings the proceedings full circle by seducing Isolde.

Despite the impression that a short narrative recap may give, *Goldfish Memory* is more than just a sequence of bed-hopping encounters. It pulls off the neat trick of both projecting a progressive sheen in its carefree depiction of pansexual relationships and ultimately endorsing the more conservative conclusion that, ultimately, happiness is to be found in some incarnation of (albeit perhaps a nontraditional one) the nuclear family. Echoing both near contemporaries ***About Adam*** (2000) and ***Cowboys and Angels*** (2003) in their depiction of Irish cities as confident, urbane, modern European locales wholly comfortable with an eclectic range of sexual identities, the film nonetheless rarely lingers on any of the relationships it depicts for long enough to imbue them with any depth. In consequence, although the film may be seen as an assertive—and liberating—intervention challenging traditional Irish mores, the ease with which characters "try on" new sexual personas is not always convincing, and the lasting impression of the film is, like some of the relationships depicted, a somewhat depthless if often enjoyable exercise.

THE GOOD MAN (2013). Informed by themes of globalization, postcolonialism, and the manner in which decisions taken in the global north trickle down with unanticipated consequence to the south, writer/director Phil Harrison assembles a morally and politically sophisticated tale around the titular "good man," played with reliable, nervous intelligence by **Aiden Gillen**.

Michael (Gillen) leads a comfortable middle-class existence in Belfast as a successful banker with a wife (Kelly Campbell) and child. However, his world is suddenly transformed when his selfish actions late one night lead to the accidental death of another man.

Halfway around the world in a South African township, politically active student Sifiso (Thabang Sidloyi) grapples with the gulf between political commitments and economic realities. The South African government has promised housing for all but lacks the financial resources to implement a building program. Sifiso becomes involved in guerrilla actions, illegally diverting electricity off the grid into a township and protesting against the building of a new factory on publicly owned land.

These two disparate existences intertwine as Michael's relationship and working life disintegrate after the accident, and he subsequently seeks to atone for his culpability by becoming involved in construction in South Africa. However, he finds that addressing the lasting consequences of colonialism and the neocolonialism of Western corporate capitalism is profoundly complex. The land on which the privately owned factory is being built by Irish workers might have been used for public housing. On the other hand, the factory brings local employment and foreign currency and creates the basis for ongoing economic activity, which may benefit the community as a whole.

Harrison's personal experiences in Africa taught him that this messiness extends to the question of Western culpability for local conditions: channeling Franz Fanon, he acknowledges that some of the difficulties of faced by African nations are beyond the influence of even the most well-meaning outsider. Thus, for Michael, identifying what it means to be "good" becomes an impossible task.

The political engagement of the narrative is reflected in *The Good Man*'s funding. The movie was made for just UK£100,000 raised through crowdsourced funding, and Harrison structured the budget in such a way as to ensure that the township where the South African sequences were shot received 10 percent of the overall budget, over and above monies expended on hiring local crew.

***GOOD VIBRATIONS* (2012).** As the Troubles in Northern Ireland escalated in the early 1970s, Tom Hooley opened a record shop on Winetavern Street, Belfast: "the most bombed half mile in Europe." This unlikely, lively biopic tells the story of Hooley's passion for punk, his promotion of local band The Outcasts, and his breakout discovery The Undertones, whose 1977 debut single, "Teenage Kicks," became the song of a generation. While the film foregrounds the music and relationships of the era, it is no exercise in nostalgia within a culture of menace and conflict. Perhaps uniquely in punk-themed films, the music emerges here as socially constructive, channeling the energies and passions of angry but passionate youth.

The film follows Hooley (Richard Dormer), whom we first meet working as a pub deejay in Troubles-torn Belfast. When he meets Ruth (Jodie Whittaker), he decides to push back against the changes in his native city and open the eponymous record shop, which becomes a magnet for young music fans and musicians across the province.

Well known locally, the story of *Good Vibrations* came to the fore with the publication of Hooley's autobiography *Hooleygan* in 2010 and a screenplay by Belfast writers Colin Carberry and Glenn Patterson. It was subsequently taken up by directors Lisa Barros D'Sa and Glenn Leyburn, who had previously collaborated on ***Cherrybomb*** (2009). Unsurprisingly, the film's sound track is a highlight, blending period music and new music by David Holmes (who is also credited as a coproducer), who returns to his native Belfast after high-profile work with Steven Soderbergh on films like *Out of Sight* (1998) and the *Ocean's Eleven* franchise. Nonetheless, even the music cannot eclipse Richard Dormer's frantically charismatic turn as Hooley, driven by a mélange of contrariness, self-destruction, and sheer joy in the transcendent possibilities of popular music.

***GRABBERS* (2012).** Having taken a stab at horror in his 2009 debut, *Tormented*, Belfast director Jon Wright moved to a comedy–sci-fi–horror hybrid for his follow-up feature.

Ambitious young Gardaí (policewoman) Lisa Nolan (**Ruth Bradley**) arrives to take up duty on Erin Island, an offshore community so small that she and recently divorced, permanently inebriated Ciaran O'Shea (Richard Coyle) constitute the full complement of the local police force. After a mysterious meteorite strikes the sea and the crew of a fishing vessel disappears, the isolated hamlet finds itself under assault from a voracious set of sharp-toothed, tentacled alien monsters intent on devouring the entire community. Aided by a motley crew of locals—including scientist Adam Smith (Russell Tovey), barfly Paddy Barrett (Lalor Roddy), and innkeeper Una Maher (**Bronagh Gallagher**)—the police quickly establish that the creatures cannot stomach (literally) alcohol-filled prey. A defensive strategy immediately suggests itself: the whole community holes up at Una's public house, determined to remain drunk until the threat is extinguished.

Grabbers is about as overtly high concept a movie as has been produced in Ireland: "rural types must get drunk to avoid alien annihilation." The transposition of sci-fi and horror tropes to a sleepy Irish fishing villages not only inevitably invokes comedy but also allows director Wright and screenwriter Lehane to create a work comprehensible to international audiences on a number of levels. Nods to classic 1970s sci-fi pepper the script, while the final sequence pretty much directly quotes the conclusion of James Cameron's *Aliens* (1986) with a backhoe doubling for Ripley's power loader. At the same time, by emphasizing alcohol as at least a temporary solution to the villagers' plight, the film does little to challenge the kind of soft primitive representations of Ireland to viewers whose familiarity with Ireland is limited to texts like **The Quiet Man** (1953).

Although hardly demanding roles, Wright extracts game performances from Bradley and others and keeps the narrative rolling along at a fair clip (though, given the buildup, the finale is something of a damp squib). Trevor Forrest's highly filtered rendition of the Donegal landscape, where the film was actually shot, is complemented by the technically highly component computer-generated imagery—belying the reported $5.3 million budget—overseen by London effects house Nvisible.

Clearly intended as a calling card movie for most of those involved, *Grabbers* succeeded in achieving wide international distribution via video-on-demand platforms, cable television, and, to a lesser extent, theatrical release.

THE GUARD (2010). When the legendary Irish columnist Myles na Gopaleen (aka Flann O'Brien) wrote about the life and times of "the brother," he invoked the always invisible and mute sibling as a model of typicality, an unpretentious and unambitious man prone to the slings and arrows of outrageous fortune. The same cannot be said of **John Michael McDonagh**—brother of widely celebrated playwright/screenwriter Martin McDonagh—who, at age 43, belatedly burst from the long shadows of his sibling's success with *The Guard*. Not only was the film a more-than-passable debut (particularly, as McDonagh suggested at its [Galway Film Fleadh (Festival)] premier, in that it was written in just 13 days), but it also went on to set a box office record as the highest-grossing Irish film ever (ca. €4.3 million) and achieved further critical and commercial success in the United Kingdom and Europe, Australia, New Zealand, and even the United States, where it was released on 200 screens. (The total box office was around $22 million on a $6 million budget.)

As Martin had done onstage with the hugely successful Leenane Trilogy, John Michael set out in *The Guard* to evoke black humor from destabilizing long-standing cultural constructions of the west of Ireland, undermining both the cozy cultural nationalism of the Celtic Revival and the "imperialist" gaze of the many travel writers and landscape painters who sought Connemara's wildness as a counterpoint to metropolitan modernity in the long 19th century. Central to this strategy is Sergeant Gerry Boyle (**Brendan Gleeson**), a highly individual "guard" in rural Connemara with a confrontational personality and an idiosyncratic attitude to the law. In all these respects, *The Guard* also displays the clear influence of Flann O'Brien's *The Third Policeman.* (Brendan Gleeson has been trying to direct an adaptation of *At Swim-Two-Birds* for years.)

When a fellow officer disappears and Boyle's village becomes key to a large drug-trafficking investigation, he is forced to surrender some of his local authority and cynicism when dealing with the humorless African American Federal Bureau of Investigation agent Wendell Everett (Don Cheadle). In a familiar genre cliché hilariously reimagined in its application to the wild Atlantic ways of the Irish, Boyle—the local law enforcement—resents the "fed" interloper and works to undermine his dull, by-the-book authority while simultaneously displaying unpredictable flashes of homespun hospitality and subversive humor. While never submitting to anything as predictable as a sentimental acknowledgment of "odd-couple" mutuality, the film's high-action finale reconciles the men as equals, and their competing tactics of law enforcement coalesce in the defeat of a mutual enemy.

While Boyle's unpredictable and often outrageous dialogue and actions are central to the film's appeal, *The Guard* can be read as an imaginative reworking of familiar elements from American rather than Irish cinema: the rural-set confrontation trope of federal versus local law has a long history in American film and TV, as does the newly arrived cosmopolitan American frustrated by the "backward" ways of the rural Irish. In this combination, it bears an unlikely comparison to the 1949 Bing Crosby vehicle *The Luck of the Irish*, in which Crosby plays a smooth New York insurance investigator sent to Ireland to investigate the theft of the Blarney Stone. Once in Blarney, his efforts are thwarted by the prosaic local knowledge and methods of Sergeant Briany McNaughton, played by the effusively "stage Irish" Barry Fitzgerald. But while that inconsequential drama proceeded to a romantic climax accompanied by a sentimental Crosby sound track, *The Guard* is altogether more postmodern in its construction of a local lawman who is both parochial and entirely worldly-wise, a "mammy's boy" who is simultaneously morally immature and a defender of the law, a dissembling bunch of contradictions that consistently keep Wendell and the audience off their "guard." It is this knowing, ironic quality, blending the familiar and the disruptive and the serious and the parodic, that has given the film the status of a "cult" classic.

GUESTS OF THE NATION (1935). Based on a short story by Frank O'Connor and set during the War of Independence, this 40-minute silent film directed by Denis Johnson traces the dawning awareness of some Irish Republican Army (IRA) volunteers that two English soldiers in their custody will have to be executed (thus anticipating **Neil Jordan**'s later script for *The Crying Game*). Made on a shoestring budget in a studio constructed in a Dublin back garden, the film enjoyed the tacit support of the then Fianna Fáil government; Minister for Defense Frank Aitken arranged for the supply of army uniforms as costumes, and he attended the premiere at the Gate Theatre in January 1936. Director Johnston was better known as a playwright associated with the Gate Theatre, and the cast (which includes **Barry Fitzgerald** and **Cyril Cusack**) relied heavily on Gate and Abbey Theatre actors. The film was warmly received on its release but represented Johnson's only dalliance with screen directing.

GUILTRIP (1995). The film traces a day in the life of a dysfunctional young couple and arrived at an apposite moment—in the middle of the referendum on the introduction of divorce to Ireland. Directed by **Gerry Stembridge**, the film follows 24 hours in the troubled relationship between Liam (Andrew Connolly) and Tina (Jasmine Russell). Conjugal relations have ceased, and it becomes clear that the whole basis of their relationship is flawed—Liam, an army corporal, has extended the behavior of the parade ground into the domestic sphere, where an atmosphere of fear and tension prevails. Thus, a subsidiary theme emerges: the contradiction between the authoritarian nature associated with the military and the behavioral norms of society at large. In short, what happens when a soldier goes home?

Stembridge's intricately structured script proceeds by comparing Tina's day and Liam's night via a series of parallel edits. During the day, quiet, nervy Tina chats or flirts with Ronnie (Peter Hanly), the hapless owner of the local electronics shop, while that night during a drinking session, the domineering Liam eyes Michelle (Michelle Houlden), who happens to be Ronnie's wife. Michelle and Ronnie's relationship also faces difficulties, Michelle clearly despising her husband's cheerful idiocy.

The use of different viewpoints in cinema often comments on the very process of representation: as one account clashes with another, so the objectivity and accuracy of both are questioned. In using this technique, the film is at least reminiscent of a European art house preoccupation with this theme and the aesthetic realism and playful debates about identity that dominate such film cultures.

GUINEY, ED (1966–). As the Irish film industry expanded in the 1990s , Ed Guiney quickly emerged as among the most astute and consistently successful executives working in the Irish audiovisual sector, having been immersed in Irish film production culture since his teens. Born into a firmly middle-class milieu (both parents were doctors), he grew up in what he describes as the "leafy suburbs" of Ballsbridge, attending the Gonzaga private school. (It was while still in school that he first encountered **Lenny Abrahamson**, with whom he would later extensively collaborate.) Having determined in his mid-teens that he wanted to be a film producer (as opposed to the perhaps more common ambition of being an actor or a director), he looked for summer jobs when he went to the university working as an intern with **Strongbow Films**.

He studied economic and social studies (ESS) at Trinity College Dublin, in part because the limited contact hours freed him to pursue his filmic ambitions. He established a filmmaking society, the Trinity Video Company, with **Stephen Rennicks** and Michael Joy. Among their first productions was a Lenny Abrahamson–directed documentary about the latter's grandfather, a Jewish refugee who had arrived in Dublin from Romania. This was quickly followed by *3 Joes* (also directed by Abrahamson), featuring Dominic West (*The Wire*'s Jimmy McNulty), comedian Gary Cooke, and actor Mikel Murfi.

On graduating, he established **Temple Films** with **Stephen Bradley** in 1993; his first feature credit was *Ailsa* (1994), directed by **Paddy Breathnach**. Notwithstanding talent and tenacity, the timing was good: the **Irish Film Board** (IFB)/Bord Scannán na hÉireann had recently been reconstituted with the remit to overhaul outmoded representations of Ireland as a rural and quaint backwater, and the young, ambitious, and cosmopolitan Guiney was exactly the kind of talent they wanted to support. With the support of the IFB (and its desire to fund companies rather than only productions), Guiney was able to establish himself at the forefront of a new era in Irish film production over the next decade, steadily building his skills and experience on a variety of projects, including *Guiltrip* (1995), *Disco Pigs* (2001; Cillian Murphy's screen debut), and *On the Edge* (2001; an ill-fated **John Carney** production also starring Murphy).

In 2001, with former IFB executive Andrew Lowe, Guiney established **Element Pictures**, which by 2015 had become the largest independent producer in Ireland (by turnover and number of productions) along with interests in film distribution (including online [**Volta.ie**]) and exhibition (**Light House Cinema**). While continuing to develop indigenous feature productions (*Boy Eats Girl* [2005] and *Isolation* [2005]), Element quickly diversified its business model to include European coproductions and Irish TV drama. Notable in the first category was *The Wind That Shakes the Barley* (2006), which won the Palme d'Or at Cannes and gave Guiney access to the prestigious international film festival scene, an arena that would prove central to the promotion and success of high-profile films like *Frank* (2014), *Room* (2015), and *The Lobster* (2015). Less glamorous but just as significant has been Guiney's involvement with "independent" TV drama miniseries, including contrasting zeitgeist representations of Ireland's Celtic Tiger in *Bachelors Walk* (2001–2006), *Pure Mule* (2005–2008), and *Prosperity* (2007). More recent credits in this format have included *Charlie* (2015) as well as executive producer credits on the BBC coproductions *Ripper Street* (2012–2013) and *Quirke* (2014). In 2014, Element successfully bid for the contract to produce a new Irish TV soap opera for TV3 to rival the long-running and hugely successful **Radio Telefís Éireann**–produced *Fair City*. Outstripping expectations, *Red Rock* became a fast success and, in a deal that demonstrated how globalized the Irish audiovisual industry had become in both format and business terms, was sold to the online digital platform Amazon Prime in November 2015.

On the big screen, Guiney has enjoyed a steady run of success in national and international art house markets. **John Michael MacDonagh**'s offbeat black comedies *The Guard* (2011) and *Calvary* (2019) attracted strong reviews and a decent box office despite the colloquial nature of their settings and characterization. *What Richard Did* (2012) and *Glassland* (2014) not only brought Hollywood looking for their young star **Jack Reynor** (*Transformers* [2013]) but also demonstrated Guiney's increasing role as a nodal point in the Irish industry, having produced both films. *What Richard Did* (2012) also marked a turning point in Guiney's relationship with director Lenny Abrahamson, whom he signed to a "first look" deal around the same time. Both had been friends since their student days at Trinity College Dublin, and while Guiney had produced Lenny's first short film *3 Joes* (1991), their professional paths did not cross again until *Garage* (2007). (Johnny Speirs was producer on Abrahamson's debut, *Adam and Paul* [2004].) By then, both men had accumulated considerable experience. Abrahamson had spent many years as a successful commercial director, and his artistic ambitions were able to take full advantage of Guiney's contacts and experience in a succession of increasingly internationally oriented films: *What Richard Did*, *Frank*, and *Room* achieved incremental critical and commercial success that clearly marked a new, more ambitious chapter in Irish film. Asked in an interview whether he has a motto, Guiney referenced Goethe: "If you move with purpose into the world, the world meets you halfway." While not wishing to simplistically reduce Guiney's success to chutzpah (a capacity to collaborate and a creative approach to financing also clearly play a role), this willingness to set and move toward goals without necessarily initially knowing exactly how to achieve them has consistently marked Guiney's career.

H

***H FOR HAMLET* (1993).** Writer/director Vinny Murphy's long commitment to community cinema has seen him operate in a huge variety of contexts, including rehabilitation centers and prisons. Having had made three short films in 1993 with the students of the Community College in Jobstown (a deprived suburb of west Dublin), he sought to expand on that experience by undertaking his first feature-length film: a screen version of Shakespeare's *Hamlet*. On any level, *H for Hamlet* is an audacious undertaking: not only does director Murphy attempt to produce a feature film on effectively no budget, but he also does so with an almost entirely nonprofessional cast of youths not traditionally exposed to high culture (though Murphy casts himself as Claudius). Furthermore, the approach to the material is radical, transposing the action from the 16th-century Danish court to the contemporary urban, alienating setting of Tallaght in Dublin. Making a virtue of its budgetary constraints, the film relies on local settings, the Betacam shoot serving to emphasize the gray concrete mise-en-scène. In keeping with the philosophy of community-based art projects, the significance of the film lies less in its on-screen achievement (though that is not inconsiderable) and more in the process that led to its production.

H3* (2001).** As one of the most brutalizing and vivid events of the Troubles, the 1981 hunger strikes by Irish Republican prisoners, resulting in the deaths of 10, have unsurprisingly inspired a steady cinematic output. Stephen Burke's *'81* (1995), **Terry George**'s ***Some Mother's Son (1996), Maeve Murphy's ***Silent Grace*** (2000), Steven McQueen's ***Hunger*** (2008), and Brendan J. Byrne's *Bobby Sands: 66 Days* (2016) have approached the events from a variety of perspectives and approaches. However, *H3* is set apart by the background of its screenwriters.

Although the film's director, Les Blair, was already renowned for his seminal television work critiquing core British institutions, such as the police (*Law and Order* [1978]) and the health service (*Our Nation's Health* [1983]), the film's singular insights owes much to the political experiences of its screenwriters: Brian Campbell and Laurence McKeown. Both were former

Republican prisoners, and McKeown spent more than 70 days on a hunger strike (the longest to keep going without dying) before his mother intervened and withdrew him after he fell into a coma. McKeown subsequently wrote a doctoral thesis at Queen's University Belfast titled "Unrepentant Fenian Bastards: The Social Construction of an Irish Republican Prisoner Community."

H3 is a fictionalized dramatization of the events between the ending of the first aborted hunger strike in 1981 and the death of Bobby Sands. The narrative follows Declan (Aidan Campbell) as he enters H3, one of the H-Blocks housing paramilitary prisoners. There, he encounters Seamus (Brendan Mackey), Ciaran (Dean Lennox Kelly), and the Republican prisoners' leader Bobby Sands (Mark O'Halloran) amid a "dirty protest" (refusing to wear prison uniforms and smearing their excrement on the walls of their cells) at the refusal of the British government to acknowledge their status as political prisoners. The narrative proceeds to argue that the hunger strikes were a last-resort response to the British government's refusal to grant political recognition (and thus to indirectly acknowledge the political dimensions of paramilitary violence in Northern Ireland). In so doing, the narrative focus is broadened beyond the usual focus of similarly themed works (Bobby Sands and the 10 men who actually died) to emphasize the wider endorsement of the hunger strikes within the Republican movement: 200 prisoners volunteered to begin the fast before the strikes were called off in October 1981.

The film prompted renewed criticism of the support by the **Irish Film Board** (IFB) for overtly nationalist projects and its failure to support other perspectives on the Troubles. For its part, the IFB responded that it could fund only those projects placed before it. In any case, the fact that the film was also supported by the **Northern Ireland Film and Television Commission** mollified some of those critics who accused the IFB of partisanship.

HALAL DADDY **(2017).** Arguably Irish cinema's first intercultural comedy and certainly the first to foreground a Muslim protagonist, this feel-good, fish-out-of-water German–Irish comedy adopts a much lighter tone than earlier efforts of both its director, Conor McDermottroe (*Swansong: Story of Occi Byrne* [2009]), and its cowriter, Mark O'Hallorhan (*Adam and Paul* [2004], *Garage* [2007], and *Viva* [2015]).

Raghdan (Nikesh Patel) lives in Sligo, having fled Bradford and his father Amir's (Art Malik) attempts to set up an arranged marriage. Living an untroubled existence with his aunt and uncle (**Deirdre O'Kane** and Paul Tylak), he passes his days with no-nonsense Irish girlfriend Maeve (**Sarah Bolger**) and stoner mates Derek and Neville (Stephen Cromwell and Jerry Iwu). This easy existence is disrupted when his father visits and spots a business opportunity arising from the closure of the town's meat-processing plant and decides to repurpose it as a halal meat factory to be run by Raghdan. To get the operation going, Amir hires the plant's former manager (and

Maeve's father) Martin (**Colm Meaney**), bringing renewed hope and vigor to the whole community. However, it emerges that Amir is motivated by more than mere altruism or commercial ambition, seeing the factory as an opportunity to redirect Raghdan down a more traditional pathway.

Although McDermottroe and O'Hallorhan's preceding films were more dramatic and darker in tone, they can be seen to have shared a common interest in socially marginalized male protagonists and themes. As a person of Asian descent living in rural Ireland, Raghdan might have slotted into a similar frame. The film, however, depicts race relations in the west of Ireland as almost entirely harmonious, signaled through Kane and Tylak's amorous interracial marriage and Raghdan's friendship with the Afro-Caribbean Neville. Even when ethnic distinctions are acknowledged, they're played mainly for laughs: a running gag sees Martin repeatedly conflate quite different Middle Eastern and Oriental cultural traditions in an effort to placate Amir.

For all its lightheartedness and ambiance of tolerance, *Halal Daddy* throws into relief the relative absence of nonwhite characters in contemporary Irish cinema, an absence that persists despite the fact that 10 percent of those recorded in the 2016 Irish census were from Traveller, black, or Asian ethnicity. Cast member Paul Tylak's deployment by Irish film and television over two decades is instructive in this regard: although of mixed Sri Lankan–Irish parentage, his background has been subsumed into nonspecific "ethnics" for two decades, resulting in his playing everything from Kurds to Aztecs or, in the case of *Halal Daddy*, an Indian uncle. Such a bundling together of "foreign" types suggests that for all its ambitions toward diversity, Irish audiovisual production and policy has some distance to travel in its recognition of and negotiation with difference, however defined.

HALL, TOM. *See* CARNEY, JOHN (1972–), AND TOM HALL.

***THE HALO EFFECT* (2002).** Having partly funded his debut picture, *Last Days in Dublin* (2001), by working as a fast-food deliveryman, Lance Daly incorporated some of those experiences into a blackly comic second picture. Fatso (**Stephen Rea**) owns and runs a Dublin inner-city fish-and-chips shop aided by less-than-enthusiastic staff Eddie (Simon Delaney), Mick (Grattan Smith), and slumming south-sider Jean (**Kerry Condon**). Generous to a fault with others, Fatso's own life is a rolling catastrophe, as a spectacularly unlucky gambling habit sees his shop visited by a succession of debt collectors (**Gerard McSorley**, **John Kavanagh**, and Willie Higgins) along with a rogues' gallery of other "characters." Over the course of a week, Fatso's fragile position becomes increasingly untenable, culminating in a poker game where he throws his entire business into the pot.

Shot over five weeks in November 2002 for a €1.1 million budget, which, though low by any standards, still dwarfed the resources available to his debut, *The Halo Effect* proved a difficult sell. Despite some diverting cameos from the solid cast, the film suffers from an uneven tone (lurching from comedy to violence via absurdist drama) and—critically for a comedy—a dearth of funny dialogue. If it illustrated Daly's assertion that the seamier side of society offered more opportunities for dramatic conflict than a more middle-class milieu, that thesis would be more convincingly supported by his follow-up *Kisses* (2008).

HANDSOME DEVIL (2017). Dumped in the prestigious Woodhill College while his father and stepmother (cameos from Ardal O'Hanlon and **Amy Huberman**) live it up in Dubai, Ned Roche (Fionn O'Shea) is a very uncomfortable fish out of water. An artsy, vintage music–loving "owl of the remove" in a school where social acceptance is almost exclusively dependent on one's prowess at rugby, Ned determines to escape by getting himself expelled. When his handsome new roommate, Conor (U.K. actor Nicholas Galitzine with a flawless middle-class Dublin accent), turns out to be a rugby star in the making, Ned initially takes him for another mindless jock. But when Conor proves to be as interested in music as Ned, an unlikely friendship develops. Both boys are encouraged to explore their artistic side by inspirational English teacher Dan Sherry (**Andrew Scott**), who commences a battle for Conor's soul with rugby coach Pascal O'Keeffe (Moe Dunford). O'Keeffe is a throwback to a less liberal age: "You can have the weird ones with the dyed hair and the banjos: I've got f**k-all use for them." This proves particularly problematic when the audience discovers—in a well-signaled reveal—that his star outhalf Conor has a secret: he's gay.

Shot at Castleknock College (alma mater of **Colin Farrell**), a year after the referendum on marriage equality saw the Irish public comfortably support the idea of gay marriage, *Handsome Devil* at times feels like a film from an earlier decade. While no one would suggest that **LGBT** identities in Irish society had become so mainstream as to be invisible or that privately educated rugby players were paragons of progressive liberalism, *Handsome Devil* still seemed to assume a social and moral milieu that was more common in the 1980s. When mentor figure Dan (who, it emerges, is also gay but is keeping at least one foot in the closet) seeks to assure Conor that things will get better when he's older, the implied social context feels like something out of Basil Dearden's *Victim* (1961).

That the filmmakers seem to recognize this is suggested elsewhere: Ned's apparently wealthy parents appear to be driving a car from the 1990s; the sound track is drawn largely from 1970s–1980s alternative bands like Big Star, The Undertones, Prefab Sprout, and so on; and the depiction of a gay bar on a dark, isolated street is hardly reflective of the contemporary Dublin gay scene. Even the film's apparently safe decision to frame rugby culture as intrinsically homophobic seems dated in an era when international referee Nigel Owens and former Welsh captain Gareth Thomas have publicly come out.

Nevertheless, there is much to engage audiences in the film. The young leads admirably carry the narrative, while Scott and Dunford embrace their roles with relish. Nonetheless, as a film made more than a decade after the likes of *Cowboys and Angels* (2000) and *Goldfish Memory* (2003) depicted an Ireland grown more tolerant of difference, the decision to maroon the text in a contemporary setting greatly undermines its credibility and wider potential relevance.

HAPPY EVER AFTERS (2009). Their brevity notwithstanding, Stephen Burke's first and second short films made quite an impact on their release in the 1990s and signaled the arrival of a potentially important voice in Irish cinema. *After '68* (1994) and *'81* looked at key moments in the Troubles in a fresh light, and subsequent works, including *No Tears* (2002), a **Radio Telefís Éireann** drama about a health scandal, and *Maze* (2017), about a mass escape of Irish Republican Army prisoners, appear to confirm Burke's serious intent. However, *Happy Every Afters*, technically his feature debut, confounds that trajectory, being as it is a frothy screwball comedy based around two wedding parties at a single venue that become increasingly interlaced with predictably farcical consequences. British actors Sally Hawkins and Tom Riley play the lead Irish roles as Maura and Freddie. Desperate to prevent the bank from repossessing her house, Maura has agreed, for a fee, to a marriage of convenience to an immigrant seeking residency status. Slacker Freddie has allowed his needy girlfriend (and her extended family) to bully him into walking down the aisle. Neither are exactly ecstatic about their situations, but when they meet at the wedding party, they suddenly recognize that they might have found the partners they actually need.

Shot on a €1.8 million budget, the film benefits from the easy chemistry between the two leads (whose attempts at Irish accents are broadly successful) and their snappy dialogue interplay. However, the film is tonally inconsistent, moving from sheer "what the hell, let's do it" bravado to a much darker mood as potentially interesting references to immigration (signaled by crudely drawn immigration officers) and banking collapse emerge. At times, it cries out for a surer directorial touch, and one wonders where the potentially interesting initial setup might have led in the hands of a professional neurotic like John Cleese.

HARRIS, RICHARD (1930–2002). Harris enjoyed a long and distinguished international acting career, appearing in more than 70 movies while remaining committed to Limerick and his homeland. On-screen, he was famous for his earthy Shakespearian qualities and for being a versatile, adventurous, intense, and richly talented all-around actor. Eulogies by his fellow actors, including **Peter O'Toole**, **Liam Neeson**, and **Gabriel Byrne**, spoke of his being a "horse of a man" and never a pampered dilettante. Born into a well-to-do Limerick farming family, he attended Crescent College, where he excelled at rugby, going on to play for young Munster and Garryowen. However, after a bout of tuberculosis in his teens ended his dreams of playing professionally, he moved to consider the theater instead. In 1954, he moved to London to study at the London Academy of Music and Dramatic Art, thereafter joining Joan Littlewood's Theatre Workshop. Smaller roles in West End theater productions followed, beginning with a production of Brendan Behan's *The Quare Fellow* in 1956. Having made a couple of small-screen appearances from 1958 (typically in one-off plays on independent television), he returned to Ireland for a small role in the first major international feature film shot at **Ardmore Studios**, *Shake Hands with the Devil* (1959). He quickly established a screen persona as a headstrong, even reckless, man of action. He quickly graduated to A movies like *The Guns of Navarone* (1961) and a year later was billed third behind Marlon Brando and Trevor Howard in *Mutiny on the Bounty* as leading mutineer John Mills. But it was his rampaging performance as professional rugby player Frank Machin in the Lindsay Anderson–directed *This Sporting Life* (1963) that made him a star. Brutal and brutalized, Harris's Machin is a star on the field but, though capable of great affection, seen as no more than a "great ape" off it. The performance won him an award at Cannes in 1963 and BAFTA and **Academy Award** nominations. Hollywood beckoned, but Harris opted instead to go east, making two films back to back in Italy, including Michelangelo Antonioni's visually (and aurally) stunning modernist masterpiece *The Red Desert* opposite Monica Vitti.

With those credentials, Harris might have established himself as a leading figure in European art house cinema, yet in practice, he looked to Hollywood, appearing in a sequence of big-budget spectaculars, including Sam Peckinpah's *Major Dundee* (1965), Anthony Mann's *The Heroes of Telemark* (1965), and John Huston's *The Bible* (1966) and, perhaps most surprisingly, as King Arthur in the screen adaptation of Alan Lerner's musical *Camelot* (1967), a role originated onstage by Richard Burton seven years earlier. (Although Harris was not previously regarded as a singer, *Camelot* apparently inspired him to explore his musical side. He released five solo albums between 1968 and 1974 and enjoyed a global hit in 1968 with his version of Jimmy Webb's "Macarthur Park.")

By this time, Harris also shared with Richard Burton a larger-than-life off-screen persona as a hard-drinking hell-raiser, along with figures like Peter O'Toole and Oliver Reed. Yet that Celtic persona was rarely overtly reflected in his on-screen roles of the 1960s and 1970s. Although he played an Irish immigrant detective in 1870s Pennsylvania opposite Sean Connery in *The Molly Maguires* (1970), his best-known roles saw him cast as leading figures from British history: in the titular role in *Cromwell* (1970), as Richard the Lionheart in *Robin and Marian* (1976), and, most notoriously, as Lord John Morgan, an Englishman captured by Sioux warriors in early 19th-century America in the *A Man Called Horse* sequence beginning in 1970.

By the start of the 1970s, Harris's star power and personality were such that he was even (ill-advisedly) permitted to try his hand at directing himself as a soccer star at the end of his career in *Bloomfield* (1971). Yet, perhaps because of his chaotic private life (his first marriage ended in 1969), his career went somewhat off the rails as the 1970s progressed. He became increasingly associated with bloated international productions featuring all-star casts such as *The Cassandra Crossing* (1977) or exploitation movies like *Orca* (a post-*Jaws* eco-horror pastiche) and *Tarzan the Ape Man* (1981), a film focused largely on Bo Derek's physical attributes. Although he reportedly dealt with his substance issues by the end of the 1970s and was largely teetotal through the 1980s, his screen career seemed doomed to peter out (although he revived *Camelot* on Broadway in 1981 to some acclaim, again taking over from Richard Burton).

Ironically, given that the absence of any kind of regular filmmaking activity in Ireland during his heyday had seen him work mainly overseas, it was an Irish film that reignited his career. When **Jim Sheridan** came to film John B. Keane's play *The Field*, it seemed preordained that **Ray McAnally**, who had defined the central role of "The Bull" McCabe onstage, would also bring it to the screen. However, when McAnally died suddenly in 1989, Harris stepped in at short notice. Harris transformed the role: where McAnally threatened through physical presence, Harris offered a more introspective, haunted portrayal, a King Lear to McAnally's Macbeth.

Nominated for both an Oscar and a Golden Globe, Harris suddenly found himself in demand again, appearing opposite Harrison Ford as an Irish Republican Army leader in *Patriot Games* (1992) and in a memorable turn as "English Bob" in Clint Eastwood's elegiac *Unforgiven* (1992). Those roles notwithstanding, his new screen incarnation was quieter and more contemplative, playing characters who, having witnessed violence, have decided that, on the whole, there are better ways of making headway.

He continued to appear in Irish productions as the local industry developed in the 1990s, first as a Traveller King in *Trojan Eddie* (1995) and then as a benevolent Presbyterian elder in *This Is the Sea* (1997). But his defining latter-day roles came at the turn of the 21st century. His Marcus Aurelius in

Ridley Scott's *Gladiator* (2000) is a compassionate figure, weary of warfare, seeking to bequeath the leadership of the empire to a figure—Russell Crowe's Maximus—who can restore democratic rule to ancient Rome. He initially turned down the role of Albus Dumbledore in the *Harry Potter* franchise, concerned at the long-term commitment it implied, but signed up for *Harry Potter and the Philosopher's Stone* (2001) at the insistence of his granddaughter. In Harris's hands, Dumbledore is a twinkly-eyed, mischievous figure who commands authority through negotiation rather than domination. Sadly, however, he was to reprise the role only once—in *Harry Potter and the Chamber of Secrets* (2002)—before succumbing to Hodgkin's disease at age 72. Fittingly, it would fall to another Irish actor, **Michael Gambon**, to shepherd the role through the rest of the franchise.

***HEAR MY SONG* (1991).** Coscripted by director Peter Chelsom (in his feature debut) with lead actor **Adrian Dunbar**, *Hear My Song* is very loosely based on the real-life narrative of Irish tenor Josef Locke, who enjoyed popular success on the British variety circuit (even appearing in a handful of films) between the late 1940s and 1950s before a reluctance to settle his tax affairs with Her Majesty's Revenue saw him relocate to Ireland for a period.

In the fictional version, promoter Micky O'Neill (Dunbar) runs a struggling nightclub venue in early 1980s Liverpool. Desperate to draw in crowds, he books "Mr. X," an impersonator who passes himself off as Locke. The gig is a sellout and draws both Chief Constable Jim Abbott (David McCallum) still hunting Locke for tax fraud and Cathleen Doyle (Shirley Anne Field), mother of Micky's girlfriend Nancy (Tara FitzGerald) and Locke's former lover. Mr. X performs to acclaim, but when he tries to embrace Cathleen, she publicly identifies him as an imposter. Blamed for the deception, Micky is fired by the venue owners and ostracized by everyone, including Nancy. Desperate to win her back, he travels to Ireland to track down the real Locke (Ned Beatty) to bring him back to Liverpool for a concert that Mickey hopes will lead to their reconciliation.

Produced during the Irish production lull induced by suspension of the **Irish Film Board** (though within months of Ron Howard's juggernaut *Far and Away*), *Hear My Song* takes a thin premise and weaves a likable, feel-good tale peopled by larger-than-life characters: Dunbar's nothing-left-to-lose Mickey, a winning turn from **James Nesbitt** as Mickey's childhood pal Fintan, and, in particular, Beatty (employing a mid-Atlantic drawl) as the rambunctious Locke. Although its depiction of the close-knit community that Locke has hidden himself away in occasionally suggests a pastoral take on another Beatty picture—**John Boorman**'s *Deliverance* (1973)—for the most part, it affirms the kind of timeless, soft, primitive depiction of rural Ireland taken for granted by international audiences familiar with *The Quiet Man* (1953) or *Darby O'Gill* (1958) (and later rehearsed by *Waking Ned* [1995]).

Yet as it draws to its whimsical "we're getting the band back together" caper comedy denouement, it also recalls the best of Ealing's postwar comedies (and, in particular, Alexander MacKendrick's *Whiskey Galore* [1949]). That the filmmakers are aware of this is evident: "We're in a shaggy dog story," Mickey wisely counsels Fintan as they drag a bull to Locke's house as part of their scheme to convince him to perform one last time.

HELL'S KITCHEN. Jim Sheridan and Arthur Lappin established Hell's Kitchen in 1993 in the wake of the critical and commercial successes of Sheridan's *My Left Foot* (1989) and *The Field* (1990), both of which Lappin line produced. For nearly a decade, the company enjoyed a first-look relationship with Universal, which, although it ended in 2000, effectively underwrote the construction of one of the few Irish production companies with experience across a broad range of production types and budgets.

Before teaming up with Sheridan, Arthur Lappin worked as a theater and stage producer for 18 years and was, for a period, drama and dance officer with the Arts Council of Ireland. Lappin has acted as a full-fledged producer on all of Sheridan's feature work from *In the Name of the Father* to *The Boxer* and *In America*. However, the company was not solely a vehicle for Jim Sheridan's talents; Lappin also produced **Terry George**'s *Some Mother's Son*, Angelica Huston's *Agnes Browne*, Peter (brother of Jim) Sheridan's *Borstal Boy*, and Paul Greengrass's *Bloody Sunday*.

The company has also developed a relationship with another major Irish producer, **Element Films**, leading to collaborations on **John Carney**'s *On the Edge* and Pete Travis's *Omagh*. The partnership was formalized with the establishment of Hell's Kitchen International, which aimed to build on the creative, technical, and financial experience of both companies by offering a complete production support structure to foreign production companies working in Ireland. Projects to date include **Irish Dreamtime**'s *Laws of Attraction* and the Paramount-funded remake of the 1950s U.S. sitcom *The Honeymooners*.

From the mid-2000s, however, production activity at the company tailed off, and the company has been effectively defunct ever since. For his part, Lappin has remained engaged with the arts, acting as the chair of the Dublin International **Film Festival** up to 2013 and temporarily working as the director of The Ark, a children's arts center located adjacent to the **Irish Film Institute** in Dublin's Temple Bar district.

HIBERNIA FILMS, 1945. Not to be confused with Tom Cooper's earlier production company of the same name, Hibernia Films was established in 1945 by Michael Scott (who would later become involved in **Four Provinces**), Stephen O'Flaherty, William Moylan, and cameraman **George**

Fleischmann. After starting operations with a documentary on Michael Davitt, the company went on to produce the Michael Scott–directed documentary short *The Silent Order* in 1948. However, considering that the company sought mainly to produce promotional and informational films for the state at a time when the state evinced relatively little interest in such activities, it was a part-time exercise for most of the partners (with the exception of Fleischmann, whose sole stock-in-trade was camera work). Indeed, by 1949, despite the company's having produced three more films—*Next Please* and *Voyage to Recovery* for the Department of Health and *Lifeline* for Irish Shipping—Fleischmann opted to take on a more secure line of work, supplying film for Movietone in London. The company appears to have effectively ceased operations after that point.

HIBERNIA FILMS, 1933. Killarney garage owner Tom Cooper established Hibernia Films in 1933 to facilitate the production of ***The Dawn***. Despite that film's commercial success, the company made one only more picture: *Uncle Nick* (of which there is no known surviving copy). By the early 1940s, Cooper had exhausted his interest in production and sought to sell Hibernia Studios (built specifically for *The Dawn*) to the state as the basis of a national film studio. Cooper's general interest in cinema was sustained, however, by a move into **exhibition**: by the end 1940s, he had acquired several theaters in Killarney, Doneraile, and Tramore.

HICKEY, JAMES (1954–). Hickey was appointed as the fourth chief executive officer of the **Irish Film Board** (IFB), later Screen Ireland, in February 2011 (formally taking it up in June) after a long career as a lawyer specializing in entertainment (mostly film), and he retired in June 2019. Unlike some of his predecessors, his tenure was marked less by impassioned expressions of the cultural or ideological importance of cinema (though he has not played these down) than by a business-like commitment to maintaining the IFB's existence and then growing the Irish audiovisual sector, goals for which his background and temperament made him ideally suited. His tenure will also be remembered for supporting the initiatives spearheaded by IFB chair Annie Doona in the implementation of schemes promoting gender equality in the industry.

As a law student at Trinity College Dublin in the 1970s, Hickey became involved in Players, the university drama society. The connections he made there would serve him well in the coming decades as his contemporaries advanced through the Irish film, television, and music industries. Before qualifying as a solicitor in 1977, he worked as administrator to the Project Theatre (and later became its chair) and was box office manager at the Dublin Theatre Festival in 1979. Having commenced practice as a solicitor, the 1980s saw him work for musicians and film producers, and he became an early member of Film Makers Ireland (later **Screen Producers Ireland**). Having acted as legal adviser on **Jim Sheridan**'s early features, he joined one of Ireland's largest and most prestigious law firms, Matheson Ormsby Prentice (MOP), in 1992 as a specialist in entertainment law, ultimately becoming a partner at the firm and head of the Media and Entertainment Law Group, whose creation he largely drove. (In 2004, Hickey was appointed to the first of two terms as chairman of the MOP partnership.) The year 1992 also saw him appointed to the chairmanship of the **Abbey Theatre** (a position he retained until 2001) and to the Taoiseach's Special Advisory Group on the Film Industry. His position at MOP saw him act as legal adviser to more than 50 film and television productions in the 2000s, ranging from the Gate Theatre's project to film the complete theater works of Samuel Beckett in 2000 to **Radio Telefís Éireann**'s hit crime series *Love/Hate* in 2010. Even while working for MOP, he remained a consistent advocate for the native film industry, intervening in public debates around Irish film policy at every possible opportunity.

By the start of the 2010s, he was the most experienced film legal adviser in the country. At a time when Irish cinema was becoming increasingly oriented toward international productions and coproductions, Hickey's grasp of the finer points of domestic, supranational, and international film regulation and his fundamental grasp of the legal/contractual structures underlying the foundation of any film project made him an ideal candidate for the role of chief executive of the IFB. That the role almost certainly meant a significant drop in salary from his MOP income also demonstrated a particular commitment to the sector.

Hickey had the misfortune to take up the role at a point when the IFB's funding was in a free fall as a consequence of the post-2008 recession. He unsurprisingly campaigned actively for the implementation of the recommendations of the 2011 **Creative Capital Report**, particularly the proposal that the administration of the increasingly significant Sound and Vision Fund be transferred from the **Broadcasting Authority of Ireland** and into the IFB. In February 2013, he brought the activities of Screen Training Ireland under the control (including budgetary authority) of the IFB and away from FAS, the state training body that was disbanded in 2011, a consolidation of training and funding that strengthened the IFB's remit and reach.

Hickey has sometimes been accused of facilitating the emergence of a creative industries discourse during his tenure at the IFB, emphasizing the economic and employment creation potential of the Irish audiovisual sector over its cultural impact. Critics also point to the IFB's increasing emphasis on projects originated from outside Ireland as a sign of a weakened commitment to cultivating local stories. He has strenuously denied such charges and convincingly argued that without an economically strong industry, there are no stories. Given the context of his appointment, culturally inflected arguments for supporting the arts during a period of austerity have tended be ignored. Additionally the IFB's two internationally oriented schemes were inheritances from an earlier administration. Nevertheless, Hickey's tenure has been associated with a more outward-directed orientation of Irish cinema and its international recognition, not least in the swath of **Academy Award** nominations in 2016 and 2017. (Against this, it has been questioned whether international audiences will have noticed the Irish dimensions of films like **Lenny Abrahamson**'s *Room* [2016], **Paddy Breathnach**'s *Viva* [2015] or Yorgos Lanthimos's *The Lobster* [2016].) Nevertheless, such successes and the consistent message and output of the IFB under his management have paid dividends. In April 2018, the Irish government announced (as part of Project 2040) that it would invest €200 million in media production and the audiovisual industry between 2018 and 2027 with IFB funding restored to its pre-2008 level.

HICKEY, KIERAN (1936–1993). Unusually for an Irish director, Hickey studied film formally in London before returning to Dublin, where, with cameraman Sean Corcoran and editor **J. Patrick Duffner** at B.A.C. Films, he produced a series of documentaries for state agencies and films about writers such as Jonathan Swift and James Joyce. In the promotional material for a festival of Irish film (The Green on the Screen) in 1984, he made some telling comments about how "Ireland on film has always been a dream country. We countered this with no filmic output of our own. So we must not complain if what films show of us is not 'real.' This was the choice we deliberately made. Ireland left the world's screens dark when it might have painted them green." Hickey wrote several books, including *Faithful Departed: The Dublin of James Joyce's* Ulysses (1982). His filmic output, which is highly regarded for its questioning of Irish patriarchal norms and innovative style, includes *A Child's Voice*, *Exposure*, *Criminal Conversation*, and *The Rockingham Shoot*.

He debuted as a fiction director with the short *A Child's Voice* in 1978. Coscripted with film critic David Thomson (who would later eulogize Hickey as "his best friend" in Thomson's *Biographical Dictionary of Film*), the film is a gothic tale about a writer (**T. P. McKenna**) who broadcasts his Le Fanu–esque tales three nights a week but one night finds his own fictional creation turning on him. The film, which pays homage to classic horror films of the 1940s, received extremely positive reviews, winning a prize at the 1978 Chicago International Film Festival.

The same year saw the production of Hickey's first collaboration with screenwriter Philip Davison: *Exposure*. Funded by an Arts Council Script award, the film deals explicitly with the reaction of Irish males to "the other"—here represented by a Continental female—while at the same time highlighting their sexual repression and the cultural insularity of Ireland in the late 1970s. The film tells the story of three male friends who are away from home on a job and become interested in a French photographer whom they meet. Their middle-class misogyny belies a deeply felt critique of Irish masculinity.

Hickey's next collaboration with Davison was *Criminal Conversation* (1980), which starred Emmett Bergin, Deirdre Connelly, and Garret Keogh and dealt with two apparently happy and secure professional married couples living in suburbia. But at a Christmas party during a game of charades, the happy facade of the couples disintegrates with alacrity. Revelations of extramarital affairs serve to irrevocably break up the comfort of their normal lives. While at a formal level the piece appears more theatrical, the visualization of the conflicts is effectively handled and well regarded, dovetailing with contemporary public debates about divorce in the country.

Attracta (1983) was considered by many to have been Hickey's most ambitious undertaking, based on a screen version of William Trevor's short story of the same name and adapted by the author. The veteran stage and screen actress Wendy Hiller was signed to play the role of the spinster teacher who visits the grave of a Belfast victim of violence, evoking her own memories. The strong supporting cast includes Kate Thompson, **John Kavanagh**, and Deirdre Donnelly. Hickey also directed a well-received adaptation of John McGahern's *The Rockingham Shoot* for the BBC in 1987.

Hickey's brother Des, a noted film critic and journalist who had been instrumental in the original establishment of B.A.C. Films in the mid-1960s, died suddenly in June 1992. Sadly, barely a year later, in July 1993, Hickey himself passed away; having survived open-heart surgery, he suffered an embolism and died almost immediately. The timing of his passing was doubly sad given that it coincided with the reemergence of regular production activity in Ireland, which would doubtless have afforded him new opportunities to work. David Thomson said of his death, "He was the best friend I'll ever have, and in a way I feel the movies are over now that he's gone."

HIDDEN AGENDA (1990). In the first of three Irish-set films, British director Ken Loach and his longtime writing partner Jim Allen constructed a conspiracy thriller exploring the involvement of British political elites in the "dirty war" in Northern Ireland. When an American human rights lawyer (Brad Dourif) is assassinated in Belfast, his girlfriend (Frances McDormand) and a senior police detective (Brian Cox) try to uncover the truth. They discover that the dead lawyer held an audiotape implicating political leaders within the highest level of the British establishment in illegal acts committed in the prosecution of the war against the Irish Republican Army (IRA). Judged purely as a political thriller, the film was thoroughly effective. However, the sight of a British filmmaker subjecting his own government's actions to scrutiny in fictional form drew intense criticism in the United Kingdom, where Loach was accused of manipulating local political realities to serve the needs of entertainment. Loach, whose career output since the 1960s constitutes a coherent leftist critique of British politics and society, was not dismayed not least because the film came in the wake of public controversy over the Stalker Inquiry, a real-life investigation by senior police officer John Stalker into the operation of a shoot-to-kill policy on the part of British forces in Northern Ireland whose findings were never made public.

***HIDEAWAYS* (*THE LAST FURLONG*) (2011).** Before collaborating with **Chris O'Dowd** on the Sky TV sitcom *Moone Boy* (2013–), screenwriter Nick Murphy scripted this dark fairy tale of troubled teens in the tradition of Tim Burton via Stephen Sondheim. Although strikingly original in conception and contemporary in setting and tone, the film's deployment of Ireland as a setting apart from modernity continues and reinforces a long-established tradition for overseas producers (the film is a French–Irish–Swedish coproduction with a French director) and audiences. It might also be grouped within the copious subgenres of Irish film dealing with residential institutions and displaced masculinities.

James Furlong (Harry Treadaway) is born into a family where the males are cursed with strange powers: his grandfather is blinded (literally) by thoughts of sex, his father causes machinery to break when scared (leading to the death of James's mother as she is driven to a maternity hospital), and James radiates Thanatos when he feels pain, killing everyone and everything in his surroundings. When he is sent to live in a reformatory, the eight-year-old James cannot control these powers. Attacked by bullies, he kills a multitude of students and even injures his best friend, Liam (Thomas Brodie Sangster). Horrified, he flees into the woods, determined not to cause further harm.

A decade later, Mae (Rachel Hurd-Wood) is a terminal cancer patient at the former reformatory now turned hospital. Straying into the woods, she encounters the teenage James living a solitary existence in a cabin surrounded by dead things. Equally cursed, the two connect amid the unadulterated beauty of the woodland, and when she returns to the hospital, staff and patients are captivated by her rejuvenated lust for life. Yet events take a darker turn when Liam, now also a teenager and still a chronically ill patient at the hospital, discovers their relationship and determines to seek revenge on James.

Although the burgeoning romance and the wooded setting grounds invoke a Brothers Grimm–like story universe, the film never quite sustains its more fantastical conceits, and director Agnes Merlet's background in visual arts can be felt in the privileging of the visual over a concern for the psychological development of her protagonists. Strikingly shot by Tim Fleming, *Hide-*

aways is frequently more interested in the flora and fauna of the quasi-mythological forest (including a dramatic, extended underwater sequence) than any meaningful development of narrative. Instead, the film arguably simply rehearses the identification of Ireland as a land of magic and fairy tales. That it appears to consider this depiction so unproblematic points to the lingering influence of older representations of Ireland, even after more than two decades of sustained indigenous filmic output.

HIGGINS, MICHAEL D. (1941–). As a published poet of some renown who came to politics from an academic background, Higgins (or "Michael D." as the Irish arts community tends to refer to him) was always an unusual figure among Irish politicians. As a politician, he was uniquely successful in pushing through a film arts agenda in Ireland and setting the tone for its legitimacy within government policy. Educated at University College Galway (UCG) and in Illinois and Manchester, he became a lecturer in political science at UCG. He became a Labour Party senator in 1973 before winning his first Dáil election in 1981. He lost his seat in 1982 and returned to the Senate before successfully contesting the 1987 general election. He was subsequently reelected in every election up to his decision not to contest the 2011 election.

Labour's spectacular success at the 1992 elections (then the party's best-ever result but eclipsed by the 37 seats secured in the 2011 election) was followed by long-drawn-out negotiations with Fine Gael and Fianna Fáil with a view to establishing the next administration. Part of those negotiations included creating a new ministry with responsibility for arts, culture, and the Gaeltacht, areas that had hitherto fallen within the bailiwick of the Department of Industry and Commerce and the Department of the Taoiseach. When those negotiations resulted in a Fianna Fáil–Labour coalition, Higgins was appointed minister to the new department, a decision that was hailed within filmmaking circles as promising the return of the **Irish Film Board** (IFB). However, initially, Higgins was somewhat cautious, suggesting that it might be 1996 before the film support structures suggested by documents such as the *Coopers & Lybrand Report* were fully in place.

However, as a pragmatic politician, Higgins seized the political opportunity gifted to him by **Neil Jordan**'s success at the 1993 **Academy Awards**, reestablishing the IFB within 24 hours of that ceremony. He subsequently drove through the establishment of the Independent Production Unit at **Radio Telefís Éireann**, encouraged his counterpart in the Department of Finance (then Minister Bertie Ahern) to overhaul the **Section 35** tax incentive, and oversaw the setting up of the Irish-language television station TG4 and the creation of the **Irish Screen Commission** as a subsidiary of the IFB. By the time he was forced to step down in 1997 after a new election returned a Fianna Fáil–led government, he could reasonably claim to have put the basic infrastructure for a sustainable indigenous audiovisual industry in place.

He has always been a great polemicist and orator, as reflected in his assertion regarding the importance of homegrown production and media literacy and the need for Irish filmmakers to make images that actively reflect and enrich national culture. Yet his success as politician also owed much to his political nous and pragmatism. Given the still-fragile state of the Irish economy in the early 1990s, he was careful to couch the need for audiovisual support measures in language that simultaneously emphasized both the cultural and the economic importance of the film industry, stressing that he was prepared to suspend such support if they proved to be a drain on state resources.

In 2004, Higgins had signaled to the Labour Party that he was interested in running as a candidate for the position of Irish president, the titular head of state. In the event, the reappointment of the incumbent president, Mary McAleese, was not contested in 2004. However, in September 2010, a month before announcing his retirement as a TD (Irish member of Parliament), Higgins again allowed his name to go forward and was ratified as the Labour Party candidate in June 2011. After a closely fought and controversial campaign, Higgins emerged as victor, taking office in November 2011. Although required to adopt a nonpartisan stance as president, his pronouncements in office remained informed by his core socialist principles, not least when critiquing the social fallout of the long recession after 2008. He was reelected for a second term in 2018.

HIGH BOOT BENNY (1993). Although director **Joe Comerford** had been working on the script for *High Boot Benny* since the mid-1970s, it wasn't until the reestablishment of the **Irish Film Board** that he was able to secure the financing to actually make it. Set in an alternative school located on the site of a former British fort near the border with Northern Ireland, the highly metaphorical narrative centers on three marginalized characters who constitute a kind of family grouping: Benny (Marc O'Shea), an emotionally damaged student, is the "son" of ex-priest Manley (Alan Devlin) and the school's Protestant matron (**Frances Tomelty**).

The border setting of the school is significant; the school attempts to forge a path outside the strictures of the politics informing the activities of the British army and Loyalist and nationalist paramilitaries. Initially, Benny tries to embrace the idealism of the school's mission, but when a naked corpse is found near the school, the entire institution is drawn into the clash between local military and paramilitary forces. Martin McLoone has noted that the tragedy of the film is that Benny is unable to escape the dogmas of Northern and Southern Irish politics and ultimately finds himself in the position of having to take sides.

HIGH SPIRITS (1988). In a desperate attempt to hold on to his ancestral home in Ireland, Lord Peter Plunkett (**Peter O'Toole**) and his staff conspire to market the castle as a haunted hotel. Among the first coachloads of American guests are Jack and Sharon (Steve Guttenberg and Beverly D'Angelo), who are on a second honeymoon to revive a flagging marriage. During the first night of their stay, the guests duly witness a motley crew of ghosts sweeping through the castle, but these are quickly revealed as the castle staff in costume. Feeling cheated, the guests decide to leave en masse the next morning. At this point, however, the castle's real ghosts step in to save the castle, prompting a mass haunting and inadvertent love affairs between the dead and the living.

On its release in 1988, **Neil Jordan**'s first U.S.-financed film came as something of a shock. After his first three films, Jordan was comfortably in the vanguard of Irish filmmakers—the early promise of *Angel* was apparently confirmed by *The Company of Wolves* and *Mona Lisa*. *High Spirits*, however, attracted almost uniformly negative reviews and, together with Jordan's next film, *We're No Angels* (1989), appeared to suggest a worrying lurch toward a more crudely commercial ambition. It was not until *The Crying Game* that *High Spirits* was reassessed as a regrettable but ultimately pardonable aberration.

That said, the film unquestionably ranks at the bottom of the Jordan canon, featuring the worst acting and dialogue of any of his films, delivered by a cast clearly chosen with an eye to the U.S. market. American stars Steve Guttenberg and Darryl Hannah are clearly unsure about where to pitch their performances. Some of the Irish cast members—**Donal McCann, Ray McAnally**, and, in particular, **Liam Neeson**—acquit themselves with more dignity, but it is nonetheless local hero Peter O'Toole who delivers the hammiest performance. That the dialogue came from an individual who had previously displayed such a gift for using ordinary language to explore political and emotional issues of extraordinary complexity was bewildering.

In his defense, Jordan has argued that the film was completed by "the studio," which imposed a feel-good style on the picture and muted the more disturbing elements. There is some evidence within the film to support this, such as a hinted discussion on the inevitable differences between the portrayal of Ireland for tourists and the reality of its everyday existence. But this too is submerged into what becomes a tourist board–approved portrayal of Ireland. There is also ample evidence of studio interference in the editing since at times there is no narrative, just a sequence of increasingly disconnected events, denying the film any meaningful sense of closure.

HINDS, CIARÁN (1953–). While never achieving the leading-man international star status of several Irish screen actors of his acquaintance and generation (i.e., **Liam Neeson**, **Pierce Brosnan**, or **Gabriel Byrne**), Ciarán Hinds's facility as a character actor has seen him cast in an extraordinary diversity of roles ranging from Irish art house material to Hollywood blockbusters, with the latter particularly coming to the fore after he passed age 50.

Born and raised in Belfast, the youngest of five children, Hinds's father hoped his son would follow him into the medical profession, but he was more taken with acting, a path he was encouraged to follow by his mother. Having appeared in several school productions at St. Malachy's College, he entered Queen's University Belfast to study law but left before completing the degree to train as an actor at the Royal Academy of Dramatic Arts in London. He then spent the best part of a decade working with the renowned Citizens' Theatre in Glasgow, with occasional forays to work onstage in London, Dublin, and Belfast with, among others, the Field Day and Druid theater companies. In 1987, Peter Brook cast him in his epic six-hour version of *The Mahabharata*, which toured internationally, and he subsequently appeared in Brook's screen version.

Hinds made his film debut in 1981 in John Boorman's *Excalibur* and was subsequently memorable opposite **Donal McCann** in **Thaddeus O'Sullivan**'s *December Bride* (1990) as Frank Echlin, an outcast from his closeted Presbyterian milieu, a man unwilling to conform to social expectations. Hinds embodied him as an outwardly stern figure torn by inner emotional turmoil. That duality, along with a physically imposing presence, made him a perfect fit for a series of late 1990s TV adaptations of classic English literature: as Captain Wentworth in the BBC's *Persuasion* (1995), Edward Rochester in *Jane Eyre* (1997), and Michael Henchard in Thomas Hardy's *The Mayor of Casterbridge* (2003). By the end of the 1990s, he was increasingly seen on the big screen as well: playing the mischievous Professor Flynn in *Circle of Friends*, a sympathetic Sinn Féin leader (clearly modeled on Gerry Adams) in *Some Mother's Son*, and the male lead opposite Julie Walters in *Titanic Town*.

By the late 1990s, Hinds was becoming increasingly familiar to international audiences, making appearances in Chris Menges's *The Lost Son* (1999) and Kathryn Bigelow's *The Weight of Water* and receiving third billing behind Ralph Fiennes and Cate Blanchett in Gillian Armstrong's *Oscar and Lucinda* (1997). He followed these with a brief but significant appearance in Sam Mendes's *Road to Perdition* (2002), playing an Irish American gangster before going the blockbuster route opposite Angela Jolie in *Lara Croft: The Cradle of Life* (2003). He has also worked twice with Joel Schumacher, playing another gangster (this time based on a real-life figure) in *Veronica Guerin* and in the poorly received musical adaptation of *The Phantom of the Opera* (2004). In 2005, he made a brief return to Northern

Ireland to star in *Mickybo and Me* before taking on the high-profile role of Julius Caesar in the BBC's €100 million drama production *Rome* (2005–2007). Confirmation of his international appeal appeared the same year when Steven Spielberg cast him in a lead role opposite Eric Bana and Daniel Craig in *Munich* (2005) as an Israeli secret service agent ordered to assassinate Palestinian guerrillas.

Since *Munich*, Hinds has appeared in more than 50 feature films and headlined a number of television series. He brought characteristic gravitas to a sequence of art house roles in the late 1990s: a restrained Fletcher Hamilton to Daniel Day-Lewis's Daniel Plainview in Paul Thomas Anderson's *There Will Be Blood* (2007), writer Dirk Koosman in Noah Baumbach's *Margot at the Wedding* (2007), and a pedophile psychiatrist in Todd Solondz's *Life During Wartime* (2009).

Hinds's roles have tended to exploit his calm yet authoritative persona. Priests (in *A Tiger's Tail* [2006], *In Bruges* [2008], *The Rite* [2011], *Last Days in the Desert* [2015], and, opposite **Liam Neeson**, Martin's Scorsese's *Silence* [2016]) loom large on his résumé, as do cops/agents (as DCI Langton opposite Kelly Relly in ITV's *Above Suspicion* [2009–2012], working for Mossad again in *The Debt* [2010], as weary MI5 operative Roy Bland in *Tinker, Tailor, Soldier, Spy* [2011], as a grizzled police chief in *McCanick* [2013], and as Russian agents in *Hitman: Agent 47* [2015] and *Red Sparrow* [2017]). He is the captain of a ship seeking the North-West Passage in AMC's *The Terror* (2017) serial and, perhaps most remarkably, gave life to DC Comics' supervillain Steppenwolf via motion capture and computer-generated imagery in *Justice League* (2017).

This list of screen roles is all the more remarkable given his commitment to work in theater. Simultaneously cast in the pivotal role of Mance Rayder (the "King Beyond the Wall" in *Game of Thrones*) and as Big Daddy opposite Scarlett Johansson in a Broadway revival of Tennessee Williams's *Cat on a Hot Tin Roof* in 2013, Hinds found himself crossing the Atlantic between Reykjavik and New York several times a week. Within the theater, he has developed a particularly close working relationship with writer/director **Conor McPherson**, appearing in five of his plays, including *The Seafarer* (2007) and *Girl from the North Country* (2017). When McPherson came to adapt Billy Roche's short story *The Eclipse* as a feature in 2013, Hinds was a natural fit for the lead role of Michael Farr, a widower who believes he is seeing ghosts.

As a young actor, Hinds looked older than his years: just 26 when he shot *December Bride*, the role required him to play Frank Echlin to middle age. On-screen, we have never seen him as truly youthful, innocent, and carefree. This plays out in his more recent roles in indigenous work. Literally haunted in *The Eclipse*, in both *The Sea* (2013) and **Terry George**'s Oscar-winning short *The Shore* (2011), Hinds's soft visage hints at how his respective characters—Max and Jim—are tormented by their personal histories, confronting demons as yet unbanished.

HIS AND HERS (2009). In a series of highly individual, award-winning documentary short films (most notably *Undressing My Mother* [2004]), Ken Wardrop emerged as a unique directorial sensibility in Irish cinema. That early potential was developed on in *His and Hers*, an unlikely yet entirely enchanting documentary feature film structured around the life cycle of women in the Irish Midlands. Eschewing the familiar features of the genre, the film does not foreground a particular character, narrative, or problem but instead composites a group portrait of women from childhood to old age and their relationship to men as daughters, wives, and widows.

His and Hers had a small but highly successful Irish cinema release in 2010 (playing for an incredible three months) and has enjoyed a significant afterlife on DVD. It won the Audience award at the Dublin International Film Festival, the Feature award at the Galway Film Fleadh (Festival), an IFTA for Best Feature Documentary, and the Cinematography award at the Sundance Film Festival in 2010.

HOW HARRY BECAME A TREE (2001). *How Harry Became a Tree* presents an awkward case for questions of national designation. Although set in Ireland and featuring an Irish cast led by **Colm Meaney**, **Cillian Murphy**, and **Adrian Dunbar**, it was directed by the Serbian filmmaker Goran Paskaljević from a script cowritten by him and Irish playwright Stephen Walsh. The screenplay was originally written in Serb based on an adaptation of a 1980s Chinese novella, *Lao Dan*, by Yang Zhengguang, read in a Serbian adaptation by Paskaljević. When a film based around the theme of warring neighbors became impossible to finance in postwar Serbia, the script was rewritten by Paskaljević's wife in French in the hopes of securing coproduction finance. When that approach also fell through, it was rewritten (again) in English and the setting transposed to post–Civil War Ireland with the production financed largely by an Italian producer and shot on location in Ireland by a mixed crew of Irish and Serbians.

The titular Harry (Colm Meaney) is a farmer battered by life: his favorite son is dead, killed in the recent Civil War. So too is his wife, having succumbed to a broken heart. He is left with his remaining son, the simpleminded Gus (Cillian Murphy), and a carefully nurtured hatred of successful local publican and matchmaker George (Dunbar). Having lost nearly everything dear to him, Harry determines to sustain himself by fomenting an artificial feud with a man he sees as the worthiest adversary since "a man is measured by his enemies." Matters are complicated when Harry avails himself of George's services to find a match for Gus: Eileen (**Kerry Condon**) is put forward and marries Gus, but the latter, sexually inexperienced, is slow to consummate the marriage, and George beds her instead. Determined to avenge this betrayal, Harry connives to shame George by seeking to drive Eileen to suicide. However, in so doing, he threatens the destruction of what remains of his own family.

The film's diversity of origins may help to explain the relative dearth of commentary on the film and its relationship to an Irish film culture. *How Harry Became a Tree* complicates the notion that the Irish nation is a coherent, unified entity and deepens this problematic status in its confounding of stereotypes, conventions, and narrative coherence. The difficulty for its consideration within a framework of national cinema is that it is neither within nor without, employing Irish linguistic, visual, and thematic tropes while never really taking these seriously enough; indeed, it constantly undermines them. The film veers between a realist and an absurdist idiom, proposing recognizable codes only to render them incomplete and insufficient to our grasp of the film's meaning. In the end, the film abandons realism entirely even as it reinforces its primacy as a historical source.

Director Paskaljević explained that although he saw the material of the short story as being applicable to the civil war in Yugoslavia and the rise to power of Slobodan Milošević, he could not return to filmmaking in his native land for fear of his personal safety. The decision to make the film in Ireland, a setting he knew little of, was suggested to him by his Italian producer. Nonetheless, he was taken by Ireland's long history of enmity with a near neighbor, which fitted the core theme of the source text. Thus, Ireland can be understood as an accidental, even metaphorical, environment for the story.

How Harry Became a Tree is an exciting and, at the time rare, instance of transnational discourse in Irish cinema, distinguished from the many coproductions that formed a core part of the **Irish Film Board**'s financing policy in the late 1990s. Its transnationalism is not merely a matter of financial expediency (though its production history is clearly important to understanding it), nor is it an instance of Irish diasporic cinema that dominates understandings of this category. Rather, it is transnational in its interest in the nation as a nonessential or an international construct: what can be said about one nation can be said about many.

HOW TO CHEAT IN THE LEAVING CERTIFICATE (1998). Shot in black and white and on an almost impossibly low budget, this short narrative is somewhat underdeveloped and suffers from sketchy character exposition. Nonetheless, as a scheme to secure exam papers for the final Irish second school exam takes off, the inevitable complications lend the narrative an agreeable caper movie quality. These are augmented by a series of cameos from well-known figures in Irish life (singer Chris De Burgh, broadcaster Joe

Duffy, and drag queen Mr. Pussy) whom neophyte director Graham Jones convinced to participate gratis. The film is punctuated by amusing vignettes, including **Eamonn Morrissey**'s performance as a nearly psychotic teacher terrifying his pupils into studying by shouting about how the Leaving Certificate is the most important thing in their lives. As such, the film works for those who recognize the real psychological trauma imposed by the test on unfortunate Irish teenagers but may be less comprehensible to audiences beyond Ireland.

HUBERMAN, AMY (1979–). Having cemented her status as Ireland's "national sweetheart" in 2010 by marrying another national treasure, former Ireland rugby captain Brian O'Driscoll, Amy Huberman's celebrity status and its accoutrements (she has both a shoe and a jewelry line in her name, published two comic novels, and has one of the largest social media followings in the country) sometimes obscure the fact that her day job is as an actor. Cast primarily in roles drawing on her blemish-free (literally and figuratively), squeaky-clean, "It girl" public image, Huberman is best known for a string of roles on Irish television, divided in roughly equal measure between straight and comedy work.

One of three children raised on Dublin's south side by her Anglo-Irish parents (her father is a London-born Jewish fashion designer, and her brother Mark is also an actor), she attended Loreto College, Foxrock, and, outside formal education, the renowned Betty Ann Norton drama school. While studying sociology at University College Dublin, she joined the Drama Society (encountering later collaborator **Chris O'Dowd**), but it was not until earning a media studies master's at the Dublin Institute of Technology that she secured her first professional acting role in *Bad Karma* (2001) in a straight-to-video U.S. genre piece shot in Galway.

However, Huberman first came to the attention of the wider Irish public across two seasons of the drama *On Home Ground* (**Radio Telefís Éireann** [RTÉ], 2001–2002), playing Diane Collins, the assertive, self-confident daughter of the lead protagonist, a small-town Gaelic football coach played by **Sean McGinley**. She quickly became a staple of RTÉ drama, appearing in two seasons of *Showbands* (2005 2006) and, most prominently, in all nine seasons of *The Clinic*, still the longest-lived nonsoap RTÉ drama and the platform for a host of Irish acting careers (including **Saoirse Ronan**, **Ruth Bradley**, and Chris O'Dowd). Introduced as dizzy, carefree secretary Daisy, the role initially played on Huberman's south-side party-girl persona. However, as the character moved up through the ranks (ultimately co-owning the medical practice in which the series was set), she acquired gravitas and was associated with story lines of much darker hues than previously. While still appearing in *The Clinic*, she relocated to London, but while securing minor roles in *Inspector George Gently* and a short-lived spin-off from Sky Television's popular soccer-themed *Dream Team* series, she struggled to secure routine work in the United Kingdom.

Stories of her waitressing in London and briefly working as a substitute primary teacher in this period point to a committed work ethic that at times has seen her choose roles in, frankly, fairly trashy low-budget genre work over not working at all. Thus, though scarcely seen in Ireland (or anywhere), her filmography includes such unlikely ventures as *Legend of the Bog* (2009), a ludicrous narrative about a resurrected 2,000-year-old man found in an Irish marsh; *Chasing Leprechauns* (2012), a Hallmark Channel piece of whimsical hokum; and *Kill Ratio* (2016), filmed in Ireland but set in eastern Europe and featuring Huberman as an American corporate executive caught up in a military coup.

An earlier appearance in **Ian Fitzgibbon**'s black comedy *A Film with Me in It* (2008) suggests that casting directors had overlooked Huberman's capacity for comedy and skill for self-deprecation. Cast as Mark Doherty's girlfriend Sally, she gave a performance that self-consciously played on her background and persona as an ambitious young woman increasingly frustrated and ultimately exasperated at her partner's utter lack of direction. This was quickly followed by a stint with the cast of director John Butler's comedy sketch show *Your Bad Self* (2010) opposite, among others, **Domhnall Gleeson** and **Hugh O'Conor**. Not only did this confirm her as a talented comedienne, but it also established a working relationship with Butler that saw her cast in his subsequent features *The Stag* (2013) and *Handsome Devil* (2016). Although her appearances were relatively brief, she offered a welcome relief in those otherwise testosterone-fueled narratives as a winsome bride-to-be in the former and a blithe trophy wife oblivious to her surroundings in the latter.

This trajectory continued when she was cast as the lead in Comedy Central's first in-house–produced sitcom, *Threesome* (2011–2012). Playing a fun-loving girl about town who finds herself pregnant as a result of a one-off ménage à trois, Huberman brought a frenetic quality to the affair, as her character faces the implications of unplanned motherhood with a steely determination. The critically well-received two seasons of *Threesome* brought her to attention of U.K. casting agents and appearances in the sitcom *Heading Out* (2013) and the police procedural *Silent Witness* (2015) and a recurring role as a wronged wife in the reboot of ITV's popular *Cold Feet* (2017).

In the meantime, a number of Irish small-screen projects offered opportunities: her turn as hippie art teacher Miss Tivnan in *Moone Boy* (2014) presaged her casting on RTÉ in the Stephanie Preissner–scripted comedy *Can't Cope, Won't Cope* (2016–) as the perennially exasperated corporate finance boss to the lead character played by Seana Kerslake. Back in dramatic mode, she anchored RTÉ's prime-time drama schedule in the stylish *Striking Out* (2017–) as a young solicitor who abandons the safety of her job to set up her own practice.

Given this profile, her absence from leading roles in higher-profile Irish feature film work is striking. Other than the titles mentioned above, her most prominent feature role to date was in the low-budget thriller **Rewind** (2010). Despite—perhaps because of—being cast against type as a working-class ex-criminal seeking to escape her murky past, Huberman's revelatory lead performance was critical to the success of the film and won her an IFTA in 2010. The apparent reluctance to cast her outside type more frequently means that she hasn't matched the impact of her television presence on the big screen. Now increasingly engaged as a screenwriter in her own right, it may be that she will have to create her own roles to find characters who fully challenge her range and talent.

HUNGER (2008). By any standards, Steve McQueen's account of the 1981 hunger strikes by Republican prisoners in the Maze prison in Northern Ireland is a remarkable undertaking. Other filmmakers have taken on the subject before—**Terry George**'s *Some Mother's Son* (1996) and Les Blair's *H3* spring to mind—but none with McQueen's singular perspective. At a glance, the appeal of the story to McQueen, a black British Turner Prize–winning artist, is far from obvious. He has written that as a black boy growing up in London's Brixton during the 1981 riots, the hunger strikes and the recurrent televisual image of the leader of the strikers, Bobby Sands, became inextricably intertwined in his youthful consciousness.

The film is divided into a triptych. The largely dialogue-free first section follows a warden at the Maze prison as he moves from his "normal" domestic existence (which involves checking under his car every morning for explosives) into the charged conflict zone that is the prison. Through the warden's perspective (but also that of a new Republican prisoner), we encounter the "dirty protests" undertaken by Republican prisoners seeking the restoration of political status. They refuse to wear prison uniforms, to wash, or even to allow bodily waste to be removed from their cells. In the middle section of the film, a bravura 17-minute sequence composed of two shots, we watch the verbal fencing match between Bobby Sands (**Michael Fassbender**) and a Republican-sympathizing priest (**Liam Cunningham**). Sands is determined to begin—and, if necessary, complete—a hunger strike for political status: though sympathetic with the objective, the priest cannot countenance the conscious destruction of life. In the final—again, almost wordless—segment, McQueen's camera lingers over Sands's body as it slowly disintegrates from within, the final battleground on which Republicans chose to face down the British government.

Given McQueen's art film background, *Hunger* is unsurprisingly a primarily visual (as opposed to a plot- or character-driven) work. At one level, this may be a strategic consideration: to even enter into the realm of the hunger strikes is to enter a political minefield. Objectively speaking, the hunger strikes led Republicanism to adopt the political strategy that gave rise to the modern Sinn Féin political party, which became part of the power-sharing Executive in Northern Ireland and an increasingly significant political force in the Republic of Ireland. McQueen's work reminds the viewer that behind the layers of symbolic meaning ascribed to the body of Bobby Sands, an essential and incarnate humanity remains, and this is the primary concern of the film.

Yet, though McQueen has sought to assert that the film is both apolitical and neutral, this is hard to sustain. Even in the Republic of Ireland, some commentators accused McQueen of aestheticizing the hunger strikers and overlooking their acts and support of terrorism. Nonetheless, although the targeting is oblique, the film critiques the manner in which the British state—represented by the voices of then British Prime Minister Margaret Thatcher and her local representatives in the Northern Ireland Office—contributed to the unique circumstances of Northern Ireland, indirectly inflicting physical and psychological scars on all who reside there. Thus, although we are afforded much greater insight to the thinking of Sands, the film is nonetheless at pains to reserve some sympathy for the position of the prison warden, who, in his own way, is also imprisoned by the unique political circumstances of Northern Ireland during the Troubles. The film clearly demonstrates how the obligation to brutally repress Republican prisoners comes at a great cost to the individual who must enact this element of the will of the state.

Nonetheless, the central figure in the film is Fassbender's Bobby Sands, whose body is used as a means of expression as much as are his voice and face. Initially, it is the site of violence visited from without as he resists the prison regime: once the hunger strike begins, the physical violence comes from within, but, though slower to take effect, it is no less dramatic. Under careful medical supervision, Fassbender dropped to 58 kilograms in weight for the final scenes: as he declines, Sands is depicted as both increasingly embodied (in the sense of being defined by his physical frame) and increasingly removed from the physical plane. In the almost unbearable concluding sequences, Sands is depicted studying the concavities and welts of his torso, his body reduced to a skin-covered skeleton.

The decision to focus on Sands is critical to understanding the film. For Irish and British audiences, the contemporary representation of the Troubles was always problematic: broadcasting restrictions in both countries severely limited the range of political perspectives that could find expression. In the Republic of Ireland in particular, those associated with paramilitary organizations were effectively banned from the airwaves between 1972 and 1994.

In consequence, the understanding of events north of the border, including the hunger strikes, could ever be only partial and in particular served to delegitimize the objectives of those associated with Republicanism. Thus, although *Hunger* is far from a pro-Republican text, the simple decision to intensely and sympathetically focus on a single Republican prisoner—to suggest why an apparently rational and intelligent individual might decide to pursue a paramilitary path—acts as a corrective to the preeminent media discourses that crudely dismiss all political violence as "terrorism."

HUNT, PETER. Although born in France, Hunt grew up in England before moving to Northern Ireland during World War II. After the war, Hunt and his wife Iris moved to southern Ireland and established a sound recording studio over May's record shop on Saint Stephen's Green in Dublin. Over the course of the next two decades, he would acquire an international reputation as a sound engineering expert, called on by technology companies like Nagra and EMI to advise on equipment design. Hunt's name would subsequently appear as sound editor or recordist on many of the key Irish documentaries of the 1950s and 1960s, often in conjunction with cameraman **George Fleischmann**. These included **Patrick Carey**'s *Yeats Country* (1965) and the occasional fiction piece, such as the **Academy Award**–nominated short *Return to Glennascaul* (1951). With his studio employee Gene Martin, he was also responsible for all aspects of sound recording on **Gael Linn**'s *Amharc Eireann* series.

In the later 1960s, he was quietly active in lobbying for state support for the industry and was one of those who encouraged **Louis Marcus** to write his seminal 1967 *Irish Times* series critiquing contemporary Irish film policy. His expertise was not limited to film sound, however; he was responsible for theater sound on productions such as Michael MacLiammoir's *The Importance of Being Oscar* and performances of *Seán O'Riada* at the Saint Francis Xavier Centre. His recording studios were also used for music recordings—the traditional group The Chieftains recorded their first album there in 1961 with a young **Morgan O'Sullivan** as the engineer. Hunt continued working into the 1970s before retiring to his home in Greystones, where he died in the mid-1990s.

HURST, BRIAN DESMOND (1895–1986). Hurst was born in Belfast to a Protestant working-class family and left Ireland for Canada in 1921, enrolling in art college. He continued to study art in Paris and got into a circle of French and émigré intellectuals and artists. As confirmed by film historian Ruth Barton, he was introduced to **John Ford** in 1928 (Barton 2004). During the 1930s and 1940s, he became a prolific filmmaker as a director for hire. His Irish films include *Irish Hearts* (1935), a romantic melodrama based on the novel *Night Nurse* by J. Johnson Abraham, which made some money, and an adaptation of Synge's *Riders to the Sea*, apparently financed by Gracie Fields, which did not. His next Irish venture, **Ourselves Alone**, is based on the play by Dudley Sturrock and is set during the War of Independence. He became a noted figure in the British film industry over the course of the 1940s and 1950s and is perhaps best regarded for *Scrooge*, his 1951 take on Charles Dickens's *A Christmas Carol*, featuring Alastair Sim.

His last film was an adaptation of J. M. Synge's **The Playboy of the Western World**, produced by the **Four Provinces** production company and starring **Siobhan McKenna**, Gary Raymond, Elizabeth March, and Brendan Couldwell. The film is a solid if conventional and sometimes staid fleshing out and visualization of the famous play and is arguably undermined by the casting of English actor Raymond in the lead role and that of 41-year-old Siobhan McKenna in the role of ingenue Pegeen Mike. Hurst's other films include his most successful wartime drama, *Dangerous Moonlight* (1941). His Irish films remain important for expressing (albeit from a British perspective) the need for reconciliation and for appreciating Irish identity from a broader point of view.

HUSH-A-BYE BABY (1989). Directed by Margo Harkin and produced by the **Channel 4**–backed **Derry Film and Video Co-Operative**, *Hush-a-Bye-Baby* very much reflects its era in its exploration of the mores of sex and extramarital pregnancy in 1980s Ireland.

Goretti (**Emer McCourt**) is a Catholic schoolgirl living through the height of the Troubles in the Derry of 1984. While some of her friends—notably Sinead (**Sinead O'Connor**, an inspired piece of casting against type)—fantasize about becoming nuns, Goretti is making out with her Republican-sympathizing boyfriend Ciaran (Michael Liebman). Against a background of British soldiers patrolling urban streets and "supergrass" trials (based on arrested paramilitaries seeking to evade a sentence by "ratting out" their associates), Ciaran is lifted by the Royal Ulster Constabulary and imprisoned. Unable to contact him, Goretti discovers she is pregnant, trapped in a conservative culture where premarital sex is abhorred and abortion simply unavailable. Unable to confide in her family or friends, she carries her secret alone until the last possible moment.

The 1980s was a period in which the taken-for-granted patriarchal nature of Irish society (north and south of the border) and profoundly repressive attitudes toward sexuality found expression in a sequence of dispiriting—indeed, often horrific—narratives. In 1983, a referendum instituted the notorious eighth amendment to the 1937 Irish Constitution, not merely upholding an existing ban on abortion but also asserting that the right to life of the unborn child was legally equivalent to that of the mother, who was effectively reduced to the status of a pregnancy-carrying vessel. In the following year,

1984 (in which the film is set), a 15-year-old schoolgirl, Anne Lovett, died along with her newborn baby, which she had delivered in a Catholic grotto: she had kept her pregnancy a secret from everyone around her throughout.

At a point in time when it seemed impossible to look beyond the binaries of Nationalist versus Unionist in any Northern Ireland–set drama, director Harkin's radical text sought to demonstrate the extent to which such dichotomies disguised the operation of other forms of domination. As Catholics living in a Republican area, Goretti and her friends are manifestly subject to the ongoing surveillance of armed representative of Her Majesty's forces. Yet the film demonstrates how, even in the absence of the British army, Irish women are subject to a patriarchal gaze that seeks to regulate their sexual behavior. That this is at least as prevalent south of the border is emphasized by an extended sequence where Goretti and her friend Majella (Jule Marie Reynolds) travel to a Gaeltacht (Irish-speaking) area to refresh their language skills. In a direct nod to the Anne Lovett narrative, Goretti is confronted by Marian grottoes, and visions of Mary begin to populate her nightmares. Despite contemplating suicide and a self-induced termination, Goretti is ultimately unable to escape her fate, but the film offers little optimism as to what the life of a single teenage mother in a Catholic enclave of an already conservative state might look like.

HUSTON, JOHN (1906–1987). A renowned film director and indeed actor—he received an Oscar nomination for his role in *The Cardinal* (1963) and a Cannes nomination for *Chinatown* (1974)—Huston lived in Ireland for more than 20 years, became an Irish citizen, was a key figure in the campaign for state support for a film industry, and made four films in Ireland. Born in Nevada, Missouri, he was of part-Irish extraction, his paternal great-grandfather having left Armagh for Canada in 1840. After working as a boxer and a journalist, his introduction to Hollywood came at the age of 27 when his father—actor Walter Huston—invited him to do a script polish on the film he was then working on: *A House Divided*. The production company—Universal—was happy enough with the polish to offer Huston a contract as a writer.

In 1938, after a sojourn in the United Kingdom, he moved to Warner Bros., where his contract stipulated that he was permitted to direct a film. He chose to adapt Dashiell Hammett's *The Maltese Falcon*—against the advice of his studio, which was concerned that two previous filmed versions had flopped. Famously, however, Huston's version went on to become a film classic and instantly cemented his reputation. In 1942, he joined the U.S. Army, which put his directorial talents to use as part of the Signal Corps. By the end of the war, he was Major Huston. He then returned to Hollywood, directing four films between 1946 and 1948, including *The Treasure of the Sierra Madre* (1948), for which his father won a Best Actor Oscar, and *Key*

Largo (1948). When his contract with Warner Bros. lapsed in 1948, he established Horizon Pictures with Sam Spiegel, for which he made *The African Queen* (1951).

Just before starting work on that film, he visited Ireland for the first time. At the invitation of the Guinness family, he attended a hunt ball in the Gresham Hotel, Dublin, staged by the Galway Blazer Hunt. This led to an introduction to fox hunting in Ireland; Huston became so enamoured with this activity that in 1953 he rented a country house near Kilcock, County Kildare, where he and his family lived for a few years before he purchased a Georgian manor house in Galway, on 100 acres of land, called Saint Clerans. Having bought the house in a state of some disrepair from the Irish Land Commission, Huston spent two years and a significant sum of money restoring it. He and his family lived there for 18 years until the early 1970s.

Two of his children later returned to Ireland to work on film projects. Tony Huston wrote the screenplay for **The Dead**, his father's adaptation of **James Joyce**'s short story "The Dead," while Angelica, who starred in *The Dead*, also directed Brendan Carroll's **Agnes Browne** in 1996. Huston's autobiographical account of life at Saint Clerans depicts him as the squire of the manor, mixing with local gentry and actively participating in the hunt season, becoming "master" of the Galway Blazers for a decade. Despite this and the fact that in 1964 he became an Irish citizen and received an honorary doctorate from Trinity College, Huston does not appear to have regarded himself as a native in the way that, for example, **John Ford** thought of himself. Although clearly very fond of the Irish, his references to Ireland and its people in his autobiography clearly position them as the "other."

However, in part as a consequence of his residence, Huston made a number of films in Ireland from the 1950s to the 1970s. His 1954 production of *Moby Dick* saw Youghal transformed into a 19th-century New England whaling town, although most of the location shooting took place at Fishguard in Wales. Part of *Casino Royale* (1967) (which he codirected) was shot in Glencree, County Wicklow, and the following year, he shot *Sinful Davey* (1967) in its entirety in Ireland (using **Ardmore Studios** for interiors). He also used Connemara as a location for that part of the Paul Newman thriller *The Mackintosh Man* (1973), which was set in Ireland.

While working on *Sinful Davey*, he was invited by then Taoiseach Jack Lynch to head a committee investigating the possibility of establishing a film industry in Ireland. Although unhappy with the committee's unwillingness to recommend extensive state support for international projects shot in Ireland, Huston nonetheless agreed to allow the resulting **Report of the Film Industry Committee** to be published under his name, and the report is generally referred to as the *Huston Report*.

Huston sold Saint Clerans in the early 1970s, finding the maintenance of the estate and the large staff required to run it increasingly difficult to finance. He opted instead for the warmer climate of Puerto Vallarta, Mexico. But his connections with Ireland did not end there. After making an extraordinary range of films in the early 1980s, including the musical *Annie* (1980) and the soccer-themed war movie *Escape to Victory* (1981), his final film was the adaptation of Joyce's short story "The Dead." Although perilously ill (he directed the film from a wheelchair), he fashioned a highly regarded swan song that successfully captured the stifling atmosphere of middle-class existence in Edwardian Dublin.

More than a decade after his death, his role in Irish cinema was commemorated by the establishment of a school of digital media at University College Galway, named the Huston School of Media.

HUSTON REPORT. *See REPORT OF THE FILM INDUSTRY COMMITTEE (HUSTON REPORT).*

I

I COULD READ THE SKY **(1999).** Circular connections abound in the narrative of the book/live performance/film mini-phenomenon that *I Could Read the Sky* has become. Renowned English photographer Steve Pyke's publishers approached Irish American writer Timothy O'Grady to narrativize a set of images captured by Pyke over several decades with a view to creating a photographic novel. O'Grady spent several years seeking a narrative, immersing himself in the works of, among others, Irish writer Dermot Healy. What eventually emerged was a narrative of emigration, memory, and the lingering connections to home. Published to acclaim in 1997, the project was then adapted for the screen by Pyke's wife, avant-garde filmmaker Nichola Bruce, who, piquantly, cast Dermot Healy in the central role of an older Irish emigrant (along with **Stephen Rea**, Brendan Coyle, and **Maria Doyle Kennedy**), near death and eking out an existence in a one-room apartment in London after a life of hard labor. The film traces his memories of growing up in rural Ireland, his departure for London in search of work, the paths followed by his siblings, and his temporary returns for the funerals of his mother and father. Resolutely nonnarrative, the film proceeds by building up layers of images, representing temporally separate moments capturing childhood, friendships, marriage, and death to create a spectral mosaic tied together by the old man's literary narration.

Although there are parallels between Bruce's film and the work of **Pat Collins** (both share a stillness that at times confounds the nature of live-action film), as her sole fiction film, *I Could Read the Sky*, stands apart from most Irish cinema in its emphasis on the form of the film. Given Bruce's background since the mid-1970s as a primarily visual artist who works as much with illustration and animation as she does film, the overtly "art house" look of *I Could Read the Sky* is scarcely surprising. Indeed, at times, in its self-conscious eschewal of a naturalistic style, it almost feels like a gallery installation. This curtailed its cinematic release, limiting the numbers who accessed via the big screen, but being picked up by art house mini-major Artificial Eye for DVD distribution, it gained an afterlife on the small screen and remains a singular moment in late 1990s Irish cinema.

I WENT DOWN **(1997).** A key moment in 1990s Irish cinema, written by **Conor MacPherson** (loosely based on his 1994 play *The Good Thief*) and directed by **Paddy Breathnach**. Git Haynes (**Peter McDonald**) leaves prison to find that his girlfriend has hooked up with his best pal, Anto (**David Wilmot**). Nonetheless, when local crime boss Tom French (**Tony Doyle**) sends his goons (including **Michael McElhatton**'s "Johner") to reclaim a debt from Anto, Git sends them packing, nursing their injuries. Now obligated by proxy for the money that Anto owes, French offers Git a way out: aid hapless henchman Bunny Kelly (**Brendan Gleeson**) in kidnapping an old associate, Frank Grogan (Peter Caffrey), from his Cork hideout, and the debt will be forgotten. A cross-country road trip ensues with the Midlands of Ireland acting as the backdrop against which Git and Bunny's odd-couple relationship develops.

On release in 1997, *I Went Down* proved something of a revelation for Irish audiences. Strictly speaking a generic blend of crime caper and road movie, the film's pleasures lie less in its thrilling narrative (which in point of fact occasionally drags) than in its well-realized cast of criminal eccentrics, razor-sharp dialogue (screenwriter McPherson's influence is felt throughout), and audience recognition of the manner in which U.S. gangster movie tropes are transposed into an Irish argot and setting. Occasional recourse to violence aside, Git and Bunny prove to be immensely likable figures, not least because of their gradually exposed vulnerabilities. As his first full-on lead role, "Bunny" proved a breakout piece of casting for Gleeson as both the main source of humor and as a catalyst for narrative progress.

Together with a less-than-prudish attitude to sex and a pulsating indie sound track, the film's brash character announced a new way of regarding Irish cinema—populist, young, and, Midlands sojourn excepted, urban— which proved popular with audiences both inside and, though hampered by limited international distribution, outside Ireland. On the flip side, it inaugurated a sequence of less-than-fully realized facsimiles, dominated by male characters and masculine preoccupations that arguably delayed the emergence of more progressive representations of gender in Irish cinema.

IN A HOUSE THAT CEASED TO BE **(2014).** Although mining the same biographical territory as Stephen Bradley's *Noble* (2014), Ciarín Scott's feature documentary on internationally renowned humanitarian Christina Noble offers a much rawer insight into a life that, on paper, reads like an impossibly dark example of Irish misery literature. Born in 1944 into a family headed by an alcoholic father and a mother who died when Christina was 10, she and her three siblings were separated into state-run orphanages and separately informed that their brothers and sisters were dead. After numerous attempts to escape the brutal regime at her industrial school, Noble found herself living rough in Dublin's Phoenix Park. After a violent gang rape, she became pregnant but was forced to give her son up for adoption. After discovering that her siblings were in fact alive, she moved to London to be near her brother and later met and married her husband. After a decade of abuse at *his* hands, she experienced a nervous breakdown but also, as the Vietnam War raged half a world away, began to have dreams where Vietnamese children fleeing the conflict pleaded with her for assistance. Two decades later, in 1989, Noble took her life savings and traveled to Ho Chi Minh City in Vietnam, where she established a children's foundation offering protection to street children. Today, the Christina Noble Children's Foundation, which has expanded its operations to Mongolia, runs medical clinics, schools, accommodations, and vocational training, offering aid to more than 140,000 children.

Coproduced by Scott and **Paul Duane**'s Screenworks, *In a House That Ceased to Be* recalls this narrative as it follows Noble through Vietnam and Mongolia but also farther afield as she raises funds to support her humanitarian activities. The film takes a distinctly darker tone when it brings her back to visit the site of the industrial schools at Letterfrack, Cliften, and Booterstown. A force of nature, Noble repeatedly emphasizes the power of love and affection as being of at least as much importance as nutrition, shelter, and education in her work to recuperate the lives of discarded children. Yet what emerges from her visit to Ireland is her lasting anger at the treatment meted out to her and her siblings by proxies of the Irish state. Scott's camera lingers as Noble repeatedly tries and fails to rein in her anger while she seeks to fathom the motivations of those who oversaw her brutal upbringing. As the film reunites her with her brother Sean and sisters Kathleen and Philomena and they individually recall their experiences, the earlier narrative of redemption is replaced by a picture of a family scarred forever and an excoriating critique of a society that treated its weakest members—infants and children—with, at best, indifference and, at worst, outright cruelty.

IN AMERICA (2004). The healing powers of faith, hope, and even magic hold sway in **Jim Sheridan**'s loosely autobiographical film cowritten with his daughters, Kirsten and Naomi, about an Irish family facing the challenges of leaving their past behind as they embark on a new life in New York City.

Johnny (Paddy Considine) and Sarah (Samantha Morton) immigrate illegally to the United States (driving over the Canadian border) with their young daughters Christy (**Sarah Bolger**) and Ariel (Emma Bolger). Like many immigrants, they seek a better life, leaving behind both a recession-hit Ireland and the memory of their baby son Frankie, who died tragically. The family finds accommodations in a run-down building in a dangerous corner of town ("Hell's Kitchen"). Among the other residents is a mysterious black man—Mateo (Djimon Hounsou)—who the unworldly Irish kids are fascinated by and afraid of in equal measure. An out-of-work actor lacking self-belief, Johnny has little luck in auditions for theater roles but nonetheless displays a quixotic tenacity in the face of defeat.

In telling its story of grief and redemption, the film posits some interesting if potentially controversial race politics linking Irish and African identities. At first a howling bogeyman, Mateo assumes a quasi-mystical function in the healing process of the parents as they conceive a child. He is revealed to be an AIDS-infected artist, and the film suggests that these attributes, combined with his outsider status in America, afford him a higher order of knowledge and empathy. In this construction, Mateo comes to function as a "magic negro/black man" in the story, a trope of American cinema especially prevalent in the 1990s that is in this case unlocked by Irish otherness and a mutual understanding of death. Mateo's eventual death is accompanied by his paying for the medical expenses for the new child, thus ensuring that the family can survive and prosper in white America, liberated from its emotional/colonial/economic past by his demise.

Fashioned from a variety of personal memories and experiences (the Sheridan family immigrated to New York in the 1980s, and Jim Sheridan's parents also lost a son named Frankie when he was young), *In America* aims for higher meanings in its construction of the United States as a place where Irish immigrants came for more than a century to escape their homeland. (Ironically, the film's interiors and exteriors were shot almost entirely on location in Dublin to save on the budget.) It thus represents a celebration of the Irish American experience and constitutes a worthy contemporary successor to the cinema of John Ford. Where so many indigenous Irish films from the 1970s and 1980s ended with the disintegration of real and symbolic families, Sheridan argues for its durability, a prognosis aided rather than defeated by modernity. Set in 1982, the year of the release of *E.T.* (its invocation being a play on the term "alien" in U.S. immigration terms), Sheridan said that his film was about getting away from the "death culture" so prevalent in Ireland since the Famine and expressed repetitively in Irish literature and art. Its success among Irish and American audiences—and the three Oscar nominations it received (screenplay and acting)—reinforced Sheridan's standing as Ireland's most intuitive film director and stands as his most personal and achieved work to date.

IN THE NAME OF THE FATHER (1993). Jim Sheridan's third film as a director saw him shift from the relatively small scale of *My Left Foot* and *The Field* into the realms of the blockbuster. Whereas those two films remained fairly parochial in scope, *In the Name of the Father* was at the time of its release easily the biggest film ever to come out of Ireland, not just in content but also in conception, production, and marketing.

Continuing the tradition of using material from other sources (*My Left Foot* and *The Field* were based on an autobiography and a stage play, respectively), Sheridan turned to Gerry Conlon's account of his 15 years in prison, having been falsely convicted, along with three others, as one of the Guilford pub bombers in 1974. The film follows Conlon (Daniel Day-Lewis) from Belfast to London in 1974, where, along with three others—Paul Hill (**John Lynch**), Paddy Armstrong, and Carole Richardson—he finds himself accused on circumstantial evidence of Irish Republican Army (IRA) membership and of carrying out the Guilford pub bombings. Traveling to England in an attempt to have Gerry released, Conlon's father, Guiseppe, and his cousins the Maguires are also arrested on suspicion of involvement in the making of the Guilford bombs. All are found guilty and sentenced to long prison terms.

Up to this point, the film is essentially a searing denunciation of the English justice system in the wake of the Guilford bombings, criticizing the willingness of the police and judiciary to deliberately ignore objective evidence in the hunt for a scapegoat. However, once Conlon enters prison, the focus shifts to a study of the relationship between Gerry and Guiseppe, who share a cell. A previously strained father–son relationship—Gerry resentful of what he perceives as his father's passivity and Guiseppe bewildered by his son's rage—is forced by proximity to change. The film is an interesting companion piece to Sheridan's earlier *My Left Foot* with its focus on a mother–son relationship. Ruth Barton suggests that the main protagonist moves from rejecting all parental authority, to a brief capitulation to the British police, to his admiration for IRA leader Joe McAndrew (Don Baker), and eventually to reconciliation with his own father, whose place he takes in prison after Guiseppe's very emotional demise.

These two themes—critique of British justice and the growing mutual respect between father and son—merge in the final third of the film, which brings the story into the 1980s and the developing momentum of the campaign to free the Guilford Four. Guiseppe dies in prison, steeling Gerry's resolve to lead the campaign to a successful conclusion and encouraging him to turn to a British lawyer, Gareth Pierce (Emma Thompson), to take up the legal challenge. A courtroom finale that sees the Guilford Four released brings the film to a rousing crescendo.

On release, *In the Name of the Father* received criticism from many quarters (particularly in the United Kingdom) for its blurring of fact and fiction for dramatic effect. The film depicts the Guilford Four and the Maguire Seven being sentenced at the same trial in the same courtroom, although, in fact, there were two separate trials. Similarly, the critical middle section of the film in which Gerry and Guiseppe share a cell could never have happened since the pair were never even in the same prison. Furthermore, a scene depicting Gareth Pierce accidentally stumbling across a vital piece of evidence withheld from the defense of the Guilford Four in 1974, although dramatically effective, is invented.

Nevertheless, the film powerfully drew attention to glaring inconsistencies in the case made against both the Four and the Maguires, inconsistencies that remain unresolved today. Ultimately, it's difficult to avoid the conclusion that what rankles about *In the Name of the Father* is the skill with which the substantive argument inherent in the Guilford Four story is made—that not only did a major miscarriage of justice occur but that also the police and judiciary were driven more by the understandable post-Guilford baying for blood of the English press and the public than by any objective notion of the pursuit of justice. Sheridan, ably assisted by his two main male leads (Day-Lewis and Postlewaite), exposes the human consequences of the injustice, skillfully manipulating the emotions of his audience with a raging sound track and occasionally sublime cinematography from director of photography Peter Biziou.

INDECON REPORT. Indecon is a large economic consultancy frequently used by the Irish state to advise on a wide range of public policy issues. In 1995, the Department of Arts, Culture, and the Gaeltacht commissioned Indecon to assess the contribution of the **Section 481** (then **Section 35**) tax relief to the Irish economy in general and to employment in the film industry. The department specifically wished to know whether Section 35 was the most cost-efficient means of creating a sustainable film industry.

Judging by the recommendations of the report (officially titled *A Strategy for Success Based on Economic Realities*), Indecon adopted a broad interpretation of the brief. The report made 24 specific recommendations, nine of which in no way related to tax relief but included the need to establish an **Irish Screen Commission**, develop postproduction facilities, and—oddly—extend artists' tax relief to film personnel who either won an award at the Cannes Film Festival or were merely nominated for an **Academy Award**.

The bulk of the recommendations, however, were focused around Section 481. Heretically, the report found that although the tax relief had undoubtedly been a contributory factor in the post-1993 increase in production activity in Ireland, the tax forgone as a result had not been recouped through increased financial activity associated with the film industry (e.g., income tax from film personnel). In short, the Section 481 tax relief was costing the exchequer approximately £5 million per annum. This went against the received wisdom that had emerged from institutions like the Audiovisual Federation of the Irish Business and Employers Confederation (IBEC), which had argued that state investment in the audiovisual sector through the **Irish Film Board** and Section 481 resulted in a net gain to the economy.

The Indecon report accepted IBEC's figures but noted that it arrived at its results by calculating the aggregate impact of all audiovisual production in Ireland, not all of which availed of the tax incentive. Indecon argued that if one separated out these productions, then the economy experienced a net loss as a result of Section 481. However, having stipulated Section 481's generally positive impact, Indecon did not suggest that the tax incentive be entirely removed. Noting that "on economic criteria it would be very hard to justify continuing the incentives in their present form," it put forward a series of recommendations designed to ensure that the tax break made a net contribution to the economy. Key among these was the decision to reduce the level of tax write-off available to private and corporation investors from 100 percent of their investment to 80 percent.

When the findings and recommendations of the report became public after its December 1995 publication, the film industry's response was extremely negative, suggesting that such changes would undermine the brief renaissance enjoyed by the sector in the previous two years. Nonetheless, faced with the report, in January 1996, the minister for finance duly altered the tax relief largely along the lines recommended by Indecon. The direct impact of the changes was hard to establish definitively: the number of investors willing to avail of Section 481 did decline, but this was an express aim of the changes, and there was little evidence to suggest that producers found it substantially harder to access such funding. There was a definitive decrease in the level of foreign activity in Ireland in the wake of the changes, but a causal link between the decline and the Section 481 alterations was harder to demonstrate, especially given the simultaneous decline in the value of the dollar vis-à-vis the punt, making it more expensive for Hollywood companies to shoot in Ireland. Nonetheless, the coincidence of the reduction in foreign activity would give pause in the future to any other suggestions that Section 481 be adjusted.

INDEPENDENT TELEVISION PRODUCTION SECTOR REPORT (FMI REPORT). Although focused on developing independent television rather than film production, the FMI report was indirectly significant for the film industry in that many of its conclusions lent weight to the case made by the Irish film industry for state support through contemporary documents, such as the ***Coopers & Lybrand Report*** in 1992.

Commissioned by Film Makers Ireland in conjunction with the Industrial Development Authority and the Irish Trade Board, the report was researched and written by Siobhan O'Donoghue, who would subsequently head MEDIA Desk Ireland. The basic thrust of the report was that deregulation and new technology were transforming the European broadcasting sector, spurring enormous market growth. This would inevitably lead to **Radio Telefís Éi-**

reann (RTÉ) facing increased competition for Irish audiences and thus pointed to the need for the Irish production and broadcast industry to gear up to compete.

However, the report argued that historically, RTÉ had made only limited use of independent production to augment its in-house production despite the requirement under EU law that it source at least 10 percent of its material from independent producers. The report also suggested that in the absence of commissions from RTÉ, independent producers in Ireland had been forced to look overseas for work and, as a result, had developed a strong export orientation. This, together with their Anglophone status, made them potentially attractive coproduction partners for other European producers.

In short, external conditions had created an opportunity for a huge expansion in the scale of the Irish independent production sector that could be facilitated by an integrated government response. Specifically, the report recommended passing legislation to ensure RTÉ's adherence to EU law on independent commissioning, appointing an independent commissioning editor with RTÉ, coordinating state policy on encouraging audiovisual production, and amending **Section 35** to allow individuals to use it and to increase the amount of money that could be invested under the scheme.

The report was published in August 1992, within a month of the *Coopers & Lybrand Report*, some of the conclusions of which it closely echoed (hardly surprising given that both were informed by interviews with either the same individuals or individuals with similar production backgrounds). In particular, the recommendations on Section 35 were virtually identical. As such, it would become a key influence on the conclusions of a subsequent *Special Working Group on the Film Production Industry* report to the taoiseach in December 1992, appointed in September 1992.

THE INFORMER (**1929**). At least three directors have brought Liam O'Flaherty's celebrated novel, winner of the 1925 James Tait Black Memorial Prize, to the screen: Arthur Robison (1929), **John Ford** (1935), and Jules Dassin, who relocated the action from Dublin to civil rights–era Cleveland in *Uptight* (1968), often credited as the first blaxploitation film. (Irish playwrights Micheál Mac Liammóir and Tom Murphy also adapted it for the stage in 1958 and 1981, respectively, the latter achieving what must be the perfect casting of **Liam Neeson** in the lead role.) Robison's treatment is perhaps closest to the novel and considered by many to be an unjustly neglected masterpiece, overshadowed by Ford's better-known version six years later. It certainly deserves wider recognition, not least because O'Flaherty (and Ford) was heavily influenced in writing the novel by the visual poetics and Manichean worldview of German expressionist film, and Robison had been right at the center of this world. Made at Elstree Studios by British International Pictures, the film was an outcome of the 1927 Film Act, designed to stimulate the quality and output of British film and help it compete with Hollywood. With ample success in adapting prestigious literary material, Robison was imported from Berlin to contribute prestige to the British industry at home and abroad, and *The Informer* was chosen as a text likely to bring out the best in his talents, even if its subject of a martyred Irish Republican Army informer during the Irish War of Independence seems an unlikely and somewhat ironic means of doing so. The casting of Swedish superstar Lars Hanson in the lead role of Gypo Nolan is similarly geared to the international market. Produced in both sound and silent versions and entirely shot in the studio, the film represents a rare Irish-themed entry in the high-water achievements of late silent cinema. Well received but somewhat lost in the transition to sound, it certainly influenced Ford's version in visual terms, even if 1930s Hollywood was more inclined to adopt a less claustrophobic and austere retelling.

INGRAM, REX (1893–1950). Born Reginald Ingram Hitchcock in Dublin, a son of a Church of Ireland clergyman, at age 18 he left Ireland for the United States, never to return. He never showed a particular predisposition to reflect his native culture, but then in Hollywood, this was never a high priority. Following the popular and critical success of *The Four Horsemen of the Apocalypse* (1921), which he directed and which made Rudolph Valentino a star, he went on to make *The Conquering Power* (1921), *The Prisoner of Zenda* (1922), *Scaramouche* (1924), *The Arab* (1926), *The Magician* (1926), *Mare Nostrum* (1927), *The Three Passions* (1929), and *Baroud* (1933), among others, becoming a very prolific and successful Hollywood filmmaker.

INSIDE I'M DANCING **(2004).** Having achieved an unexpected hit with his debut feature comedy, *East Is East* (1999), director **Damien O'Donnell** returned to Ireland with this second and, to date, only other feature film, an unusual buddy movie centered on two physically disabled young men. Although set and shot in Dublin, the film eschewed local casting in the lead roles in favor of up-and-coming British actors and despite strong local signifiers came across as an offbeat comedy that its primary producers— StudioCanal and Working Title Films—specialize in.

Rory O'Shea (James McAvoy) is a young man with muscular dystrophy and a spiky attitude. When he moves into the Carrigmore Home for the Disabled ("a special home for special people") run by the formidable Eileen **(Brenda Fricker)**, he forms an unlikely friendship with long-term resident Michael (Steven Robertson), whose speech is affected by cerebral palsy. Uniquely, Rory is able to understand comprehend Michael's utterances and acts as his translator. Nevertheless, he refuses to accept the dull conformity of Carrigmore and repeatedly applies for a grant that would allow him to live independently. When he is repeatedly turned down, Michael applies instead and is successful. With the help of his estranged father, they find a flat, and Michael insists that Rory be allowed join him to work as his interpreter. The young men then hire Siobhan, a young, able-bodied woman, as their living assistant (Romala Garai), and the trio embark on a bittersweet quest to create an existence within a society that is indifferent, not to say hostile, to the needs of the disabled.

Although the screenplay is by veteran British screenwriter Jeffrey Caine, the story was originated by Galway-based writer Christian Reilly based on his experiences working at the Centre for Independent Living, a nonprofit institution providing services that "facilitate an individual's choice to live independently in their home and participate in their community." Confronting traditional attitudes to disability head-on, Reilly's story advocates the creation of structures and a transformation in attitudes that facilitate people with disabilities to lead fully independent lives while also exhorting them to reject institutionalization. In the film, Michael and Rory do not seek a caretaker per se but rather an employee who can afford their personal agency. In the event, both also seek affection and romantic fulfillment from Siobhan, and her rejection of their overtures brings a painful reminder of their limits of their agency.

The film displays O'Donnell's gift for character and blending comedy with heartache and successfully articulates its objectives. Furthermore, its unsentimental depiction of the obstacles faced by the two leads is entirely convincing and far removed from the "Supercrip" stereotype found in popular representations of disability, such as *Rain Man* (1988), *Avatar* (2009), and even **Jim Sheridan**'s *My Left Foot* (1987). Michael and Rory succeed because they assert an alternative framework for thinking about disability, not because they exhibit remarkable intrinsic capacities.

Given this, however, it is notable that both lead roles are played by able-bodied actors, and the decision not to use actors with disabilities (though the producers asserted that they did try to do so) arguably reinforces the very message the film seeks to undermine. When Christian Reilly returned to the subject of disability with his well-received film *Sanctuary* (2016), he would insist that the intellectually challenged central characters be played by actors with similar conditions.

INTER-DEPARTMENTAL COMMITTEE ON THE FILM INDUSTRY. In 1938, **Sean Lemass**, as minister for industry and commerce, established a three-man committee with a broad remit to examine and report on every aspect—actual and putative—of the Irish film industry. The report was a response to two sets of pressures. The first was the trickle of private proposals relating to the establishment of Irish film industry (most of which centered on the building of a film studio) that the department had been in receipt of since 1928. Second, Lemass appeared to have been exercised by the increasingly vocal call from the influential Jesuit priest Father Richard Devane for a government inquiry into all aspects of cinema. Lemass might conceivably have ignored Devane's calls were it not for the fact that on the 22 April 1937, the priest wrote to Prime Minister Eamon De Valera requesting a meeting to pursue the idea of an inquiry. Seeking to head off any possibility that the de facto determination of cinema policy might fall to Devane, Lemass established a small interdepartmental committee (representing Industry and Commerce together with the Departments of Finance, Education, and Justice) to examine difficulties standing in the way of a national film production enterprise. Lemass further suggested to De Valera that any meeting with Devane should await the conclusions of that committee.

Those conclusions were long in coming. The Department of Finance refused to sanction expenditure for the committee, fearing that their report would be used to justify state subsidies for a putative film industry. However, it acceded to the committee's creation when assured that in fact the primary function would be to collate information that would allow the Department of Industry and Commerce to deal with (and implicitly reject) private appeals for subsidy.

The three-man committee, made up as it was of three middle-ranking civil servants from Industry and Commerce, Finance, and Education (Justice declined a role), was far from expert in the field of the cinema. None of its members had ever been inside a film studio, for example. This ignorance would delay the completion of the report by years: the committee had planned to travel to London to witness the work of British studios but had to first postpone and then cancel the trip when war broke out in September 1939. Consequently, the committee's deliberations were informed by evidence or representations received from bodies or individuals associated mainly with either the film industry in Ireland or the Catholic Church. The committee finally submitted a completed draft in March 1942.

The report was divided into chapters dealing with **exhibition**, **distribution**, production, and **censorship** of films in Ireland. The penultimate chapter discussed how the establishment of a national film institute could address some of the problems discussed in the earlier chapters. As a result, it represented a comprehensive oversight of (and offered a profound insight into) official thinking on the role of cinema in Irish cultural affairs. Furthermore, the fact that it was written on the understanding that it would not be made public led the committee to express its views in relatively unguarded terms.

The opening chapter on exhibition noted a growing concentration of cinema ownership and recommended placing a ceiling on the total number of seats cumulatively held by an exhibitor or group of exhibitors. It also described the increasing Jewish ownership and control of Irish cinemas as "undesirable" given the part played by cinema in the social and cultural life of the community.

Similar concerns were voiced with regard to distribution and the fact that "alien" film distributors could determine the extent and nature of films available to the Irish public. This was particularly significant for the committee's core interest: production. Noting that even low-budget films could not recoup their costs within Ireland, the report concluded that access to international distribution was a prerequisite for a commercially successful indigenous industry. However, the committee was tentative in discussing how this might be achieved. Although suggesting that the Irish state could "encourage" American distributors to acquire one or two Irish features a year by threatening import restrictions on Hollywood films, it cautioned that such a move might provoke a punitive response from Hollywood, such as entirely withholding film supplies from Ireland. Thus, the committee recommended that the state adopt at most a "*reasonably* firm attitude" with regard to distribution.

Moving to production, the report cited far more prosaic difficulties, chief among these being the absence of any substantial studio facilities or of any company regularly producing films on any scale. Since neither gap looked likely to be filled by private capital, the committee proposed building a modest (£25,000) studio. The committee concluded that further state assistance in the form of partial reimbursement of actual production costs would be essential. The committee further recommended that initial domestic production be concentrated on newsreels, where it felt there was a gap in market provision.

In sum, however, with regard to production, the conclusions of the report were somewhat gloomy:

> A native film industry could never hope to replace to any large extent imported films by native films. . . . Its prospects of ever becoming self-supporting would depend on the extent to which a foreign market could be secured. . . . Obstacles in the way are so great that it would be wise in considering the question of the establishment of a small-scale film industry to proceed on the assumption that its products would seldom procure exhibition outside the country. The greater portion of the cost of films produced in this country would in these circumstances have to be met from public funds. (*Report of the Inter-Departmental Committee on the Film Industry*, 1942)

The question of precisely how those public funds might be dispensed was addressed via discussion of a national film and cinema board. It was envisaged that the board would regulate the exhibition sector and act as a focus for production activity, offering encouragement, advice, and, on occasion, funding for prospective producers. Finally, the board would advise on the question of a state-funded film studio and on encouraging overseas producers to film in Ireland. In short, the board would take day-to-day responsibility for defining film policy in Ireland.

What is striking about the report, viewed from a distance, is the persuasive power that the committee explicitly and tacitly ascribed to cinema. The committee argued that the promotion of film for purposes of education, culture, and general propaganda would be the most important function of the **Irish Film Board**, suggesting that there was no subject that could not be dealt with via cinema. The Irish language in particular was singled out as a subject that could be mainstreamed by cinema.

Yet if cinema's power for good was stressed, so too was its darker side. The report's final chapter—reflecting representations from the Catholic hierarchy and other Catholic organizations—addressed the practice of film censorship. The report referred to films informed by a materialist philosophy that threatened Ireland's values as a small Christian nation. Particular attention was drawn to the cumulative negative impact on young people of watching such films. Despite these views, the committee advised against making any substantive changes to the existing censorship code. Ironically, it did so on the grounds that such changes might have the opposite outcome to that sought by the hierarchy, that is, that forcing the censor to operate within a more strictly defined code might restrict the freedom permitted under the existing code to cut or ban films.

Lemass's immediate response on receiving the report is not recorded. However, he can hardly have been encouraged. The conclusions on production effectively confirmed what the Department of Finance had long asserted—that a commercially viable Irish film industry was impossible. Thus, Lemass strategically "parked" the report lest its gloomy conclusions be seized on by others (in particular, Finance) as definitively closing the question.

Nonetheless, some of the report's recommendations relating to the educational potential of cinema were passed on. In December 1943, another inter-departmental committee (this time representing Education, Finance, Industry, and Commerce; Agriculture and Local Government; and Public Health) considered the original report's recommendations relating to educational films and films in the Irish language. This committee would ultimately recommend the advancing of funds to the **National Film Institute of Ireland** (NFII), which was established under (ironically) Father Richard Devane in July 1943. Thus, from 1945 to 1946, the NFII was voted £2,000 via the annual science and art vote of the Department of Education for the purposes of acquiring a library of educational films and producing films on behalf of government departments.

However, the report would ultimately have a much more substantial impact on the shaping of the state's longer-term policy on film production. By impressing on Lemass the difficulties entailed in creating an Irish film industry, it led him instead to consider how to encourage the development of a *film industry in Ireland*, that is, one based on foreign direct investment from American and British production companies.

INTERMISSION (2003). Combining elements of post-*Trainspotting* (1996) "new lad" cinema with a nod in the direction of "smart film" (signaled through a complex intertwining of a multitude of characters and story lines), *Intermission* marked an extremely ambitious—but also highly popular—debut for both director John Crowley and screenwriter Mark O'Rowe.

After an unexpectedly violent opening featuring petty thief Lehiff (**Colin Farrell**, then emerging as a Hollywood star) and an unsuspecting shopgirl (**Kerry Condon**), the narrative switches to John (**Cillian Murphy**) and Oscar (**David Wilmot**), two wastrels working dead-end jobs as shelf stackers in a supermarket. John's relationship with Deirdre (*Trainspotting*'s Kelly MacDonald) has recently ended, and she has moved on to bank manager Sam (**Michael McElhatton**), who in turn has left his wife Noeleen (**Deirdre O'Kane**). (Noeleen in turn has a brief fling with Oscar.) Meanwhile, bus driver Mick (Brian F. O'Byrne) loses his job when he crashes his vehicle after a feral kid hurls a brick through his windshield. Short of cash and with nothing to lose, John and Mick team up to rob Sam's bank with Lehiff, while the latter holds Deirdre hostage. However, when John, Mick, and Sam arrive at the bank, they are assaulted by Noeleen and flee. Discovering that Lehiff has hit Deirdre, John in turn attacks him. Taking flight, Lehiff is pursued by his nemesis, Detective Lynch (**Colm Meaney**), the subject of a reality documentary filmed by director Ben Campion (Tomas O'Suilleabhain). The complicated denouement sees most of the characters back in the relationships where they started albeit on a much-altered basis.

The whiff of testosterone off *Intermission* is at times so overwhelming that one might easily dismiss it as mired in a hypermasculine fantasyland: Noeleen aside, the female characters display little agency. The stunning violence visited on the innocent shopgirl by Farrell's Lehiff immediately after the opening credits sits uneasily with audiences, unsure whether to recoil or stifle laughter at the sudden display of naked male brutality. When Deirdre hooks with up Sam, John berates her behavior as that of a "whore" (though he has initiated their breakup). Peak machismo arrives in the form of New Age Celtic music–loving cop Lynch, a man so self-consciously performing the role of a "screw-the-rulebook" cop that he literally creates his own sound track and goads director Ben, whose television bosses refuse to sanction a series about Lynch, into making his own guerrilla-style show with Lynch as the star.

Yet Lehiff and Lynch (two sides of the same coin) aside, the multiplicity of masculine types in *Intermission* offers an opportunity to explore a number of male roles. John, Sam, and Oscar all undergo "learning experiences" that see them emerge as at least marginally more progressive figures than they start off as. Indeed, Colm Meaney's no-holds-barred performance as Lynch is so over the top that it's difficult to regard it as anything but a (deliberate?) caricature whose presence, if anything, underscores the absurdity of the traditional male archetypes that populated U.K. and Irish new lad cinema in the late 1990s and early 2000s.

For all that, at the time of its release, the film was the most successful independently produced Irish film released by the second **Irish Film Board**, taking in €2.3 million at the Irish box office by the close of 2003 (though it would subsequently be eclipsed by *The Guard* [2011]). Buoyed by Colin Farrell's increasing currency as a Hollywood star (not to mention the emerging status of Cillian Murphy and Kelly MacDonald alongside the more established Colm Meaney), it was acquired by U.S. distributor Independent Film Company and released in March 2004. Although achieving a respectable U.S. release by art house standards, the film's "Restricted" rating in the United States limited the scope of its potential audience, and its final U.S. take—just under $900,000—dashed hopes of a breakout international hit for Irish cinema.

INTO THE WEST (1992). Produced by **Little Bird** with **Parallel Films**, from a **Jim Sheridan** screenplay and directed by Mike Newell, *Into the West* made an important and internationally well-received contribution to the early phase of the second wave of Irish cinema and the ascent of Sheridan's career. Blending mythic and contemporary modes of storytelling, it represents a relatively successful effort to mobilize Ireland's oral story traditions in the service of film (see also *The Secret of Roan Inish*, *Ondine*, and so on) This has as much to do with Newell's experience and skill as a cinematic storyteller as it does with Sheridan's novel concept.

The film opens with **Traveller** Grandpa Ward (**David Kelly**) being followed from the beach to his Ballymun encampment by an enormous white horse. There, he encounters his son-in-law, Papa Riley (**Gabriel Byrne**), a former Traveller "King" who has lived among the settled community with his two sons, Ossie (Ciaran FitzGerald) and Tito (**Rúaidhrí Conroy**), since the death of their mother. The horse forms an instant attachment to Ossie and moves into their Ballymun flat. When the neighbors complain, the police remove the horse and then illegally sell it to a racehorse owner. Ossie and Tito then steal the horse back and set off across the country, pursued both by the police and by their father, who enlists the help of the Traveller community. They race through the Midlands before the boys and the horse are cornered by the police on the edge of the Atlantic Ocean. Papa arrives just in time to see Ossie and the horse dive into the sea to evade capture. Both disappear under the waves, apparently drowned, but while the horse disappears, Ossie reemerges, having magically encountered his mother under the sea. The film concludes with Papa vowing to return to the Traveller community, his sense of self-worth reinvigorated by his rediscovery of his old life.

Into the West faces several hurdles from the outset: not only is the screenplay carried largely on the backs of two children and a horse, but the film must render sympathetic an element of the Irish population at best generally ignored by the mainstream media and at worst actively pilloried. The film successfully hurdles the first of these obstacles with a combination of a well-chosen cast and skillful direction. As Ossie and Tito, Fitzgerald and Conroy successfully convey the essential innocence of their characters that lies behind their necessarily outwardly tough appearance and demeanor. As for the horse itself, clever shot framing and editing combine to give it a dramatic physical presence and even the illusion of acting.

The film's portrayal of Traveller culture itself, however, is less credible. In casting cuddly **Colm Meaney**, friendly Johnny Murphy, and, most awkwardly, sultry Ellen Barkin, the film suggests that members of the community are pretty much the same as everyone else and that only blind ignorance prejudices the settled community against them. The film is unwilling or unable to explore the possibility that Traveller society is culturally distinct, an endeavor subsequently taken up in a film such as *Pavee Lackeen*.

Into the West is concerned primarily with its pursuit of a more universally accessible story, a tack signaled by Papa Riley's gnomic comment that "there's a bit of a Traveller in everybody. . . . Only a few of us know where we're going." Hence, the film unashamedly weaves generic elements into its narrative, and its referencing of the western genre in particular is evident not only from the title but also by explicit references within the text to *Butch Cassidy and the Sundance Kid* (1969) and the identification of Ossie and Tito during their flight across the country as "desperadoes." More surprisingly, the film also borrows elements from magic realism, arguably the mode in which the film is most successful. The scenes of the horse in a Ballymun flat and Ossie's aquatic encounter with his mother are easily the most affecting. When this mode is abandoned, as it is for most of the latter half of the film, *Into the West* loses its distinctive appeal.

***IRISH DESTINY* (1926).** Written and produced by Dr. Isaac "Jack" Eppel (1892–1942), a Jewish doctor who ran a general practice and a pharmacy on Mary Street in Dublin, and directed by George Dewhurst, *Irish Destiny* is a love story set against the backdrop of the War of Independence. Interweaving actual newsreel footage of the Black and Tans, the burning of Cork, and the burning of the Customs House in Dublin with dramatized scenes filmed in Enniskerry, Wicklow, and Dublin, the film was produced to mark the 10th anniversary of the Easter Rising. As such, it constituted the first feature film produced in the Irish Free State and is one of only three Irish-set feature films (along with **Knock-na-Gow** and *Ireland, a Nation*) produced during the silent era.

The film opens with the arrival of the Black and Tans in the village of Clonmore, home of Irish Republican Army (IRA) man Denis O'Hara and his fiancée, Moira. When O'Hara learns of a plan to raid a secret IRA meeting, he travels to Dublin to warn his colleagues. On arriving, he is shot and captured by British soldiers. People in Clonmore believe that O'Hara has died, and the shock of this news leads his mother to lose her sight, while local poitín maker Beecher (who is in league with the British) takes the opportunity to kidnap Moira. O'Hara is in fact imprisoned at the Curragh Camp in Kildare. Despite his injury he escapes, arriving in Clonmore just in time to rescue Moira. The film concludes with the dramatic burning of the Customs House in Dublin and the signing of a truce with the British.

Determined to make a movie about the War of Independence, Issac Eppel used his own funds (along with additional borrowings) to hire an English director, George Dewhurst, and cameraman Joe Rosenthal to shoot the film. Dewhurst had established a modest reputation since his feature debut in 1917 and his 1922 version of the stage play *A Sister to Assist 'Er*. Exteriors for the film were shot on location in Ireland, while Shepherd's Bush Film Studios in London were used for interior scenes. The all-Irish cast was mostly amateur, and several had never acted before. For example, Paddy Dunne Cullinan, who played O'Hara, was employed largely because of his equestrian skills. Eppel's son Derek and his brother Simon also appeared as extras, while Kit O'Malley, formerly of the IRA's Dublin Brigade, played the local IRA commandant.

Released on Easter Saturday in 1926, the film was reviewed in glowing terms in the domestic press and was retained for a second week in the Corinthian cinema, where it set a new box office record. Overall, however, it was not a financial success. Because of its subject matter, it was initially banned in the United Kingdom before being reedited (removing the IRA and the Black and Tans confrontations) and then rereleased as *An Irish Mother*. Eppel also released the film in the United States, where, although Irish Americans warmly embraced it, reviewers compared it unfavorably with the more polished Hollywood product. As a result, *Irish Destiny* was Eppel's only film production, and the enormous debts he incurred in making it took him years to clear. He later emigrated to England, divorced, and remarried, and when he died in 1942, he was largely forgotten in Ireland.

For decades, the film was believed lost and largely forgotten. In 1988, an original poster for the film turned up under the linoleum of a Dublin house (and is now on display in the **Irish Film Institute**). This prompted a search for the film itself, which led to the Library of Congress in Washington, D.C.

The library had retained an original nitrate print for copyright purposes from which a new print was struck and given to the **Irish Film Archive**. In 1993, the National Concert Hall in Dublin saw the first Irish screening of *Irish Destiny* in nearly half a century, with a specially commissioned score by Micheál Ó Súilleabháin.

IRISH DREAMTIME. Both the initial financing and the rationale for Irish Dreamtime's existence owe much to **Pierce Brosnan**'s stint as James Bond. The Los Angeles–based company was formed in 1996 by Brosnan (with producing partner Beau St. Clair) on the back of a first-look deal struck with Metro-Goldwyn-Mayer (MGM) after his successful debut as Bond in *GoldenEye*. Motivated by a concern that Bond would typecast him, Irish Dreamtime was designed to ensure access to roles beyond 007. This has indirectly benefited the Irish film industry: although Irish Dreamtime's highest-profile production was *The Thomas Crown Affair* remake, the company had also shot three Brosnan vehicles in Ireland by 2005. Brosnan's role in the first of these, *The Nephew* (1998), was relatively low profile since that story focused on a young black American man returning to Ireland to scatter his mother's ashes and find her roots. However, in *Evelyn* (2002), he took on the main role, playing against type as a down-at-the-heels, drunk, and despairing single father taking on the courts and the Irish Catholic Church to get his three kids out of children's homes. Finally, in 2004, Brosnan again starred (opposite Julianne Moore) as a shabby but effective lawyer in Dreamtime's *Laws of Attraction*.

Although the Irish films received generally positive reviews, their financial performance in their primary English-language markets was mixed. *The Nephew* was never released in the United States and earned less than half a million dollars in Britain and Ireland. The generally well-received *Evelyn* took in just over $1.4 million at the U.S. box office compared to the $2.2 million in the much smaller British and Irish market. However, the also favorably reviewed *Laws of Attraction*, boosted by a setting and cast more familiar to American audiences, earned $17 million in the United States.

Since 2005, the company has operated primarily as a vehicle for producing Brosnan-headlined work (although it also produced *My Father Die* [2016], a revenge-horror written and directed by Brosnan's son Sean). These include familiar roles, such as the ex–Central Intelligence Agency operative in *The November Man* (2014), but have also allowed Brosnan the freedom to work against type: a self-parodying turn as a washed-up hit man in *The Matador* (2005), a Northern Irish blackmailer in *Shattered* (2007), and, most affectingly, the patriarch of a family grieving over a deceased son in *The Greatest* (2009). Although Brosnan has played Irish roles in recent years (channeling Gerry Adams opposite Jackie Chan in *The Foreigner* [2017] and an Irish tech mogul in *I.T.* [2014]), Irish Dreamtime has not produced an explicitly Ireland-set film since *Laws of Attraction*. Nonetheless, Brosnan's continued desire to shoot in Ireland when possible (evinced by the fairly successful decision to use Dublin as a double for New York in *Laws of Attraction*) is attested to by the 2014 filming of the Washington, D.C.–set *I.T.* largely on location in Dublin.

IRISH FILM AND TELEVISION ACADEMY. The Irish Film and Television Academy (IFTA) was established in August 1998 to promote Irish film and television nationally and internationally. Although the academy nominally existed to facilitate dialogue between film and television practitioners and to provide an independent forum for debate and discussion of those issues affecting the industry, its highest-profile activity has been the organization of the annual IFTAs, an awards ceremony rewarding excellence in Irish screen production, since 1999.

Eligibility for the awards reflected the composition of the governing body, which included representatives of the Irish film and television industry from both Northern and Southern Ireland. **Radio Telefís Éireann, TV3**, TG4, UTV, and BBC Northern Ireland were all represented on the academy's council, which also included professional bodies, such as the **Irish Film Board**, the **Irish Film Institute**, the **Northern Ireland Film and Television Commission, Screen Producers Ireland**, and the Royal Television Society.

IRISH FILM ARCHIVE. Although an "official" national film archive in the sense of a dedicated space came into being only with the opening of the **Irish Film Centre** in 1992, the idea of an archive has a much longer history.

As early as the mid-1930s, it is apparent that the then film censor, James Montgomery, had amassed a collection of newsreel material from J. Gordon Lewis, the local manager of Pathé Frères in Dublin, that covered the period of revolutionary struggle from the early 1910s to the Civil War. Montgomery made a proposal to Eamon de Valera that newsreels should be edited into a single narrative of the period but also stressed the need to preserve the films so as to maintain a historical record of the events leading up to the foundation of the state. Although de Valera apparently approved of the project, civil servants in his department balked at the cost of assembling the film, and the associated preservation project was also sidelined in 1938.

Other than this abortive proposal, the little archiving that did occur in Ireland prior to the 1980s was carried out largely by dedicated individuals. Notable examples of this include the cataloging undertaken by George Morrison in assembling material for *Mise Éire* and *Saoirse?* and **Liam O'Leary**'s single-handed crusade to preserve as much Irish film–related material as possible (although the bulk of O'Leary's material was in the form of documents rather than actual film stock).

Speaking at the Dublin Arts Festival in 1976, O'Leary complained that the absence of a national film archive had created a situation whereby a new generation had little or no knowledge of cinema's contribution to shaping the life of the nation. Some moves to address this were made in 1984 when the **Irish Film Institute** (IFI) received some funding from the **Irish Film Board** to conduct research on the practicalities of creating an archive. This subsequently led the IFI to create a post for an individual to promote the need for an archive: to produce a profile of a putative archive and complete a report on the technical aspects of actually building an archive space.

The first moves to coherently preserve material commenced in 1986, when the IFI officially established an archive section and began to isolate Irish material on celluloid from the film-lending library it had built up since the 1940s. By the mid-1980s, the library was infrequently called on, as educational institutions increasingly switched to using videotape for in-class screenings rather than 16-mm films. The Irish material culled from this source would constitute the core collection of the embryonic national film archive. The work was initially carried out by two IFI staff members. Although third-level qualifications in archiving did not exist at the time, both were sent for training at the National Film and Television Archive in Britain.

The Irish Film Archive proper came into being in 1992, when the IFI moved to its premises to Dublin's Eustace Street, and four vaults were commissioned specifically to house the archive's collections. As of 1986, the archive held perhaps 800 films. An active film search commencing in 1986 unearthed chunks of additional material from sources such as **Bord Fáilte**, the Department of Foreign Affairs, the National Safety Council, indigenous production companies, and individual filmmakers like Vincent Corcoran. As of 2006, the 20,000 items held by the archive appeared to constitute a comprehensive collection of extant indigenous production in and about Ireland. Holdings ranged from full prints of commercially released films that were released commercially (the Irish Film Board, the Broadcasting Authority of Ireland [BAI], and the **Arts Council** require that any film receiving their support deposit a copy in the archive) to advertising footage and home movies.

The archive's vaults in the IFI building are temperature- and humidity-controlled at optimal levels for long-term preservation. These vaults are in turn protected by a sophisticated system of fire and flood alarms. Two vaults store master material, which is acquired solely for preservation. However, there is also a viewing vault that houses all "access material," film, and tape, which can be accessed by external researchers. The archive also has a climate-controlled paper vault housing documents, posters, stills, scripts, press packs, production-related correspondence, and other paper material. However, with the expansion of the archive's holdings, the original vaults were quickly filled and by the mid-2000s were effectively full. Hampered by a lack of finance—almost uniquely in Europe, the Irish Film Archive receives no direct state funding—the archive launched an Archive Preservation Fund campaign in November 2011 to partly fund a new archive. Fronted by **Saoirse Ronan**, the campaign sought to raise €300,000, and in 2012, the archive announced an agreement with Maynooth University to develop a second archive on its Kildare campus.

At the same time, the 2000s also saw the archive increasingly move into restoring key works in Irish cinema history, including *Guests of the Nation* (1935), *Beloved Enemy* (1936), *She Didn't Say No* (1958), and, perhaps most notably, the Isaac Eppel–produced *Irish Destiny* (1926). These restorations formed part of a larger project to improve public access to the archive's holdings. In 2007, the archive organized the "Reel Ireland" project, curating works for international screenings via minifestivals. Following a redevelopment of the IFI building between 2009 and 2010 (which included a redevelopment of the archive space), the IFI commenced the "Archive at Lunchtime" series, free screenings drawing on the archival collection. In 2010, the "Irish Film Archive on Tour" project saw material brought from the archive and screened at arts festivals around Ireland. In a similar vein, the IFI began making archival material available in DVD format, including *The O'Kalem Collection*, *Seoda* (a collection of acclaimed but short films dating from 1948 to 1970), and a collection of **Thaddeus O'Sullivan**'s often-referenced but rarely seen early work.

Work on the Maynooth facility coincided with moves by the archive to exploit the potential of digital technology. Although the mid-2000s had seen the archive begin creating low-resolution digital files from amateur footage, it was the acquisition of first a 2K digital scanner in 2016 followed by a higher-resolution 4K scanner in 2017 (both associated with BAI-funded projects) that allowed the archive to create preservation-quality digital files. In 2014, the archive had installed new digital infrastructure, including a fiber-optic network, high volume digital storage, and an upgrade of the archive's existing digital restoration capabilities. This was followed in 2015 by the launch of a Digital Preservation and Access Strategy with an emphasis on the use of digital technology not only to preserve content (and obviate the risks associated with the possible obsolescence of specific digital formats) but also to exploit it to make that content available to the widest possible audience. This goal was realized in September 2016 with the launch of the "IFI Player," a Web player affording free, global access to a wide range of archival material, including early Kalem films, material from the Gael Linn collection, and a number of films associated with religious and government institutions. Starting with 20 hours of material, the archive subsequently released new content, such as the Irish advertising collection in May 2017 and, in a neat nod back to James Montgomery's plans in the 1930s, the Irish

Independence collection in April 2018. Between these releases, access was further improved by the August 2017 launch of the IFI Player as a smartphone app.

In March 2018, the new Maynooth facility was officially opened, tripling the archive's capacity. Measuring 180 square meters, the facility contained 120 square meters of climate-controlled vault space to house a collection that had reached nearly 30,000 cans of film. Yet just a month later, in April 2018, the launch of the archive's Moving Image Survey report suggested that there remained a significant array of largely uncataloged audiovisual material held in private collections around Ireland that lacked preservation strategies. This suggests not only a need for ongoing active measures to retrieve such content from oblivion—on film and videotape and in digital formats—but also a need for recurrent state funding of the archive's work.

IRISH FILM BOARD. Although an Irish Film Board was inaugurated in 1981, proposals for such a body date back to the 1942 *Report of the Inter-Departmental Committee on the Film Industry*. In 1954, after his attempts to establish a National Film Studio had been frustrated by the refusal of the Department of Finance to countenance such a facility, **Sean Lemass** instead proposed the establishment of what he termed a film board. Although nominally influenced by the example of the National Film Board of Canada, the body he proposed was to do the following:

- Produce films, including films in Irish
- Encourage and coordinate filmmaking by other Irish producers
- Encourage the making of feature films in Ireland by outside organizations
- Foster the general development of a film industry in Ireland

In effect, Lemass proposed not only a single institution that would perform the functions of a film board but also a production company and a screen commission. In any event, the proposal lapsed after Fianna Fáil lost the May 1954 general election.

The idea was revived, however, by the 1968 *Report of the Film Industry Committee*, which, in the course of proposing the creation of a fund to finance low-budget feature and short-film production, suggested that the fund be administered by a putative film board. The idea was incorporated into a 1970 bill, simply entitled the Film Bill. Unfortunately, the bill was never passed, and it was not until the late 1970s that the idea of a film board was revisited.

The return to the notion of a film board was an unintended consequence of attempts to deal with the ongoing question of how to make the National Film Studios of Ireland (NFSI) at **Ardmore** viable. In 1977, the new minister for industry and commerce, Des O'Malley, commissioned the London office of the U.S. consulting firm Arthur D. Little to examine why the studios were consistently losing money. The consultants acknowledged that the studios were hindered by the absence of any state-funded financial incentive for filmmaking in Ireland as was common in other European nations. They recommended creating a fund of IR£2.8 million to be disbursed over four years to incentivize foreign producers to shoot at Ardmore. Ardmore itself expressed an interest in administering such a fund but was rebuffed by the Department of Industry and Commerce, which instead recommended the creation of a separate, independent body . O'Malley also made it clear that it would be politically difficult to continue supporting the NFSI without also making some gesture toward indigenous filmmakers. Thus, he proposed ring-fencing an additional £1.3 million for indigenous productions, whether shot at the NFSI or not. The resulting 1980 Film Board Bill was thus aimed primarily at an industrial objective—sustaining Ardmore for use mainly by international productions—with support for indigenous work as a secondary consideration.

The board commenced its work in 1981 despite the fact that only three of the seven board members had actually been appointed. Controversy immediately surrounded it when the partially constituted board awarded half of its first year's funding (£200,000) to a single picture—**Neil Jordan**'s debut, *Angel*—before returning the rest of the year's allocation to the state. The **Association of Independent Producers** interpreted this as effectively suggesting that there were no other Irish projects worthy of support. The controversy was fueled by the fact that one of the board members, **John Boorman**, was also the executive producer on the film (though his role in this regard came at the insistence of **Channel 4**, the main source of funds for the film). Eventually, board chairman Louis Heelan resigned in frustration at the response to *Angel*'s funding, and five new board members were appointed.

Over the next six years, the board would go on to put money into 10 feature projects as well as a number of short and experimental works. The full list of features was *Angel, **The Outcasts**, The Country Girls, **Anne Devlin**, **Pigs**, **The End of the World Man**, **Eat the Peach**, **Budawanny**, **Reefer and the Model**,* and ***The Courier***.

Several of the features supported by the board would have been regarded as avant-garde: the films made by **Joe Comerford, Cathal Black**, and **Pat Murphy** with Film Board support were textbook examples of national cinema. However, their culturally specific nature arguably constrained their capacity to travel, and the films failed to sell widely overseas. Indeed, with the exception of *Eat the Peach*, neither did they perform well at the Irish box office, and the original idea that the board would eventually become self-funding, using profits from earlier films to fund investment in later ones, never came to fruition. Thus, although technically the board gave soft loans rather than grants, in practice, the loans were rarely repaid. As late as 1992, of the IR£1.247 million advanced to the 10 feature films, only IR£106,000 had been reimbursed to the board. Consequently, in 1987, a new Fianna Fáil government, facing a national economic crisis, suspended the operation of the board, arguing that it constituted an unsustainable drain on the economy. Filmmakers retorted that the direct return to the board failed to fully reflect its economic impact. Former board chair Muiris Mac Conghaile argued that the IR£1.2 million in loans had jump-started work with a total budget of IR£6.1 million, 20 percent of which (IR£1.2 million) had been returned to the state by way of direct and indirect taxes. The government was unmoved, however, pointing to the introduction weeks earlier of the **Section 35** tax break and the promise of the European Union's MEDIA program as more than compensating for the loss of the board.

As a result, the board remained in stasis, not actually closed down but not operating either for a six-year period. During this time, the number of indigenous film projects declined significantly (just one Irish film was made in 1991), demonstrating how important the development function of the board had been.

In 1992, however, several factors led to a revival of the board: the lobbying of industry groups such as Film Makers Ireland was supplemented by a series of reports (most notably the *Coopers & Lybrand Report*) pointing to the economic potential of the audiovisual sector in Ireland. Most significant, in January 1993, **Michael D. Higgins** became minister at the new Department of Arts, Culture, and the Gaeltacht. Two months later, Higgins declared that he had secured cabinet approval for the immediate reactivation of the board, which, in keeping with a (usually only rhetorical) commitment to administrative decentralization, was given new head offices in Galway. Veteran producer **Lelia Doolan** was appointed chair, and former Channel 4 commissioning editor **Rod Stoneman** became the chief executive and thus assumed day-to-day responsibility for running the board.

By 2003, a decade after its reestablishment, the Film Board was receiving around €12 million per annum in capital and administration funding from the state. This was used to fund loans and equity investment for independent Irish filmmakers to assist in the development and production of Irish films. In this way, the board was a critical driver of the explosion in production activity that took place in the 1990s. Nearly 100 Irish features and television series and 300 short films received funding in the decade after 1993, and another 500 projects received development funding. The board also funded **animation** and **documentary** projects and promoted a series of initiatives with **Radio Telefís Éireann**, TG4, and **Film Base** intended to allow neophyte filmmakers to develop their craft (mainly via the production of shorts). These schemes included Short Cuts, Short Shorts, Frameworks, Oscailt, and Irish Flash.

The second board in particular adopted a broad interpretation of Section 4 of the Film Board Act, outlining its general functions. The section notes that the board may "assist and encourage by any means it considers appropriate the making of films in the State." In practice, this saw the board cooperate with a range of other Irish semistate agencies (notably the **Arts Council**, FAS [the state training body], and the **Northern Ireland Screen**) with a view to improving the marketing, sales, and distribution of Irish films and promoting training and development in all areas of filmmaking. (It should be noted that the employment of Irish film workers and the use of ancillary Irish services are usually regarded as a crucial considerations in the board's assessment of applications.)

Furthermore, the 1980 act empowered the board to establish subsidiaries (technically committees) to carry out functions that the board considered might be "better or more conveniently performed by a committee. Consequently, the board established the **Irish Screen Commission** in 1997 to promote Ireland as a film location. Initially, the commission was established as a separate entity with its own offices in Dublin. However, in 2001, the commission was replaced by a Location Services unit, which was folded back into the main board and which now provides comprehensive information about all aspects of filming in Ireland, from tax incentives to locations, casting, crews, equipment, and facilities.

In terms of the films supported by the Stoneman board, it has been argued that, notwithstanding the chief executive's expressed policy of "radical pluralism" (i.e., supporting the widest range of films possible), it was somewhat more commercially minded than its 1980s predecessor. Some critics noted an increasing trend toward more formally conservative filmmaking, especially in comparison with the culturally engaged, critical cinema of the 1980s. However, while it seems undeniable that most of the board-funded films since the 1990s adopted more universally comprehensible narratives (e.g., *Circle of Friends*, *About Adam*, or *Dead Bodies*), the Stoneman board undeniably also supported a more critical cinema. Moreover, it was largely due to the board that there was constant production activity in Ireland after 1993 in contrast to the previously stop-and-start nature of production.

In 2003, Stoneman resigned as CEO to become director of the Huston School of Film & Digital Media at NUI Galway. His successor, **Mark Woods**, came to the position having been head of acquisitions and investment for the Showtime and Encore film channels in Australia. Woods's background brought a new emphasis on marketability, but he was unfortunate in arriving at a point when the board was experiencing cuts to its budget (the first since 1993) as the Irish economy was buffeted by the impact of the post–dot-com global recession. At the same time, the overall Irish film policy model—which had prevailed since the early 1990s whereby large-scale international productions shooting in Ireland were implicitly used to cross-subsidize losses on indigenous (often board-supported) productions—began to fall asunder. Fluctuations in the exchange rate between the euro and the dollar made Ireland an increasingly expensive location for U.S. productions, while changes to the U.K. film tax code made it harder for overseas productions to simultaneously "double-dip" into Irish and U.K. funding. Confronted by this and a degree of hostility to his pro-market approach from elements of the Irish production industry, Woods departed in April 2005, and a seven-month interregnum followed in which the board effectively had no chief executive. In November 2005, **Simon Perry**, former head of British Screen Finance, was appointed to take over the position.

It was during that interregnum that then Minister for Arts **John O'Donoghue** decided to respond to the changing terms of international trade by increasing the board's funding from 2005 on. This was done with the understanding that the additional revenues would be ring-fenced for incoming *international* productions, thus overtly repurposing the board as an industrial development body. Not coincidentally, in October 2006, the board opened a regional office in Los Angeles—"The Irish Film Commission U.S."—headed by a former Enterprise Ireland executive tasked with promoting Ireland as a location to Hollywood producers. And, even as an increasing number of large-scale incoming TV productions in Ireland were supported on a recurrent basis by the board's International Production Fund, a second initiative in 2007—the "Creative Co-Production Fund"—was introduced to allow Irish producers to become a minority partner in any European film as long as they were involved as a "creative collaborator." Under Simon Perry's direction, between 2007 and 2014, the board supported nearly 50 features from this fund, and, though notionally prioritizing projects that "utilize Ireland as a film location, depict Ireland for Ireland [*sic*], and where a number of key Irish HODs and/or Irish cast are employed," many of the supported projects did not meet at least the first two criteria. In sum, after 2005, there was a marked shift in the state's overall policy toward the audiovisual sector and thus in the manner in which the board was expected to operate: a new emphasis on encouraging foreign capital to invest in Ireland was firmly established.

Such pressures would be amplified as the post-2008 recession took hold. As part of a strategy to reduce state spending, the board's very existence was threatened by a proposal to shut it down. Critically, it was also suggested that the board's function could instead be taken on by Enterprise Ireland (the national industrial development body), again privileging the economic rationale for supporting audiovisual activity over a more culturally inflected line of reasoning. Although the board survived, it saw its funding halved by 2013, and the threat in 2008 to close the board made it clear that, in an era of austerity, the state would not support screen production simply for sociocultural reasons or even because it indirectly supported economic growth through encouraging tourism. Instead, state support for screen production would be countenanced only if the latter constituted economic activity in and of itself. This was reflected in the manner in which the board increasingly came to be regarded. A "Culture 2025" discussion document published by the Department of Arts, Heritage, and the Gaeltacht in late 2015 explicitly framed the board as an industrial development body and—for the first time since its existence—entirely omitted any reference to its potential cultural function. Faced with this context, **James Hickey**, the board's fourth chief executive (appointed in 2011), appears to have had little choice but to embrace the "creative industries" discourse and proceed accordingly.

Taking over at the board at a point when its funding was being persistently cut must have been something of a poisoned chalice for Hickey. Looking over the period from 1993 to 2013 and adjusting for inflation, the board's average per film investment had gradually risen from €280,000 in 1993 and 1994 to €610,000 between 2005 and 2008. Thirteen individual films received investments of more than €1 million from the board in that same period (2005–2008). By contrast, Hickey had to oversee a decline in average production funding to less than €500,000 by 2013, and just two films received €1 million or more in investments between 2010 and 2013. Despite this, the audiovisual sector as a whole bucked the spiraling decline of the rest of the Irish economy after 2008. The combined value of Irish and international production activity in Ireland averaged €154 million per annum between 2007 and 2009. This would nearly double to €300 million between 2013 and 2015, driven in no small part by board-funded U.S. television projects, such as *The Tudors*, *Vikings*, and *Penny Dreadful*. Yet, although the board continued to support locally engaged, indigenous and *popular* feature film activity (e.g., **The Young Offenders** and **A Date with Mad Mary**), it was also apparent that Irish producers seeking board support had themselves internalized the exhortation to look to international markets. In 2016, the board could look with some pride on the clutch of Golden Globe, Cannes Festival, and **Academy Award** nominations secured by Irish-produced (and board-supported) films such as John Crowley's **Brooklyn**, **Lenny Abrahamson**'s *Room*, and the **Element Pictures**–produced *The Lobster* and *The Killing of a Sacred Deer*. Yet the last titles were helmed by a Greek director and not overtly set within Ireland, while Abrahamson's *Room* looked, for all intents and purposes, like a U.S. film in setting and cast.

Over its existence, then, the organization has had to continually adapt itself to the vagaries of shifting economic and political forces. While the 2010s witnessed a recognizable shift toward a rhetoric of economic return— the "monetization" of culture and the introduction of a "creative industries" paradigm—the board has also succeeded in maintaining a generally consistent rate of production (an average of 12 films per year) and an output that has continued to develop and mature. Equivocation between cultural and economic arguments might thus be seen less as a failure to clarify an ideological agenda than as a national cinema understood as an expression of a dynamic conception of the nation. But it also points to a splintering of concerns within government policy, with employment gradually taking precedence over a cultural emphasis, which, as long as there is occasional international recognition of demonstrably Irish "product" (e.g., *Once* and *The Guard*), has become increasingly secondary within the board's discourse.

IRISH FILM CENTRE. The concept of the Irish Film Centre (IFC) dates from an **Irish Film Institute** (IFI) proposal in the early 1980s to create a physical nexus for the often disparate activities of film-related bodies in Ireland. In 1985, the IFI drew up plans for a center on the corner of Trinity Street and Andrew Street in Dublin, but these were abandoned the following year when the IFI acquired most of what was then the Friends (Quakers) Meeting House at 6 Eustace Street in Dublin's Temple Bar. Architect Sheila O'Donnell drew up an award-winning plan to rework the interior in line with the IFI's requirements for a space containing two cinemas, a film archive, and a library (to which a bar and restaurant and a bookshop were later added). The project was given a political fillip in January 1987 when the government's first white paper on cultural policy, "Access and Opportunity," singled out the Film Centre project as deserving support, and later that year, the **Arts Council** provided a £95,000 capital grant to the IFI (over and above a direct grant of £20,000) to allow it to complete the purchase of the building. The building was then occupied on an interim basis by the institute along with **Film Base**, the MEDIA program's EVE initiative, and the Traditional Irish Music Archive. In 1989, the Arts Council established the Irish Film Centre Building Ltd (IFCB) to oversee the development of the project. Having raised £350,000 of National Lottery funds via the Arts Council in December 1989, with another £600,000 of EU structural funds in November 1990, the IFCB commenced a major redevelopment of the building in June 1991.

The newly refurbished building, redevelopment of which ultimately cost £2.25 million, eventually opened in September 1992, following the merger of IFI and the IFCB. Although logical administratively, the merger was not an entirely happy one, as it led to "rationalization" of staff numbers and initial tensions between staff from the formerly separate organizations. Nonetheless, the main public focus of the center, the two cinemas, enjoyed early success. Around 15,000 people became members in the first 12 months—three times the targeted figure. This was financially significant given that Arts Council support to the IFI was limited to supporting education and archival and informational work but not the operation of the cinemas. Furthermore, a policy that generally limited cinema runs to no more than two to three weeks and that reserved a percentage of screenings for repertory and archival material imposed programming constraints that a purely commercial cinema would have eschewed.

The financial limitations imposed by the remit would become a pressing issue for a period in the mid-1990s as membership—and therefore the cinemas' income—dropped off. When in March 1995 the IFC announced plans to screen Oliver Stone's *Natural Born Killers*, which the film censor had banned on an open-ended basis, it was suggested that the decision was driven less by ideological objections to **censorship** and more by the need to keep the cinemas afloat. In any event, the screenings were prohibited by the Department of Justice, which threatened intervention by the Gardaí (police). The financial position of the cinemas improved after 1996, when the **Light House Cinema** closed.

In addition to the cinemas, by the mid-1990s, the IFC was home to MEDIA Desk Ireland, EVE, Film Base, the Federation of Irish Film Societies, the Junior Dublin Film Festival, Film Makers Ireland, and Hubbard Casting. By the first decade of the 21st century, the center was widely recognized as being at the heart of film culture in Ireland, and it has become a model for proposed similar initiatives in other Irish cities.

IRISH FILM FINANCE CORPORATION. The Irish Film Finance Corporation (IFFC) was established in 1960 as a response to changes in the operation of the British Cinematograph Films Act of 1957. Prior to 1959, films made by Irish citizens or companies were considered British under that legislation and could thus avail themselves of Eady levy funding, derived from a tax on cinema admissions in Great Britain. It is apparent that the promoters of **Ardmore Studios**—the building of which started in 1957—assumed that such funding would be available for productions shot at the studios. However, in 1959, the British Board of Trade amended the operation of the levy so that only films made by British residents or by companies registered, managed, and controlled in the United Kingdom qualified for funding.

The absence in Ireland of any alternative organization offering to provide risk capital for producers wishing to make films at Ardmore posed a serious threat to that operation's viability. However, within six weeks after the changes to the Eady levy went into effect, the state-owned Industrial Credit Company responded by establishing a subsidiary, the Irish Film Finance Corporation Ltd.

Between 1960 and 1967, the IFFC would invest £506,317 of public funds in 15 films. Of these, however, only two dealt with Irish subjects. More significantly, Irish employment on all of these films was limited to carpenters, plasterers, and canteen and office workers at Ardmore. This was because, surprisingly, the IFFC was explicitly established not to support Irish film production but rather to consider applications from *film producers in Ireland* for financial assistance by way of loans. Indeed, neophyte Irish film companies were virtually unable to access IFFC funding for two reasons. First, the IFFC required that any project they considered had previously secured distribution guarantees—that is, a commitment from a distributor to pick up the film once completed. Second, the IFFC preferred to provide "end money," the remaining capital required by a producer to finance a film after the producer received credit from commercial institutions. Both of these conditions meant that IFFC funding was of use only to those producers with a track record impressive enough to convince distributors, banks, or building societies to invest in their films. Since there was no history of consistent feature production in Ireland, there were effectively no such producers based in Ireland. Not surprisingly, a 1967 civil service assessment of the IFFC concluded that "the IFFC is serving no useful purpose as a credit institution for regular film production in Ireland." As a consequence, the IFFC effectively ceased operations in that same year, although it was not formally closed until the 1980s.

IRISH FILM INSTITUTE. The origins of the Irish Film Institute date back to the mid-1930s, when Jesuit priest Father Richard Devane's interest in cinema was piqued by an *Irish Press* campaign castigating elements of the **exhibition** industry for its effect on public morality. Although supporting the campaign, Devane's critique of cinema was more nuanced: he called for a government inquiry into all aspects of cinema to enable a fuller understanding of its cultural, educational, and "national" potential. He would repeat this call in April 1937, notwithstanding the publication in the interim of Pope Pius XI's encyclical on cinema, which advocated a censorious approach to the medium. For Devane, by contrast, the establishment of an inquiry would enable Ireland to use cinema as a powerful instrument of cultural development. Ultimately, he expected the inquiry to recommend that this be achieved through the establishment of a national film institute.

Devane's call for an enquiry was indirectly answered by the decision of **Sean Lemass** to establish the **Inter-Departmental Committee on the Film Industry** in 1937. In its eventual 1942 report, the committee considered the pros and cons of a national film institute, which it envisaged (among other functions) as acting as a focus for production activity, funding prospective producers, and advising the state on running a putative state-funded film studio. In short, the committee envisaged a body that would effectively bear de facto responsibility for defining film policy in Ireland.

However, the committee described as "perhaps the most important function" of the institute the promotion of film for purposes of education, culture, and general propaganda. Demonstrating almost limitless faith in the power of the medium, the report asserted that there was no subject of the school curriculum that did not lend itself, in a greater or lesser degree, to film treatment. Similarly, with regard to cinema's cultural potential, the report suggested that

> an important contribution could be made towards the development of national culture by the exhibition of films dealing with the history and institutions, traditions and customs, literature, music, games and pastimes of the people.

Although many of the committee recommendations were not acted on, the one exception to this related to a national film institute, in part because other actors took a hand in the matter. In July 1943, Devane (with the imprimatur of Archbishop John Charles McQuaid) announced the intention to establish the National Film Institute of Ireland (NFII). The following December saw another Inter-Departmental Committee representing the Departments of Education, Finance, Industry and Commerce, Agriculture and Local Government, and Public Health revisit the original committee's comments on educational films and films in the Irish language. This new committee recommended state funding of the institute to facilitate the acquisition of a library of education films and the production of films on behalf of government departments. Thus, beginning in 1945–1946, the NFII was in receipt of funding via the annual science and art vote of the Department of Education.

In effect, the state co-opted the Film Institute, imposing on it the dual responsibilities of a national film unit and a film education board without giving it sufficient funds to properly fulfill either remit. However, from the perspective of the Catholic hierarchy, it seems likely that state funding was interpreted as a tacit endorsement of the institute as the state's "official" film body, thus obviating the possibility that a more secular body, such as the **Irish Film Society**, might occupy that role.

In general terms, the institute identified its function as being to direct and encourage the use of the motion picture in the national cultural interests of the Irish people. However, the approach adopted by the institute to realizing this broad objective changed dramatically in the late 1970s, so much so that the NFII's history can be divided into two periods—its "Catholic" phase from 1945 to 1979 and its secular one since 1979.

The Catholic phase was inaugurated by the initial grant of state funds, which permitted the institute to begin a concerted program to acquire a substantial library of educational films. By 1950, it had already amassed 800 films, although at the time, relatively few schools were equipped with projectors. These were augmented by a range of films commissioned by the state in the 1940s and 1950s. Key among these were *A Nation Once Again* (1945), a documentary commemorating the centenary of Thomas Davis's death, and

W. B. Yeats—A Tribute (1950), although most of the films commissioned were more mundane public information shorts relating to subjects like road safety and hygiene.

In 1948, the institute launched a journal that would remain in existence in one form or another until the late 1960s. *Irish Cinema Quarterly* (1948–1949) became *National Film Quarterly* (1950–1956), then *Irish Film Quarterly* (1957–1959) before eventually being retitled *Vision* (1965–1968).

Beyond film library, production, and journal functions, the institute operated some sporadic education outreach programs, initiating a course on educational films for teachers in 1946, and in theory, it acted as an advisory committee on state film policy. In practice, the institute's influence in this regard was limited by its resources. In 1955, Minister for Industry and Commerce William Norton requested that the NFII look into the whole question of a film industry. Although the institute did hold some meetings to attempt to devise some kind of film strategy, the resulting document, only a few pages long, obviously fell well short of what Norton had been expecting. However, the poverty of the document reflected the limited financial resources made available to the institute by the state. In 1967, for example, the Department of Education grant to the institute was £5,250, only slightly greater than the 1945 grant in real spending terms.

However, even if such resources had been adequate, it was unlikely that the institute would have undertaken a more ambitious program of action. At the institute's annual meeting in 1965, during a speech intended to compliment its members on their Catholic character, Archbishop McQuaid made comments that indirectly acknowledged how he perceived the relevance of the organization in the wider society:

> I invite you to be glad at being treated with a sardonic contempt. If you had not standards of Christian Reverence, you would not be regarded as uneducated, illiberal, and inexperienced.

Hence, by 1978, **Kevin Rockett**, although noting that the institute had a library of 6,000 films and two traveling projectors touring the country, described the institute as ineffectual and largely dormant, operating outside contemporary developments in film screening and writing. Nevertheless, Rockett would be one of the key individuals in the cultural revolution that transformed the institute at the close of the 1970s. In 1978, Rockett had noted that the institute's connections with what remained a largely Church-run education system placed it in a unique position to drive forward a film education policy through the appointment of a film education officer. This coincided with **Arts Council** thinking on encouraging the institute to modernize and professionalize through financial incentives.

A first step in this direction was taken when the board of the institute (some of whose members had been in situ for two decades) invited Kevin Rockett to join the board. He was later followed by figures like Ciaran Benson (later chair of the Arts Council) and renowned cultural theorist Luke Gibbons. In 1979, the Arts Council responded by increasing the institute's grant from £200 to £7,400, an increase conditional on the appointment of a dedicated film education officer, Martin McLoone (who has written extensively on Irish film). By 1983, the grant went to £21,000, permitting the appointment of a full-time director. Thus, when David Kavanagh became director of the institute in 1983, he inherited a staff of six and an annual turnover of £130,000.

This purging of the board of its old guard continued through the early 1980s. By the time Kevin Rockett became chair in 1984, it had become possible to secularize the institute's articles of association, a shift reflected in the redesignation of the body as the Irish Film Institute.

In practical terms, these changes led to a dramatic transformation in the way the institute went about its business. Film education changed from merely screening approved material in schools to a more progressive, pedagogically informed approach typified by publications like *Every Picture Tells a Story* (1985) and *Roll It There, Colette* (1986), which were visual culture and media studies texts for secondary schools. This followed logically from a broader call for changes in the curriculum to reflect the growing influence of the mass media articulated in institute publications like Martin McLoone's *Media Studies in Irish Education*. Third-level education was also addressed in the 1984 copublication (with **Radio Telefís Éireann**) of *Television and Irish Society*.

From 1984, the institute began to receive seed funding from the Irish Film Board to develop an **Irish Film Archive**. However, arguably the most ambitious activity of the institute in the 1980s was the quest to find a new home, one that would allow the institute to operate a permanent cinema. The institute had had a taste of the exhibition business in 1983, when it was called in by the Arts Council in an attempt to revive the flagging fortunes of the **Irish Film Theatre** (IFT). Although the IFT closed in May 1984, the institute pursued an exhibition strategy, curating the well-received *Green on the Screen* season of Irish and Irish-related material as part of the 1984 Contempor-Eire festival. In 1985, the institute announced plans for an **Irish Film Centre** (IFC) but, acknowledging that it would take some time to raise the necessary funds, engaged in a partnership with Neil Connolly to establish the **Light House Cinema** as an interim measure to maintain some kind of continuity in art house exhibition. This relationship came to an amicable conclusion with the opening of the IFC in September 1992.

Kevin Rockett stood down as chair of the IFI in 1991, to be followed by Niamh O'Sullivan (who was in turn followed by Martha O'Neill and later **Alan Gilsenan**). Yet despite the opening of the IFC and a spectacular increase in Arts Council funding (reaching £330,000 by 1995), the early 1990s were a politically difficult period for the board. In early 1993, the IFI and Irish Film Centre Building Ltd, the ad hoc body charged by the Arts Council with the establishment of the IFC, merged, bringing two sets of staff together and creating a new entity, the Film Institute of Ireland (FII). This led to a period of "rationalization" and redundancies and an internal dispute over the appointment of a chief executive, which ultimately led former IFI director David Kavanagh (who by 1994 oversaw 45 staff and a turnover of £1.5 million) to resign from the organization. Matters were compounded by the fact that the center as a whole lost money in 1994, in part as a result of the initial failure of the IFC's bar and restaurant to earn the profits that had been earmarked to cross subsidize more overtly cultural activities.

In September 1994, however, a new chief executive, Sheila Pratschke, was appointed, and with the aid of substantial ongoing funding, the environment at the FII became more settled. In 1999, in part driven by the Arts Council publication of a three-year arts plan, the FII published its own five-year plan, identifying the organization's core functions. These included the operation of the IFC cinemas, the promotion of the education department, supporting the Irish Film Archive, and performing a research and information function for all aspects of film and filmmaking in Ireland. Most of these mapped neatly onto the film policy emphases laid out in the Arts Council document, and they have subsequently remained the main foci of institute activity.

In 2003, driven by a concern that there was a lack of public appreciation of the institute's activities (many people were unaware that the IFC housed much more than its cinemas), the FII board voted to revert to the Irish Film Institute (IFI) name. As part of this shift, the IFC building became the IFI. By 2004, the IFI employed 70 people and had an annual turnover of approximately €2.6 million (including a €600,000 Arts Council revenue grant and €14,000 for education from the Department of Education). For a period, in the mid-2000s, the institute actively pursued the acquisition of "national cultural institute" status, a move that would put it on a par with other national cultural bodies, such as the National Library, the National Gallery, and the **Abbey Theatre** and perhaps lead to a more secure funding base. However, the issue was allowed to drop, perhaps reflecting the calculation that the cultural institute status might come with golden handcuffs, limiting the institute's de facto independence.

In 2009, the IFI building underwent a substantial refurbishment, adding a third cinema to its exhibition capacity, thus permitting it to run additional events, such as free lunchtime screenings from the Irish Film Archive. By the mid-2010s, the IFI's operations were clearly focused around three core activities: exhibiting, preserving, and educating. With regard to exhibition, still the function most publicly associated with the institute, the cinemas typically show more than 300 films a year across 5,000 screenings and in 2016 achieved an overall attendance of 170,000 admissions. In addition to regular screenings, the IFI schedules family-friendly screenings and work aimed at older audiences under its "Wild Strawberries" brand. It also operates four annual festivals around family films, documentary, horror, and French cinema. That exhibition work also reaches beyond the bounds of the IFI building and indeed the Irish border. IFI National organizes local screenings around Ireland under the Local Films for Local People scheme, often drawing on holdings from the Irish Film Archive. Similarly, IFI International liaises with overseas festivals to showcase Irish film abroad, collaborating with 56 such events in 2016. The Preservation function is discussed at length in the entry on the Irish Film Archive and the Education function in the **Education** entry. To these foci, the institute's 2017–2022 strategy document added an emphasis on promoting the importance of film culture among Irish policymakers and funders. To some extent, this is related to the question of the institute's longer-term funding. Although as of 2016 the institute needed around €3.5 million to conduct its various activities, its Arts Council budget of €800,000 accounts for less than a quarter of the sum required. Thus, the IFI must sustain itself largely from within its own revenues, including ticket sales and revenues from the bookshop and from the institute's café/bar. Such revenue sources are inherently unpredictable (indeed, the IFI recorded a small deficit of €15,000 in 2016). Thus, notwithstanding the decision to park the question of national cultural institute status, a key concern for the IFI going forward is securing a reliable and predictable source of funding.

IRISH FILM SOCIETY. The Irish Film Society (IFS) was founded in 1936 by **Liam O'Leary**, Edward Toner, Sean O'Meadhra, and Patrick Fitzsimons. Membership grew quickly, and branches were set up around the country. Although the main objective of the society was to exhibit classical and foreign films, by 1943, the work of the society had expanded to include a School of Film Technique, a Children's Film Committee (which trained teachers to use film as a pedagogical tool), and working with elements of the Irish cinema trade to sponsor children's matinee screenings. In addition, the society was responsible for publishing *Scannán*, the only regular indigenous film journal. The school collapsed in 1948 as the society struggled to find adequately trained instructors in a country lacking a professional film industry. Before this, its members produced a series of short films, including the well-received *Foolsmate*, a 20-minute fiction piece directed by Brendan Stafford (who later pursued a directorial career in the British film industry), and

Aiséirghe, directed by Liam O'Leary, which, in critiquing the nation's practical commitment to the ideals of 1916, arguably prefigured O'Leary's 1948 film *Our Country*.

However, the society's most important cultural contribution was to bring to Ireland foreign language films, which had largely disappeared from mainstream cinemas since the introduction of sound and the ensuing Anglo-American dominance of the Irish **distribution** sector. And while side projects, such as the film school and *Scannán*, gradually came to a conclusion, the society's core function of exhibition has persisted into the modern era. Although with the advent of the **Irish Film Theatre** in 1976 (and subsequently the **Light House Cinema** and the **Irish Film Centre**) the society was no longer the sole avenue for art house material in Ireland, it remained crucial for audiences based outside Dublin or Cork who lacked access to a dedicated art house venue.

In 1977, the IFS was superseded by the Federation of Irish Film Societies (FIFS), which acted as an umbrella body for all of the country's local film societies. The FIFS provided a centralized film-booking agency for its members from its head office in Dublin. Typically, the FIFS organized biannual screenings of new material on offer (especially in the 16-mm format, which was then the preferred option for societies) to allow local societies to draw up seasonal screening programs. By the early 1990s, the federation was bringing in approximately 250 titles annually for 25 societies with aggregate membership of around 4,500 people. It was also arguably developing an audience for more permanent art house venues. As of 1990, the society at the Triskel Arts Centre in Cork City was operating four days a week for 25 to 30 weeks of the year, a consideration that indirectly influenced the decision to open a permanent commercial venue (the Kino) in the city in November 1996.

By the end of the 1990s, the widespread availability of material for home consumption in VHS and DVD formats and doubts over the long-term availability of 16-mm material (along with the emerging possibilities of digital cinema) began to raise serious questions over the future role of the federation. In addition, an increasing number of regional arts centers were using their theater spaces to screen art house material alongside the operation of local film societies. In response, in 1998, the federation commissioned a development plan to outline new directions for the organization.

This in turn led to the rebranding of the organization in 2001 as ACCESS Cinemas. ACCESS continues to advise local societies on film selection, technical issues (including those relating to Digital Cinema screenings), presentation standards, and event promotion as well as negotiating with distributors to block-book and ship films (and related promotional materials) on behalf of local film societies. However, these activities take place within a broader remit to promote regional cultural cinema programming in general, which sees ACCESS also work in partnership with arts centers, other local cultural organizations, and, on occasion, permanent cinemas interested in adding art house content to their programs. In the main, however, as of 2018, the clients of ACCESS Cinemas are roughly evenly drawn from "traditional" film clubs and "MPVs" (mixed program venues).

ACCESS Cinemas has a particular remit to promote the screening of Irish content to their members, and overall, around 60 percent of titles accessed via the network are sourced from Europe (including Ireland). This emphasis facilitated ACCESS's acceptance as a member in 2004 by the Europa Cinemas Network, making it the first network of part-time venues to be included in that wider network. Similarly, in the 2010s, ACCESS Cinemas has increasingly moved to effectively act as a quasi distributor within Ireland, acquiring international titles on behalf of member organizations (occasionally with financial assistance from the **Creative Europe** program) and facilitating their national distribution via their member network.

Remarkably, notwithstanding the increased accessibility of film content via a variety of home entertainment avenues, ACCESS Cinemas has seen its membership rise throughout the 21st century, servicing some 80 groups (including three in Northern Ireland) as of the beginning of 2017. In 2016, nearly 80,000 people watched 1,300 screenings of more than 400 film titles via the various film clubs operating around the country. In addition to the long-established annual Viewing Days, when clubs can congregrate to view and select titles in advance of screening seasons, ACCESS offers direct training on film marketing (with an increasing emphasis on the use of social media tools) and curates touring programs on behalf of its members in conjunction with cultural institutions such as the Alliance Francaise or various embassies and consulates based in Dublin.

Although partially supported by both the **Arts Council** and the Europa Cinemas network (to the tune of €120,000 and €16,000, respectively, in 2016), the bulk of ACCESS's revenue (€470,000 in 2016) comes from renting films to member organizations.

IRISH FILM THEATRE. In many ways a forerunner of the **Irish Film Centre** cinemas, the Irish Film Theatre (IFT) was established in March 1976 after the success of the European Film Fortnight held in January of that year in Dublin's International Cinema. The aim was to satisfy the demand for films that would not otherwise receive commercial release. In effect, the IFT represented the nearest thing Ireland had at the time to a national film theater. Despite this and the fact that the European Film Fortnight had been run by the **Arts Council**'s film and literature officer, **David Collins**, and that the IFT was legally a subsidiary of the Arts Council, it received no Arts Council funding. Encouraged by the success of the European Film Fortnight, the council felt that the IFT could be financially self-sufficient, particularly in light of the fact that it would be constituted as a club and thus would not have to pay **censorship** fees. Despite this view, David Collins summed up the section on film in the 1976 Arts Council report by stating that the council's overall level of finance for film was still inadequate.

However, the initial success of the IFT seemed to confirm the Arts Council's view. By 1980, membership had reached 12,000 people, and annual admissions topped 100,000—an extraordinary figure considering that there were only two screenings a day, all taking place in the single-screen, 240-seat Earlsfort Terrace cinema. The initial success owed much to the availability of product, as there was a huge backlog of art house material that had never been screened in Ireland.

Such was the euphoria that, in 1980, a second cinema was leased from the **Ward Anderson** group in Limerick. It was intended to be the first stage in an ambitious plan to establish a national circuit of IFTs. However, the 1982 Arts Council annual report made it clear that all was not rosy: plans to establish a third IFT in Cork were abandoned when a disturbing trend of diminishing audiences in the Dublin IFT during the last quarter of 1982 prompted the IFT board to introduce a change in programming policies and discard the membership requirement for admission. The ongoing lack of subsidy was exacerbated by several other factors. The Limerick IFT was a disaster from the start: poorly located, it had never broken even financially. Furthermore, by 1980, the Dublin IFT had exhausted the backlog of blue-chip art house material and was increasingly forced to rely on newer material, which proved less reliable in drawing audiences.

As a result, in 1983, the IFT administrative offices were closed, and the Arts Council was forced to pay out £105,953 to cover the debts of its subsidiary. Despite handing over programming policy to the **Irish Film Institute**, attendances continued to drop from their peak of 2,000 per week in 1979 to 500 per week in 1984. In May of the same year, £50,000 was provided to conclude the IFT's affairs. The 1984 annual report concluded with the hope that "a new way of providing for the public who wish to see and support a programme of art-house films will emerge."

The significance of the IFT as a model (particularly for the Irish Film Centre cinemas) cannot be overstated: its spectacular rise and fall made explicit the possibility of screening art house material but also drew attention to the commercial pitfalls of doing so.

IRISH-LANGUAGE CINEMA. Although notionally the official language of Ireland, the vast majority of indigenous Irish films are shot through the de facto main language: English.

At the beginning of the 19th century, Irish remained the majority language on the island of Ireland, but the ban on teaching the language through primary schools, combined with the devastating effects of the Famine of the 1840s (which had a disproportionate impact on the mainly Irish-speaking western counties) plus a perception that English was, under imperial rule, the language of both administration and commerce, undermined its day-to-day use. Although the cultural revival movement of the 1880s and 1890s included a strong emphasis on sustaining the language, by the time the Irish Free State came into existence in 1922, Irish had, at best, a marginal status. Notwithstanding a strong emphasis on the language in primary and secondary education—Irish remains, along with English and mathematics, a core subject for all students from age four up to 16—the failure to find a means of integrating it into daily discourse saw its use continue to dwindle over the course of the 20th century. Although 1.7 million people described themselves as able to speak the language in the 2016 census, fewer than 80,000 asserted that they used it on a daily basis, and of these, more than a quarter lived in Gaeltacht regions (areas specifically designated by the state as Irish-language speaking). (Indeed, more people speak Polish on a daily basis in Ireland than Irish.)

These are clearly not fertile conditions for a commercial Irish-language cinema. Nonetheless, not only is the landscape of Irish film production dotted with Irish-language texts, but such texts have been among the most critically acclaimed indigenous films produced by filmmakers like **Bob Quinn**, **Tom Collins**, and **Pat Collins**.

The failure of the state to step in and generate any sustained filmmaking activity until the 1970s clearly militated against the emergence of a subgenre of Irish-language cinema. The sole gesture made in that direction in the interwar period was the grant of £200 made to filmmaker **Robert Flaherty** to make *Oidhche Sheanchais* (The Night of Storytelling) as he worked on the postproduction for *Man of Aran*. The short film (Flaherty's first synchsound project) placed famed Aran Island storyteller Seáinín Tom Sheáin in a Gainsborough Studio set re-creating a cottage hearth as he regaled an audience with the tale of Máirtín 'ac Conraoi, a fisherman whose family encounters the fairy folk. The film received a limited release and, though positively (if somewhat earnestly) reviewed failed to make much of an impact with audiences. Earnest Blythe, a lifelong champion of efforts to revive Irish, criticized its failure to engage its audiences with a more contemporary story. (Long believed lost, a copy turned up in the Harvard Library in 2013 and was painstakingly restored.)

When the state did begin more consistent funding of filmed work after World War II, the resulting films—driven by the public information needs of various government departments and the international outreach goals of the **Cultural Relations Committee**—were shot primarily in English. Convincing local audiences to sit through exhortations on protecting against tuberculosis and the importance of road safety was difficult enough without adding the additional hurdle of a language most audiences had little working knowledge of. That said, there were exceptions, such as *Gnó Gach Éinne* (Everybody's Business) (1951) and *Na Fiacla Sin Agat* (Keep Your Teeth) (1951). For the most part, however, it was left to Comhdáil Náisúnta na Gaeilge (the National Gaelic Congress) to take up the cause. Originally established in 1943 by the state, the organization had argued that the revival of the language might be pursued on three fronts: publishing, cinema, and promoting economic activity in Gaeltacht regions. In 1950, the Comhdáil published *Films in Irish*, a booklet outlining how Irish-language filmmaking might be promoted. However, government support proved hard to secure, and in 1953, Comhdáil decided to proceed under its own impetus, establishing **Gael Linn** both to raise funds (via Gaelic Athletic Association–linked football pools) and to, among other cultural activities, oversee the production of films in Irish. A grant of £100 from Ernest Blythe, the former government minister and then chair of Comhdáil Náisúnta na Gaeilge, jump-started the production of the *Amharc Eireann* newsreel series. The initial 36 reels (34 of which were directed by Colm O'Laghaire and the remaining two by George Morrison) were produced on a monthly basis, focusing on one topic per film. Thereafter (from 1959), the series moved to a weekly production schedule. Typically running four minutes in length, each weekly "issue" had to convey news but also had to be entertaining—with a view to maintaining the interest of a broad-based cinema audience and rejuvenating the Irish language. Thus, an individual issue might cover fashion, church ceremonies, or sporting fixtures alongside politics.

However, although the newsreels worked to normalize the use of Irish as a linguistic medium, Gael Linn's best-known contribution to Irish-language cinema was unquestionably the mammoth work, largely undertaken by **George Morrison** from 1952 on, to trawl through newsreel footage with a view to constructing a filmic narrative of the struggle for independence and the subsequent establishment of the Irish Free State. Morrison's *Mise Éire*, with its famed **Sean O'Riada**–composed score, was first shown at the Cork Film Festival in 1959 before going on general release in 1960, when, the Irish language notwithstanding, it was met with enormous and widespread acclaim. Almost entirely composed of found footage, the film depicted a heroic narrative of the struggle against imperialism, focusing on the 1916 rebellion and concluding with Sinn Féin's near clean sweep in the 1918 general election. Originally conceived of as a trilogy, a second film, *Saoirse*, was released in 1961. Much more somber in tone due in no small part to the need to negotiate its representation of the post-treaty split and the ensuing Civil War, the second film received a much more muted public response, and as a result, the third film in the sequence, detailing post–Civil War Ireland, was never completed.

Although Gael Linn persisted with the *Amharc Eireann* series, the arrival of **Radio Telefís Éireann** (RTÉ) in 1961 and the availability of television news in an increasing number of homes somewhat undermined the rationale for newsreels, and the sequence was discontinued in 1964. Yet though RTÉ was nominally charged with promoting the Irish language, the first directors general and governing authorities were reluctant to devote too much time to material that audiences might well have regarded as linguistically difficult. (RTÉ's radio predecessor, Radio Eireann, had long noted how audiences switched off in droves when confronted with Irish-language material.) RTÉ's caution was exacerbated by the state's emphasis on the need for the new service to be financially self-sustaining. Thus, although RTÉ did include some Irish-language material in its schedules, Gael Linn also continued supporting some short-film work in Irish through the 1960s and early 1970s. **Louis Marcus**, who had worked on the *Amharc Eireann* newsreels and as an editor on *Mise Éire*, was a key figure in this regard, solo directing a sequence of Irish-language shorts, ranging from *Peil* (1962), on Gaelic football, to *Paisti ag Obair* (Children at Work) (1973). Beautifully shot and often light-hearted in their approach, Marcus's films were widely acclaimed: he won the Silver Bear at the Venice Film Festival in 1967 with *Flea Ceoil* and was twice nominated for an **Academy Award**. (Marcus would actively continue making documentaries into the 21st century, but, though he continued to have recourse to the Irish language, these were increasingly outnumbered by English-language projects.)

Appropriately for a maverick figure who had turned his back on what he saw as the increasingly commercial direction taken by RTÉ in the late 1960s, Bob Quinn would make extensive use of Irish in his film work form the 1970s on. Quinn's decision to do so clearly reflected a larger project to create a countercinema, one that repudiated in particular the soft romantic lens through which Ireland—and in particular the western seaboard—had been represented by overseas filmmakers like **John Ford** and **David Lean**. His first large-scale Cinegael production *Caoineadh Airt Ui Laoire* (1975) offered a critique of colonialism, with its protagonists actively using the Irish language as a point of resistance against external oppressors over several centuries. Quinn's next film, *Poitín* (1978), one of the first long-form films supported by the **Arts Council**, used Irish to emphasize the distance between the idealized pastoral vision of the west of Ireland, which appealed to a European bourgeois sensibility, and the harsh reality of the more brutal aspects of the Celtic identity still prevailing in that region.

The creation of state-financed, noncommercial funding routes in the 1970s and 1980s—the Arts Council from 1973 and the first **Irish Film Board** from 1981—might have been expected to support a flowering of Irish-language production. Yet, *Poitín* aside, this did not bear out in practice: none of the 10 features supported by the Film Board in its first incarnation featured the language, although Bob Quinn's *Budawanny* (1987), the title of which bastardized the Irish for "priest's penis," was silent, reliant on intertitles that might as easily have been written in Irish as in English. This absence appears to have reflected not any animus toward the language on the part of such funders but rather the simple absence of a cohort of filmmakers sufficiently versed in the language so as to be able to contemplate such production.

Nor did the revival of the Film Board in 1993 particularly address this lacuna notwithstanding that one of the first films it supported was *An Goban Saor* (1994), Liadh ni Riad's witty transposition of an Irish legend to a contemporary setting. In 1998, the board established the Oscailt scheme to encourage short film production through Irish as a stepping-stone toward longer-form productions. Although successful in its own terms, supporting the production of some 30 Irish-language shorts up to its suspension in 2007 (ostensibly because of concerns over the "ghettoization" of Irish-language shorts), this didn't necessarily lead to a flood of feature productions. The scheme did, however, support the filming of work that highlighted the absurdity of the position of the official language in modern Irish society. Daniel O'Hara's *Yu Ming Is Ainm Dom* (2003) and *Fluent Dysphasia* (2004) played on the incapacity of most Irish people to speak their native language. In the first, a Chinese student, determined to see the world, prepares for a trip to Ireland by using language tapes to become fluent not in English but in Irish after his preparatory research identifies the latter as his destination's official language. On arrival, he is disappointed when it appears that no one can understand him, initially blaming his poor pronunciation. For their part, most of the Irish people he encounters are so disconnected from their own tongue that they assume he is speaking in Mandarin. In *Fluent Dysphasia*, Murph (**Stephen Rea**) awakens after a night of heavy drinking to find not only that he can speak and read Irish fluently but also that he entirely has lost his capacity to understand English, a situation that—again perversely given the notional status of the Irish language—makes it impossible for him to function in Irish society.

Yet such productions have not translated into a significant body of longer works. A key issue in this regard is the obvious concern over the limited market for minority-language production in general. Although director Robert Quinn was able to make his adaptation of Mairtin O'Cadhain's classic Irish text *Cre na Cille* (2007) with some private capital raised via **Section 481**, he also looked to the **Broadcasting Authority of Ireland**, the Irish-language broadcaster TG4, and direct state support via the Department of Community, Rural, and Gaeltacht Affairs. The advent of the Irish-language television channel TG4 in 1996 might have leveraged some funding for Irish-language fiction features, but, though the station unquestionably jump-started an unprecedented wave of television fiction through Irish (including the long-running soap *Ros na Rún* and serial dramas such as *Rasaí Na Gaillimhe*, *Scúp*, and *An Klondike*), this did not generally extend to support for cinema-bound work. Beyond the inclusion—for reasons of historical accuracy—of some Irish in works, such as ***Hunger*** (2008), ***Pilgrimage*** (2017), and *Black*

'47 (2018), long-form Irish-language films have been limited to a handful of Film Board–supported works. These have included some documentary work through Irish, including *Rocky Ros Muc* (2017), a documentary about Connemara boxer Sean Mannion, which had the distinction of becoming the first Irish-language feature-length film to be long-listed for an Academy Award. It has also funded a sequence of documentaries and one fiction feature from Pat Collins, including *Oilean Thoraí* (2002), a study of a year lived on Tory Island off the coast of Donegal; *Taibhsí i mBéal na Gaoithe* (2011), his profile of the Irish-language poet Nuala Ní Dhomhnaill; and **Song of Granite** (2017), his extraordinary docu-fiction study of the *sean-nós* singer Joe Heaney. Indeed, since 1993, there has arguably been just one fiction filmmaker consistently working through Irish: Derry's Tom Collins. Collins has cleverly parlayed TG4 support for short drama series into fiction feature production by dint of reediting multipart television drama into two-hour features. His 2014 Irish noir crime feature *An Bronntannas* first saw the light of day as a five-part thriller series for TG4 before being recut in a two-hour version for cinema. Yet Collins has also won Film Board support for straight feature work, including *Aithrí (Penance)* (2018) and, most notably, **Kings** (2007), an adaptation of Jimmy Murphy's 2001 play *The Kings of the Kilburn High Road* featuring **Colm Meaney**. The first primarily Irish-language drama to get a general release at the Irish box office in Ireland and also the first to be entered by the **Irish Film and Television Academy** in the Best Foreign Language Film category for the Oscars, *Kings* also had the distinction of securing a North American theatrical release, a hitherto unprecedented occurrence.

In 2017, in a somewhat belated acknowledgment of the relative omission of Irish-language works, TG4, Bord Scannán na hÉireann/Irish Film Board, and the Broadcasting Authority of Ireland launched the Cine4 Development scheme, a joint-funding initiative to support the development and production of feature films with budgets of up to €1.2 million in the Irish language.

IRISH SCREEN COMMISSION. When, in January 1996, the minister for finance introduced changes to **Section 481**, they were—to the consternation of both the state and the Irish film industry—reported in international film industry journals as signaling a shift away from encouraging international productions to shoot in Ireland. Although in the longer term Hollywood companies continued to arrive in Ireland, the changes drew attention to the absence of any state mechanism for countering the effect of such stories. The response in March 1997 was the creation of an Irish Screen Commission as a subcommittee of the **Irish Film Board**. The new body was charged with promoting Ireland internationally as a filmmaking location. In addition, the commission was to facilitate both incoming and indigenous productions by acting as a one-stop information source for filmmakers, offering advice on liaising with local authorities and on potential locations for filming.

The commission did not commence actual operations until Roger Greene was appointed chief executive in August 1998. Greene had previously worked as a public relations consultant to **Strongbow** film and television productions, **Ardmore Studios**, and the **Irish Film Institute** in the 1980s and had founded his own production company—Charlemont Films—in 1987. Immediately before taking on the commission position, he had worked in England, lecturing in media at the University of Lincolnshire and Humberside and directing television coverage of horse racing.

Although officially constituted as a subcommittee of and funded by the Irish Film Board, the Screen Commission had its own offices in Dublin (120 miles from the Film Board's headquarters) and from February 1999 maintained an office in Los Angeles. However, the commission proved relatively short lived as a stand-alone body. In November 2000, as part of a package of measures growing out of the *Kilkenny Report*, it was decided to fold the commission's activities back into the Irish Film Board, a decision that took effect in September 2001. Much of the responsibility for the commission's activities fell to the location services unit within the Film Board's new marketing department. In 2001, the role of location services manager was renamed screen commissioner to reflect the broad range of activities that come under the rubric of the position. These included maintaining a database of potential locations, offering information on financial incentives for shooting in Ireland, maintaining a database on local production personnel, and acting as a hub for the developing network of regional film commissions and Film Dublin, which works to facilitate film production in the capital city.

In May 2005, Government Minister **John O'Donoghue** announced that the Irish Film Board would appoint a deputy film commissioner, based in Los Angeles, to liaise with the major studios there and to effectively link these studios with the services and supports available in Ireland. In 2006, the board appointed Jonathan Loughran, a former Enterprise Ireland employee who had worked with Irish technology companies in the entertainment industry, to the U.S. role. The one-person U.S. operation acted as a stopping-off point for Irish producers and directors visiting the United States, facilitating meetings between them and U.S. studio development executives. However, the office also actively promoted Ireland as a location for U.S.-originated works with *The Tudors* paving the way for a succession of large-budget U.S. television productions using Ireland as a double for other locations: *Camelot* (2011), *Vikings* (2013–), *Penny Dreadful* (2014–2016), and *Into the Badlands* (2017–). (It also saw Dublin included amid a host of international locations for Steven Soderbergh's actioner *Haywire* [2011].)

However, the impact of the post-2008 Irish economic recession on the Film Board's finances curtailed the commission's overseas activities. When Loughran stepped down in 2012 to set up his own production company, the board essentially shut down the Los Angeles office, using routine U.S. visits by the board's new chief executive, **James Hickey**, to fill in the gap. Further reorganization followed the 2015 departure of Naoise Barry (who had filled the role of screen commissioner in Ireland since 2001) to head the new Irish operation of Pinewood Studios. Barry's replacement was styled "inward productions manager" with that office taking on responsibility for the myriad set of functions required to facilitate incoming productions. This includes providing information on financial incentives, international coproduction agreements, Irish coproducers and facilities companies, local (county-level) film commissions, the increasing variety of guilds representing Irish crew, liaising with the local police force, and maintaining the ever-expanding database of Irish filming locations.

ISOLATION **(2005).** An early entry in the Irish horror genre, writer/director Billy O'Brien's feature debut struck a serious tone, playing on the kind of body horror, "terror from within" tropes evoked by the early work of David Cronenberg or Ridley Scott's *Alien* sequence.

Dan Reilly (**John Lynch**) is a cash-strapped cattle farmer eking out a precarious existence on his isolated rural homestead. He lives alone, though two Travellers—Jamie and his pregnant girlfriend Mary (Sean Harris and **Ruth Negga**)—are squatting on his land, a presence that Dan barely tolerates. When Orla, Dan's veterinarian ex-wife (Australian actress Essie Davis), offers him an opportunity to make some money by allowing his cattle to be used as test subjects for a new growth hormone, he reluctantly accepts, allowing corporation scientist John (Romanian actor Marcel Iures) to recode his herd's DNA. It soon becomes clear that this Promethean interference with nature has produced unanticipated effects: when one of the cows goes into labor, the calf delivered by Dan with Jamie and Mary's assistance is mutated and, perversely, is itself already pregnant with decidedly nonbovine fetuses.

The idea that the humble dairy cow, a placid staple of the Irish rural landscape, could be framed as a potentially malevolent force might easily have been played for laughs. (Within 12 months of *Isolation*'s release, the New Zealand comedy *Black Sheep* did just that with ovine predators.) Yet, made in an era of bovine spongiform encephalopathy (mad cow disease) and genetically modified crops and coming just four years after an outbreak of foot-and-mouth disease threatened to devastate the Irish dairy herd, *Isolation* successfully tapped into wider concerns about the dangers of applying scientific innovation to agricultural practices widely, if erroneously, coded as "natural." Such fears are given voice through the alternately desperate and coolly sinister performances from Lynch and Iures, but it is Negga's character, Mary, who comes to signify the ultimate threat to bodily integrity. Already carrying a pregnancy that, the film suggests, may not be entirely welcome, the narrative further hints that Mary may have been indirectly infected by something infinitely more horrific via sexual congress with Jamie. Cinematographer **Robbie Ryan**'s washed-out palette imbues every scene with existential, at times postapocalyptic dread, and the doubtless budget-determined decision to use animatronic creature effects rather than computer-generated imagery complements the low-tech feel of the work as a whole. Although the payoff in the last act is somewhat underwhelming, director O'Brien certainly hinted at hitherto-undreamt-of generic possibilities for Irish cinema that a plethora of others would subsequently seek to explore.

J

JIMMY'S HALL (2014). Ken Loach's portrait of Jimmy Gralton—from a screenplay by regular collaborator Paul Laverty—sets out to reclaim a largely forgotten figure of Irish social history. Set in rural Ireland of the 1930s, the film acts as something of a successor to Loach's Palme d'Or–winning *The Wind That Shakes the Barley* and centers on Gralton's ambition to reopen a community hall and the ensuing ferocious opposition by hegemonic social forces.

Jimmy Gralton, from Effrinagh in County Leitrim, emigrated to New York in 1907 and became an active supporter of Irish republicanism and a follower of the ideas of James Connolly. He joined the Communist Party USA in 1919 and returned to Leitrim just before the truce in 1921. The local parish hall had been burned to the ground by the Black and Tans a year previously, and Gralton set about building a new community hall. Pearse-Connolly Hall opened on New Year's Eve 1921, weeks after the signing of the treaty. However, his political views gained him several enemies at a delicate time in the formation of the state, and he fled back to New York in 1922.

The film takes up the story when Jimmy (Barry Ward) returns home in 1932 to help his mother run the family farm after 10 years away. Returning in the midst of the Great Depression, his commitment to socialist beliefs has intensified, and, stirred by the poverty and fragmentation of his community, he sets about renovating and reopening the hall as a community space for dancing, reading poetry, and debate around the issues of the new Ireland. In so doing, he manages to annoy several powerful forces, including parish priest Father Sheridan (Jim Norton, who, despite a nuanced performance, cannot quite shake Bishop Brennan from Father Ted), influential Catholics, conservative Irish Republican Army leaders, and local fascist militia. With his commitment to Stalinism and a love of jazz, Grattan is a major threat to their collective vision of and control over the new Ireland (themes present but less developed in *The Wind That Shakes the Barley*). At one point, he declares, "We need to take control of our lives again. To live to celebrate, to dance as free human beings," but it can end only one way.

On Christmas Eve 1932, the hall that Grattan had worked to invigorate was burned to the ground by unidentified persons. But that wasn't the end of the matter. In August 1933, he was deported as an undesirable alien on the basis that he held a U.S. passport, and there was precedent for such an expulsion. He never returned to Ireland, and he died in New York in 1945.

Jimmy's Hall was adapted as a musical for the **Abbey Theatre** stage by the theater's codirector, Graham McLaren, in the summer of 2017.

JORDAN, NEIL (1950–). Born in County Sligo but raised by his national school father and painter mother in the middle-class Dublin suburb of Dollymount, Jordan studied English literature and history at University College Dublin. Marrying young and with a family to support, he toyed with a variety of careers, including teaching, but committed to writing from the mid-1970s. He made his initial impact as a writer of literary fiction, establishing the Irish Writers' Cooperative in 1974 and winning the Guardian Fiction Prize in 1976 for *Nights in Tunisia*, a collection of short stories. He has subsequently published eight novels, many of which have garnered critical praise and awards. He began his film career with a documentary on **John Boorman**'s *Excalibur* (1981). Having scripted **Joe Comerford**'s *Traveller* (1981), he was very unhappy with the finished film, which he claimed lacked narrative cohesion. His first feature film, *Angel* (1982) (funded in controversial circumstances by the new **Irish Film Board**), began his preoccupation with representations of violence and the Northern Irish Troubles as well as an enduring creative relationship with actor **Stephen Rea**. A well-produced revenge narrative, it opened doors for the fledgling director beyond the barely existent indigenous industry. In films such as *Angel*, *Michael Collins* (1996), and *The Crying Game* (2002), Jordan was in the forefront of Irish artists dealing with the political division of Ireland and the violence accruing from it in the pre–Good Friday Agreement period. Other films, such as *The Butcher Boy* and *Breakfast on Pluto*, have made equally important contributions to debates around Irish history and culture. Throughout his work, Jordan has displayed a repeated fascination with the gothic theme of the double, reworked in different ways and contexts to investigate and problematize the fixity of borders and constructions of identity, whether gendered, sexual, national, or otherwise.

Joining up with British producer Stephen Woolley and Palace Pictures, Jordan directed a number of successful small-scale films in the mid-1980s, beginning with the rites-of-passage horror narrative *The Company of Wolves* (1984), adapted and coscripted from a short story by feminist English writer Angela Carter. The film is a surreal take on the Little Red Riding Hood fairy tale with men morphing into wolves. Critics reviewed the film very favorably, which belied its relatively small budget to include several spectacular special effects sequences. Coproduced by George Harrison's Handmade

Films, Jordan's next feature was the British neo-noir *Mona Lisa* (1986), which greatly enhanced his standing and gained him his first critical attention in the United States. Bob Hoskins plays a recently-released-from-prison petty criminal rehired by his former boss (Michael Caine) to chauffeur chic prostitute Cathy Tyson between jobs in London. The film was nominated for multiple awards, with Hoskins winning the Golden Globe and BAFTA Awards for Best Actor in a Leading Role.

This success led to **High Spirits** (1988). Although made from Jordan's own script and equipped with what was then his biggest budget (more than $12 million), it was poorly received. The haunted house farce, set in an Irish castle, featured an A-list Hollywood cast, including Daryl Hannah, Steve Guttenberg, **Peter O'Toole**, and Beverly D'Angelo alongside Irish actors **Donal McCann**, **Liam Neeson**, **Ray McAnally**, and Tom Hickey. The cringing and stilted comedy lacked overall pace and narrative drive, and Jordan complained at his lack of postproduction input or control. The film was a resounding critical and commercial failure. *We're No Angels* (1989) followed, again with an A-list cast of Robert De Niro, Sean Penn, and Demi Moore. This story of two escaped convicts proved a conventional reworking of Michael Curtiz's 1955 movie of the same name and was again not positively reviewed.

Chastened by the experience of making Hollywood fare and the loss of creative control that accompanied it, Jordan returned to a more intimate and less expensive form of filmmaking with **The Miracle** (1991), set in a seaside town of Bray, County Wicklow. Two teenagers spend their time inventing imaginary stories about the local townfolk who pass them in the street, but when a glamorous actress (Beverly D'Angelo) comes to town, the boy, Jimmy, soon becomes obsessed with her. Only as the film progresses is the truth about her particular relationship to him revealed.

This romantic rites-of-passage narrative was followed by career highlight **The Crying Game** (1992), which, beyond its commercial and critical success, became a staple within academic analysis of gender and queer theory. The crossover appeal of the film—from U.K. art house to U.S. mainstream—had seemed unlikely. How could a film mixing Northern Irish politics and violence with debates around ethnicity and a controversial gender-bending twist be attractive to a mass audience? Certainly, the myriad funding bodies that passed on the original screenplay—then known as *The Soldier's Wife*—didn't believe it could. Having secured last-minute financing from **Channel 4**, producer Stephen Wolley sold the U.S. distribution rights to Miramax, which transformed the film's fortunes. Foregrounding the sexual tensions at the heart of the story, Miramax marketed the film as a noir thriller and borrowed a tactic from B-movie distribution to trade on the film's gender twist and teaser: "The movie that everyone's talking about, but no one is giving away its secrets." Between its release in November 1992 and the

Academy Awards the following March, more than 1,000 release prints were issued, and the film was nominated for six Academy Awards, including Best Film and Best Director. It won the award for Best Screenplay and grossed more than $60 million at the U.S. box office alone.

Riding high on this success, Jordan returned to Hollywood to make *Interview with a Vampire* (1994), an adaptation of Anne Rice's cult gothic novel starring Brad Pitt, Christian Slater, Tom Cruise, and Antonio Banderas. The film was well received critically and commercially and gave him the creative leverage to get funding for a long-held ambition to produce a biopic on the life of Michael Collins (*Michael Collins*). Working with a budget unprecedented in Irish cinema, he weighed into and changed forever debates around the 1916 rebellion, the Irish Civil War, and the great "what if" of modern Irish history through the life and death of Collins, rousingly played by **Liam Neeson**. The Irish film censor initially intended to give the film an Over-15 certificate but later decided that it should be released with a Parental Guidance certificate so that it could be seen by as many Irish citizens as possible. Unsurprisingly, debates raged over the historical accuracy of the story, with many objecting to Neeson's heroic portrayal of guerrilla violence and the film's suggestion that de Valera (slyly personified by Alan Rickman) was directly involved in Collins's assassination. The British press was generally hostile to the film's portrayal of the old Irish Republican Army and its sympathetic representation of Irish nationalism generally. Thanks to its ubiquity in public discourse, the film broke box office records in Ireland and went on the achieve a global box office of $28 million. It remains a touchstone of Irish historical filmmaking.

With *The Butcher Boy* (1997), Jordan was again able to leverage funding from the Geffen Film Company/Warner Bros. to attempt something quite different: an art house adaptation of Pat McCabe's much-feted novel. Irish critics regard the resulting film as Jordan's crowning achievement, citing its successful retention of the novel's unique authorial voice, its toying with the clash between tradition and modernity in early 1960s Ireland, and the extraordinary visual tropes used to depict that clash. However, the difficult terrain of violent childhood imaginings made it hard for the film to attract a wider audience, especially since the film's release coincided with widely reported real-life stories of violence meted out by dysfunctional children.

In Dreams (1998) was a supernatural psychological thriller that remained overly generic and formulaic but maintained Jordan's presence and profile within the U.S. industry. This preoccupation with generic material continued with *The Good Thief* (2002), starring Nick Nolte, his stylish remake of Jean-Pierre Melville's *Bob le Flambeur*. He completed his second adaptation of a McCabe novel, ***Breakfast on Pluto*** (2005), a slyly humorous treatment of an Irish transvestite in London during the 1970s featuring **Cillian Murphy** that has all but disappeared from critical consciousness but is worthy of reassessment. There then followed several bumpy years for Jordan, development hell intermittently broken by a variety of projects produced against the backdrop of a rapidly transforming industry. *Ondine* (2005) was a low-key retelling of the Irish selkie myth starring **Colin Farrell**, while *The Brave One* (2007) was a largely unseen New York–set revenge thriller starring Jodie Foster. *Byzantium* (2012) saw a return to supernatural/coming-of-age narratives, this time a mother–daughter vampire story starring **Saoirse Ronan** and Gemma Arterton, and was seen as something of a return to form. Again, however, it failed to perform at the box office. A long-gestating Borgias project finally saw the light as a three-season TV series for Showtime (2011–2013) for which Jordan wrote every script, a highly unusual level of commitment. In 2017, Jordan and fellow scribe John Banville were credited as cocreators of the Sky Atlantic series *Riviera*, but both quickly disowned the project, saying that the scripts they submitted to producer Paul McGuinness had been substantially rewritten and reimagined.

Although not life threatening, an accident in 2013 put him out of commission as a director for a number of years, leading him to concentrate on writing again. To his first five novels (*The Past* [1980], *The Dream of a Beast* [1983], *Sunrise with Sea Monster* [1994], Shade [2004], and *Mistaken* [2011]), he has more recently added *The Drowned Detective* (2016) and *Carnivalesque* (2017). It remains unclear whether the mature Jordan considers himself as primarily a writer or a director. Jordan has noted how his experience of watching another director take his script for *Traveller* and transform it in a manner he didn't approve of left him determined to direct his own material thereafter, suggesting that the world of direction was something he entered into in order to "protect" his words. He has spoken positively of his experience working on television drama, emphasizing how that medium canonizes one of those identities—the writer—over the director. There has even been talk of adapting his own novel *The Drowned Detective* for the screen. And yet, in 2018, he returned to the big screen (and to the United States) as a director with *Greta* (which he also coscripted), a kitsch (indeed, at times, outright camp) take on the psycho-thriller starring Isabelle Huppert as a psychotic mother figure to Chloe Grace Moretz's ingenue character. Far more playful than his more recent big-screen works, *Greta* points to a filmmaker contemplating the third act of his career with a certain relish.

JOYCE, JAMES (1882–1941). Joyce is the most recognized Irish modernist writer, one whose expansion of literary form has been seen as both contiguous with the emergence of cinematic apparatus and resistant to the conventions of cinematic adaptation. Joyce famously managed and operated one of Ireland's first cinemas—The Volta on Mary Street—from 1909, having convinced a group of Italian businessmen (Joyce and his family were then domiciled in Trieste) that there was a market for a permanent **exhibition** venue in

Ireland. And while he protested that his novel *Ulysses* could not be realized in film, he later told Eugene Jolas that the only ones who could possibly film it were the über modernists of European cinema Sergei Eisenstein or Walter Ruttmann. Eisenstein had visited Joyce in Paris in 1929 and discussed the possibility of filming *Ulysses.* In a lecture on Joyce at the State Institute of Cinematography in November 1934, he expressed his admiration for the book's ability to "hold the process of disintegration in stylistic unity."

While there were to be no cinematic adaptations or collaborations during his lifetime, there is nevertheless a small Joycean filmography that includes two adaptations of *Ulysses*—**Joseph Strick**'s formally ambitious 1967 British–American adaptation and *Bloom* (Sean Walsh, 2003), Strick's 1977 take on Joyce's more naturalist *A Portrait of the Artist as a Young Man* (1977), *Passages from James Joyce's Finnegans Wake* (1965) by American experimental filmmaker Mary Ellen Bute, and **John Huston**'s masterful adaptation of *The Dead* drawn from Joyce's short story "The Dead" from the *Dubliners* collection of short stories. (The last also forms the basis of *Voyage in Italy* [1953], directed by Roberto Rossellini.) Alongside countless documentaries on the writer, we can also count the biographical texts *Nora* (2000) (directed by **Pat Murphy** and based on Brenda Maddox's biography of his wife) and Robert Mullan's *James and Lucia* (2017) featuring **Aidan Gillen** as the writer.

JOYRIDERS (1988). Directed by Aisling Walsh and set in contemporary Dublin, the film tells the story of a woman, Mary (Patricia Kerrigan), forced to abandon her home with her two kids and facing the prospect of homelessness. She decides in the opening sequences to have them taken into care, abandoning them at a main train station and calling the police to pick them up. Alone and distressed, her troubles worsen when two sailors looking for a good time in an all-night café harass her. She is rescued by car thief ("joyrider") Perky Rice (Andrew Connolly), who brings her to a public house where, despite or because of her seething anger at her situation, he becomes attracted to her. However, his situation becomes more complicated when gangsters track him down and demand a payoff for an earlier misdemeanor. He decides to escape the city and asks her to accompany him. So begins a road movie romance—he steals a car that she chooses, and they head off to the coastal town of Killeel, where she had her honeymoon, a source of fond memories. However, all has changed when they reach their destination, and she finds a town peopled by bachelors and a seedy hotel proprietor (**John Kavanagh**). Nonetheless, the pair form a friendship with washed-out dance hostess Tammy (Billie Whitelaw).

The joyride shifts to the west and a farm on which Daniel, an aging widower (**David Kelly** in another outstanding performance), lives, more asleep than awake. In this rural refuge, the city dwellers find redemption in hard work on the farm, while Daniel realizes his need for a family. The film's closure follows the protagonists as they return to the city en famille. The film's attempt to merge the gangster movie conventions that characterize the opening section of the story with the romantic road movie of the latter section does not always fully succeed, but the core love story relationship sustains the overall narrative.

JUMP (2011). Kieron J. Walsh (*When Brendan Met Trudy*) takes Lisa McGee's stage play (McGee later wrote the hit **Channel 4** comedy *Derry Girls*) and weaves a heady mix of thriller, drama, and comedy set on a New Year's Eve night in Derry. Three separate story lines converge over the course of its narrative. The first sees Greta (Nichola Burley) dissuaded from leaping off the Derry Peace Bridge by Pearse (Martin McCann). In the second, Greta's mobster father Frank (Lalor Roddy) coerces retired criminal Johnny (Richard Dormer) into a mission to track down stolen money. The final comedic element follows Greta's pals Marie and Dara (Charlene McKenna and Valene Kane) as their night on the town goes south after a car accident. The gradual intertwining of the three strands demands some impressively intricate plotting on the part of Walsh and co-screenwriter Steve Brooks, but the tonal shifts between genres become increasingly difficult to suture over as the narrative progresses. Nonetheless, the film remains a notable instance of post—Good Friday Agreement Irish cinema: not only is Derry/Londonderry depicted in a hitherto unseen manner (as an exciting cosmopolitan urban center), but references to both religion and/or politics are conspicuous by their absence.

KALEM. The Kalem Film Company was formed in the United States in 1907 by George Kleine, Samuel Long, and Frank Marion and produced the first film made in Ireland, *The Lad from Old Ireland* (1910), which is also the first fiction film produced by an American company outside the United States. Ex-Biograph director/actor **Sidney Olcott** (whose mother hailed from Howth, County Dublin) and scenarist/actor Gene Gauntier were the driving forces behind the 1910 Irish expedition, which initiated the production of almost 30 films over four annual visits between 1910 and 1914 before being halted by World War I and a transformed American film industry that had by then moved to Hollywood. (Olcott and Gauntier stopped working for Kalem in 1912 but continued to come to Ireland, first as Gene Gauntier Feature Players and then Sid Films.) Along with immigrant romances, Olcott and Gauntier repeatedly returned to Irish historical themes concerning mostly Robert Emmet and the rebellion of 1798. While these likely grew out of Kalem's experiences and expertise in American Civil War films (they pioneered location shooting in Florida before coming to Ireland), they are significant not only in their pioneering use of the Irish landscape (in and around Killarney, County Kerry) but also as reminders of how potent this period of history was for Irish audiences at home and abroad in the pre-1916 period. While these films proved attractive at the U.S. and U.K. box offices, they attracted the condemnation of authorities on both sides: the local parish priest in Beaufort, County Kerry, denounced the visiting production company from the pulpit, and the British complained to Kalem directly about the romantic representation of Irish nationalism at a moment of fomenting political unrest. As the American film industry began to seek longer subjects, Olcott turned to the hugely popular melodramas of the playwright Dion Boucicault, producing one of the very first (if not, *the* first) three-reel film with *The Colleen Bawn*. This was followed by *Arrah-na-Pogue* and *The Shaughran*. The landscape in and around Beauford, County Kerry, remains virtually unchanged to this day, and the Beaufort Bar where Olcott, Gauntier, and fellow filmmakers stayed is still in the same family hands. Several of their Irish films have been restored and are viewable on YouTube.

KAVANAGH, IVAN. Strikingly independent in his production practices and story material, Kavanagh might be simultaneously one of the most prolific and least well known of contemporary Irish film directors. A self-taught cinephile who began making Super 8 films while in his teens, Kavanagh epitomizes the do-it-yourself ethos of independent digital filmmakers, working as writer/director/editor on an ever-expanding filmography of shorts and feature-length films across a wide range of genres.

While a traditional pattern for emerging talents has been to develop short films and screenplays with the assistance of **Irish Film Board** funding, Kavanagh determined to get his material on-screen as quickly and frequently as possible from the beginning of his career. This ethos was greatly facilitated by the digital revolution, which ensured that while his early films were often of uneven quality, a palpable sense of progress and sophistication can be felt across his filmography. There is a discernible creative energy and curiosity within his work that seems unlikely to dim or suffer discouragement anytime soon. On the other hand, his relative independence from traditional structures of production and distribution often makes it difficult to see his films outside the festival circuit. This seems to have recently changed with a number of video-on-demand services buying rights to his earlier films and his more recent productions receiving wider media attention.

His early shorts (shot on "low-fi" DV tape) include *Bandage-Man* (2003) and *Reflections* (2004), both of which established his practice of widespread film festival exhibition, a strategy that has resulted in multiple awards in many countries. Kavanagh directed his first feature film, *Francis*, in 2005, followed by *The Solution*, both also low-fi DV efforts that toured the festival circuit worldwide before "breaking through" with the grotesque apartment horror *Tin Can Man* (2007), which won a raft of awards, including Boundary Breaking Best Feature at the Sydney Underground Film Festival, Best Foreign Film and Best Foreign Director at the Melbourne Film Festival, and Best Cinematography at the Strasbourg International Film Festival in 2008. A Lynchian horror set over the course of a single night, the film produces an impression of extreme violence that is largely imagined by the audience and generated from an oppressive and cleverly designed sound track.

More conventional in their settings and family-centered narratives, *Our Wonderful Home* (2008) and particularly **The Fading Light** (2009) signaled a considerable advance in technique and themes and again disturb the viewer through emotionally uncompromising and harrowing scenes. According to Kavanagh, this derives from rigorous background work on each character undertaken by the actors before the plot is revealed to them step-by-step during filming.

More recent work suggests a shift toward (though perhaps still not firmly within) the mainstream. Kavanagh's earlier work was often characterized by nods to German expressionism with its stark contrasts of light and dark. If this suggested a predilection for the uncanny, Kavanagh's *The Canal* (2014) was much closer to a straight horror, though it retained his trademark concern for the psychological stability (or otherwise) of its central protagonist. Widely praised and securing berths in a multitude of festival programs, Kavanagh parlayed its success into support for his follow-up, *Never Grow Old* (2018), a western shot in Connemara (doubling for the Oregon Trail ca. 1849) featuring the talents of U.S. stars John Cusack and Emile Hirsch.

KAVANAGH, JOHN (1946–). Born into a Dublin family, Kavanagh grew up in the suburb of Milltown. As a teenager, he was determined to work in cinema albeit as a technician rather than an actor. After leaving school at age 16, he worked as a caddy at a local golf club, later returning to a technical school to complete his Leaving Certificate. He then trained as an actor at the Brendan Smyth Academy and in 1967 joined the **Abbey Theatre**, where he would remain for a decade before becoming a freelance actor.

He made his film debut with a small part in *Paddy* (1970), based on a play by Lee Dunne, but it was his performance more than a decade later as the Bowser Egan in **Pat O'Connor's** *Ballroom of Romance* that established him as a screen actor. Kavanagh was well cast in the adaptation of the William Trevor short story, his peevish visage embodying the cautious rural culture in which the heroine of the story finds herself trapped. He worked with O'Connor on several subsequent features, including *Cal*, *Fools of Fortune* (another William Trevor adaptation), *Circle of Friends*, and *Dancing at Lughnasa*. Kavanagh also became a familiar face to British audiences although mostly for roles in single dramas or miniseries set in Ireland or with an Irish theme. He is perhaps less well recognized outside the United Kingdom and Ireland, although American audiences would know him from roles in Neil Jordan's *Michael Collins* and *The Butcher Boy* and for his recurring roles as roles of the Ancient Seer and Pope Leo X in the History Channel's *Vikings* and the role of Arturo Toscanini in Stephen Frears's *Florence Foster Jenkins*.

Like many Irish actors of his generation, Kavanagh has combined screen appearances with a busy stage career, winning acclaim for playing Magwitch in *Great Expectations* and Astrov in Anton Chekhov's *Uncle Vanya* and becoming inextricably associated in the minds of Dublin theater audiences with the role of Joxer in Sean O'Casey's *Juno and the Paycock*—especially in a 1980s production opposite **Donal McCann**. He has also worked onstage in London's West End and on Broadway in New York.

KELLEGHER, TINA (1967–). Born in Dublin, Kellegher became a household name with her powerful role as working-class Sharon Curley in *The Snapper*, Stephen Frears's adaptation of the eponymous Roddy Doyle novel.

She had subsequent roles in *Widows' Peak* and *The Disappearance of Finbar* and several well-reviewed performances in Irish television miniseries, such as *The Hanging Gale* (1995), *Ballykissangel* (1996), *Sinners* (2002), and *Showbands* (2004, 2006).

KELLY, DAVID (1929–2012). Born in Dublin and educated at the famous Synge Street School, Kelly started acting at the age of eight with the Gaiety Theatre, going on to become the grand old man of Irish theater and film until his death in 2012 at age 83. After making a strong impression in British TV comedy—including 50 performances as the one-armed dishwasher Albert Riddle in *Robins' Nest* and as the hapless builder O'Reilly in *Fawlty Towers*—he attained immortality through his touching performance as the down-and-out Rashers Tierney in the landmark seven-part adaptation of James Plunkett's historical novel *Strumpet City* (1980), adapted by Hugh Leonard for **Radio Telefís Éireann**. Among his extensive film credits are an adaptation of Brendan Behan's *The Quare Fellow* (1962), Edna O'Brien's *The Girl with the Green Eyes* (1964), James Joyce's *Ulysses* (1967), *Joyriders*, *Into the West*, *Waking Ned* (aka *Waking Ned Devine*), *Ordinary Decent Criminal*, *Mystics*, and his penultimate screen role in *Charlie and the Chocolate Factory* (2005). Kelly received a Lifetime Achievement Award from the Irish Film Industry in 2005.

KENNEDY, MARIA DOYLE (1964–). After beginning her show business career as a singer for the Hothouse Flowers and subsequently as lead singer for the Black Velvet Band, Doyle came to wider public attention when she was cast as Maria in Alan Parker's *The Commitments*, making a strong impression in a large cast. She has continued to work in music as a recording artist and performer (releasing nine albums of material to date) interspersed with a wide variety of roles in feature films, such as *A Further Gesture*, *The General*, *I Could Read the Sky*, and *Tara Road* (2005) and more recently as maternal characters in **Neil Jordan**'s *Byzantium* (2012), **John Carney**'s *Sing Street* (2016), and *The Conjuring 2*. Her versatility and strong screen presence has led to sustained work in international TV projects with memorable recurring roles in *Dexter* (2010), *The Tudors* (Showtime, 2007), *Downton Abbey* (2011), *Orphan Black* (BBC, 2013–2017), and *Redwater* (BBC, 2017).

KEOGH, GARRETT. Garret refined his acting skills while doing the fringe and theater circuit in Dublin during the 1970s, performing in a wide range of genres and acting styles. This variety has served him well in work spanning film, television, and especially theater. On television, he has been a constant presence in recurring roles that include the hit BBC/**Radio Telefís Éireann**

series *Ballykissangel*, the very popular soap *Fair City*, the medical-themed series *The Clinic*, and the short-lived contemporary-set drama *Legend*. More recently, he had a recurring role in the Jack Taylor detective series for **TV3**. In film, he had important parts in ***The Bargain Shop*** (1992) and ***Veronica Guerin*** (2003), in which he played inner-city Dublin independent TD (Irish Member of Parliament) Tony Gregory. Other films include ***Excalibur*** (1981), on which many Irish actors got a start in film, alongside ***Widows' Peak*** (1994), ***Angela's Ashes*** (1999), ***Saltwater*** (2000), and ***Evelyn*** (2002).

KEOGHAN, BARRY (1992–). Having experienced an unstable upbringing after his mother died from a heroin overdose when he was just 12, Keoghan's nomination by the *Hollywood Reporter* as "the next big thing" in 2016 marked an remarkable and meteoric career trajectory for the talented young Dublin actor. After securing small roles in a number of independent projects, the ambitious Keoghan got his breakthrough in **Radio Telefís Éireann**'s crime series *Love/Hate* (2013) and made his big-screen debut in **Lance Daly**'s lost Lotto comedy *Life's a Breeze* (2013). **Rebecca Daly**'s *Mammal* (2015) revealed an altogether more enigmatic quality to his talent—capable of being simultaneously innocent and calculating—that was put to fine use in Yorgos Lanthimos's *The Killing of a Sacred Deer* (2017) and followed with Christopher Nolan's World War I big-budget epic *Dunkirk*, in which he starred alongside acting heavyweights Cillian Murphy and Mark Rylance. Keoghan's boyish looks, strong physical presence, and an ability to communicate such ambivalence has made him a hot draw, and a rapidly escalating range of credits includes *'71* opposite Jamie Dornan, *Trespass Against Us* (2016) alongside **Michael Fassbender** and **Brendan Gleeson**, and *Black '47* (2018).

KILKENNY REPORT. *See* STRATEGIC DEVELOPMENT OF THE IRISH FILM AND TELEVISION INDUSTRY (2000–2010).

KILLANIN, LORD (1914–1999). Born Michael Morris, he inherited the title Killanin when the previous lord—his uncle—died in 1927. Having been educated at Eton, the Sorbonne, and Cambridge, he went to work as a reporter first for the *Daily Express* and then for the *Daily Mail* in the 1930s. During this period, he came into contact with Irish director **Brian Desmond Hurst**, for whom he began writing scripts. While on assignment in Hollywood, he encountered director (and apparently his distant cousin) **John Ford** for the first time. Anticipating the coming conflict with Germany, he joined the British army in 1938. During the war, he was decorated on several occasions, took part in the D-Day landings in Normandy, and by 1945 had been promoted to brigade major. With the fighting over, he returned to his ancestral home in Spiddal, County Galway, which he rebuilt in 1945. In 1951, his relationship with Ford moved onto a professional plane when he played a substantial role in location scouting and production work on *The Quiet Man* (1951). In the same year, he established **Four Provinces** films, through which he produced a number of films. The first of these was *The Rising of the Moon* (1957), followed a year later by another Ford-directed picture, *Gideon's Day* (1958). This was followed by Hurst's adaptation of *The Playboy of the Western World* (1962). In 1965, he acted as associate producer on Ford's *Young Cassidy*, based loosely on Sean O'Casey's early life. His final film credit came in 1969, when he again acted as associate producer, this time on Clive Doner's *Alfred the Great*.

In addition to his film work, he engaged in an extraordinary range of other activities. Most notable among these was his work with sporting organizations. Having been president of the Olympic Council of Ireland since 1950, he became a member of the International Olympic Committee (IOC) in 1952. In 1972, he effectively became the most powerful man in international sports when he was appointed IOC president, a position he retained until 1980, when Juan Antonio Samaranch replaced him. Meanwhile, in Ireland, in addition to a number of commercial directorships, he sat on a range of state bodies, several of which had a cultural dimension, including the **Cultural Relations Committee** from 1949 to 1972, the Film Industry (Huston) Committee in 1968, and the Dublin Theatre Festival, which he chaired from 1958 to 1970. Indeed, he was an active campaigner for state support of the film industry, especially in the 1950s, when he made a series of suggestions in that regard to the Department of Industry and Commerce. He had four children, one of whom, Redmond Morris, himself became a producer working on most of **Neil Jordan**'s films since the 1990s. *See also REPORT OF THE FILM INDUSTRY COMMITTEE (HUSTON REPORT).*

KING OF THE TRAVELLERS **(2012).** In the immediate post–World War II period, French artist Dubuffet coined the term *art brut* (literally "raw art" but since 1972 translated into English as "outsider art") to describe art produced by those outside the art establishment by nonprofessionals. It is tempting to classify **Mark O'Connor**'s *King of the Travellers* as a form of "outsider cinema," combining as it does sequences of some poetry and an undeniably breakneck pace with an almost cavalier disregard for narrative development and plausible characterization.

As a child, John Paul Moorehouse (John Connors) witnesses the murder of his father Black Martin (David Murray), the "King of the Travellers." Although the assassins are unknown, John grows up believing that a rival Traveller family, the Powers, are responsible. In Martin's stead, his brother (and John's uncle) Francis takes over as head of the family. Under Francis, a temporary peace reigns: he negotiates with the local police and uses the legal system to defend the Moorehouse clan's claim to occupy their site in the face of threats from thuggish local landlord Mick Lafferty (Mick Foran). However, tensions arise when the Powers reappear, settling land on the far side of Lafferty's estate. After an arranged fight between John and one of the Powers fails to settle matters, friction between the families is exacerbated by John's adopted brother, the loose cannon Mickey Moorehouse (Peter Coonan), who leads a series of sorties against the Powers. The relationship is further complicated when John secretly rekindles an old flame with Winnie, daughter of the scion of the Power family.

An ultra-low-budget project shot over four weeks, the script was developed by director Mark O'Connor in conjunction with Michael Collins, an actor of Traveller ethnicity best known to Irish audiences from his role as Traveller Johnny Connors in now defunct **Radio Telefís Éireann** soap *Glenroe*. Using a cast of nonprofessional actors drawn largely from the Traveller community, the screenplay notionally sets out to offer a truthful albeit warts-and-all depiction of Traveller life. Only someone from within that community could properly assess how successful the film is in that regard, but there's little evidence that O'Connor and Collins sought to sugarcoat their representation: the community is presented as patriarchal, aggressive, and drink sodden. (To this, one might add quasi-criminal in their disregard for private property, although the film makes oblique reference to the Traveller community's philosophical refusal to accept the idea that land can ever be regarded as property.) These negative traits are somewhat alleviated by the emphasis on the strength of internal family bonds and the fact that—representatives of the Irish police force aside—settled characters are exclusively depicted as crude, venal, and prone to violence themselves.

On one level, *King of the Travellers* is almost fatally undermined by its crudeness. Performances from the more minor characters vary widely in quality. The plot is so absurdly dense with incident (especially in the final act) and so eager to sprint to its somewhat farcical denouement that individual characters and the relationships between them have no time to develop.

And yet this is a project of undeniable gusto and verve that sustains a degree of narrative integrity by overtly borrowing from story structures established elsewhere. There's a touch of *Romeo and Juliet*, a heavy sprinkling of *Hamlet* (right down to the ghostly appearance of John's father), and a more or less direct rehearsal of Brando's "I could have been a contender" scene from *On the Waterfront*. (Even the camera work directly quotes previous works: Martin Scorsese's *Raging Bull* is a clear influence on the camera movement in the fight scenes.) It even succeeds in at least occasionally conjuring a mythic elemental tone, situating its protagonists as descendants of much older tribes in a manner that work that is much better resourced, such as *Into the West* (1992), never quite achieves. As such, though an honorable failure, *King of the Travellers* points to reserves of untapped potential on the part of director O'Connor.

***KINGS* (2007).** Based on Jimmy Murphy's play *Kings of the Kilburn High Road*, **Tom Collins**'s film *Kings* tells the story of a group of Irish male émigrés who meet after 30 years living in London. The tragic end met by Jackie (Seán Ó Tárpaigh) brings them together again at his wake and forces them to briefly and inconclusively face their respective pasts.

Joe (**Colm Meaney**) has made a huge success of his career but is plagued by a drug habit and various insecurities. The others—played by Donal O'Kelly, Barry Barnes, Brendan Conroy, and Donncha Crowley—have barely survived three decades of booze and building sites, but despite their deep yearning for the place they left behind, they are too proud and too disillusioned to return home. Modest in its scale and narrative, *Kings* nonetheless offers an all-too-rare and poignant perspective on 1950s Irish (male) immigration to England, a subject that had long remained largely ignored by Irish culture and society back home.

A bilingual production, *Kings* was selected in 2007 as Ireland's Foreign Language contender for the 80th **Academy Awards** but missed out on a final nomination.

***KNOCK-NA-GOW* (1918).** The first feature film "Produced by the Film Company of Ireland in Ireland by Irish Men and Women" (as it puts it in its opening title), *Knock-na-gow* represents both an auspicious beginning and an unfulfilled ambition. Adapted from Charles Kickham's eponymous novel, it marked a dramatic scaling up of ambitions for the recently established **Film Company of Ireland**, which had made just nine short films in the previous 18 months. Inspired by the wider political and cultural revolution surrounding 1916 as well as the Dublin release of D. W. Griffith's landmark epic *Birth of a Nation* (1915), producer James Mark Sullivan and director Fred O'Donovan (along with others in a cast and crew of notable future talents) sought to create a story capable of expressing distinct yet enduring Irish values through the modern medium of cinema.

Knock-na-gow was an apt and obvious choice of material on which to base such an endeavor. Its author was Charles Kickham, a lifelong Fenian and contemporary of O'Donovan Rossa (with whom he had shared prison time), and his book—a portrait of Irish peasant life set in 18th-century rural Tipperary—was the most widely read novel in Ireland since its publication in 1879. By the time it was brought to the screen, *Knock-na-gow* still had enormous recognition, having been translated into Gaelic by Micheál Breathnach in 1906 and touring Ireland as a stage adaptation by R. G. Walshe as recently as 1915.

In the summer of 1917, a crew of actors and technicians led by Sullivan and O'Donovan (working with a British newsreel cameraman) traveled to Clonmel and then to Mullinahone in County Tipperary, the village where Kickham had lived, worked, and set his story. Contemporary accounts of the filming describe the emptying of the village for an afternoon, the burning down of a cottage, and the presence of thousands of curious onlookers. Following the earlier example of the Kalem film company in its adaptation of *The Colleen Bawn* and other stories, the resulting film was distinguished by its use of "authentic" locations and its deep sympathy for the people and landscape in which it was conceived. The task of adapting the massive novel seems to have fallen to O'Sullivan's wife Nell. (Court documents show that the initial company was closed in June 1917 and reestablished with Nell and her husband as directors.) It was not entirely faithful to its source (it couldn't be); Kickham's book was Dickensian in scope and structure, and the film sought to find a story among its copious scenes and episodes.

Knock-na-gow premiered to great excitement and acclaim in Dublin on 22 April 1918—the 60th anniversary of the 1848 Young Ireland Rebellion (during which it is set) and the second anniversary of the 1916 Easter Rising—and jump-started careers in film and TV for several of its participants: actors J. M. Kerrigan (*The Informer* [1936] and *Gone with the Wind* [1939]) and Arthur Shields (*The Quiet Man* [1951] and *She Wore a Yellow Ribbon* [1949]), who had long careers in Hollywood; Micheál Mac Liammóir, cofounder of the Gate Theatre; and its director, Fred O'Donovan, who would go on to pioneer the filming of live drama on British TV in the 1950s.

The film had some success inside and outside Ireland, and while some British reviewers expressed suspicions about its politics, Irish American audiences thrilled to see their homeland, even if the narrative was not quite up to the exciting and efficient standards of Hollywood. It enjoyed a long domestic run, and for almost two years, cast members traveled around Ireland with the film, introducing it to audiences and singing songs by Kickham (notably his famous poem "Slieve na mBan"). Foremost among these was Breifne O'Rorke, accompanied by his young stepson **Cyril Cusack**, whose screen career would stretch from *Knock-na-gow* to *My Left Foot* (1987). The latter would finally achieve what J. M. Sullivan had hoped to but didn't manage 70 years earlier: produce an international hit using Irish men and women to tell an Irish story and create the impetus for an indigenous film industry.

***KOREA* (1985).** The capacity of the past to send shock waves through time lies at the core of *Korea*, director Cathal Black's densely layered and richly visual adaptation of a John McGahern short story. Set in a small Cavan village in 1952, the film opens with the funeral of Luke Moran, who, having immigrated to the United States, is killed in the Korean War. The Moran family receives scant sympathy from John Doyle, a widower who fishes the freshwater lake with his son Eamonn. Doyle still nurses a feud with Luke's father Ben, born of choosing opposite sides in the Civil War three decades earlier. Luke's death coincides with change in the community: the rural electrification scheme is reaching the village, promising to "sweep away inferiority complexes"; tourism is developing as a local industry; and two of the "first generation born in freedom," Eamonn and Ben's daughter Una, are entering their first romance.

The historical setting of *Korea* is critical, for if the years from 1959 to 1963 are widely recognized as the era in which modern Ireland was born, it was the economic and demographic crises of the preceding decade that forced change. In *Korea*, John Doyle becomes the vehicle through which the dawning of this transformation is shown. The opening shot follows him rowing on the lake while Eamonn casts out a fishing line. As the camera angle disguises any progress across the water, Doyle is represented as a man literally going nowhere. Thus, director Black eloquently establishes his role: John Doyle remains the defeated anti-treatyite for whom change is not synonymous with progress. He is already suspicious of the advent of electricity, which will bring both literal and figurative light to the village. The emergent tourist industry invasion threatens the withdrawal of Doyle's fishing license so that fish stocks might be built up for tourists. Faced with an uncertain future, he clings to the dark ages of his own past despite the pain engendered by his memories—atrocities witnessed in the Civil War and the death of his wife.

By focusing on the experience of one individual, Black makes comprehensible the persistence of Civil War politics in Ireland, which can be obscured by explanations that refer to the nation as a whole. *Korea* offers a complex study of the nature of memory and, both in content and in form (re-creating the Ireland of the 1950s), examines the re-creation of the past. In *Korea*, Civil War iconography pervades the Doyles' home. A photo of John Doyle as a young man in his Civil War uniform brings him back, recalling images of reprisal executions. But the process works two ways: the photo has the power to stare back, his past self challenging his present. Doyle, however, is unable to answer that challenge: his loyalty to the cause has won him little. Indeed, if anything, the cause has betrayed Doyle: it is, after all, a political party led by Eamon de Valera (three decades earlier, Doyle's comrade in arms in the Civil War) that threatens to withdraw his fishing license. The Ireland that emerged from the ashes of war bears scant resemblance to his romantic and patriotic visions of it. Betrayed by his own nation, he looks to send Eamonn to the United States, away from "this fool of a country." Yet Eamonn, educated, in love with Una, and part of the generation that will lead Ireland into the 1960s, is unwilling to leave. The resulting confrontation between the old and the new forces Doyle to face his own past and so come to terms with the present.

L

LALLY, MICK (1945–2010). After graduating from University College Galway, Lally became a teacher before establishing the Druid Theatre Company in Galway with Garry Hynes and Marie Mullen in 1975. Druid would subsequently become a major force in Irish theater responsible for many notable touring and omnibus productions (e.g., DruidSynge and DruidMurphy) as well as launching the career of **Martin McDonagh**, among other achievements. With and beyond Druid, Lally solidified his reputation as a formidable presence on the Irish stage while becoming a household name for his role as bumbling farmer Miley in the long-running **Radio Telefís Éireann** television soap *Glenroe*. Alongside career-defining roles in the plays of John B. Keane and J. M. Synge, he also had numerous character roles in films as diverse as *The Fantasist* (1986), *The Outcasts* (1982), *Fools of Fortune* (1990), *A Man of No Importance* (1994), *The Secret of Roan Inish* (1993), *Circle of Friends* (1995), and *Alexander* (2004). Among his final performances was the voice of the sagacious Brother Aidan in the **Academy Award**–nominated animation *The Secret Of Kells* and a courageous turn as a homeless man in Carmel Winter's *Snap*. The home location of Druid Theatre in Galway is named the Mick Lally Theatre in his memory.

LAMB **(1986).** Adapted from Bernard MacLaverty's eponymous novel, *Lamb* is a moving account of the relationship between kindred spirits of starkly contrasting character. Owen Kane (**Hugh O'Conor**), an eight-year-old offender with epilepsy, is brought by his mother to Saint Killian's, a school for difficult children, run by the Christian Brothers. There, he is taken under the wing of Michael Lamb (**Liam Neeson**), a brother facing a crisis of faith. As he learns about Owen's life—the absence of any father figure and the consistent abuse at the hands of his drunken mother—Michael despairs at the world at large and questions his own faith. Owen is trapped in a miserable life not of his own choosing, while Michael is unable to legitimately escape the control of his religious order. In short, neither has much to look forward to. The impact of their age difference is somehow mitigated since life has forced Owen to become streetwise, growing up faster than most, while Michael, by contrast, has never really been without a father figure—be it actual or spiritual.

Michael's father dies, leaving him money and a way out. His order, however, seeks to claim his father's estate by invoking Michael's vow of poverty. Michael flees to England with Owen only to find that the order has reported his act as a kidnapping. With £2,000 from his father's estate, Michael and Owen are able to live comfortably for a while. Thus, for both characters, the escape from the boy's home represents an escape from fates that would otherwise be set in concrete. However, this all comes to a sharp end when Owen suffers an epileptic fit at a football match. Soon after, the pair are conned out of their money, forcing them to return to Ireland. Pursued by the police, Michael ultimately takes both their fates into his own hands with terrible consequences.

The film is almost entirely carried by its two leads, Neeson and O'Conor, both of whom used the film as a launching pad for their subsequent careers. The performances are matched by careful direction from Colin Gregg, who opts for an unobtrusive style that allows the story to unfold at its own pace. Indeed, it is a tribute to the skill with which actors and filmmakers work to convey the characters' inner emotional lives that the terrible final act in the film is rendered almost merciful—"almost" because the film also allows the possibility that Michael's act is not the correct choice but that the pressure of the situation has caused an essentially good man to carry out an evil act.

THE LAST BUS HOME **(1997).** Readable as a critique of Celtic Tiger Ireland and its obsessive focus on fiscal success, the film follows the rise and fall of a punk band from 1979—in a kind of darker reflection of the narrative of *The Commitments*. As in *The Bargain Shop*, director **Johnny Gogan**'s concerns are with the compromises that come with success and the realizations that come with failure. It is tempting to read the apparent suicide of Petie (John Cronin), the gay punk band member, as motivated by his parents' narrow-minded, "old Ireland" fear of queer sexuality. Extensive use is made of the deserted streets of Dublin when most of the population attended the papal mass of the late Pope John II's only visit to Ireland in Phoenix Park, which contrasts with later scenes in dark venues as frustrated teenagers connect with the music.

THE LAST DAYS ON MARS **(2013).** Readers will be hard pressed to find a less overtly Irish text in this volume than director Ruairi Robinson's feature debut. Six Anglo–North American astronauts/scientists, led by Commander Dalby (Elias Koteas), have spent six months on a mission to find life on Mars—without success. However, within sight of their departure window, they encounter a Martian bacterium that "infects" them, transforming them into indestructible zombielike monsters. The dwindling survivors, led by Liev Schreiber and Romola Garai, struggle to escape the Mars base and return to the spaceship that will bring them home.

There are, in effect, no textual clues as to the national origin of the film. Nonetheless, *The Last Days on Mars* is revealing of Irish cinema's place in the international audiovisual markets of the early 21st century. Director Ruairi Robinson became involved in the project at draft script stage, brought in as director for hire by U.K.-based Qwerty Films on the strength of his experience directing the VFX-heavy short *Silent City* (2006). Reportedly made for UK£7 million (a limited budget in the best of times), Robinson had only eight weeks to shoot *The Last Days on Mars*: two on location (Jordan doubling for Mars) and the rest at Shepperton Studios in London. As a consequence, much of the film was created in postproduction with Robinson taking on the task of creating 60 VFX shots himself.

Indeed, it was the flawless visual effects shots, peppered throughout the 95-minute running time, that constitute the most Irish element of the production (Robinson himself aside). The **Irish Film Board**'s contribution to the original core funding for the film was predicated largely on the decision to use Dublin postproduction company Screen Scene for the special effects shots. There is something profoundly ironic in the fact that board's involvement was conditional on the involvement of a company that worked to distance the film from an Irish (or even earthbound) setting.

Ultimately, then, if his earlier *Silent City* was a calling card to suggest that Robinson could make features, *The Last Days on Mars* feels like a calling card demonstrating a capacity to make even bigger films.

***THE LAST OF THE HIGH KINGS* (1997).** Based on a novel by Ferdia MacAnna and adapted for the screen by writer/director David Keating on a budget of IR£2.25 million, *Last of the High Kings* is a lighthearted coming-of-age picture that follows Frankie (Jared Leto) as he awaits his Leaving Certificate results through the summer of 1977. With his actor father (**Gabriel Byrne**) working overseas and his mother (Catherine O'Hara) involved in ultranationalist activities, Frankie is left to pursue local girls (loss of virginity is identified as synonymous with coming of age) and plan an end-of-summer beach party. The film was reasonably well received at the Irish box office, but despite careful cameo casting (Christina Ricci, **Colm Meaney**, and **Stephen Rea**), it failed to travel successfully.

***THE LAST SEPTEMBER* (1999).** Based on the novel by Elisabeth Bowen, the film was directed by Deborah Warner and stars Maggie Smith, **Michael Gambon**, **Fiona Shaw**, and Keeley Hawes and is set in Danielstown, somewhere in the south of Ireland. This is the country town of the Anglo-Irish Sir Richard Naylor (Gambon) and his wife, Lady Myra (Smith). Set against the backdrop of the Irish War of Independence in the early 1920s, the protagonists know that—the facade of dinners, tennis parties, and dances aside—their way of life is coming to an end. Lady Myra's niece Lois (Keeley Hawes), who is being courted by a captain in the British army, is lured by the menacingly playful and violent young man who has taken up residence at the bottom of the garden. What unfolds is a portrait of the demise of a way of life and a young woman's coming of age in a brutal time.

This story outline hints at the period-costume nature of the film. National conflicts serve as a conventional backdrop for a story that includes a police officer who is indecently stripped before being shot in the head and a head of the household who attempts to protect his beloved. Ultimately, the characters escape back to "civilization" and Britain before the natives' "animalistic" passion breaks loose.

LEMASS, SEAN (1899–1971). Lemass, who became taoiseach (prime minister) in 1959, was minister for industry and commerce for 21 of the 27 years from 1932 to 1959. For much of that period, he pursued the goal of developing if not an Irish film industry, then at least a film industry in Ireland.

The Department of Industry and Commerce was receiving private proposals to establish a film studio at least as early as 1928, but these had generally been rebuffed on the grounds that the Irish market was too small to support such an industry. However, in 1938, apparently prompted by a concern that other (specifically, Catholic Church–driven) agendas might seek to drive film policy, Lemass began to push for some official consideration of film in Ireland. In the face of stiff opposition from officials in the Department of Finance, he succeeded in establishing the **Inter-Departmental Committee on the Film Industry** with a remit to examine all the difficulties standing in the way of a national film production enterprise. Lemass was unhappy with the pessimistic appraisal the committee offered of the possibility of jump-starting a domestic film industry when it finally reported in 1942, and he effectively mothballed their report.

Once the war was over, Lemass returned to the subject of film policy. Now, however, rather than focusing on the creation of an indigenous industry, his attention shifted to the possibility of attracting overseas producers to use Ireland as a location for their films. Key to this strategy was the building of a national film studio. Over a period of 17 months in 1946 and 1947, the Department of Industry and Commerce prepared a series of memos to the cabinet seeking more than £250,000 (later revised to £500,000) to build two soundstages, an administrative building, and a laboratory. Another £70,000 was sought for the annual administrative costs of the studio. Draft legislation was even prepared to put this into effect. Lemass's film policy at this point worked around the gloomy conclusions of the Inter-Departmental Committee's 1942 report. If American and British companies dominated the English-language film **distribution** market, then the most pragmatic means of generating filmmaking activity in Ireland was to attract film production companies from those countries. Such companies would require studios that could accommodate larger-scale productions.

Lemass's confidence in the spin-off benefits of such a studio was not widely shared by the rest of the cabinet. Even his own department expressed doubts about the viability of the scheme. But the most substantive critique of the proposals came from the Department of Finance, where Minister Frank Aitken, in addition to expressing doubt over the economic viability of the putative studios, argued that it would be most undesirable, nationally and culturally, that the shape and character of an Irish film industry should be determined on the basis of the needs of wealthy foreign industrialists. Thus, although Lemass twice submitted his national film studio proposals to the cabinet, they were dismissed on both occasions.

In the mid-1950s, Lemass returned to the subject of film in a more sporadic fashion (at least in part because he was out of power between 1948 and 1951 and 1954 and 1957). In 1951, he briefly raised the possibility of creating a film production fund along the lines of the Eady levy in the United Kingdom (a levy on cinema tickets that was used to fund domestic film production), and in 1954, he directed that a memo be drawn up outlining a proposal to establish a national film unit. This was to be a much more modest enterprise than his earlier studio plans and returned to the idea of setting up a native film industry, starting with the production of **documentaries** and shorts on a limited scale. The proposal was set aside, however, when Fianna Fáil lost the May 1954 election.

However, by the time Lemass returned to the Department of Industry and Commerce in 1957, there was a newer prospect in the offing. **Louis Elliman** and **Emmet Dalton** had established Dublin Film and Television Productions Ltd to film **Abbey Theatre** plays for the American television market. In August 1957, apparently convinced that there was a substantial market for this material, Elliman and Dalton acquired a site for a film studio at Ardmore Place, Herbert Road, in Bray, County Dublin.

The studios were completed by March 1958. A month later, Lemass officially presided over the opening of the studios, where he praised the enterprise as generating exports and employment and training Irish citizens in the complex processes of the industry. He acknowledged that when Elliman and Dalton had initially approached him, he had promised the greatest possible aid that the Department of Industry and Commerce could give.

The nature of this aid was largely financial. Ardmore's construction was initially budgeted at £161,000, of which £45,000 was raised from an Industrial Development Authority (IDA) grant. Furthermore, the Industrial Credit

Corporation (ICC) advanced another £217,750 to Ardmore by way of a debenture loan. ICC assistance to the studios did not cease there. In 1960, in an effort to encourage production at Ardmore, the ICC established the **Irish Film Finance Corporation** (IFFC) to consider applications from film producers in Ireland for financial assistance by way of loans. Between 1960 and 1962, the IFFC would invest IR£385,000 of public funds in 15 films.

Although Lemass had no overt hand in these funding decisions, it would seem unlikely that he was entirely out of the loop given that both the ICC and the IDA were very much creatures of the Department of Industry and Commerce. Thus, in many respects, it is arguable that **Ardmore Studios** was an explicit realization of Lemass's national studio plans from the 1940s. Indeed, the extent of state funding to Ardmore meant that the studios were de facto state owned (via the ICC), even if Elliman and Dalton were nominal owners. When, in 1964, the studios ran into financial difficulties, it was the ICC that appointed a receiver. Yet if Ardmore represented a secret victory for Lemass, it was not an entirely straightforward one. It would be 20 years after his death before the studios were consistently used for indigenous production and longer still before overseas productions shot in Ireland began to use local talent in creative production roles.

LGBT CINEMA. Homosexuality remained a taboo subject in Ireland until relatively recently due largely to religious and cultural factors. However, since the 1990s in particular, there has been a remarkable shift in attitudes. In 1993, the Criminal Law (Sexual Offences) Act granted parity before the law to homosexual citizens and introduced a common age of consent of 17 years for both heterosexual and homosexual relations. While homophobia remains a problem, the overwhelming public support (expressed through a 2015 referendum) to extend the right to marry to same-sex couples illustrates how homophobic attitudes have become less acceptable than previously.

Although cinematic treatment of all forms of sexuality has been subject to severe **censorship** in Ireland until relatively recently, there has of late been some implicit and even explicit exploration of homosexuality on film in Ireland. Film shorts that foreground homophobia and its effects on teenagers growing up in Ireland include Orla Walsh's *Bent Out of Shape* (1995) and Eve Morrison's *Summertime* (1995). Feature films that deal with the topic include **Cathal Black**'s highly regarded *Pigs* (1984), which explores, among other characters, the life of a gay man living in an abandoned building in Dublin, and **Johnny Gogan**'s *The Last Bus Home* (1997), which, though set mainly in the 1970s, features a coda set during a period when homosexuality had just been decriminalized in Ireland. Capturing the mood of the 1960s, *A Man of No Importance* (1996) most notably explores the dilemma for a gay man, played by Albert Finney, who tries to come out by staging a play by Oscar Wilde—almost a synonym for homosexuality—and gets beaten up as a result.

The Crying Game (1993), of course, represents a major breakthrough with its famous gender twist in the narrative. It became internationally successful as a case study of homosexuality and spawned a huge international industry in gender and queer studies. Similarly, **Neil Jordan**'s *Breakfast on Pluto* (2006), adapted from the novel by Pat McCabe, also foregrounds gay characters and themes.

The modest domestic success of *Cowboys and Angels* (2003) suggests that the mainstreaming of homosexuality in Irish society has been at least partially achieved given that although one of the two protagonists is openly—in fact, flamboyantly—gay, the film was received more as a youth picture than as a story about a homosexual character. Similarly, although **Alan Gilsenan**'s *Timbuktu* (2004) is much darker in tone, the homosexuality of its leading male, although important to understanding the character's background and motivations, does not constitute the subject of the film.

Recent chick-flick and art house lesbian films include *Goldfish Memory* (2003) and *About Adam* (2000), where open sexual experimentation and sometimes even playful subversion of "normative" heterosexuality are used with comic effect—a long way, one might conclude, from the heavily censored society that existed in Ireland for many years. More radical and less mainstream avant-garde narratives include *2by4* (1998), which deals most explicitly with homosexuality as a lived experience rather than as a narrative device.

The Crying Game aside, narratives featuring trans characters were relatively scarce in 20th-century Irish film. Since 2000, however, one can point to a minigenre of such works, including **Neil Jordan**'s adaptation of Pat McCabe's novel *Breakfast on Pluto* (2005); *Albert Nobbs* (2011), starring Glenn Close as a cross-dressing lesbian in Victorian Dublin; Conor Horgan's popular documentary *The Queen of Ireland* (2015) about Ireland's best-known drag queen, Panti; and *Viva* (2016), **Paddy Breathnach**'s remarkable Spanish-language narrative set in the milieu of the Havana drag scene.

Although LGBT identities are thus more visible than in the past in Irish cinema, it remains the case that such identities are rarely mainstreamed (i.e., the fact of a character's homosexuality is rarely considered incidental to his or her narrative role). Thus, while in the 1980s the depiction of the kiss between an Irish Republican Army man and an Irish soldier featured in **Joe Comerford**'s *Reefer and the Model* (1988) clearly pointed to the progressive and emancipatory potential of Irish cinema, it is arguable that more recent cinematic output has, if anything, failed to keep pace with the real-world shifts in Irish cultural attitudes toward LGBT identities.

LIGHT HOUSE CINEMA. Neil Connolly established the Light House in 1988 to fill the programming gap left by the collapse of the **Irish Film Theatre** (IFT) in 1984. Connolly, a former accountant at **Ardmore Studios**, had acted as IFT programmer in its last year of operation, when the **Arts Council** drafted the **Irish Film Institute** (IFI) in an unsuccessful attempt to save the IFT. The IFI saw in the Light House the possibility of an interim solution to the lack of a national film theater that could exhibit nonmainstream material. Accordingly, it took a 50 percent interest in the cinema, which was situated in the shell formerly occupied by a mainstream cinema (the Curzon) on Dublin's Abbey Street. It had two auditoriums, the main cinema having a capacity of 280 seats and the other 80 seats.

The films that were screened on the opening night of the cinema—Eric Rohmer's *4 Adventures of Reinette and Mirabelle* (1987) and Pedro Almodovar's *Law of Desire* (1987)—set the tone for subsequent programming policy: a mixture of "mainstream" and more adventurous art house titles. In the autumn of 1991, with the construction of the **Irish Film Centre** (IFC) finally under way, the IFI amicably severed its links with the Light House, leaving it as an independent commercial cinema. Thus, in a single move, the cinema lost a sponsor and acquired a competitor. Remarkably, however, despite the added presence of the IFC in the Dublin market, the finances of the Light House remained in the black.

Indeed, in part, the significance of the Light House lay in the simple fact that it remained in existence, exhibiting exclusively art house material in a period when most independent cinemas faced dwindling audiences and when even the **Ward Anderson** group was facing the possibility of retrenchment in the face of competition from globe-spanning competitors such as United Cinemas International. More important, however, the Light House introduced Dublin audiences to work that was simply inaccessible elsewhere—one-off screenings at **festivals** aside—and thus made a unique contribution to the artistic life of the city.

However, in September 1996, the screens at the Light House on Abbey Street went dark for the last time. The closure reflected not a downturn in business but rather the opposite: the building was leased from Arnotts, a major Dublin department store that, amid the mid-1990s economic boom, decided to expand its premises, taking in the site of the Light House and another former cinema, the Adelphi.

At the time of the cinema's closure, it was assumed that the two directors—Connolly and Maretta Dillon—would reestablish in a new shopping development on Dublin's O'Connell Street, but when that development failed to come to fruition, the cinema plans were also abandoned. Over the next decade, Connolly and Dillon attempted to find a suitable alternative site in a runaway real estate market without success. However, in May 2005, the cultural cinema consortium, a joint initiative of the Arts Council and the

Irish Film Board and charged with the task of expanding the range of cinema exhibited in Ireland, announced that it was offering €750,000 in capital funding to two groups, one of which—Lighthouse@smithfield—was headed by the directors of the Light House. (The other was the long-delayed and controversial development of Galway's Picture Palace.) With total state grants of €1.75 million, a new and very attractive four-screen, 600-seat Light House opened in Smithfield, Dublin, in May 2008. This appeared to be the happy ending that Connolly and Dillon, as well as devoted audiences of the original Light House, had long hoped for, yet the history of the Light House was to take another twist in 2011 when it was forced to close once again after its rent was doubled from €100,000 to €200,000 and was briefly put under the control of the National Asset Management Agency. Unwilling to subsidize a private venture any further but keen to keep the cinema functioning as a venue for alternative—or at least nonmultiplex—film, the Department of Arts and Culture brokered a deal with **Element Pictures** to take over the running of the cinema in early 2012. Although not expected to pay back any of the substantial state funding, Element was required to keep with the spirit of the original "cultural cinema" vision for the cinema. Key elements of their business strategy therefore included attracting the Dublin International Film Festival to use the facility as its central venue but also offering a wider range of programming than traditional art house fare, including cult and revival seasons, premieres, guest events, and live cinema. Driven by more obviously commercial imperatives than the IFI (which continues to receive substantial Arts Council funding) and exploiting its vertically integrated relationship to Ireland's most successful production and distribution companies, this cosmopolitan approach has substantially revived the fortunes of the Light House, which attracts a wide range of audiences from its hinterland of the center and north of the city as well as farther afield.

LINEHAN, ROSALEEN (1937–). Born to a middle-class Dublin family of 13 (her father Daniel McMenamin was a barrister and later TD [Irish member of Parliament] for Donegal—under various party affiliations—from 1927 to 1948), the highly esteemed and much-loved Linehan has had a long, varied career on onstage and on-screen. She got her taste for music at Loreto College on Stephen's Green before going on to study economics and politics at University College Dublin (UCD), an uncommon achievement for Irish women in the 1950s. At UCD, she joined Dramsoc and began a career in entertainment almost immediately. She quickly became a household name through her collaborations with Des Keogh, and the duo collaborated on a wide variety of comedic musical material over the following 40 years. She also made a number of appearances in films in the late 1960s, including **Joseph Strick**'s adaptations of **James Joyce**'s *Ulysses* (1967) and *A Portrait of the Artist as a Young Man* (1977).

In the mid-1980s, Linehan successfully shifted toward more dramatic roles in Irish theatrical productions of, among others, Anton Chekov's *The Seagull*, Federico Garcia Lorca's *House of Bernardo Alba*, Peter Sheridan's *Mother of All the Behans*, Brian Friel's *Dancing at Luchnasa*, the Young Vic production of **Martin McDonagh**'s *The Beauty Queen of Leenane*, and Enda Walsh's *The New Electric Ballroom*. Key among these was her performance as Winnie in Beckett's *Happy Days*, for which she received critical plaudits and which she would reprise on-screen in Patricia Rozema's contribution to the **Beckett on Film** project. Among her other screen credits are character roles as mother figures in films such as *Snakes and Ladders* (1996), *About Adam* (2000), and *The Butcher Boy* (1997).

LITTLE BIRD. One of the first significant production companies to be established in Ireland, over its 27-year existence, Little Bird quietly became one of the most prolific screen production entities in Ireland. Indeed, having established offices in Dublin and London and built partnerships with British, German, and South African companies, it could at one point legitimately claim to be in the second tier of leading European film and television production companies.

The company was established in 1982 by James Mitchell, an entertainment lawyer based in the United Kingdom, and his business partner, Jonathan Cavendish, to produce the light comedy *The Irish R.M.* for **Channel 4** in the United Kingdom. The show, which eventually ran to three seasons, was sold to more than 50 territories worldwide. Thereafter, the company continued to produce a regular output of television drama. It complemented this work with a semiregular output of feature film titles through the difficult years of the late 1980s, commencing with *Joyriders* (1988). This was followed by a sequence of films in Ireland, including Mike Newell's *Into the West* (1994), Suri Krishnamma's *A Man of No Importance* (1996), and three **Thaddeus O'Sullivan** pictures: *December Bride* (1991), *Nothing Personal* (1995), and *Ordinary Decent Criminal* (2000).

Regularly cited by industry journals as among the most powerful figures in the Irish film industry, Mitchell and Cavendish also gained substantial overseas clout. The London branch of Little Bird produced Mike Hodges's *Croupier* (1997) and Paul McGuigan's *Gangster No. 1* (2001) in partnership with FilmFour, and it coproduced the two highly successful film adaptations of Helen Fielding's Bridget Jones novels with Working Title films. In 2001, the company established a distribution entity (Zephir Films) in Germany with local coproduction partner TatFilm. Finally, in 2002, Little Bird established a financial services company to raise funds for international film projects shot in South Africa with South African financial services company Coronation Capital.

The company owed much of its success to its (unusual by Irish standards) careful nurturing of distribution that went well beyond the establishment of Zephir, referred to above. In 1993, James Mitchell and Little Bird producer Jane Doolan established Clarence Pictures to distribute not only Little Bird material in Ireland but also a wider range of nonstudio pictures and indigenous films. Clarence, which later spun off from Little Bird and was rebranded as Eclipse Pictures in 2002, developed distribution relationships with FilmFour and Mel Gibson's Icon Production and Distribution Company, the latter leading to the reciprocal distribution by Icon of *Ordinary Decent Criminal* in Britain.

However, the company experienced a series of losses between 2000 and 2004 from which it struggled to recover. Although it limped on for half a decade, difficulty accessing equity finance after the financial crash of 2008 saw the company fold in 2009 with debts of €3.5 million. In 2010, James Mitchell would go on to establish Soho Moon productions, which has sustained a connection with Ireland, filming sequences from the 2012 documentary *Dreams of a Life* in Dublin, coproducing the series *Acceptable Risk* for **Radio Telefís Éireann** in 2017, and producing *Citizen Lane* in 2018, on the life of the Irish art dealer Sir Hugh Lane. For his part, Jonathan Cavendish set up The Imaginarium with actor Andy Serkis in 2011. Part production company, part high-end motion capture facility, the company has produced two feature films (*Breathe* [2017] and *The Ritual* [2017]) and provided postproduction work on a number of high-profile blockbusters, including the *Planet of the Apes* sequence, the most recent *Star Wars* reboots, and *Avengers: Age of Ultron* (2017).

THE LOOKING GLASS (2009). For cinematographer/director Colin Downey, unfathomably prolific (including four features in 2007 alone) and working with no-budget funding levels, *The Looking Glass* was the first of his films to secure **Irish Film Board** funding.

The narrative returns to familiar territory for Downey: lead protagonist Paul (frequent collaborator with Patrick O'Donnell) exemplifies a masculine figure in crisis, one directly confronted by the monstrous feminine in the form of Agnes (Sanne Hulst), mother of his heavily pregnant girlfriend Claire (Natalia Kostrzewa). Agnes, a doctor, taunts Paul with regard to his unreadiness for fatherhood, screening visceral footage of childbirth and clinically recording his dismayed response. Paul is already a haunted figure: mysterious figures drift through the woods of a park near the home he shares with Claire, encounters with male prostitute Max (Rodrigo Rodrigues) point to his repressed homosexuality, while Agnes's tale of the self-immolation of a former patient recalls a similar childhood trauma experienced by Paul.

Downey's work is rarely if ever characterized by straightforward narrative, and *The Looking Glass* is no different: though fear of paternity—à la David Lynch's *Eraserhead* (1977)—is a major theme, the significance of other threats (the pyromaniac British soldiers visiting Max) are, though unnerving and bringing the film into horror genre territory, deliberately left vague, inviting the audience to actively construct meaning. That the film, though notionally set in Ireland, is better understood as occupying the landscape of the imagination further complicates viewer comprehension. With budgetary constraints doubtless negating the possibility of closing down public spaces, Downey relies heavily on interior settings or tightly shot exterior setups obscuring the background. The resulting abstract diegesis simultaneously alienates the viewer who is determined to read the text as reflective of modern Ireland while opening up the possibility of a more universally accessible—if still oblique—commentary on contemporary masculinity.

A LOVE DIVIDED (1998). Directed by Sydney McCartney and set in Fethard-on-Sea in County Wexford, the film is based on a true story of religious sectarianism that divided the area in 1957. Catholic Sean (**Liam Cunningham**) marries Sheila (**Orla Brady**), who is a Protestant, but when their eldest child reaches school age, Sheila decides to send her to the local Protestant school. The Catholic parish priest forbids such a move, claiming it violates a pledge that Sheila signed on her wedding day stating that she would bring up her children in the Catholic faith. Outraged at the priest's interference and her husband's inability to change matters, she flees to Belfast and then Scotland, where she takes refuge on a farm. Meanwhile, back at home, her family and the other Protestant villagers become the victims of a boycott initiated by the Church. Eventually, Sheila returns (after Sean travels to Scotland), and the boycott is ended by the intercession of the more politic local bishop, but the bitterness continues as Sean and Sheila educate their children at home.

LYNCH, JOHN (1961–). Lynch grew up in Corrinshego outside Newry as the eldest of five children (including his sister, actress **Susan Lynch**). His parents met in London, where Lynch spent his earliest years, but returned to Northern Ireland in 1968, just as the Troubles were breaking out, and as a consequence he grew up in what he has described as an oppressive atmosphere. On leaving school, he was offered a place at the Central School of Speech and Drama in London. He secured his first major role—the lead in *Cal* opposite Helen Mirren—while still attending the school. He was cast as a young Irish Republican Army recruit who falls in love with the widow of a member of the Royal Ulster Constabulary. *Cal* was an instant breakthrough for Lynch after the film received critical plaudits and achieved modest box office success. Despite this, it was another six years before he would appear in a second feature film: the roles offered in the wake of *Cal* were mainly Northern Irish, and fearing typecasting, Lynch retreated to concentrate on theater work for the rest of the 1980s, including an 18-month spell with the Royal Shakespeare Company in London.

When he did return to film, however, it was precisely in Northern Irish parts that he drew critical praise. He played Paul Hill opposite Daniel Day-Lewis's Gerry Conlon in *In the Name of the Father* (1994), a Catholic father caught up in sectarian violence in *Nothing Personal* (1995), and Bobby Sands in *Some Mother's Son* (1996). Indeed, for a period, Lynch's haunted visage with its piercing eyes became synonymous with representations of the Northern Irish.

In 1994, he appeared in **Mary McGuckian**'s *Words upon the Window Pane* (1994) and collaborated on three more films: *This Is the Sea* (1997) (for which he also acted as second unit director), *Best* (2000) (the biopic of legendary soccer player George Best, which he cowrote), and McGuckian's Hollywood debut, *The Bridge of San Luis Rey* (2004). Their frequent collaborations are in part explained by the fact that they have been romantic partners for more than a decade and married in 2002.

While appearing mostly in Irish films during the 1990s and 2000s (including *Evelyn* [2002], *Puckoon* [2002], and, with his sister Susan, *The Secret of Roan Inish* [1994]), he also began to be cast farther afield: in Derek Jarman's *Edward II* (1991); the Australian art house hit *Angel Baby* (1995), for which he won and AFI award; and opposite Gwyneth Paltrow in the comedy *Sliding Doors* (1998). In addition to a variety of character roles in international film productions, he has turned to writing with the novels *Torn Water* (2005) and *Falling Out of Heaven* (2010) and appeared in prominent roles in the TV dramas *Retribution* (aka *One of Us*, Netflix, 2016), *The Fall* (**Radio Telefís Eireann**/BBC, 2013–2016), and *The Terror* (AMC, 2018–).

LYNCH, SUSAN (1971–). Born in Newry in Northern Ireland, she is best known for a career-defining performance in **Pat Murphy**'s *Nora* (2000), in which she played the title role of the Galway-born wife and muse of James Joyce. With an innate sensuality, intelligence, and directness, Lynch brought life to a figure that had long been relegated to secondary status in literary history in the third of Murphy's unofficial trilogy of Irish "herstories" (along with *Maeve* [1981] and *Anne Devlin* [1984]).

Although she first came to public attention in the early 1990s for her stage work—a reputation revived in a memorable performance as Hester Swain in the 2015 Abbey Theatre revival of *By the Bog of Cats*—Lynch quickly moved to the screen and shone in a variety of film roles, including *The Secret of Roan Inish* (1994), *Waking Ned* (1998), *The Mapmaker* (2001), and *Mickybo and Me* (2004), garnering a raft of IFTA nominations and awards in the process, as well as appearing in British productions such as

Beautiful Creatures (2000), *From Hell* (2001), and *Enduring Love* (2004). Since moving to the United Kingdom in the early 2000s, she has established a solid and highly respected career in quality TV drama, including *Great Expectations* (BBC), *Happy Valley* (BBC), and *Apple Tree Yard* (BBC). She made an all-too-brief return to Irish film in **Jim Sheridan**'s *The Secret Scripture* (2016) (in which she was chronically underused) and more prominently as a glamorous but psychotic crime boss in *Bad Day for the Cut* (2017), a fun if uneven Northern Irish genre film that found a limited release on Netflix.

M

MACAVIN, JOSIE (1920–2005). Born in 1919, set designer Josie Mac-Avin learned her trade with touring theater productions. These included pantomimes with Irish stage actress Maureen Potter, a European tour with *Joan of Arc*, and a production of Michael Mac Líammoir's *Playboy of the Western World* in Edinburgh. She began her film work in 1959 on Michael Anderson's ***Shake Hands with the Devil***, one of the first films shot at **Ardmore Studios**.

MacAvin's employment on that film was unusual for the era: typically, films shot in Ireland by overseas production companies (as was the case for *Shake Hands with the Devil*) did not employ local talent in senior creative positions. Her employment reflected an appreciation of her abilities. This was confirmed in 1964 when she was nominated for an Oscar for her work on the Albert Finney version of *Tom Jones* (1963). Two years later, she was nominated again for her work on Martin Ritt's adaptation of John Le Carré's *The Spy Who Came In from the Cold* (1965), which used Dublin as a double for East Berlin.

From that point on, MacAvin was employed on virtually every major film shot in Ireland: David Lean's ***Ryan's Daughter*** (1969), **John Huston**'s ***The Dead*** (1986), Ron Howard's ***Far and Away*** (1991), and **Neil Jordan**'s ***Michael Collins*** (1996) (she was also set designer on Jordan's later ***Butcher Boy*** [1998]). Nor was she averse to working on smaller films; during the period of the first **Irish Film Board**, she worked on ***Eat the Peach*** (1986), and in the early 1990s, she was the set designer on two low-budget films by director **Ronan O'Leary**: ***Diary of a Madman*** (1990) and ***Hello Stranger*** (1992). Her work was not confined to films shot in Ireland, however; her non-Irish shoots included Michael Cimino's *Heaven's Gate* (1980), and she won an **Academy Award** for her contribution to Sydney Pollack's *Out of Africa* (1985), which entailed her living in Africa for nine months.

Remarkably, MacAvin continued working into her 80s. At the age of 75, she won an Emmy for Outstanding Individual Achievement in Art Direction for her work on the *Gone with the Wind* sequel *Scarlett* (1994) and was 82 when she completed work on her last major production, ***Evelyn*** (2002), produced by **Pierce Brosnan**. She died in January 2005 at the age of 85.

MACBRIDE, TIERNAN (1933–1995). When Tiernan MacBride died in 1995, Michael Dwyer wrote that no other individual had campaigned quite so vigorously and so ceaselessly for the Irish film industry. At his funeral, **Lelia Doolan** called him the father *and* the mother of Irish film.

MacBride was a son of Sean MacBride and grandson of Maud Gonne MacBride. In addition to his work for the Irish film industry, he was an activist on various political issues, including campaigns to release the Birmingham Six and the Guildford Four. He went to University College Dublin to study architecture in 1951 and subsequently worked in an agricultural company before moving to the Arks Advertising Agency. Starting as a projector operator, he progressed through the film department before moving to the United States for half a decade to work as a commercial director in Detroit and New York.

On his return to Ireland, MacBride joined the television department at McConnells Advertising and then established his own company, Advertising on Film, which built up a substantial national and international client list. During this period (1978), he also directed his only fiction film, a short titled *Christmas Morning*. In 1985, Advertising on Film closed, and MacBride shifted his considerable energies to feature films by establishing Roebuck Moving Pictures (the company was named for the house MacBride grew up in). He would subsequently act as executive producer on **Bill Miskelly**'s *The End of the World Man* and on Vinny Murphy's *H for Hamlet* and received a posthumous production credit for his partner **Pat Murphy**'s *Nora*.

However, it was in the field of lobbying and campaigning for support for Irish film that MacBride's impact was felt the most. He was on the board or a member of virtually every film-related organization included in this volume. In the 1970s, he was a pivotal figure in the establishment of a Film Section in the Irish Transport and General Workers Union and was chairman of the **Irish Film Theatre**. He was a member of both the Association of Irish Producers (AIP) and the Association of Irish Film Makers and as such was one of several key figures in lobbying then Minister for Industry Desmond O'Malley to revive the idea of an **Irish Film Board**. Ironically, he subsequently led the AIP's boycott of **Neil Jordan**'s *Angel* at the 1982 Celtic Film Festival (in protest of the manner in which the Irish Film Board and **John Boorman** had funded the film). In another twist, he himself was subsequently appointed to the Film Board.

MacBride was also one of the prime movers behind the 1986 establishment of **Film Base**, going so far as to personally finance the purchase of video equipment for the organization. When the Film Board closed in 1987, MacBride was at the forefront of the campaign to reestablish it and as a member of Film Makers Ireland was vociferous in his criticism of **Channel 4** when in 1989 the channel abruptly canceled its *Irish Reel* documentary series.

When the European Union's MEDIA program commenced, MacBride was appointed to the board of MEDIA Desk Ireland and was Irish representative on the Madrid-based MEDIA Business School. Finally, by the time of his death, he was one of the longest-serving members of the board of the **Film Institute of Ireland**.

Happily, MacBride lived to see his campaigning bear fruit: When **Michael D. Higgins** became minister for arts, culture, and the Gaeltacht in January 1993, MacBride led a group of placard-wielding filmmakers not to protest but, uniquely, to welcome his appointment. He was famously combative in pursuing his lobbying objectives but was equally renowned for his generosity of spirit and his willingness to assist younger filmmakers as they attempted to break into the industry. Given this, it was fitting that, after his death, the Film Institute of Ireland renamed their annual script-funding award in his name.

MAEVE (1982). *Maeve*, directed by **Pat Murphy** (with **John T. Davis**), remains one of the most sophisticated films ever made about the Troubles in Ireland, developing a coherent analysis and critique of the stifling stasis imposed by the past (real or imagined) on the present.

The film opens when Maeve Sweeney returns from London to visit her Catholic family in Belfast, a trip that brings up memories of her childhood in Northern Ireland. The story cuts back and forth between three temporal planes: Maeve as a young girl, as a teenager, and in the present. She recalls her family leaving their home in a Protestant area of Belfast in the face of threats from the locals. However, the family's move to a Catholic area means living amid people on the other side of the political spectrum: nationalist Republicans. She remembers, too, traveling around the north with her determinedly neutral father, selling cakes from their van, all the time encountering hostility from Republicans, Unionists, and the British army. As Maeve enters her later teenage years, even her sympathetic boyfriend pressures her to take a stance on the "Northern Question." Unwilling to take sides in a conflict that she sees as based on a mythologized version of the past, Maeve is finally unable to find a place for herself in Northern Irish society.

The protagonist Maeve has moved beyond national politics, which she perceives as rooted in conflicts of the past, memories of which have been reimagined and reshaped and selectively edited to suit the current mind-set.

The film argues that it is memory that provides the framework that allows the older generation (particularly of Irish Republican Army leaders) to retain their sanity in the face of decades of violence. However, memory frequently depends on reference to events that have been mythologized out of all recognition. These past events then trap those living in the present in imposed categories: for those unwilling to accept the label "Unionist" or "nationalist," the past offers them no identity. By being neither, one has no option but to leave. For those seeking to go beyond this, as Maeve does by embracing feminism, there is simply no place to exist: the dominant (indeed the only permissible) discourse is Unionist against nationalist, Protestant against Catholic. Other struggles—women against patriarchy—are subsumed into this. So Maeve escapes to England, a country so turned in on itself that "people can grow up here without being imprisoned by the history. . . . They've disconnected themselves from their own neuroses."

***THE MAGDALENE SISTERS* (2002).** Based on the horrific true story of the incarceration of over 30,000 women over the course of the 20th century in Ireland who had been disowned by their families because they were pregnant or in some way regarded as "fallen women." They were dispatched into the hands of Catholic nuns who used their labor to run a number of laundries throughout the country until their closure in the 1970s. The ethos of the institutions was that hard work would help make up for the alleged sins the girls committed. Scottish filmmaker and actor Peter Mullan brought the story to the big screen, filming in an unused Benedictine convent in Dumfries, Scotland.

The composite story of three girls, generically framed as a "prison movie" in the tradition of *The Shawshank Redemption* (1994), ensured its wide appeal to audiences. It opens with a close-up of a priest, building to a crescendo as he plays traditional Irish music on a bodhran at a wedding celebration. The party initially appears to replicate a stereotypical *craic*, but this is thrown into sharp relief by intercuts to the scene in an upstairs bedroom of the attack and rape of one of the protagonists, Margaret (Anne-Marie Duff), which proceeds as the music grows more raucous. The impressively choreographed opening scene concludes with the priest being told in hushed tones of what has happened. It becomes obvious, however, that it is the female victim who will suffer most as a consequence in this regressive paternal and religious community, and the following day, Margaret is taken away with the quiet consent of her family. We next encounter Bernadette (Nora-Jane Noone), who has a healthy eye for the boys, at Saint Attracta's Orphanage. When the nuns running the orphanage note this, they move her to the laundry in a bid to temper her sinful flirtations. Finally, we meet Rose (Dorothy Duffy), who has just had a baby. A priest working for an adoption agency informs her that a child born out of wedlock is a bastard and convinces her to sign away her child, a decision she immediately regrets. After this preamble, the camera tracks through a long list of names of such unfortunate girls, reminiscent of a memorial plaque for war victims. As the three new recruits enter the laundry, the evil head nun (Geraldine McEwan) informs them that eternal salvation will come only by doing penance in this life.

Throughout their incarceration, the girls endure numerous indignities, especially if they refuse to accept their situation or try to escape. Serious misdemeanors receive the strongest punishment, including having all their hair ceremoniously cut off. Their pariah status in the outside world is exemplified by the laundry man warning his young apprentice not to look at or talk to them.

Although the film ends on an upbeat note as the other two lead characters hatch and carry out an escape plan, a postscript telling of their subsequent lives outside the institution is countered by the knowledge that most inmates were not so lucky. With strong performances by all the leading actors and character-centered direction from the Catholic-raised actor/director Mullen, *The Magdalene Sisters* proved to be one of the most important as well as one of the most commercially successful Irish films of its era. Casting a well-researched light on an extended phase of Irish history long suppressed and overlooked, the film was very successful at the box office, passing the €1 million mark in Ireland and almost £2 million in the British market.

MAMMAL (2016). **Rebecca Daly**'s second feature, cowritten with Glenn Montgomery, retains the passive, observational quality characteristic of her debut, *The Other Side of Sleep* (2011). Margaret Brady (Australian actress Rachel Griffiths) has carved out an existence that holds the outside world and close relationships at bay. Having divorced her husband Matt (**Michael McElhatton**) years earlier and left their son Patrick entirely in his care, she has retreated to a two-bedroom home while running a charity shop where she maintains minimal contact with her employees. Her days are punctuated by visits to the local swimming pool, where she lurks under the surface, external stimuli muffled by the dense medium of water. When Matt arrives with news that Patrick has disappeared, she barely reacts.

Yet her self-imposed solitude is disrupted, and her maternal instincts are rekindled when she encounters Joe (**Barry Keoghan**), a homeless boy whom she finds stabbed outside her shop. Patching his wounds, she offers him her spare room and Patrick's remaining old clothes. Joe is a feral creature, depicted as akin to the wild cats that roam around Margaret's home. At night, he sporadically roams with his old gang, careening through nights of chaos and drugs. Yet as the weeks pass, a bond emerges between the pair, blurring the lines between a motherly and a more carnal connection.

Mammal is a film that largely refuses to embrace classic narrative structure and is more interested in exploring themes of loss and grief through the various facets of its dysfunctional characters: even Margaret's ex-husband Matt is depicted as crippled by barely suppressed anger. Unburdened by extensive dialogue, Griffiths is left plenty of space to convey Margaret's state of mourning (though for what exactly is left unclear) through discreet shifts of expression. These are relentlessly observed by director Daly's static camera, which also dispassionately presents Joe's headlong embrace of disaster. This is a sober work, then, one reluctant to tell its audience how to interpret its central characters.

MAN ABOUT DOG (2005). Directed by **Paddy Breathnach**, the film stars Allen Leech, Tom Jordan Murphy, and Ciaran Nolan as Mo Chara, Scud Murphy, and Cerebral Palsy, respectively, three luckless losers from Northern Ireland whose main aim in life is simply to survive while having the best time possible. However, whether running a mobile shop, selling dope, or gambling, the trio—initially at least—are no match for the crooked bookie (**Sean McGinley**), who thwarts their ambitions.

The comic road movie caper charts their revenge as they travel down south with a thoroughbred greyhound that they hope will bring them luck. When the dog initially fails to perform, they sell it to a group of Travellers (led by the comic **Pat Shortt**), at which point the dog suddenly demonstrates a remarkable turn of speed. Stealing their dog back, they head for the "holy grail" of dog racing in Clonmel, County Tipperary, where the story culminates and all their newfound enemies congregate.

The film was dismissed by most Irish critics, but despite this, it became the most successful indigenous film in Ireland in 2004. Its success is not hard to fathom: constructed as an Irish take on the "new lad" pervading British cinema in the 1990s, the dialogue throughout is scattered with risible colloquialisms and scatological references. It eschews the traditionally squeamish approach of Irish films to sex scenes and, to the extent that it makes references to politics at all, plays them for laughs. (One sequence sees the boys fantasizing about how well-known political figures like Gerry Adams or Ian Paisley would look if they were drugged sufficiently.) Its generic appeal, fused with the preference of local audiences for local stories, especially those told using a universally accessible narrative structure, made it a top-ten box-office hit.

MAN OF ARAN (1934). This landmark ethnodocumentary (sometimes described as fictional documentary) from American director Robert Flaherty, inspired by J. M. Synge's *The Aran Islands* and made during a two-year residency on Inis Mór off the coast of Galway, remains a defining portrait of primitive endurance and romantic representation of a premodern Irish identity. When the film was first seen by the political elite, it was said that Eamon de Valera—the leader of the Fianna Fáil political party who helped define a post–Civil War identity that continued well into the 1950s—wept at its heroic portrayal of his people. Although its "myth" was subsequently debunked, it has occupied a defining importance to both cinematic representations of the Irish and the local tourist economy (and arguably survival) of the Aran Islands ever since.

As in all his films—from *Nanook of the North* (1922) to *Louisiana Story* (1948)—Flaherty, the son of an Irish prospector, remained preoccupied with "discovering" primitive societies embodying the universal human trait of endurance and the ability to survive against all odds. The fact that the family in the film was cast by Flaherty and his wife Frances after extensive photographing of locals and that the central activity of the film—the hunting of basking sharks for oil—had not actually being carried out for years remains problematic for many critics, as the film claimed to reflect the truth of the island they encountered. While filmmakers such as Flaherty's erstwhile friend John Grierson wanted to capture the specific truth of 1930s poverty and social deprivation, Flaherty was more focused on valorizing man's struggle with nature and was willing to "shape" the truth to this end. As Grierson caustically wrote, "I imagine they shine as bravely in pursuit of Irish landlords as in the pursuit of Irish sharks."

Man of Aran prefers instead to portray the enormous hardship the natives have to endure on the island in order to eke out a living. Flaherty's filming method involved living for an extended period in the environment with his subjects and producing extensive footage in an attempt to capture the essential tenor of their lives. (George Stoney's *How the Myth Was Made: A Study of Robert Flaherty's Man of Aran* [1984] offers indispensable insight into Flaherty's methods.) Even if one took issue with the film's evocation of "reality," it is impossible to dismiss the cinematic sweep and effect of the work achieved through extended shooting and experiments with lenses of different focal lengths and editing (influenced by early Hitchcock and Soviet films). Finally, it is little wonder that the story of the islanders' attempts to fight the wild but beautiful sea and the poetic hardship of breaking up rocks and carrying seaweed up the cliff face to make precious fertile soil was co-opted as an enduring testament to an idealized Irish rural mythos, picking up and giving visual "proof" to themes found in the nationalist revivalist writings of Synge and Yeats.

Nonetheless, it is also noteworthy that when anthropologist John Messenger interviewed islanders in the late 1950s and mid-1960s, *Man of Aran* was consistently identified as the most distorted representation of their place and history. Somewhat puritanically, Messenger cited more than 50 "abuses of reality" in the film and also noted that many of the islanders bitterly resented the indelible image of their home the film created.

In 2014, a presumed lost film by Flaherty was rediscovered at Harvard University. The 11-minute *Oidhche Sheanchais* (A Night of Storytelling) was produced at the end of the *Man of Aran* production and features the famed local *seanachaí* (storyteller) Seáinín Tom Ó Dioráin telling a story in front of a hearth to other members of the cast. Shot in a London studio rather than an Aran cottage, it features an Aran *seanachaí* telling a fireside story to fellow islanders. Although of limited cinematic merit, *Oidhche Sheanchais* is Flaherty's first work in direct sound and is acknowledged to be the first "talkie" in the Irish language.

A MAN OF NO IMPORTANCE (1994). Screenwriter Barry Devlin's adaptation of Terence McNally's novel is set in Dublin of the early 1960s. It centers on the life of a bachelor bus conductor, Alfie Byrne (Albert Finney), forced by a conservative and Catholic culture to conceal his homosexuality at a time when it was a criminal offense. He finds a temporary outlet for his instincts in directing an amateur dramatic group (often drawing his cast from bus passengers) and occasionally cross-dressing within the home he shares with his sister Lily (**Brenda Fricker**), who clings to the notion that 60-year-old Alfie is simply waiting for "the right girl." He later attempts to stage Wilde's *Salome* in his local church hall, allowing his secret to be revealed, with potentially tragic consequences.

We stress "potentially" because in U.K. director Suri Krishnamma's hands, the depiction of Alfie's journey to self-knowledge (effectively coming out) offers a relatively cozy take on everyday expression of homophobia in 1960s Dublin (a point amplified in the film's subsequent adaptation as an off-Broadway musical in 2002). Dubliners are presented as benevolently ignorant of the very idea of homosexuality (and sexuality in general), responding to Alfie's last-act revelation more with bewilderment than with revulsion. (Indeed, his passengers ultimately band together to defend Alfie when he is verbally attacked by his leading man, Camey [**Michael Gambon**], after he has been outed.) This display of solidarity with Alfie from his immediate circle notwithstanding, the film's conclusion fails to fully deliver on its central premise: though Alfie's status is accepted, this appears to be conditional on somewhat neutering his sexuality. In the conclusion, though surrounded by friends, Alfie lacks a romantic partner, his sexuality acceptable only as long as it remains an abstract concept rather than a clear and present reality.

***THE MAPMAKER* (2001).** When cartographer Richie Markey (Brian F. O'Byrne) travels to a border area of County Fermanagh to make a hill-walking map, his arrival arouses the suspicion of locals. The landscape holds secrets, particularly in relation to the disappearance of a local farmer 10 years earlier who was suspected of being a police informer. It emerges that completing the map will require Markey to discover the fate of the missing farmer.

Framed as a crime thriller and intended for a mainstream audience (in keeping with the tendencies of "second-wave" Irish cinema), **Johnny Gogan**'s imaginative film can also be read against the backdrop of mapping/naming Ireland, beginning with the Ordinance Survey of 1829–1842 (just in time for the Great Famine), a project greatly revised and increased in scale between 1893 and 1913 that served to impose modernity on an ancient landscape. As with Brian Friel's celebrated play *Translations*, Gogan's film links Ireland's political and colonial history to themes of buried local knowledge and secrets.

MARCUS, LOUIS (1936–). Born in Cork, the son of a picture framer, he completed an English and French degree at University College Cork before George Morrison took him on as assistant editor on *Mise Éire*. He also worked on *Saoirse?* (*Mise Éire*'s sequel) before the Irish-language cultural organization **Gael Linn** hired him to make documentaries. As a result, Marcus was one of the very few individuals working outside **Radio Teleffs Éireann** (RTÉ) who was able to make a full-time career of filmmaking in the Ireland of the 1960s. Noted films from this period include *Peil* (1962), on Gaelic football; *Rhapsody of a River* (1965), commissioned by the **Cultural Relations Committee**; and arguably his best work of that decade, *Fleá* (1967), a cinema verité record of the Kilrush, County Clare, music festival. This last film was widely screened internationally, won Marcus the Silver Bear award at the Berlin Film Festival in 1967, and was nominated for an **Academy Award** the following year.

By the late 1960s, however, Marcus was becoming as well known for his lobbying on behalf of an as-yet-nonexistent film industry as he was for his creative work. As early as 1959, he had written articles for the *Irish Times* critiquing government film policy and arguing that organizations like **Ardmore Studios** were contributing little to the development of an indigenous production sector. In 1967, he wrote another series of articles for the same newspaper that the **Irish Film Society** subsequently republished as a single pamphlet, decrying the failure of Ardmore and, more generally, of successive governments to treat cinema seriously. The articles drew Marcus to the attention of then Irish resident **John Huston** and indirectly led to the establishment of the Film Industry Committee and the publication of the *Huston Report* in 1968.

Marcus was also a member of that committee, and it is apparent that he had a substantial influence on its conclusions and recommendations. Unfortunately the Dáil never passed the legislation that was to have put those recommendations into action in 1970, and the emergence of an Irish film industry was delayed by at least a decade as a consequence. This was particularly damaging for Marcus himself, as Gael Linn, the major sponsor of his output in the 1960s, withdrew from filmmaking activity in 1973 (though not before Marcus completed his 1971 documentary *Dubliners: Sean agus Nua*).

From the 1970s on, Marcus produced a mix of promotional documentaries, such as *The Heritage of Ireland* (1978) and *Discovering Ireland* (1983), and more aesthetically engaged work. His 1973 film *Paistí ag Obair*, made for RTÉ, looked at a Montessori school in Dublin and was nominated for an Academy Award. This was followed in 1975 by the stunning cinematography of *Conquest of Light*, a documentary about Waterford Crystal. Later in the decade, he made the first of his (very) occasional forays into drama, with his production of *Revival*, a drama-documentary about the life and thinking of one of the 1916 martyrs, Padraig Pearse. He remained an active filmmakers well into the 21st century, producing more than 80 documentaries and short films. He was appointed chair of the **Irish Film Board** when **Lelia Doolan** retired in 1996 and in 2005 was the subject of a lifetime tribute at the film festival in his native city of Cork.

MARY BREEN FARRELLY PRODUCTIONS. Mary Breen Farrelly Productions (MBF) is included in this volume not because of an impressive track record as a production company but rather because of its central role in the production of the sci-fi movie *Space Truckers* (1996), the near collapse of which led to a substantial tightening up of the administration of the **Section 481** tax incentive. MBF Productions was launched in May 1992 with the promise that it would revitalize the Irish film industry by way of an IR£70 million film production package. The company was launched by the eponymous Mary Breen Farrelly and her partner John Avery. Farrelly's experience in the industry derived from her work in the accounts departments of a range of British film companies in the two decades preceding the establishment of MBF Productions. The IR£70 million never materialized, but with the expansion of the Section 481 tax incentive, the company acquired funding for an animation series based on Bible stories (*Sign of the Fish*) and for the **Ronan O'Leary** feature *Driftwood*.

In 1994, MBF came into contact with U.S. producer Peter Newman, who was seeking a location to shoot *Space Truckers*. Promised by MBF that £7 million could be raised via Section 481, the production duly came to shoot at **Ardmore Studios** in July 1995. In fact, however, only £4.1 million had been raised by the time the film commenced production, and the project soon ran into financial difficulty. The minister for arts, culture, and the Gaeltacht,

Michael D. Higgins, whose department had originally certified the project for Section 481 funding, called in producer **Morgan O'Sullivan**, film lawyer **James Hickey**, and ACCBank to attempt to retrieve the film. Mary Breen Farrelly resigned as producer of the film and was replaced by Morgan O'Sullivan, who succeeded in securing more Section 481 funding to complete it.

However, while salvaging the finances of *Space Truckers*, ACCBank found that of the £4.1 million raised under Section 481 for the film, only £1.5 million had actually gone into its production budget. Of the remaining £2.6 million, £850,000 had been diverted to *Driftwood* and another £250,000 to *Sign of the Fish*. The remaining money was simply unaccounted for. This was bad news for the original Section 481 investors who had put money into *Space Truckers*: since not all of their money had gone into that film, they were no longer entitled to avail themselves of a tax break on their investment and found themselves faced with an unexpected tax bill.

The film effectively marked the end of MBF Productions in Ireland, although the company was granted another Section 481 certificate for a film called *Feeney's Rainbow*. That project never came to fruition, and the collapse of the *Sign of the Fish* project meant that *Driftwood* was the only film begun and finished by MBF. However, the impact of MBF Productions lingered in the way in which investors and Irish tax officials subsequently viewed Section 481. For investors, Section 481 no longer appeared to promise a guaranteed return. For the revenue commissioners, the project offered evidence that unscrupulous producers were using the tax break in an illegal fashion. More concretely, in the January 1996 budget, the minister for finance announced that, henceforth, Section 481 certification would be granted only to films made by production companies established solely for the purpose of the production of one and only one film. Furthermore, tax relief for investors would commence only from the date of principal filming of the project (i.e., when production actually commenced).

MAZE **(2017).** Writer/director Stephen Burke's return to the thematic territory he first visited in his superb early half-hour dramas *After '68* (1994) and *'81* (1997) was almost inevitably going to cause controversy, focusing as it did on the 1983 breakout of 38 Republican prisoners from the Maze prison in County Down. Even before the film was released, Unionist politicians felt compelled to critique the very notion of portraying the escape on the predictable grounds that the Irish Republican Army prisoners would, they assumed, be represented as heroes.

In point of fact, Burke's film offers a more nuanced approach. Tom Vaughan-Lawlor plays the real-life figure of Larry Marley, a Republican prisoner more than a decade into his sentence. Two years after the end of the Maze hunger strikes (the focus of *Hunger* [2008], *H3* [2001], and *Some Mother's*

Son [1996], among others), there is a palpable sense of defeat among the prisoners. Visited by his wife Kate Marley (Eileen Walsh), Larry is reminded that his family is growing up in his absence. As a seasoned escapee, Marley determines to assert the prisoners' ongoing resistance by hatching a plan to break out from what was then widely regarded as the highest-security prison in western Europe.

To advance this, Marley develops a relationship with prisoner officer Gordon Close (Barry Ward). Although Close is initially suspicious, a relationship—perhaps even something approaching a friendship—begins to emerge. The film is careful to establish that, like Marley, Close is a family man, a parallel that underwrites their growing rapport. Marley exploits this to gradually amass bits of key information—passwords, architectural drawings, and work schedules—critical to an escape plan designed to free more prisoners in a single event than any post–World War II jailbreak.

Although initially focused on the interpersonal relationship between jailer and prisoner while also deftly establishing the wider political context of Northern Ireland in the 1980s, Burke's film really comes alive in the second half as the tension builds toward the escape. Fusing the local context with the generic demands of the prison breakout movie (both *The Great Escape* and *Stalag 17* are invoked), the film transcends its specific setting and offers an involving procedural narrative of men coming together to flee incarceration by a "foreign" power. As such, it clearly encourages identification with the escapees and elides their wider political motivations as well as less savory elements of the story, such as the death of a prison officer stabbed during the escape and Marley's own brutal murder four years later at the hands of the Ulster Volunteer Force. Ultimately, however, it transcends politics and concentrates on individuals on both sides of the conflict, bookending Burke's earlier films while becoming an exemplar of post-Troubles Irish cinema.

MCANALLY, RAY (1926–1989). Although hardly unknown to cinema audiences (especially in Ireland, where his big-screen career stretched from 1957 to 1989), Ray McAnally's film career prompts a series of what-ifs. What if his talent on both film and television had been recognized by international cinema earlier? What if he had won (as he probably should have) the **Academy Award** for his performance in Roland Joffe's *The Mission* (1986)? And, most important, what if he hadn't died prematurely of a heart attack in 1989 just as his international stature was in the ascendant?

McAnally was born in Buncrana in County Donegal and grew up a few miles down the road in Moville. He became involved in theater production while at secondary school (St. Eunan's College in Letterkenny) but, on leaving school, initially considered a religious vocation, entering the seminary at Maynooth. However, he quickly reconsidered and in 1947 joined the **Abbey Theatre**, where he met actress Ronnie Masterson, whom he married in 1951.

(The couple, who would go on to have four children, separated in the early 1980s.) McAnally became a familiar figure on the Abbey stage, ultimately appearing in more than 150 productions over nearly two decades. These included works from virtually every Irish playwright of note from that era: Tomas MacAnna, Louis d'Alton, Hugh Leonard, Brian Friel, and Denis Johnston. Perhaps seeking a wider repertoire, in 1963, he took the risk of departing the Abbey and, with Ronnie Masterson, would subsequently establish Old Quay Productions, which concentrated on staging contemporary U.S. and British theater in Ireland. However, he also continued to appear in Irish productions, notably embodying the role of Bull McCabe in the original 1965 production of John B. Keane's *The Field* for Gemini Productions. Although many actors subsequently took on the role, McAnally's embodiment of Bull's alternately bullying and poetic character remained definitive. The Keane family reportedly considered him as *the* Bull, and he would reprise the roles in several revivals over the following decades.

His position with the Abbey Players brought him his first big-screen roles in adaptations of Abbey adaptations and other early films shot at Ardmore: he was the lead in *Professor Tim* (1957) as the cash-strapped Hugh O'Cahan and in *She Didn't Say No* (1958) was near the top of the bill as Jim Power, one of five men in a small Irish village who father children with the same woman. Other, smaller roles in U.S. and British films followed (**Shake Hands with the Devil** [1959] and *Billy Budd* [1962]), but as the 1960s progressed, it was the small screen that more often beckoned. These included high-profile **Radio Telefís Éireann** productions as diverse as the 1916 Easter Rising–set *Insurrection* (1966) and as the lead detective investigating a Dublin crime family in *The Burke Enigma* (1978). However, the bulk of his work was constituted by an extraordinary variety of usually one-off guest roles in British television, including the array of single dramas curated within ITV's *Armchair Theatre* and *Playhouse* series. He was usually cast as English, often playing characters with working-class or regional accents, into which he slipped with apparently effortless ease. Typical of these was North London crime boss Alec Spindoe, who, having been sent to prison by the protagonists of *The Fellows* (1967) (a crime series based around two academic sleuths), reemerged in *Spindoe*, a 1968 series following the eponymous criminal as he struggled to secure dominance of his patch. However, he was equally at home playing upper-class and professional roles, such as doctors (*Man in a Suitcase* [1968]), wealthy benefactors (John Pendleton in the BBC's 1973 adaptation of *Pollyanna*), and priests (a recurring role opposite Milo O'Shea in the Hugh Leonard–scripted BBC sitcom *Me Mammy* [1968–1971]). He would even appear as the resolutely middle-class Gabriel Conroy in **The Dead**, a 1971 Granada Television adaptation of **James Joyce**'s "The Dead," some 15 years before **Donal McCann** essayed the same role for **John Huston**.

As he entered his 50s (and the 1980s loomed), big-screen casting directors seemed to suddenly notice McAnally's screen presence, and, some heart-related ill health notwithstanding, he entered a halcyon phase. Many of these roles related to the Troubles: he played Bloom, a cynical detective investigating a sectarian murder in **Neil Jordan**'s *Angel* (1982), a hard-edged Protestant employer in **Pat O'Connor**'s *Cal* (1984), and part of a group of Protestant partygoers who inadvertently double book a Liverpool bar with a counterpart Catholic group in the Alan Bleasdale–scripted *No Surrender* (1985). In 1986, British director Roland Joffe cast McAnally opposite Jeremy Irons and Robert de Niro in the key role of Cardinal Altamirano, a Spanish Jesuit sent to survey the work of his order among South American natives as a prelude to the sale of their land to the Portuguese. As the moral (but also amoral) core of the narrative, McAnally's Altamirano exuded a quiet charisma, charmed by the spiritual purity of the natives but equally mired in (and implicated by) the realpolitik of colonialism. He won the first of three BAFTAs for the performance but was criminally overlooked in that year's Academy Award nominations.

However, *The Mission* presaged a sequence of award-nominated and award-winning roles in U.K. and Irish film and television. Although also appearing in his share of dross (*The Fourth Protocol* [1987] and the execrable *Taffin* [1988], both opposite **Pierce Brosnan**, stand out in this regard), he excelled in three completely different roles. He was eye-twinkling charm personified as the enigmatic con man Ron Pym in the BBC's adaptation of John Le Carre's *A Perfect Spy* (1987) before tackling the role of Harry Perkins, a steelworker turned politician, in **Channel 4**'s take on the Chris Mullins novel *A Very British Coup* (1988). As a working-class prime minster confronted by the forces of the establishment when he seeks to unilaterally disarm the United Kingdom of its the nuclear arsenal, McAnally's shrewd intelligence shined through, deftly navigating Perkins through the infinite duplicity of Whitehall personnel. But it was his role as Paddy Brown, father to Christy Brown in **Jim Sheridan**'s debut, *My Left Foot* (1989), that made the greatest impact. Although Sheridan considered the film as being primarily about Christy's relationship with his long-suffering mother (played by **Brenda Fricker**), McAnally brought warmth and even empathy to what could so easily have been a one-note portrayal of an individual who was often drunk and brutish. McAnally is central to the key scene where the young Christy struggles to spell out the word "M-O-T-H-E-R" with a piece of chalk wedged between his toes. Paddy's slowly dawning recognition of his son's fierce intelligence, long disguised by his cerebral palsy, is profoundly moving. (The next scene sees Paddy barging into the local pub with Christy over his shoulder to declare, "This is Christy Brown. My son. Genius.") Although Fricker would win the Academy Award for her role, McAnally took home another BAFTA for his performance.

Tragically, that award would be given posthumously. Although he made several screen appearances after *My Left Foot* (including *We're No Angels* [1989] for Neil Jordan and the critically acclaimed Scottish film *Venus Peter* [1989]), he died suddenly of a heart attack at the home he shared with actress Britta Smith in June 1989. At the time of his death, he had been working with Jim Sheridan on the preproduction of *The Field* to reprise the role of Bull McCabe, nearly a quarter of a century after he had first created on it. The British film critic Barry Norman noted of his passing that "if anyone died at the height of their powers, it was Ray McAnally," a fair assessment of an actor who had looked set to enjoy a glowing autumn in his career.

MCARDLE, TOMMY (1939–). An eclectic scriptwriter and film and theater director, McCardle produced three small-scale but nonetheless highly innovative films in close collaboration with his twin brother John. All three—*The Kinkisha* (1977), *It's Handy When People Don't Die* (1980), and *Angela Mooney Dies Again* (1997)—drew on various aspects of Irish myth, superstition, and history.

Raised in Monaghan in a family of seven, both Tommy and John played Gaelic football at the county level and qualified as teachers. But from the mid-1970s, both eschewed teaching in favor of careers in the arts: the twins had moved into amateur acting, and their company, Ballintra Players, was critically lauded from its debut 1969 production (which saw the twins memorably cast as Gar Public and Private in Brian Friel's *Philadelphia, Here I Come*). John subsequently moved to work as a writer with the **Abbey Theatre**. For his part, Tommy's background in education led him to produce a school program for **Radio Telefís Éireann** (RTÉ) before progressing into radio programming and ultimately joining RTÉ on a full-time basis as a producer and director (working on popular children's programming, such as *Wanderly Wagon*, until his retirement in 2004). Tommy would also intersperse his broadcast work with theater production, adapting two Eugene McCabe Troubles-themed teleplays for the stage as *Heritage* in 1980 and directing an Irish-language version of John McGahern's *The Power of Darkness* (itself based on a Tolstoy story) at Galway's Taibhdhearc theater in 2007.

The brothers would collaborate again on Tommy McArdle's three independently produced films, all of which were scripted by John (who also wrote the collection of short stories, published in 1981, on which *It's Handy When People Don't Die* was based). Although to some extent able to draw on the financial security offered by their respective jobs, the first two films were financially challenging, undertaken as they were in the absence of support structures, such as the **Irish Film Board**. Shot on 16 mm for a rock-bottom IR£14,000 (personally funded by the brothers and their families), McArdle's debut, *The Kinkisha*, came out a 60-minute "long short." Drawing on an obscure Irish superstition, namely, that a child born on Whit Sunday will either kill or be killed unless he or she in turn kills a robin, the film demonstrated a willingness to play with established cinematic codes that belied the director's neophyte status. The film received mixed reviews, and McArdle expressed frustration at the critical focus on the film's mythic elements rather than, as he saw, its more central themes of religion, superstition, motherhood, and misogyny. Although receiving a run in the **Irish Film Theatre**, the McArdles were unable to secure wider distribution, and the film earned just IR£7,000 from its various short theatrical runs and television sales. Undeterred and determined to establish their production company Kinship Films on a commercial basis, the McArdles secured IR£21,000 (of a final budget of IR£40,000) in funding from, variously, RTÉ, the **National Film Studios of Ireland** (which donated studio equipment in kind), and **John Boorman** to produce the full-length feature *It's Handy When People Don't Die*. Drawing parallels with contemporary events in Northern Ireland, the film explored how ordinary people inadvertently (and unwillingly) caught up in key moments of history cope with radical change (and the process of mythmaking that often follows such events). **Garret Keogh** played Art, an innocent caught up in the Irish Rebellion of 1798 Wexford, his personal odyssey puncturing the kind of historical myths of glorious revolution invoked to legitimate political violence during the Troubles. Screened at the 1980 Winter Festival at the Irish Film Theatre, the film was praised for its intellectual ambition, but its two-hour duration was also considered too long (a point subsequently addressed by McArdle, who removed 20 minutes from the running time). Again, it failed to achieved widespread distribution, and, perhaps as a consequence, the McArdles withdrew from production for the big screen for a period.

Partly funded by the Irish Film Board, *Angela Mooney Dies Again*, McArdle's most recent and, to date, last film was constructed as a satire on the disappearance of mysticism from an Ireland gearing up for the financial excess of the Celtic Tiger period. Mia Farrow played the titular character, a woman determined to draw public attention to the need for a life lived through spirituality by repeatedly engaging in increasingly eccentric—and highly public—suicide attempts. Despite the film's obviously satirical intent, its deployment of self-harm in a quasi-comic mode sat uncomfortably with some audiences, and Farrow's one-note performance undermined the rich dialogue of the script. Although the McArdles' most technically accomplished work, it again failed to find purchase with audiences, even with the, relatively speaking, star power accorded to the project by Farrow's presence.

MCCABE, RUTH. An enduring presence in Irish theater, film, and TV who is equally effective in dramatic and comedic roles, McCabe began her career in the mid-1970s. She amassed a large number of stage successes (including her performance in the 1989 **Abbey Theatre** production of *King of the Castle* written by her celebrated father, Eugene McCabe) before being cast in *My Left Foot*, in which she played Mary Carr, Christy Brown's nurse and future wife, with a blend of no-nonsense earthiness and romance that has defined her best work. She has since made memorable appearances in a wide range of Irish films, including *The Snapper* (playing Kay Curley), *Philomena*, *Stella Days*, *Circle of Friends*, *Intermission*, *Inside I'm Dancing*, and **Neil Jordan**'s *Breakfast on Pluto*, among others.

McCabe's versatility, vocal distinctiveness, and ability to work in both English and Irish have also provided the basis of a long and wide-ranging career on the small screen. Among her many small-screen credits are *Catastrophe*, *Damo and Ivor*, *The Clinic*, *Any Time Now*, and *No Tears*. On the Irish-language channel TG4, she played the mother in her father's Famine-set *Tales from the Poorhouse* miniseries and provided voice-over work for TG4's long-running "súil eile ident."

MCCANN, DONAL (1943–1999). When McCann died, the *Irish Times* devoted an editorial to his passing, describing him as the best Irish actor of the 20th century (and possibly the best ever). Although it is widely acknowledged that his best performances were reserved for the stage and that filmmakers had largely failed to take advantage of his talents, he remains a mesmerizing figure on both the small and the large screen.

He acquired his zest for acting from his father, a former TD (Irish member of Parliament) and lord mayor of Dublin who wrote plays for the **Abbey Theatre** in the 1950s. McCann debuted onstage in 1962, appearing in a Terenure College past pupils' production of one of his father's own plays: *Give Me a Bed of Roses*. In college, he studied architecture but left to work as a copyboy at the *Evening Press*, a job that allowed him to moonlight as an actor. He received formal acting training at the Abbey School of Acting and made his first professional stage appearance with the Abbey company in Padraic Colum's *Thomas Muskerry*. He continued to receive second billing, however, until he was cast in the Abbey's enormously successful 1968 production of Dion Boucicault's *The Shaughraun*, which both revived the playwright's reputation and ensured that McCann was subsequently offered only lead stage roles.

By this time, he had already broken into cinema, appearing in a 1966 Disney take on early modern Irish history, *The Fighting Prince of Donegal*, and in 1969 in **John Huston**'s *Sinful Davey*. However, his first successful screen role was in the BBC's serial adaptation of Anthony Trollope's novel *The Pallisers*, in which he played the dashing Phineas Finn. He followed this the following year with another successful screen role, this time as Gar Public in an adaptation of Brian Friel's *Philadelphia, Here I Come!* (1975).

However, for a period in the late 1970s and early 1980s, his work rate dropped due in part to disenchantment with the world of acting but due also to chronic alcoholism. Nonetheless, he turned in another striking performance as the menacing Sleamhnan in **Bob Quinn**'s *Poitín* opposite **Cyril Cusack** and **Niall Toibin**, and he achieved local fame with his role in the successful **Radio Telefís Éireann** series *Strumpet City*. Onstage, he produced what is still regarded as one of the most astounding Irish theatrical performances of that decade as Captain Boyle (opposite **John Kavanagh**'s Joxer) in Sean O'Casey's *Joxer and the Paycock*. He would later be equally mesmeric in Brian Friel's *Faith Healer*.

However, one of his screen roles from the mid-1980s is arguably the equal of either of these frequently cited performances. John Huston cast him opposite his daughter, Angelica Huston, in his 1986 feature adaptation *The Dead* of **James Joyce**'s short story "The Dead." McCann's performance as Gabriel, Joyce's most enigmatic outsider, is the core of the film. Everything that occurs is observed through his impeccably mannered but impassive gaze, and his soliloquy at the close, following on the story's climatic revelation, is heartbreaking in its evocation of a heart that cannot break.

He did make other impressive screen appearances in that decade, most notably in **Pat O'Connor**'s *Cal*, **Neil Jordan**'s *Angel*, and *The Miracle* (he also appears in *High Spirits*, but, like the film, this is best forgotten) and as the tortured but defiant priest in Bob Quinn's *Budawanny* (later refilmed as *The Bishop's Story*). The nature of that last film—at least in its original silent version—offered something of an insight into McCann himself: self-effacing and almost entirely without ego yet carrying with him the constant threat of anger when he found fault with others. Something of the same character is also evident in the screen performance that capped off the 1980s for McCann—the brooding Hamilton in **Thaddeus O'Sullivan**'s *December Bride*.

By the 1990s, he had won his battle with alcohol, and it was reflected in the quality of his work, especially onstage. In 1995, he was awarded the London Critics Circle Theatre award for his tormented portrayal of Thomas Dunne in Sebastian Barry's *The Steward of Christendom*, a play that toured both sides of the Atlantic and won McCann extensive praise everywhere. Arguably, his cinema work in that period was a little less interesting, although he was increasingly called on by internationally renowned directors, such as Bernardo Bertolucci and Phillippe Rousselot for *Stealing Beauty* (1996) and *The Serpent's Kiss* (1997), respectively. One can only speculate as to where his career might have gone had not pancreatic cancer brought him to an early grave at age 56.

MCCOURT, EMER. Northern Irish actress McCourt came to prominence with her endearing and empathetic performance as Goretti in *Hush-a-Bye Baby* alongside a young, unknown cast, including the singer Sinead O'Connor. After roles in **Johnny Gogan**'s *The Bargain Shop* and Ken Loach's *Riff-Raff* (1990), she had roles in *Boston Kickout* (1995) and *Sunset Heights* (1997). In 1999, she turned producer for the film *Human Traffic* (1999), which featured **Lorraine Pilkington**, and in 2003 switched roles again when Virago published her warmly received first novel, *Elvis, Jesus and Me*.

MCDONAGH, JOHN MICHAEL (1967–). While the global success of brother Martin's plays and films may have eased his entry into film production, John Michael has been understandably keen to stress that he is very much his own man, even if his first two films featured a central actor (**Brendan Gleeson**) and surreal constructions of rural Ireland familiar from his sibling's celebrated reworking of the plays of Synge. Born in London to Irish immigrant parents, like many of his background and generation, he grew up, in Morrissey's memorable phrase, with "Irish blood and an English heart." That is to say, through his immediate family and extensive periods on vacation with relatives in the west of Ireland, he encountered the place and its people with a mixture of affection and wry detachment.

Whatever leverage his sibling's success might have afforded him (Martin takes an executive producer credit on *The Guard*), McDonagh's path was not smooth, and success eluded him until well into his 40s. He wrote five novels, but none of them found a publisher. After deciding he would try to write movies, he won a scholarship to a screen-writing course at the University of Southern California and soon after secured the rights to a biography of legendary Irish Australian outlaw Ned Kelly. He seemingly got his break when his adapted screenplay was made into a 2003 film of that name, starring Heath Ledger and Orlando Bloom. Disgusted by what he described as the mutilation of his script by the film's director, he pledged to direct all future screenplays himself. His first two films—*The Guard* (2011) and *Calvary* (2014)—were set in the west of Ireland and used Brendan Gleeson to brilliant effect in communicating his ambivalent attitude toward his Irish heritage. The first built on the actor's unique talent in playing criminals who combine sociopathic tendencies with sensitivity and stupidity (familiar from films such as *I Went Down* and *In Bruges*), while the latter brilliantly flipped this in the role of a priest living under a death threat from one of his crazed parishioners. Despite a highly parochial tone and off-color humor, both not only were commercial successes in Ireland but also received hugely positive reactions in British and American markets. *The Guard* was the most successful Irish film ever, with a box office in excess of €4 million, and earned $20 million when its U.S. receipts were added, while *Calvary* earned around $17 million—enormous figures for highly local stories. However, despite domestic success, both might be said to have garnered greater critical plaudits abroad, where close-to-the-bone elements of racism, misogyny, and stereotyping in west-of-Ireland settings sailed close to the colonial representations that an indigenous cinema was supposed to counteract. Indeed, were it not for the anchoring presence of Brendan Gleeson, both films seemed to be mischievously working to test the tolerance of what **Irish Film Board** funding might support. Such an impression was enhanced by a now infamous 2014 interview in which McDonagh claimed that "I'm not a fan of Irish movies, I don't find them to be that technically accomplished and I don't find them that intelligent. . . . So I'm trying to get away from the description of the movie as an Irish film in a way." Explaining in less incendiary terms elsewhere that he set the films in Ireland only for pragmatic reasons (casting or funding) seemed either disingenuous or myopic: without its Irish setting and the recent history of the Catholic Church, *Calvary* loses much of its meaning, while *The Guard* offers a brilliant postmodern take on the troubled history of Irish emigrants and African Americans and the fetishization of the west of Ireland for the Celtic twilight. In any case, having (like Martin) attained recognition through the debunking of Irish cultural myths, John Michael set off for the United States.

He followed the controversy and inevitable backlash (critic Donald Clarke suggested that he return his IFTA award) with the appropriately titled *War on Everyone*, a U.S.-set black comedy set around two corrupt cops trying to blackmail criminals, starring Alexander Skarsgard and Michael Peña, which he again wrote as well as directed. The film was shot in New Mexico, and McDonagh again claimed that the location was incidental and pragmatic. Perhaps, but the film again offered an imaginative and punchy postmodern rethread of the western and buddy-cop genres, though the familiarity of the settings offered a less striking endeavor than *The Guard*—for Irish audiences anyway. While some critics liked the film, the sub-Tarantino screenplay was often directionless and relentlessly challenged political correctness, resulting in wildly mixed reviews. Despite an increase in production budget from his first two films to $8 million, the film's box office return was a dismal $700,000.

In interviews, McDonagh again displayed an oddly contemptuous attitude to his creative impulse. Declaring himself to be tired of writing, he claimed, "Now I want to find books where other authors have done all the work. In fact I don't want to work at all. That's what I aiming towards. I'm trying to save up enough money to go and retire to Australia at about the age of 55. . . . I just don't want to engage any more with anybody." True to his word (sort of), his next film was an adaptation of Lawrence Osborne's critically acclaimed novel *The Unforgiven*. Set in Morocco and featuring an international cast led by Ralph Fiennes and Rebecca Hall, the film's story is a "Graham

Greene meets Paul Bowles" thriller-drama around themes of First World guilt, sexual betrayal, and decadence. More literary than his preceding efforts, *The Forgiven* (2014) nevertheless reveals new dimensions to McDonagh's often disguised (Catholic?) interest in moral themes if also an uncertainty about exactly where and if he wishes to creatively explore them. Thematically, it represents a step forward even if it represents a temporary shuttering of his undeniable writing talents.

MCDONALD, PETER (1972–). McDonald considered attending acting college after secondary school but opted to study English at University College Dublin instead. He was very active in Dramsoc, the college drama society, and it was there that he first met **Conor McPherson**, with whom he has subsequently worked on several occasions. In 1992, McDonald and McPherson were key figures in the establishment of the Fly by Night theater company, which concentrated on the production of original plays.

McDonald concentrated on stage work for the first five years of his career, but his film debut, when it came, made a major impact. The film *I Went Down* was directed by **Paddy Breathnach** and scripted by Conor McPherson. Cast opposite **Brendan Gleeson**, McDonald made an instant impression as Git, conveying a winning mixture of steadfastness, intelligence, and vulnerability. After the film became a hit in Ireland, McDonald (like Gleeson) was offered a series of screen roles, and for several years his stage work took a backseat. *I Went Down* was followed by roles in Atom Egoyan's *Felicia's Journey* (1999) and **Pat Murphy**'s *Nora*, playing **James Joyce**'s brother Stanislaus in the latter film. He would work with Breathnach again in the poorly received *Blow Dry* (2001) but received better reviews for his next McPherson collaboration, *Saltwater* (2000). Adapted from McPherson's own play *This Lime Tree Bower* (in which McDonald had already performed in a British radio adaptation), McDonald played the key role of Frank, the oldest son in an Irish Italian family who resorts to desperate measures in an attempt to save his father's (Brian Cox) fish-and-chips shop from financial ruin. The same year, he took the lead role in *When Brendan Met Trudy*, playing an ineffectual secondary school teacher whose life is turned upside down when he meets a cocky petty criminal. The self-referential comedy was a major success at home and, along with *I Went Down*'s Git, is the early role for which McDonald is best known.

After appearing in a lead role opposite Christopher Walken in the poorly received independent U.S. picture *The Opportunists* (2000), he collaborated with actor/writer Michael McIllhatton in the **Radio Telefís Éireann** comedy series *Paths to Freedom* (2000). McDonald played Tomo, the long-haired guitarist in a no-hope Dublin band fronted by recidivist criminal Rats (McIllhatton). The series ran for just one short season but spawned a spin-off feature film in 2003, *Spin the Bottle*, and McDonald appeared in another McIllhatton-scripted sitcom, *Fergus's Wedding*, in 2002.

McDonald then worked to carve out a career in British television, beginning with a recurring role in the BBC series *Sea of Souls* (2004), followed by roles in *Your Bad Self* (2010) and *Titanic* (2012) and as the father Liam Moone in **Chris O'Dowd**'s delightful comedy *Moone Boy* (Sky, 2012–2015), among many others. This, in turn, has led to roles in recognizably British films, such as *The Damned United* (2009), the Morrissey biopic *England Is Mine* (2017), and the 17th-century period drama *Fanny Lye Deliver'd* (2017). In 2011, McDonald wrote and directed the short film *Pentecost*, which was nominated for an **Academy Award** for Best Short Film (2012)—a not inconsiderable achievement for a directorial debut. He returned to familiar Irish comedic territory in *The Stag* (aka *The Bachelor Weekend* [2013]), which he also cowrote with director John Butler.

Since commencing his career among the company of the "second wave" of Irish filmmakers to emerge with the reconstitution of the **Irish Film Board** in 1993 (McPherson, Breathnach, and others), McDonald has shown versatility, talent, and a flexible attitude to a career in the film and TV sectors while remaining creative and curious. Although he is now less well known as a big-screen actor than he might once have been (and certainly not beyond Ireland and the United Kingdom), his adaptability beyond the once narrow confines of "Irish film" marks him out not merely as a survivor but also as an example of how to navigate opportunities across a range of production contexts in building a sustainable career.

MCELHATTON, MICHAEL (1963–). Although more often than not Michael McElhatton's big-screen appearances see him billed fifth or sixth in the cast list, he has been a staple of Irish cinema since the 1990s, and in the shape of Rats, the inner-city rapper who graduated from the small-screen mockumentary *Paths to Freedom* (2000) to **Ian Fitzgibbon**'s *Spin the Bottle* (2004), he has created at least one modern on-screen folk hero. Born in 1963 to a middle-class Dublin family, McElhatton's first forays into acting were at Terenure College, a secondary school with an established track record in encouraging the thespian arts (other alumni have included **Donal McCann**). On leaving school, McElhatton moved to the United Kingdom, where he spent eight years training with the Royal Academy for Dramatic Arts (RADA) and working in theater. Returning to Ireland in the early 1990s, he found work onstage (he continues to intersperse theater work with his screen commitments) before making his feature debut in the **John Carney/Tom Hall**–directed *November Afternoon*. As the émigré brother who rekindles an incestuous relationship with his sister, McElhatton brought a brooding intelligence tinged with a suppressed desperation to the role.

His screen ubiquity since 1995 owes much to his versatility: a gay gangster in *Perrier's Bounty* (2009), a weaselly Republican politician in *Shadow Dancer* (2012), and the hapless banker Sam in *Intermission* (2003). This is augmented by his manifest gift for comedy as both a performer and a writer. His cocreation (with Ian Fitzgibbon) of the hapless Rats and the **Radio Telef's Éireann** series that showcased him—*Paths to Freedom*—brought something hitherto almost unknown to Irish screens: a genuinely funny comedy series. More recently, he appeared in and contributed sketch material for John Butler's underrated *Your Bad Self* (2010), which also prominently featured **Domhnall Gleeson** and **Peter McDonald** among the cast.

Since 2012, much of his screen work has been for television, often in one of the range of shows currently filmed in Ireland by overseas broadcasters. These include recurrent roles in the BBC's *The Fall* (2013), Commissioner Monro in the BBC/Amazon coproduction *Ripper Street* (2013), and, most notably, the recurring role of the malevolent Roose Bolton in *Game of Thrones* (2012–2016). That last role brought him to much wider international attention; thus, while he remains a fixture in indigenous work (see *The Hallow* [2015], *Mammal* [2016], and *Handsome Devil* [2016]), he is more likely to be encountered in an increasingly eclectic range of overseas work, including in the Norwegian drama *Mammon* (2016) (as a Central Intelligence Agency agent), as a small-town U.S. sheriff in Andre Ovredal's *The Autopsy of Jane Doe* (2016), and even a cameo in Zack Synder's *Justice League* (2017).

MCGARVEY, SEAMUS (1967–). Twice nominated for an **Academy Award** (*Atonement* [2007] and *Anna Karenina* [2012]), McGarvey is one of the most in-demand cinematographers working today and a trailblazer for the profession in Ireland. While working with still photography at school, McGarvey was encouraged by his art teacher to experiment with Super 8 film. In 1985, he left his native Armagh to do a three-year film and TV arts course at the Polytechnic of Central London, where he produced a short road movie. This attracted the attention of **Thaddeus O'Sullivan**, who offered him a camera trainee job on *December Bride*. From this, he began shooting a series of low-budget shorts funded by the British Film Institute and **Channel 4** before graduating to working with some of the emerging talents of early 1990s British cinema. These included Michael Winterbottom, on whose directorial debut, *Butterfly Kiss* (1995), McGarvey acted as cameraman, and actor/directors like Alan Rickman (*The Winter Guest* [1997]) and Tim Roth (*The War Zone* [1999]). In the late 1990s, he moved to larger-budget pictures with Stephen Frears's *High Fidelity* (2000) marking a significant step up in terms of recognition and budgets, leading to *Enigma* (2001) and *The Hours* (2003), for which he won the Evening Standard British Film Award for Best Technical/Artistic Achievement.

Atonement (2007) marked a breakthrough into next-level international recognition for McGarvey and the first of several collaborations with Joe Wright, including *The Soloist* (2008), *Anna Karenina* (2012), and *Pan* (2015). By the 2010s, he was in the front line of Hollywood cinematographers, lensing Joss Whedon's mammoth *The Avengers* (2012), another franchise reboot in *Godzilla* (2014), Sam Taylor-Wood's take on the notorious *Fifty Shades of Grey* (2015), and the turn-of-the-century spectacle *The Greatest Showman* (2017). These were interspersed with smaller, art house–inflected works, including Tom Ford's sumptuous thriller *Nocturnal Animals* (2015) and **Neil Jordan**'s *Greta* (2018).

MCGINLEY, SEAN (1956–). Born and raised in Ballyshannon, County Donegal (where his mother taught at the local primary school), McGinley trained to be a teacher at University College Galway. While working on a university theater production, he was spotted by Garry Hynes and Marie Mullen (whom McGinley later married), looking for actors to work with their new company, the Druid Theatre. McGinley duly became a key element of what was the first professional Irish theater company set up outside Dublin. He stayed with the company for nearly a decade (and has intermittently returned), helping build its studio and—in stark contrast to his subsequent screen career—was frequently cast in the role of the quiet simpleton.

In 1986, Garry Hynes, who had become director at the **Abbey Theatre**, cast him against type in a production of Tom Murphy's *Whistle in the Dark*. The role proved revelatory: McGinley was violent and domineering in a production that won him awards and toured the United Kingdom. The role dramatically altered the trajectory of his career, and he quickly secured roles in production of Eugene O'Neill's *The Iceman Cometh* and Anton Chekhov's *Three Sisters* at the Gate Theatre. This was followed by a nine-month stint at the National Theatre in London.

Although rarely receiving first billing in features, McGinley secured a steady line of small- and big-screen work throughout the 1990s as the Irish film industry gained momentum, making his first screen appearance as Father Doran in **Jim Sheridan**'s film ***The Field***. While he was subsequently cast in guest appearances in a wide range of British TV dramas, including *Minder*, *Cold Feet*, and *Waking the Dead*, his most memorable work during this period was on Irish television, where he played leading roles in three key dramas: *Family*, *Making the Cut*, and *On Home Ground*. *Family* in particular—directed in 1994 by English director Michael Winterbottom from a **Roddy Doyle** script—seared McGinley's screen persona into the consciousness of Irish audiences. He played Charlo, a seductive but spectacularly violent patriarch of a working-class Dublin family, capable of switching from apparent calm to untrammeled fury in an instant, and McGinley imbued him with a sense of constant menace.

The role made McGinley a household name in Ireland and exerted a heavy influence over his subsequent screen career. When **Radio Telefís Éireann** (RTÉ) came to produce *Making the Cut* in 1997, the station's highest-profile drama undertaking for some years, McGinley was cast in the lead role of a Waterford-based detective, and he was again the obvious choice for the station's prime-time Gaelic football drama, *On Home Ground*, in 2001.

Family also led to many offers of feature film work. Many of these played on the air of danger if not psychosis established with Charlo: his detectives in **Michael Collins** and **Dead Bodies** are alternately savage and sinister, while his sidekick roles in **Trojan Eddie** and **Resurrection Man** carry more than a whiff of menace. He was more than capable of playing outside these confines, however, playing a gentle Gardaí (police) sergeant in **The Butcher Boy** and demonstrating fine comic timing as Gary opposite **Brendan Gleeson** in **The General**. In 2002, he was cast (along with Brendan Gleeson and **Liam Neeson**) in Martin Scorsese's *Gangs of New York*, playing one of the gang leaders.

As the Irish industry shifted into a new generation of talents and production patterns (moving away from the subjects and genres in which he made his name), McGinley's career moved more toward British and Irish TV drama. His extensive small-screen credits include *Single Handed* (RTÉ, 2010), *Love-Hate* (RTÉ, 2012–2013), *Clean Break* (Acorn, 2015), *Fir Bolg* (a widely overlooked 2016 TG4 comedy series about aging traditional musicians), and the **Conor McPherson**–scripted thriller *Paula* (BBC, 2017), among others. In 2017, he returned to Druid for a critically acclaimed production of Eugene McCabe's *King of the Castle*.

MCGUCKIAN, MARY (1964–) The daughter of a well known agricultural entrepreneur, McGuckian graduated from Trinity College with an engineering degree. She subsequently moved into theater, becoming an actress and then a producer, beginning with *Macbeth*, which she devised with **Alan Gilsenan**. Since 1994, she has produced and directed more films than most Irish directors and has worked with some of the biggest stars in Hollywood. Unfortunately, many of the resultant films have had mixed reviews and limited distribution, and her work has thus often remained unseen and overlooked in critical considerations of Irish film. This is all the more notable given the status accorded to many (male) directors with a fraction of her output and ambition.

McGuckian's film debut, **Words upon the Window Pane** (1994), featuring Geraldine Chapman and Ian Richardson, is reminiscent of classic European art cinema, and she was apparently encouraged to direct the film by **Pat O'Connor** as well as **Jim Sheridan**, taking more than three years to raise the €3 million budget. Based on a W. B. Yeats one-act play, it focuses on Jonathan Swift's (Jim Sheridan) relationship with his two lovers: Stella (**Brid Brennan**) and Vanessa (**Orla Brady**). The stories of these historical figures are told by a medium, Mrs. Henderson (Geraldine James), using flashbacks.

Her next feature, *This Is the Sea* (1997), is a conventional "love across the barricades" story dealing with the Troubles and set in contemporary Belfast—a romance between Protestant Hazel (Samantha Morton) and Catholic Malachy (Ross McDade). *Best* (2000) recounts the life and career of the famous football player George Best, portrayed by McGuckian's partner, **John Lynch**. In 2004, she adapted Thornton Wilder's classic novel *The Bridge of San Luis Rey*, with the phenomenal cast of Harvey Keitel, Kathy Bates, F. Murray Abraham, and Robert De Niro. Unfortunately, the film got a roasting from American critics and did not receive a theatrical release in Ireland. *Rag Tale* (2005) focused on the activities of a down-market tabloid newspaper and its preference for celebrity gossip over more conventional news. The film used striking camera angles and staccato editing to emulate the brash style of the tabloid world and was described by one unnamed critic as "*Natural Born Killers* on speed." *Intervention* (2007) was a drama set in a rehab clinic and attracted an ensemble cast that included Charles Dance, Andy McDowell, and Kerry Fox and won the Best Feature Film award at the 2007 San Diego Film Festival but failed to secure a U.K. release. *Inconceivable* was a 2008 satirical drama about the test-tube-baby industry that McGuckian both wrote and directed. It again starred McDowell alongside Jennifer Tilly, Kerrie Fox, and Geraldine Chaplin. *The Making of Plus One* was also a satire (the third of this loose trilogy), this time centered on the independent film industry. All were critically panned.

In 2011, she remade the French hit *The Man on the Train*, with Donald Sutherland and U2 drummer Larry Mullen Jr. (making his screen-acting debut) taking the role earlier played by Johnny Halliday, and while it had a very limited release, it attracted positive press and reviews. In a change of direction, McGuckian next turned to Irish-themed biopics of very different women: *The Price of Desire* (2014), an account of the life of modernist designer Eileen Gray's life and fractious relationship with architect Le Corbusier (rekindling a working relationship with **Orla Brady**), and *A Girl from Mogadishu* (2018), the story of Ifrah Ahmed, the Somalian-born (Irish resident) campaigner against female genital mutilation in Africa who in 2010 established the immigrant support nongovernmental organization United Youth of Ireland.

As a director/producer of more than a dozen titles, McGuckian has displayed ambition—a work ethic and capacity to attract casts and to raise funds that eludes many. It remains to be seen whether she will attain the commercial and critical recognition that thus far has been beyond her grasp.

MCKENNA, SIOBHAN (1922–1986). Born in Belfast, she grew up in County Monaghan speaking fluent Gaelic and got involved with the theater in her early teens. Over the years, she became a well-known and respected actress in Ireland and Great Britain as well as in off-Broadway classics, such as *Saint Joan*. She even appeared on the cover of *Life* magazine. Although primarily a stage actress, she appeared in a number of films, including *King of Kings* (1961), *Of Human Bondage* (1964), and *Doctor Zhivago* (1965). Her most significant Irish role was in **Brian Desmond Hurst**'s 1960s version of *The Playboy of the Western World*, although at age 42, she was arguably too old to play the ingenue role of Pegeen Mike.

MCKENNA, THOMAS PATRICK (T. P.) (1929–2011). Born the son of the local auctioneer in Mullagh, County Clare, McKenna was educated in Saint Patrick's College, near Cavan Town, where he developed keen interests in Gaelic football (he would play at the county minor level) and politics. His family was staunchly Fine Gael—typical of his class and background—but although McKenna's own politics proved more flexible, he would later be a card-carrying member of the British **Labour Party**. While at school, he developed something of a reputation as a boy soprano and in his first stage performance played the female lead in a production of Gilbert and Sullivan's *The Yeoman of the Guards*. He initially worked in the Ulster Bank in Granard, Longford, and on transfer to Trim, County Meath, he became active in the local musical society. Later transferring to Dublin, he again pursued semiprofessional acting and in 1954 spent a season at the Gaiety Theatre, working under Irish theater legend Anew McMaster before becoming a full-time actor the following year when he joined the **Abbey Theatre** company, with which he remained until 1963 (frequently appearing opposite **Ray McAnally**).

His first film roles were bit parts in films shot at **Ardmore Studios**, including *A Terrible Beauty* (1960) and *The Quare Fellow* (1962), before securing more prominent roles in the Sean O'Casey biopic *Young Cassidy* (1964) and in **Joseph Strick**'s *Ulysses*, in which he memorably played Buck Mulligan. Over the course of the 1960s and 1970s, McKenna became a well-known face on British TV. This included playing three different roles in episodes of the hit show *The Avengers* between 1964 and 1968. By the mid-1960s, he was also increasingly in demand for theater productions and in 1969 spent a year in David Storey's famed Royal Court play *The Contractor*. He was also frequently cast in British roles, testimony to his talent, looks, and urbane demeanor.

By the 1970s, he was an established character actor and appeared in a number of notable films, including Sam Peckinpah's *Straw Dogs* (1971) and Lindsay Anderson's *Britannia Hospital* (1982). Although he rarely worked in Irish cinema—an eye-catching role in **Kieran Hickey**'s haunting short *A*

Child's Voice (1978) apart—he has frequently been cast in Irish roles in films produced by other countries. He worked with Joseph Strick again in 1977, playing Simon Daedalus in *Portrait of the Artist as a Young Man*. He appeared opposite Sterling Hayden in *The Outsider* (1979), in which a Vietnam veteran joins the Irish Republican Army, and he worked with **Pierce Brosnan** in *The Mannions of America* in 1981. Although TV was his least favorite medium, it was there that he found the most work with memorable roles in *The Year of the French* (**Radio Telefís Éireann** [RTÉ], 1982), *Bleak House* (BBC, 1985), and Stendhal's *The Scarlet and the Black* (BBC, 1993). He returned to RTÉ in 2004 for a stint in *Fair City*.

He made stage appearances in Dublin throughout the 1980s and 1990s in such plays as Stewart Parker's *Nightshade* at the Peacock and Anton Chekhov's *Uncle Vanya* at the Gate. His last big-screen credit was in *The Libertine* (2004) opposite Johnny Depp.

MCMAHON, CONOR. Having made horror films since he was a teenager (shooting and editing in camera on VHS), McMahon went on to study at the National Film School (Institute of Art, Design, and Technology [IADT]) before writing and directing his feature film debut, *Dead Meat*, a low-budget zombie/gore-horror film whose tiny budget and exploitation pedigree belie its significance within considerations of Irish national cinema. Not only was the film the first to link mad cow disease with zombie contagion (tagline: "It's not what you eat, it's who you eat!"), thereby overturning any lingering pastoral associations of the Irish landscape, but it was also the first Irish horror film to receive support from the **Irish Film Board**, thanks to the enthusiasm of Brendan McCarthy, then head of development (and later of **Fantastic Films**, which also specializes in horror.)

In 2010, McMahon wrote and directed the Web series *Zombie Bashers* (winning the **Radio Telefís Éireann** Storyland scheme). *Stitches* (2012), starring British comedian Ross Noble, represented something of a breakthrough in terms of budget and profile, winning Best Film at the Midnight Xtreme section of the prestigious Sitges Film Festival. *From the Dark* (2015) dealt in more familiar tropes of the horror-thriller genre, centering on a young couple who encounter an ancient force of evil while on a road trip through the Irish countryside.

MCPHERSON, CONOR (1970–). McPherson grew up on the north side of Dublin. As a teenager, he dabbled with music, playing in a number of bands before studying English and philosophy at University College Dublin (where he encountered future collaborator **Peter MacDonald** in the Drama Society). Although he began as an actor, he gradually came to concentrate more on writing and, citing David Mamet as a key influence (both share an enduring interest in the male psyche and its demons) established the Fly-by-Night theater company with MacDonald in 1992. By his mid-20s, he had already established himself at the forefront of a new generation of Irish writing talent (along with Mark O'Rowe, Martin McDonagh, and Enda Walsh) with internationally successful plays like *The Weir* (his breakthrough at just age 25), *Port Authority*, and *Shining City*, performing to full houses in London and New York, often before they even opened in Dublin. Success was not without its pressures, and in 2001, at age 29, he was hospitalized with a ruptured pancreas as a consequence of four years of heavy drinking. He kicked the alcohol habit and went on to ever greater success, driven by a prodigious work rate and unique voice.

While he has always written for film and TV, he never quite matched the success and accolades he has received in theater, where his deft wordplay has distinguished his work. His screenplay for *I Went Down* (clearly drawn from his 1994 monologue play *The Good Thief*) represented his first entry into filmmaking, and he subsequently directed an adaption of his play *This Lime Tree Bower* as *Saltwater* in 2000 starring Peter MacDonald opposite Brian Cox. He undertook one of the more substantial elements of the project to film all of **Samuel Beckett**'s works in 2000, when he directed *Endgame* with **Michael Gambon** and David Thewlis. This was followed by the much-lighter-in-tone *The Actors* (2003), a crime caper starring Michael Caine and Irish comic Dylan Moran that McPherson wrote and directed. In the meantime, he continued to score success after stage success with plays such as *The Seafarer* (2006), *Dublin Carol* (a 2008 play about alcoholism), a 2013 revival of *The Weir* (again starring Peter McDonald), and *The Night Alive* (another male ensemble about loneliness), which won the New York Drama Critics Circle Award for Best Play in 2014. *Girl from the North Country* (2017) was a drama set in Duluth, Minnesota, during the Great Depression, structured around 20 Bob Dylan songs. Initiated by Dylan himself, the endeavor has been widely and favorably compared to Thornton Wilder's *Our Town*. (By coincidence, David Bowie approached another young Irish dramatist, Enda Walsh, to write the stage play *Lazarus* the same year.)

Lately, he has turned to TV, with some success. *The Eclipse* is a 2009 supernatural drama set in Cork and produced for **Radio Telefís Éireann** with **Ciarán Hinds**, **Aidan Quinn**, and Danish actress Iben Hjejle. He wrote a well-received episode of John Banville's *Quirke* featuring **Gabriel Byrne**, but *Paula* (BBC, 2016) represented a new departure—a noir TV series in the tradition of *The Killing*—which he wrote from scratch and which achieved widespread praise. Whether this represents a new direction for the ever-inventive and busy McPherson remains to be seen.

MCSORLEY, GERARD (1950–). With one of the most familiar faces and voices in Irish film and TV, McSorley's range—and legacy—is perhaps best illustrated by two contrasting roles: the grieving Michael Gallagher, whose son has been killed in the bombing of *Omagh* (2004), and the mysterious and possibly psychotic Father Todd Unctious in *Father Ted* ("A Christmassy Ted," 1996). To these and other roles, he brought a glint-eyed intensity that seemed of a piece with his Northern Irish background and made him a ubiquitous presence in the "second wave" (1993–2005) of Irish film and TV.

A native of Tyrone, McSorley attended the famed St. Columba's school in Derry (past pupils include Seamus Heaney, John Hume, and Brian Friel), and it was there that he first considered acting before attending Queen's University Belfast and then moving to Dublin, where he was cast in the stage drama *The True Story of the Horrid Popish Plot*, directed by Hilton Edwards at the Gate Theatre. More work with the Gate followed, but he was also involved in the **Project Theatre** during the mid-1970s during the tenure of **Jim Sheridan**—who would memorably cast him in several feature films—and his brother Peter. He joined the **Abbey Theatre** in 1981 but left before his contract ended, finding it too confining.

He had in any case already begun to branch into screen work; he appeared in **Joe Comerford**'s *Withdrawal* (1982) and had a small role in **Neil Jordan**'s *Angel*. He also made appearances in the British television programs *The Irish R.M.* and *Bergerac*. Given the sporadic nature of screen production in Ireland in the 1980s, the bulk of his work in that decade remained on the stage. However, when Irish film production began to take off in the early 1990s, McSorley quickly established himself as a key talent in the indigenous industry. In 1995 alone, he appeared in eight major productions, including *Moondance*, *Braveheart*, and *Nothing Personal*, but a well-honed cameo in Jim Sheridan's *In the Name of the Father* was the most important of these roles. Although his screen time was limited to a couple of minutes, his portrayal of the psychologically subtle policeman was among the most memorable in a film heavily populated with impressive performances.

But it also led to a measure of typecasting, and McSorley subsequently seems to have appeared in virtually every film made relating to the Troubles, including *Michael Collins* (as Cathal Brugha), *Bloody Sunday*, and, again for Sheridan, *The Boxer*. In *Omagh*, he played the real-life figure of Michael Gallagher, who lost his son in a terrorist bombing that killed 28 people in 1998. In a remarkably sympathetic performance, McSorley's character becomes a proxy for the other grieving relatives, and much of the picture is carried on his shoulders.

Gallagher could hardly have been more different from the character McSorley portrayed in his previous performance in Joel Schumacher's *Veronica Guerin*. McSorley had already appeared in two productions about Dublin gangster Martin Cahill—a BBC production called *Vicious Circle*

(1999) and **Thaddeus O'Sullivan**'s *Ordinary Decent Criminal*—but in *Veronica Guerin*, he took on the role of John Gilligan, the Dublin criminal who was ultimately imprisoned for his role in Guerin's murder. His portrayal of a career criminal is horribly fascinating, repulsive yet compelling, especially in a scene where he threatens harm to Guerin's young son.

With the arrival of the new millennium, McSorley became a less visible screen presence. Although he remained busy and found work in larger-budget work, such as *Blood Creek* (2009), *Robin Hood* (2010), and *War Horse* (2011), he was more often cast in small roles and increasingly in episodic Irish-language television and short films. We might speculate a combination of professional and personal influences on such developments. First, in the aftermath of the Good Friday Agreement, the industry moved on from the topics on the Troubles with which he was closely identified and most lauded. Additionally, long-form TV took over much of the space taken by dramatic Irish film in the 1990s, and he has not pursued that shift in practices in the way that some other actors have. Finally, newspaper headlines revealed that he was experiencing an ongoing series of personal difficulties, including bad health, financial troubles, and treatment for alcoholism. Nevertheless, he remains in demand and clearly relishes working across a variety of smaller-scale projects. For many, however, he will always be Todd Unctious, the interloper and false friend of Father Ted, intent on stealing the Golden Cleric Award.

MEANEY, COLM (1953–). Sometimes referred to as the "first Irishman in space," Meaney is most popularly associated with *Star Trek*, holding the unique distinction of having appeared in 14 seasons of the *Next Generation* and *Deep Space Nine* series between 1987 and 1999. Relying a hale and hearty Dublin persona, he is also one of the busiest and hardest-working screen actors to have come out of Ireland, with a range and recognition that encompasses Irish, American, and European big- and small-screen credits.

He grew up in Finglas on the north side of Dublin and attended both the Dublin Drama Centre and the **Abbey Theatre** Training School in the late 1960s and early 1970s. Based in London for most of the 1970s, he developed an impressive stage curriculum vitae and toward the end of the decade made a number of smaller television appearances, beginning with a role in the classic British police series *Z-Cars*. In 1982, he moved to New York and worked on Broadway, as well as making appearances in several TV series, including *Moonlighting* and *Remington Steele* (opposite **Pierce Brosnan**) before securing the recurring role of Miles O'Brien on *Star Trek: The Next Generation*. When *Deep Space Nine* began in 1993, he negotiated the right to do feature film work while working on the television series. As a result, he was able to appear in two or three features a year through the mid-1990s.

Although he had appeared in an American Public Broadcasting System production of J. M. Synge's *The Playboy of the Western World* in 1983 (opposite then wife Bairbre Dowling), his first significant Irish feature role came in 1987, when he was cast in a minor role in **John Huston**'s *The Dead*. Smaller Hollywood roles followed in *Dick Tracy* (1990), *Die Hard 2* (1990), and Alan Parker's *Come See the Paradise* (1990) before he took on the role of Jimmy Rabbitte Sr. in Parker's adaptation of **Roddy Doyle**'s novel *The Commitments*. The boisterous working-class father with a heart of gold seemed tailor made for him and remains the role with which he is most readily associated in Ireland. Although he played a minor part in *The Commitments*, he was the unquestioned star of the show when he reprised the character in *The Snapper* and *The Van*.

Although based for a long period in the United States and more recently in Spain, Meaney has always maintained a home on the north side of Dublin, and this dual residence is reflected in a long career in Irish film stretching back to *Into the West* and *Last of the High Kings* and included a classic comic turn as a New Age Irish music–loving detective in *Intermission*. One of his most substantial Irish roles is also one of his most overlooked: playing the eponymous Harry Maloney in the surreal *How Harry Became a Tree*, a man obsessed with besting his rival (**Adrian Dunbar**).

A long list of roles in low-budget U.K./Irish feature comedies includes *Alan Partridge: Alpha Papa* (2013), *Halal Daddy* (2017), *The Yank* (2014), *The Stand Off* (2012), and *Get Him to the Greek* (2010), among many others. Although he has generally played comic characters in his Irish work (with notable exceptions in films such as *Kings* and *Parked*, both of which he carries with great skill), he has secured a broader range of work in the United States. Thus, he has played a Federal Bureau of Investigation agent in *Con Air* (1997), a small-town mayor in *Mystery, Alaska* (1999), and a pimp in *Claire Dolan* (1998). He has also maintained a presence on American television screens, playing an occasional role in *Stargate: Atlantis* and appearing in *Law and Order: Criminal Intent*. Illustrative of his range and of the demand for his services in the United States are turns as H. L. Mencken in the Scopes trial drama *Alleged* (2010), in *Hell on Wheels* (AMC, 2011–2016), and as theater impresario James Burbage in *Will* (2017), the TNT steampunk period drama that imagines William Shakespeare's early years in London.

MERLIN FILMS. John Boorman and well-known accountant Kieran Corrigan founded Merlin Films in 1989 as a production company and vehicle for raising **Section 481** funds for other production companies. Corrigan (b. 1954) studied economics and law at Trinity College, later qualifying as a barrister. From Trinity, he joined Arthur Andersen, trained as an accountant, and specialized in tax law, a field in which he subsequently established his own consultancy.

By the 1990s, he had an established profile in Irish business circles and was appointed to the board of the Industrial Development Authority, sat on the Custom House Docks Development Board, and chaired the National Building Agency. In many respects, Corrigan can be seen as a pioneering figure in Irish film finance, and although he has retained an interest in non-film activities since 1989 (unsuccessfully bidding as part of a consortium for the controversial national mobile phone license that was won by Denis O'Brien in 1995), he is widely recognized for his skills and influence as a film financier and producer.

Corrigan became involved with film and John Boorman when he advised the director on the funding of *Excalibur* in 1981. In 1987, Corrigan and two partners, Philip King and Nuala O'Connor, set up Hummingbird Productions to produce a major documentary series on the impact of Irish music overseas, *Bringing It All Back Home*. Two years later, he and Boorman created Merlin Films, through which Boorman has produced the bulk of his films, including *I Dreamt I Woke* (1991), *Two Nudes Bathing* (1995), and the John Le Carré adaptation *The Tailor of Panana* (2001) with **Pierce Brosnan**. From an Irish perspective, Merlin's most notable Boorman production has been *The General*. Unusually for an Irish production company, Merlin financed the film largely independently (as opposed to funding it through presales), borrowing much of the budget from a bank on the basis of estimates of box office sales and Corrigan's own reputation. As a consequence, the company owned the rights to the film when it was completed and was able to sell it across a number of territories. Subsequent credits include *In My Country* (2004) starring Samuel L. Jackson and Juliette Binoche and *The Tiger's Tail*, a Celtic Tiger satire also starring **Brendan Gleeson**. Numerous Merlin/Boorman projects have been announced but failed to materialize; in 2002, it was announced that Boorman would make *Knight's Castle*, a $35 million family fantasy movie, while in 2012, it was reported that Corrigan and Boorman had secured financing for a €20 million *Wizard of Oz*–based film to be made in France.

In addition to producing non-Boorman pictures such as **Angela Mooney Dies Again** and **This Is My Father**, Merlin actively sought to expand its interests into a range of media-related areas. In 1992, in a joint venture with finance firm Media Assets, Merlin became co-owner of the Dublin-based Don Bluth Animation Studio, which, although in financial difficulty at the time, was the largest non-Disney feature **animation** production company in the world. (In 1994, Merlin unsuccessfully attempted to purchase the studios outright.) The group also includes a music division—Hummingbird Records—and in 2001, the group acquired the long-established Dublin publisher Wolfhound Press, which became part of Merlin Publishing. In 2003, Corrigan became a director of Concorde Anois Teoranta, **Roger Corman**'s low-budget film studio located in Connemara. Corrigan largely engineered Corman's decision to establish in Ireland, helping to access an initial $10 million line of credit for the "king of B movies."

For a time, the company maintained offices in Dublin, London, Los Angeles, and Shannon. The last of these is explained by Corrigan's involvement with Alliance International Releasing, a Shannon-based film distribution company owned by Canadian film production company Atlantic Alliance. Shannon was also a base for Corrigan's dealings with Cinar, one of the largest animation producers in the world.

METROPOLITAN FILMS. *See* OCTAGON FILMS.

MICHAEL COLLINS **(1997).** The film that consolidated **Neil Jordan**'s status as Ireland's premier national filmmaker. It traces Collins's involvement in the establishment of the state from the 1916 Easter Rising to the War of Independence (1919–1921), the Civil War (1922–1923), and the establishment of the border between Northern Ireland and the Irish Free State. Any discussion of history in Ireland almost inevitably has a resonance for modern-day politics, but these moments in particular are regarded as central in modern Irish history and have particular significance for the subsequent conflict in Northern Ireland.

The film's release during the nascent Northern peace process unsurprisingly prompted much debate about its historical accuracy and its meaning for contemporary national politics. According to some critics, not since *The Dawn* (1936) and its historical representation of rebellion has Irish nationalist history been visualized so effectively, while for others, the film represents a revisionist history designed to validate contemporary political perspectives and obfuscate difficult historical issues.

Certainly, Jordan takes some liberties with historical accuracy to make the story fit the classic narrative structure. Some of these are relatively minor, such as the amalgamation of several real-life individuals to create **Stephen Rea**'s character, Ned Broy. Others are more open to question: the Croke Park killings of 1920, although terrible, did not involve armored cars, as depicted in the film, but rather were carried out as the army and police searched for Irish Republican Army assassins.

In any case, Jordan's masterly use of the narrative techniques of Hollywood cinema and the gangster genre lends a dynamic energy and emotional depth to complex historical events. In particular, the relationship between Collins (**Liam Neeson**) and his friend Harry Boland (**Aidan Quinn**) is the film's principal affective drive, functioning to personify the two opposing sides that fought over the partition of the island in the Civil War.

At a glance, the real Collins is arguably the most cinematic figure of modern Irish history: a young warrior and lover who took on a massive empire and forced it to the negotiating table before being tragically killed in his prime. Thus, the Collins of Neeson and Jordan is a likable, rabble-rousing man more comfortable with the gun than the pen. The Collins of history, however, was also the first Dail's minister for finance, whom historians widely regard as the most effective member of that first Irish cabinet. In part, the film's portrayal of him seems prompted by the need to contrast him with his eventual nemesis, de Valera, portrayed by Alan Rickman as an ascetic, aloof, and intellectual figure. It is only when the plot seeks to address modern politicians by stressing Collins's attempt to take the gun out of Irish politics after the treaty that a more bucolic figure emerges.

Similarly, although the casting of Julia Roberts as Kitty Kiernan, Collins's fiancée, was clearly done with an eye to the American market, it indirectly resulted in an underwriting of her character. In the final scene, while Kitty is shopping for her wedding dress, her fiancé is being ambushed. This can be read as symbolizing, albeit through a highly conventional Hollywood cliché, selfless sacrifice by all who loved this enigmatic rebel hero. Collins was sent to negotiate a peace settlement against his wishes. He believed that the treaty, which included the partition of Ireland and having to swear an oath of allegiance to the British monarchy, was the best deal Ireland could get from Britain at that time. While accepted by a majority of the people in a vote, this set in train a violent civil war. De Valera and his followers were unable to accept such a compromise or stepping-stone, while Collins pleaded for the resolution in Anglo-Irish conflicts. The working out of this schism has taken a number of violent decades. Many critics assert that the film remains an important representational and historical marker of the national political struggle.

However, taking the story as just that—a story—and judging *Michael Collins* simply as a piece of filmmaking, one cannot but be impressed by Jordan's sweep and verve. *Michael Collins* is arguably the first epic of Irish cinema, dwarfing even Jim Sheridan's passionate *In the Name of the Father* by dint of its scope of ambition, which recalls the mythmaking ability of a David Lean.

MICHAEL INSIDE (2017). Joe Comerford's *Down the Corner* is worth invoking as a precedent when approaching the films of Frank Berry: his 2011 documentary *Ballymun Lullaby*; his feature debut, *I Used to Live Here* (2014); and, in particular, his latest film, *Michael Inside* (2017). Each has also emerged from workshops arranged by Berry with working-class community groups, combining an open and respectful attitude to his subjects with skillful and effective storytelling. His films thus both take up and diverge from that earlier moment in Irish film history, displaying an admirable and all-too-rare commitment to the issues and social circumstances of the communities he depicts (and from which draws some of his nonprofessional actors) while eschewing the fragmentary and more formally experimental elements of first-wave cinema.

With *Michael Inside*, Berry turns to themes of crime and punishment among urban youth, developed through the Irish Prison Service's "Pathways Programme." Borrowing tropes from the prison drama genre and recalling Jacques Audiard's *A Prophet* (2009), among other intertexts, the narrative centers on a young male protagonist, Michael McCrea (Dafhyd Flynn, a nonprofessional actor also seen in *I Used to Live Here*), who lives with his grandfather Francis (Lalor Roddy) and, through a combination of naïveté and circumstance, finds himself minding drugs for his friend's older brother. Following a police raid, he is caught and sentenced to three months in prison, to the profound upset of Francis. The film's second act takes place "inside," where the inexperienced and vulnerable Michael is marked by the seductive and dangerous David (Moe Dunford), who grooms him as an accomplice by offering protection from other prisoners. The conditionality of that "protection" is revealed when David stages an attack on another prisoner but insists that Michael inflict extreme violence on the helpless inmate. In this brutally Darwinian environment, roles of perpetrator and victim are reversed, and Michael's relative blamelessness for his earlier crime as well as his grandfather's hopes for him emerging unscathed become irredeemable. A brief third act plays out the fated consequences of this sordid slide from innocence to experience.

Nuanced yet entirely accessible, with compelling performances from all three leads but especially Flynn, *Michael Inside* was an ethical and increasingly necessary act of empathy and understanding at a time of deepening social inequality, highly gendered and violent criminality, and class-coded social media outrage.

***MICKYBO AND ME* (2005).** Starring **Adrian Dunbar** and **Ciarán Hinds**, the Terry Loane–directed film tells the story of two young boys in 1970s Belfast at a critical time during the Troubles. The two escape the confines of their urban world by becoming their heroes: Butch Cassidy and the Sundance Kid. Micky Boyle, otherwise known as "Mickybo" (John Joe McNeill), plays a kid who is always up to some mischief and striving for attention in a large Catholic family, particularly from his mother (Julie Walters) and father (Dunbar). Johnjo (Neill Wright), on the other hand, is an only son who receives lots of attention from his guilt-ridden father (Hinds), who is having an affair. Through their imagination, they flee the imploding city for the freedom of the Australian Outback with dramatic results. While the ending might seem out of place in such a lighthearted children's adventure, it still serves to underscore the pervasive influence of the Troubles in Northern Ireland on all the characters' lives as it disrupts the possibility of community solidarity.

THE MIRACLE (1991). Made in the aftermath of Neil Jordan's ill-fated efforts to "crack" Hollywood with *High Spirits* and *We're No Angels*, this modest story successfully evokes the tone and mood of a small seaside town near Dublin where a young man, Jimmy Coleman (Niall Byrne), is trying to resolve family tensions. His home life is difficult with his musical father (**Donal McCann**) unfulfilled in life and unable to engage with his son's ambitions. When a glamorous older woman, Renee Baker (Beverly D'Angelo), arrives in town, Jimmy follows her with his girlfriend Rose (Lorraine Pilkington) and quickly becomes infatuated. Renee is eventually revealed to be Jimmy's mother, who his father had claimed was dead. Based on Jordan's short story "Night in Tunisia" (1976), *The Miracle* is thwarted by a heavy-handed Oedipal subtext, but in spite of its shortcomings, the film's atmosphere remains memorable and engaging, marking a development in Jordan's skills and a return to more personal subjects.

MISE ÉIRE (I AM IRELAND) (1959). Directed by **George Morrison**, *Mise Éire* was the first of a projected trilogy of films on Irish history (and, in particular, the struggle for independence) covering the period 1896–1939. A second film, *Saoirse?* (Freedom?), was released in 1961, but the third film was shelved. Produced by **Gael Linn**, an independent but state-aided Irish-language and cultural organization, *Mise Éire* was the first feature-length (90 minutes or longer) Irish-language film.

The film traces the development of Ireland's revolutionary movement between 1896 and 1918, exclusively relying on found footage from the period (most of which had to be sourced outside Ireland). The film divides its treatment into three sections: "Awakening" (1896–1915), "The Rising" (1916), and "The Dawning of the Day" (1917–1918). While the film makes widespread use of newspaper headlines and an Irish-language voice-over (the former functioning as a sort of intertitle system for non-Irish speakers), a knowledge of Irish history is presumed on the part of the filmmaker that may not be there for the contemporary or nonnative viewer. This history is well known, but in brief, it follows the rise of Sinn Féin in the first decade of the 20th century against the waning power of the Irish Parliamentary Party (IPP), noting too the rise of (unsuccessful) revolutionary wars against the British Empire in the same period (most notably the Boer War). As the narrative enters the 1910s, the Unionist reaction to the passing of the Third Home Rule Bill (setting up the Ulster Volunteers) is mirrored by the establishment of the Irish Volunteers. While the bill is shelved with the outbreak of World War I and the majority of the Irish Volunteers join the British army, two years later, in 1916, the Easter Rising breaks out in Dublin. The rising is swiftly crushed, but Irish public opinion, initially hostile to the rising, turns to support the rebels when their leaders are summarily executed by the British in its aftermath. In the closing segment of the film, Sinn Féin's political success in the 1918 general election is interpreted by the film as offering strong evidence that the tide of history is turning the way of Irish nationalism.

The film's release coincided with a key moment in modern Ireland with the publication of the Whitaker Report (1958) and the election of Sean Lemass, and, seeming to coincide with such modern impulses, the film made it possible to celebrate the foundation of the state in a way that would have been harder to imagine previously. As a piece of **documentary**, *Mise Éire* is far from the objective recording of actuality ideal held up by many. Although **Louis Marcus**, who acted as one of the assistant editors on the film, argued that the raw footage had not been slanted politically, this is hard to square with the film's mode of representation, which nails its political colors to the mast. While the Sinn Féin movement is venerated as holding the torch of "true nationalism," it is implied that the IPP was a dupe of the British Empire, especially in the wake of IPP leader John Redmond's call to the Irish Volunteers to join the British army. Meanwhile, the Ulster Unionist case is simply not put forward: they remain characterized as the "invaders."

Judged as a piece of propaganda (or nation-building exercise), *Mise Éire* is pretty effective. The painstakingly assembled footage is cleverly used to tell a linear narrative: in the absence of Irish material from the 1890s, the film instead uses contemporaneous Boer War footage to suggest a parallel struggle against the empire. Furthermore, director Morrison was clearly a student of the Eisensteinian school of symbolism: while the British Empire in Ireland is represented by stone statues of snarling lions, the image of Ireland as timeless and indomitable and indeed the persistence of the "Irish revolutionary spirit" are symbolized by footage of waves crashing and breaking against rocks on the Irish shore. Composer **Seán Ó Riada** was at the peak of his abilities, his score an integral part of the film's meaning, effect, and success. *Mise Eire* has subsequently become one of the classic pieces of 20th-century Irish music, classical in form yet undeniably Celtic in tone.

MISKELLY, WILLIAM (BILL) (1940–1991). Born in Belfast, Miskelly joined the BBC in 1967 initially as a film editor. He later moved to directing and, before parting company with the broadcaster, in the early 1980s directed more than 40 documentaries and dramas. In 1983, he and Marie Jackson established Aisling Films as an independent production company.

The first Aisling production was *The Schooner* (1983), a one-hour drama for television based on a short story by Michael McLaverty. The story followed an elderly woman's final coming to terms with the loss of her husband at sea many years before, a process brought about by her encounter with her young nephew.

In 1985, the company produced **The End of the World Man**, an ecologically themed children's film partially financed by the **Irish Film Board**. Well made from an intelligent script with its heart in the right place, the film is most impressive for the absence of any sense that the filmmakers are talking down to children. However, perhaps the most remarkable fact about the film is the almost total absence of any comment or explicit reference to the political environment of Northern Ireland. Perhaps inevitably, the Troubles do have an impact on the narrative, but they do so in an almost incidental manner. *The End of the World Man* reminded viewers that life in the six counties had another side and that shooting and bombings did not represent the only normality.

As was the case for so many Irish filmmakers, the closure of the Irish Film Board made it difficult for Miskelly to continue in feature production. Sadly, by the time the board was reestablished in 1993, he had prematurely passed away. The **Northern Ireland Film and Television Commission**, together with Miskelly's family, has commemorated his work by establishing an annual film script award in his name.

MISTER JOHN **(2013).** Writer/director/editor/producer team Desperate Optimists (Christine Molloy and Joe Lawlor) construct a contemporary variation on Conrad's *Heart of Darkness*. Unusually for an Irish film but in keeping with its producers' background as visual artists, it takes a highly aestheticized approach to its subject and mode of address. Jerry (**Aidan Gillen**) travels to Singapore, where his brother John has died in a drowning accident. There, he encounters, for the first time, John's wife Kim and their daughter. Jerry begins to inhabit his brother's life: wearing his clothes, sleeping in his bed, and taking responsibility for John's escort bar business. Jerry's immersion in this new identity is driven partly by circumstance—his luggage has gone astray—and partly by unhappiness with his old life, including a marriage damaged by his wife's infidelity (itself a response to Jerry's introspection).

Mister John (the title is taken from the name of his brother's bar) visually reflects Jerry's inner state through formally constructed static shots focusing on motionless characters. Gillen's trademark taciturn screen presence creates a stillness that is less a depiction of calm serenity than it is of a character in stasis. As the days and weeks pass, Jerry gradually comes to occupy his brother's persona, becoming both more emotionally expressive and finding the distance to reflect on his own dysfunctional character in the process. As he peers into the depths of a tropical rain forest, the camera adopts a Lynchian perspective, moving farther and farther into his inner darkness. This movement is accompanied by flashbacks to Jerry's former domestic life: repeated shots show him descending the staircase from his sleeping daughter's room into the darkness of the ground floor occupied by his wife.

Although clearly played as Irish by Gillen (as is the character of his brother heard in flashbacks), the film makes little of Jerry's specific origins beyond his status as a white male westerner in a postcolonial setting. Like a character from Conrad or Greene, he is a man adrift geographically, culturally, and existentially. Although the film makes much of the lush beauty of rural Singapore (whose national film commission partly funded it), it resists becoming enthralled by its exoticism. Singapore is presented as far from a paradise: the legacy of colonialism is hinted at, as Jerry's progress is lubricated by the omnipresence of, in addition to Mandarin and Malay, English-language speakers. Postcolonial exploitation persists in other forms. Although Jerry clearly contemplates swapping his old existence for a new one in the Orient, he is ambivalent about the manner in which the urban economy seems oriented around the exploitation of young women by both locals and middle-aged Europeans, a business his brother also engaged in. Even if, as the bar employees emphasise, John was a relatively benign boss, Jerry realizes that he was something akin to a pimp.

The film's treatment of the sexual economy operates on a number of levels. Although discreet about the precise nature of the transactions between the girls and customers in Mister John's bar, the film touches on a discussion over the legitimacy of sex work as a form of labor. It also engages in a parallel discussion of sex as currency in its exploration of Jerry's marriage: for Jerry's wife, sexual infidelity functioned as a means of agency, forcing her husband to confront the nature of their relationship.

Built largely around Gillen's subtle but compelling central performance, the film offers little in the way of a narrative resolution. Jerry has come through an emotional voyage, but it remains unclear as to what the final destination may be.

MONTGOMERY, FLORA (1974–). Born in Northern Ireland and for a period considered a rising star, she is most recognized for her commanding role as Trudy in *When Brendan Met Trudy*. Her feisty performance and ability to creatively speak to a new generation has made her marketable. She also had a major role in *Goldfish Memory* and made numerous appearances in television films and series, such as *The Bill*. An appearance in the 2006 sequel to *Basic Instinct* hinted at the possibility of a Hollywood breakthrough, but that film's poor critical reception dampened such prospects. Although still active in U.K. and Irish television drama (with appearances in the Inspector Morse spin-off *Endeavour* [2012] and briefly opposite **Gabriel Byrne** in *Quirke* [2014]), her subsequent feature film work has been limited to smaller roles in *Speed Dating* (2007) and *The Daisy Chain* (2008).

MOONDANCE (1994). This rite-of-passage story, based on *The White Hare* by Francis Stuart and directed by Dagmar Hirtz, stars Ian Shaw, **Rúaidhrí Conroy**, and Jasmine Russell. Two brothers, 21-year-old Patrick and 14-year-old Dominic, lead an idyllic existence, living alone in a rambling country house together with their greyhound. They spend endless days swimming, fishing, and hunting while their mother is in Africa. Eventually, they make the acquaintance of a young German girl, Anya, who becomes their tutor and eventually comes to Dublin with them. The film was not critically well received: the German–Irish production was perhaps overly focused on presenting local (admittedly magnificent) scenery to the detriment of developing the main characters. The overall story is certainly fascinating, but ultimately the film reads as unfinished.

MOORE, JOHN (1970–). Born in Dundalk, he developed a fascination with film while pursuing a production course at the Dublin Institute of Technology, after which he set up the ClingFilms Production Company with several graduates, including **Damian O'Donnell**, going on to produce several award-winning short films and commercials. Moore got his big break when Hollywood executives saw his Sega games advertisement during the 1999 MTV Music Video Awards and was invited to direct *Behind Enemy Lines* (2001), a taut war story based on the recent Bosnian struggle, starring Gene Hackman and Owen Wilson. This represented an unprecedented career leg up for a young Irish director at the time, and Moore embraced the opportunity with obvious relish and energy. *Behind Enemy Lines* went on to recoup more than twice its production budget at the box office. Despite access to enormous production and advertising budgets by Irish standards, his fortunes since then have been somewhat mixed. The $60 million remake of *Flight of the Phoenix* (2005), starring Dennis Quaid, was a flop, although the remake of *The Omen* (2006) fared significantly better, notwithstanding the fact that it was drawing on a cult classic. *Max Payne* (2008) was a high-concept neo-noir action film based on a video game of the same name that did reasonably well at the global box office in the face of poor reviews from critics and fans. However, ambitions for a franchise failed to materialize. This run led to an offer to direct *A Good Day to Die Hard* (2013), the fifth and final installment of the iconic Bruce Willis franchise and the zenith of opportunities for any action director. It could not fail to pull in massive box office, but reviews again were poor, with many judging it the weakest of the storied franchise for a perceived lack of characterization and uninspiring action sequences. The cautionary thriller *I.T.* (2016) (again a remake of *Firewall* [2006]) starring **Pierce Brosnan** (playing Mike Regan in the angry middle-aged mold of late **Liam Neeson** with an Irish accent) failed to make any critical or commercial impact.

MORRISON, GEORGE (1922–). Born in County Waterford, George Morrison became interested in still photography in the mid-1930s and shot his first film in 1942 with a never-completed 16-mm adaptation of Bram Stoker's *Dracula.* After the war, he became involved in documentary production, working with the film company run by Michael MacLiammoir and Hilton Edwards of the Gate Theatre. After attending the 1952 meeting of the International Federation of Film Archives in Amsterdam, his pioneering work on cataloging Irish-related archival material began. This would constitute the basis of his most famous work, *Mise Éire*, produced for **Gael Linn** and completed in 1959. Although Morrison described the technique of using exclusively "found footage" to recount the Irish struggle for independence in the film (and its 1961 sequel *Saoirse?*) as entirely novel, there were arguably several antecedents for this, most notably Esfir Shub's seminal 1927 documentary *The Fall of the Romanov Dynasty* (also the first film of a projected trilogy—celebrating the rise to power of the Bolshevik party—using existing footage).

Morrison continued to work as a filmmaker and archivist after these montage films. Subsequent productions included Rebellion (1963), *These Stones Remain* (1971), *Two Thousand Miles of Peril* (1972), *Look to the Sea* (1974), and *Dublin Day* (2007), the last a celebration of Joycean Dublin that he produced at the age of 83. In 2007, Morrison was the subject of Ciarin Scott's tender film biography *Waiting for the Light*. In 2012, he was awarded an Industry Lifetime Contribution Award by the **Irish Film and Television Academy**, which also named its annual documentary feature film award in his honor. In 2017, President Michael D. Higgins bestowed on him the title of Saoi of Aosdána, the highest honor in the Irish arts world, in recognition of his work as "an archivist, a writer, a photographer and, above all, a great pioneer and innovator."

MORRISSEY, EAMON (1943–). Morrissey made a household name for himself as a comic actor working on series like *Hall's Pictorial Weekly* on **Radio Telefís Éireann** and, more recently, *Father Ted*, *Ballykissangel*, and *The Irish R.M.* Major roles in film include his well-honed comic persona in *Eat the Peach*, *Philadelphia, Here I Come*, *How to Cheat in the Leaving Certificate*, *This Is My Father*, and, most recently, *The Trouble with Sex*

(2005). Since 2005, he has again become a staple on the small screen, most notably in his five-year stint (2012–2017) as Cass Cassidy on the popular Irish soap *Fair City*.

***THE MOST FERTILE MAN IN IRELAND* (2001).** Eamonn Manley, a Catholic, lives in post–cease-fire Belfast, working in a dating agency, and is in love—initially unrequited—with a local Protestant girl, Rosie, who works in a funeral parlor. Meanwhile, Eamonn finds that his loins are unusually productive: each of his romantic encounters leads to conception. This light-hearted comedy, directed by Dudi Appleton, challenges conventional representations and perceptions of Northern Ireland by placing Eamonn's fertility against the backdrop of a conflict in which the Catholic nationalists are "outbreeding" their Unionist counterparts. This film is particularly interesting for its sympathetic representation of Loyalist culture; for example, the "Glorious Twelfth," generally understood by nationalists as an exclusivist demonstration of triumphalism, is depicted here as more akin to the St. Patrick's Day celebration.

MOXLEY, GINA. Originally from Cork, this multitalented actor/writer began her film-acting career with Fergus Tighe's 1987 production *The Clash of the Ash* and went on to various roles in *Joyriders*, *Hear My Song*, *The Sun, the Moon and the Stars*, *The Butcher Boy*, *This Is My Father*, and *Snakes and Ladders*, the last of which was written around two characters created by Moxley and her costar, Pom Boyd. However, although she still appears on small and big screens, the focus of her career since 1996 seems to be the stage. In that year, her debut as a playwright in *Danti-Dan*, a tale of sexual awakening in 1970s Cork, produced by the Rough Magic company, became a massive critical hit, winning a Stewart Parker award and transferring to London after a successful Irish run. A film version of the play—apparently to be directed by Moxley herself—has long been in gestation. Meanwhile, she has continued to write plays, including *Tea Set* for Fishamble Productions and *A Heart of Cork* as part of that city's 2005 Festival of Culture, and has appeared in a variety of often small but memorable character roles in film and TV, including *Out of Here* (2011), *Stay* (2013), *Small-town* (TV3), *Titanic: Blood and Steel* (BBC, 2011), and *Game of Thrones* (HBO, 2016). In 2002, her work was included in the *Field Day Anthology of Irish Writing*.

MULDOWNEY, BRENDAN (1969–). A graduate of the Institute of Art, Design, and Technology, Muldowney directed nine award-winning short films between 1994 and 2006, including *The Ten Steps* (2004) and *Final Journey* (2006), before finally making his low-budget fiction feature debut with the psychological thriller *Savage* in 2008. While not entirely convincing as a narrative and noticeably weak in its female characterization, this tale of male revenge was striking in theme and visual execution. It centers on a shy press photographer, Paul (Darren Healy), who is viciously assaulted by youths as he makes his way home one night. (In an ironic metanarrative, Healy was convicted of assaulting and causing the death of a man in Dublin in 2003 and sentenced to four years' imprisonment soon after the film's release.) The assault utterly changes Paul's outlook, and he submits to a rigorous physical and character transformation in its wake: shaving his hair, working out, and cultivating aggression and fearlessness. This leads to an inevitable though still shocking climax with clear debts to the ultraviolence of 1970s films, such as *Taxi Driver*, *A Clockwork Orange*, and *Straw Dogs*. Shot in steel-gray hues by Tom Comerford, *Savage* engages with the cinematic legacy of such films from an Irish perspective by understanding Paul's path to violence as a "manning up" (a term given currency through Kay Hymowitz's 2011 book) born of necessity in the mean streets of contemporary Dublin. In this underexplored and troubling account of Irish masculinity, he is victim turned perpetrator, and his narcissism is a survival mechanism in the new millennium.

It was another five years before Muldowney was able to bring his macabre second feature, *Love Eternal* (2013), to the screen, a delay perhaps attributable to the unusual nature of its story and source: the cult novel *Loving the Dead* by Japanese horror-supernatural author Kei Oishi. Eventually financed as an Irish–Luxembourg–Dutch–Japanese coproduction, the film again centered on an estranged young male (Robert de Hoog) who has watched his father die and discovered a female classmate who had hanged herself, triggering a withdrawal from the world and a fascination with online suicide forums that, inevitably, leads to his own death wish. Having decided to kill himself by inhaling exhaust fumes, he encounters a family embarking on a similar path and attempts to rescue one of them. Although he is unsuccessful, this brings him back into the world and leads to a subsequent encounter with a grieving young mother (Pollyana McIntosh) of a similarly dark outlook with whom he forms an unusual and uncertain relationship. While the film's story remained recognizably Japanese in tone, its international financing led to casting and location decisions that robbed it of any sense of cultural specificity or resonance. In this sense, it might be grouped with similarly "transnational" Irish films of the period, such as *Room*, *Glassland*, and *Mammal*, that aimed at reducing markers of Irishness in an effort to both placate financiers and attract international audiences. Nevertheless, it was highly original in conception, displayed characteristic delicacy by talented cinematographer Tom Comerford, and marked a clear development in Muldowney's skills as a filmmaker. Despite being largely ignored at the box office, it won the Dublin Film Critics Circle Best Irish Feature Award in 2014.

Ever ambitious, Muldowney's third feature as writer/director was unambiguously Irish in its setting and themes but aimed for a scope few if any indigenous filmmakers had previously attempted. *Pilgrimage* (produced in 2015 but not released until 2017) tells the story of a group of monks in 13th-century Ireland who must escort a sacred relic to Rome across a treacherous landscape. Developed from an idea by writer Jamie Hannigan, it is an ambitious action-adventure set in the distant past. Owing a debt of influence to male-centered religious epics, such as *The Mission* and *Aguire, Wrath of God*, *Pilgrimage* features characteristically desaturated cinematography of the western landscape by Tom Comerford (their third collaboration) and a guttural, violent sound track by Stephen McKeown (who won an IFTA for Best Original Soundtrack), aiming to look and sound different from any Irish film before. If it shares commonalities with the director's previous work, it is in his persistent interest in overlapping themes of masculinity under pressure, lawlessness, and the male body. The ambition of the film was reflected in its casting of international stars Tom Holland (United Kingdom, *Spiderman*), Richard Armitage (United Kingdom, *The Hobbit*), and Jon Bernthal (United States, *The Waking Dead* and *Daredevil*). However, despite being premiered at the Tribeca Film Festival and being picked up by a number of international territories, the film fared poorly in distribution relative to its evident ambitions for international accessibility.

MURPHY, CILLIAN (1976–). Cillian Murphy grew up in Cork and became interested in theater and acting while studying at the Presentation Brothers College. He enrolled in law at University College Cork but left midway through his degree to pursue acting and was soon after cast in the original stage production of Enda Walsh's *Disco Pigs*, which received universally positive reviews when it toured internationally. Murphy's performance as the near psychotic "Pig" was singled out for attention, and when Kirsten Sheridan came to film the play in 2000, he reprised the role. His screen performance was equally impressive, alternately seductive and terrifyingly unpredictable, and quickly led to a successful international career in a variety of roles for film and TV.

He was subsequently seen in similarly challenging roles as a suicidal psychiatric patient in **John Carney**'s *On the Edge* and as the unresponsive son in the often overlooked *How Harry Became a Tree*. He found a wider range in the lead role of Danny Boyle's contemporary horror *28 Days Later* (2002), which became a crossover hit in the United States and brought Murphy to the attention of a much wider audience. This has led to a series of more classic roles in **Academy Award** fodder such as *Girl with a Pearl Earring* (2003) and *Cold Mountain* (2004) before returning to characters on the edge in Wes Craven's thriller *Red Eye* (2005) and as the deranged super-villain Dr. Johnathan Crane/The Scarecrow in *Batman Begins* (2005). His success in that role initiated a long and fruitful working relationship with writer/director Christopher Nolan that has kept him highly visible in international cinema: *Inception* (2010), *The Dark Knight Rises* (2012), and *Dunkirk* (2017).

While he has given memorable performances in a number of Irish films, including *Intermission*, in the main role as a transvestite prostitute in **Neil Jordan**'s undervalued *Breakfast on Pluto* (2005), and Mark O'Rowe's *The Delinquent Season* (2017), Murphy's career today is decidedly transnational without being "Hollywood." Alongside his work with Nolan and other directors of note on a variety of big-budget and interesting art house projects—including *Free Fire* (Ben Wheatley, 2016), *Anthropoid* (Sean Ellis, 2016), and *The Party* (Sally Potter, 2017)—Murphy has become most closely associated with his recurring role as Thomas Selby in the BBC period crime drama series *Peaky Blinders* (2013–2018), which experienced an exponential growth in popularity on both sides of the Atlantic with each successive season. In 2017, he and his family moved back to live permanently in Ireland after many years in London.

MURPHY, PAT (1951–). Murphy has been an influential feminist film director and teacher and an important artistic force for explicating radical ideas within Irish film. Born in Dublin, Murphy graduated from the Ulster College of Art and Design, followed by earning a BA in fine art at the Hornsey College of Art and an MA in film and television from the Royal College of Art in London. In 1977, she was the first European to receive a scholarship to spend a year at the Whitney Museum of American Art in New York.

She began her film career on her return with the formally experimental and highly innovative *Maeve* (1981)—jointly directed with **John T. Davis**—which explored the themes of republicanism and feminism within the political vicissitudes of Troubles-era Belfast. The film centers on the titular character (Mary Jackson), who returns to Belfast from London, staying with her sister (**Brid Brennan**) and father (Mark Mulholland), and meets up with her old boyfriend (John Keegan). These encounters precipitate a range of conversations and flashbacks to Maeve's experiences in England that foreground her as a dissenting feminist voice, formally articulated through the rejection of linear personal or political narratives or a single, fixed point of view. Similar themes are dealt with from a historical perspective in Murphy's next film, *Anne Devlin*, based on the diaries of Robert Emmet's housekeeper. More conventional in style, the film had a "balladic structure," according to Murphy, and went on to represent Ireland at myriad international festivals.

After *Anne Devlin*, Murphy experienced a 16-year hiatus in filmmaking, struggling to find funding for her next project, *Nora*, a period film focused on Nora Barnacle, the wife of James Joyce and a critical influence on his work. Murphy did eventually make *Nora* (2000) based on Brenda Maddox's acclaimed biography of **James Joyce**'s Galway-born wife with Susan Lynch in the lead role and Scottish actor Ewan McGregor—whose company Natural Nylon coproduced—as Joyce. Visually lush and conforming to the production standards of international art house cinema, Lynch in particular gives a stirring and memorable performance. While it received mixed reviews, it remains an important work, a valuable corrective to Joycean myth, and a fitting final part to Murphy's feminist trilogy of Irish women occluded by a patriarchal view of history.

After many years teaching film at universities in Ireland and Singapore, Murphy converted to Buddhism and in 2015 made *Tana Bana*, a visually striking documentary on the disappearing craft of female silk weavers in Varanasi on the banks of the Ganges River in India.

***MY BROTHERS* (2010).** Best known as a screenwriter for his collaborations with his childhood friend, British director Shane Meadows, on the latter's early works (*TwentyFourSeven* [1997] and *A Room for Romeo Brass* [1999]), Paul Fraser's debut as a director in his own right takes as its source Irish writer Will Collins's debut feature script. Set in 1987, the episodic road movie narrative follows three brothers on a quest to replace the watch won by their father (**Don Wycherley**) years earlier on a family holiday in Bally-bunnion in Kerry. The watch symbolizes time running out: Dad is dying (of an unspecified respiratory condition). "Borrowing" a decrepit bread truck, 17-year-old Noel (Tim Creed); flatulent, asthmatic Paudie (Paul Courtney); and *Star Wars*–obsessed Scwally embark on a road trip across a beautifully lensed (by cinematographer P. J. Dillon) rural southeast landscape, encountering the inevitable mix of eccentrics (and one less predictable encounter with Terry McMahon's pedophile) and narrative hurdles (not least of which is the unreliable mode of transport).

As such, though convincingly anchored in its geographical and temporal setting, *My Brothers* rarely strays from road movie conventions and offers little in the way of innovation. The decision to set the film during what was arguably the nadir of the economic recession of the 1980s ensures that the good-humored tone set by the younger siblings is undercut by a sense of melancholy that pervades not only the family home but also the wider society. Ballybunnion is remembered as a site of happiness for the family, but the boys encounter it in autumn as a twilight town, empty save for a few locals. Although this somber atmosphere is counterpointed by the often comic development of the relationship between the introspective Noel and his younger siblings (all three of whom are portrayed in convincingly naturalistic fashion by the young cast), the film ultimately seems unsure as to where it stands on the value of familial bonds as a bulwark against life's vicissitudes.

MY LEFT FOOT (1989). Often cited as having single-handedly revived the faltering and underfunded domestic film industry, the critical and commercial success of *My Left Foot* can certainly be identified as a key event in persuading an Irish government to take an interventionist role in developing a national audiovisual sector. In some respects, the film came as a bolt out of the blue: director **Jim Sheridan** and producer Noel Pearson, fresh from collaborating at the **Abbey Theatre**, came up with the idea to make a feature film—with Sheridan as writer and Pearson as producer—about a locally known disabled Irish writer who had published just two books and who had died nearly 15 years earlier. On paper, this cannot have seemed an especially easy proposition to fund, and, indeed, although initial reviews of the finished film were universally positive, public reaction was muted. Even in Ireland, the film failed to set the box office alight on its first release. Then came the 1989 **Academy Awards**. Nominated in four categories, the film astonished the world by winning twice: Daniel Day-Lewis and **Brenda Fricker** for Best Actor and Best Supporting Actress, respectively. Rereleased on the strength of that performance, the film did enormous trade on both sides of the Atlantic and in doing so raised the possibility of making films in Ireland that could be internationally successful in both financial and creative terms.

Examined on its own merits, the film remains far superior to many of the Irish pictures that followed in its wake. It opens in 1963 when Christy Brown (Day-Lewis) is a guest at a fund-raising gala held in his honor. As he waits to be presented to the crowd, he recounts his life to the nurse (**Ruth McCabe**) assigned to look after him. Born with cerebral palsy into an impoverished and large working-class family in 1932, his parents are informed by the doctors that he will remain a "vegetable" for the rest of his life. This defines his father's (**Ray McAnally**) initial rejection of him, although his mother (Brenda Fricker) is not convinced by the diagnosis. Ten years pass, however, before Christy, compellingly embodied as a child by **Hugh O'Conor**, is able to communicate his fierce intelligence: in a pivotal scene, he picks up a piece of chalk with his left foot to write the single word "M-O-T-H-E-R" on the ground. Thereafter, Christy begins to explore his artistic side: although almost his entire body is affected by the palsy (including his mouth, which slurs his speech), he retains control over his left foot, which he uses to paint with. At the age of 19, he enters a new clinic for cerebral palsy patients. There, he meets Eileen (**Fiona Shaw**), a specialist in treating palsy who works with Christy to overcome his speech impediment. When she announces her engagement to Peter, the gallery owner who exhibits Christy's first public exhibition of art, Christy is heartbroken, and he abandons painting as a means of expression in favor of writing.

As the story returns to the present, Christy asks Mary, his nurse, if she'll go out with him. Initially reluctant, she eventually agrees. The film closes with the pair on Killiney Hill, drinking a toast with champagne to "Dublin, where Christy Brown was born." As the credits close, a postscript tells us that Christy and Mary married in 1972.

The performances through the film are extraordinary and rightly recognized. Day-Lewis imbues his highly disabled character with an extraordinary charm, intelligence, and physicality: unable to easily and rapidly express his frustrations with life through speech, his Christy communicates with his entire body, most notably in a confrontational restaurant scene where Eileen announces her engagement. Nor is his Christy an always sympathetic character: given to fits of depression, he also allows himself to wallow in self-pity. And it is this warts-and-all portrayal that lies at the center of the picture. Equally impressive in less showy roles are Fricker and McAnally as Christy's parents. While Fricker's performance was recognized with an Oscar, McAnally, given the difficult job of embodying a character unable to communicate with his own flesh and blood and frequently taking refuge in the bottle, nonetheless skillfully gives the audiences an insight into his character's frustrations with his own failings. After a long and distinguished career in theater, this was McAnally's final and most memorable appearance in Irish film, one that just managed to record his talent before his death in 1989.

The film revealed director Sheridan as a consummate storyteller. He altered the original autobiographies of Christy Brown (*Down All the Days* and *My Left Foot*) on which the film was based so that, for example, Christy's father, although still gruff, was rendered a far less brutal figure than in Brown's own depiction. But it is Sheridan's unerring ability to make such judgments in the pursuit of a universally comprehensible narrative knowledge that has often been cited as a critical factor in the international success of his pictures.

Although *My Left Foot* helped create the circumstances in which an indigenous industry could emerge, it also raised the stakes for those Irish films that followed. No longer was it sufficient to make an artistically accomplished film in Ireland: to match *My Left Foot*, it should also be a financial and critical success on an international stage. It is notable, then, that much of the criticism leveled at the post–*My Left Foot* crop of Irish films often focused less on the actual quality of the films themselves than on their financial performance, and over time, these two criteria tended to blur into one another so that commercial failures were often automatically dismissed as critical failures. This situation has changed in more recent years as Irish film has ridden high on international awards and reached wide art house audiences on relatively modest production budgets.

If there was a downside, it might be that *My Left Foot*—despite its highly local character and superb performances—followed an all-too-familiar narrative arc of personal will overcoming adversity (it was produced the same year as *Born on the Fourth of July*). In so doing, it created an orthodoxy that only "universal" narratives could succeed commercially overseas, contributing to a noticeable tendency in 1990s Irish cinema to increasingly eschew cultural specificity and to embrace genre production. That the film's success cast a long shadow for both Irish filmmakers and audiences is hardly surprising; it remains as fresh and engaging today as it did in 1989 and has long taken its place in the front rank of Irish film achievements.

MYSTICS **(2003).** This caper comedy was directed by David Blair and features veteran actors **Milo O'Shea** and **David Kelly** as Dave and Locky, who, unable to secure thespian employment, run fake séances above a Dublin public house to earn cash. The story is complicated when a recently deceased Dublin gangster (played by Ronnie Drew of the traditional band The Dubliners) begins using Locky to communicate with his family. This slender comedy can be seen as an attempt to revisit the success of *Waking Ned* (1998), in which David Kelly played opposite Ian Bannan in a similar "ould fellas" on-the-make caper comedy.

N

NATIONAL FILM INSTITUTE OF IRELAND. *See* IRISH FILM INSTITUTE.

NATIONAL FILM STUDIOS OF IRELAND. *See* ARDMORE STUDIOS.

NEESON, LIAM (1952–). Neeson was born to a working-class Catholic family in staunchly Loyalist Ballymena in Northern Ireland. As a child, he nurtured ambitions to be a priest, although he also joined the local All Saints Boxing Club at an early age. He attended Ballymena Technical College, then spent an abortive year at Queen's University Belfast studying physics and mathematics before taking up a place in an actors' training course in Newcastle-upon-Tyne in England. He then returned to Northern Ireland, approached the Lyric Theatre, and was immediately cast in their next play. While touring, Neeson was spotted by Peter Sheridan (brother of Jim and a cofounder of the **Project Arts Centre**), who offered him a part in a play called *Says I, Says I*. This led him to move to Dublin, where he worked onstage with, among others, **Brid Brennan** and **Gabriel Byrne**, appearing in several plays at the Project, **Abbey Theatre**, and the Peacock. His breakthrough into film came with his casting in the role of Gawain in **John Boorman**'s *Excalibur* (1981), an important precursor to Ireland's indigenous industry.

In 1982, he moved to London, where he worked on a succession of American miniseries and the occasional British film, including *The Bounty* (1984) and *The Mission* (1986). **Pat O'Connor**'s *Lamb* (1986) brought his name to the attention of a popular audience in Ireland. His casting as gentle giant Michael Lamb played on his large frame (Neeson is six feet four inches tall), and his powerful physique stood in marked contrast to the sense of impotence that the character experiences in the face of the corruption and unfairness of life. In 1987, Neeson moved to Los Angeles, where he made an immediate impact in Peter Yates's *Suspect* (1987), playing a deaf-mute homeless man opposite Cher and Dennis Quaid.

419

In 1988, Neil Jordan cast him in *High Spirits*; while both men knew each other from Neeson's time in Dublin, it was the first of several collaborations between the two. Leading roles in Sam Raimi's *Darkman* (1990) and Woody Allen's *Husbands and Wives* (1992) followed, but it was his role as Oskar Schindler, the charismatic wartime profiteer turned Holocaust hero, in Steven Spielberg's *Schindler's List* (1993) (based on a Thomas Keneally novel) that placed him in the firmament of A-list Hollywood stars. Such was his star status that his casting by Jordan in *Michael Collins* not only facilitated its funding by Warner Bros. but also imposed itself on the narrative to the extent that it would focus on a single, heroic figure in exploring the complex politics underlying the foundation of the Irish state. His portrait of Collins comes from the well-established conventions of the biopic: a highly individual, physical, and vigorous man of action, unafraid to use any means necessary to achieve his political ends. The fact that the real 1920s Republican rebel Collins had among his responsibilities the more sedate role of minister for finance was not one easily accommodated by this casting.

Neeson's performances in *Schindler's List* and *Michael Collins* were to have lasting influences on the actor's career and resulted in a degree of stereotyping as strong male figures on the right side of justice. He was subsequently cast in a variety of mentor roles, playing Qui-Gon Jinn opposite Ewan McGregor's Obi-Wan Kenobi in *Star Wars: The Phantom Menace* (1999), Henri Ducard in *Batman Begins*, and even the voice of Aslan in *The Chronicles of Narnia: The Lion, the Witch and the Wardrobe* (2005). Even in *Breakfast on Pluto*, an art house collaboration with Jordan that was at the opposite end of the spectrum from Hollywood blockbusters in scale and subject, Neeson played a priest guiding the young "Kitten" (Cillian Murphy) through his formative years.

In 2009, Neeson's life took a tragic and unexpected turn with the death of his wife Natasha Richardson (aged 45) in a skiing accident, leaving him to care for their two young children. (The accident happened while Neeson was filming Atom Egoyan's *Chloe*.) He subsequently threw himself into work as a means of dealing with grief (according to interviews), resulting in an unexpected and late career turn as an action star. This came about through his casting in *Taken* (2008), a kinetic, transnational thriller typical of its writer and producer, Luc Besson. Brilliantly cast against type, Neeson played a retired Central Intelligence Agency agent who travels across Europe and relies on a "particular set of skills" to save his kidnapped daughter. The surprise international success of the film (a whopping $230 million) led to a highly lucrative franchise (a rarity for actors of Neeson's vintage in the Netflix era), several other action films, and a host of imitation revenge thrillers starring actors of his generation (Sean Penn in *The Gunman*, Denzel Washington in *The Equalizer*, **Pierce Brosnan** in *The November Man*, and Keanu Reeves in *John Wick*).

The Grey (2011) was superior to most of these, a meditation on grief wrapped in a genre piece that echoes and illuminates Neeson's personal circumstances during this period. Clearly energized, his late career demonstrates an actor of astonishing range and productivity. Notable and diverse credits include Martin Scorsese's *Silence* (2016), *A Monster Calls* (2016), *The Lego Movie* (2015), and *Mark Felt: The Man Who Brought Down the White House* (2017). Past official retirement age and protesting that it was time to hang up his avenging persona, Neeson had not only transformed his career and legacy but also sparked discussions about the cultural meaning and resonance of the angry-old-white-dude persona that anticipated the election of Donald J. Trump.

NEGGA, RUTH (1982–). Born in Ethiopia to an Irish mother and an Ethiopian father, Negga lived in Addis Ababa until she was four and then moved with her mother to Limerick. (Her father was supposed to join them but subsequently died in a car crash, leaving her mother to raise her alone albeit among her extended Irish family.) She spent her formative years in Ireland and undertook drama studies at Trinity College Dublin before moving at age 24 to London, where she has since been based. These facts are worth rehearsing since Negga's background has been repeatedly invoked in media discussions around her achievements and status as an Irish actor to such an extent that, after she received an **Academy Award** nomination for her performance in *Loving* (2017), an *Irish Times* article under the headline "With Ruth Negga, We Have Disgraced Ourselves Again" argued that knee-jerk complaints about her being claimed as "British" revealed more about "neurotic nationalism" and "infantile pettiness" than they do about Negga's success and right to identify herself as she wishes. The subtext to such comments, of course, is Negga's uncertain place within Irish cinema as a highly mobile actor of color who has not allowed herself to be typed as "other" or played the Irish card in pursuit/support of international recognition. Regardless, she is in the front rank of Ireland's female actors, one whose achievements across stage and international small- and big-screen productions bear comparison on multiple levels with contemporaries such as **Saoirse Ronan**, **Kerry Condon**, and **Sarah Bolger**.

Certainly, Negga's early Irish film roles invoke a thematic of race in interesting if often unintentional ways. Her film debut was in *Trafficked* (2004), an Irish feature by Ciaran O'Connor that didn't receive a release—under the new title, *Capital Letters*—until 2010. One of several contemporary efforts wrestling with the new phenomenon of inward migration, she was cast as Taiwo, a trafficked African migrant who escapes but remains firmly subaltern within the sleazier quarters of Dublin, where she is "saved" by a con man with a golden heart (Karl Shiels). Her turn as Orla in *Isolation* (2005) allowed greater range, even if once again race was a subtext in a rural-set Irish horror in which her character becomes pregnant with a potentially monstrous child. The same year, she was again cast as the pregnant best friend (Charlie) of **Cillian Murphy**'s transvestite Kitten in ***Breakfast on Pluto*** (2005). Following the death of her boyfriend Irwin, active in the Irish Republican Army, they become a happy postnationalist and queer Irish family under the initial protection of **Liam Neeson**'s renegade priest Father Liam. That led to castings for a wide variety of TV projects in the United Kingdom and Ireland, including *Criminal Justice* (2008), **Channel 4**'s *Misfits* (2010), a BBC 2 Shirley Bassey biopic (*Shirley*), a rare appearance on Irish screens in *Love/Hate* (2010–2011), and opposite **Gabriel Byrne** in *Secret State* (2012), a four-part Channel 4 political drama.

While she remained busy and in demand during the first half of the decade, moving between quality TV drama, video game voice-overs, and well-received stage performances (including an inspired piece of casting as Pegeen Mike in the Old Vic production of *The Playboy of the Western World* [2011]), her profile and career exploded in 2016 when she was cast in the recurring role of Tulip O'Hare, the resourceful ex-girlfriend to the titular *Preacher* in the hit AMC TV series (adapted from Garth Ennis's cult comic books), then as Lady Taria in Duncan Jones's big-budget *Warcraft* and, most notably, as Mildred in *Loving*, based on a true story of interracial marriage and bigotry in 1950s Texas. This performance brought her widespread critical plaudits and attention (including the cover of *Vogue*) and an Oscar nomination in the highly contested Best Actress category.

Still, her outsider status continues to dominate perceptions in Ireland albeit with greater imagination and maturity. This is best expressed in her casting as the Dane in the September 2018 production of *Hamlet* at Dublin's Gate Theatre. Shakespeare's most coveted role, centered on questions of identity and mutability and based on the premise of returning home after years of experience and education abroad (not to mention the context of recently exposed sexism at the theater), represented a timely and worthy follow-up to Negga's U.S. successes and a recognition of her value to a paradigm of global Irishness.

THE NEPHEW **(1998).** Produced by **Pierce Brosnan**'s **Irish Dreamtime**, the film, directed by the Irish-born, U.S.-based Eugene Brady, mobilizes a mythic rural narrative aimed squarely at the American market, playing on stereotypes of the Irish as quirky yet welcoming. Hill Harper plays Chad, the dreadlocked mixed-race nephew of Uncle Tony (**Donal McCann** in his final film appearance) who has come back to the place of his mother's birth. Chad finds himself at the center of an ongoing conflict between his uncle and the charming local bar owner Joe Brady (Pierce Brosnan), who have been at loggerheads since Chad's mother left. Although the film plays its "stranger comes to town" narrative sympathetically, its narrative delight in constructing a closed, monoracial culture seems extraordinary from today's vantage point, marking a late and regressive contribution to a narrative trope stretching back to *The Quiet Man*. Although the film seeks to posit the Irish as open to outside cultures, it is striking that Chad succeeds in achieving acceptance into the wider local community only by singing a song in Irish at a wake, thereby securing his cultural lineage.

NESBITT, JAMES (1965–). Although known primarily for a seemingly endless succession of lead roles in U.K. television drama since the late 1990s, the Northern Irish actor has been a stalwart of Irish cinema since as far back as 1986, when he appeared down the cast in **Bill Miskelly**'s *The End of the World Man* (1988).

From a Protestant background but raised in apolitical circles in Ballymena, County Antrim, Nesbitt originally studied to become a teacher before dropping out of college to pursue acting. He joined the local Riverside Theatre before moving to drama school in London. Small roles, often in BBC Northern Ireland drama productions, began to accumulate from the mid-1980s before he made an apparent breakthrough as theatrical agent Fintan O'Donnell aiding **Adrian Dunbar**'s Micky O'Neill in his quest to track down a reclusive singer in *Hear My Song* (1991). Yet the big roles didn't quite follow, and Nesbitt found himself stuck in a series of one-off roles— often as a policeman or soldier—on U.K. television for much of the 1990s (although his appearance in the Michael Winterbottom–directed drama *Love Lies Bleeding* [1993] was followed by big-screen appearances in three of the director's subsequent features: *Go Now* [1995], *Jude* [1996], and *Welcome to Sarajevo* [1997]). He finally secured a recurring role in the BBC's *Ballykissangel* from 1996, but it was ITV's hit drama *Cold Feet* (1997–) that made him a household name. Initially running for six seasons between 1997 and 2003 (before a successful revival in 2016), Nesbitt's character Adam was a serial womanizer given to living the high life before settling down with ad executive Rachel (Helen Baxendale). The casting reflected something of a recurring type for Nesbitt: the good-hearted opportunist with a touch of the manic about him.

Although the TV roles kept coming after *Cold Feet* began its lengthy hiatus in 2003, for a period, he interspersed these with more film work, appearing down the cast in Danny Boyle's *Millions* (2004) and Woody Allen's *Match Point* (2005). Although these included appearances in Irish features, he has rarely played the lead even in these. Notwithstanding his recurring role as the dwarf Bofur in Peter Jackson's *Hobbit* trilogy (2012–2014) (easily the highest-profile film work that Nesbitt has done), since 2010, he has remained primarily a small-screen star with a remarkable run of lead roles in seven separate U.K. television series up to 2017, including turns as the eponymous headstrong surgeon in ITV's *Monroe* (2011–2012), a beleaguered metropolitan police chief in *Babylon* (2014), and a distraught father seeking his kidnapped son in *The Missing* (2014).

Arguably, his screen roles have allowed to work against type: though once again playing the lovable Irishman in Emilio Estevez's *The Way* (2010) (joining grieving father Martin Sheen on a pilgrimage) and in the Australian-backed *Matching Jack* (2010), they are eclipsed by a sequence of much darker roles. He played real-life nationalist politician Ivan Cooper in Paul Greengrass's account of the **Bloody Sunday** murders in 2002 and was outstanding in Oliver Hirschbiegel's **Five Minutes of Heaven** (2008) as Joe Griffin, a Catholic retraumatized by the opportunity to meet the Loyalist gunman (**Liam Neeson**) who murdered his brother 30 years earlier. Even when the work has a lighter feel, Nesbitt demonstrates a relish for less-than-pleasant characters—from the smarmy politician in *Wild About Harry* (2000) to the uptight father in **Cherrybomb** (2009) and the control freak husband in **Gold** (2014).

However, if there is one consistent element in Nesbitt's casting, it is his recurrent identification as not simply Irish but also specifically Northern Irish (even when the character was not explicitly written as such). In *Cold Feet*, Adam is notionally from Manchester, his accent justified by childhood holidays in Northern Ireland. Cast as the lead in Sky Television's adaptation of an original concept from Stan Lee's *Lucky Man* (2016–) as a detective with a supernatural ability to control luck, he became the first figure connected to the Marvel Universe to speak with an Ulster accent. While his Northern Irish contemporaries (and occasional costars), such as Dunbar and Neeson, have frequently adopted other nationalities on-screen, the exuberance, belligerence, and haunted qualities of Nesbitt's roles are arguably anchored by his on-screen commitment to his local identity.

NIGHT TRAIN (1998). Directed by John Lynch (not the actor of the same name but, rather, a former **Radio Telefís Éireann** director) from a script by playwright and author Aodhan Madden (*Fear and Loathing in Dublin*), this charming, low-key two-hander stars Brenda Blethyn as Alice, an older single woman who feels trapped by life and eventually takes in a lodger, Poole, played by John Hurt. It transpires that while Poole spends most of his time operating his beloved model train set in his room, he is on the run from a Dublin criminal gang. The somewhat unrealistic plot developments that lead the pair to flee from the capital do not hamper a solid study of character and romance. The film is also an all-too-unusual—and welcome—narrative exploration of the lives and loves of older people rounded out with excellent performances from both leads. Hurt won Best Actor award at the Verona Film Festival in 1999, and the film was nominated as Best European Feature at the Brussels Film Festival.

NILAND, MARTINA. A native of Westport, County Mayo, Martina Niland is among the most successful of a growing cadre of female producers in the Irish film industry. After graduating with a BA in communications (film and broadcasting) at the Dublin Institute of Technology in the late 1990s, she joined **Samson Films**, where she initially developed a series of low-budget features, including *The Honeymooners* (2003), ***Pavee Lackeen*** (2005), and Carmel Winter's ***Snap*** (2010). Acting as coproducer on **Radio Telefís Éireann**'s *Bachelor's Walk* Christmas special (2006), she began an enduring working relationship with director **John Carney**. When she left Samson in 2014 to cofound **Cosmo Films**, she maintained the relationship with Carney by producing the Golden Globe–nominated ***Sing Street*** (2016). Other credits include several films by female directors: *Dollhouse* (Kirsten Sheridan, 2012) and the medium-budget coproductions ***Run and Jump*** (Steph Green, 2013) and ***Stay*** (Wiebke von Carolsfeld, 2013). She was selected as European Film Promotions Irish Producer on the Move in 2007 and is a member of the European Film Academy.

NORA **(2000). Pat Murphy**'s long-gestating film sets out to do justice to the woman behind the myth that surrounds **James Joyce**'s wife Nora Barnacle, a constant muse to his writing, immortalized through the character of Molly Bloom. Based on Brenda Maddox's acclaimed biography, with a script cowritten by **Gerry Stembridge**, the story begins with their meeting on a Dublin street in 1904 and follows the couple's testy and unconventional relationship (they didn't marry until 1934) as they leave Ireland for a nomadic life on the European continent. In a surprising piece of casting, Ewan McGregor plays Joyce; however, without him as star and producer, the film would likely not have been made. **Susan Lynch** takes the titular role and brings a rare combination of elegance, love, exasperation, and a forthright sexuality to her performance as an uneducated girl from rural Ireland married to the spendthrift and impractical genius who adored her earthy sensuality. Their marital struggles serve to affirm Nora's distinctive character and an atypical embodiment of Irish motherhood. While some critics judged the film an abandonment of the radicalism that marked Murphy's earlier feminist histories by embracing the conventions of romantic period drama, others have more generously suggested that *Nora* represents a commercially determined realignment of strategies without sacrificing that wider critique. It marked the final film in Murphy's loose trilogy of studies of Irish women and history and indeed the end of her career (to date) as a maker of feature-length fiction.

NORTHERN IRELAND SCREEN. Northern Ireland Screen (NIS) is a rebrand of the Northern Ireland Film and Television Commission (NIFTC), which in turn grew out of the Northern Ireland Film Council (NIFC). The

NIFC was established in 1989 as a voluntary body following recommenda-tions in the **Derry Film and Video Co-Operative**'s 1988 *Fast Forward* report. In 1991, the NIFC published its own *Strategy Proposals* outlining its ambition to create a vibrant film and video culture and industry in Northern Ireland. From the mid-1990s, the NIFC was in receipt of British National Lottery funds, which it used for film project development. In July 1997, the NIFC became the NIFTC with a much broader remit and more substantial funding from the Department of Culture, Arts, and Leisure; Invest Northern Ireland; and the British Film Council. In addition, the commission adminis-tered lottery funding for films in Northern Ireland on behalf of the Arts Council of Northern Ireland. The rebrand to the NIS, which reflected another expansion of the organization's remit to include digital media, including games, occurred in 2007.

In many respects, the responsibilities of the NIS mirror those of its counterpart in the Republic of Ireland, the **Irish Film Board**. However, while both institutions bear responsibility for funding film development and production and both operate screen commissions in their respective jurisdic-tions, the NIFTC's remit is much broader. The commission focuses on eight objectives: production and development of film, television and digital games, business development (focused on developing production companies rather than simply individual productions), skills development and training, educa-tion (embedding audiovisual study into the primary and secondary school curricula), heritage (archiving), exhibition, and marketing and information.

In addition to funding short-film and television production, the NIFC/NIFTC/NIS have been involved in financing virtually every feature shot in Northern Ireland since 1997 from *Sunset Heights* (1999) and *Titanic Town* (1998) to *Good Vibrations* (2012) and *Maze* (2017). All three iterations of the NIS have had close working relations with the Irish Film Board, with which they have cofunded several productions (especially—and appropriate-ly—those with cross-border or community themes, such as *The Most Fertile Man in Ireland* [2000], *A Love Divided* [1999], and *Puckoon* [2002]). The 2005 creation of linguistically focused schemes supporting production in Irish and Ulster Scots also supported cross-border coproductions on work like the Tom Collins–directed *Kings* (2007). Northern and southern institu-tions have also collaborated on exhibition issues, jointly funding research into an island of Ireland art house cinema network and cofunding the pur-chase and running of the Cinemobile, a mobile cinema.

The redevelopment of the former Paint Hall of the Harland and Wolff shipyard as a studio space since 2007 created an opportunity for the NIS to promote Northern Ireland as a hub for international filmmaking activity. Commencing operations with the filming of the sci-fi spectacular *City of Ember* (2008) featuring **Saoirse Ronan** and Bill Murray, the Paint Hall was subsequently renamed Titanic Studios as the total floor expanded from four

16,000-square-foot soundstages in 2011 to eight stages with a combined area of 250,000 square feet by 2014. In 2010, Northern Ireland Screen achieved what remains its signature breakthrough, attracting the producers of HBO's *Game of Thrones* (2011–) to base their shoot in Northern Ireland. The mammoth production directly contributed more than UK£200 million to the local economy by the end of its sixth series in 2016. However, its larger impact was in putting the region on the map for international producers. By the early 2010s, Northern Ireland was actively vying with the Republic of Ireland to attract footloose international productions and succeeding in winning high-profile work, such as the Natalie Portman–James Franco medieval comedy *Your Highness* (2011), Ben Wheatley's adaptation of J. G. Ballard's dystopian novel *High Rise* (2014), and the Brad Pitt–produced *Lost City of Z* (2016).

Buoyed by this success, in 2014, the NIS launched "Opening Doors," a four-year plan to generate €250 million worth of screen production, leveraged by £42 million in funding from the NIS itself. As of 2017, the bulk of the NIS's total funding of UK£16.5 million comes from Invest NI (the regional economic development agency) with the remainder coming from the Department of Culture, Media, and Sport (via the British Film Institute) as well as the Department of Communities and the **Arts Council**.

NOT AFRAID, NOT AFRAID (2001). Left by her husband of 25 years and convinced she is dying of cancer, Paula (Dianne Wiest) summons her son (Jack Davenport) and his wife to inform them of her impending demise and of her decision to embark on a nostalgic journey to visit her ex-lovers. Her journey is complicated when she brings her grandson, who has Down syndrome, along for the ride. Produced by an independent American production company in conjunction with **World 2000 Entertainment** and directed by Annette Garducci, the film has never received a theatrical release in the United States or Europe, suggesting a degree of unhappiness with the finished product on the part of potential distributors.

NOTHING PERSONAL (ALL OUR FAULT) (1995). **Thaddeus O'Sullivan**'s Troubles-era drama unfolds over the course of a single evening in Belfast in 1975. Republican and Loyalist leaders Cecil and Leonard (**Gerard McSorley** and **Michael Gambon**) meet to negotiate a cease-fire on behalf of their organizations. Leonard's lieutenant Kenny (James Frain) and his fanatically anti-Catholic sidekick Ginger (Ian Hart) are uncomfortable with the negotiations, and when they are subsequently caught up in a riot that breaks out on the Peace Line dividing Catholics and Protestants, Ginger sadistically burns a Catholic teenager to death. At the same time, Liam (**John Lynch**), a Catholic injured during the riot, finds himself trapped on the wrong side of the Peace Line. He takes refuge in the house of Anne (**Maria Doyle Kennedy**), a Protestant nurse (and, it turns out, the former wife of Kenny). Picked up by Ginger, Liam is subjected to interrogation until Kenny arrives, recognizes Liam as a childhood friend, and orders him released. Despite this, events continue to spiral out of control, leading to the deaths of not only Kenny and Ginger but also Liam's daughter Kathleen.

The look and feel of mid-1970s Belfast is so effectively rendered by the skillful production and costume design of Mark Geraghty and **Consolata Boyle**, respectively, that one might be forgiven for assuming that the film's representation of the era's politics is equally faithful. Yet it arguably offers a somewhat reactionary take in its identification of the roots of the "long war." The political context is sidelined in favor of a criminal-terrorist-madman discourse especially with regard to the motivations of the Loyalist side. Cecil, the Loyalist leader, is willing to contemplate a cease-fire because the conflict is interfering with the operation of his extortion racket. Ginger's rabid sectarianism is so deeply rooted in psychosis that even his own comrades can envisage dealing with it only by having him killed. This approach reaches its zenith during Kenny and Liam's brief reconciliation: its soft-focus recall of shared childhood experiences emphasizes the humanity they have in common, positing the subsequent post-1969 sectarian division as an irrational wave of madness. By the 21st century, it had become common to discuss the Troubles as a "war," thus acknowledging its political dimension. Perhaps because of its temporal proximity to the era of violence (the film was shot after the initial Irish Republican Army cease-fire of 1994 but before the signing of the Good Friday Agreement in 1998), *Nothing Personal* seemed unable to evade further mythologizing the then still prevalent—and in some quarters politically useful—"terrorist-madman take" on Northern Ireland.

NOTHING PERSONAL **(2009).** Less an Irish film than a film set in Ireland (and, briefly, Amsterdam and Spain), Polish director Urzsula Antoniak's contemplative debut follows Anne (Lotte Verbeek), a young Dutch woman, as she leaves a failed marriage in Amsterdam to seek isolation in the west of Ireland. Reticent to a point of silence, she encounters a similar figure in Martin (**Stephen Rea**), a loner living in a rural cottage, eking a living from the land. Anne agrees to live and work with Martin on the condition that they ask nothing about one another. Despite this, as both orbit around one another, a connection emerges, and they increasingly seek emotional sustenance from the other as well as food and shelter.

Coproduced by **Fastnet Films** with some financial support from the **Irish Film Board**, *Nothing Personal* nonetheless "feels" very different from most Irish work (although there are obvious points of connection with the work of **Pat Collins** and, arguably, **Gerard Barrett**) in its active eschewal of exposition. Narrative progress is limited to occasional oblique intertitles: knowing nothing about the past of the two characters, the audience is forced to read them based only on their present actions. Nonetheless, both leads offer a strong sense of their characters' interior lives, of who (and why) they are.

Overall, then, *Nothing Personal* makes very different demands of its audience than most "mainstream" Irish work, the contrast suggesting in passing that it may yet be possible to identify some coherence in the Irish national cinema "project."

NOVEMBER AFTERNOON (1997). **John Carney** and **Tom Hall** shot their stylish no-budget feature film debut in black and white on the Hi8 format. Tracing an incestuous relationship between a brother and sister, the film's aesthetic nodded at the early work of John Cassavettes as well as French art house cinema of the 1950s and 1960s, deploying handheld cameras, overlapping dialogue, and extreme close-ups against a jazz sound track background (composed and performed by Carney himself).

The story is structured in three acts that play out over a long weekend as Karen (Jayne Snow) and her husband John (Mark Doherty) arrive home from London to stay at her brother Robert's (**Michael McElhatton**) flat in Dublin. Reversing conventional stereotypes, the English husband is very fond of alcohol, while Robert is a connoisseur of jazz. The returning emigrant narrative (a recurring trope in Irish cinema since *The Lad from Old Ireland* [1910]) is reimagined through a claustrophobic, cinema verité aesthetic and a sensational sexual subtext. The pacey and engaging narrative marked the filmmakers out as fresh and thoroughly cosmopolitan new voices in Irish cinema, even if the overall effort feels a little callow overall. Although highly distinctive, *November Afternoon* can be seen as anticipating elements of Carney's later work in *Once* (2007), *Bachelor's Walk* (2001–2003), and *Sing Street* (2016), notably a preference for low-budget narratives set in and around Dublin, handheld cameras that circle and reveal characters' shifting emotions, and a unique talent for composing and integrating music into film.

O'CONNOR, MARK. Writer/director O'Connor has produced four feature films to date, and while each has been distinctive there is a discernible unity of vision in his socially marginal characters; a kinetic, realist shooting style; use of gritty (mainly urban) locations; and recurring preoccupations with contemporary Irish masculinities and violence.

Displaying a debt to Martin Scorsese (notably *Mean Streets*), O'Connor made his debut with the entertaining *Between the Canals* (2011)—a loose-limbed story of a raucous and sometimes violent 24 hours in Dublin during St. Patrick's weekend. The film featured a charismatic debut performance from O'Connor's friend and collaborator Peter Coonan that would inaugurate his still-rising career. His second feature, *King of the Travellers* (2012), proposed a revenge drama set within the Irish Traveller community and drawing on the traditions of that much-maligned subculture. The film was uneven in its narrative development—although a significant improvement on *Between the Canals*—but is distinguished by committed performances again from Peter Coonan and John Connors, one of several impressive nonactors from the Traveller community cast in the film.

O'Connor's third feature film, *Stalker* (2012), was again centered on themes of violence and masculinity and developed further his highly mobile, location-based style of shooting. It followed Oliver (John Connors), a seriously troubled homeless man, and his relationship with teenager Tommy (**Barry Keoghan**). Having appointed himself as protector to the young drug dealer, Oliver finds himself in conflict with Tommy's immediate family and criminal fraternity. Finally, *Cardboard Gangsters* (2016), his most successful film to date, reimagined the gangster genre in the underprivileged Dublin suburb of Darndale.

O'Connor is impressive for his clear passion for film and his courageous commitment to exploring settings and themes that rarely find their voice in "official" Irish cinema. However, his films to date have been marred by narratives that are often underdeveloped and occasionally implausible—a particular issue given his unstinting stylistic commitment to realism.

O'CONNOR, PAT (1943–). Born and raised in County Waterford, O'Connor enrolled in a liberal arts program at the University of California and then continued his education in Canada, returning in 1970 to work with **Radio Telefís Éireann**, where he learned the craft of directing. He served his apprenticeship in television production and was particularly acclaimed for his adaptation of John McGahern's short story *The Ballroom of Romance* (1982), a narrative that dealt with frustrated gender relations in a rural society where the only respite was the mating rituals of a local dance hall. It went on to win a BAFTA for Best Television Drama in Britain and acted as a springboard for a feature film career.

His first feature, *Cal* (1984), was produced by highly regarded British producer David Puttnam. He followed this in 1987 with *A Month in the Country*, based on the novel by J. R. Carr. The film, which helped to establish the film careers of Colin Firth and Kenneth Branagh, is set in Britain after World War I. Firth and Branagh play two traumatized and shellshocked war veterans who get summer jobs in a beautiful English country village—one to uncover a mural in a local church and the other to uncover the grave of a famous luminary. They become friends as they unearth secret Muslim influences in the area and discover the religious tensions between churches. They also become attracted to Natasha Richardson's Alice, who is locked in an unhappy marriage to the pastor. O'Connor's adaptation successfully transposed the complexity of the novel and paved the way for more international work. However, his star was dimmed somewhat by his subsequent features, namely, *Stars and Bars* (1988) and *The January Man* (1989), although he returned to form with another instance of heritage cinema in *Fools of Fortune* (1990), an adaptation of a William Trevor novel following the fortunes of a wealthy Anglo-Irish family during the War of Independence.

Drawing on the large readership already secured by the author, Maeve Binchy, the adaptation of *Circle of Friends*, with its all-star cast, was an enormous commercial success—certainly the biggest that the **Irish Film Board** had been involved with up to that point. O'Connor subsequently moved to theatrical adaptation, directing Frank McGuinness's screenplay based on Brian Friel's hugely popular *Dancing at Lughnasa*. The play—set in the small village of Ballybeg in rural County Donegal in the summer of 1936—had been highly successful for the **Abbey Theatre** abroad as well as in Ireland. The film was a sensitive and evocative transcription, giving free rein to its all-star cast, which included Meryl Streep.

Although the size of his output compares with that of **Jim Sheridan** and **Neil Jordan**, critics have generally afforded O'Connor less critical analysis and credence, judging that his extensive output lacks authorial distinctiveness and is perhaps characterized by a generic approach to his material. There is certainly a sense that he has been happy to work as a director for hire: half of his 10 features are not merely textually unconnected with Ireland but suggest relatively little in the way of consistent thematic concerns, although there is a consistent preference for period work and, in particular, the 1910s as evinced by *A Month in the Country, Fools of Fortune* and his last film (to date), an adaptation of Michael Murpago's World War I novel *Private Peaceful* (2012).

O'CONNOR, SINEAD (1966–). While she is best known as a performer, O'Connor's distinctive vocals have contributed to the soundscapes of a long list of films, particularly during the 1990s, as Irish film sought to establish itself though a blending of local and global textures. (IMDb lists some 80 credits as singer.) *The Butcher Boy*, *Michael Collins*, *When the Sky Falls*, *Angela's Ashes*, and *In the Name of the Father*, among many others, benefited from her contribution, the last memorably featuring "Thief of Your Heart" over the end credits. Indeed, directors have shown a peculiar preference for deploying her music at the denouement of the narrative: in *Michael Collins*, she performs "She Moved Through the Fair" over the final montage and contributes a haunting ballad to the close of *Veronica Guerin*.

O'Connor's strong and often controversial beliefs and her internationally publicized criticism of the Catholic Church in particular have framed her two notable Irish film roles to date. In *Hush-a-Bye Baby* (for which she again sang the theme), she plays a young girl growing up during the Northern Troubles. Although her character makes a relatively brief appearance, a scene where she dresses up as a nun resonates with her larger public persona. Clearly playing on this, **Neil Jordan** cast her as a blasphemous Virgin Mary in *The Butcher Boy*. The performance effectively and intertextually reflected her real-life persona, and the film explores the range of contentious debates over sacred divinity within the country and its contemporary traumatized sexual politics.

O'CONOR, HUGH (1975–). In *Red Hot* (1993), Hugh O'Conor plays a teenager living in 1950s Russia who attempts to set up a rock-and-roll band. He was well equipped for such a musical role: the actor is the son of John O'Conor, the internationally acclaimed pianist and director of the Royal Irish Academy of Music. Hugh O'Conor himself plays guitar, piano, and clarinet. He made an arresting debut at the age of nine opposite **Liam Neeson** in *Lamb* (1986). A role in *Da* (1988), an adaptation of a Hugh Leonard play, followed before he took on the role of the young Christy Brown in *My Left Foot* (1989). His performance as the palsied writer was again remarkable, and several critics cited it above even Daniel Day-Lewis's Oscar-winning performance as the older Christy.

From 1993 to 1995, he studied drama at Trinity College Dublin but continued to make films, such as the acclaimed *The Young Poisoner's Handbook* (1995). This last, a British-French-German coproduction, suggested a willingness to work in European cinema: he has subsequently made films in Turkey, Italy, and France. By contrast, his appearances in Hollywood productions have been few and far between: he played King Louis in the 1993 version of *The Three Musketeers* and appeared in *Chocolat* (2000), but the majority of his other screen appearances have been in Irish or British productions. These include a winning turn as the older brother in **The Boy from Mercury** (1996) and, in a definitively adult role, as Stephen Dedalus in **Bloom** (2003). More recently, he turned to directing with the debut feature *Metal Heart* (2019).

O'DOMHNAILL, RISTEARD. O'Domhnaill is that rare beast in contemporary Irish cinema: a filmmaker activist. Just as unusual is the fact that, for someone born and raised in the agricultural landscape of County Tipperary, his primary focus to date has been on the coastal communities of the west of Ireland.

After graduating in theoretical physics from Trinity College Dublin (and then a degree in Irish and history from the National University of Ireland), he commenced his career in film as a news cameraman before shooting *Shtax: A Homecoming* (2009) about Galway fiddle player and comedian Aindreas De Staic. He was propelled to national recognition when a news story he was sent to cover became *The Pipe* (2010), a film about the establishment of the Corrib Gas Project in Rossport, County Mayo—or, rather, a David-versus-Goliath story about local resistance to Shell Oil's attempts to build an onshore refinery. For four years, O'Domhnaill was granted access to follow three members of the community: Willie Corduff, one of five protestors (the "Rossport Five") jailed for refusing to stop interfering with Shell's work; Monica Muller, who controversially refused to join protests but whose court action delivered a major blow to Shell; and Pat "The Chief" O'Donnell, a local fisherman who is repeatedly arrested for sailing his small fishing boat into the path of the gigantic pipe-laying ship *Solitaire*. Produced by Rachel Lysaght, the film received a domestic theatrical release—unusual for a documentary feature on a subject such as this—and was a huge hit on the film festival circuit.

O'Domhnaill's next project, *Atlantic* (2016), was more ambitious but still rooted in a deep concern for the environment and the local. Narrated by **Brendan Gleeson** and financed through a crowdfunding campaign, it tells of the deeply depressing decline of coastal communities in County Donegal, Newfoundland, and Norway as a consequence of the rapacious actions of big oil and industrial super-trawler fishing. As with *The Pipe*, the power of the film lies in O'Domhnaill letting the people of these small communities tell their stories. While the film again received a theatrical release, O'Domhnaill also traveled far and wide to screen it anywhere people wished to have it screened. That kind of effort displays the depth of commitment to both topics and communities that makes his films shine.

O'DONNELL, DAMIEN (1967–). A native of Dublin, O'Donnell came to the fore during the "second wave" of Irish cinema in the 1990s with an impressive run of intelligent comedies. His first film *35 Aside* (1995), one of the all-time-great Irish short films and winner of multiple awards, was produced under the umbrella of production company ClingFilms, which he co-founded with other Dublin Institute of Technology film school graduates: Paul Fitzgerald, Harry Purdue, and **John Moore**. Another highly original short film, *Chrono Perambulator* (1998), preceded his feature debut, the British-Asian drama-comedy *East Is East* (1999), set in Manchester in 1971 and starring the great Om Puri as the unbending patriarch of an immigrant family. Produced for Film4, this unusual subject for the young Irish director won the 2000 Alexander Korda Award for Best British Film and BAFTA Awards and rapidly established his reputation in the United Kingdom and internationally.

After this stellar debut, O'Donnell seems to have stumbled in finding his next project before returning to Irish subjects with *Inside I'm Dancing* (aka *Rory O'Shea Was Here*) in 2004, produced by **Octagon Films**. This odd couple drama-comedy centered on physical disability, and while the screenplay felt somewhat compromised (the original story by Irish writer Christian O'Reilly was rewritten by Jeffrey Caine [*GoldenEye* and *Rules of Engagement*]), its direction clearly benefited from his deeply humanist sensibility. Again, however, his career seemed to stall, apparently due to successive development difficulties, as he continued to burnish a reputation as a commercial director (his quirky and optimistic outlook can be felt in many of his ads, viewable online) and in TV comedy (*The Savage Eye* [**Radio Telefís Éireann**]). His next film credit was *How Was Your Day* (2016), another award-winning short (based on a short story), funded by the **Irish Film Board**. It marked a significant shift in tone from O'Donnell's early films (although coincidentally returning to the themes of *Inside I'm Dancing*) in its story of a mother (played by the excellent Eileen Walsh) navigating the excitement and subsequent grief she feels after given birth to a child with disabilities. O'Donnell referred to it as "the most rewarding piece of work" he had ever done, and it received several awards, including Best Narrative Short Award at the 2016 SXSW (South by Southwest) film festival in Austin, Texas.

O'DONOGHUE, JOHN (1956–). O'Donoghue succeeded Sile de Valera as the minister with responsibility for film policy in June 2002. Born and raised in Caherciveen, County Kerry, O'Donoghue was a solicitor by trade and was elected TD (Irish member of Parliament) for the Fianna Fáil party in 1987 (and in each subsequent election). In 1997, O'Donoghue was appointed minister for justice, having campaigned on a hard-line "zero tolerance" policy in that year's election. He remained in that department until 2002 when, in a move widely regarded as a demotion, he was appointed to Arts, Sport, and Tourism, a new department that took on elements of the previous Department of Arts and Culture and Department of Tourism.

O'Donoghue's bullish public persona prior to this appointment made him a surprising choice. Despite this, he was generally regarded as having been an effective defender of state support for the film industry during a period when there was substantial pressure from the Department of Finance to withdraw all film support.

In the autumn of 2002, an independent estimates review committee, brought in to advise then Minister for Finance Charles McCreevy on the budget for the next year, recommended the abolition of the **Irish Film Board**. O'Donoghue intervened to ensure that the board was retained, and he was able to make an announcement to that effect in December 2002. Similarly, when McCreevy then announced his intention to end the **Section 481** tax incentive at the end of 2003, O'Donoghue employed **PriceWaterhouse-Coopers** to write a report recommending the retention of the incentive (as subsequently occurred). In 2005, when production levels fell to their lowest in five years, he intervened to augment the level of funding available to the Film Board, and in the summer of 2005, he announced the appointment of a Los Angeles–based screen commissioner to promote Ireland as a filmmaking location.

However, these achievements were entirely overshadowed by revelations in the *Sunday Tribune* in 2009 of O'Donoghue's profligate use of expenses during his time as minister and later as Ceann Comhairle. It was discovered that he ran up expenses of €550,000 during his tenure at Arts, Sport, and Tourism, including a lavish six-day visit to the Cannes Film Festival (in the company of his wife) for which he borrowed the government jet as well as car rental costs of €10,000. The detailed exposé of similar extravagances came to illustrate the hubris of the Celtic Tiger and brought about his resignation from office and politics in 2009.

O'DOWD, CHRIS (1979–). Although not quite an internationally recognizable "leading" man, Chris O'Dowd has, in a short period of time, transitioned from a comedy actor known only to U.K. and Irish audiences to one whose name is increasingly likely to receive third or fourth billing in Hollywood comedies (most notably those associated with Judd Apatow). He has also become something of a regular on the Hollywood chat show circuit, where his self-deprecating charm and ability to extemporize comedically make him a natural fit. As his star has risen in Hollywood, he has acquired a certain industry heft on the other side of the Atlantic: not only has he appeared in a series of Irish film roles, but he also created (and starred in) a Golden Globe–winning sitcom for Sky television.

O'Dowd grew up in Navan, County Meath (also the home of **Dylan Moran**), and studied politics and sociology at University College Dublin. Although not completing his studies, he was actively involved in the university drama society (Dramsoc), and he subsequently attended the London Academy of Music and Dramatic Art. His first screen role was a bit part in the ITV drama *Red Cap*, quickly followed by the more substantial role of the shy accountant Brendan in the first three seasons of **Radio Telefís Éireann**'s medical drama *The Clinic* (something of an incubator for a roster of Irish screen talent, including **Saoirse Ronan** and **Amy Huberman**). He interspersed this work with appearances in a number of British films, including a Scottish BAFTA award–winning turn as an Irish stand-up comedian in *Festival* (2005). Despite this last role, Irish audiences were so used to O'Dowd as a straight actor that it came as something of a surprise when his first substantial post–*The Clinic* role turned out to be one of the three leads in Graham Linehan's **Channel 4** comedy *The I.T. Crowd* (2006–2010).

O'Dowd played lowly IT support technician Roy Trenneman as a nerdy slacker Irishman opposite Richard Ayoade and Katherine Parkinson throughout the show's four seasons. Although returning to the United Kingdom for filming, O'Dowd moved to Los Angeles during the show's run and began to appear in U.S. comedy features, such as *Gulliver's Travels* (2010) and *Dinner for Schmucks* (2010). In 2011, director Paul Feig cast O'Dowd in *Bridesmaids* as Rhodes, a patrol car cop and Kristen Wiig's love interest. The film's critical and box office success brought O'Dowd to the attention of a much wider audience. Strikingly, at Feig's insistence, O'Dowd played the role in his native accent: in contrast to so many actors from this country who initially appear indistinguishable from their U.S. counterparts when they first appear in Hollywood productions, O'Dowd was clearly identified as Irish from the outset. This contributed to a U.S. perception of O'Dowd as slightly exotic and, more surprisingly, as a somewhat unlikely eccentric sex symbol. (O'Dowd himself downplays this, describing himself as more of a "spoon symbol: I think women just want to spoon me.")

Bridesmaids immediately led to a lead role in *Friends with Kids* (2011) (also featuring much of the *Bridesmaids* cast) and another role in *Bridesmaids* producer Judd Apatow's *This Is Forty* (2012). (In 2018, he appeared in yet another Apatow production, an adaptation of Nick Hornby's novel *Juliet, Naked*.) However, in a somewhat unexpected turn, O'Dowd was also cast in a straight role as the male lead in the BBC's 2011 production of *The Crimson*

Petal and the White, an adaptation of Michael Faber's novel set in 19th-century London. Although the switch back to a serious role initially perplexed U.K. critics, his performance was nonetheless acclaimed.

After 2012, O'Dowd's career seemed to go in several directions at once. On television, he remained primarily a comedy actor (and clearly primarily regards himself as such), appearing in a quasi-comedic recurring role on Lena Dunham's *Girls* and as lead in Christopher Guest's HBO comedy *Family Tree* (2013). However, on the big screen, although still playing comedy in *The Sapphires* (2012), his characters in *Thor: The Dark World* (2013), Richard Ayoade's *The Double* (2013), and, perhaps most notably, John McDonagh's **Calvary** (2014) have been not only serious but at times actively sinister. A recognition of this aspect of his star persona appears to have underlined the decision to cast him as Lenny (opposite James Franco's George) in Anna Shapiro's 2014 Broadway revival of John Steinbeck's *Of Mice and Men*. His first theater role since college officially confirmed his chops as a straight actor and earned O'Dowd a Tony nomination.

However, arguably his greatest on-screen success (off-screen he married U.K. TV host Dawn Porter in 2012 and became a father in 2015) has been his creation of the comedy series *Moone Boy* (2012–) for Sky Television. The sitcom mines O'Dowd's own biography to create 11-year-old Martin Moone as he grows up in the late 1980s in Boyle, County Roscommon (O'Dowd's real-life home), with his parents and three sisters (O'Dowd appears as Martin's imaginary friend Sean Murphy). Over the course of three series, pivotal events in Irish history of the period—the Irish soccer team at the World Cup in 1990, the election of a female president, and so on—acted as a backdrop to Martin's coming of age. Despite its cultural specificity (a recurring joke is the use of the theme music from a now defunct Irish radio show), the show proved remarkably popular with U.K. audiences and in the United States (by 2012 familiar with O'Dowd's work) via the Hulu platform. As writer and executive producer of the series, O'Dowd won an international Emmy Award for Best Comedy Series in 2013.

Although postpaternity O'Dowd would return to television comedy (albeit of a macabre nature) for his lead role in the Epix cable reboot of *Get Shorty* (2017), he has appeared mainly in straight dramas thereafter. He plays real-life journalist David Walsh as he investigates Lance Armonstrong in *The Program* (2015), the son of bereaved mother Andie McDowell in *Love After Love* (2016), and an insecure poker player whose actions lead to the titular character's downfall in *Molly's Game* (2017). His willingness to essay flawed (often profoundly so) characters (see his toxic male Douglas Downey in *Molly's Game* but especially Duncan in *Juliet, Naked*) suggest an actor happy to experiment with his screen persona.

O'HARA, MAUREEN (1920–2015). Remembered for her striking beauty and feisty roles—most notably as Mary Kate Danaher in John Ford's *The Quiet Man* (1952)—O'Hara was born Maureen FitzSimons in the middle-class Dublin suburb of Ranelagh as Ireland was going through the birth pains of civil war. Later known as the Queen of Technicolor for her green eyes and red hair in color adventure films such as *The Black Swan* (1942) and *At Sword's Point* (1952), her career began when she screen-tested for actor/director Charles Laughton in London. Laughton was first a mentor, recommending her for roles in *Kicking the Moon Around* (1938) (her screen debut) and *My Irish Molly* (1938) and later to costar in three films: Hitchcock's *Jamaica Inn* (1939), *The Hunchback of Notre Dame* (1939), and *This Land Is Mine* (1943). It was Laughton who suggested she change her name, and she got her breakthrough as Maureen O'Hara in John Ford's Oscar-winning *How Green Was My Valley* (1940). It was the first of five films made with the director who defined her legacy, even though—as she later revealed in her autobiography—she had a fractious and often abusive relationship with the director. He subsequently cast her in *Rio Grande* (1950), *The Quiet Man* (1952), *The Long Gray Line* (1954), and *Wings of Eagles* (1957), and in all, she came to define a Fordian ideal of womanhood: strong and dutiful but also passionate and devoted.

While John Wayne (with whom she made seven films) was jokingly referred to as "the greatest guy I ever met," O'Hara spoke in a 1945 interview of her reputation as a "cold hunk of marble" and a "cold potato without sex appeal" for her refusal to let Hollywood producers and directors "paw" her. In a declaration that was years ahead of its time and all too prescient, she remarked, "If that's Hollywood's idea of a woman, I'm ready to quit now."

She didn't, of course, and although she worked throughout her long career, it was during the 1940s and 1950s that she shined brightest. She retired to Ireland in the 1970s and was delighted by the appreciation and recognition that she received in later years when she was celebrated as a feminist icon. After quarrels with her caregiver, however, she returned to the United States in her 90s to be near her nephew (son of her beloved brother Charles Fitzsimons) and died there at age 95. She is buried in Arlington National Cemetery next to her husband, who was a U.S. Navy pilot.

O'HERLIHY, DAN (1919–2005). O'Herlihy studied architecture at the National University of Ireland and worked as a theater set designer before turning to acting with the Abbey Players and Radio Éireann—the forerunner of **Radio Telefís Éireann**. His first film role was in Carol Reed's 1947 classic *Odd Man Out*. Later moving to the United States, he joined Orson Welles's Mercury Theater and was cast as McDuff in his 1948 film version of *Macbeth*. Other notable film roles included those in *Imitation of Life* (1958) and *McArthur* (1977), and though rarely returning home to work, he did appear in **John Huston**'s adaptation **The Dead** (1987) of James Joyce's classic story "The Dead." In all, he starred in more than 60 cinema and television films and was nominated for an Oscar in 1955 for his intense portrayal of the title role in *The Adventures of Robinson Crusoe*, directed by the great Spanish director Luis Buñuel.

O'LEARY, LIAM (1910–1992). Liam O'Leary was arguably the single most active and influential figure in the establishment of a film culture in Ireland. Over the course of his life, he was an author, an actor, a filmmaker, and the cofounder of the **Irish Film Society**, and in his later years, he almost single-handedly gathered and preserved the nucleus of what would become the **Irish Film Archive**.

He was born in Youghal, but his formative cinema experiences were in Wexford, where his family moved when he was a child and where he became an avid cinemagoer. While studying at University College Dublin, he expanded his interests to include theater, and in 1934, he cofounded the Dublin Little Theatre Guild. While still a student, he partook in an extraordinary protest at the screening of *Irish Eyes Are Smiling* in the Savoy Cinema in Dublin. The protestors (who included **Cyril Cusack** and later president of Ireland Cearbhall O'Dalaigh) demanded the removal of the film, which, they argued, represented the Irish as stupid and backward. In O'Leary's account (O'Leary 1945), the cinema manager then called for the aid of armed detectives before agreeing to discuss the film with protestors. The protestors achieved their end, however, and the film was removed.

He was formally employed as a civil servant, but his interest in and commitment to film were evident in his extracurricular activities, which included working as film critic for *Ireland Today* and cofounding the Irish Film Society in 1936. After a decade in the civil service, he was seconded to the **Abbey Theatre** as a producer but left to freelance in radio and journalism and as an occasional actor for director Brendan Stafford. He played a priest in the latter's *Men Against the Sun* (1953) and a gangster in *Stranger at My Door* (1956).

This period also saw the publication of O'Leary's *Invitation to the Film*, the first book written on Irish cinema. Published in 1945, the book argued passionately for the establishment of an indigenous industry, pointing to the need for a well-equipped national studio (thus coinciding with **Sean Lemass**'s contemporaneous ambitions) and a native newsreel service. Contending that film had a unique role to play in "national renaissance," he argued that "not to use it would be almost an acknowledgement of terrible failure" (O'Leary 1945).

In that same book, he argued that "cinema must be used to open the eyes as well as the hearts of our people." That philosophy clearly informed his own work in the 1940s, when he became a director of short films in his own right. The most notable of these was his production of *Our Country*, commissioned by Sean MacBride as part of Clann na Poblachta's 1948 election campaign. The eight-minute film dwelled on national poverty, unemployment, and emigration and implicitly cited the incumbent Fianna Fáil administration as the cause of these ills. Certainly, Fianna Fáil regarded the 100-print release of the film as a factor in their loss of the election.

Sean MacBride became minister for external (foreign) affairs in the government that followed the election, and he appointed O'Leary to sit on the newly established **Cultural Relations Committee**, which immediately began to commission a series of films on Ireland. O'Leary and Brendan Stafford collaborated on *Portrait of Dublin*, the third of these. However, by the time the film was completed in 1952, Fianna Fáil had returned to power, and *Portrait of Dublin* was effectively suppressed.

Effectively deprived of the only realistic means of making a film in Ireland, in 1953, O'Leary moved to London, where he was appointed acquisitions officer of the British National Film Archive. This indirectly benefited Irish cinema culture since O'Leary negotiated an arrangement with the British Archive that allowed him to use their facilities to preserve any historic Irish films. As a consequence, several crucial productions from the **Kalem Company** and **Film Company of Ireland** were held for a period by the British National Film Archive.

O'Leary returned to Dublin in the 1960s, finding employment with **Radio Telefís Éireann** as a film reviewer, a job he held until his retirement in 1986. However, it was his leisure activities during this period that had a much more lasting impact. In 1976, he organized an elaborate exhibition on the history of film in Ireland at the invitation of the Dublin Arts Festival. He also researched and wrote a major biography of the Dublin-born silent-era director **Rex Ingram** that was published in 1980. Most important, he continued collecting a vast range of rare and valuable material relating to Irish cinema that he stored in his Dublin flat until 1986, when the National Library gave him an office and a room for his archive.

Fittingly, his efforts led him to become the subject of a documentary celebrating his life and times: **Donald Taylor Black**'s *At the Cinema Palace—Liam O'Leary*. More tacit acknowledgment of his key place in Irish cinema history came when—only months before passing away—he was invited to preside over the opening ceremony of the **Irish Film Centre** in 1992. This was especially apt given that the center was home to the then **Irish Film Institute**'s archive.

O'LEARY, RONAN. The most notable thing about Ronan O'Leary's career was perhaps not so much the quality of the films he has made but the fact that he made them at all. Between 1987 and 1992, widely acknowledged as the most barren period for Irish production in three decades, O'Leary managed the not inconsiderable feat of completing four drama productions: ***Riders to the Sea***, ***Fragments of Isabella***, ***Diary of a Madman***, and ***Hello Stranger***. Ironically, however, since 1993, the period during which the Irish production sector took off, his output has dwindled to virtually nothing: just one feature (***Driftwood***). However, viewed in its totality, his work arguably lends itself more to an auteurist analysis than that of many Irish directors, with his films invariably set in a single location (in part for budget reasons) and, as a result, characterized by an occasionally overwhelming sense of claustrophobia.

Ronan O'Leary began his career as a drama producer/director for the Public Broadcasting Service (PBS) in Los Angeles in 1983, making a number of drama-documentaries and some profiles on filmmakers like Oliver Stone and David Puttnam. His "Irish" debut with an adaptation of J. M. Synge's play *Riders to the Sea* in 1987 was heavily criticized at home, but its small budget meant that even the modest TV and video sales it achieved in the United States were enough to allow O'Leary to move to his next production, *Fragments of Isabella*, in 1989. Both this and his third film in 1990 (a film version of Gogol's *Diary of a Madman*) received more positive reviews that focused mainly on the manner in which O'Leary had managed to transcend the limitations imposed by what were obviously low budgets.

His fourth film—*Hello Stranger*—was nominated for four awards at the 1993 Monte Carlo Television Festival. After *Hello Stranger*, O'Leary took on screen-writing duties, working with Michael Lindsay-Hogg and Chet Raymo to adapt the latter's novel *The Dork of Cork* into the screenplay for ***Frankie Starlight***. However, when **Mary Breen Farrelly Productions** (MBF) set up shop in **Ardmore Studios** in 1992, O'Leary became a part of that operation, working as an editor on *The Sheltering Desert* (1992), a film that the company picked up and completed when the original production company—Kusier Films—went bust.

It was thus with MBF Productions that O'Leary made *Driftwood* (1997). Although he was operating with his largest budget to date, the resulting film was poorly received internationally, and virtually all reviews cited Rob Reiner's *Misery* as an obvious—and superior—influence.

His work since 1997 has been much more sporadic; most recently, he directed a documentary—*Hold the Passion*—in 2003. It is worth noting that over the course of his films, O'Leary has managed to assemble quite remarkable casts and crews. He has worked with four Oscar winners—actress Geraldine Page, cinematographers Walter Lassally and Billy Williams, and set designer **Josie MacAvin** (who worked on three of his films). Similarly, James Spader, who appeared in *Driftwood*, had previously won a Best Actor award at the Cannes Film Festival for *Sex, Lies and Videotape* (1989). If nothing else, this demonstrates a remarkable capacity to sell his projects, one perhaps not entirely reflected in the finished products.

Ó RIADA, SEÁN (1931–1971). Widely regarded as the most significant Irish composer of the 20th century, Ó Riada first came to wide public attention through his score for the **Gael Linn** film *Mise Éire*. Born in Cork, Ó Riada grew up and was schooled in Limerick before going to University College Cork to study arts. He graduated with first-class honors in music in 1952 and in 1953 was appointed assistant director of music at Radio Éireann (later to become **Radio Telefís Éireann** [RTÉ]). Although he enjoyed aspects of the job—namely, concert arranging and the occasional opportunity to have his own music recorded—he was less interested in the administrative side and in 1955 resigned his post. This led Ó Riada to approach the recently formed **Gael Linn** for work, initially writing a few articles on music for *Comhar*, the organization's magazine. In 1959, he visited the Kerry Gaeltacht on the Dingle peninsula and for the first time experienced what he termed *An Saol Gaelach* (literally "the Irish life"). On his return to Dublin, he encouraged Gael Linn to record two of the singers he had encountered in Kerry, and when the organization subsequently decided to make its first long-playing record of Irish music, Ó Riada was invited to produce it.

When Gael Linn turned its focus to the production of a major Irish film based on archival material (*Mise Éire*), the organization naturally turned to Ó Riada to compose the music for it. The film's director, George Morrison, agreed despite his misgivings about Ó Riada's youth. The resulting score remains a high point in the history of not merely Irish film music composition but arguably of all 20th-century Irish music. The score drew heavily on arrangements of traditional Irish songs but arranged them in the kind of lush romantic style that characterized mainstream European composition. At a stroke, then, Ó Riada conjured up an Irish classical tradition informed by a nationalist vision. He also, it is worth stressing, created a fantastically emotive score: the "Roisín Dubh" sequence, where the music swells to a crescendo as independence is achieved, is as stirring as any moment in film music history.

Ó Riada continued to work with Gael Linn on *Saoirse?* (the 1961 sequel to *Mise Éire*) and on Louis Marcus's 1966 film (also for Gael Linn) *An Tine Bheo*. He was also commissioned to score the **Four Provinces** production of *Playboy of the Western World* (1962); **John Ford**'s thinly disguised Sean O'Casey biopic *Young Cassidy* (1965), which permitted Ó Riada a brief sojourn in Hollywood; and *Kennedy's Ireland*, a documentary made in the wake of President John F. Kennedy's 1963 visit to Ireland.

He went on to work with the **Abbey Theatre** through the 1960s and made a major contribution to the revival of Irish traditional music through the establishment of the Ceoltóirí Cualann musical group; a recording of their performance at the Gaiety Theatre in the late 1960s became the best-selling Gael Linn record *Ó Riada sa Gaiety* (Ó Riada in the Gaiety).

Less well known is the fact that Ó Riada set up his own production company—Draíon Films—in the mid-1960s to make short films for some of the RTÉ television shows with which he was involved. He had planned to make an Irish-themed feature-length film for the American market but was forced to abandon the scheme when he realized that color television had become the norm in the United States: his own equipment was exclusively for black-and--white production.

Sadly, Ó Riada's life and work were cut short in his 40th year. Decades of drinking had contributed to cirrhosis of the liver, and in 1971, he was admitted to a Cork hospital, and from there he went to King's College Hospital in London, where he died after a series of heart attacks.

O'SHEA, MILO (1926–2013). O'Shea was an outstanding Irish character actor recognizable for his bushy eyebrows, a resonating baritone, and impish smile. Born in Dublin, he attended the Christian Brothers in Synge Street (the setting for **John Carney**'s *Sing Street*), where he met his lifelong friend and fellow screen character actor Donal Donnelly. He began acting on the Dublin stage during the 1960s—appearing in plays at the **Abbey Theatre** and The Gate—before moving to TV and stage in London.

He then rapidly established his reputation and career on-screen and on-stage. He was highly effective in a diverse range of screen roles that included Leopold Bloom in **Joseph Strick**'s 1967 film version of *Ulysses*, as Dr. Durand Durand in Roger Vadim's counterculture classic *Barbarella* (1968), and as Friar Laurence in Franco Zeffirelli's *Romeo and Juliet* (1968). In 1968 also, he scored a major success in the United States when he was cast and secured a Tony Award nomination in the New York production of *Staircase*, a two-character play about an aging gay couple who own a barbershop in London's East End.

His long career included many memorable if usually secondary roles in film, including *The Verdict* (1982) with Paul Newman, the Chris Columbus comedy *Only the Lonely* (1991) (also starring **Maureen O'Hara**), and a late turn as a Catholic priest in **Neil Jordan**'s *The Butcher Boy* (1997) along with a constant stream of U.S. TV: *Cheers*, *Frasier*, *The West Wing*, *Oz*, and so on. He died in 2013 at age 86.

O'SULLIVAN, MAUREEN (1911–1998). Born in Boyle, County Roscommon, O'Sullivan attended a convent school in Dublin before attending the famous high class finishing school in Roehampton in England, where the actress Vivien Leigh was one of her classmates. After a successful screen test, she got a role in *Song o' My Heart* (1930), which also starred the Irish tenor Count John McCormack. After completing this film in the United States, she went on to appear in six more movies and in 1932 signed with

Metro-Goldwyn-Mayer (MGM) studios. She later appeared as Jane Parker in *Tarzan the Ape Man* (1932) opposite Johnny Weissmuller and in five sequels. Her marriage to John Farrow produced seven children, several of whom—most notably Mia—became actors in their own right. She also starred in *The Thin Man* (1934), *Anna Karenina* (1935), and *Pride and Prejudice* (1940). When John Farrow contracted typhoid while in the navy, O'Sullivan requested that MGM release her from her contract in order to nurse him. This effectively marked the end of her career as a leading actress, although she enjoyed something of a renaissance in the decade following her reappearance in the noirish *The Big Clock* in 1948 (under the direction of her husband) and would work with directors as diverse as Douglas Sirk (*All I Desire* [1953]) and Bud Boetticher (*The Tall T* [1957]). These later films included one Irish-themed curio, *No Resting Place* (1951). Shot in County Wicklow by renowned documentary director Paul Rotha (in his fiction debut), the film included O'Sullivan as part of an Irish Traveller family, pursued by the police after one of their number (Alec Kyle played by Michael Gough) accidentally kills a gamekeeper. Drawing on the thespian resources of the **Abbey Theatre** and the **Radio Telefís Éireann** Players, the film's realist style, echoing the work of Italian contemporary work from Vittoria da Sica and Roberto Rossellini, won plaudits, although its clumsy conclusion somewhat undermined the overall impact. By the mid-1950s, however, O'Sullivan increasingly moved to work in television, her big-screen appearances diminishing to almost nothing. She made a couple of cameo appearances in higher-profile works during the mid-1980s, including Francis Ford Coppola's *Peggy Sue Got Married* (1986) and, playing mother to her own daughter Mia, in Woody Allen's *Hannah and Her Sisters* (1986).

She was widowed in 1963, when Farrow died at just 58 years of age. She would remarry in 1983 to an American businessman, James Cushing, to whom she remained wed until her death at age 87 in 1998.

O'SULLIVAN, MORGAN. *See* WORLD 2000 ENTERTAINMENT.

O'SULLIVAN, THADDEUS (1947–). O'Sullivan was born in Dublin on 2 May 1947 but moved in 1966 to London, where he received his early film training at the Ealing School of Art and the Royal College of Art. As with contemporaries like **Pat Murphy**, **Joe Comerford**, and **Bob Quinn**, his earlier films were influenced by avant-garde practices, and in the late 1970s, he made two experimental films about the life of the Irish immigrant in London: the short *A Pint of Plain* and the feature-length *On a Paving Stone Mounted*. Using a combination of documentary footage and fictional re-creation, both films explore the place of the exile and encapsulate O'Sullivan's position as a filmmaker caught between Britain and Ireland, "in the crack between cultures" as he put it. In 1985, he made his first foray into drama filmmaking when he produced one of the all-time great Irish short films, *The Woman Who Married Clark Gable* (1985), commissioned by **Radio Telefís Éireann** (RTÉ) and adapted from Sean O'Faolain's short story about a woman whose humdrum existence is transformed by the imaginative power of the movies on her sheltered but deeply impressionable Irish Catholic imagination. The BAFTA-nominated film featured memorable performances from Bob Hoskins and **Brenda Fricker**.

During the 1980s, O'Sullivan established himself primarily as a cinematographer and worked on many important Irish films of the period, including Joe Comerford's *Travellers*, Bob Quinn's TV series *Atlantean*, **Cathal Black**'s *Pigs*, and Pat Murphy's *Anne Devlin*. His first fiction feature as director was *December Bride* (1990), an adaptation of Sam Hanna Bell's 1951 novel about a young woman who goes to work for two brothers in a tight-knit turn-of-the-century Presbyterian community and falls in love with both of them. The film was exceptional in many ways, not least for offering a sympathetic depiction of an element of the Northern Irish Presbyterian community in the early (pre–Anglo-Irish Treaty) 20th century.

In a very different tone and social context, he revisited Northern Ireland, making one of the first explorations of Loyalist paramilitaries in the thriller *Nothing Personal* (1995). Set in 1975, it offered a detailed portrait of a paramilitary unit over a 24-hour period at the height of the Troubles. The film's invocation of gangster movie tropes and 1970s pop sound track led to an offer to direct the Robert de Niro–produced *Witness to the Mob* series in the United States, and he continued this line of enquiry with *Ordinary Decent Criminal* (2000), a crime-comedy portrait of Dublin gangster Michael Cahill (earlier the basis of **John Boorman**'s *The General*), scripted by **Gerry Stembridge** and, perhaps not entirely successfully, with U.S. actor Kevin Spacey in the lead role and Linda Fiorentino as his "moll." The film was not well received by critics.

The Heart of Me (2002), starring Helena Bonham Carter, Paul Bettany, and Olivia Williams, reprised the love-triangle theme of *December Bride* set in 1930s middle-class England to lukewarm reviews, but O'Sullivan was by this stage finding the majority of his work in TV crime drama in Britain and Ireland. Credits here include the little-seen Acorn TV series *Single Handed* (2010) and the second series of the RTÉ television gangster thriller *Proof* (2005) along with the four-part RTÉ drama *Amber* (2013) and, for the BBC, *Silent Witness* (2017–2018) and *Call the Midwife* (2015). His 2009 portrait of Winston Churchill's immediate prewar wars *Into the Storm* (2009) was widely acclaimed and nominated for a plethora of Emmy and Golden Globe awards (with **Brendan Gleeson**'s central depiction of Churchill securing the Emmy nod for Best Actor). He made a return to the big screen in 2011 with

Stella Days (2011), a well-realized if familiar portrait of tensions between cinema and the Catholic Church in 1950s rural Ireland in the tradition of *Cinema Paradiso*, starring Martin Sheen.

Citizen Lane (2018) is one of O'Sullivan's most unusual projects, dealing, as many of his films have done, with the vagaries of Irish history but in a very different vein. Mark O'Halloran's screenplay takes a docudrama approach to the story of Hugh Lane (played by Tom Vaughan Lawlor), who fought a project to establish a public modern art gallery in Dublin before his untimely death on the USS *Lusitania*. The drama is intercut with interviews from historians, including Roy Foster, Paul Rouse, and Morna O'Neill, who offer a narrative of his life that is illustrated by the paintings of his outstanding collection and the campaign to recover for Ireland Lane's bequest of 39 great works of impressionism, among them paintings by Monet, Renoir, and Manet.

O'TOOLE, PETER (1932–2013). O'Toole is often remembered as part of a generation of "hell-raiser" British actors who came of age in the 1950s and 1960s alongside the likes of **Richard Harris**, Richard Burton, Oliver Reed, and Albert Finney. Certainly, he had an enduring and lifelong friendship with Harris, grounded in their shared Irish roots, an appetite for alcohol and women (including a long affair with Princess Margaret), and an apparently reckless attitude toward their prodigious talent. However, his long and productive career suggests that this reputation also contained large elements of myth, and (unlike many of those he was associated with) he was highly regarded for his professionalism and worked consistently up until his death in 2013 at age 81.

Born in Leeds (not Connemara, as he proclaimed throughout his life) to a Scottish mother and Galway-born bookmaker, O'Toole early on cultivated a Celtic flair alongside aristocratic manners that belied his background as working-class English Catholic. Like others of the postwar generation, his greatest performance was perhaps himself. Handsome and debonair, he won a scholarship to attend the Royal Academy of Dramatic Arts in London and came to prominence as a stage actor in the heyday of postwar British drama, first as a member of the Bristol Old Vic and then in the Royal Shakespeare Company. However, he shot to international attention and immortality when David Lean cast him as *Lawrence of Arabia* (1962) (after Albert Finney and Marlon Brando had turned it down). In 1966, he appeared on an Irish stage for the first time in the Gaiety production of O'Casey's *Juno and the Paycock* (Jack Boyle) and three years later made his sole appearance on the **Abbey Theatre** stage, opposite **Donal McCann**, in the first Irish production of Beckett's *Waiting for Godot*.

Among his most appreciated screen performances were *The Lion in Winter* (1968), *Goodbye Mr. Chips* (1969), *The Ruling Class* (1972), *The Stunt Man* (1980), *My Favorite Year* (1982), and *Venus* (2006). He appeared in few Irish roles, a notable exception being **Neil Jordan**'s *High Spirits* (1988). On being notified by the Academy that he was to be a recipient of an Honorary Oscar at the 75th (2003) awards, he initially rejected the offer (for fear of receiving no more work), only to relent and accept the accolade.

O'Toole maintained his association with Ireland to the end of his life, building a beautiful stone house outside Clifden, where he bred Connemara ponies and became a great supporter of the annual Connemara Pony Show. When he died, the president of Ireland, **Michael D. Higgins**, offered this appreciation: "I imagine Peter's soul still walking the Sky Road in Clifden, on guard against the return of the rabbits, still coaching cricket and still shouting at the television. . . . To be in his company was not an experience in the raising of hell—as some tabloids would have it—rather it was about the witness of a great talent, mischief and genius too."

OCTAGON FILMS. One of the busiest and most business savvy of Irish production companies, Octagon was founded by James Flynn (previously business manager at the **Irish Film Board** [1993–1997] and head of development at **John Boorman**'s **Merlin Films**) and **Juanita Wilson** in association with **Morgan O'Sullivan**. Originally known as Metropolitan Films, the company initially combined with **World 2000 Entertainment** as a coproducer and to service incoming productions, many of which were big-budget Hollywood feature films. These included *Reign of Fire* (2002), *The Count of Monte Cristo* (2002), *King Arthur* (2004), and *Tristan and Isolde* (2006). However, responding to changes in British film tax incentives and wider industry production trends, the company was forced to reevaluate its business model and shifted to hosting the production of long-form TV drama. Notable successes in this area include three seasons of the Victorian horror drama *Penny Dreadful* (Sky Atlantic and Showtime, 2013–2016), the hugely successful *Vikings* (History Channel, 2013–), **Neil Jordan**'s *The Borgias* (Showtime, 2011–2013), and *Love/Hate* (**Radio Telefís Éireann**, 2010–2013). Octagon has also coproduced a number of Irish-set feature films over the years—described by Flynn as "passion projects"—including *Inside I'm Dancing*, *Cowboys and Angels*, *H3*, *Nora*, and **John Michael McDonagh**'s *Calvary* (2014).

The somewhat opaque relationship between Octagon and World 2000 came to a head in 2016 when Berlin-based investment firm W2 Filmproduktion Vertriebs sued Morgan O'Sullivan and James Flynn, claiming that the producers diverted funds, profit, and income from international productions to other companies, resulting in estimated losses of €25 million for W2, which, it claimed, owned 49 percent of Octagon. At the Irish High Court in

November 2017, the Irish producers claimed that Octagon Films was a development company, not a production one, and as such did not owe any revenues to its German partner since that part of their business had not made any profits. Arguing that the case was spurious and opportunistic, Flynn and O'Sullivan eventually agreed to repay more than €300,000 to W2 Filmproduktion acquired in start-up funding over 16 years previously. The case resulted in a request by the Irish producers to close the company.

***ODD MAN OUT* (1947).** This Irish-themed film noir classic is part of a trilogy from the British director Carol Reed that deals with various forms of fatalism, including later adaptations from stories by Graham Greene, *Fallen Idol* (1948), and the better-known *The Third Man* (1949). *Odd Man Out* explores the character of Johnny (James Mason), a disaffected leader of the "Organisation"—an old Irish Republican Army unit—who emerges from prison full of doubts about the continued use of violence to further republicanism. Still loyal to his ideals, however, and unwilling or unable to accept the pleadings of his girlfriend, Kathleen (Kathleen Sullivan), he goes ahead with one last robbery to replenish resources for the movement. Inevitably, things go awry: a man is killed, and Johnny is seriously injured while attempting to steal a textile mill payroll in Belfast.

Johnny finds himself wandering the mean streets of Belfast, which are filmed using expressive low-key, chiaroscuro lighting that effectively captures the postwar blitzed-out buildings in the docks area of the city. Most people ignore the wounded man as he tries to find his destiny, but Kathleen, following her heart and in spite of all entreaties not to do so, hatches an escape plan for both of them. Trying to capture the escaped convict in this divided city is the Royal Ulster Constabulary inspector (Denis O'Dea), who embodies the forces of reasoned law and order, as he seeks to discover where Johnny is hiding. At one stage, in a scene reminiscent of the famous child and ball sequence in Fritz Lang's *M* (1931), the children playing in the street notice the outlaw, which ensures that he will be discovered. Kathleen unwittingly leads the police to her beloved, accompanied by her priest, Father Tom, who wants to save his immortal soul. Following some engaging meanders into public houses and scenes of artists trying to capture the soul of such a terrorist, the spiral of the story eventually moves to its inevitable fatalistic conclusion.

As snow begins to fall—reminiscent of the ending of *The Dead*—Kathleen eventually locates Johnny. While ostensibly trying to escape on an emigrant ship at the docks, their fate together is sealed as the police surround them and Kathleen decides to draw their fire. After both are shot dead in a hail of bullets, the camera majestically swoops around their bodies in the snow as the priest blesses them and the camera tilts to a close-up of a clock—time has finally run out for them—and the sound of the horn of the ship that could have taken them away is heard on the sound track. The critic John Hill speaks of the fatalistic evocation of atavistic violence in such narratives that corresponds to an attitude toward the political problems in the North. Generic or stylistic conventions implicit in film noir can also promote an attitude and approach toward ethical questions about human agency that are universal, beyond local or political explications. Either way, *Odd Man Out* has remained a canonical text for Irish studies.

OLCOTT, SIDNEY (1873–1949). Born in Toronto to an Irish mother who emigrated from Howth and an unknown father, "John Sidney Alcott" moved to New York as a young man to further his acting career. After some years on the stage, he became a performer with the fledgling American Mutoscope and Biograph Studios in 1904 before graduating to directing films. Energetic, talented, and handsome, he subsequently moved with Biograph managers Frank Marion and Samuel Long (with funding from Chicago distributor George Klein) to establish **Kalem**, which would become one of the most important and pioneering U.S. producers of American cinema's transitional era (ca. 1906–1914). (His resignation caused Biograph to promote another of its actors, D. W. Griffith, to directing with enduring consequences for American film history.) His first film was *Ben-Hur* (1907), which made use of sets erected as part of an existing outdoor re-creation of Lew Wallace's famous and widely adapted novel. More action than narrative, the film made legal history after being sued by Wallace's estate for breach of copyright.

During New York's savagely cold winter months—making location shooting difficult—Olcott, along with a stock company that included leading Kalem actress and scenarist Gene Gauntier and cameraman George Hollister, moved production to the warmer climes of Florida. The setting—along with the 50th anniversary of its commencement in 1911—inspired the development of American Civil War–themed adventures, and soon Kalem became synonymous with the genre, which included the pioneering girl-spy serial (starring Gauntier). Soon, however, other production companies came to Florida, sending the Kalems farther afield in search of novelty, beginning with an overseas trip to Ireland, England, and Germany (where Gauntier had a sister) and later as far as Egypt and Palestine. The first of these voyages took place in 1910, and Olcott and Gauntier—at first with Kalem and later independently—would return to Ireland annually until 1914, shooting at **Beaufort** near Killarney. (The Beaufort Bar, where they shot and stayed, remains open to this day and in the hands of the same Sullivan family.) The "O'Kalems" became justifiably synonymous with Irish subjects, becoming the first company to ever shoot drama subjects in Ireland, a location that, as Florida had previously, inspired the themes of their 28 films ranging from *The Lad from Old Ireland* (1910) to *Bold Emmet, Ireland's Martyr* (1915). The first told the story of an Irish immigrant in the United States who pines for and then returns to marry his sweetheart. Although it may have been aimed primarily at Irish American audiences, its story had universal appeal and made Kalem a lot of money, spurring future visits and innovation.

In 1912, Olcott took the company to Palestine to film *From the Manger to the Cross*. Budgeted at $35,000, the film took in an incredible $1 million in U.S. theaters. However, despite being president of the company, Olcott's share in the earnings amounted to no more than $350, and he received no credit. In 1912, Olcott and Gautier left the company to form the Gene Gautier Feature Players in keeping with the brief vogue whereby female actresses created their own production companies. It was this company that returned to Beaufort in 1913 and was followed in 1914 by Olcott's own Sid Films (with his wife Valentine Grant). The outbreak of World War I brought his Irish sojourns to a conclusion (newspapers reported that he was "trapped" in the country as war broke out) and put an end to his stated ambition to build a permanent studio in Ireland.

The body of work left behind ranged from romantic melodrama, such as the popular three-reel adaptation of Dion Boucicault's *The Colleen Bawn* (1911), to more overtly politicized material, such as *Rory O'More* (1911), which drew the ire of the British authorities in Ireland during a period of political unrest that would eventually lead to 1916. Historians have tradition-ally argued that the films were produced primarily for the large diasporic Irish audience in American cities: several identify the United States as a potential haven for those forced by economic or political circumstances to flee Ireland, and the end titles of *For Ireland's Sake*, for example, posit the West (in this case, the United States) as "the land of the free." However, as Gary Rhodes and others have shown in researching film exhibition of the period, Kalem films played all over the United States and Europe, indicating that Olcott's success and significance cannot be reduced simply to immigrant nostalgia. Nevertheless, the Kalem company literally put Ireland on the cine-matic map through a combination of Olcott's leadership and energy, Gauti-er's photogenic looks and canny use of existing popular sources (stories, plays, and poems), and George Hollister's brilliant and pioneering use of the Irish landscape. Their legacy is everywhere in Irish and Irish-themed film—from the opening sequences of *The Quiet Man* (1952) to films as diverse as *Leap Year* (2010) and *The Wind That Shakes the Barley* (2006).

OMAGH* (2004).** Directed by Pete Travis, *Omagh* re-creates a horrific chap-ter in the Troubles when a bomb killed 29 people in the small northern town of Omagh on 15 August 1998. Based on a screenplay by Paul Greengrass, who had previously directed ***Bloody Sunday (and would later channel his capacity for frenetic filmmaking in the Bourne films), the film stars **Gerard McSorley** as Michael Gallagher, whose 21-year-old son died in the blast. Gallagher becomes a spokesman for the victims' families and thus the focal point for the narrative. The semidocumentary style of the film has become a very common format for addressing such traumatic events of late. The film is a visceral and sincere endeavor to capture the authenticity of events, from the terrible bomb scene (as shot in Navan, County Meath) to the families' immediate reactions and later their coming to terms with the grief following their—still unresolved—pursuit of justice.

***ONCE* (2007).** In some respects, *Once* may be the greatest-ever success in Irish film history—and the most unlikely. Written and directed by **John Carney**, whose idiosyncratic career had threatened to blossom on several earlier occasions, the microbudget film (approximately €150,000) spent years in development with the **Irish Film Board** and was turned down by several film festivals before gaining acceptance by the prestigious Sundance Film Festival in January 2007 (having been viewed at the previous year's Galway Film Fleadh [Festival]).

A simple plot follows an unnamed busker ("the Guy," played by Glen Hansard, lead singer of The Frames, for whom Carney had previously played bass guitar) as he encounters Marketa Irlgova's musically gifted Czech immigrant ("the Girl") selling newspapers in Dublin. Carney deliberately and pointedly avoids the temptation to structure the film around the development of a romantic connection (their relationship remains ultimately platonic). Instead, the narrative arc of the film builds around their musical connection, which climaxes in the production of a demo album. Thus, the film depicts two souls briefly intersecting to produce something beautiful before parting ways (a journey subsequently paralleled by the real-life relationship between Hansard and Irlgova). Beyond the music, much of the film's appeal lay in its nostalgia: although set in the 21st century, it seems to hanker for the simpler days of the 1980s, to which Carney would return in *Sing Street* (2015). Somewhat anachronistically, the busker works as a vacuum cleaner repairman and records his songs in the already obsolete cassette format. Set during the heyday of the Celtic Tiger, this presents the leads as representing those left behind by the era's dash for cash while suggesting that a commitment to art for its own sake can achieve its own rewards.

This certainly proved true for the filmmakers and lead cast. A positive audience reception at Sundance gave rise to a limited U.S. release that, accompanied by a U.S. tour by its musical leads, saw the film steadily gain momentum, ultimately resulting in an **Academy Award** for Best Original Song: "The little film that could," as **Colin Farrell** memorably introduced it at the 2008 Oscar ceremony. This contributed to a global box office of $20 million, which, if modest in absolute terms, nonetheless represented a remarkable profit relative to its initial budget.

While Hansard and Irlgova successfully toured as "The Swell Season," the film was adapted into a stage musical (based on the "book" written by ***Disco Pigs*** playwright and screenwriter Enda Walsh). Having received a workshop premiere in April 2011, it moved to an off-Broadway run in New York in December of the same year. By February 2012, it moved to Broadway proper, where it began a critically acclaimed three-year run: it was nominated for 11 Tony awards in 2012 and won in eight categories. The production subsequently transferred to Dublin and London's West End: subsequent runs have been produced in Australia, Korea, and Toronto. Indeed, the success of the musical has arguably eclipsed the reputation of the original film.

ONE HUNDRED MORNINGS **(2009).** Working on a miniscule budget awarded under the **Irish Film Board**'s Catalyst scheme, *One Hundred Mornings* is the debut feature film of writer/director Conor Horgan. Set in an unspecified rural Irish location (but shot in Wicklow), its postapocalyptic narrative unfolds in and around a "cabin in the woods" that Mark (Rory Keenan) and his wife Katie (Kelly Campbell) are sharing with another couple, Jonathan (Ciaran McMenamin) and Hannah (Alex Reid). The nature of the calamity that has struck society, driving the principals to take refuge in the countryside, is deliberately unspecified, thwarting audience expectations as to how the narrative may develop. However, it becomes clear that the protagonists are equally in the dark as to what the future may hold. A powerful sense of stasis pervades, as the couples, already lacking electricity, await the next sign of societal collapse. Despite its dystopian premise, interpersonal dynamics are more to the forefront than the usual challenges of survival, and the psychological rivalries of this couple-centered drama owe more to Ingmar Bergman than *Mad Max*. Indeed, the futuristic element works principally to explore the ways in which tensions arise between individuals forced to exist in a situation of inescapable necessity. That the film does not submit to its inherently claustrophobic setting is largely due to Suzie Lavelle's somber cinematography, which renders the otherwise stunning natural setting as stark and foreboding.

ONE MILLION DUBLINERS **(2014).** An affecting and involving feature-length documentary dealing with Dublin's famed Glasnevin Cemetery, which opened in 1832 and has become the final resting place for some 1.5 million individuals, including some of Ireland's most revered historical and political figures. First-time director Aoife Kelleher (*Strange Occurrences in a Small Irish Village* [2016] and *We Need to Talk About Dad* [2017]) brings curiosity as well as visual grandeur to its storied history, qualities that ensured that the film was a surprise commercial as well as critical hit during its limited theatrical and subsequent DVD release. The film's central figure is

Shane Mac Thomáis (who died tragically soon after shooting), who guides the viewer through the history of its famous and not-so-famous inhabitants. Along with segments on other aspects of the cemetery, such as florists and regular visitors (e.g., the "mysterious French lady" who regularly visits Micheal Collins's grave), the film offers a multifacted look at Dublin's famed north-side necropolis. The film won the Silver Medal for Documentary at the 2016 New York Festivals Awards, was the joint winner of the Best Irish Feature Documentary at the 2014 Galway Film Fleadh (Festival), and was voted Best Irish Film of the year in a competition held by the *Irish Times*.

***ON THE EDGE* (2000).** An unusual entry in **John Carney**'s pre-*Once* filmography (and a film he has subsequently distanced himself from), this sensitive and uncommon treatment of teenage suicide and self-harm (a theme explored later in **Frank Berry**'s *I Used to Live Here*) features strong performances from **Cillian Murphy** and Tricia Vessy as well as excellent support from a number of other young actors. Jonathan Breech (Murphy) is unable to accept life and, sparked by the death of his father, drives a stolen car off a cliff. He survives and ends up in a mental hospital alongside other emotionally damaged young people. The psychiatric environment is controlled by the undemonstrative **Stephen Rea**, who tries to get these patients to understand their problems. However, Jonathan and a few others try to subvert this form of behavior analysis and rebel in various ways. A process of bonding between the inmates—who have to wear their pajamas at all times—eventually helps the main characters discover and face up to themselves. While at times the narrative is somewhat clunky and uneven, the film is not without its powerful moments. Produced by **Ed Guiney** and Arthur Lappin under **Hell's Kitchen**'s briefly lucrative deal with Universal, the film marked an important early effort in **Cillian Murphy**'s fledgling career.

***ON THE NOSE* (2000).** This comedy, produced by **Subotica** and directed by Irish director David Caffrey (*Divorcing Jack* [1998], *Love/Hate* [2010–2014], *Prime Suspect 1973* [2016], and *Peaky Blinders* [2017]), suffers from a confusion of tone and ambition and seems better suited for television than for a cinema audience. (Along with the similarly small-scale *Rat*, it was produced by **Sky Pictures** and represented a brief effort by the broadcaster to develop Irish filmmaking talent.) It stars Scottish actor Robbie Coltrane as Brendan, a university janitor with a betting addiction. Having gambled away his daughter's college fund, he is forced to earn it back when she accepts a university place in Trinity College. Happily, Brendan discovers the preserved head of an aboriginal tribesman, which has the power to pick racehorse winners. The outsized cast for this caper also includes Dan Aykroyd and Brenda Blethyn.

***ORDINARY DECENT CRIMINAL* (2000).** Following a spate of gangster movies based on the notorious Dublin gangster "The General," this all-star cast, directed by **Thaddeus O'Sullivan**, milks the story for generic laughs. Kevin Spacey plays a lovable rogue who dreams up robberies with a panache that rarely fails to endear him to the public. The last is a prestigious art gallery theft that dumbfounds the police, Interpol, and the rest of the criminal fraternity generally. As the blurb for this underdeveloped narrative asserts, the main character is driven by two fundamental beliefs: loyalty to his own and to hell with everyone else.

OSCARS. *See* ACADEMY AWARDS.

***THE OTHER SIDE OF SLEEP* (2011).** Feted on its screening as part of the Director's Fortnight series at the Cannes Film Festival, **Rebecca Daly**'s debut feature at times invokes the work of David Lynch and Scandinavian noir in its suggestion that dark secrets lurk even in the most banal of settings. The film commences with somnambulist Arlene (Antonia Campbell-Hughes) awaking in the woods outside an Irish Midlands town. Beside her is the murdered body of Gina, a young local woman. Although herself a suspect in the death, as the police investigation proceeds, Arlene insinuates herself into Gina's life, connecting with her sister and her boyfriend. As Arlene obsessively collects press clippings about the murder, she recalls the still-unexplained disappearance and death of her own mother decades earlier.

Although this setup suggests a suspense thriller, with Arlene gradually unveiling the truth behind both deaths, the film consciously avoids this route. Instead, Daly opts for a more ambiguous path, focused on the psychic impact on her central protagonist of years of grief over another's death, the unexplained nature of which denies her the closure necessary to complete the process of mourning. It is suggested that Arlene not only engages in literal nocturnal sleepwalks but also, at a more figurative level, has sleepwalked through her young adulthood, though her trauma occasionally—and unpredictably—emerges in moments of irrational, bordering on violent, behavior.

However, though film successfully evokes a somber, melancholy tone throughout, the relative absence of dialogue and long, static silent shots make for a piece that, though mesmeric at times, can veer toward the ponderous. Suzie Lavelle's cinematography successfully conjures a compelling atmosphere of mystery, but overall, the filmmakers' decision to more or less exclusively focus on character at the expense of story somewhat neuters the overall impact of the work.

OURSELVES ALONE (1936). Codirected by Brian Desmond Hurst and Walter Summers, the film recounts how, during the Irish War of Independence, Inspector Hannay (John Lodge) of the Royal Irish Constabulary takes responsibility for the killing of a Republican leader to allow the real killer— an English officer—to develop a relationship with the victim's sister. The cast includes Maire O'Neill (Nanny), Clifford Evans (Commandant Connolly), Antoinette Cellier (Maureen Elliott), and Niall MacGinnis (Terence Elliott). A pioneering and sympathetic portrait of the human cost of conflict, the film was banned in Northern Ireland on its release. The line "I'm as Irish as you are," from Hannay to Terence, signals an effort by the Protestant Hurst to enlarge the concept of Irishness in the decade following independence. Nevertheless, the film ultimately sides with Hannay's legitimacy and point of view.

OUT OF HERE (2013). Donal Foreman (1985–) wrote and directed this feature debut after a decade of well-received short films, produced during and after his time as a film student at the Institute of Art, Design, and Technology. Developing themes and a personal style evident in some of those works, *Out of Here* is an open-ended and wistful narrative centering on a genial twenty-something Irish guy, Ciaran (Fionn Walton), who returns home to Dublin after a year of traveling the world. Staying with his parents in their middle-class suburban home, Ciaran looks up some old friends and hooks up with a girl he meets at a disco. Displaying the influence of maverick independent directors such as John Cassavettes and Jim Jarmusch as well as sharing low-budget aesthetics and in-between characters of the mumblecore "movement," the film ends as inconclusively as it begins with Ciaran both changed by his experiences and pulled back into familiar patterns and circles.

While *Out of Here* demonstrates clear points of contact with American independent cinema, it is recognizably set and conceived of in contemporary Ireland. This sense of place, along with Foreman's clear and consistent sense of tone, contributes to a film that is surprisingly engaging while being dramatically unremarkable. The director is especially good at capturing suburban Dublin locations (many previously unfamiliar on film) and pays notable attention to geographical consistency in following his central character. Walton, in that role, is just as unremarkable but equally convincing, as are his various interactions and encounters. The film conveys a moment of transition in the life of a young person who is both at home and a stranger, no longer a child but not fully yet an adult. It seeks to offer neither no more nor no less than this and in so doing offers us a contemporary counterportrait of Dublin a century on from Joyce's *Ulysses* (set in 1904), with Ciaran wandering through town at night but without any pretenses toward epic parallels.

Foreman's script was turned down by a number of production companies, and he eventually produced the film without the support of the **Irish Film Board** through a crowdfunding campaign. After some early contact with the board, this was a deliberate decision made to protect the film from the imposed narrative/storytelling conventions that Foreman felt such support came with. Foreman maintained his dogged independence with his subsequent feature, *The Image That You Missed*, a highly accomplished memoir of his absent father, Irish American documentary director Arthur MacCaig (1948–2008).

THE OUTCASTS (1982). This unusual film was directed by Robert Wynne-Simmons and was cofinanced by a combination of the **Arts Council** Script (1981) and **Channel 4**'s Film on Four Award. Set in mid-19th-century Ireland, the film follows Maura's (Mary Ryan) relationship with Scarf Michael (**Mick Lally**), a man cast out of the local community because of his dealings with the world of the supernatural. Maura seeks to leave the community to be with Michael, but he refuses her company, and a series of catastrophes subsequently befalls the locality. Believing this to be Maura's fault, the locals move to drown her, but Michael intercedes and takes her away. The film is uneven in tone and direction but fascinating nonetheless. Its originality lies in the straightforward manner in which it fuses the natural and the supernatural, constructing a quasi-pagan Ireland that draws little distinction between religion and superstition.

Despite Wynne-Simmons's status as a British writer/director and the obvious narrative links to the British folk-horror genre, the film has often been identified as marking the debut of the so-called first wave of indigenous Irish cinema made possible through Arts Council funding and the subsequent formation of the first **Irish Film Board**.

PARALLEL FILM PRODUCTIONS. Established in 1993 by Tim Palmer and Alan Moloney, Parallel has remained one of the most consistent and ambitious of indigenous production companies to have emerged with the reestablishment of the **Irish Film Board**. The company debuted with *Into the West* (1992), coproduced with **Little Bird**. This was followed by *The Last of the High Kings* (1996) and the well-received *A Love Divided* (1997). Other notable productions include *The Escapist* (2008), ***Breakfast on Pluto*** (2005), ***Intermission*** (2003), and the John Banville–scripted adaptation of *Albert Nobbs* (2011), featuring an award-winning turn by Glenn Close. More recently, the company has been involved in productions such as the **Academy Award**–nominated ***Brooklyn*** (2016), Aisling Walsh's *Maudie* (2016), and playwright Mark O'Rowe's directorial debut, *The Delinquent Season* (2017).

Parallel is also significant as one of the first Irish production companies to specialize in quality TV drama, which, as a far more reliable source of cash flow than the extended feature film production process, came to form the backbone of the company's business model. In 1998, it produced two BBC/**Radio Telefís Éireann** (RTÉ) television miniseries: the superb *Amongst Women* and *Falling for a Dancer*, based on books by John McGahern and Deirdre Purcell, respectively. These were followed in 1999 by *DDU* (District Detective Unit), a pioneering Irish-set police series produced for RTÉ. Debuting in 2003, *The Clinic* became RTÉ's flagship Sunday night drama series and ran for seven seasons before it was axed in 2009, one of the first indigenous projects to ensure multiannual employment for those involved and paving the way for subsequent long-running TV series shot on Irish soundstages, such as *Penny Dreadful* and *The Tudors*. *The Clinic* was shot in the former John Player cigarette factory on Dublin's south side, which became an unofficial studio space for the duration of its production and facilitated smaller-budget projects for Parallel (such as *The Escapist*) during its annual hiatus.

In 2000, Alan Moloney, in partnership with Michael Colgan of the Gate Theatre, undertook the ambitious "Beckett on Film" project, adapting all 19 of **Samuel Beckett**'s works for the screen. Funded by RTÉ, the project attracted an exceptional group of international behind- and in-front-of-camera talent to the project, including Anthony Minghella, Karel Reisz, Damien Hirst, David Mamet, Atom Egoyan, Julianne Moore, Kristin Scott Thomas, and Jeremy Irons, as well as younger, local talent, such as **Damien O'Donnell**, **Conor McPherson**, Kieron J. Walsh, and Enda Hughes. The completed project was broadcast on RTÉ and **Channel 4** and later sold as a DVD box set.

***PARK* (1999).** A quasi-experimental and self-consciously small-scale film, directed by **John Carney** and **Tom Hall**, *Park* opens with a woman seeking a psychiatrist's aid in interpreting a recurring dream in which she stabs a man in the street for no apparent reason. Later under hypnosis, she eventually regresses back to when she was a teenager to reveal the truth. The re-creation of the park of her dreams is very rich and evocative. The film captures a sense of innocence and escape from the rigors of school as she walks around in her school uniform, only to be met by Adam, the park keeper. Eventually, he entices her to have a meal with him after he teases her about whether she had a boyfriend. The borderline between friendly banter and seedy talk is very carefully maintained. Apparently, she likes to lead him on and be nice to him, while he appears to look after her and pay attention to her. The first part of her remembering process ends with her going through the black door of his hutch, and she seems to be heading toward a space where more traumatic memories are deeply buried.

Evidence of what eventually happened and its tragic consequences are withheld as the story moves forward to an old people's home, where the keeper is still enjoying the pleasures of female attention. This realization leaves a very bad taste for the audience when the full revelation of what happened is finally dramatized. Overall, in spite of some odd narrative lapses, the piece, with its art house format, remains memorable.

***PARKED* (2013).** The directorial debut of Darragh Byrne, *Parked* stands out from many low-budget Irish features by virtue of an original and topical premise and a characteristically grounded and convincing performance from its star, **Colm Meaney**. Its narrative centers on Fred Daly (Meaney)—a fastidious middle-aged man—who is forced to live in his car when he loses his home. Set mostly in a parking lot facing Dublin Bay, the film offers a novel twist on the familiar "odd couple" structure in its development of the relationship between Fred and Cathal (Colin Morgan), a dope-smoking 21-year-old with a positive attitude who is also "parked" in the similar circumstances. While the younger man at first seems to represent all that Fred resents and despises in the modern world, each comes to restore dignity and hope to the other.

While it avoids any sociological comment and remains primarily a character-driven narrative, *Parked* might be read in relation to a number of other urban-set films from this period (such as **Adam and Paul** [2004], **Out of Here** [2013], *Our Wonderful Home* [2008], or **Glassland** [2014]) that link unstable identities and themes of home. Made in the midst of the property "crash" and news coverage about mortgage arrears and repossessions, the film's theme of homelessness was timely and topical, stressing self-respect and the precarious nature of an individual's living circumstances. Nevertheless, the fact that Fred is ultimately redeemed by the romantic attention of a middle-class female character established and defined by her substantial red-brick house advances a vision of cross-class solidarity that is utopian and that reasserts the status value of (middle-class) home ownership in Irish society, which contributed to Fred's fall in the first place. Unwittingly, however, the film anticipated real-life media stories around families living in cars and a chronic shortage of housing following the economic crises that put homelessness front and center on the Irish political agenda.

Although a modest success in Ireland, *Parked* toured widely at film festivals and won a number of awards, including Best Film at the Foggia Independent Film Festival and at the Mannheim-Heidelberg Festival, audience awards at the Brussels Film Festival and the D'Annonay festivals, and Best First Feature at the Galway Film Fleadh (Festival).

PATRICK'S DAY **(TERRY MCMAHON, 2014).** Patrick (Moe Dunford) is a gentle young man in his mid-20s with schizophrenia. Permitted to leave the institution in which he resides on a day pass, Patrick takes a trip into Dublin with his mother Maura (New Zealand actress Kerry Fox) for his birthday (17 March, St Patrick's Day). Having protected Patrick all his life, Maura is deeply concerned when he encounters Karen (Catherine Walker), an older flight attendant. Karen has her own issues: introduced as someone determined to end her own life, she seduces Patrick as a final fling before oblivion. However, Patrick's uncorrupted nature prompts her to reconsider her self-destructive path. Meanwhile, Maura, convinced that Karen poses a danger to Patrick's health, hires policeman John Freeman (Philip Jackson) to disrupt their burgeoning relationship and eventually convinces Karen to break things off. She devises a scheme to convince Patrick that the entire relationship was a fiction, a product of his schizophrenia.

Representations of mental health have been a recurring theme in Irish cinema since the 1980s, reflecting a growing social and medical awareness and understanding around issues such as depression and suicide. Notwithstanding the recurrence of the terrorist "madmen" characterization of political violence, especially in pre-cease-fire cinema, local explorations of mental illness—including **Eva Birthistle**'s Nicole in *All Souls Day* (1997), Eamon

Owen's Francie in *The Butcher Boy* (1998), *The Gift* (2013), *Property of the State* (2017), and *I Used to Live Here* (2016)—have sought to see past the caricatures of mental health commonly found in popular cinema.

In keeping with director McMahon's often proclaimed and wide-ranging critique of the failures of Irish society, *Patrick's Day* frames mental illness as a response to wider social conditions. While the medical model regards mental illness as innate to the individual and treats them accordingly, *Patrick's Day* invokes a social model not only to highlight the practices through which those with mental health conditions are actively "othered" but also to call into question the boundaries between normal and abnormal. Although Patrick is medically and institutionally diagnosed as schizophrenic, Karen is equally shaped by her less externally obvious mental health issues. And, as the film progresses, even the so-called normal characters are demonstrated to operate somewhere on a continuum of ill health. Maura's commitment to her maternal responsibilities borders on the obsessive, while policeman John has retreated into a world of black humor in response to the darkness his job routinely exposes him to.

Given the critical mauling meted out to his debut, *Charlie Casanova* (2011), there was a certain curiosity about what Terry McMahon might do next, especially given that he had used the platform offered by the promotion of that debut to roundly criticize the **Irish Film Board**. Nevertheless, the writer/director succeeded in securing board funding for his second film and ultimately produced a critically acclaimed, award-winning exploration of mental illness. Much of the success of the film rests, unsurprisingly, on the excellent cast. As the suffocating Maura, Fox not only brings art house star power to the project but also offers a nuanced performance that retains audience empathy even as Maura contemplates ever more extreme measures to "protect" Patrick. Moe Dunford's channeling of man–child innocence is at the emotional and narrative core of the film. His Patrick is not reduced to his condition: never a caricature "schizophrenic," he remains a fully recognizable "person *with* schizophrenia."

With this second feature, McMahon also defied expectations. Although still given to placing essaylike dialogue into the mouths of his characters, this was a far more restrained and thoughtful work than his debut. Working with a larger budget, he also demonstrated a stronger grasp of camera and movement than previously hinted at, and a bravura third-act sequence depicting the impact on Patrick of Maura's nefarious scheme is as innovative as anything seen in 21st-century Irish filmmaking.

***PAVEE LACKEN: THE TRAVELLER GIRL* (2005).** The first and, to date, only feature film directed by photographer Perry Ogden offers an unaffected portrait of Winnie Maughan, a 10-year-old member of Ireland's Traveller community who lives with her family in a caravan in Ringsend on the outskirts of Dublin. Forgoing drama for documentary realism, the film (shot entirely on handheld video) follows its young protagonist as she moves between her impoverished family (including her imprisoned brother) and contemporary Dublin with little to motivate or guide her. Displaying something of the style and social consciousness of Ken Loach's *Kes* (1969), *Pavee Lackeen* is a significant contribution to the small but significant corpus of Irish films dealing with the Traveller community. However, unlike the majority of such representations, it stays close to the point of view of Winnie, lending the film an empathy and freshness that endures. The scenes shot around Dublin put Winnie into contact with Ireland's (at the time) new immigrants (notably around Moore Street), forging a link between their mutual marginality within contemporary Irish society. On its release, the film toured festivals widely and won the Best Feature Film award at the Galway Film Fleadh (Festival).

PEACHES (2000). This Irish-produced film, directed by Nick Grosso, is set in London but was shot in Dublin. It follows student Frank (Matthew Rhys) as he prepares to leave college and face up to living in the real world and in particular to dealing with real women rather than the fictional ones he has hitherto boasted of to his friends. Production Company Stone Ridge Entertainment, which made the film, was associated with **Ward Anderson**, a fact that helped ensure that the film received an unusually wide domestic release.

PEARSON, NOEL. Ferndale managing director and producer Noel Pearson has been an impresario figure in Irish entertainment since the 1960s. Born in 1943, he initially considered the priesthood, but after graduating from the seminary, he rejected the idea and went to work in the Dublin fruit markets. He began his career as manager of the Chessmen, a Dublin pop group, before taking on the internationally renowned traditional folk group The Dubliners. In 1972, while still their manager, he produced an adaptation of Brendan Behan's *Richard's Cork Leg* at the **Abbey Theatre** as part of that year's Dublin Theatre Festival, which subsequently transferred to London's Royal Court. However, it was Pearson's subsequent success with lavish theatrical productions of *Joseph and the Amazing Technicolour Dreamcoat* and *Jesus Christ Superstar* that established him as Ireland's leading theatrical producer.

From the late 1970s, he began to bring stage productions to the United States, including a New York run in 1979 for a ballet version of J. M. Synge's *Playboy of the Western World*. His first direct contact with the world of film came in 1982 when, despite having never made a film, he was appointed to the neophyte **Irish Film Board** (IFB), a position he maintained until the board's activities were suspended in 1987. Ironically, the closure of the IFB meant that Pearson was unable to secure state funding for what would become Ferndale's first film, *My Left Foot*. Pearson had nursed the idea of a film adaptation of Christy Brown's two-volume autobiography since the 1960s and approached **Jim Sheridan** and Shane Connaughton to adapt it as a screenplay. As the project underwent development, Sheridan also emerged as the director.

Although the film was shot on a shoestring budget, Pearson's experience as a producer seems to have been very positive, bringing the UK£1.5 million project (which had been substantially funded by Granada Television) in on time and under budget. The phenomenal success of the film secured Pearson and Sheridan a deal with Universal, under which they were due to produce at least two films over a three-year period. The first of these was another Ferndale production, an adaptation of John B. Keane's play *The Field*. Citing personality differences this also proved to be the last Pearson–Sheridan collaboration until *The Secret Scripture* in 2017. (Sheridan **subsequently** established **Hell's Kitchen** with Arthur Lappin, and Pearson focused on theatrical production.)

Pearson had in any case been chair of the Abbey since 1987 and was appointed artistic director, replacing Vincent Dowling, in 1989. He stepped down from the latter position in 1991 (to be replaced by Garry Hynes) but remained as chair until 1993. This led indirectly to his triumphant multi–award-winning Broadway production of Brian Friel's *Dancing at Lughnasa*, and he subsequently brought two more Friel plays—*Wonderful Tennessee* and *Translations*—to Broadway.

Pearson returned to filmmaking in 1994 with *Frankie Starlight*, an adaptation of the Chet Raymo novel *The Dork of Cork*, but without the support of Universal, which—by Pearson's own account—had passed on every project he put their way after *The Field*. This was quickly followed by another novel adaptation, *Gold in the Streets* (1997). In 1998, he returned to Friel, choosing **Pat O'Connor** to direct a screen adaptation of *Dancing at Lughnasa* with Meryl Streep as one of the leads. However, the lukewarm response to the film version led to another screen production hiatus. It was 2005 before Pearson's next film, an adaptation of Maeve Binchy's *Tara Road*. Like *Lughnasa*, it was clearly designed for the export market, in particular the United States, where the source novel had sold 5 million copies. He followed this with another Binchy adaptation, *How About You . . .* (2007).

Over the years, Ferndale has also produced a number of documentaries, most of which emerged from Pearson's long career in Irish theater and the arts. These include *Maeve Binchy: At Home in the World*, *Ronnie Drew: September Song*, and *Bram Stoker's Dracula*.

PERRIER'S BOUNTY (2007). With the exception of Roddy Doyle's hugely critical and commercially successful Barrytown trilogy, comedy has been a relatively uneven and halting genre within contemporary Irish cinema that has attracted surprisingly little critical commentary. Distinctive among its characteristics is a predilection for farce and narratives centered on male vanity and humiliation. *Perrier's Bounty* suggests an uncommon measure of continuity within the genre, employing talents associated with a number of moderately successful Irish film comedies over the previous decade in its director (**Ian Fitzgibbon**), writer (Mark O'Rowe), and starry cast (**Brendan Gleeson**, **Cillian Murphy**, **Michael McElhatton**, and the voice of **Gabriel Byrne**). Fitzgibbon has form in Irish comedy, with a number of notable credits, including the TV shows *Paths to Freedom* (2000), *Fergus' Wedding* (2002), and *Moone Boy* (2013), and the features ***Spin the Bottle*** (2003), *A Film with Me in It* (2008), and ***Death of a Superhero*** (2011).

Perrier's Bounty opens with Michael (Murphy), a small-time operator on the fringes of Dublin criminal circles, receiving a pointed reminder that his debt to local kingpin Perrier (Gleeson) is within hours of falling due. In a bid to pay it off, Michael becomes embroiled in the lives of Brenda (his doomed in love neighbor for whom he holds an unrequited candle, played by *Doctor Who*'s Jodie Whittaker), Mutt (another local criminal played by Liam Kavanagh), and his estranged father Jim (Jim Broadbent), who reveals at the outset that he is terminally ill. Burdened with such allies, Michael's best-laid plans inevitably go astray, leaving him to confront Perrier and his gang directly.

It is revealing of the extent to which criminality has become a key trope in post-1993 Irish cinema that *Perrier's Bounty* can be discussed in the context of such a wide range of antecedents (many of which also feature Brendan Gleeson in a leading role): *I Went Down* (1997), *The General* (1998), *In Bruges* (2008), and so on. *Bounty* shares many of the genre's local characteristics: it is set in an unrelentingly masculine environment populated by unusually philosophical (given their metier) characters who adhere to strict codes of conduct. The film suggests that the world of Michael, Mutt, and Perrier is characterized by a kind of "honor among thieves." There is a flair for dialogue as well, imbuing most of the characters with a level of intelligence that raises questions as to how they found themselves operating in this world in this first place.

Yet these are not questions the film (again like most of its antecedents) is interested in addressing. This is an efficient genre piece—a comedy-thriller—cast in a manner that suggests at least modest ambitions for international distribution. Such an undertaking is not interested in offering an in-depth exploration of the social context in which individuals are formed: in *Perrier's Bounty*, criminals are criminals, the violent are violent.

Yet in some respects, the script is almost too efficient. The plotting leaves no loose ends but rather relies on a series of coincidental encounters that, as they accumulate, increasingly draw attention to themselves. Perhaps as a consequence of the emphasis on plot, characterization suffers: the Michael–Jim father–son relationship never quite comes off in part because it is difficult to fully identify with Michael and thus to empathize with his plight. As virtually the only female character, Brenda is a cypher, exclusively defined by her relationships with men whose deficiencies she seems determined to repeatedly overlook.

Overall, then, the knowing, sardonic tone of *Perrier's Bounty* may well appeal to a cine-literate audiences, but the film begs the question as to how far the template established by **Conor McPherson**'s *I Went Down* can be refashioned.

PERRY, SIMON (1944–). Chief executive officer of the **Irish Film Board** (IFB) from 2005 to 2011, (the third holder of the role since its reconstitution in 1993), Perry brought stability to the organization following the resignation of Mark Woods and the existential threat to the organization in the aftermath of the 2008 Irish financial crisis. His most lasting contribution perhaps was substantially increasing coproduction agreements and encouraging an increasingly outward focus for Irish film. In common with his predecessor **Rod Stoneman**, Perry came with a broad range of industry experience from his native England, having worked for *Variety* for three years as London editor before serving as the head of the British National Film Development Fund. He then set up his own production company, Umbrella Films, which produced/coproduced 10 feature films, including *1984* (1984) and *White Mischief* (1987), before returning to administration as chief executive of British Screen prior to joining the IFB.

Early in his tenure, Perry gained an unexpected bounce in profile and leverage for the industry at home and abroad as **John Carney**'s *Once* gained widespread critical and commercial momentum and eventually went all the way to the **Academy Awards**, where it won Best Original Song. Although *Once* predated his stewardship, its success led to Perry's endorsement and encouragement of a transnational, auteur cinema as the cornerstone of Irish film policy and identity, the legacy of which can still be felt. A second key element of his time in the role was the development of bilateral coproduction agreements with a range of countries, including Canada, Luxembourg, New Zealand, and South Africa. The effect of these treaties is to confer national status on a production in more than one territory, thereby allowing it to receive incentives from both. These have had mixed success, although the agreement with Canada has proven notably active and produced a wide range of fiction and nonfiction content for big- and small-screen productions.

To considerable surprise, the IFB did not renew Perry's contract when it came up for renewal in 2011, and after a recruitment process, he was replaced by **James Hickey**.

***PHILADELPHIA, HERE I COME!* (1975).** Directed by the British direc-tor/producer John Quested (owner of Goldcrest Productions and assistant director on John Ford's final film, **Young Cassidy**) and adapted from the 1964 stage play that marked **Brian Friel**'s breakthrough, the film takes place on the night before and morning of its protagonist Gar's (**Donal McCann**) departure to the United States. The drama uses the theatrical device of pre-senting "public" and "private" versions of the main protagonist (played by different actors) to outline the surface and interior life of this troubled man as he debates whether to leave his dull hometown. Gar must leave his taciturn father and cannot himself express any emotion, even with his few male friends, who lack the courage to escape their tedious rural backwater.

Donal McCann delivers a characteristically strong performance in the title role as he mocks the lack of sophistication in his American cousins, who revel in not having a past and in a culture that endorses material wealth. At the same time, Gar celebrates their vibrant popular culture. Without such an outlet, he would become like his drunken old teacher, who speaks of dreams of escape. But we know this will never happen, as the teacher presents his former pupil with a self-published copy of his "cries from the heart" poetry.

The theatrical device of two actors playing the same role is a less disrup-tive device within the formal conventions of film than theater. Des Cave, as Gar's extrovert alter ego, is effective enough without communicating any complexity in the characterization. The great **Siobhan McKenna** is more convincing as the surrogate mother figure who helps out in the home and tries to bring father and son together, though it becomes clear that this is an impossible task as this often humorous yet nonetheless tragic story reaches its inevitable dénouement.

***THE PIER* (2011).** Having left Ireland at age 17 to work in a variety of jobs across Europe, lead actor/writer/producer and director Gerard Hurley worked in film production in the United States from the 1990s, seeing a succession of scripts optioned but never progress beyond development. Determined to pro-duce his own work, he funded his debut, *The Pride* (2008), an exploration of Irish Traveller culture in the United States through credit card debt before moving to shoot *The Pier* over eight days on a meager budget of €100,000 in West Cork.

The narrative follows Jack McCarthy (Hurley), an immigrant who returns from New York after 20 years because his father Larry (Karl Johnson) has fallen ill. On his arrival, however, Larry is revealed to be hale and hearty, his illness a ruse to bring his son home. As the two men struggle to reestablish their relationship, Jack meets Grace (American actress Lili Taylor), a vaca-tioning American divorcée with whom he strikes up a platonic relationship.

Although rehearsing well-established tropes of the returned Irish emigrant, *The Pier* is a likable undertaking. Its shoestring budget works to reflects the economic desolation of post–Celtic Tiger rural Ireland, and the performances (the cast, apart from the three leads, are nonprofessional locals) lend a folksy quality to the undertaking. Despite its shortcomings, the film's main appeal lies in the plausible characterization of the father–son relationship, two figures lacking the emotional resources to properly communicate and bond.

PIGS **(1984).** Directed by **Cathal Black** from a story by Jimmy Brennan (who also plays its protagonist), *Pigs* is both brilliantly pessimistic but also a deeply sensitive story of marginal masculinities sharing a squat in Dublin. As the film opens, Jimmy takes up residence in a decrepit but once elegant Georgian building in the city ("home sweet home") and is soon joined by other squatters—George (George Shane), an erstwhile businessman trying to retain some dignity, along with Tom (Maurice O'Donoghue) and Ronny (Liam Halligan), the latter a drug dealer. These are joined by Orwell (the Ghana-born writer/actor/poet Kwesi Kay), a Jamaican pimp, and his prostitute, Mary. The film was ahead of its time in many respects, not least in the suggestion that its central character may be gay and/or transvestite, communicated through an aborted pickup in a bar (when Jimmy and another man are chased by homophobic thugs) and Jimmy's status as the film's primary "homemaker" for the motley collection of men who come and go. (Jimmy also prefers to wear a towel around the rambling house.) Not the least of the film's achievements is its evocation of a decrepit and now disappeared inner-city Dublin through the cinematography of **Thaddeus O'Sullivan** underpinning Black's delicate and nonjudgmental storytelling.

PILGRIM HILL **(2013). Gerard Barrett**'s fiction feature debut is so understated and low-key that one could be forgiven for at times imagining it to be a piece of cinema verité, passively documenting the quiet desperation of its bachelor farmer protagonist.

Shot for a scarcely credible budget of €4,500 and set in rural Kerry, the film follows Jimmy (amateur actor Joe Mullins) as he ekes out a subsistence existence on his isolated 30-acre holding. Trapped by the need to care for his elderly and ailing on-screen father, Jimmy leads a lonely existence, going for days without speaking to another person, his social life limited to occasional single-drink excursions to the local pub. Sequences dispassionately tracing his humdrum routine are occasionally interrupted by almost-but-not-quite-direct addresses to camera, monologues where Jimmy laments the path his life might have taken (e.g., having had a family of his own) if not for his externally imposed obligations. Already on the precipice of survival at the film's beginning, the narrative proceeds through a series of events that render his position even more marginal, a downward spiral from which there appears to be no return.

Although released at a point when the entire country was facing a social and economic malaise, *Pilgrim Hill*'s depiction of an Ireland that was never touched by the Celtic Tiger might have seen it released at any point in the previous three decades. That the film's budgetary constraints limit the variety of settings works to underscore the limits of Jimmy's existence. Tommy, a younger man with whom Jimmy occasionally interacts, encourages him to emigrate or go back to college, but these are naive suggestions, literally impossible for Jimmy to contemplate. Overall, then, Barrett's remarkable film depicts a rural Ireland in crisis, one borne not of official acts of commission (the various representatives of the state, though potentially tipping Jimmy's already precarious position into full-on disaster mode, are not in and of themselves represented as malevolent) but rather of omission, leaving a geographical and social setting unable to maintain a hold on 21st-century Irish modernity.

***PILGRIMAGE* (2017).** Although Irish cinema took a definitive turn toward genre work in the 21st century, the costs associated with action-adventure seemed to have put the kibosh on any locally produced instances of that particular variety of work. This was reflected screenwriter Jamie Hannigan's initial ambitions for his *Pilgrimage* script, which saw the narrative limited to short-film duration (and initially, unsuccessfully, submitted to the now defunct "Lasair" support scheme operated by **Radio Telefís Éireann** and **Filmbase**). However, when the script fell into the hands of producer Conor Barry of Savage Productions, he brought it to the attention of intrigued director **Brendan Muldowney**. An expanded script treatment secured **Irish Film Board** development support and later production funding from the Broadcasting Authority of Ireland and two Belgian film schemes.

Headlined by an international cast (Richard Armitage [Thorin in *The Hobbit* franchise], Marvel alumni Jon Bernthal [*The Punisher*], and Tom Holland [*Spiderman*]), *Pilgrimage* commences in a 13th-century Irish monastery to which papal envoy Brother Geraldus (French actor Stanley Weber) has been sent by the pope. Geraldus requests that the monks release into his care a holy relic—a rock used to dispatch an early Christian martyr a millennium earlier—that he might return it to Rome. Acceding to this, a group of monks embark on their journey to cross a lawless Irish landscape and then onto the continent. Among their number are the sagacious Ciaran (**John Lynch**), "The Mute" (Bernthal's vow-of-silence muscle), and the youthful Diarmuid (Holland), the core character through whose perspective the audience witnesses events. These include an encounter with Norman troops with whom the monks establish a tentative alliance to defend the passage of the relic against assaults from local tribes. Yet it emerges that the Normans have their own politically motivated ambitions for the relic.

Budgeted at just under €5 million, *Pilgrimage* is arguably one of the most ambitious projects—in terms of cast, production design, and sheer visceral visual thrills—ever undertaken by an Irish filmmaker. That it also manages to raise provocative questions about the wisdom of (blind) faith bestows it with an intelligence not always associated with action-adventure work. The decision to cast Holland and Bernthal just as they were on the brink of international stardom was both fortunate but also perceptive on Muldowney's part: as the youthful but not naive Brother Diarmuid, Holland evinces open discomfort at the manner in which the relic is deployed for secular, political objectives rather than treated as an object of veneration. Yet he also conveys his character's doubts about the manner in which Geraldus actively seeks to imbue the relic with quasi-miraculous properties, not least the suggestion that the Mute's rediscovery of his fighting prowess is driven by the rock's qualities.

Muldowney also demonstrates a sustained commitment to verisimilitude: director of photography Tom Comerford offers a stunning vision of the Connemara landscape (though much of the film was also shot in Belgium) drawn from a muted palette of grays and browns set against the aural background of Gregorian chants. Then there is the decision to at least partially respect the linguistic realities of the era: English, French, Gaelic, and Latin are all peppered across the narrative.

But arguably, it is the cleverly choreographed action sequences—painstakingly storyboarded by Muldowney over several months of preproduction work—that constitute the film's strongest visual element. Despite working with limited camera resources and lacking the hordes of extras available to contemporaneous productions such as *Game of Thrones* or *Vikings*, Muldowney's decision to utilize handheld cameras, getting up close and personal with severed limbs, gouged eyes, and disembowelments, lends the film a primal quality that recalls the spirit if not quite the epic grandeur of better-resourced productions.

As a consequence, *Pilgrimage* became one of the more widely distributed Irish films of recent years, picked up by Studio Canal in the United Kingdom and Ireland, RJL Entertainment in the United States (reportedly for a seven-figure sum), and other distributors in Europe, Asia, Australasia, and the Middle East.

PILKINGTON, LORRAINE (1975–). Raised in the middle-class Dublin suburb of Malahide, Pilkington maintained a consistent presence on the large screen during the decade following the 1993 reestablishment of the **Irish Film Board**. She made a striking debut as a spiky 15-year-old in **Neil Jor-**

dan's modestly budgeted but warmly received *The Miracle*. That role established a template for her early career. At age 21, she was still playing a rebellious 17-year-old in *The Last of the High Kings*, but after a series of less demanding roles in *Gold in the Street*, *The Disappearance of Finbar*, *The Boxer*, and *The Nephew*, she left Dublin to live in the United Kingdom, where she was cast as the brash Irish clubber Lulu in the Welsh independent hit *Human Traffic* (1999). As she reached her late 20s, bad-girl roles gave way to more subdued characters. A turn in the BBC hit *Monarch of the Glen* (2000) and opposite **Richard Harris** in the *King Lear*–esque *My Kingdom* (2001) preceded a career hiatus driven in part by marriage to director Simon Massey and becoming a parent. A confident comeback in a lead role the **Radio Telefís Éireann** drama *The Clinic* (2003–2009) presaged a move to a sequence of recurring roles on U.K. television, including *Waking the Dead* (2003), the Irish-set equestrian drama *Rough Diamond* (2007), and *Britannia High* (2008). These have been interspersed with lead film roles on the big screen, but—a smaller role in *What Richard Did* (2012) aside—these have tended to be concentrated in low-budget U.K. and European productions that have made little impact.

THE PLAYBOY OF THE WESTERN WORLD (1962). Produced by **Lord Killanin**'s **Four Provinces** company and directed by **Brian Desmond Hurst**, the film adaptation of J. M. Synge's renowned comic play began as a stage production during the 1960 Dublin Theatre Festival. The production would assume landmark status as a consequence of the performance of the formidable Belfast-born actress **Siobhan McKenna** in the role of Pegeen Mike. It then moved to several European theater festivals before playing for four months in London, then to Belfast, after which McKenna took a break to play the Virgin Mary in the MGM extravaganza *King of Kings* (1961). This validation by Hollywood secured McKenna's international reputation at this time and ensured the play's viability as a film adaptation.

English actor Gary Raymond plays Christy Mahon ("the son of a strong farmer"), who escapes his family and finds shelter in a small town in rural County Mayo, where he meets Pegeen Mike and recounts his story of how "I killed my poor father, Tuesday was a week." This "lie" earns him respect and indeed sex appeal but will eventually prove his undoing.

While Pegeen Mike becomes romantically attracted by his notorious deed—comparing him to the great Irish poet Owen Roe O'Sullivan—the voracious Widow Quin is also interested in this heroic outsider but later, sarcastically, dubs him the "walking Playboy of the Western World." For all is not as it seems, as the supposedly deceased father of Mahon returns, seeking out his son. Although it captures something of the famed theatrical production from which it was drawn, particularly McKenna's performance, Hurst's adaptation has been criticized both for excising significant portions of Synge's texts and for not being cinematic enough, missing a clear opportunity, most obviously, to more effectively evoke the setting that is so crucial to its meaning (notwithstanding the sporting montage shot on Inch Strand, Dingle, later the location for *Ryan's Daughter*). Shot on a meager budget of £130,000, the film finds itself compromised between reverence for its source text and a desire to appeal to audiences not familiar with Synge's cadences and poetry.

THE PLAYBOYS **(1992).** Based on the writings of Shane Connaughton and filmed in County Cavan, like *The Run of the Country*, the film is directed by British director Gillies MacKinnon. Albert Finney plays Brendan Hegarty, a strong-willed local sergeant in a small rural community. A former alcoholic now trying to control his life and his excesses, his secret tryst with local girl Tara (Robin Wright) results in the birth of a son. Sworn to secrecy by Tara regarding their connection, Hegarty is tormented by the truth, as he dearly wants a family. Competing for Tara's affection is Mick, a local farmer (**Adrian Dunbar**) who, affected by incessant rain and his cows dying, along with rejection in a marriage proposal, soon commits suicide. This brings matters to a head, and the local priest calls on Tara from the pulpit to name the father, affirming how "one sinner can infect us all." The local priest pleads with her to realize that "scandal is a contagion." But far-too-modern Tara will not be forced to marry and is well able to withstand the bile of the community, affirming how "if everyone around here owned up to their sins—there would be a queue at confessionals a mile long!"

An outside force arrives in the shape of a traveling theater company ("playboys"), led by **Milo O'Shea** and including among its number the dashing Tom Casey (**Aidan Quinn**). The outsiders bring excitement but also raise doubts about the moral center of the enclosed community. At one stage, the outsiders describe themselves as a "bunch of cut price Tinkers" (Travellers). Now faced with a much more potent competitor for Tara's favors in the form of the outsider playboy, the sergeant loses his grip on reality, leading finally (after some engaging theatrical spectacle) to a rather too neat narrative closure.

THE PLOUGH AND THE STARS **(1936).** Produced a decade after Sean O'Casey's play caused riots at the **Abbey Theatre** through a perceived disrespect for the Irish flag (and exactly two decades after the events it depicts), screenwriter Dudley Nichols's adaptation attempts to turn a biting socialist critique of the Irish revolution into Hollywood melodrama.

The origins of the adaptation lie in the 1934–1935 Abbey Theatre tour of the United States, when the company performed four plays by Synge and two by O'Casey, including *The Plough and the Stars*, despite initial opposition by the Irish government. (The irony of Taoiseach Eamon de Valera's opposition was that the company was compelled to tour the United States several times during the 1930s due the cutting of its government subsidy.) Given his Irish background and nationalist sympathies, it is not surprising that **John Ford** should have pursued O'Casey's drama, an ambition that found favor with RKO studios in the aftermath of Ford's Oscar and box office success with Liam O'Flaherty's *The Informer* (1935), also scripted by Dudley Nichols. (RKO similarly retained cinematographer Joe August.)

Ford originally proposed transposing the Abbey production to film, using the entire original cast and having O'Casey do the adaptation himself. RKO refused both requests—although four members of the Abbey company took part—and instead Brooklyn-born Barbara Stanwyck—at the time one of Hollywood's greatest actresses—was cast as Nora Clitheroe with Preston Foster as Jack. (Ironically, Foster gives one of the weakest performances in the film despite having been born in Ireland.) Ford succeeded in retaining **Barry Fitzgerald** in the iconic role of Fluther Good, thus beginning one of the most successful careers by an Irish actor in studio-era Hollywood. While the adaptation remains superficially faithful to the tone and dialogue of O'Casey's play and contains signature Fordian elements of humor, community. and atmosphere (thanks to August's stunning cinematography), its differs notably in emphasis and effect, particularly in its closing scenes. Where O'Casey had seen only death and human anguish, Ford's production concludes with a rousing rallying cry. Additionally, RKO meddled with the film after Ford had finished and gone on vacation to Hawaii, making several changes, including, inexplicably, altering Nora and Jack's relationship from marriage to lovers. This resulted in at least two versions—one for the U.S. market and one for the United Kingdom—and even allegedly a third containing newsreels from the period, although this has never been conclusively proven. Nevertheless, the film was highly praised by American critics who cared little for or who knew little of the source material and achieved a comparable box office to *The Informer*.

***POITÍN* (1978).** In **Bob Quinn**'s second feature, Michil (**Cyril Cusack**) hands over his latest batch of illegally distilled poitín to his "agents," Labhcas (**Niall Toibin**) and Sleamhnan (**Donal McCann**), to sell on his behalf. The local police confiscate the poitín, but the two agents retrieve most of the consignment after the police are rendered unconscious by sampling the drink themselves. However, Labhcas decides to hide the retrieval of the poitín from Michil, and after selling the lot, he and Sleamhnan keep the money for themselves. Having squandered the proceeds on more drink, they return to Michil demanding more poitín. Michil proceeds to calmly extract revenge for their betrayal.

Poitín, Bob Quinn's follow-up to ***Caoineadh Airt Uí Laoire*** (1975), was financed largely by the first **Arts Council** Script Award in 1977. Quinn, who at the time was based in Connemara in County Galway, had been approached by local writer Colm Bairéad with a story that reminded Quinn of Guy de Maupassant. Certainly, the film's direction is informed by a Maupassantian simplicity and economy of expression. In interviews, Quinn has spoken of his desire to portray something of the "terrible bleakness" of existence on the economically depressed western seaboard during the 1970s, and the film certainly succeeds in that respect. The world of *Poitín* is one of casual cruelty where alcohol offers what is apparently the only escape—however brief—from the harshness of existence.

It also makes compelling viewing despite the fact that it was shot in a language—Irish—of which most natives have a poor working understanding. That much of narrative requires no understanding of any spoken language is a tribute to Quinn's quiet mastery of visual grammar. In this respect, he was clearly aided by the work of a crew that reads like a who's who of first-wave Irish cinema: **Cathal Black**, **Joe Comerford**, and **Seamus Deasy**, among others, were all involved in the production of the film.

POWER, IAN. A native of Dublin and graduate of University College Dublin, writer/director Ian Power came to prominence with the award-winning short films *The Wonderful Story of Kelvin Kind* (2004) and *Dental Breakdown* (2009). His feature debut, ***The Runway*** (2011), was an entertaining "stranger-comes-to-town" story of a Columbian pilot who crash-lands in rural Ireland in the mid-1980s that, despite strong reviews and international distribution, foundered at the box office due, perhaps, to its narrative mildness. With his second film, *The Guarantee*, Power again worked with a true story from recent Irish history (adapted from Colin Murphy's eponymous play) but changed tone substantially in a drama focusing on the events of 28 September 2008, when the Irish government guaranteed the funds of the entire banking system—with disastrous consequences. In these films, Powers displays a genuine feeling for character and situation, sensibilities that work well on the stage or small screen but can underwhelm on the big screen, which requires greater dramatic depth and/or complexity. Nevertheless, Power is a clearly developing talent who is committed and ambitious.

PRICEWATERHOUSECOOPERS REPORT **(2003).** In the wake of the ***Kilkenny Report*** (named for Ossie Kilkenny, who had chaired the **Film** Industry Strategic Review Group [1999]), Minister for Finance Charlie McCreevy extended the operation of **Section 481** until the end of 2004. In December 2002, however, he indicated that it was not his intention to renew the tax incentive after the December 2003 budget. This prompted a major campaign on the part of the film industry, spearheaded by Film Makers Ireland, to convince him to change his mind. With these competing discourses at loggerheads, it fell to Minister for Arts, Culture, and the Gaeltacht **John O'Donoghue** to commission the international accountancy firm PricewaterhouseCoopers to address the question of whether there was an economic or competitive justification for maintaining fiscal support for the Irish film industry after 2004. Less overtly, the report was also intended to address the perception that unscrupulous "producers" had been abusing the Section 481 mechanism.

The report identified the key role played by overseas productions in the post-1993 boom in the industry, the importance of Section 481 in attracting those productions, and the extent to which Ireland now faced international competition for such productions.

The report noted that hitherto, large-scale offshore productions had been attracted by a combination of Section 481, production infrastructures, and personnel. Reflecting their larger scale, the report concluded that such offshore productions were more likely to result in a net gain to the exchequer than indigenous productions with budgets of less than €5 million. However, many of the overseas productions were "location neutral"; that is, they could be shot in any number of countries, and the filmmakers would tend to choose the location that offered the most attractive financial incentives. In this respect, Section 481 was key: the report therefore concluded that had Section 481 not been in place between 1999 and 2001, around €150 million in offshore funds would have been lost to the Irish economy.

However, the report also noted that while Section 481 had constituted a major advantage in attracting offshore productions in 1993, the introduction by other countries of competing incentives in the interim had eroded Ireland's competitiveness. In particular, the report concluded that limiting the amount in Section 481 funds that could be raised for any single picture to €10.48 million did not facilitate its use by large-scale offshore productions. Given this, the report recommended not only retaining the tax incentive but also substantially increasing the amount that could be raised for any individual film to €50 million. However, the report also recommended that the Department of Arts employ budget experts to review budgets before allowing a producer to raise Section 481 funds and that the commissioners be allowed to audit the level of Section 481 spent on randomly selected productions after they were complete.

The report was delivered to Minister O'Donoghue in September 2003 and formed a key element in his submission to the minister for finance on the future of Section 481. It had the desired impact: in December 2003, McCreevy announced that rather than prematurely ending Section 481, he would instead extend it until 2008. Furthermore, he announced an increase in the sum of money that could be raised per picture via Section 481. However, rather than the €50 million figure suggested by the report, he limited the increase to €15 million. The other recommendations were also largely implemented: as of 2004, primary responsibility for overseeing the operation of Section 481 shifted from the Department of Arts, Sports, and Tourism to the revenue commissioners.

PROJECT ARTS THEATRE/PROJECT CINEMA CLUB. The Project Arts Centre emerged from a three-week festival at the Gate Theatre in November 1966 that included avant-garde theater, experimental music, and visual arts. The success of the festival led to the establishment of the Project Gallery on Lower Abbey Street as a permanent venue for alternative takes on performing and visual arts. In 1969, the gallery became the Project Arts Centre and provided a venue for the early work of writers and directors like Jim and Peter Sheridan and **Neil Jordan**. After a two-year sojourn on South King Street, the project moved to a former print works on East Essex Street (a building that was purchased outright with **Arts Council** assistance in 1977).

Although regarded as alternative, the early project was only nominally radical until July 1976, when a new board committed to an oppositional cultural policy was elected. Driven by a **Kevin Rockett** manifesto stressing the need to look at cinema in a wider critical and cultural context, the Project Cinema Club operated from 1976 to 1980 in a 70-seat theater within the Project Arts Centre in Dublin's Temple Bar. (Rockett also programmed the cinema.) Screenings began in October 1976 with seasons of new German cinema, some previously unscreened Irish material, and other noncommercial films. From the winter 1977–1978 program, the club also ran a series of screenings followed by talks and discussions to overtly situate films in a critical context. The series were organized around themes such as feminism and cinema and avant-garde cinema, and cutting-edge theorists, such as Laura Mulvey, traveled to Dublin to give lectures.

In 1978, the club programmed *Film and Ireland*, a pioneering and landmark endeavor that screened more than 100 Irish and Irish-themed films, organized into loose groupings, such as Family, Foreign Images of Ireland, and Irish Literary Traditions on Film. It was the largest assembly of Irish films hitherto gathered together and influenced later events in London and the even more ambitious 1984 **Green on the Screen** season by the **Irish Film Institute** (IFI).

The project also planned more ambitious ventures, such as a film workshop and a 16-mm distribution organization, but these proved difficult to achieve in the absence of sustained funding. In any case, with the development of the **Irish Film Theatre** and the (partially Rockett-inspired) revamp of the IFI, the club's screening and education functions were gradually usurped, and the club's operations ceased in the early 1980s. Nonetheless, the club represented a key moment in the emergence of an Irish film culture and created a space in which the early work of pioneers like **Bob Quinn** and **Joe Comerford** could find an audience.

PUCKOON **(2001).** A British–Irish coproduction directed by Terence Ryan, *Puckoon* is based on Spike Milligan's surrealist first novel. Set during the work of the 1925 Boundary Commission (which was to finally agree on how Northern Ireland and the Irish Free State would be geographically divided), *Puckoon* traces the consequences of their efforts for one village that finds itself split down the middle by the new border. There was an unintended though happy irony in the film being the first project to be shot on the massive stages of **Titanic Studios**, a direct dividend of the peace process, where *Game of Thrones* would later transform the Northern Irish film economy. Despite an international star cast (including Sean Hughes, Elliott Gould, Richard Attenborough, and Gryff Rhys Jones), the film's producers found it difficult to secure a release, and it sank without a trace domestically and internationally.

PURCELL, NOEL (1900–1985). With his long beard and gravelly working-class accent, Purcell was long characterized as the definitive Dubliner who, during a prolific career in theater and film, kept Ireland and the Irish in the international public gaze. Born in inner-city Dublin, Purcell began his acting career at the Gaiety, having begun there as a messenger boy at age 12 thanks to his mother's friendship with the stage manager. Later, he toured Ireland in a vaudeville act with the famed Jimmy O'Dea. His breakthrough came after he was cast in the historical drama *Captain Boycott* (1947), which sufficiently impressed Pinewood Studio executives that they made him a contract player, and he spent much of the 1950s appearing in British films. He was frequently called on to play stock Irish roles in films such as *Talk of a Million* (1951), *Rooney* (1958), and **John Ford**'s anthology of Irish stories *The Rising of the Moon* (1957). His old sea dog appearance led to his being cast in a disproportionate number of nautical roles, including Lew Milestone's *Blue Lagoon* (1949) (his American debut), **John Huston**'s *Moby Dick* (1956), *Mutiny on the Bounty* (1962), and *Lord Jim* (1965). He also starred in two other films for the Irish-resident Huston: *The List of Adrian Messenger* (1963) and *The Mackintosh Man* (1973). By the 1960s, he was an internationally recognized screen actor, although he increasingly began to appear in television roles as that decade progressed. In his last feature roles in the early 1970s, he played a ferry boat captain in *The McKensie Break* (1970) and a singing and dancing Dublin rabbi in the fanciful *Flight of the Doves* (1971).

***THE PURPLE TAXI (UN TAXI MAUVE)* (1977).** A rarely seen oddity, this French–Irish–Italian coproduction directed by Yves Boisset is based on the award-winning novel (*Grand Prix du roman de l'Académie Française*) by longtime French-born County Galway resident Michel Deon (1919–2016). The book is considered Deon's masterpiece and was written after the writer relocated to Ireland following the introduction of the Artists Tax Exemption scheme in 1969 by the then Minister for Finance Charles J. Haughey.

Philippe (Philippe Noiret) is a French journalist who relocates to Connemara in the wake of his son's death. There, he encounters a group of troubled expatriates, including Jerry (Edward Albert), a young American and heir to a family fortune, and his sister, Sharon (Charlotte Rampling), with whom he becomes infatuated. The cosmopolitan group is completed by Taubelman (Peter Ustinov), a Russian exile, and his ward, Anne, who is apparently mute. The film also, bizarrely, features Fred Astaire (his second role as an Irishman after ***Finian's Rainbow*** [1969], in which his accent is just as unconvincing) as a local doctor.

Unusually, the film was partially financed by the **National Film Studios of Ireland** (**Ardmore Studios**), where the film was partially shot. The studios paid £260,000 for a 7 percent stake in the film's profits from English-language territories. This proved a poor investment, but nevertheless the film was entered into the 1977 Cannes Film Festival and became a box office hit in France. A Gallic counterpart to **Heinrich Böll**'s **Irisches Tagebuch**/*Irish Journal* (1957), arguably no other work of literature or cinema has so shaped the French idea of Ireland.

Q

***THE QUIET MAN* (1952).** In the same way that *The Purple Taxi* played a seminal role in constructing the French view of Ireland, **John Ford**'s 1952 film remained a dominant representation of a romantic Ireland for postwar America and beyond. For many years, it was a source and touchstone of offense to those who, still prickly from the centuries-long experience of colonialism, saw in it a perpetuation of stereotypes that cast them as primitive, premodern, and equally prone to violence and drink ("that ridiculous film . . . wifebeating, priest-ridden, blather talking gombeen men getting drunk. . . . No true Irish person takes pride in that low class insult to Ireland," Malachy McCourt ranted in a 2015 Facebook post). However, such responses have undergone radical popular and critical revision in recent years as Ireland became a wealthier and more cosmopolitan country and the ironic distance of Ford's vision became easier to discern and appreciate. It remains a keystone of cinematic representations of Ireland and Irish screen studies.

Adapted from Maurice Walsh's short story (published in the *Saturday Evening Post* in 1933 and later revised for inclusion in his 1950 collection of stories *Green Rushes*), the property was a pet project for Ford, who optioned it in 1936 and spent many years trying to convince someone to finance it before Herb Yates at Republic Pictures reluctantly agreed after *Rio Grande* (1950) (also starring John Wayne and **Maureen O'Hara**) had been a big hit.

The narrative focuses on an Irish American's—Sean Thornton (Wayne)—return to his homeland of Innisfree and his attempt to recapture the imagined innocence and beauty of his lost Irish childhood (Yeats via Henry David Thoreau's *Walden*). In the Ford version—adapted by Frank Nugent—Sean is not merely returning but actively fleeing the United States, having killed an opponent in a boxing match that, despite the brevity of its representation in flashback, functions as an allegory of capitalism as a culture of death. The drama of the film follows his attempt to begin his new life, caught between a desire to be left alone (with his memories of his mother and home) and a powerful sexual attraction to local beauty Mary Kate Danaher (O'Hara) that drags him into the customs and company of the community. Viewed this way, the film can be read as an Oedipal journey toward sexual maturity, coded in terms of the Irish immigrant experience.

While Walsh's story attempted to locate its action in a recognizable historical context, the film has only a very tendentious relationship with the period in which it ostensibly takes place, sometime in the 1920s in the aftermath of the Irish Civil War. However, while many have dismissed this as an excess of nostalgic or stage Irishness, others have read the film more positively as a playful fantasy that is closer to the tradition of the "Green World" comedies of Shakespeare than the contrived realism of **Robert O'Flaherty**. Luke Gibbons, who has written more than anyone about the film, speaks of its influence in creating a picturesque exoticism of Ireland—as evidenced by a cover for *National Geographic* in 1961 with a **Maureen O'Hara** look-alike—and its foregrounding of a soft romanticism, especially when compared with the "hard primitivism" of works such as Flaherty's *Man of Aran* (Gibbons, *The Quiet Man*, 2002). (Indeed, that visual iconography persisted into the 21st century, as evinced by Annie Leibovitz's 2013 West of Ireland shoot for *Vogue* magazine.)

Making broad use of **Abbey Theatre** actors and influences (notably Lady Gregory and Synge's *The Playboy of the Western World*), the film was coproduced by **Lord Killanin**, a (reportedly distant) relative of Ford who was long active in trying to set up an Irish film industry and developed a lifelong relationship with Ford. Local lore reports that Killanin and Ford originally hoped or intended to shoot the film entirely in Spiddal, from where Ford's father had emigrated (from lands owned or adjacent to the Killanin's estate) in the aftermath of the Irish Famine. While a lack of local facilities prohibited this (particularly the absence of a hotel of the scale of Ashford Castle), Ford and members of the company frequently visited during the shoot, and the film used locations from all over County Galway from Yeats Tower (Thorr Ballylee) in Gort to the "Quiet Man bridge" in Oughterard to Ballyglunin railway station near Tuam.

Despite the initial reservations of Republic Pictures, *The Quiet Man* received seven **Academy Award** nominations, winning in two categories—Best Director and Best Color Cinematography (Ford's fourth Oscar for Best Director)—and taking nearly $4 million in the United States alone in its first year, his largest-grossing picture to date. The film's enduring significance and influence is demonstrated, for example, by its playing in the background on television during a domestic scene in Steven Spielberg's *E.T.* (1982) and in Martin Scorsese's frequent referencing of its boxing scene for *Raging Bull*—not to mention its enduring importance to the economy of the west of Ireland, particularly Ashford Castle and Cong, where tourists can pose beside a statue of John Wayne and gaze across the pastures where he once wondered, "Is that real?"

QUINN, AIDAN (1959–). Although a recurrent presence in Irish cinema since the early 1990s, Aidan Quinn is not the only member of his family to be preoccupied with filmmaking. His brother Declan is a noted cinematographer, with films like *Leaving Las Vegas* (1995), **Neil Jordan**'s *Breakfast on Pluto* (2005), and **Jim Sheridan**'s *Get Rich or Die Tryin'* (2005) to his credit. Quinn's younger sister, Marian, is a successful actress, appearing in a number of Irish films, including *Broken Harvest* and *When the Sky Falls* and directing *32A* (2007). Finally, another brother, Paul Quinn, directed *This Is My Father*, which featured both Aidan and Marian and on which Declan acted as cinematographer.

Aidan Quinn spent most of the first two decades of his life living on both sides of the Atlantic, with his academic father getting work in the United States and commuting back and forth from their Irish home in Birr, County Offaly. He attended St. Joseph's College in Blackrock, where he excelled at sports, history, and English. On leaving school, however, he did not pursue an academic career and for a period worked as kitchen porter. His interest in acting was piqued by lunchtime plays he would attend in Dublin's city center, although, concerned that his American-tinged accent would prove a hindrance, he never considered pursuing an acting career in Dublin. In his early 20s, he returned to the United States, where he took acting classes. Two years of stage acting followed before he secured his first screen role opposite Darryl Hannah in *Reckless* (1984). The following year, he appeared as the male lead in his breakthrough film, *Desperately Seeking Susan*, opposite Rosanna Arquette and Madonna. He also made an indelible impression in *An Early Frost* (1985), one of the first pieces of popular drama to address the impact of AIDS on American society.

By the start of the 1990s, he was an acknowledged star on U.S. screens, typically third or fourth on the cast list but occasionally, as in *Benny and Joon* (1993), *Blink* (1994), and *Legends of the Fall* (1994), receiving equal lead billing alongside actors such as Johnny Depp and Brad Pitt. His first Irish role did not come until 1992, when he played the amorous traveling player in *The Playboys*. Indeed, until the late 1990s, he was perceived in Ireland largely as an American actor with a facility for Irish accents. However, his de facto dual citizenship and his star status in the United States became increasingly useful for casting directors working in Ireland as production activity there took off in the mid-1990s. Quinn's Irish work has frequently had a "heritage" element and sought to leverage his popularity in the U.S. market—the lead role in *This Is My Father*, in which James Caan's character attempts to trace his family history back to Ireland; his role as Harry Boland in *Michael Collins*; and opposite **Pierce Brosnan** in *Evelyn*. His most affecting role in an Irish film to date arguably remains that of

William Franklin, the idealistic teacher in the brutal *Song for a Raggy Boy* (Aisling Walsh, 2003), an unsentimental *Dead Poets Society* story set in 1950s rural Catholic Ireland.

In more recent years, Quinn's star status has dimmed, a combination of circumstances, the onset of middle age, and a changed industry, where the mid-level films for which his skill set is best suited are no longer produced. But he has remained busy, working like many in a similar situation in smaller roles and quality TV, including *Elementary* (CBS, 2012–2017), *Prime Suspect* (BBC, 2011–2012), and *Weeds* (Showtime, 2011). A late entry to his Irish-set filmography is the largely unseen Canadian–Irish coproduction *Stay* (2013), where he gives a moving performance as a middle-aged academic who wants to avoid the demands of the modern world, including impending fatherhood with a much younger girlfriend (Taylor Schilling).

QUINN, BOB (1939–). Although beginning his media career as a trainee studio operator with **Radio Telefís Éireann** (RTÉ) in 1961, Quinn moved upward to become a director by the mid-1960s. As a salaried director, Quinn's work took him where the broadcaster sent him, from arts documentaries (*Backstage* and *On the Road*) to religious-themed programming, such as the Horizon series, and broader current affairs territory via Discovery. In 1969, Quinn, along with colleagues **Lelia Doolan** and Jack Dowling, famously parted ways with the broadcaster, complaining of its lurch toward commercialism. He left to take up residence in his beloved Connemara, a Gaeltacht (Irish-language–speaking) region in Galway, and in 1973 set up Cinegael with Seosamh Ó Cuaig and Toni Cristofides in a bid both to create a means of reflecting contemporary life in the west of Ireland through a Gaelic-language idiom and to construct a sustainable production infrastructure for that part of the country. (He would become a longtime campaigner for Irish-language and Gaeltacht civil rights and was a key mover in the campaign to establish an Irish-language television station, leading led to the establishment of Teilifís na Gaeilge [later TG4] in 1996.) He made his first feature, *Caoineadh Airt Uí Laoire*, in 1975, its self-conscious use of various modes of representation emulating the experimentation of Jean-Luc Godard's polemical work and, by drawing audience attention to the constructed nature of the text, inviting viewers to actively participate in the process of meaning making. Next, he made a full-length feature entirely in Gaelic, *Poitín* (1978), starring **Cyril Cusack, Niall Toibin**, and **Donal McCann**, which was financed by the **Arts Council**. The story demonstrates the brutality of this insular community in the west, which has been hampered by centuries of emigration and underdevelopment.

In 1986, Quinn made *Atlantean*, a three-part television series that sought to question the founding myth of Celtic mythology and its suggestions of a pure, rural, self-sufficient race that is uncorrupted by foreign influence. Focusing on the various extensive trade links between the sea people of Britain, France, Spain, and North Africa, together with Ireland and, in particular, the Port of Galway, the director presented a convincing dramatic thesis of at least possible blood relations between these various seafaring trading countries.

The line between his 1987 film *Budawanny*, adapted from the novel *Súil le Breith* by Connemara priest Padraic Standún, and his 1993 reworking of this same material in *The Bishop's Story* is somewhat unclear. But both deal with a Catholic priest, played by **Donal McCann**, on Clare Island, off the west coast, and his sexual relationship with his housekeeper (Margaret Fegan). The story has strong echoes of several real-life scandals in the Catholic Church, most notably the story of Bishop Eamon Casey and his illegitimate son, which has subsequently come to light.

Quinn's feature film output trailed off by the end of 1990s, but he has long been an outspoken critic of new Irish cinema, arguing that younger Irish filmmakers are being seduced by the outside world while being led to believe through various government film agencies that they can and should become international cinema figures rather than simply setting their sights on working toward a distinct—and critical—voice for a native audience. He has remained a vocal critic of aspects of Irish and international society and politics, often resorting to other media—literature and still photography—to express his views. In 1995, he became the first filmmaker to be inducted into Aosdana, the Arts Council body that assists artists in maintaining their commitment to artistic production. The same year saw him—to his own surprise—appointed to the board of RTÉ, the organization he had walked out on 36 years previously. He remained an outspoken critic of the organization (though also, at times, a supporter), though his tenure was cut short when he resigned in 1999, citing frustration at his failure to have the broadcaster remove advertising aimed at children and to increase the level of regionalization within RTÉ. (He would later recount his experiences on the board in his autobiography *Maverick* [2001].) Now in his 80s, Quinn remains a trenchant critic of commercial culture and, in particular, its impact on the environment.

QUINN, MARIAN. Part of the Irish American Quinn family (writer/actor Paul [d. 2015], cinematographer Declan, and **Aidan Quinn**). Born in Chicago, Marian migrated back and forth from Ireland, living in Birr, Illinois, and Dublin. As an adult, she settled in New York, although after *This Is My Father* (1998), she returned to Ireland again with her husband and children to live in County Leitrim. She has starred in several other Irish films—including *When the Sky Falls* (2000) and *Evelyn* (2002)—as well as the Irish American narratives *Broken Harvest* (1994) and *2by4* (1998). In 2007, she wrote and directed her feature debut, *32A*, a charming coming-of-age story set in Dublin of the 1970s.

R

RADIO TELEFÍS ÉIREANN. Radio Telefís Éireann (RTÉ) is the national public service broadcaster owned by the state and run by a state-appointed governing authority. Although sound broadcasting began in 1926, the move to television was not seriously explored until the mid-1950s. Government policy throughout that decade worked on the assumption that television would be run on a commercial basis, but in 1959, the cabinet decided that the existing public service broadcaster, Radio Éireann (Radio Ireland), should expand its operations to encompass television. This was given legal effect via the 1960 Broadcasting Authority Act.

The act was relatively unspecific with regard to RTÉ's programming obligations beyond Section 17 of the act, which stated that "in performing its functions, the Authority shall bear constantly in mind the national aims of restoring the Irish language and preserving and developing the national culture and shall endeavor to promote the attainment of those aims."

Thus, RTÉ faced no particular obligations to engage in drama production or more particularly to support filmmaking activity. Nonetheless (indeed inevitably), RTÉ did engage in fiction production, the bulk of which were single dramas, until the 1980s. Some serial production commenced as early as 1964 with the production of the first Irish television soap opera, *Tolka Row* (which ran until 1968). A year later, in 1965, it was followed by a second soap, *The Riordans*, which ran until 1979 and which generated two spin-off dramas: *Bracken* (1981–1982) and *Glenroe* (1982–2001). As the 1970s and 1980s progressed, drama series came to dominate RTÉ drama production, although this took place in the context of an overall reduction in output, especially in the decade from 1985 to 1995.

Direct support of Irish film production did not take place until the 1980s, when the station partially funded **Joe Comerford**'s first feature-length drama, *Traveller*. Film finance remained patchy for the remainder of that decade, although the station did put some funds into **Pat Murphy**'s *Anne Devlin* and **Jim Sheridan**'s *My Left Foot*. Typically, RTÉ came late to these projects, committing funds only once it was clear that the rest of the budget was already in place. Ironically, then, Irish filmmakers were more likely to receive funding from British broadcaster **Channel 4** than from their local channel.

But this situation changed somewhat after 1993 with the passage of that year's Broadcasting (Amendment) Act, which transposed into Irish law that part of the European Union's 1989 "Television Without Frontiers" directive, which required European broadcasters to reserve 10 percent of their broadcast time for independently produced work. This resulted in the establishment of a new unit within RTÉ—the Independent Production Unit (IPU)—charged with commissioning work from production companies outside RTÉ. At the same time, the station came under increasing criticism for the decline in its commitment to drama production in previous years.

Happily for RTÉ, the establishment of the IPU coincided with the expansion in indigenous feature production that followed on the re-establishment of the **Irish Film Board** (IFB), with the result that it could become involved in a plethora of extant projects in development while simultaneously fulfilling its obligations to independent production and drama output. Thus, in 1994, RTÉ partially funded **Cathal Black**'s *Korea* and **Bob Quinn**'s reworking of his earlier *Budawanny* into *The Bishop's Story*. IPU involvement with feature production continued through the 1990s; it partially funded (among other titles) *I Went Down* (1997), *A Love Divided* (1999), *Nora* (2000), and *Borstal Boy* (2000). However, from 2000 on, support for feature production dried up as RTÉ began to actively commission independently produced drama series. As hit shows like *Bachelor's Walk* and *Paths to Freedom* came onstream, RTÉ was able to fulfill its drama commitments without recourse to feature film funding.

However, RTÉ did not entirely abandon independent film production. From 1994 on, it developed a series of schemes in collaboration with the IFB aimed at supporting short-film and animation production. These included Short Cuts (1994–2007), which funded six- to 15-minute dramas; Oscailt (1998–2008), which was supported by TG4 (then an RTÉ subsidiary) together with the Film Board; and the still extant Frameworks (1995–), which supports animation.

It might also be argued that the simple fact of RTÉ's existence has indirectly (and unintentionally) supported Irish filmmaking by offering at least some small space for writers, directors, and actors to practice their craft. Producer **Lelia Doolan** worked as a drama director and current affairs producer in the 1960s, as did **Bob Quinn**, before both left dramatically in May 1969 in protest of what they characterized as the station's stifling of creativity. Both, however, acknowledged their professional debts to the organization. Farther down the line, in 1979, RTÉ director **Pat O'Connor** directed single dramas penned by both **Jim Sheridan** (*Mobile Homes*) and **Neil Jordan** (*Miracles and Miss Langan*). Indeed, RTÉ cofinanced (with **Channel 4**)

Pat O'Connor's BAFTA award–winning drama *The Ballroom of Romance*, which led to O'Connor's first feature work on **Cal**. **Eat the Peach** director Peter Ormrod worked as a director for RTÉ, most notably on the 1983 series *Caught in a Free State*. Even **Lenny Abrahamson** worked with the station on his 2007 series *Prosperity*.

However, Abrahamson has also publicly critiqued what he characterizes as RTÉ's passive attitude to developing drama production. And it remains the case that, in contrast with many other public service broadcasters in Europe, RTÉ's engagement with film can at best be described as sporadic and unstructured. In contrast to countries like Denmark, France, and the United Kingdom, where public service broadcasters face a legal requirement to invest in feature film production, RTÉ has no such obligation, although the 2009 Broadcasting Act explicitly permits it to invest its funds in such a fashion. Irish producers have consistently complained that the lack of local broadcaster support places them at a disadvantage relative to their European counterparts. This is reflected in a 2016 policy document from **Screen Producers Ireland** that proposed a requirement that RTÉ set aside 1.5 percent of its television expenditures (or a at least €2.5 million) to film production. To date, that measure has not been taken up by RTÉ or the Irish government.

THE RAFTERS (2011). Rose (Marcella Plunkett) is a psychologically disturbed young woman, haunted by unspecified events in her past. Seeking to confront them, she travels to a guesthouse on the Aran Islands that, it is hinted, holds the key to her condition. There, she encounters two backpacking Americans (Irish actors Killian Scott and Sean Donegan) who make bets as to who will bed her first. In their respective rooms that night, they hear indistinct movements in the attic, perhaps footsteps, an object being lifted. Although the boys are undeterred in their pursuit of the ever more somnolent Rose, it becomes clear that there is a sinister hidden presence pervading the building.

Shot during the interregnum between director **John Carney**'s sci-fi romp **Zonad** (2009) and *Begin Again* (2013), the middle section of his music trilogy, *The Rafters* feels incomplete or, at best, as a short film thinly stretched to feature length. Performances are fine, and cinematographer P. J. Dillon emphasizes the gothic quality of the Aran scenery, but Carney seems uncertain whether to pitch the narrative as a straight horror or—echoing his earlier film **On the Edge** (2001)—as an exploration of Rose's psychosis. Although the film ultimately plumps for the former territory, the conclusion is frustratingly inconclusive.

That verdict seems confirmed by the—even by the standards of Irish cinema—narrow release afforded to the film. Although screened at the Galway Film Fleadh (Festival) in 2012, it received such an excoriating review in *Variety* that it appears that the producers decided then and there to abandon any further distribution plans.

RAT **(2000).** This is a quirky comedy, somewhat reminiscent of Kafka's story "Metamorphosis," concerning a lazy working-class man (Peter Postlethwaite) who one day wakes up to find himself transformed into a rat. Remarkably, his family, including his wife (Imelda Staunton) and Uncle Matt (**Frank Kelly**), quickly accept these unusual circumstances and proceed to bring him around to his usual haunts. This absurd comic-fantasy directed by Steve Barron and scripted by Wesley Burrows, who is remembered for the long-running rural television soap *The Riordans*, has the unforgettable tagline "He might eat maggots and live in a cage but he's still our Dad." The resultant film remains engaging.

REA, STEPHEN (1946–). Born in Belfast, Rea was the only boy in a Protestant family with four children. While studying English at Queen's University Belfast, he joined the politically driven Young Irish Theatre Company before moving to Dublin to work with the **Abbey Theatre**. From there, he moved to the London stage, where he worked in virtually every major theater, including the Old Vic, the Royal Court, and the English National Theater. In the course of this, he worked through the canon of modern theater from Henrik Ibsen through Anton Chekov to Bertolt Brecht. In 1980, Rea returned to Northern Ireland, where, with playwright Brian Friel (and later internationally renowned poet Seamus Heaney and academic and writer Seamus Deane), he founded the Field Day theater company, which sought to create a cultural space to interrogate a more constructive historical identity from within the specter of the Troubles. This is reflected in Rea's own career choices on-screen and onstage, which, his nominal Protestant background notwithstanding, has seen him essay both Loyalist and Republican roles. (That ambiguity was reflected in his private life given his two-decade-long marriage to convicted Irish Republican Army bomber Dolours Price and, piquantly, his work as "the voice" of Sinn Féin leader Gerry Adams during the period [1988–1994] of his ban from U.K. broadcast television.)

Rea first became known as a screen actor with *Angel* (1982) and has maintained a close relationship with **Neil Jordan** ever since, making seven appearances in the director's subsequent films. These include ***Breakfast on Pluto*** (2005); an adaptation of the Graham Greene novel *The End of the Affair* (1999), in which he plays the cuckolded Henry Miles; and *The Company of Wolves* (1984), *Interview with the Vampire* (1994), ***Michael Collins***

(1996), *The Butcher Boy* (1997), *In Dreams* (1999), *Ondine* (2009), and *Greta* (2018). Rea often brings a quiet, understated quality to his roles, appropriate for an actor often cast as characters who, torn between competing moral positions, escape to avoid scrutiny (see his Danny in *Angel*, Fergus in *The Crying Game*, and Ned Broy in *Michael Collins*). This perhaps reaches its apotheosis in *Nothing Personal* (2009) as Martin, a Connemara-dwelling hermit who agrees to take in a young woman on the condition that she ask him nothing about himself. This self-effacing tendency can sometimes obscure the intensity of his performances, although he was **Academy Award** nominated for his starring role in *The Crying Game* (1992).

Beyond his work with Jordan, he has also appeared in numerous other Irish films—often in cameo roles—including *Black '47* (2017), *Stella Days*, *The Halo Effect*, *Bloom*, *Evelyn*, *On the Edge*, *This Is My Father*, *A Further Gesture*, *The Last of the High Kings*, and *Trojan Eddie*. He is also in steady demand for roles in smaller-scale European and U.S. films, especially since the *Crying Game* Oscar nomination. These include *Life Is Sweet* (1990), *Prêt-a-Porter* (1994), and *Fever Pitch* (1997).

Although he has occasionally returned to stage—most notably for the Broadway run of Frank McGuinness's *Someone to Watch Over Me* and in several Sam Shepard plays written with him in mind—the bulk of Rea's recent work has been on the small screen in British serial productions, such as *The Shadow Line* (2011), *Utopia* (2013), *The Honorable Woman* (2014), *War and Peace* (2016), and *Dickensian* (BBC, 2016).

***REEFER AND THE MODEL* (1988).** **Joe Comerford**'s second feature film is an unconventional road movie set off Ireland's west coast and begins when Reefer (Ian McElhinney), a former Irish Republican Army (IRA) man, a gives a lift to Teresa (Carol Scanlon), the homeless and pregnant "model" returning to Ireland in the hope of kicking her heroin habit. When he takes her to live on his boat, an occasional ferry between the mainland and the islands, we are introduced to his crew—Spider (Sean Lawlor), who is on the run from the British authorities, and Badger (Ray McBride). Together, this group of misfits and marginals form a rough kind of community in a narrative that reworks American outlaw stories on a number of levels. Produced by **Lelia Doolin**, the film won the Europa Prize at the Barcelona Festival and Best Feature at the Celtic Film Festival in Wales, but its wider achievement may be that it was the film that inspired the establishment of the Galway Film Fleadh (Festival) as a showcase for new Irish cinema—a legacy that endures to this day.

One can possibly better understand *Reefer and the Model* by ignoring specific elements of the narrative (which can be confusing and overdidactic) and focusing instead on the impact of the whole. Here, the film is somewhat more successful, particularly if one is mindful of the political context in which the film was made in the mid-1980s, a period characterized by occasional news stories about shoot-outs between IRA members on the run and the Gardaí (police). Reefer is portrayed as an IRA man who is attempting to put the past behind him but who is thwarted both by the tendency of his past to catch up with him and by an unwillingness to completely abandon past methods in moments of crisis. While this somewhat humanizes a figure who for many was simply a media and political bogeyman at the time, he remains shallowly drawn overall and often contradictory, as does the film as a whole, which, while suggesting interesting ideas about representation and political themes, emerges as an incoherent if spirited effort to construct a distinctly Irish cinematic idiom.

RENNICKS, STEPHEN. One of a growing list of Irish composers of film music who, along with the likes of Stephen McKeon and Brian Byrne, has made acclaimed contributions to the sound tracks of the industry's "third wave" (after 2004).

A contemporary and friend of **Ed Guiney** and **Lenny Abrahamson** at Trinity College Dublin in the late 1980s, he began his career composing music for the latter's debut short film *3 Joes* (1991) and has worked with Abrahamson on all his films since: *Adam and Paul* (2005), *Garage* (2005), *What Richard Did* (2012), and *Frank* (2013). His contribution to *Frank* was distinguished by the songs sung by the film's Frank Sidebottom character (played by **Michael Fassbender**), which managed to combine both the sincerity of his musical ambitions and their incongruity within a commercial music industry.

Rennicks has also contributed to a wide variety of other Irish fiction projects, including *Man About Dog* (2004), *Pure Mule* (2005), *Boy Eats Girl* (2005), *Eden* (2008), *The Stag* (aka *The Bachelor Party*) (2013), *A Date for Mad Mary* (2016), and *Viva* (2016) as well as a number of documentaries, including *The Pipe* (2010) and *African Pride* (2014).

More recently, Rennicks has extended his talents internationally with commissions for the Spanish horror feature *Muse* (2018) and the documentary *Forever Pure* (2016).

***REPORT OF ENQUIRY INTO THE SUPPLY AND DISTRIBUTION OF CINEMA FILMS* (1977).** In 1970, the Fair Trade Commission (FTC) received a number of complaints from independent cinema owners to the effect that they were experiencing difficulties in getting access to films. The complaints clearly implied that **Ward Anderson** and the **distribution** sector were colluding to give Ward Anderson cinemas preferential access to prints. As a result, the commission engineered the establishment of the Cinema Trade Complaints Committee in May 1970 to deal with such complaints.

However, in 1976, faced with an ongoing flow of complaints, the examiner of the Restrictive Practices Commission (which superseded the FTC in 1972) met with the Irish Cinemas Association, which represented independent cinema owners. The association asserted that Dublin suburban cinemas had to wait two to 14 months for products due to the privileged status of Ward Anderson's Green Cinema and, further, that Ward Anderson–controlled provincial cinemas got all the first runs outside Dublin.

The examiner proceeded to examine the exhibition patterns of 17 films and concluded that priority was indeed given to the Adelphi-Carlton group, Rank Odeon, and Ward Anderson's Green Group and that effectively the major distributors had established Ward Anderson in a monopoly position throughout the country outside Dublin.

The examiner's report led the commission to establish a major inquiry into the supply and distribution of cinema films in Ireland. The enquiry received 23 submissions from distributors and exhibitors and heard evidence from 26 witnesses (five of whom were barristers or senior counsel: Ward Anderson were legally represented by Peter Sutherland, who would later become an EU commissioner and head of the World Trade Organization).

With regard to the dominant position enjoyed by Adelphi-Carlton and Rank Odeon in Dublin's city center, the distributors argued that this was driven purely by commercial motivations. Faced with a limited number of prints for any given film, they had to employ some form of priority in distributing them, and the system they employed was based on the revenue-generating capacity of individual cinemas (which in turn was based on the comfort, quality of presentation, and likely run length associated with individual cinemas). The distributors further asserted that the performance of a given film outside Dublin was affected by the success of the Dublin release. In short, the distributors argued that the position enjoyed by Adelphi-Carlton and Rank derived from the financial advantages they offered to distributors.

In response to assertions about their dominance outside Dublin, Ward Anderson pointed out that, in addition to the fact that they owned 13 of the 15 cinemas based in Cork, Limerick, and Galway (which, although placing them in a dominant position, was not in itself illegal), it was easier for distributors to book films into Ward Anderson's 40-strong circuit than to make 40 individual bookings with independent cinema owners. They also argued that they had invested more money in their cinemas than their independent counterparts, thus enhancing the revenue-generating capacity of their cinemas.

The enquiry largely accepted these assertions and effectively overturned the examiner's report. With regard to the position enjoyed by Adelphi-Carlton and Rank Odeon, it did suggest that some procedures might be adopted that would moderate their dominance, suggesting that the distributors establish a Product Allocation Committee. However, the enquiry found no evidence of any collusion between the Ward Anderson group and the major distributors, citing instead the group's investment in cinemas and skillful exploitation of commercial opportunities as explaining its growth. Indeed, while stating that it would be desirable from the perspective of competition to have more than one major cinema circuit in Ireland, the enquiry found that it was nonetheless in the interest of the consumer to have at least one circuit capable of investing in facilities and offering a counterbalance to the power of distributors.

REPORT OF THE FILM INDUSTRY COMMITTEE (HUSTON RE-PORT). Arguably, the most important development, as well as the greatest missed opportunity, in the long and tortured history of state funding for Irish film. In 1967, Hollywood maverick and Irish resident **John Huston** invited **Louis Marcus** to the Gresham Hotel Dublin to discuss the possibility of state support for filmmaking in Ireland. This was provoked by a series of *Irish Times* articles by Marcus lamenting the absence of such support. Following this discussion, Huston invited Taoiseach Jack Lynch to Glencree, County Wicklow, to visit the set of his current production *Sinful Davey* (1969). In a canny political maneuver, Huston made a public speech—directed at Lynch—suggesting that the time was ripe for the establishment of an Irish film industry. Huston's status and clear enthusiasm for Ireland guaranteed that Lynch would have to act, and in November 1967, Minister for Industry and Commerce George Colley established a committee, chaired by Huston and including representatives from all sectors of film production (including Marcus and **Lord Killanin**), **distribution**, and **exhibition** in Ireland. The 24-person committee also included five civil servants representing the Departments of Finance, Industry, and Commerce; Education; and External Affairs.

In its final report, the committee acknowledged that state support for industry was usually justified by an expectation of contribution to employment and the economy in return for that support. Crucially, however, it also noted a "lack of a potent means of presenting Ireland, its heritage and its people to the world and of keeping the people in touch with their distinctive environment." Finally, it pointed out that—outside the United States—all countries with a film industry were financially aided either by the state or by a fund formed from proceeds of a levy on box office receipts.

According to Louis Marcus's later recollections, two competing perspectives drove—and, to an extent, divided—the committee's work. Huston argued that the state should concentrate any support it might be willing to offer on funding the preproduction of films (i.e., development funding) to be shot in Ireland. A cynical view might suggest that this approach would clearly have most benefited Huston's own approach to filmmaking, one that relied on international sources of finance. Intriguingly, according to Marcus, Huston rejected the idea that the state should fund the actual production of films and threatened to resign as chairman if the final committee report made any reference to short films.

When Marcus wrote an internal report for the committee, he pointed out that the cost of developing an international-scale feature film could be anything from £100,000 to £250,000—money that would be lost if the film did not succeed in attracting production finance. Furthermore, in an indirect response to Huston's position (while not wishing to give offense), C. J. Byrne from the Department of Finance argued that the state was unwilling to support preproduction finance for international producers beyond the sum of £10,000 per film. However, the state *was* interested in aiding the development of Irish filmmakers through 100 percent funding of fiction shorts and modestly budgeted (less than £50,000) features. Byrnes's farsighted ideas appear to have formed the basis for the key financial recommendations emerging from the final committee report.

Perhaps the most far-reaching recommendation of the report and its legacy was its recommendation for the creation of an agency (effectively an Irish film board) to disburse these funds. However, rather than simply re-creating the **Irish Film Finance Corporation**, this agency would have a broader responsibility to take action not merely through the provision of financial assistance but also by becoming involved in distribution, marketing, the negotiation of coproduction agreements, and offering training facilities. The agency would also act as a screen commission, offering international producers advice on locations, the availability of technicians, extras, and other elements of filmmaking in Ireland. Finally, the agency would be charged with establishing a national film archive. In its conclusion, the committee report insisted on the cultural function of such an agency in incubating a local pool of creative talent:

> The agency will have failed if its efforts lead merely to the establishment here of branches of international film companies, producing films that have no significant Irish creative, artistic and technical content. It will have achieved success when Irish creative endeavour, technical ability and artistic talent are combined in making, on a continuing basis, films of a quality and a standard acceptable to audiences in Ireland and throughout the world.

The committee submitted its report in the autumn of 1968 with Huston's name attached (despite his personal misgivings about its content). By November 1969, Colley had announced that legislation to implement the main recommendations of the film industry committee was in the course of being drafted. In July 1970, Colley's successor at the Department of Industry and Commerce, Patrick Lalor, introduced the first stage of the Film Industry Bill, which he declared would establish a film board charged with developing a film industry in the state. Although the bill was due to go to a second reading a week later, the fallout from an unrelated political scandal (the arms crisis) saw the legislation shelved. It would reemerge only a decade later in the guise of the 1980 **Irish Film Board** Act.

REPORT ON INDIGENOUS AUDIOVISUAL PRODUCTION INDUS-TRY. *See COOPERS & LYBRAND REPORT.*

RESURRECTION MAN (1998). Tapping into serial killer and new gangster conventions, director Marc Evans's film focuses on the sectarianism of a real-life Loyalist paramilitary who led a maverick Ulster Volunteer Force gang known as the Shankill Butchers, who were responsible for several brutal, ritualistic murders of Catholics (and even Protestants deemed disloyal to the cause). While the film made no claim to historical accuracy, Pierre Aim effectively photographed 1970s gritty Belfast urbanism, while the ambient sound track also succeeds in capturing the mood of the time. **Stuart Townsend** plays the eponymous "resurrection man," Victor Kelly, who is brought up by an overzealous and protective mother (**Brenda Fricker**) and a weak father (George Shane). As a child, the boy is seen to identify with the seminal image of Jimmy Cagney in *Public Enemy* (1931) and, prompted by his dysfunctional sexual nature, seeks the recognition of the media for his evil deeds. The film probes how individual psychosis is intimately connected with the normality of a dysfunctional society, such as the heavily militarized and surveillance-pervaded Northern Ireland of the 1970s. Others suggest that such a film contributes to the popular perception of Loyalist paramilitaries as essentially monstrous.

Some British critics walked out of previews of the film, and it was very critically reviewed in the south of Ireland. Both this film and **Thaddeus O'Sullivan**'s *Nothing Personal* (1995) appropriate Loyalist agency and the Troubles to explore violent **masculinity**.

REWIND (2011). Noted Irish cinematographer P. J. Dillon turns director and cowriter for this taut and suspenseful thriller. Leads **Amy Huberman** and Allen Leech are cast against type as, respectively, a former junkie turned housewife and a malevolent criminal. Karen (Huberman) has put her wild past behind her and settled down to a humdrum but contented suburban existence with her businessman husband Brendan (Owen McDonnell) and daughter. Karl (Leech), her lover from a reckless youth, reappears in her life, presenting himself to her husband as a long-lost cousin. But Karl is in serious trouble and needs Karen's help to deal with it. Karl threatens to reveal all about Karen's past if she fails to cooperate, and they commence a headlong plunge into violence and betrayal.

It's hard to avoid clichés in describing a film so firmly rooted in generic conventions. But *Rewind* has few pretensions to be more than that and is remarkably effective, especially given that as part of the **Irish Film Board**'s Catalyst scheme, it was made for just €250,000. Director Dillon fashions a visually arresting work drawing from a palette of blues and grays and, as cowriter with Ronan Carr and Roger Karshan, pens an intelligent script. However, the real revelation is the acting: Allen Leech's previously affable turns in *Man About Dog* (2002) and *Cowboys and Angels* (2003) are overtaken by a sinister and memorable performance as Karl. (In the same year, he was cast as Tom Branson in *Downton Abbey*, a role that would continue to grow and bring him international attention over the following five years.) Huberman's performance is even more startling: her previous typecasting as a squeaky-clean, South Dublin "It girl" offered little to suggest the grit of this working-class ex-criminal capable of murder, a darkness she has infrequently explored since.

REYNOLDS, EMER. One of Ireland's most respected film editors, now increasingly working as a film director in her own right, Reynolds was part of the cadre of talent that emerged from Trinity College Dublin in the late 1980s and early 1990s (from non–film-related degrees) who would go on to be key figures in second wave of Irish cinema (see also **Ed Guiney**, **Lenny Abrahamson**, **Stephen Bradley**, **Rob Walpole**, and **Alan Gilsenan**). She began exploring editing in the context of Trinity's film society before working as a trainee with **Martin Duffy** and later **Sé Merry Doyle**. Having worked on Orla Walsh's politically charged short *The Visit* (1992), she edited her first feature, **Paddy Breathnach**'s feature debut, *Ailsa* (1994). Since then, she has accumulated a long and distinguished range of credits, frequently working with directors on multiple occasions. She has collaborated on several occasions with Walsh, Breathnach, **Cathal Black**, **Conor McPherson**, and **Dearbhla Walsh**, among others. Her collaborations with **Alan Gilsenan** stand out in this regard—between 2001 and 2006, she edited five of his productions, including a short, a feature (*Timbuktu*—for which she won an IFTA in 2004), and three documentaries. After an interregnum of more than a decade, they again collaborated on *Unless* (2016) starring Catherine Keener. Other notable projects include Terry McMahon's *Patrick's Day* (2014) and Simon FitzMaurice's extraordinary achievement *My Name Is Emily* (2015). Although her work as an editor has generally been concentrated in Ireland, from 2005 on, she was also increasingly in demand overseas, working on **Channel 4**'s *Shameless* (2005) and *Funland* (2005) for the BBC.

Not content with such achievements, Reynolds has gradually turned her hand to directing, with two shorts in 2001 and the **Radio Telefís Éireann** two-part drama *Trouble in Paradise* (2007), and has come to assume a more public identity. Her feature documentaries have thus far centered on

American narratives. The first, *We Went to War* (2012), focused on the recollections of Vietnam veterans, while the second, *Here Was Cuba* (2013), recounted the events of the Cuban missile crisis. *The Farthest* (2017) brought an even bigger audience: a masterfully told story of literally cosmic dimensions recounting the story of the Voyager space exploration missions of the 1970s, combining archival footage, interviews with key players in the mission (with a notable and welcome emphasis on female participants), and computer-generated imagery visualizations of the Voyager planetary flybys. While *Here Was Cuba* and *The Farthest* might be said to demonstrate Reynolds's origins as an editor in their use of judiciously selected archival material (although both were edited by her husband Tony Cranstoun), they equally demonstrate strong storytelling skills and a sharp intelligence capable of blending a sensitive perspective on people's lives with complex historical and scientific data.

REYNOR, JACK (1992–). Jack Reynor's ascent to the cusp of international stardom was so rapid that, from the outside, it appeared all but predestined. Playing the titular role in **Lenny Abrahamson**'s *What Richard Did* (2013) brought him to the attention of international critics and talent agents, not least because of the visibility afforded to the film by its high-profile inclusion at the Toronto International Film Festival.

While some critics assumed that Reynor brought to the role a deep familiarity with middle-class privilege (evidenced by a stereotypically South Dublin accent), the actor's background is far from gilded. He was born in the United States, where his mother and her siblings had been brought by their father at the end of the 1980s after his business in Ireland failed. Reynor was raised in Colorado, and his parents separated soon after his birth. The years in the United States were filled with financial hardship, and Reynor and his grandparents returned to the village of Valleymount in County Wicklow in 1994, followed seven months later by his mother and uncle. Reynor's accounts of his childhood suggest that, notwithstanding a middle-class background, the financial circumstances of his family remained tight. He demonstrated an interest in acting in primary school and appeared as an altar boy in Kevin Liddy's *Country* (1999) at the age of seven. After securing a place in Dublin's Jesuit-run Belvedere College, Reynor's commitment to the thespian arts fully developed, and he actively participated in the school's drama program in a range of support and leading roles.

From secondary school, he was more or less immediately cast in his first full film role in Kirsten Sheridan's *Dollhouse* (2012) as the charming Robbie, who happens on a gang of teenage misfits as they rampage through an empty South Dublin modernist mansion. The role brought him to the attention of casting director Louise Kiely, who suggested him to Lenny Abrahamson, then searching for the lead in his contemporary Dublin morality tale.

The role was a gift: Richard appears in virtually every frame of the film, and Reynor's education afforded him insight into the mind-set of the privileged classes the film represents. The result was a performance of nuance, a largely understated portrayal of a handsome and likable young man who nonetheless commits a violent act and then—with the tacit support of his friends and family—covers it up. While the film was not a financial success, Reynor's performance was widely praised.

By the time the film was selected for Toronto, Reynor already had representation at the William Morris Agency, and U.S. roles began to arrive. The first was as one of Vince Vaughan's sperm-donor character's more than 500 children in *Delivery Man* (2013) (where Reynor plays a struggling actor) before action director Michael Bay cast him in the reboot of the *Transformers* franchise. (Bay had apparently spotted him in *What Richard Did* on TV.) Despite what was, almost by definition, a career-making role, Reynor did not pursue a traditional Hollywood trajectory. Indeed, one has the impression of an actor content to take his time and explore his range. In what once might have been seen as a backward move (but clearly no longer given the critical cachet of independent Irish film), he immediately followed *Transformers* with the lead role in **Gerard Barrett**'s no-budget Irish drama *Glassland* (2014) as a Dublin taxi driver struggling to aid his alcoholic mother (Toni Collette). If this suggested a capacity to move beyond the class confines of Richard, those that followed—a young British soldier on VE Day in *A Royal Night Out* (2015), the key role of Malcolm in Justin Kurzel's *Macbeth* (2015) (opposite **Michael Fassbender**), and an in-over-his-head cop in Kathryn Bigelow's *Detroit* (2017)—confirmed his range. While he did his best as Rooney Mara's lover in **Jim Sheridan**'s poorly conceived *The Secret Scripture*, his performance as the cynical older brother Brendan in **John Carney**'s warmly received *Sing Street* (2015) saw him in more comfortable territory and demonstrated a knack for comedy that director Ben Wheatley subsequently exploited in his freewheeling *Free Fire* (2016). While Reynor has not yet quite enjoyed the recognition of peers such as **Domhnall Gleeson** or **Saoirse Ronan**, these decisions suggest a young and intelligent actor still finding his voice and a transnational industry still curious to hear it.

RHYS MEYERS, JONATHAN (1977–). Born Michael Francis O'Keefe, biographies of the actor frequently allude to his troubled and turbulent childhood following his father's abandonment of his mother and three siblings by way of accounting for his sporadic lapses and benders. Expelled from school at age 16, he was spotted by a casting agent and auditioned—unsuccessfully—for *The War of the Buttons*, which was being shot on location in his home county of Cork. The experience—and a lack of options—left its impression, and he had his first small role in *A Man of No Importance* (1994) before being cast as a dissatisfied youth who disappears in *The Disappear-*

ance of Finbar, his first and, to date, only leading role in an Irish film. Aided by his striking physical beauty (he has fronted several international campaigns for clothing and fragrance brands) and a mercurial on-screen presence, he made fast progress in his career following short but important scenes in **Neil Jordan**'s *Michael Collins*, working with Ang Lee in *Ride with the Devil* (1999), Mike Figgis in *The Loss of Sexual Innocence* (1998), and Todd Haynes in *Velvet Goldmine* (1998). His performance in Gurinder Chadra's surprise crossover hit *Bend It Like Beckham* (2002) brought him even wider attention, and he was cast in a leading role in Woody Allen's *Matchpoint* (2005), for which he received strong reviews. In 2006, he received a Golden Globe for his performance in a U.S. television miniseries on the life of Elvis Presley, a role that led to his casting as Henry VIII in Showtime's *The Tudors* (2007–2010), a worldwide hit filmed in Ireland that spawned a legion of historically themed TV dramas blending big budgets, gruesome violence, and copious sex. (Rhys Meyers's casting was clearly designed to reinvent Henry for the 21st century, actively playing on his unpredictable, wild-man public persona.) He followed that with *Dracula* (2013–2014) and *Vikings* (2017). He remains busy and in demand as a feature film actor with leading roles in a wide variety of international productions, including *Black Butterfly* (2017), *Damascus Cover* (2017), and *The Aspirin Papers* (2018).

RIDERS TO THE SEA (1987). This is the second (after **Brian Desmond Hurst**'s 1935 version) adaptation of Synge's classic play, which explores themes of paganism, fatalism, and the lingering vestiges of tradition in a modern world through the narrative of a woman who has lost her husband and her six sons to the sea. **Ronan O'Leary**'s directorial debut was made on a shoestring budget (even considering the play's short 45-minute duration) of £95,000, with support from the Public Broadcasting Service in the United States, and pulls off a remarkable casting coup in securing the services not of not only Barry McGovern and Amanda Plummer but also Oscar winner Geraldine Page in what would prove to be her penultimate screen performance. Although widely criticized after its premiere at the Cork Film Festival, it nonetheless succeeded in achieving modest TV and video sales in the United States, sufficient to allow O'Leary to move to his next production.

RIPPLE WORLD. Having previously established Subotica in 1998 with Tristan Orpen-Lynch, United Kingdom–born and Oxford-educated Dominic Lynch partnered with Australian Jacqueline Kerrin—formerly of Nine Network Australia—to establish Ripple World in 2007. Although the company debuted with **Ivan Kavanagh**'s *Our Wonderful Home* (2008), much of their early output had relatively little connection with Ireland beyond elements required to access **Irish Film Board** (IFB) and **Section 481** funding. *Lap-*

land Odyssey (2010) typifies this: set in Finland and featuring an all-Finnish cast, Irish involvement was limited to postproduction work, including music composition. Similarly, *Iztambul* (2011) was set in Hungary and Turkey and filmed in Turkey, and *Ghosthunters* (2015) was set in the United States but filmed largely in Germany and Austria. (Conversely, the IFB did not support a funding application for Ripple World's *Retreat*, a 2011 thriller featuring Jamie Bell and Thandie Newton, because the eventual third lead, **Cillian Murphy**, was not attached to the project at the time of the funding application.)

Subsequent international projects have been characterized by increasing levels of Irish crew involvement and even overt Irish content. Although set in Italy, *Controra (House of Shadows)* (2013) was partially filmed in Ireland and featured an Irish cast (Antonia Campbell-Hughes and Fiona Glascott) and several senior heads of departments. A succession of film and television collaborations with the Norwegian-based company Cinenord Kidstory, notably the *Little Grey Fergie* (2016–) series, also used Irish locations and made extensive use of local production crews. While *Earthbound* (2012) centers on British actors Rafe Spall and David Morrissey, it is clearly set in a Dublin milieu populated mostly by local characters, while *Zoo* (2017) (again casting British stars Toby Jones and Penelope Wilton as leads) is set in Belfast during World War II. Ironically, it was Ripple World's second collaboration with *Lapland Odyssey* producer Helsinki Filmi Oy that led to the company's most recognizably localized text to date: Darragh Byrne's post–Celtic Tiger tragicomedy *Parked* (2010), in which **Colm Meaney** plays a man forced by economic vicissitudes to take up residence in his car.

THE RISING OF THE MOON (THREE LEAVES OF A SHAMROCK) (1957).

The film was the first production of **Lord Killanin**'s **Four Provinces** company and was designed to showcase the possibilities of shooting in Ireland. It also emanated from **John Ford**'s deep sense of romanticism, which his biographer Joseph McBride (2001) described as so extravagant that it could come only from a first-generation American. In the opening sequence of the film, we hear an Irish tenor singing with laconic passion, "The Garden of Eden has vanished, they say, but I know the lie of it still."

The film is made up of three vignettes of Irish country life that are based on a series of short episodes, with the Hollywood star Tyrone Power, in his last movie, introducing all three stories. In the first voice-over, he describes the story as being "about nothing, yet, perhaps it's about everything." Frank O'Connor's "The Majesty of the Law" tells of the reluctant visit of a Galway police inspector (**Cyril Cusack**) to serve a search warrant on an old man (**Noel Purcell**) who makes his home next to the ancient ruins of his family castle. Another story, "A Minute's Wait," based on Martin J. McHugh's 1914 one-act comedy, can be appreciated, according to some critics, as

Ford's paean to the irrepressible anarchy of the Irish spirit while also reinforcing the idea of Ireland as a backward island with lovable incompetents, indulging the director's dreamlike romantic vision of his childhood. The final element, based on the playwright Lady Gregory's 1907 play "The Rising of the Moon," traces the first stirrings of nationalism within a venal police sergeant as he contemplates whether to betray an Irish nationalist to the British authorities. The resultant stereotypical Irish blarney caused offense in some quarters when the film was released, but the overall wit and good-natured camaraderie of the production displays the talents of many fine **Abbey Theatre** actors. However, although the film's modest performance at the box office ended longer-terms plans to establish a private production infrastructure in Ireland, the construction of **Ardmore Studios** (with covert but considerable state support) largely obviated the need for such investment.

ROCKETT, KEVIN (1949–). With the possible exception of **Liam O'Leary**, it would not be too contentious to say that, through his extensive scholarship and widespread public contributions, Rockett has done more to develop a coherent idea of Irish film history and culture than any other single individual. Through his curation of the Irish Film & TV Index and myriad Irish film festivals in the 1970s and 1980s, his influence is felt throughout Irish film studies and programming and laid the groundwork for generations following—or contesting—his foundational scholarship.

While studying architecture in London in 1973, he came across the first university video studio. Gradually, his interest shifted from his nominal subject toward film, and he became involved in community video. After he returned to Dublin in 1976, Rockett was invited to join the board of the **Project Arts Centre** by its administrator, John Stephenson, at a point when the center was undergoing something of an artistic revolution under the direction of **Jim Sheridan** and his brother Peter. Rockett immediately outlined a film policy for the Project, realized through the establishment of the **Project Cinema Club**. His work at the Project was informed by his annual attendances at the British Film Institute's residential summer schools at Stirling and the Edinburgh Film Festival, where he encountered such luminaries of early British film theory as Laura Mulvey, Peter Wollen, and John Hill (with whom he would later collaborate).

In 1978, he became a lecturer on the fine arts course at the National College of Art and Design (NCAD). Although he was initially employed to teach video production, his duties soon expanded to include the first third-level modules on film history and theory taught in Ireland. Within a year, this work, combined with his Project activities (and an influential 1978 *Screen* article on constructing a film culture in Ireland), led the then moribund **National Film Institute of Ireland** to invite him to join the board (this despite the fact that institute board members had publicly criticized the explicit content of some of the films he had screened at the Project). His appointment was the first of a series that would revolutionize the role of the institute, changing it from an extension of the Catholic hierarchy to an advocate for film culture in Ireland. By 1984, he had become the chair of the institute board, in which capacity he oversaw the efforts to establish an **Irish Film Centre**, including the decision to sell the institute's old building on Harcourt Street and acquire new premises on Eustace Street in Temple Bar.

Rockett left the NCAD in 1983 to begin work on his doctoral dissertation (under John Hill), Cinema in Ireland. Large elements of this would find their way into the seminal *Cinema and Ireland* (1987), cowritten with Hill and Luke Gibbons. It is impossible to overstate the impact and influence of this tome, which at a stroke established a template for subsequent academic study of Irish film culture and policy. When dedicated film studies courses began to emerge in the early 1990s, *Cinema and Ireland* was usually the key text on reading lists, and Rockett's contribution on political economy in particular remains essential reading for understanding the industrial and policy dimensions of Irish film culture.

After completing his thesis, "Cinema in Ireland: A Study of Production, Distribution, **Exhibition** and Censorship" (1989), Rockett remained at the institute for another two years before moving to University College Dublin to lecture in 1992. During this period, he assembled and published the massive *Irish Filmography*, an index of more than 2,000 films that not only included virtually every feature and short ever made in Ireland but also referenced all overseas films that even referred to Ireland or the Irish. In 2000, he was offered a post at Trinity College Dublin, where his publishing activities continued. He collaborated with his wife Emer on a critical study of the films of **Neil Jordan** (2003), and in 2004, he published *Irish Film Censorship*, another massive undertaking that entailed examining censors' reports on 18,000 films. Appointed associate professor of film studies at Trinity College in 2005, his subsequent projects included a two-volume history of Irish cinema exhibition as well as an expanded and updated Irish filmography made available on the Internet at the end of 2006 as the Irish Film & TV Index database, which documented all fiction films made in Ireland and about Ireland and the Irish produced worldwide since the beginnings of cinema. In 2010, he (again in collaboration with Emer Rockett) published the third and final pillar of his PhD research on Irish film, a two-volume study of the history of exhibition: "Magic Lantern, Panorama and Moving Picture Shows in Ireland, 1786–1909" and "Film Exhibition and Distribution in Ireland, 1909–2010." His retirement from Trinity College in 2016 was marked by a Festschrift-style symposium featuring contributions from both former colleagues and a generation of scholars influenced by his work.

***THE ROCKY ROAD TO DUBLIN* (1968).** A landmark documentary resulting from a collaboration between Irish journalist Peter Lennon and Raoul Coutard, a cinematographer of the French nouvelle vague, *Rocky Road* has the distinction of being the last film screened at the 1968 Cannes Film Festival before it was shut down by Jean-Luc Godard and accomplices. (When Lennon complained, Godard accused the director of missing the point: "We are speaking about revolution and all you are talking about is close-ups and tracking shots.") Although it disappeared for many years, the film underwent a revival in the 2000s thanks to several screenings at the **Irish Film Institute** (in the presence of its director) and the release of a DVD and a "making-of" featurette.

In the late 1960s, Irish-born—but Paris-based—journalist Lennon had caused controversy in Ireland after he produced a series of pieces for *The Guardian* newspaper severely criticizing the Irish establishment. The response inspired him to make a film along the same lines. He secured financing from an American businessman and persuaded legendary French cinematographer Raoul Coutard (*400 Blows* and *Contempt*) to film the documentary. The premise of Lennon's thesis was, "What do you do with your revolution once you've got it?" Recounting the revolutionary period of 1916 and the struggle for independence, the director's polemical voice-over argues that the nation had been locked into a backward, Catholic Church–controlled republic that did not follow through on the heroic struggle of the revolutionary's vision of the past.

To dramatize his thesis, the director interviewed a Gaelic Athletic Association (GAA) official who justifies the outright ban on their members playing English games while focusing on Catholic priests and their influence on society. Lennon got permission to film one well-known "singing" (or swinging) priest, Father Michael Cleary—who later caused a scandal for fathering several unacknowledged children with his "housekeeper." With the benefit of hindsight, Cleary's insights and contributions appear outrageously hypocritical, especially when he discusses how the Church is not against "sex" per se but does extol the virtues of celibacy for the priesthood. Older schoolchildren spout their religious indoctrination for the camera. Yet the documentary concludes with one of the most engaging scenes in Irish film history. which chimes with the conclusion of *The 400 Blows*, as many of these kids in their school uniforms are filmed running toward the motorcycle-mounted camera, symbolically innocent and escaping the clutches of their repressive society.

Furthermore, the changing pleasures of the adult society are beautifully dramatized through the cinema verité–style observation of various dance hall sequences alongside the diegetic use of traditional and popular Irish music. Only in voice-over are we presented with a counterdiscourse. A young married woman explains how she had several children and did not want more, but the Church's advice on contraception was limited to abstinence and accepting her lot in life. Well-spoken middle-class male university students discuss the inequality in Irish society and their inability to express their political views, while a leading dissident writer of the time, Sean O'Faolain, refers to the control exerted by the Church with great passion and conviction.

The reception of the film probably ensured its cult status. Even though despised by the censor's office, the documentary could not be banned since there was no sex in it. Nevertheless, after a limited run in one Dublin cinema, it was effectively buried and its—by 21st-century standards—mild critique of Ireland failed to receive further exposure through television screenings, with **Radio Telefís Éireann** refusing to screen it. In Europe, however, after Cannes in 1968, the documentary was taken to heart by the revolutionary movement in Europe and shown widely. It remains a provocative exposé of an important period in Irish cultural history. In 2006, **Paul Duane** made a companion piece: *The Making of the Rocky Road to Dublin*.

RONAN, SAOIRSE (1994–). Given the relative dearth of Irish women who have succeeded in reaching the status of internationally recognized screen actresses, Saoirse Ronan is remarkable not merely because she has been the lead figure in a number of Hollywood and international productions but also because she had already achieved this before she was out of her teens.

Born in New York, her U.K.-born father and Irish mother moved the family to County Carlow in the Irish Midlands when Saoirse was three years old. There, she went to the local primary school, her dramatic talents initially finding expression through creating mini-plays with her Polly Pocket dolls. Her father, Paul Ronan, is a jobbing actor, appearing mainly in U.K. and Irish television shows, such as *Ballykissangel, The Clinic,* and *The Tudors*. Although this meant that as a toddler Ronan was brought on set to films like *The Devil's Own*, this was not her route to casting agents (nor did she attend stage school). Instead, her father sent videos of her reading parts directly to casting agents. At the age of eight, she secured a small but recurring role in **Radio Telefís Éireann**'s *The Clinic* and again two years later in the second series of the crime drama *Proof*.

She unsuccessfully auditioned for the role of Luna Lovegood in *Harry Potter and the Order of the Phoenix* (2007) but secured roles in three other features released in 2007. *The Christmas Miracle of Jonathan Toomey* and *I Could Never Be Your Woman* made little impact, but the third, Joe Wright's adaptation of Ian McEwan's novel *Atonement*, made her a star overnight. On hearing that Wright was to film the novel, Paul Ronan taped Saoirse reading scenes in which, demonstrating the ear for accents that characterizes much of her work, she replaced her native Irish intonation with a clipped English Home Counties accent. Wright found the taped audition "extraordinary" and cast her as the precocious 13-year-old would-be novelist Briony Tallis, whose naive actions propel the main protagonists into catastrophic circumstances. Ronan's performance was remarkably compelling. In her hands, Briony's motivations and actions, despite their terrible consequences, appear understandable, even sympathetic. In a cast that included James McAvoy, Keira Knightley, Vanessa Redgrave, Brenda Blethyn, and Benedict Cumberbatch, hers was the performance that secured **Academy Award**, Golden Globe, and BAFTA nominations.

This guaranteed more work, but Ronan had already secured Hollywood representation (with the Creative Artists Agency) and two further lead roles before *Atonement*'s August 2007 premier at the Venice Film Festival. These included one of the two teen leads in sci-fi adaptation *City of Ember* and the central role of Susie Salmon in Peter Jackson's adaptation of Alice Sebold's macabre best seller *The Lovely Bones*. It was a demanding role, playing a character who is brutally murdered at the outset and spends most of the film observing how her family copes with their bereavement from the afterlife.

However, although again impressive in Peter Weir's *The Way Back* (2010) opposite **Colin Farrell**, it was arguably her role as the eponymous *Hanna* in 2011 that placed her at the forefront of young actors in Hollywood. Cast before a director was brought on board, Ronan herself suggested that the producers consider *Atonement* director Joe Wright, who was ultimately hired for the role. *Hanna* centers around a genetically enhanced teenager raised in the wilderness by her ex–government agent father in an attempt to keep the agency from exploiting Hanna's remarkable mental and physical capabilities. The Jason Bourne–esque role required Ronan to learn martial arts for the film's innumerable fight scenes, but the film avoided becoming a by-the-numbers actioner due mainly to Ronan's otherworldly performance—at once innocent and impossibly knowing. Shot on a relatively low budget ($40 million), the film outperformed expectations at the box office and established Ronan as a go-to actor for leads in tentpole movies. She topped the bill in the 2013 adaptation of Stephanie ("Twilight") Meyer's *The Host*, was considered for the role of Katniss in *The Hunger Games*, and was due to play the lead in Disney's aborted megabudget reimagining of Snow White, *The Order of the Seven*. (She also met with J. J. Abrams for talks about *Star Wars: The Force Rises*.)

Despite the blockbuster clamor, her discrimination in choosing roles after *Hanna* suggest a desire to avoid pigeonholing: *The Host* aside, most of her work has been in high-profile independent work. Signing up for *Violet and Daisy*, the directorial debut of *Precious* screenwriter Geoffrey Fletcher, saw her play one of a pair of teenage assassins in a visually arresting (if commercially disappointing) character study. This was followed by the closest thing to an Irish film she had yet done: the **Neil Jordan**–directed modern vampire tale *Byzantium*. In 2013, Wes Anderson included her among her cast of eccentrics for *The Grand Budapest Hotel*, and a year later, she completed filming on Ryan Gosling's ambitious debut, *Lost River*. These were rounded out by her role as Leia in *Stockholm, Pennsylvania* as a young woman who, after spending years as the captive of a kidnapper, finds it impossible to reconnect with her family when released. Taken together, these more recent roles suggest a desire to focus on roles that are intrinsically interesting rather than lucrative.

Studies of star personas are usually predicated on the assumptions that their private lives are public and that the public persona informs how their on-screen roles are interpreted. However, beyond the duties of film promotion, Ronan's private life has remained just that: private. Her family has sought to allow her a relatively normal upbringing in Ireland (albeit as her fame grew, it apparently became impossible for her to continue in secondary school, and from age 14, she was homeschooled), and the kind of incident often associated with growing up in public (e.g., Miley Cyrus) has been completely absent from Ronan's life. The public face she presents while promoting her films—composed, funny, and unselfconscious—seems totally disconnected from the weirdly mature, oddly compelling outsider roles she is often cast in. It may be significant that the children she has played appeared in films addressing primarily an adult audience, demanding performances beyond her years. (It was not until her appearance in the postapocalyptic *How I Live Now* that she played a role that situated her among other children.) Her Briony is remarkably precocious, eager to join the adult world, while Susie Salmon is at once innocent but also—given her omniscient perspective—almost infinitely knowing. Similar observations could be made about *Hanna* and her dual role in *The Host* as Melanie Stryder and as Wanda, an alien who comes to share her body.

In interviews outside Ireland, she actively identifies herself and is heavily coded as Irish—there are repeated discussions of how difficult her name is to pronounce, and constant surprise is expressed at her native accent (in contrast to her voice on-screen as British or American). Even the decision to wear an emerald dress to the Oscars was interpreted as a declaration of national affinity. Indeed, outside Ireland, her star persona is almost entirely constituted by her work. (Within Ireland, she does have a public persona, albeit a limited one that aligns her with progressive causes. She works as an ambassador for the Irish Society for the Prevention of Cruelty to Children, lending her name and her tear-streaked visage to a high-profile campaign against bullying. She is also the public face of a campaign for sustainable food production in Ireland.)

Given this and the fact that she remains domiciled in Ireland, it is remarkable that virtually all of her feature film work has been done outside the country. However, this finally came to an end in 2015 with the production of John Crowley's adaptation of Colm Tobin's novel ***Brooklyn***, in which she plays the central role of Eilis Lacey (opposite **Domhnall Gleeson**), an Irish emigrant in 1950s New York. Hitherto, Ronan had played roles far removed from her day-to-day reality. In *Brooklyn*, she played something closer to herself: a young Irish woman finding her way in a new culture. Her performance was acclaimed, and a multiplicity of Best Actress nominations again ensued at the Academy Award, Golden Globe, BAFTA, and Screen Actors Guild ceremonies. Although empty-handed at the close of the awards season (ironically, often beaten out by Brie Larson's performance in another Irish film, **Lenny Abrahamson**'s *Room* [2015]), she didn't have to wait long to secure another slew of nominations for her role as the titular *Lady Bird* (2017) in director Greta Gerwig's semiautobiographical account of growing up in Nowheresville, California.

***RUN AND JUMP* (2013).** Although she has subsequently established a career and reputation in U.S. serial television directing (*Preacher* [2017], *The Man in the High Castle* [2017], and *Luke Cage* [2018]), American-born director Steph Green established her early career credentials through her Oscar-nominated **short film** *New Boy* (2009), adapted from a short story by Roddy Doyle. As with that film, Green shares cowriting credit on her debut feature with Kerry writer Ailbhe Keogan.

Thirty-eight-year-old carpenter Conor Casey (Edward MacLiam) returns home to his wife Vanetia (Maxine Peake) and their two teenage children, having suffered a debilitating stroke that has left him confused and withdrawn. The ebullient and optimistic Vanetia invites visiting American neurophysiologist Ted (Will Forte) into their rural home to study her husband's recovery. The uptight Ted finds himself becoming the third point in a triangular relationship with Vanetia and Conor. As the film progresses and Conor slowly begins to reemerge from his solipsistic state, Ted finds himself increasingly—if reluctantly—occupying the role of the family's paternal figure as well as charting a hesitant romance with Vanetia.

Widely screened and acclaimed at international festivals, *Run and Jump* offers a study of a family under pressure that is unusual in tone and themes for Irish cinema. The film was shot mainly in and around Dingle in West Kerry, and director Green adopted a painterly eye to fully exploit the visual appeal of the area. Primary colors loom large in landscape shots, on building exteriors, but in particular within the home, serving to amplify Vanetia's optimistic worldview. This visual intelligence is matched by the deft characterization. Loyal to her husband, Vanetia's dalliance with Ted feels curiously apt, less a betrayal than a working through of a transformed family context. Conor's earlier self is recalled in fleeting glimpses even as he and the family come to regard Ted as a pivotal element in their new dispensation. Although the piling up of emotional incidents at the film's conclusion threatens to overwhelm the narrative, the film ultimately succeeds in tying together its complex elements, achieving a compassionate yet unsentimental conclusion.

THE RUN OF THE COUNTRY (1995). This adaptation of Shane Connaughton's semiautobiographical novel of Cavan in the 1950s stars Albert Finney, Mat Keeslar, Victoria Smurfit, and **David Kelly**. Danny (Keeslar) argues with his father, the local Gardaí (police) sergeant, and moves in with his friend Prunty (Anthony Brophy), who "has the run of the country" and was mixed up with the old Irish Republican Army. Taking confidence from his friend and mentor, Danny finds courage to talk to Annagh Lee (Smurfit), a girl he has long been attracted to who lives across the border. When she becomes pregnant, however, Prunty offers to give them money to pay for an abortion (a switch from the source novel, in which she has a miscarriage). Danny initially wants to follow her to the United States and decides to emigrate with the support of his father, but he eventually goes to college in Ireland instead. This story of impossible love across the border is particularly notable for the evocation of place and the unique drumlin landscape of County Cavan.

Directed by Peter Yates (*Bullitt* [1968] and *The Friends of Eddie Coyle* [1973]) and produced by Sony-owned Columbia Pictures (locally coproduced by **Morgan O'Sullivan**'s **World 2000**), the film is symptomatic of the impulses of the second wave of Irish cinema in its (literary) themes—rural, period set, father–son conflicts, emigration, and Catholic sexuality—and is addressed to an international Anglophone audience by means of casting, genre, and production values. It also makes an interesting point of comparison with the later *Brooklyn* as a mid-century emigration narrative centered on a female protagonist and romance in rural Ireland.

THE RUNWAY (2010). Writer/director **Ian Power** set out for Spielberg territory with this ambitious debut feature, a sweet-natured family film centering on a crash-landed pilot and his developing friendship with a local boy set in rural Ireland. Inspired by the true story of a South American pilot who crashed his plane near Mallow, County Cork, in 1983, the film is seen through the eyes of nine-year-old Paco Thomas (Jamie Kierans), who believes that his absent father is Spanish and may one day return to him and his mum (**Kerry Condon**).

This belief seems fulfilled when Paco finds what he thinks is the shell of a rocket while playing in the woods. When a Spanish-speaking man emerges from it, Paco happily invites him home. Paco has been teaching himself Spanish in case his father should return and translates Ernesto's story. With the enthusiasm of a local engineer (James Cosmo), the villagers set about trying to help Ernesto repair his plane and construct a makeshift runway from which he can take flight.

The Runway skillfully blended national and international cinematic idioms on a very tight budget through casting, family-friendly themes, and stylistic choices. The charismatic presence of Oscar-nominated Mexican actor Demian Bichir in the leading role achieved a measure of attention for the film in the United States, where it received a limited theatrical release.

RYAN, ROBBIE (1970–). A native of Dublin, Ryan is an Irish cinematographer of growing international stature who is particularly well regarded as a collaborator with Anglophone art house directors. After completing a degree at the Dún Laoghaire Institute of Art, Design, and Technology, Ryan began shooting short films, commercials, and music video. Although his feature debut as director of photography came with the ultra-low-budget *How to Cheat in the Leaving Cert*, his star properly ascended with the beginning of his long working relationship with Andrea Arnold on her **Academy Award**–winning short film *Wasp* (2004). He won several awards for his work on the Irish horror *Isolation* (2005) the following year before returning to work with Arnold on what is an ongoing and highly creative collaboration with *Red Road* (2006), *Fish Tank* (2008), *Wuthering Heights* (2010), and *American Honey* (2016). The last two secured further cinematography awards, including a British Independent Film nod for Outstanding Achievement in Craft in 2016 and the Golden Osella (an award granted only sporadically) for Outstanding Technical Contribution to *Wuthering Heights*. This success led to a second working relationship with veteran English director Ken Loach, beginning with *The Angel's Share* (2012), returning to Ireland for Loach's Irish-themed *Jimmy's Hall* (2014) and Loach's Palme D'Or–winning *I, Daniel Blake* (2016).

Now highly in demand as director of photography, working with directors as diverse as Sally Potter, Stephen Frears, Yorgos Lanthimos, and Noah Baumbach, Ryan nonetheless sporadically works with Irish directors and is well known for his approachability and commitment to helping new talents make short films. In 2008, he shot Nick Ryan's CGI-heavy short *The German* and collaborated with Ryan again in 2011 on *The Summit*, a documentary about climbing-related deaths on K2 in 2008. In 2012, he worked with Ruairi Robinson on another computer-generated imagery–dependent feature, the sci-fi/zombie genre picture *The Last Days on Mars* (2013), and more recently has collaborated with *Isolation* director Billy O'Brien on the latter's midwestern U.S.–set *I Am Not a Serial Killer* (2016). Expressing a marked preference for working on film (as opposed to digital), Ryan is an easygoing and self-effacing craftsperson in person, preferring to concentrate on how he can serve his collaborators and denying any ambition to direct himself.

***RYAN'S DAUGHTER* (1970).** After the enormous success of *Lawrence of Arabia* (1962) and *Doctor Zhivago* (1965), David Lean considered several subjects for his next film. However, when Robert Bolt produced a script version of Gustave Flaubert's novel *Madame Bovary*, this was eventually turned into a script for this film. Set in County Kerry in 1916, the film cost more than $6 million and used more than 115 hours of film stock. Initially, the film was a great success with Irish audiences but was critically ridiculed in Great Britain and elsewhere. Stung, Lean withdrew from filmmaking entirely for more than a decade.

As a historical romance, the story is concerned with issues of love, passion, revolution, betrayal, heroism, and cowardice. All of these are evocatively framed by the magnificent Kerry landscape, and extremes of weather correspond to changing emotional states in the chief protagonist, Rosie (Sarah Miles). Rosie is the daughter of an ambivalent patriot and local publican and marries well-mannered schoolteacher Charles Shaughnessy (Robert Mitchum), an older widower and far from spontaneous and romantic. Sexually unsatisfied, she has a passionate affair with a troubled and shell-shocked young British officer, Major Doryan (Christopher Jones), who has been temporarily transferred from the trenches to the relatively minor disturbances in Ireland. Rosie's personal betrayal of her husband is mirrored by her father's betrayal of the old Irish Republican Army (IRA), whose men are captured as they land guns on the shore, with the active support of the community, for a future rebellion. In the dénouement of the long, episodic film, Major Doryan shoots the IRA leader, and the villagers take their revenge on Rosie by tarring and feathering her, assaulting her, and cropping her hair.

Many critics focus on the representation of the "village idiot," Michael, played by John Mills, who serves as an important narrative driver for the film. His exaggerated grotesque features deliberately represent, according to some critics, the simian caricature of Victorian cartoons, which seek to affirm a colonial discourse. In spite of much criticism, the film has helped promote a touristic image of Ireland and remains a classic archetypical representation of Irish identity at a specific period in time.

S

SALTWATER **(2000).** Based on his 1995 play *This Lime Tree Bower*, comprised three overlapping monologues, Conor McPherson's directorial debut, *Saltwater*, follows the experiences of three members of the Beneventi family (played by Brian Cox, **Peter MacDonald**, and Laurence Kinlan) who run a fish-and-chips shop in a small east coast Irish town. Frank (MacDonald) is determined to free his father from the fiscal clutches of the local gangster/gombeen ("wheeler-dealer") (played by **Brendan Gleeson**), while Joe (Kinlan) must defend himself from the (as it emerges unfair) charge of date rape. These stories are juxtaposed with that of Ray (Conor Mullen), a University College Dublin lecturer experiencing an early midlife crisis.

Critical reaction to the film was mixed: the film's humor deriving from McPherson's knack for the pithy one-liner and his eye for the absurd was welcomed, but the busy nature of the script, which saw often only tangentially related plotlines vying for screen time, suggested a reluctance to reconfigure the original stage script for the big screen.

SAMSON FILMS. One of Ireland's pioneering and longest-established production companies, Samson was founded by David Collins, former film officer with the **Arts Council** of Ireland, in 1984. Collins was responsible in 1976 for setting up the film festival that would ultimately lead to the establishment of the **Irish Film Theatre** before moving into production in the 1980s, when he established Samson to produce **Cathal Black**'s 1984 feature *Pigs*. A year later, he cofounded **Strongbow Film and Television Productions** with John Kelleher—which produced two major TV series and the feature *Eat the Peach* in 1986 and *The Woman Who Married Clark Gable*, directed by **Thaddeus O'Sullivan**. Collins subsequently cofounded Radius Television with Bill Hughes, an early innovator in Irish independent TV production. In 2003, he cofounded **Accomplice TV** with **Ed Guiney/Element**, which for a time produced some of the most innovative indigenous TV drama, including three series of **John Carney**/Tom Hall's *Bachelor's Walk*, Eugene O'Brien's *Pure Mule*, and *Hide and Seek*.

Although Strongbow subsequently folded, Samson continued becoming a key indigenous production entity during the first years after the 1993 revival of the **Irish Film Board** with an early filmography that included *The Disappearance of Finbar* (1996), *A Further Gesture* (1997), *I Went Down* (1997), and *The Most Fertile Man in Ireland* (2000).

As his résumé amply demonstrates, Collins had, from the outset, recognized that to be effective, an Irish production company must also be adaptable and sustainable. As coproducer of *The Governor* (ITV, 1996), Samson embraced work on the kind of overseas-funded long-form TV drama that would become a central element of the Irish audiovisual production sector from the mid-2000s. Similarly, although certainly one of the busiest Irish-based production companies, Samson has consequently often been less oriented toward originating projects than it is in acting as a coproduction partner/executive producer (with particular experience in accessing the **Section 481** tax investment scheme) on projects developed by other companies on big and small screens, developing links with film and television funding agencies in Ireland, Great Britain, the wider Europe, and the United States. Thus, Samson has been involved in projects entirely lacking textual connections to Ireland, such as the New York–set *Babygirl* (2013) and *Coming Home* (2014). It has also actively engaged in multilocation coproductions, such as *Milo* (2012), *Mister John* (2013), and *Stay* (2013). Nonetheless, Irish-originated material also continues to play a role in the company's roster, including **John Carney**'s hit *Once* (2007), Declan Recks's speculative fiction *The Truth Commissioner* (2015), and Liam Gavin's well-received debut horror, *A Dark Song* (2016).

SANCTUARY (2012). A Polish–Irish coproduction from first-time feature director **Norah McGettigan**, *Sanctuary* follows Jan (Jan Frycz), a former plastic surgeon who now leads a globe-trotting existence, speaking at conferences about the dangers of his former previous profession. Although estranged from his wife, they continue to share a home in the Polish countryside, but, returning from a trip abroad, he finds her dead in their garden. Racked by guilt, Jan is unable to connect with his daughter Nadia (Agnieszka Zulewska) and flees to another conference in the Midlands of Ireland. There, he encounters hotel manager Marie (Anne-Marie Duff), who recalls his deceased wife and compels him to reflect on the decay of that earlier relationship.

A slow-paced, emotional character study, *Sanctuary*'s roots in an eastern European storytelling tradition are evident throughout. Although director McGettigan grew up in Ireland's northwest (*Sanctuary*'s Irish scenes were shot in Cavan), she moved to Poland after completing a degree at the University of Ulster. On completing an MA at the Polish National Film in Lodz, she began short-film production. Although her earliest projects—*The Water*

Fight (2003) and *A Song for Rebecca* (2007) (which also deals with mourning)—were also set in Ireland, their tone and aesthetics are (refreshingly) derived from a different cinematic tradition. *Sanctuary* at times recalls the work of Ibsen in its recurring depictions of characters in unlit rooms staring out windows, seeking to reconcile their inner turmoil with the routine patterns of the world outside.

The film's deployment of Ireland—and in particular the Irish countryside—as a safe haven is a recurring trope in both international and Irish cinema. **The Quiet Man** is perhaps the quintessential example in American film, but the Irish **horror** genre also often plays on this theme, as apparently idyllic rural settings prove to be hiding places to malevolent forces. As the title suggests, in *Sanctuary*, Jan also comes to Ireland seeking escape, but, as his relationship with Marie develops in an uncertain manner (he is attracted to her yet weighed down by a mixture of grief and guilt), he finds himself confronted with his own failings as a husband and father.

Sanctuary was cofinanced by the **Irish Film Board** and the Polish Film Institute (through **Venom** films) and developed in the frame of EKRAN: the Media-supported program based on creative preproduction process and run by Wajda Studio and Wajda School.

SANCTUARY (2017). Having provided the source story line for Damien O'Donnell's **Inside I'm Dancing** (2004), writer Christian O'Reilly returned to the subject of disability for his second feature after an interregnum working on U.K. and Irish television drama. The script was initially developed between 2012 and 2014 as a stage play with Galway's Blue Teapot Theatre Company, a drama initiative for people with intellectual disabilities. Although previously better known as a writer on U.K. prime-time dramas like *Eastenders*, *Holby City*, and *The Bill*, first-time feature director Len Collins had also worked with Blue Teapot from 2011. Encountering O'Reilly's play, Collins brought it to the attention of Zanzibar Films' Edwina Forkin, who in turn secured funding from the **Irish Film Board**'s low-budget Catalyst scheme.

With a cast drawn largely from Blue Teapot's cadre of actors, *Sanctuary* focuses on Larry (Kieran Coppinger) and Sophie (Charlene Kelly), both of whom attend a center for the intellectually disabled. Larry and Sophie are in love, but because of their respective conditions—Larry has Down syndrome while Sophie is severely epileptic—they are legally prohibited from having sex unless married to one another. (Although repealed in the same year the film was released, the 1993 Criminal Law [Sexual Offences] had blocked such contacts on the grounds that those with intellectual disabilities were considered unable to give meaningful consent.) Undeterred, Larry ropes in sympathetic worker Tom (Robert Doherty) to book a hotel room and cover for the couple while bringing a larger group on a trip into Galway city. While the couple engage in their romantic tryst, a parallel narrative emerges in which the rest of the group commence a screwball comedy careen through the heart of the city.

Judged purely as a caper movie, *Sanctuary* is a minor triumph: genuinely funny and peopled by characters carefully honed in collaboration with the actors who play them on-screen. Although largely lighthearted in tone, *Sanctuary* makes a number of discreet political points along the way, highlighting a wider social and legal tendency to infantilize the intellectually disabled. By contrast, *Sanctuary*, in its content *and* form, takes the opposite tack and emphasizes the abilities of its protagonists, not least in its still-rare decision to exclusively use actors who are actually intellectually disabled to play such roles.

SCANNAIN.IE. Initially growing out of editor Niall Murphy's writings for the University of Limerick student publication *An Focal* and subsequent work for culch.ie, the first online incarnation of Scannan (minus the "i") appeared online in 2002 as a broad pop culture–oriented website offering an Irish perspective on, in particular, Hollywood releases. Although pressure of Murphy's day job saw the project sidelined for a period, trips to the Cannes and Toronto film festivals in 2007 rekindled his interest in cinema in general and—especially after witnessing **Lenny Abrahamson**'s *Garage* (2007) in Canada—in Irish film in particular. Recognizing that the newly launched (2009) Scannain was somewhat swamped among the myriad similar online sites, Murphy leveraged his nomination as Blogger of the Year in the 2010 Sky Movies awards to become part of the press junket circuit for large-scale Hollywood releases, traveling to London to film interviews with high-profile international directors and stars.

However, in 2011–2012, the site took on a markedly more Irish focus, in part addressing the gap in the market left by **Film Ireland**'s cessation as a print journal. As currently structured, Scannain operates as a portal for Irish writers working on all aspects of cinema (moderated by Murphy) but augmented by a comprehensive Irish film production news stream, again populated largely by Murphy exploiting careful monitoring of Google Alerts, key Twitter accounts (associated with Irish production companies and personnel), and a network of contacts within the Irish industry cultivated since 2012.

As if this was not sufficient (Murphy does all this on top of a full-time position in an unrelated sector), in the autumn of 2018, Murphy launched a print edition, called *CinEireann*, to create an outlet for longer-form pieces subjecting Irish cinema output to sustained critique. Although primarily a labor of love for Murphy, the combination of Scannain and *CinEireann* now, along with the **Irish Film and Television Network**, constitute a primary port of call for anyone interested in comprehensive, up-to-the-minute information about developments within the Irish industry.

SCOTT, ANDREW (1976–). Andrew Scott's career can be neatly divided in terms of pre- and post-*Sherlock* (2010–2017) phases. Cast as Sherlock Holmes's nemesis Moriarty in BBC's modern-day reimagining of Conan Doyle's iconic detective (Benedict Cumberbatch), Scott's performance reimagined his character as a menacing psychotic and became an instant screen villain classic. The role brought him widespread praise and attention on both sides of the Atlantic and propelled him to the forefront of screen actors. Although he almost always performs using his native accent, Scott has forged a singular career that transcends traditional associations of Irish masculinity.

The middle of three children born to a comfortably-off close-knit family in Dublin's Churchtown, by the time Scott began attending the private secondary school Gonzaga, his face was already familiar to Irish audiences through work in commercials. He briefly attended Trinity College Dublin but abandoned university to work with the **Abbey Theatre** before making his screen debut in the **Irish Film Board**–supported short film *The Budgie* (1995). The same year, **Cathal Black** cast him in the leading role of Eamon Doyle in *Korea* (1995), a young man struggling to assert his own identity in the face of a father (Donal Donnelly) consumed by memories of the Civil War. Scott's vulnerable yet ultimately defiant characterization was perfectly in harmony with the unobtrusive tone of Black's direction, and career success seemed destined to follow. However, although he racked up credits in a diverse slate of productions (*Sweety Barrett* [1998], *Nora* [2000], *Saving Private Ryan* [1997], and, again with Steven Spielberg, *Band of Brothers* [2001]), the roles were generally minor.

He gave a convincingly smug performance as Tommy McGann in **Robert Quinn**'s neo-noir *Dead Bodies* (2004), a wastrel twenty-something who inadvertently kills his girlfriend and becomes embroiled in a murky cover-up. A pivotal role in the short-lived BBC sitcom *My Life in Film* the same year saw him named as a "Shooting Star" by the EU MEDIA program's European Film Promotion initiative. However, despite leading roles in HBO's *John Adams* (2008) and **Radio Telefís Éireann**'s *Little White Lie* (2008) opposite **Elaine Cassidy**, Scott's most prominent roles in the 2000s were onstage. He was nominated for an award for his 2006 Broadway debut in David Hare's *The Vertical Hour* opposite Bill Nighy and Julianne Moore, having already won a Laurence Oliver Award for his role as Alex, a narcissistic gay man in *A Girl in a Car with a Man* (2004). By the end of the decade, playwright Simon Stephens had written the gut-wrenching tragic monologue *Sea Wall* (2008) specifically for Scott, a performance that won him countless plaudits.

Then came *Sherlock*. Scott's take on Moriarty is alternately seductive, feminine, brilliant, and infinitely cold, driven by an implacable commitment to the idea of committing (perfect) crime for crime's sake. The massive global success of the series owed much to Scott's ability to match Cumberbatch's charismatic star turn, and the role created previously unimagined career options for him.

His choices since have been eclectic: although offered plenty of TV roles (he fronted BBC's *The Town* [2012]), he has leveraged his popularity primarily in high-profile big-screen productions. Moriarty's malevolence is echoed in his casting as "C," nemesis to Daniel Craig's James Bond in *Spectre* (2015), and to a lesser extent as asylum doctor Addison Bennett in Tim Burton's *Alice Through the Looking Glass* (2016). His "outing" as a gay man in 2013 (after he publicly criticized Russia's introduction of antigay legislation) might be cited as accounting for his roles in *Pride* (2014) (playing the reserved boyfriend of a gay activist [Dominic West]) and **Handsome Devil** (2016), in which he plays an in-the-closet Irish secondary school teacher. However, Scott had never really been "in the closet" himself, simply choosing not to discuss his sexuality or relationships in public. Nonetheless, his affecting performance as Dan Sherry in *Handsome Devil* is one of the film's strongest elements, a boisterously enthusiastic English teacher in the "Oh Captain, My Captain" *Dead Poets Society* mode, exhorting his students to express their individuality while actively suppressing his own nature.

The public revelation of his sexuality didn't noticeably affect his casting (although it did heat up the homoerotic subtext in later series of *Sherlock*). He plays a widowed, religiously devout policeman tracking James McAvoy in the period film *Victor Frankenstein* (2015), and in Ken Loach's **Jimmy's Hall** (2014), he portrays the forward-looking Father Seamus, who attempts to moderate between the traditionalist, orthodox views of Jim Norton's Father Sheridan and the socialist leanings of Jimmy Gralton (Barry Ward). Indeed, in **The Stag**, it is Scott's character Davin who is entrusted with establishing the masculine credentials of his best friend, Fionan (Hugh O'Conor), by leading a group on a catastrophic hill-walking adventure.

If *The Stag* confirmed Scott's gift for comedy, the work in which that was subsequently exploited to best effect was his mercurial interpretation of the coveted role of *Hamlet* at London's Almeida Theatre in 2017. Running for 220 minutes over 150 performances, praise for the acclaimed production centered on Scott's capacity to transcend the constraints of iambic pentameter and make readily comprehensible to a modern audience even the most archaic of *Hamlet*'s more than 1,500 lines of dialogue. Filmed for television and broadcast by the BBC in March 2018, audiences thrilled to Scott's revelation of the character's inner consciousness, a performance that was grief stricken, furious, resolved, and also very funny.

SCREEN PRODUCERS IRELAND. Screen Producers Ireland (SPI) is the latest incarnation of a filmmakers' representative body and first emerged in 1978. Such bodies had existed before this date—for example, it was in large part due to lobbying from the Society of Film-Makers in Ireland that the state acted on the recommendations of the *Huston Report* and brought the Film Industry Bill to the Dail in 1970. In 1977, the Association of Independent Producers (AIP) was established in the United Kingdom. The following year, an AIP representative came to Ireland to address a group of Irish producers, leading directly to the establishment of an Irish AIP. The major achievement of the AIP was to successfully lobby for the introduction of a state board to support the film industry, culminating in the publication of the Film Board Bill by Minister for Industry and Commerce Desmond O'Malley in 1979. In 1980, the AIP, together with the Irish Film and Television Guild and the Irish Transport and General Workers' Union, lobbied for changes to the proposed legislation—specifically demanding that the bill prohibit any **Irish Film Board** funding of overseas projects. Although unsuccessful in this regard, the AIP did succeed in broadening the board's responsibilities to include responsibility for an *Irish film archive* and for training.

However, the AIP clashed almost immediately with the board following its decision to award half of its initial funds to **Neil Jordan**'s *Angel*. The tension between the two institutions came to a head during the Third International Festival of Celtic Film and Television held in Wexford in 1982, during which *Angel* was premiered. The AIP effectively boycotted the film, calling a committee meeting that coincided with the premiere.

In fact, the *Angel* protest was simply the culmination of tensions between those individuals, such as **John Boorman**, who were associated with the **National Film Studios of Ireland** (NFSI) and members of the AIP, such as **Tiernan MacBride**. The AIP, echoing **Louis Marcus**'s 1967 *Irish Times* articles on **Ardmore**, had long argued that the NFSI was a drain on state funds that might otherwise have been available for investment in independent production and consequently regarded Boorman's chairmanship of the studios as a missed opportunity. Boorman, for his part, argued that he had consistently acted in a manner designed to serve Irish film best, citing his formation of the Motion Picture Company of Ireland as a case in point.

Given the AIP's position, however, Boorman's appointment (along with that of Louis Heelan and Robin O'Sullivan) to the Irish Film Board in 1982 was likely to provoke a confrontation. When the three-man board (technically, the full board had seven members, but these were yet to be appointed) decided to fund *Angel* to the exclusion of any other applications (including several from AIP members), a clash became inevitable. Thus, the Celtic festival witnessed AIP member **Bob Quinn** delivering a scathing attack on Boorman, followed by a formal AIP statement to the effect that the decision to fund *Angel* was "at best improper." The statement acknowledged that a full board might well have made the same decision, but in the absence of such a board, there was at least the appearance of impropriety.

The long-term effect of the Celtic festival incident was to create a rift between Boorman and Jordan on the one hand and the AIP on the other, one that was only partially healed when AIP chair Tiernan MacBride and Irish Film and Television Guild chair **Michael Algar** were appointed to the board in 1982.

In the mid-1980s, the AIP became the Association of Independent Film-Makers (AIFM) in an attempt to reflect the fact that the membership was made up of not merely producers but also directors. With the closure of the Film Board in 1987, the AIFM was effectively replaced in November of that year with Film Makers Ireland (FMI). It was funded by membership subscriptions and in its initial years driven by a clear objective to lobby for the restoration of the Film Board or a similar institution. Initially chaired by film lawyer **James Hickey**, the FMI committee also included **David Collins**, **Tiernan MacBride**, **Alan Gilsenan**, and Jane Gogan.

FMI's establishment was significant in that it expressly aimed to educate political representatives as to the nature of the film industry with a view to initiating a public debate about film policy that could occur outside the confines of the Department of the Taoiseach, which had taken responsibility for arts policy in 1986. In particular, FMI began to advance the argument that, especially given the high level of unemployment that characterized the Irish economy in the late 1980s, film should be supported as a manufacturing industry capable of creating employment. However, FMI also acknowledged that, as of 1990, the industry was still in a developmental phase and would require some nurturing from state agencies like the Industrial Development Authority. Thus, for example, FMI argued that the state venture capital company NADCorp should fund if not production, then at least the development costs for films to be shot in Ireland. This kind of thinking found its most advanced expression in a major report commissioned by FMI in 1991. The resulting *Independent Television Production Sector Report*, published in 1992, would become influential in shaping the variety of film policy decisions that occurred after 1992, including the decision to join **Eurimages**, the reestablishment of the Film Board in 1993, and the alteration of **Section 481** that same year. Another 1993 decision placed FMI on an entirely new financial footing. Although FMI had employed a full-time administrator for some years, the body's income relied entirely on production companies taking out membership. However, the vagaries of the production climate in the late 1980s and early 1990s meant that income fluctuated from year to year. This was in large part addressed as a by-product of the establishment of the Independent Production Unit (IPU) at **Radio Telefís Éireann** (RTÉ) in 1993. As part of the IPU's establishment, it was agreed that a sum equivalent to 1 percent of the value of independent commissions would be apportioned to FMI. This was subsequently augmented by funding from TG4 and a levy on Section 481–funded projects.

Consequently, FMI was able to broaden and professionalize its activities, and as of 2018, the body had a permanent staff of four. In 2003, the organization adopted a new moniker, Screen Producers Ireland, to reflect the fact that the activities of many of its members—and therefore the focus of SPI's negotiations—related to the television sector. Although SPI continues to act as a lobbying group on behalf of Irish production companies, campaigning for the retention of Section 481 and an increase in funding to the Irish Film Board, it has also become a de facto trade body, negotiating terms of trade with both RTÉ and TG4 on behalf of producers and drawing up collective agreements with trade unions related to the crewing of feature film and television drama production. SPI also acts an information resource for producers on upcoming commissioning opportunities and organizes seminars allowing producers to meet and exchange views with domestic and European commissioning bodies.

THE SECRET OF KELLS (2009). Long in gestation, *The Secret of Kells* is a remarkable demonstration of the extent to which the **animation** form, one long dominated by U.S. and Japanese artists, can be definitively and successfully localized to reflect an Irish visual idiom.

Brendan (Evan McGuire) is a young monk living at the monastery of Kells in eighth-century Ireland. His uncle, the stern abbot Cellach (**Brendan Gleeson**), is determined to build a defensive wall around the community in anticipation of raiding parties from the north. However, Brother Aidan (**Mick Lally**), a refugee from an earlier Viking attack on the monastery of Iona, argues that the monks should instead concentrate on completing a sacred text (the Book of Kells), an "illuminated" depiction of the Gospels that promises to turn darkness into light. Although loyal to his uncle, Brendan is drawn to the powerful images already adorning the incomplete text. Determined to help Aidan, Brendan defies his uncle to sneak into the surrounding forest to seek out oak tree berries from which to make colorful inks. Although pursued by wolves, Brendan is saved by Aisling (Christen Mooney), a forest sprite who helps him secure the berries but also warns Brendan to avoid the lair of the "dark one," Crom Cruach, a quasi-mythical creature who slumbers beneath the woods. Returning to the monastery, Brother Aidan mourns the disappearance of "eye of Columbcille," a crystal essential to the completion of the book. Recognizing it as identical to the image of Crom Cruach's eye, Brendan determines to confront the monster, aided by Aisling and Aidan's mischievous cat Pangur Ban.

By any standards, *The Secret of Kells* is a remarkable undertaking. Although feature animation production in Ireland goes back to the presence of Sullivan Bluth and others in the early 1990s, the films of that era were heavily influenced by the classical (read Disney) animation mode of the 20th century. While director Tomm Moore has cited as influences the early work of Studio Ghibli founder Hayao Miyazaki, Russian American artist Genndy Tartakovsky, and British animator Richard Williams, *The Secret of Kells* is unmistakably Irish at the level of narrative but also, much more overtly, in its extensive quotation from traditional Irish arts in building the film's mise-en-scène. Eschewing the realist mode of popular American 2-D animation, directors Tomm Moore and Nora Twomey opt for a far more stylized approach. For example, the background of the abbot's dark chambers consists of an abstraction of Celtic images; the trees of the forest appear in impossibly symmetrical alignments, as do the forest wolves when pursuing Brendan, reflecting the manner in which the original illuminators of the Book of Kells introduced flowing patterns into their Gospel images. Composed largely of 2-D work (though with occasional recourse to 3-D elements), the film acts as a contemporary analogue of its eighth-century source text.

Although visually tied to a specific setting, Moore worked with Fabrice Ziolkowski, a French American screenwriter, to ensure that the story was comprehensible to an international audience. Moore has overtly cited Joseph Campbell's work (also a key influence on George Lucas) as shaping the film's hero's journey structure. Yet the final film adopts a much darker tone than commonly found in animations targeting a young audience. When the Viking attack on the monastery finally occurs, it is stunningly brutal, the Norsemen depicted as dark, horned, geometric shapes slaughtering without mercy. Although the epic scale of the film suggests that, ultimately, the Book of Kells will indeed "turn the darkness into light," it does not shirk from acknowledging the overwhelming, if temporary, victory of evil.

Ultimately, however, the film operates at a metatextual level, exploiting the affordances of the animated and illustrated forms to illuminate how the Book of Kells symbolized the survival and ultimate triumph of knowledge (scientific as well as sacred—Aidan is depicted as creating his inks with laboratory-style implements) during the Dark Ages. That the film enjoyed widespread international acclaim, including an **Academy Award** nomination, paving the way for production company **Cartoon Saloon**'s equally lauded subsequent features, suggested that Irish illustrators retained the power to influence audiences far afield.

***THE SECRET OF ROAN INISH* (1994).** The career choices of U.S. director John Sayles have been nothing if not eclectic. Best known for issue-oriented films like *City of Hope* (1991) and *Matewan* (1987), his decision to follow his acclaimed 1992 disability drama *Passion Fish* with a lyrical children's tale set in 1940s Ireland somewhat blindsided critics. Based on Rosalie K. Fry's 1957 Scottish-set novel *The Secret of Ron Mor Skerry*, Sayles's decision to relocate the slim text to Ireland was driven in part by ready access to favorable tax breaks for film funding, such as **Section 481**, but also by the opportunity to mine the extensive early 20th-century literature stemming from Ireland's offshore islands.

The film opens with a distraught father who, having lost his wife and child, sends his remaining daughter to her grandparents' house in a rural region of Ireland to seek solace and a new beginning. The 10-year-old girl, Fiona (Jeni Courtney), becomes enchanted by the local folktale of the selkie, a magical creature that is a seal by day and a human by night, and persuades her grandfather (**Mick Lally**) to explore the myth by going to Roan Inish [the island of seals).

From the opening sequences, a very clear opposition is established between the beauty of the island and the west and the impurity of the east and the city. This is witnessed through the innocent eyes of a young girl with the camera framed at her eye level: as she searches for her father in a Dublin pub, the voice of the barmaid affirms that this is no place to raise a child, suggesting that she be sent to the fresh air of the countryside, where her grandparents reside. The child functions as a conduit to a lost past through the sea and wild landscape.

The girl's sojourn in this primitive but beautiful place is framed by a number of stories told by her grandfather and her cousin. The first of these narrates the shocking primal story of how her cousin's little brother was washed out to sea in his distinctive baby cradle. A flashback shows the islanders preparing to leave the island. As they do, a malevolent force of nature expresses its displeasure at this abandonment. The islanders are attacked by everyday seagulls, while unbeknownst to them, the cradle is being taken by the tide out to sea. As they try to rescue the boy, the elements suddenly take a turn for the worse, with strong rain and winds and a darkening sky. Subsequently, the islanders superstitiously believe that the sea had taken the infant because it was angry with them for leaving their homeland. The trajectory of the fable works through this imbalance in nature as the islanders realize their loss, and the story finally resolves—after the intervention of the little girl—with their return to their island.

SECTION 481/SECTION 35. Section 481 of the Consolidated Finance Acts of 1997 (formerly Section 35 of the 1987 Finance Act) initially incentivized private investment in audiovisual production in Ireland (though not necessarily in Irish films) through the mechanism of a tax break but was switched to a tax credit model in 2015. It has been significant because it is by far the largest single source of indigenous capital for filmmaking in Ireland. Introduced in 1987 just as the activities of the first **Irish Film Board** (IFB) were being suspended, its arrival represented a philosophical shift in state film policy away from direct state support toward providing incentives for the investment of private capital in the industry.

In its first six years of operation, the impact of the incentive was relatively modest—only corporate entities could avail themselves of the tax write-off, and the maximum annual investment was initially capped at IR£100,000. Consequently, between 1987 and 1993, a relatively modest IR£11.5 million was raised by using the incentive. However, in 1993, as part of a package of measures aimed at developing the audiovisual sector in Ireland (which included the revival of the IFB), Section 481 was radically overhauled. The scale of the tax write-off was increased, as was the ceiling on individual investments. Perhaps most significantly, the tax break was extended to individual investors: from 1993, individuals could write off film investments of up to IR£25,000 against income tax, a strong incentive to invest at a time when the marginal rate of personal income tax was 46 percent. The subsequent impact of the incentive on filmmaking activity in Ireland is almost impossible to overstate. Between 1993 and 2003, some €640 million in private capital was raised through the scheme, and virtually every film shot in Ireland since 1993 has availed itself of it.

Nonetheless, that €640 million figure arguably overstated the mechanism's impact since Section 481 investors expected the majority of their investment to be secured against income from presales (a commitment from a distributor or television company to buy rights to a film once it is completed). Since the producer was effectively required to hand over the presales income to Section 481 investors as soon the production was completed, the actual gain to an average film's budget was on the order of 12 to 13.5 percent of the total production cost. (It should be noted that presales were not a legal prerequisite for the mechanism to operate; indeed, the legal structure of Section 481 notionally discouraged such risk-averse strategies on the part of investors given that the very existence of the incentive was predicated on the assumption that any investment in film production involves a high degree of risk and thus required a concomitant incentive.)

Nonetheless, Irish producers insisted that Section 481 was a key ingredient in maintaining production activity in Ireland and actively mobilized to argue for the retention of the scheme whenever the Department of Finance discussed ending it. In December 2002, then Minister for Finance Charlie McCreevy announced a decision to suspend the tax break from 2004. His thinking was shaped by the deliberations of the Tax Strategy Group within his department, which argued that the expansion of the Irish audiovisual sector since 1993 made it impossible to continue citing an infant industry rationale as a basis for retaining Section 481. McCreevy's announcement prompted a yearlong campaign coordinated by lobby group **Screen Producers Ireland** (with the support of the Department of Arts, Sports, and Tourism), which argued that Section 481 was a key element of the Irish audiovisual financial infrastructure without which large-budget overseas productions in particular would have little incentive to contemplate shooting in Ireland. One study, the *PricewaterhouseCoopers Report*, commissioned by the IFB and the Department of Arts in 2003, concluded that the removal of Section 481 would lead to a 65 percent drop in the value of audiovisual production in Ireland and a 60 percent drop in related employment. Even the head of the Hollywood lobby group Motion Picture Association of America, Jack Valenti, when visiting Ireland in October 2003, was pressed into service to call for the retention of the tax break.

As a result, not only was the tax break retained after 2003 (and extended to 2008), but the amount of money that could be raised under its auspices was consistently increased as well. This expansion grew out of debates emerging in the late 1990s about the aims and objectives of the tax incentive and in particular whether Section 481 was intended primarily to support indigenous production or simply to incentivize audiovisual production in Ireland regardless of a given production's national origins. In 1996, faced with the perception that large-scale foreign projects such as Mel Gibson's *Braveheart* were sucking up the bulk of Section 481 investment, the minister for finance at the time altered the operation of the incentive to target investment on indigenous productions. Working on the assumption that domestically originated projects were typically characterized by low (less than IR£10 million) budgets, the minister capped at IR£7.5 million the amount of Section 481 money that could be raised for any individual film.

By 2003, however, the *PricewaterhouseCoopers Report* concluded that the cap was beginning to seriously undermine Ireland's capacity to attract larger-budget productions from overseas. The report noted that the introduction of competing tax incentives in other countries (e.g., the United Kingdom, the Isle of Man, and Luxembourg) meant that Ireland was no longer "competitive" for projects with budgets in excess of €15 million. As a consequence, the report recommended that the per-project cap on Section 481 finance be dramatically increased to €50 million to allow Ireland to continue drawing in projects on the scale of *Reign of Fire* and *King Arthur*. The cap was raised in December 2003 initially to €15 million and subsequently to €35 million in 2006 and €50 million in 2008, figures clearly targeting the incentive at large-scale overseas-originated projects.

However, after 2008, as the Irish economic recession deepened and the cost to the state of Section 481 relief grew (to "almost €50 million" by 2011), the tax incentive was subjected to further scrutiny. A May 2012 Department of Finance consultation was of particular concern to the local production sector. While inviting submissions from interested parties as to the retention (or otherwise) of Section 481 after 2015, the consultation noted a 2007 Indecon finding that "the benefits of the scheme to the Irish economy were . . . low and declining." More pointedly, the consultation pointed to Indecon's finding that, on average, "for every €100 raised under Section 481, the exchequer cost was €34 but that only €19 accrued as a subsidy to the producers with the balance being returned to investors or accounted for in administration costs." These figures were altered somewhat—to the benefit of producers—by the 2007 decision to allow investors to write off 100 percent of their investment at the marginal rate of tax relief as opposed to the 80 percent then permitted in 2007. Thus, by 2012, for every €100 of a Section 481 investment made by an individual, the state lost €41 (given that the marginal rate of tax was then 41 percent) in income tax, yet the production company benefited only to the tune of €28.

By 2012, the state was unwilling to accept this kind of leakage to Section 481 investors and their financial intermediaries (typically banks and accountancy firms). Instead, it began to explore a producer-led tax credit model designed to maintain the net benefits hitherto enjoyed by producers while ending the leakages. The industry initially expressed dismay at this, asserting that the new system could not seamlessly replace Section 481. The primary reason for this related to cash flow: the investor-led form of Section 481 finance was particularly appealing for producers because it was available on day one of principal photography. The value of a typical tax credit, by contrast, would become available only at the end of the tax year in which the production was shot. In Ireland in 2012, the obvious model for a tax credit system was the producer-led Film Tax Relief system, which had been adopted in the United Kingdom in 2007, superseding the older investor-led Film Partnership Relief system. The U.K. Film Tax Relief system was explicitly crafted as a repayable tax credit; thus, investment in filmmaking could be claimed as a deduction only at the end of the tax year when film production companies come to calculate their taxable profits.

Irish producers acknowledged that the delay in realizing the benefit of a tax credit was less problematic for international productions, which, being typically financed by companies with the capacity to self-fund, could afford to wait for the benefit of the tax credit to become available. However, Irish producers also stressed that the delay would potentially be critical for indigenous productions, especially in a changing banking context. (Banks that before 2008 had been heavily engaged in film finance were far less interested in cash-flowing production finance in the dramatically changed financial context of 2012.)

In practice, when the details of the new scheme finally emerged in 2015, producers appeared to adopt it with relatively little pain. The tax credit approach allowed production companies to claim relief against their corporation tax bill. In the event that the relief exceeded the corporation tax bill faced by individual production companies, the Revenue Commissioners make a direct payment to the production company to cover this excess.

Furthermore, early concerns about cash flow were largely mollified by the Irish Revenue Commissioners' decision to allow production companies claiming a tax credit to receive up to 90 percent of the credit in advance of production.

To date, there seems little evidence that either local or international productions have encountered significant difficulties in using the new mechanism. Furthermore, it appears that the cost of the tax break to the exchequer has been substantially reduced.

SENSATION (2010). *Sensation* qualifies as one of the oddest films of recent years and is evidence, if needed, that the Irish cinematic imagination continues to be dominated by a male mind-set concerned with themes of sex and the crisis of masculine identity. Although not overtly presented as satire, its tone and topicality serve to suggest that the outlandish plot should not be taken entirely seriously even if its sexual politics veer more toward the misogynistic than the comic. Reflecting a Celtic Tiger obsession with the sale price of agricultural land for redevelopment, the film centers on Donal (**Domhnall Gleeson**), who inherits his father's farm after his death. In a satirical nod to the rejection of rural identities and traditions and the contemporary cult of "entrepreneurship," he decides to sell the farm and go into the sex business with Kim (Luanne Gordon), an unsentimental Australian prostitute he meets through an escort service. The remainder of the film charts the rise and fall of their personal and professional relationship in a "saucy" coming-of-age narrative for its 26-year-old protagonist.

Sensation reflects its era in exploring themes and visuals that would have been unimaginable even a decade earlier. It reflects not only the replacement of a traditional agricultural economy with one based on service-industry capitalism and a rapid growth in the illegal sex industry in Ireland but also the rapid secularization within Irish society and media more generally. However, it makes little effort to analyze any of these themes in any meaningful way and simply uses them as a backdrop for its central narrative of male self-realization. This is particularly problematic in relation to the film's treatment of the brothel business established by Donal and Kim, where exotic young women in underwear are seen but remain largely unheard, unintentionally reflecting a wider social ill of sex trafficking and coercion.

THE SHADOWS (2011). Even by prolific writer/director **Colin Downey**'s typically efficient budgets, the decision to adapt this fairy tale by seminal 19th-century Scottish fantasy writer George MacDonald for a microbudget of €100,000 was ambitious. Recounting the story of a young boy's journey into the "World of Shadows," the film is at once charming and disturbing even if the necessarily limited visual effects make it slightly reminiscent of a 1980s children's TV drama.

Exploring his grandmother's garden, Matthew (Lorcan Melia) discovers a strange structure built by his now deceased grandfather. His grandmother dismisses it as a rubbish heap, but when Matthew discovers a map, he realizes that it is a portal to the subterranean world of the Shadows. Entering the structure, he tunnels through to encounter Yorrick (Michael Parle) and Alice (Emma Eliza Regan) and the centuries-old struggle of the Shadow People to defend the crown of their ancient kingdom from wicked witch Geldren (Natalia Kostrzewa). Learning that he is destined to become king of the underground kingdom, Matthew embarks on an adventure to defeat Geldren and her human henchman, the treasure hunter Alexander (Eddie Webber).

Creative as always within constrained resources, Downey ekes the most out of his budget. For example, Geldren's spectacular icy lair to the north is constructed from stock footage of snowcapped mountains—a smattering of computer-generated imagery and model shots. Recognizing that there are limits to what even he can achieve, Downey relies mainly on his cast (drawn from his and **Ivan Kavanagh**'s stock company) to convey the requisite sense of wonder. To their credit, they are broadly successful in this regard, conjuring into existence a parallel world and suggesting to a younger audience that whole other realms lie tantalizingly close to even the most banal of settings.

***SHAKE HANDS WITH THE DEVIL* (1959).** The first major international production shot at **Ardmore Studios**, director Michael Anderson's adaptation of Reardon Conner's War of Independence–set novel starred Irish American legend James Cagney in the twilight of his career.

An Irish American medical student, Kerry O'Shea (Don Murray), hopes to stay above the conflict but gets sucked in while trying to save a wounded friend. He is eventually drawn into an Irish Republican Army (IRA) unit headed by his former professor, Sean Lenihan (Cagney), who, medical background aside, has "shaken hands with the Devil" and embraced the armed struggle.

The story becomes more complicated when Kerry falls in love with a beautiful English hostage, Jennifer Curtis (Dana Wynter). When a cease-fire between the IRA and the British forces is called, the leader of the IRA (clearly based on Michael Collins but played by the much older Michael Redgrave) is sent over to broker a treaty in London. However, many at home, including the professor, cannot stomach the resulting deal, and civil war ensues.

Shake Hands with the Devil is notable for the manner in which, despite being produced by a U.K. company, it suggests that in the long history of Anglo-Irish violence, atavistic tendencies were characteristic of both sides: Kerry O'Shea's allegiance to the cause is clearly driven by repeatedly witnessing the depredations of the auxiliary British military force the Black and Tans. However, in its depiction of the central nationalist figure of Sean Lenihan, the film appears to consciously downplay a political rationale for his violence. Instead, Lenihan appears as pathologically driven by a puritan motive to "purify" Ireland of not only British influence but also, as his repeated assaults on a succession of female characters suggest, the threat of female sexuality. The film's conclusion, which sees Kerry shoot Lenihan to prevent the latter killing Jennifer, thus becomes the only means of addressing Lenihan's (and, by extension, nationalism's) recourse to violence.

SHAW, FIONA (1958–). Although like many Irish actresses of her generation Shaw is celebrated primarily for her stage work, her recurring—and now iconic—role as Aunt Petunia in the adaptations of the *Harry Potter* series between 2001 and 2010 made her face familiar to international and intergenerational cinemagoers. Recurring roles in the HBO series *True Blood* (as Marnie Stonebrook), *Channel Zero* (2016), and BBC America's *Killing Eve* (2018) have maintained her U.S. screen profile thereafter.

Raised in Cork's middle-class Montenotte suburb, she studied philosophy at University College Cork in the late 1970s before moving to London (still her main residence) to study at the Royal Academy of Dramatic Art (RADA). From RADA, she became a key member of the Royal Shakespeare Company (RSC), her angular visage and crisp delivery being admirably adapted to a range of classical female protagonists. Initially associated with lighter roles on the Shakespeare canon—Beatrice in *Much Ado About Nothing* and Katherine in *The Taming of the Shrew*—her brother's death in car crash preceded a shift to darker, often tragic characters. In 1989, Deborah Warner, then one of the RSC's youngest directors, cast her in the title role of Sophocles' *Electra*. The production was the making of Shaw, and her performance won her a first Lawrence Olivier award. (She would win a second in 1994 for *Machinal*.) The Warner connection has endured onstage and on-screen: Shaw performed in *Richard II* (a much-maligned production), T. S. Eliot's *The Wasteland*, and Euripides' *Medea* (for which both earned Tony nominations in 2003), among many others, for the director and had a relatively minor role in Warner's 1999 film version of Elizabeth Bowen's *The Last September*. In 2013, Shaw even stepped in for Warner as director of the New York Metropolitan Opera when the director couldn't continue due to medical reasons.

Her intelligence and diction have frequently seen her cast in adaptations of classic plays and novels—*Jane Eyre, Persuasion,* and *Anna Karenina*—although she has also appeared in a number of contemporary Hollywood dramas—*Three Men and a Little Lady* (1990) and *Undercover Blues* (1993). Although usually cast as English, Shaw has essayed Irish roles on-screen. Her first was in **Jim Sheridan**'s *My Left Foot* as Eileen Cole, cast against type as Christy Brown's unrequited love interest. In **Neil Jordan**'s *The Butcher Boy*, she memorably played the ill-fated returned emigrant Mrs. Nugent, the object of the eponymous protagonist's envy and hatred. Her suburban, well-intentioned, but overbearing characterization can be seen as a precursor to her casting as Aunt Petunia. She has also made recurring appearances on the Irish stage, appearing in **Abbey Theatre** adaptations of Samuel Beckett's *Happy Days* (2007) and in Henrik Ibsen's *John Gabriel Borkman* (2011). Still combining directorial duties on operas with stage appearances, her most recent Irish theatrical connection came with her acclaimed 2014 New York and London performances in Irish writer Colm Tobin's stage adaptation of his novel *The Testament of Mary*, wherein she played the mother of Jesus.

SHEEHAN, ROBERT (1988–). Doe-eyed and equipped with a mop of curly hair and an ebullient persona, Robert Sheehan is probably the closest thing to a teenage heartthrob Irish screens have seen since **Colin Farrell** burst onto the scene in 2000. Although best known to audiences in the United Kingdom and Ireland for his television roles, he has also appeared in a wide variety of feature films, ranging from low-budget horrors to blockbuster-scale would-be franchises like *The Mortal Instruments* (2013). Although, to date, these big-screen excursions have proved less than commercially successful, since 2013 in particular, Sheehan's résumé suggested a conscious decision to focus on work for the cinema rather than the small screen.

Born and raised in the Midlands town of Portlaoise, Sheehan's first break came when his mother drove him to Dublin for the casting call for *Song for a Raggy Boy* in 2003, having read about it in the paper. Despite having no acting experience (beyond the occasional school play), Sheehan was plucked from hundreds of auditioners and cast as "O'Reilly 58," one of the inmates of an Irish reformatory school in the 1930s. This was quickly followed by the first of a series of roles in largely forgettable (and quickly forgotten) television series: as an Irish schoolboy in the Australian–Irish coproduction *Foreign Exchange* (2004) and as a young King Louis XIV in a Canadian drama, *Young Blades* (2005), centering on the early exploits of Dumas's Three Musketeers. More television and one film role (in **Martin Duffy**'s *Summer of the Flying Saucer* [2008]) followed, but Sheehan was not convinced that his future lay in acting and began a college degree in film production. However, in 2009, he was cast in the pivotal role of BJ, a male prostitute, in *Red Riding*, **Channel 4**'s adaptation of David Wearing's novels about the search for the Yorkshire Ripper serial killer. Sheehan played his character as alternately seductive and innocent, putting his good looks to good effect.

The role won him plaudits and brought him to the attention of the producers of the sci-fi series *Misfits* (Channel 4, 2009–2013) and *Love/Hate* (**Radio Telefís Éireann** [RTÉ], 2010–). *Misfits* made him a star in Britain—as the anarchic, loud-mouthed, and ludicrously charismatic Nathan, who, along with four other young offenders on community service, miraculously acquires superhuman powers (immortality in his case) when struck by lightning during a storm. Hugely popular in the United Kingdom, the show reached U.S. audiences via Hulu beginning in October 2012. Sheehan left the show after three series but not before taking on the role of Darren in RTÉ's hugely popular gangland drama *Love/Hate*. Darren represented a radical change of pace—arguably the pivotal character in an ensemble cast that included **Aiden Gillen** and **Ruth Negga**, Sheehan's Darren is, despite being part of gangland milieu, a reluctant criminal, a gentle character driven to violence only in extreme circumstances.

Love/Hate was acquired by Netflix in 2013 and has since become part of its global package, available in the United States and beyond. More television followed, including a dalliance with comedy in the BBC's short-lived but well-regarded *Me and Mrs Jones* (2012). In 2012, he won one of the three leads in the first film of an envisaged franchise based on Cassandra Clare's successful *Mortal Instruments* novels. Cast against type as, at least initially, a bookish type in unrequited love with Lily Collins's Clary, his first *Mortal Instruments* film failed to capture a public imagination perhaps already sated with the likes of *Harry Potter* and *The Hunger Games*, and any further extension of the franchise seems unlikely.

Unthwarted, Sheehan has turned to theater in London (appearing as Christy Mahon in the Young Vic's 2013 adaptation of Synge's *Playboy of the Western World*) and appeared in a flurry of indie projects (*The Road Within* [2014]), comedy (*Moonwalkers* [2015]), and horror (*The Messenger* [2015]) as well as turning producer on *Jet Trash* (2015). These are interspersed with high-profile television work (as the Russian Vladek Klimov in Sky Television's *Fortitude* [2017–] and as Pablo Picasso's doomed friend Carles Casagemas in National Geographic's mammoth *Genius* [2018] series) and a return to franchise-friendly material, such as the 2018 adaptation of Philip Reeves's literary sequence *Mortal Engines*.

SHERIDAN, JIM (1949–). As the eldest of seven children born into a working-class area of Dublin, Jim was no stranger to poverty. Key incidents in his lifetime include the death of his brother Frankie in 1967 when he was only 11 years of age. This traumatic incident informed the personal script written by Jim and his daughters, Naomi and Kirsten (who directed ***Disco***

Pigs), for *In America* (2003). He graduated from the university in 1972 and married the same year. Between 1973 and 1974, he toured Ireland with **Neil Jordan** and their children's T Company. Following several theatrical performances and helping to develop the Project Theatre company with his brother Peter (who later directed *Borstal Boy*), he left Ireland in 1981 to manage the Irish Rebel Arts Centre in New York.

It was not until 1989 that Sheridan made his first film, *My Left Foot*, based on the autobiography of Christy Brown, a physically disabled writer with cerebral palsy who wrote and painted with his foot. The film celebrates Christy's individual determination to overcome physical limitations and lead a creative life while at the same time highlighting his belligerent and complex personality. Most especially, the importance of a close-knit community is dramatized through scenes of football (soccer) in the street and drinking in the local public house, personified by his drunken and authoritarian father (**Ray McAnally**). *My Left Foot* was nominated for five **Academy Awards**, and both Daniel Day-Lewis and **Brenda Fricker** won for Best Actor and Best Supporting Actress, respectively, with their deeply moving performances. This enormous first success had a strong influence on Sheridan's career path and on Irish filmmaking generally.

Sheridan's subsequent Irish films deal with emotive issues, often structured allegorically in terms of familial conflict. In 1990, he directed *The Field*—adapted from the play by John B. Keane—which tells the story of Bull McCabe (**Richard Harris**), a tenant farmer who has spent his life cultivating a small rented field in a barren and inhospitable landscape. Then, in 1992, he wrote the screenplay for Mike Newell's film *Into the West*, a fable of two **Traveller** children escaping from Dublin to the mythic west.

Sheridan and his producer Arthur Lappin subsequently set up **Hell's Kitchen** to produce *In the Name of the Father*, a film that explores the narrative of the so-called Guilford Four, falsely accused of carrying out the 1974 Guilford Pub bombings and wrongfully imprisoned for 15 years. The film marked a massive step forward for Sheridan, who, equipped with a Hollywood-scale budget, brought considerable visual bravura to the prison experiences of one of the Guilford Four, Gerry Conlon (Daniel Day-Lewis), and their impact on his relationship with his father, Guiseppe (Pete Postlethwaite). The film was nominated for seven Oscars but did not win any. In 1996, Sheridan cowrote the **Terry George**–directed *Some Mother's Son*, which dealt with the 1981 hunger strike in Northern Ireland's Long Kesh prison. In 1997, he directed another Northern Ireland–themed film, *The Boxer*, again starring Daniel Day-Lewis as a recently released former Irish Republican Army member who seeks to escape his sectarian community by embracing the world of boxing, establishing a cross-community gym. Made during the nascent years of the real-life Northern Ireland peace process, the film won plaudits for its core performances (from not only Day-Lewis but also Emily Watson, Brian Cox, and **Gerard McSorley**) but failed to make the same impact internationally as his previous work. Sheridan also worked as producer and second director on *Agnes Browne* (1999), directed by Anjelica Huston, and **John Carney**'s *On the Edge* (2000), for which he had helped secure funding through his first-look deal with Universal Pictures.

Audiences had to wait until 2003 for his semiautobiographical *In America*, which he cowrote with his daughters about their experiences as a young immigrant family in 1980s New York. The film marked a high point in Sheridan's career, long gestating and drawn from deeply personal circumstances, including the death of his brother Frankie and his own artistic crises. In production when the Twin Towers collapsed on 11 September 2001, its New York–set story of grief and redemption was particularly timely. Despite a very modest budget (the majority of the film was shot in and around Dublin, doubling for New York City), *In America* was nominated for a host of awards, including three Academy Awards—Best Original Screenplay for the Sheridans, Best Actress for Samantha Morton, and Best Supporting Actor for Djimon Hounsou—and went on to earn more than $25 million at the box office. It also launched the career of **Sarah Bolger**, who has since gone on to forge a steady career in American TV.

Sheridan has long been associated with strong performances from his actors—notably Daniel Day-Lewis, with whom he made three early films that propelled both to international acclaim. Indeed, actors in Sheridan films, particularly men, have an unrivaled record in awards and nominations, although this success has dimmed in recent years. In contrast to Irish filmmakers of the "first wave," Sheridan sought from the outset of his career to craft emotionally strong stories that would appeal to mass audiences in and beyond Ireland. A charismatic, intelligent, and highly opinionated figure, he frequently spoke during the 1990s about the need to make Irish stories "universal," and by pursuing this as well as using the leverage gained from his success in the United States, he arguably did more to inspire and achieve a viable Irish film industry than anyone.

Since *In America*, Sheridan's career has faltered, as if, having told his most personal story, he hasn't been sure where to look for inspiration (although it must also be acknowledged that the market space within which his career took shape has changed out of all recognition as streaming services have moved to become the center of gravity of the U.S. screen industries). His biopic of American rapper 50 Cent—*Get Rich or Die Trying* (2005)—seemed an odd choice, and while it received generally positive reviews, it made no impression at all at the white-dominated Academy Awards. (However, in box office terms, it achieved his biggest box office of $46 million). Frequently associated with a variety of projects, *Brothers* (2009) was a remake of a Danish film by Susanne Bier, and while it had strong creative credentials (and an A-list cast that included Tobey Maguire, Jake Gyllenhaal, and Natalie Portman), it made little lasting impression, although Maguire received a Golden Globe nomination. Sheridan's experience with the psychological thriller/ghost story that was *Dream House* (2011) was so bad (he claimed that the film released bore little relationship to the one he made) that he sought—unsuccessfully—to have his name removed from the credits but has disowned it publicly. *The Secret Scripture* (2016) represented a return to Irish themes (certainly a return to working with producer Noel Pearson, who produced *My Left Foot* and *The Field*). The film was an adaptation of the prize-winning novel by Sebastian Barry starring Vanessa Redgrave, Rooney Mara, Eric Bana, and the cream of young Irish talent, including **Jack Reynor** and Aidan Turner. Despite this cast and the obvious importance of its subject—dealing with the incarceration of a young woman by various Irish institutions for the crime of childbirth outside marriage—the film lacked the urgency of Sheridan's best work and felt, for all its sincerity, too crowded and polished to be truly engaging. Reviews were tepid, as was the box office.

SHORT FILMS. Inevitably perhaps, given the delayed absence of an infrastructure for indigenous filmmaking, short films constituted the vast majority of Irish cinema output prior to the 1990s. Pre-1970, such films were almost exclusively in the **documentary** mode, as exemplified by filmmakers like **Louis Marcus** and **Patrick Carey**. Notable exceptions to this generalization include the fiction films *Foolmate* (1940) and Hilton Edwards's Oscar-nominated *Return to Glennascaul* (1951) starring Orson Welles.

At an official level, the short was regarded early on as a crucial stepping-stone on the path to developing an indigenous industry. The 1942 ***Report of the Inter-Departmental Committee on the Film Industry*** assumed that, initially at least, the main scope for domestic production would be confined to short films and was concerned with the practicalities of establishing such production. It conceded that the tendency toward double features and cinema verité had had a deleterious impact on the market for short films but noted that the majority of cinemas still required such films to complete single-feature programs.

This was no longer the case a quarter of a century later when the 1968 ***Report of the Film Industry Committee*** was published. Although the report also emphasized the need to support short production, it regarded shorts as a stopgap measure. Thus, although Irish fiction shorts could "provide the domestic audience with a reflection of themselves in that special way that only fiction can achieve," this was to be resorted to only "in the absence of a significant volume of Irish *feature* films." The report further noted that short films provided filmmakers "*with potential for making feature films* practical, technical and creative training and experience which a small country could not as readily provide in any other way" and recommended that a fund (worth between IR£55,000 and IR£75,000) be provided annually to support short production in Ireland.

Although ultimately nothing came of that report, the beginning of **Arts Council** film funding in the early 1970s saw the start of more consistent short-fiction production. Not surprisingly, the same individuals who would later produce the first wave of indigenous features were associated with many of the shorts produced in this era. **Joe Comerford** directed his first short—*Swan Alley*—in 1969 and followed it with *Emtigon* a year later. In 1976, aided by an Arts Council grant, **Cathal Black** directed *Wheels* from a John McGahern story. A year later, **Bob Quinn** directed the comic *Self Portrait with Red Car* featuring painter Brian Bourke, and in 1978, **Kieran Hickey** made his fiction debut with the well-received gothic horror *A Child's Voice*.

From 1981 on, the presence of the **Irish Film Board** began to complement the Arts Council's activities. In 1984, the two bodies cofounded Joe Comerford's *Waterbag*, an experimental film that acted as a pilot for his later feature *Reefer and the Model* and a year later partially financed **Thaddeus O'Sullivan**'s *The Woman Who Married Clark Gable*, based on Sean O'Faolain's short story. Other beneficiaries of Film Board support included **Alan Gilsenan** for *Eh Joe* (1986), City Vision's *Sometime City* (1986), and Siobhan Toomey's *Boom Babies* (1987).

As the 1980s progressed, third-level institutions also became key players in increased short production. Trinity College's film society had been involved with shorts to varying degrees since the late 1960s—Comerford's *Swan Alley* received its premiere at the Film Society—while **Alan Gilsenan**'s first short, *Shelia* (1986), was credited as a coproduction involving the Film Society. However, it was not until the advent of formal education courses in film production at the National College of Art and Design, Dún Laoghaire, and the Dublin Institute of Technology (DIT) in the 1980s that levels of short-fiction production really took off. In 1987 alone, DIT students produced seven shorts, a level of output that Dún Laoghaire matched and surpassed in the following years. Between 1987 and 1989 in particular, Dún Laoghaire shorts showcased a number of directors who would go on to become significant figures in film and television production, including Liam O'Neill (*Frankie and Johnny* [1987]), Kieron J. Walsh (*Goodbye Piccadilly* [1988]), and Declan Recks (*Big Swinger* [1989]). The last of these, a comedy starring Tom Hickey as a pirate radio station owner and operator, became a minor hit on the festival circuit and—unusually for the time—was broadcast on domestic television. The early 1990s saw **John Moore**'s debut when he worked on graduation films at DIT and then directed the well-received *Jack's Bicycle*. Indeed, by the early 1990s, the tropes of student films were sufficiently well established to allow one DIT student, Alan Duffy, to make a student film parodying other student films. The appropriately titled *Student Film* took as its subject the production of a student film called *Belly of a Convent Girl*.

The closure of the Film Board in 1987 severely curtailed both short and feature activity, and as a result, directors who might have expected to be making their first long-form projects found themselves concentrating on shorter but no less ambitious shoots. **Paddy Breathnach** made an immediate impact with *A Stone in the Heart* in 1991, as did **Lenny Abrahamson** with *3 Joes*, which won the Best Irish and European Short awards at the 1991 Cork Film Festival.

However, in 1995, short production received another boost when the re-formed Film Board instituted the Short Cuts scheme, which provided relatively generous funding for short production. In part as a consequence, in 1995, approximately 40 short films were produced in Ireland. Ironically, then, short production in Ireland has been at its healthiest in an era when there is virtually no commercial market for such films. This raises the question of what the role of the form is for contemporary Irish cinema. The invariable answer is that they are calling cards, a response that exacerbates the tendency—noted in the 1968 report discussed above—to regard them as a stepping-stone to feature production rather than as an end in themselves.

However, if this is true of the majority of shorts produced, Irish filmmakers have continued to produce work that acknowledges the short as a legitimate form in its own right characterized by a unique aesthetic. Examples of this include Kieron Walsh's *Shooting to Stardom* (1992), Robert Quinn's *Detour* (1994), John Moore's *He Shoots, He Scores* (1994), Damien O'Donnell's *35 Aside* (1994), Alan Gilsenan's *Zulu 9* (2001), and Martin McDonagh's *Six Shooter* (2004), the last of which won an **Academy Award** for Best Short Film. Beyond their value in providing valuable production experience to emerging filmmakers, shorts have become something of a shop window for the Irish film industry through a variety of festivals and awards. Notable successes over the past decade include *New Boy* (Steph Green, based on short story by **Roddy Doyle**, 2009) (Oscar nominated), The Door (**Juanita Wilson**, 2009) (Oscar nominated), *Pentecost* (**Peter McDonald**, 2011) (Oscar nominated), *The Shore* (**Terry George**, 2012) (Oscar winning), *Irish Folk Furniture* (Tony Donoghue, 2011) (winner, Best Animation at the Sundance Film Festival), *Stutterer* (Benjamin Cleary, 2016) (Oscar winning), and *Wave* (codirected by Benjamin Cleary and T. P. O'Grady, 2017). **Brown Bag** films began its path to international animation powerhouse thanks to Oscar nominations for its breakout short films *Give Up Yer Aul Sins* (2002) and **Granny O'Grimm's Sleeping Beauty** (2008). Other notable animation shorts from recent years include *The Boy in the Bubble* (Kealan O'Rourke, 2011), *The Missing Scarf* (2013) (Oscar nominated), *Somewhere Down the Line* (Julien Regnard, 2014), and *A Coat Made Dark* (Jack O'Shea, 2016).

Many Irish filmmakers have used the short format to work through subjects in a manner that the feature form cannot. Orla Walsh and Stephen Burke provide good examples of this approach. Both have worked in other forms—Walsh, for example, has directed television comedy, and Burke has directed drama for **Radio Telefís Éireann** and the feature film *Maze* (2017). Walsh directed three shorts in the 1990s—*The Visit* (1992), *Bent Out of Shape* (1995), and *Blessed Fruit* (1999)—all of which explored various aspects of sexual politics in contemporary Ireland in a much more nuanced fashion than contemporaneous features generally achieve. *The Visit*—which follows the wife of a Republican prisoner as she visits her husband to inform him that she is pregnant with another man's child—stands out in this regard, raising and exploring a range of ideological issues related to nationalist and feminist politics.

Stephen Burke's two shorts *After '68* (1993) and *'81* (1996) are more overtly connected. The first follows events in Northern Ireland from the civil rights marches in 1968 to Bloody Sunday in 1972, while the second follows the 1981 hunger strikes through the eyes of a French camera crew covering the story. Both films (especially *After '68*) engage more directly with the complex realities of living through the Troubles than better-known long-form counterparts, such as **High Boot Benny** and **In the Name of the Father**.

SHORTT, PAT (1967–). One of 13 children from a Thurles, County Tipperary, family, Pat Shortt was raised by his father and older siblings after his mother passed away when he was just seven years old. Creatively inclined from an early age, Shortt developed an interest in music (he has played saxophone professionally) and attended art college after secondary school. Encountering comedian Jon Kenny after college, Shortt initially joined him onstage as a saxophonist before becoming his cowriter and ultimately one-half of what remains Ireland's most successful comedy double act: the D'Unbelievables. Building their shows around extreme—but recognizable—versions of provincial archetypes, their work was sometimes derided as populist (especially when compared with contemporaries like Dylan Moran or Tommy Tiernan). Yet, embraced and given a platform by Gay Byrne, then host of Ireland's top-rated *The Late, Late Show*, they built up a huge and loyal live following, and both they and their characters were household names in Ireland by the end of the 1990s. This also translated into small-screen success, with videos of their shows enjoying strong sales in the Irish home entertainment market.

The strongly character-driven nature of Shortt's work with Kenny pointed to potential as a "straight" actor, a potential that was partially realized when Shortt appeared in Druid Theatre's production of Martin McDonagh's *The Lonesome West* (1998). (He would work with McDonagh again in *The Cripple of Inishmaan* [opposite Daniel Radcliffe] on the West End and on Broadway in 2014 and 2015 and in *A Skull in Connemara* in Dublin's Olympia Theatre in 2018.) He also appeared—in small roles—in the occasional film, including *Angela Mooney Dies Again* (1996) and *This Is My Father* (1998).

However, Shortt's career was unexpectedly transformed when Kenny was diagnosed with Hodgkin's lymphoma in 2000, forcing him to step back from live performance. Although Kenny subsequently recovered—and performed in D'Unbelievables reunion tours—Shortt, with a young family, was prompted to strike out on his own. After a stint playing saxophone with Galway band the Saw Doctors, he returned to live comedy as a solo artist and increasingly looked to big- and small-screen roles. He followed his cameos as rural grotesque Tom in **Channel 4**'s *Father Ted* (1996–1998) with a lead role (alongside Jon Kenny, **Eamon Morrisey**, **Bronagh Gallagher**, and **Ruth McCabe**) in the short-lived *The Fitz* (BBC, 2000). Thereafter, he became increasingly prevalent in—again initially minor—feature film roles, including *Saltwater* (2000) and *Inside I'm Dancing* (2004) and an eye-catching performance in *Man About Dog* (2004), bringing a degree of comic menace to Fergie, leader of a **Traveller** gang.

None of this prepared audiences for *Garage* (2007). Josie, the simple, innocent, small-town garage attendant, was a million miles away from some of Shortt's earlier over-the-top characters. Shortt brought a quiet dignity to an intellectually challenged figure swept aside by the Celtic Tiger gold rush and ill equipped to deal with a more cosmopolitan Ireland. In a performance of utmost restraint, he deploys cautious laughter and uncertain nods as Josie attempts to feign comprehension of his increasingly tenuous circumstances. Indeed, though director **Lenny Abrahamson** apparently never looked past Shortt for the role, even he seems to have been surprised by the power of the performance: an initial 150-minute cut of the film was whittled down to 85 minutes to concentrate on Shortt's footage. The film won the CICAE award at the Cannes Film Festival that year, and Shortt's performance won three more elsewhere.

Yet comedy remained his day job. His country-and-western parody song "Jumbo Breakfast Roll" was the best-selling song in Ireland in 2006, and between 2003 and 2008, he wrote, produced, and played five distinct roles in the mainstay of the television comedy schedule for **Radio Telefís Éireann** (RTÉ), *Killinaskully*. An absurdist comedy set in a rural village, its broad humor proved immensely popular (it routinely secured more than 700,000 viewers by its final season) and allowed Shortt scope to pilot two follow-ups for RTÉ, one of which became the 2009–2011 series *Mattie*, another comedy following a rural guard as he relocated to Dublin. Similarly, on the big screen, his lead roles in *Life's a Breeze* (2013) and *The Flag* (2016) were played primarily for laughs.

Nonetheless, *Garage* opened a door to more serious work that Shortt has continued to walk through. In Shimmy Marcus's *Soulboy* (2010), he played Brendan, an Irish delivery van driver living in 1970s England, simultaneously mentor to the main protagonist, the butt of anti-Irish aggression, and agonized by his love for a married—and therefore untouchable—woman. **John Michael McDonagh** deploys a rogues' gallery of locals (**Aidan Gillen, Chris O'Dowd**, Dylan Moran, and so on) to act as foils to *Brendan Gleeson*'s protagonist in *Calvary*, but it is Shortt's Church-hating pub owner Brendan Lynch who snaps first and actually assaults the priest. And in 2016, Shortt twice portrayed fathers in turmoil: in *Gerard Barrett*'s three-part *Smalltown* for TV3, playing a man watching his wife suffer through illness, and, no less effectively, in Tom Ryan's *Twice Shy* (2016), watching his daughter face a crisis pregnancy.

***SHROOMS* (2007).** Even before the release of *Shrooms* (a contraction of "mushrooms"), there was clear evidence that a horror subgenre was emerging within Irish cinema. There were the hurley-wielding zombie killers of *Dead Meat* (2003) and the eco-horror *Isolation* (2005), while the years since 2007 have confirmed this trend. *Shrooms* closely follows the conventions of that genre: a youthful group (mainly an American cast) travels to a forested park somewhere in southern Ireland to take magic mushrooms. They are chaperoned by upper-class Jake (Jack Huston), who primes them for consuming the fungi with stories of a now derelict industrial school and the psychotic cleric who used to run it. Under the influence of the shrooms and increasingly unable to distinguish reality from imagination, the "trippers" become convinced that they are being watched by the deranged spirit of the cleric and—as the genre demands—meet their grisly ends one by one.

This description may suggest that the script successfully mobilized the specter of industrial schools—by 2007, universally understood in Ireland as sites of irredeemable evil for thousands of young men and women. Such a reading would credit the script with absent depths but also obscure how *Shrooms* was expressly designed to eschew any cultural specificity that might confuse overseas audiences. *Shrooms* clearly reflected an increasing concern on the part of Irish cinema in general (and institutions like the **Irish Film Board**, which supported the production, in particular) to demonstrate the commercial viability of the industry.

In that regard, the film was a success: a wide release in U.K. and Irish cinemas earned $2 million at the box office in the first three weeks of its release. Although less successful in U.S. cinemas, this is likely to have been compensated for by its performance in ancillary markets: *Shrooms* was custom-built for the kind of sci-fi–fantasy–horror channels long characteristic of the U.S. cable market and, by 2007, increasingly prevalent in Europe.

The film was received poorly in Ireland, the response of Irish critics predicated largely on the assumption that the genre was something that Irish filmmakers shouldn't get involved with. It certainly marked a shift in the career trajectory of **Paddy Breathnach**. His 1997 collaboration with **Conor McPherson** on *I Went Down* (which itself followed the warm critical success of *Ailsa* in 1994) had suggested that it was possible to contemplate a career in making Irish films. Thus, it seemed particularly disappointing that a decade later, Breathnach was back to making a calling-card movie. In that respect, however, it was a success: even with a limited budget, the film efficiently showcases Breathnach's grasp of the visual aspect of the genre and led directly to Breathnach's work as director for hire on *Freakdog* (2008) (aka *Red Mist*), a U.S.-shot, hospital-based horror, the following year.

SILENT GRACE **(2001).** Like *H3*, partially funded by both the **Irish Film Board** and the **Northern Ireland Film Commission**, Maeve Murphy's *Silent Grace* traces the experiences of Republican female prisoners in Armagh Prison during the early 1980s (the period of the hunger strikes). The narrative follows Eileen (**Orla Brady**), the leader of the Irish Republican Army's women prisoners, as she encounters the apolitical Áine, imprisoned for car theft, and subsequently traces the development of their friendship. However, in contrast to *H3*, *Silent Grace* is a much more evenhanded take on the politics of the period. Thus, although prison officers are represented as brutal, this is implicitly accounted for by the backdrop of an assassination campaign being waged by Republicans against those officers. Meanwhile, the prison governor (Conor Mullen) is portrayed as concerned and even mildly sympathetic toward the women.

SITUATIONS VACANT **(2008).** Coproduced by noted Irish comedy production company Grand Pictures, *Situations Vacant* marks the feature debut of director Lisa Mulcahy (*The Legend of Longwood* and *Red Rock*) and scriptwriter Steven Murray in a lad-centered comedy of manners set in contemporary Ireland.

Dave (Diarmuid Noyes), Vinny (Shaun Dunne), and Tom (Sam Corry) are in their late 20s and unhappy with their lot. While Dave and Vinny are looking for work and love, Tom has both, but neither are making him fulfilled. The thinly plotted narrative is structured around Dave's increasingly desperate job interviews, a pursuit not aided by his strategy of relaxing himself with a few pints in advance; henpecked Tom, who struggles to assert himself in the face of his equally domineering wife; and boss and laborer Vinny, who unsuccessfully pursues his coworker Janice (Lorna Dempsey).

Although one must applaud anyone who can assemble a feature production for €200,000, *Situation Vacant* is skewered by an underdeveloped script, unsympathetic characters, an incoherent theme, and—most critically for a comedy—unfunny dialogue.

SNAKES AND LADDERS (1996). A relatively conventional, almost soap-style story about two young roommates in search of love, framed against a well-conceived social realist urban environment that includes a strong comic performance by **Rosaleen Linehan** as Nora. Most of the film's energy comes from the relationship between the two women (Pom Boyd and **Gina Moxley**) and their attempts to succeed as street entertainers alongside a male love interest played by stand-up comic Sean Hughes. An amiable farce, Trish McAdam's very light comedy confidently tells its engaging story but lacks the dramatic intensity necessary to elevate it above a regular episode of a soap story.

SNAP (2011). A disturbing yet sensitively told narrative centering on child abduction and dysfunctional family dynamics, *Snap* marked the cinematic debut of Cork-born writer/director Carmel Winters. While the plot echoes a number of contemporary headline horrors, its origins were as a training exercise, written by Winters, for student psychiatrists. This context and its subsequent development as part of the **Irish Film Board**'s Catalyst scheme (for which it was ultimately rejected) clearly benefited the final film, which is notable for complex characterization, strong performances from its leading actors (particularly Aisling O'Sullivan), and sensitivity of the scenes between the abducted toddler Adam (Adam Duggan) and his kidnapper, Stephen (Stephen Moran).

The film's fractured narrative, moving back and forth in time, is threaded by a TV interview with Stephen's brittle mother Sandra (O'Sullivan) in her apartment. As the interviewer attempts to uncover the background to Stephen's abduction of Adam, Sandra's bitter dismissals and a self-conscious performance of indignation and anger gradually give way to a dysfunctional but nevertheless sympathetic personality that cannot be reduced to easy explanations. O'Sullivan manages to express several competing motivations within her character at once, and the filmmaker and actress clearly worked hard and with a great deal of trust in constructing such an Irish maternal figure of such complexity. The film screened at the prestigious Tribeca Film Festival and won *Variety*'s Critic's Choice Award at the Karlovary International Film Festival as well as the Best Irish Film and Best Irish Director awards at the Dublin Critic Circle Awards. It also marked the final appearance of Irish acting legend **Mick Lally** in a small but deeply courageous performance. Winters subsequently reworked the piece for the stage as *Witness*.

***THE SNAPPER* (1993).** Adapted from Roddy Doyle's trilogy of Barrytown novels (which also includes *The Commitments* and *The Van*), the film stars Tina Kellegher as Sharon, the eldest daughter of a large working-class family in Dublin who stuns family and friends with the news that she is pregnant. Sharon asserts to her family that the pregnancy is a consequence of a one-night stand with a Spanish sailor, but the actual father is revealed to be middle-aged neighbor Georgie Burgess (Pat Laffin), who took advantage of Sharon's inebriated state outside a pub one night. **Colm Meaney**'s turn as Sharon's father is a tour de force, especially in his reaction to his daughter's refusal to reveal the true identity of the father. While the sexual politics look decidedly suspect from a 21st-century vantage point, the use of vernacular language and humor and the evocation of working-class family and community are surprisingly effective, all the more so given that the film was directed by English director Stephen Frears, who brought little prior knowledge of the milieu to the task. The film was unusual in that, having been screened on BBC television (which had initially commissioned it), public demand in Ireland led to a subsequent and successful cinema run, rendering it an instant classic of contemporary Irish cinema.

SOCIETY OF FILM-MAKERS IN IRELAND. *See* SCREEN PRODUCERS IRELAND.

***SOME MOTHER'S SON* (1996).** A widowed teacher and lifelong pacifist, Kathleen Quigley (Helen Mirren), is shaken out of her middle-class existence when her son (played by **Aidan Gillen**) is captured after a shoot-out with the British army during the Northern Troubles. Along with the mother of another prisoner, Annie Higgins (**Fionnula O'Flanagan**), whose husband was killed by the British and hence accepts her son's political stance, Kathleen finds herself suddenly brought into the middle of Northern Ireland's political conflict. Both women find common purpose when their sons go on a hunger strike demanding political recognition for their armed struggle.

The film, directed by **Terry George** and cowritten with **Jim Sheridan**, is an imaginative attempt to humanize the Northern conflict from a Republican perspective through a modern-day evocation of the Virgin Mary–Jesus Christ story. Informed that she has the right to end her son's hunger strike, the broader political arguments between the clergy, leaders of the Irish Republican Army (IRA), and others become secondary as the mother asserts her primal apolitical privilege and signs the document to take her son out of danger of imminent death.

Made in the period between the Provisional IRA cease-fire (1994) and the Good Friday Agreement (1998), the film unsurprisingly came in for criticism for failing to critique the actions that led to the hunger strikers' imprisonment in the first place. This response reflected the extent to which popular discourse still refused to accept representations of members of groups such as the IRA as anything other than murdering psychopaths. As a counterview, *Some Mother's Son* sought to play a role in the unfolding peace process by imagining the hunger strikers not as martyrs but as mortals whose deaths had impacted families but also brought little immediate political change. The film bravely sought to reposition the strikes for a new era by remembering the social and human context of the deaths and arguing for the legitimacy of another approach imagined in terms of maternal intervention.

***SONG FOR A RAGGY BOY* (2003).** Directed by **Aisling Walsh** and adapted from playwright, poet, and former Royal Air Force member Patrick Galvin's autobiography (1990), the film can be contextualized within an emerging anti-Catholicism in Irish society and popular culture in the 1990s and first decade of the 2000s, driven by a series of scandals and revelations of abuse. Set in an era when corporal punishment was the norm in most Irish schools, the story is based on the violence inflicted on boys incarcerated in a Cork borstal/reform school run by Oblate religious brothers and priests during the late 1930s and 1940s.

We are introduced to William Franklin (**Aidan Quinn**), who lost his lover while fighting for the International Brigade in the Spanish Civil War. His psychological fragility is revealed through flashbacks of atrocities and by his need for solitude and resignation. The only job he can get in the Ireland of 1939 is teaching English to poor and troubled children in a boys' reformatory school. The adaptation is reminiscent of Peter Weir's *Dead Poets Society* (1989) and other films in the subgenre of inspirational teacher narratives. William tries to spark his charges to find their voice through literature, in this case, Spanish love poetry.

The story line offers strong, if simplistic, character conflicts, particularly the evil Brother John (Iain Glen) as dean of discipline, who has been appointed by the bishop and pedophile Brother Mac (Marc Warren), who molests and rapes "Patrick Delaney 743" (Chris Newman) (all students are issued with numbers) in the school's bathrooms. Following the murder of student "Liam Mercier 636" (John Travers), both men are taken away by church authorities. Franklin decides he must leave the school, and in a touching final scene, Delaney runs toward Franklin and hugs him while all the other boys gather round in admiration and love.

SOUTHPAW **(1997).** The feature-length documentary, directed by Liam McGrath, follows the experiences of Francis Barrett, a 19-year-old **Traveller** from Galway who trains as a boxer and dreams of going to the Olympic Games. Against all the odds, especially as an outsider in Irish society, he eventually succeeds in his ambition. The film follows Barrett through the qualification rounds, culminating in the final trip to Atlanta in the United States, where the Olympics are hosted. In particular, the story explores his personal relationship with his trainer and close friend, Chick Gillen. In an era when the documentary form had almost exclusively become the province of television, *Southpaw* was groundbreaking in that it was expressly intended for cinematic release, presaging a later (ca. 2005–2006) turn toward supporting theatrical documentaries on the part of the **Irish Film Board**.

SPIN THE BOTTLE **(2002).** Directed by Ian Fitzgibbon, *Spin the Bottle* revives the character of Rats for the big screen, having been first introduced in the hit **Radio Telefís Éireann** comedy *Paths to Freedom*. Newly released from prison, Rats (**Michael McElhatton**, who also cowrote the series and film) enlists members of his former band (**Peter MacDonald** and Donal O'Kelly) in a farcical attempt to cure his aunt's terminal obesity by raising money for a trip to Lourdes. The re-formed band eventually gate-crashes a national television talent show, leading to another spell in prison. In contrast to other films set in contemporary working-class Dublin, *Spin the Bottle* is played strictly for laughs: although the character Rats is ultimately portrayed as sympathetic, there is little attempt to place his recidivist behavior in any kind of larger social or political context.

THE STAG (*THE BACHELOR WEEKEND*) **(2013).** Clearly intended as a "localized" expression of contemporary Anglo-American "laddism" in film in general and of the lucrative popularity of *The Hangover* franchise in particular, *The Stag* can be filed alongside *The Hardy Bucks* (2013) and more idiosyncratic titles such as *Paths to Freedom* (2000) and *Intermission* (2003) in its portrayal of an Irish masculinity liberated from the sexual and moral strictures of Catholic Ireland. In common with international "lad" films, it features an isolated group of "men" (including **Andrew Scott** and **Hugh O'Conor**) run amok in a masculine fantasy space free of feminine supervision and censure while (following a tendency of Irish cinema evident from the mid-1990s) it calls into question the coherence of masculine identity and agency. Directed and cowritten by John Butler (along with **Peter McDonald**, who also stars), it simultaneously deconstructs Irish manhood as a monolithic construct—thereby debunking the Catholic-nationalist paradigms of an earlier era—while reinforcing an accidental camaraderie predicated on "male bonding." As such, it rejects a (politicized) postcolonial understanding of

Irish masculinity while reaffirming its distinctiveness as a nonhegemonic but distinctive and enriching category of masculine belonging. Many reviews reflected this double consciousness in describing the film as "good-hearted" and "charming," epithets redolent of an earlier era of cinematic representations.

STANDBY (2014). Directing team Rob and Ronan Burke, previously best known for their work on children's drama and comedy for **Radio Telefís Éireann**, made the move to feature production with a romantic comedy based on a script by Pierce Ryan. Alan (Brian Gleeson, brother of Domhnall and son of Brendan)—a stuck-in-a-rut, late-twenty-something man, jilted at the altar and fired from his job in finance—is reduced to living at home with his dad and working with his mother at Dublin Airport's Tourist Information kiosk. But one day, Alice (Jessica Pare fresh off a starring role as Don Draper's second wife in *Mad Men*) appears at his kiosk, her flight from Paris to New York having been grounded overnight in Dublin. Eight years earlier, she and Brian were an item during his summer working in the United States as a student. It emerges that she had even been willing to marry him to get him a green card and thus an extended stay in the United States For old times' sake, he offers to show her Dublin before her flight home the next day. After a bid to impress her by paying a colleague to act as his girlfriend falls through, he apologizes and asks for a second chance, and the pair embark on a nighttime odyssey through the city.

Given Irish cinema's ongoing dalliance with other generic forms, it was perhaps simply a matter of time before it threw its hat at romantic comedy. Unfortunately, the film fails to sufficiently deliver either element of its generic makeup. In terms of romance, the film never convincingly establishes Alan as an object of desire for Alice: the film attempts to hint at an artistic soul dwelling beneath his self-deprecating black humor, but two scenes showing him belt out country standards are less than convincing in this regard. The dialogue contains nuggets of real humor, as both leads, especially Gleeson, prove adept at delivering a comic line, but the film is overly reliant on farcical setups: a three-way meal on St. Valentine's night, performing the Heimlich maneuver on a randy septuagenarian (and subsequently being invited to the latter's wedding), and getting onstage in a gay bar to perform a Hank Williams number. Stripped of these, the film is reduced to a single—overly long—conversation about "what went wrong" for the couple eight years earlier (and indeed in their separate lives since).

Given the film's post–economic crash setting, it might have used the malaise of the post–Celtic Tiger to explain Alan's status in life: certainly, plenty of his contemporaries found that the apparently unending economic boom and its associated opportunities suddenly evaporated just as they were on the cusp of adulthood. However, far from foregrounding that context, the film seems more eager to disguise it. Fittingly, perhaps, given Alan's day job, nighttime Dublin is represented through a touristic gaze, most prominently in a sequence where the pair gaze over the new developments on Dublin's dockside from atop an illegally entered building. Generic conventions demand that the couple pair up at the conclusion, but the final denouement is almost depressing, the viewer left with an uncomfortable feeling that Alice's decision to stay with Alan in Ireland is motivated more by pity than by romance.

STAPLETON, FRANK (1962–). It is easy to forget just how difficult it was for the first wave of Irish directors who attempted to launch a career in the 1980s. Frank Stapleton was part of that vanguard. Like others from the period, his work is defined by daring and determination: balanced between an ambition to create a personal cinema and the need to make a living. At first glance, his oeuvre seems characterized by an eclecticism of topics and formats, but on closer consideration, continuities can be traced through a portfolio of creative documentaries, TV drama, short-film and feature film output, and a TV documentary series. Across these works, we encounter an intellect that is both limpid and ludic, a visual sense that is ambitious and original, and a commitment to exploring the condition of Irishness that is imaginative, engaged, and wide ranging.

A native of Churchtown in Dublin's southern suburbs, he attended the distinguished Belvedere College, where, like the impressionable **James Joyce** before him, he came under the spell of the Jesuitical mind-set. However, unlike Stephen Daedalus, he did not initially choose an artistic vocation over a priestly calling and spent several years studying within the Society of Jesus. While still appending an "SJ" to his director credit, Frank commenced a career in film, directing the subversive and inventive *A Second of June* (1984), a contemporary drama-documentary inspired by *Ulysses* focusing on a day in the life of two ordinary Dubliners against the backdrop of Ronald Reagan's 1984 visit to Ireland. Two years later, Frank finally uttered "non servium" and left the Jesuits. After a few years in London (where he developed an interest in R. D. Laing's psychoanalytical techniques), he returned to Dublin and formed Ocean Films with producer Catherine Tiernan in 1989.

The absence at that point of either a film board or state funding structures for independently produced television saw Ocean Films apply for funding wherever it could. Its first success was a prestigious but controversial commission—*The Whole World in His Hands*—a documentary made for U.K. broadcaster **Channel 4** about what Ireland had become in the 10 years since the visit of Pope John Paul II. Several similarly polemic documentaries followed, including two with Noel Browne (*Requiem for a Civilisation* [1991] and *Dr. Browne Also Spoke* [1992]) and two in collaboration with **Michael D. Higgins** just before he became Ireland's first minister for arts, culture, and the Gaeltacht.

Moving away from documentary and able to secure funding from **Radio Telefís Éireann**, Frank directed the short film *Poorhouse* (1996), an evocative adaptation of a Michael Harding story set during the Famine that featured strong central performances and memorable visuals. Its success paved the way for what proved to be the creative high point of Frank's career as a filmmaker, *The Fifth Province* (1997), an artfully realized, unclassifiable feature from a script that Frank cowrote with the late Pat Sheeran and Nina Witoszek (aka Nina FitzPatrick). Attracted by its startling originality, it was British Screen (**Simon Perry**) that first offered funding to the project, with the **Irish Film Board** subsequently contributing to its production. Evocatively shot by celebrated French cinematographer Bruno de Keyzer (who contributed a European sensibility to the film's quirky tone), the film is set in the Irish Midlands and is a worthy cinematic successor to the surrealistic perspective of that liminal zone inaugurated by Flann O'Brien. Once again, it offered an alternative view of Ireland and its culture, challenging official or sanctioned narratives (notably in an amusing but pointed scene about what makes a successful Irish screenplay), and centers on a maverick and dreamer in the figure of Timmy Sugrue (Brian F. O'Byrne).

The Fifth Province was well received at film festivals (winning Best First Feature at the Galway Film Fleadh [Festival] and the Audience Prize at the Fantasporto Festival) but didn't manage to find a distributor outside of the United Kingdom and Ireland, perhaps because it was not perceived as "Irish" enough. In its aftermath, Frank worked on a range of documentary series before the onset of multiple sclerosis prematurely ended his career. These included *Irish Dreamtime* (2000), an ambitious six-part series exploring concepts of Irish heritage at the turn of the millennium. Each, in different ways, continued the work of his fiction and nonfiction films in seeking to interrogate and articulate the distinctive qualities of the Irish condition at a specific moment in time with a bias toward the marginal, the excluded, and the unorthodox.

STARFISH (2004). This quirky narrative directed by Stephen Kane tells the story of Ella (Ailigh Symons), whose relationship with her boyfriend begins to collapse after he is laid off from his software engineering job. In the café where she works as a waitress, she befriends a lonely science fiction writer (Pat McGrath) who is obsessed with a fish tank (and the starfish in particular) in the restaurant. The narrative subsequently degenerates into a series of comic vignettes involving a hitchhiking nun and shoplifting as the unlikely trio escape the city with their fish to release it into the sea.

***STAY* (2013).** In adapting Canadian novelist Aislinn Hunter's 2004 Irish-set novel, German director Wiebke Von Carolsfeld adjusts the setting to facilitate structuring the project to avail himself of the 1989 Irish–Canadian coproduction agreement.

Abbey (an immediate pre–*Orange Is the New Black* Taylor Schilling), a 20-something Canadian woman, finds herself in a relationship with a man two decades her senior, ex–archaeology professor Dermot (**Aidan Quinn**). Having moved to a small Connemara village to flee a dark secret from his past, Dermot is content to live a quiet, somewhat directionless existence. For Abbey, village life offers few prospects, and the locals are not entirely welcoming of her. When she becomes pregnant, Dermot is horrified, having previously made clear his abhorrence of fatherhood. Distraught, Abbey leaves for Montreal to contemplate whether to proceed with the pregnancy while rekindling a fraught relationship with her own father (Michael Ironside). Meanwhile, Dermot becomes—not entirely willingly—embroiled in the lives of local teenagers Deirdre (Nika McGuigan) and Sean (**Barry Keoghan**), the first a heavily pregnant lone parent-to-be and the latter a secondary school dropout. While apart, both Abbey and Michael excavate their own histories, debating on how and whether to stay together.

Low on narrative incident and hampered somewhat by a failure to establish a convincing chemistry between the two leads, *Stay* struggles to escape its literary origins as a novel focused on the interior lives of its characters. Indeed, though Quinn and Schilling are fine, it is telling that both are eclipsed by Ironside (cast against type as an unintentionally humorous, eager-to-please patriarch) and Keoghan, further establishing his credentials as a star of the future.

***STELLA DAYS* (2011).** Adapted from Michael Doorley's 2011 memoir *Stella Days: The Life and Times of a Rural Irish Cinema*, the film marked a welcome return to Irish subjects by **Thaddeus O'Sullivan**. Its themes and setting are familiar: Martin Sheen plays a parish priest working in a community undergoing social and cultural transformation. The rural electrification of Ireland in the mid-1950s functions to anchor the film historically and thematically, setting up familiar oppositions between modernity and tradition and corresponding forces of liberal thinking and closed-mindedness centered around the Catholic Church.

Martin Sheen plays the progressive, intellectual priest and amateur filmmaker Daniel Barry, who is sent to the backwater parish of Borrisokane after 20 years in the United States. With money needed to build a new church, Bishop Hegarty (Tom Hickey) asks for Father Barry's help in fund-raising, and he suggests opening a cinema. The bishop reluctantly agrees on the condition that it will screen only spiritually uplifting material, but inevitably,

Father Barry runs up against conservative forces—here incarnated by **Stephen Rea**'s local politician, who strives to keep Ireland free from foreign influences.

Stella Days was likely pitched as "John McGahern meets *Cinema Paradiso*," and, to an extent, it works, but Sheen's thoughtful and committed performance outshines the screenplay and suggests that buried underneath a busy set of subplots, there hides a film more along the lines of French films like *Leon Morin: Priest* (1961) or *Diary of a Country Priest* (1951). In this respect, it resembles *Calvary*, another "post-Catholic" tale of Irish clerical isolation with a strong central performance. Like that film, it chooses to introduce a colorful variety of local parishioners rather than commit to a sparer—and no doubt riskier—narrative of troubled male spirituality and vocation.

STEMBRIDGE, GERRY (1960–). A native of Limerick, Stembridge is a singular voice in Irish culture with a prolific output across various media. If there is a unifying vision to this output, it lies in its pointed topicality and an often wry or satirical deconstruction of social constructions of gender (particularly masculinity) and class.

After studying at University College Dublin, Stembridge joined **Radio Telefís Éireann** (RTÉ) as a producer/director in the early 1980s and remained for five years, writing and performing the now legendary satirical radio show *Scrap Saturday*. Having written and directed a major one-off TV drama for RTÉ—*The Truth About Claire*—which examined the politics of the abortion debate in Ireland, he made his debut as a feature writer and director with the domestic abuse drama *Guiltrip*, produced by **Ed Guiney** in 1995. Stembridge followed *Guiltrip* with *Bad Day in Blackrock*, another issue-based drama for RTÉ exploring racism and multiculturalism in Ireland.

In a dramatic and successful shift of tone and audience appeal, he conceived of the romantic comedy *About Adam* (2000), a genre rarely seen in Irish film that, channeling Pasolini's *Theorem* (1968), offered an iconic and ironic representation of Celtic Tiger Ireland and one that delightedly rejected every shibboleth of a "national cinema" project in favor of postmodern globalized sheen. During this period, Stembridge also worked as screenwriter on **Thaddeus O'Sullivan**'s *Ordinary Decent Criminal* (2000) and **Pat Murphy**'s *Nora* (2000).

After another interregnum, Stembridge returned to the big screen with his third (and, so far, last) feature film as director in 2008 with *Alarm*. Once again, the film demonstrated Stembridge's knack for capturing the zeitgeist, this time reflecting the transformation of the status of "home" in Irish society—from bulwark against external threats to a commodified investment that came to constitute a threat in itself.

Frustrated by the long periods of development common in film production, Stembridge has apparently given up on film and turned to writing novels, carrying on his interest in pryingt apart contemporary social norms, including *What She Saw* (2017), *The Effect of Her* (2013), *Unspoken* (2011), and *According to Luke* (2006). Each, in different ways, makes manifest his undiminished Swiftian impulse, a rare gift to turn inside out the assumptions and presumptions of Irish society at a given moment.

STITCHES (2012). Having shot his previous feature *The Undistributed* for just over €1,500, schlock-horror specialist **Conor McMahon** moved significantly upscale for *Stitches*, spending more than €1 million on a comedy-horror built around a feature debut performance from British stand-up comedian Ross Noble.

At a birthday party populated by a particularly obnoxious set of kids, foulmouthed, unenthusiastic clown Stitches (Noble) is fatally wounded when a prank goes wrong. On the night of the clown's funeral, birthday boy Tommy sneaks out to spy on a bizarre posthumous ceremony carried out by Stitches's fellow clowns. It emerges that each clown's spirit is preserved in the form of an egg recording their unique facial makeup.

Flash forward six years, and Tommy (*Doctor Who* alum Tommy McKnight) is now an awkward teenager, surrounded by the same friends (and less than friends) who attended the fateful party. When his mother's work demands that she leave him home alone for his 16th birthday, his mates seize the opportunity to invite the school to Tommy's for a house party. Initially reluctant, he is brought around by the calculation that it may offer him an opportunity to woo his childhood sweetheart Kate (Gemma-Leah Devereux). However, the anniversary reanimates the body of Stitches, who arrives at Tommy's determined to complete his performance with a bloody revenge.

The charm of McMahon's earlier work owed much to the creative ingenuity exercised to overcome the limitations of his often absurdly low budgets. Gifted with a more substantial (though, by almost anyone else's standards, still low) budget for *Stitches*, McMahon's touch is less sure. Although the geographical location is recognizable to anyone familiar with North Wicklow, the film scarcely introduces the setting, and the characterization of the teenage characters is thin: as a child who has apparently grown up in Ireland, Tommy's English accent surely demands some explanation. The inexperienced cast seems underrehearsed and are in any case ill served by a script that is heavily reliant on the indiscriminate spraying of expletives for comedic impact. (Even Noble, a gifted comedian, is too often forced to take recourse to Anglo-Saxon for laughs.) The sole raison d'être of the narrative is to shift events along from one set-piece slaying to the next. To be fair, considerable imagination is expended on the conception and execution of what must rank among the most gory deaths in recent cinema history. However, the film appears to confuse gore for horror and, by dwelling on every tiny detail, dilutes the visceral impact of each death. This is disappointing because elsewhere McMahon demonstrates a particularly impressive grasp of how to exploit the visual nature of film for comic effect, and visual puns abound.

These flaws may not deter hard-core fans of the genre, but less committed audiences may find it harder to stomach.

STONEMAN, ROD (1953–). Appointed chief executive officer of the reestablished **Irish Film Board** (IFB) in 1993, Rod Stoneman was a key figure in Irish film production for the next decade. Born in London, he grew up in Devon, going on to study English literature at the University of Kent before completing a postgraduate diploma with the film unit at the Slade College of Art in London. Having spent some years teaching film in art colleges, working for the British Arts Council, and compiling catalogs for film exhibition, he then managed the Arnolfini art house cinema in Bristol.

In 1982, Stoneman joined the fledgling **Channel 4**, initially on a consultative basis but then as a deputy commissioning editor with the channel's groundbreaking Independent Film and Video section, sometimes referred to internally as the "channel within the channel" because of its budget and the wide range of material made there. During his time there, he commissioned a number of Irish-themed documentaries and low-budget fiction projects, including Margo Harkin's teenage pregnancy drama *Hush-a-Bye Baby* (1990) and **Joe Comerford**'s *High Boot Benny* (1993).

At the IFB, Stoneman sought to find a middle ground between, on the one hand, offering funding on a purely commercial basis and, on the other, acting as a purely cultural agency funding film "artists." This philosophy found expression in the phrase *radical pluralism*, a concept borrowed from the early days at Channel 4. In practice, this meant supporting the widest possible range of films. Thus, the first review of the IFB's activities included a (Stoneman-penned) (mis)quote from Mao Tse Tsung: "Let a thousand flowers bloom and a thousand schools of thought contend."

However, this was more than an abstract philosophy: Stoneman argued that the best means of ensuring both the development and the sustainability of Irish cinema was through a proliferation of content and output. Additionally, the strength of artisanal filmmaking lay in its unpredictability, which, theoretically, increased the chances of capturing the public imagination in a fashion that did not require the huge production and marketing resources brought to bear by Hollywood. In practice, Stoneman's approach was exemplified by the early simultaneous funding of the low-budget Irish-language feature *An Gabhan Saor* (1994) and **Pat O'Connor**'s more overtly commercial Maeve Binchy adaptation *Circle of Friends* (1995). Certainly, the remarkable recoupment rate enjoyed by the IFB during its first year of existence (£200,000 from an investment of £945,000, or 25 percent—an unusually high rate of return for an arts funding body) suggested a certain commercial savvy, although such a high rate of return inevitably diminished over his decade-long tenure.

Stoneman adopted a broad interpretation of the IFB's legal mandate to assist and encourage filmmaking in Ireland "by any means it considers appropriate." Recognizing that production was only one of the issues faced by Irish filmmakers, Stoneman commissioned research on the distribution of Irish (and other European) films in the United States, prepared an analysis of rural cinema exhibition (and of the viability of an art house cinema network), and examined the Irish facilities and postproduction base. By 1998, Stoneman was laying increasing emphasis on the marketing and development of Irish films while defending the cultural and artistic role of cinema against the *Kilkenny Report*'s emphasis on developing the audiovisual sector as a mainly business undertaking.

By the time Stoneman resigned from the IFB in 2003, he could point to its involvement in the production of more than 100 features, 60 documentaries, eight television series, and 150 short films. The IFB had grown from a three-person, £1 million operation in 1993 to a staff of 16 and a €12 million budget in 2003. However, perhaps his most significant achievement lay in the simple fact of the IFB's continued existence, the result of a successful gauging of how to reconcile the pressure to create audiovisual activities that have significant economic and employment outcomes with the need to support cultural effects.

On stepping down from the IFB, he remained engaged both with Ireland (domiciled in Clare, he became a fully fledged citizen in 2017) and with Irish cinema. He became founding director of the Huston School of Film and Digital Media at the National University of Ireland and was subsequently appointed full professor, a position he retained until his retirement in 2016.

STRATEGIC DEVELOPMENT OF THE IRISH FILM AND TELEVISION INDUSTRY (2000–2010). The Film Industry Strategic Review Group was appointed by Minister for Arts and Culture Síle de Valera in June 1998 to assess strategies for the ongoing development of the audiovisual sector in Ireland in the context of the anticipated expiration of **Section 481** in April 1999. However, in addition to that short-term question, de Valera tasked the group (which she characterized as a "think tank") with the development of a decade-long road map for the development of the industry. It was originally envisaged that the report would address the Section 481 question by September 1998, well in advance of the April 1999 deadline, but as the work of the group expanded, the minister decided to extend Section 481's existence by one year to allow the group to complete its full report.

The ambition of the final report was reflected in the scale of activity that informed it. Chaired by accountant Ossie Kilkenny (who would subsequently be appointed chair of the **Irish Film Board**), the group had 17 members, representing groups such as **Radio Telefís Éireann**, **TV3**, Film Makers Ireland, the **Film Institute of Ireland**, and the Department of Arts and Department of Finance. Independent producers were particularly well represented, accounting for six of the positions. Furthermore, in the course of drawing up its own report, the group would commission two more of its own: one from consultant **Indecon**, which three years earlier had written a report casting doubts over the efficacy of Section 481, and a second comparing the costs of film production in the United Kingdom and Ireland.

Despite these efforts, for the most part, the resulting report made unsurprising reading—its recommendations could best be summarized as "more of the same." It proposed an expanded, better-resourced Film Board with a greater emphasis on strategic business development and marketing. These additional activities were to be funded by a levy on cinema tickets and the sale and rental of videos and DVDs. Similarly, the report recommended extending Section 481 for seven years, although it also suggested increasing the tax relief on such investments from 80 to 100 percent for investments in projects with a budget of IR£4 million or less (i.e., for indigenous films).

The most notable innovation was in the stress laid on the development of stronger production companies characterized by greater scale, capitalization, business acumen, and editorial expertise. While acknowledging the role played by smaller companies, the group emphasized the need to create companies capable of competing in the international market. Implicitly pointing to the Hollywood model, the report stressed the importance of supporting companies that developed libraries that could be exploited over a period of time. This support would be funded by the introduction of a special equity fund that would be established along the lines of Section 481. Private investors would be encouraged to make equity investments in production companies by being allowed to write off such investments against tax.

The report was published in August 1999, but despite the status theoretically accorded to its conclusions, it had little practical impact. Given that the group envisaged that most of the developments recommended would be funded from taxation, the Irish filmmaking community awaited the December 1999 budget (the first after the report's publication) with anticipation. To their dismay, virtually none of the recommendations were adopted, although Minister for Finance Charlie McCreevy did extend Section 481 for another five years. Filmmakers were particularly incensed at the failure to increase to 100 percent tax relief on Section 481 projects with budgets of less than £4 million. In the longer term, the Film Board did receive an increase in exchequer funding that allowed it to broaden its activities in a manner that at least in part reflected the report's recommendations, although the idea that this might be funded by a film and video levy was never instituted. Ultimately, then, the main long-term effect of the report was the intangible impact of its emphasis on developing film production as a business. Although the report did acknowledge the cultural significance of cinema—and interviewed a number of cultural commentators on that subject—it devoted only three of its 122 pages to that perspective.

STRICK, JOSEPH (1923–). Although as a director he has made only 11 films in nearly 40 years, those he has made—including two **James Joyce** adaptations—have rarely been less than interesting. Born in Philadelphia to Jewish immigrants from eastern Europe, his earliest filmmaking experience was gained as an aerial photographer with the U.S. Air Force. In 1948, while working at the *Los Angeles Times*, he made his first short film, *Muscle Beach*, a satire on the bodybuilder culture.

From 1954 to 1959, he worked on *The Savage Eye*, an award-winning semidocumentary study of the emptiness of Los Angeles culture. In 1963, Strick directed his first adaptation, *The Balcony*, based on Jean Genet's novel set in a brothel before, in 1967, turning to Joyce's *Ulysses*, a text widely considered to be unadaptable.

Strick later recalled that his father bought a copy of *Ulysses* in Paris in 1929, and it "was around the house as a holy cultural artefact." After reading it at age 16, he considered it as a potential film. The film rights had become available in 1964, and despite competition from 20th Century Fox, Strick secured them for $75,000. Although he initially planned to make an 18-hour film, which would have included every episode from the book, financial constraints saw the running time cut to just over two hours. By Strick's account, the shooting of the film was almost prematurely ended when British Lion, which was financing the film, informed Strick that it was withholding funds despite the fact that shooting had begun. Happily for Strick, the threat coincided with a three-week bank strike in Dublin, so he continued to write checks in the knowledge that the recipients could not attempt to cash them.

Although the screenplay was nominated for an Oscar in 1967, *Ulysses* was refused a certificate by both the censor and the Film Appeals Board in 1967. In the United Kingdom, it was rated "X" after extensive cuts were demanded by the British Board of Film Classification censor for bad language. Strick replaced the offending dialogue with a series of screeches and sounds, thus rendering the scenes unintelligible. (Resubmitted to a new censor, Dermot Breen, in 1974, it was promptly banned again.)

Through the 1970s, Strick continued to direct films looking at the underside of the American Dream, including an adaptation of Henry Miller's *Tropic of Cancer* (1970) and the critically well-received *Road Movie* (1974), a

Cassavettesean tale of two truckers and a prostitute. Ironically, his more radical work was subsidized by his work as a producer on more wholesome fare, such as *Ring of Bright Water* (1969).

In 1977, he returned to Joyce to film *A Portrait of the Artist as a Young Man* with Bosco Hogan as Stephen Dedalus, **T. P. McKenna**, John Gielgud, **Rosaleen Linehan**, Maureen Potter, and Niall Buggy.

Strick would make another visit to Ireland in 2000 to direct Aristophanes' *Ladies Day* at the Granary Theatre in Cork. Happily, this coincided with the decision of film censor Sheamus Smith to finally pass *Ulysses*, which received its first public screening at the **Irish Film Centre** in February 2001.

STRONGBOW FILMS. Despite having already established **Samson Films** in 1983, David Collins partnered with John Kelleher the following year to establish Strongbow in large part with a view to raising funds for what would prove to be the company's only feature film, **Eat the Peach**. Strongbow was designed to take advantage of the recently introduced **Business Expansion scheme** (BES), which allowed private individuals to buy shares in BES-registered companies and to claim tax relief on that investment. Using the BES, Strongbow was ultimately able to raise IR£1.4 million for *Eat the Peach* from 300 investors, a sum that was subsequently augmented by IR£600,000 from **Channel 4** and another IR£100,000 from the **Irish Film Board**.

Buoyed by the success of *Eat the Peach* in the domestic market, the company went on to produce a number of drama series for television and succeeded in finding a U.S. distributor (Skouras Pictures, which had previously enjoyed some success with Peter Greenaway's *A Zed and Two Noughts*) for *Eat the Peach*. However, although the film's initial single-print release in 1987 was considered a success (in its first week, the film's per-screen take was well in excess of the top movie in the United States at the time—Paul Verhoeven's *Robocop*), when the release was broadened to 11 screens at the height of the release, it failed to sustain its performance and was pulled from the U.S. market after six weeks, having earned just over $200,000.

Thereafter, although Strongbow was involved in coproducing at least one more feature (*Innisfree* [1990]), it focused mainly on television production, especially after partnering with Green Apple productions, which brought a track record in popular, mass appeal to the joint enterprise.

STUDS **(2006).** Two decades after its initial outing as one of the most popular plays emerging from the Passion Machine theater company, writer/director Paul Mercier (and former artistic director of the theater company) transposed his own work to the big screen. Emmet Rovers is a catastrophic Sunday League football (soccer) team, routinely having double-figure defeats inflicted on them. Captain Bubbles (**David Wilmot**) is ready to throw in the towel, especially when it emerges that the team's field looks set to fall prey to local developers. Salvation arrives in the form of Walter Keegan (**Brendan Gleeson**), a mercurial figure, rumoured to have semiprofessional footballing experience, who offers his managerial services. Although initially put off by his unconventional—not to say blunt—approach, the team gradually warms to his methods, not least when results start to go their way, both on the field and off. Whipping boys no more, the team finds itself progressing into the later stages of the league cup and begins to dream of hitherto unimagined glory.

Long in gestation—producers Brothers Films originally commissioned Mercier to adapt his play for film in 1996—*Studs* makes a somewhat awkward transition to the cinematic form. In the original play, the mid-1980s setting saw the team composed of a ragtag group of unemployed losers for whom football offered a faint hope of escape from a dreary, quotidian existence. Transposed to the peak of Celtic Tiger excess in 2006, there is, almost by definition, far less at stake for the players and thus for the watching audience. Although the original's humor still shines through, the film—necessarily—drops the stage version's various self-consciously hilarious workarounds prompted by the need to re-create an entire football field within the constraints of a theater space, and Mercier's screen direction, though workmanlike, sees the film rely on cast performances for comic impact rather than exploiting the affordances of the medium.

SUBOTICA ENTERTAINMENT. Named after a city in northern Serbia, Subotica Entertainment Ltd grew out of Subotica Films, which was established in 1994 by Tristan Orpen Lynch, who had worked as a television and commercial producer since 1989. Subotica Films' first major feature production was *Night Train*, starring John Hurt and Brenda Blethyn and directed by Lynch's father, John, himself a former **Radio Telefís Éireann** (RTÉ) director. In June 1999, Lynch and British producer Dominic Wright, along with Paul Moore, the managing director of the **Ardmore Studios** sound postproduction facility, became directors of Subotica Entertainment, a new company set up to produce feature films and large-scale television dramas. Wright had worked in broadcast television since the late 1980s, first on **Channel 4**'s *Week in Politics* program and then as production manager of the **Strongbow**-produced Spanish–Irish coproduction *Innisfree* (1990). He subsequently worked with London-based financiers Film Trustees before moving to Dublin to coproduce *Spaghetti Slow* in 1995. He has subsequently been based in Ireland and began working with Subotica in 1996 while maintaining an occasional sideline as a film and television actor.

Since the establishment of Subotica Entertainment, the company has produced a series of features and large-scale television dramas. These include David Caffrey's *On The Nose* (2001) and the eight-part period drama *Random Passage*, directed by John N. Smith. In 2003, Subotica released Aisling Walsh's ***Song for a Raggy Boy***, which became a major festival hit, followed by Niall Heery's *Small Engine Repair* (2006) and the horror ***The Daisy Chain*** (2008), again directed by Aisling Walsh. Arguably, however, their highest-profile early work within Ireland was their production of two political thriller series for Irish television—*Proof* and *Proof 2*—which aired in 2004 and 2005, respectively, and achieved impressive ratings for RTÉ.

In 2007, Dominic Wright parted ways with the company in order to set up **Ripple World**, a company whose business strategy very much focused on acting as an Irish partner on projects that were usually set overseas. Perhaps driven by the same broader pressures on the Irish industry to internationalize, Subotica appears to have subsequently adopted a similar approach, making non–Irish-themed coproductions a central element of its business model. These productions include the thriller *Terminal* (2018); a Norwegian fantasy adventure film, *The Ash Lad: In the Hall of the Mountain King* (2017); Liv Ullmann's *Miss Julie* (2014) starring Jessica Chastain and **Colin Farrell**; the science fiction film *Young Ones* (2014) starring Nicholas Hoult and Elle Fanning; and **Alan Gilsenan**'s *Unless* (2016), set and shot entirely in Toronto.

THE SUN, THE MOON AND THE STARS **(1996).** This film was a rarity in 1990s Irish cinema in that it was written and directed by a woman, Geraldine Creed, and is because it is a coming-of-age film focusing on young women rather than men. Mo (**Gina Moxley**) abandons her job and her home in Dublin, bringing her two daughters, Dee (Aisling Corcoran) and Shelly (**Elaine Cassidy**), to live in a small seaside resort to escape the unreliable men in their lives, namely, the children's father and Mo's employer. Moderately well received by local critics who were bemused by the casting (which included U.S. actress Angie Dickinson and then Aussie soap heartthrob Jason Donovan), the film received a short and limited Irish release.

SWANSONG: STORY OF OCCI BYRNE **(2009).** Adapted from writer/director Conor McDermottroe's 2004 stage show *Swansong*, this German–Irish coproduction follows the experiences of Austin "Occi" Byrne (Oisin Geraghty as a child and Martin McCann as young adult). Something of an outlier in style and setting and overlooked in terms of critical and audience impact, the film nevertheless revisits recurring themes in Irish cinema of the "long 1990s" in its concern with small-town Ireland, a vulnerable and socially marginal young male protagonist, and the setting of a mental institution.

Occi is child to single mother Bridget (Jodie Whittaker), who is cast out by her conservative father (**Gerard McSorley**) after becoming pregnant. Having initially traveled to the United Kingdom for an abortion, Bridget is unable to go through with the termination and returns to 1970s Sligo. Bullied and stigmatized as a child born out of wedlock, Occi becomes a mentally fragile teenager prone to outbursts of violence and eventually finds himself confined to a mental institution. There, he finds solace and acceptance in the company of another inmate, Mary (Marcella Plunkett), who suffers from depression. He remains driven by an obsession to identify his father and to understand the nature of his parents' relationship.

Debutante director McDermottroe is not afraid to take risks with his material: the film's temporal setting is left vague and ambiguous, voice-over narration from Occi is sporadically dropped into the narrative, and the fourth wall is occasionally broken as the lead character addresses the audience. However, such decisions make for a tonally and stylistically uneven film, the episodic nature of which at times betrays its theatrical origins. Additionally, some of the episodes arguably weaken rather than add to the coherence of the narrative. Nonetheless, McDermottroe's intimate familiarity with the text allows him to coax a sequence of compelling performances from his large cast, including Whittaker as a mother determined to make the best life for her son, Plunkett's sensitive embodiment of melancholy, and both McSorley and Owen Roe as Occi's grandfather and psychiatrist/father figure, respectively, in the institution. But it is Martin McCann's central performance that lingers most: rarely off-screen, he is magnetically watchable, inhabiting the role whether called on to express one of Occi's psychotic outbursts or to wordlessly convey his inner turmoil.

***SWEETY BARRETT* (1999).** Barrett (**Brendan Gleeson**) is a giant of a man with the mind of a child. Having lost his job with the traveling circus, he arrives in the seedy port of Dockery looking for work. He befriends a local woman and develops a close bond with her six-year-old son, Conor, who loves his new playmate. An easy target in this corrupt town, Sweety becomes embroiled in a smuggling operation that unleashes a spiral of dangerous and unexpected events. In a final twist, Sweety triumphs as the unlikely hero against the evil machinations of Detective Bone (**Liam Cunningham**). Writer/director **Stephen Bradley**'s feature debut was heavily criticized for being narratively unconvincing, a criticism frequently aimed at early second-wave Irish film.

T

TEMPLE FILMS. *See* ELEMENT PICTURES.

32A **(2008).** Given the quantity of Irish coming-of-age dramas centered on young men, *32A* stands out because of its focus on four teenage girls dealing with puberty and their changing relationships with friends, boys, and parents. In her feature debut as a director, actress Marian Quinn (sister of **Aidan Quinn**) successfully re-creates the look and feel of 1970s middle-class Dublin suburbia in images of off–lime green/brown-orange interiors, period cars and clothes, and poured-concrete roads.

The narrative follows two strands: 14-year-old Maeve (the wonderfully cast Ailish McCarthy) encounters local Lothario Brian Power (Shane McDaid, a convincing ringer for *Tommy*-era Roger Daltrey) at a party she shouldn't be at. They immediately hit it off, aided by a lying-on-the-ground-staring-at-the-stars sequence lifted straight from Bill Forsyth's *Gregory's Girl*. Girl having met boy, girl then falls out with friends over boy, boy drops girl (nicely enough), and girls make up. The reappearance of the estranged father of one of these friends (and his equally rapid disappearance) constitutes the film's subplot, suggesting that even adult relationships are not always straightforward.

What it is (or was) to be a pubescent girl in Ireland is potentially rich territory and certainly underexplored in Irish cinema. Although *32A* toys with a number of thematic possibilities—teenage sexuality and the unreliability (and even mortality) of parents—it fails to explore them in significant depth. For example, it is unclear as to whether Maeve's stoicism at being dumped in her first "relationship" points to remarkable self-control or signals the performative nature of early courtships. And while 1970s Dublin is created with great attention to detail, the film's portrait of teenage romance remains decidedly chaste.

That the film seems reluctant to explore the very real and intense heat and passion generated by teenage lust is disappointing given parallel depictions of U.S. youth in the films of Larry Park or Catherine Hardwicke's *Thirteen* (an obvious point of comparison for *32A*). Although there are clearly very real differences between Irish teenagers in the 1970s and their 21st- century U.S. or U.K. counterparts, *32A* exhibits tentativeness around approaching representations of teenage sexuality. Thus, while offering a pleasingly nostalgic account of a time that has passed, *32A*'s portrait of Irish teenage girls at a time of dramatic social transformation (Vatican II and large-scale suburbanization) is rather banal and unconvincing.

***THIS IS MY FATHER* (1998).** In this well-regarded Irish American film directed by Paul Quinn, James Caan plays Kieran Johnson, a burned-out American high school teacher whose mother is dying. The depressed son makes the decision to go back to her homeland in Ireland on a pilgrimage of discovery. Accompanying him is his wayward nephew, who will not knuckle down at school. Back in the bogs of Ireland and framed initially by an incongruous symbol of modernity—a powerhouse chimney spewing out steam in the background of their bed-and-breakfast accommodation—he tries to discover the true story of his mother's past. Mrs. Kearney (Moira Deady), the mother of the proprietor of Kieran's hotel, recounts the narrative of the impossible romance between Kieran's mother Fiona Farrelly and the "poorhouse bastard" Kieran O'Day (played in flashback sequences by Moya Farrelly and **Aidan Quinn**, respectively) in rural Galway in 1939. Although they are passionately in love, the wider community—and, in particular, Fiona's mother (the "Widow Flynn" played by Gina Moxley)—disapproves of their relationship and conspires to end it. Although leavened by moments of levity—such as an inexplicable scene featuring John Cusack as a pilot who crash-lands near the village—and a quasi-happy ending in the modern-day time line, the film mainly trades in the screen equivalent of "misery literature" driven by themes of religious morality exploited for personal gain, fear of social nonconformity, and sheer class prejudice. As the film's tagline announces, "When actions were ruled by guilt, fear and prejudice, their love could not flourish."

***THIS IS THE SEA* (1997).** Directed by **Mary McGuckian**, the film is set in Northern Ireland shortly after the 1994 cease-fire and addresses a conventional romance "across the barricades" between a Protestant woman, Hazel (Samantha Morton), and a Catholic man, Malachy (Ross McDade). Both experience personal pressures that threaten to thwart their relationship: Hazel from her religiously conservative mother, who disapproves of Catholics, and Malachy from associates in the Republican movement (embodied in the character of Rohan [**Gabriel Byrne**]) still committed to the use of violence. Reflecting the narrative's Shakespearian template, their relationship seems doomed to failure as they try to affirm their private love within the context of the Troubles.

THIS MUST BE THE PLACE **(2011).** While the rise in coproductions in recent years has forced demands on casting and shooting locations on "Irish" films with variable consequences, *This Must Be the Place* (an Italian–French–Irish coproduction) belies its title to use Ireland as a largely contextless backdrop to a generally daft but oddly engaging story of a middle-aged American rock star escaping his past. Directed and cowritten by Italian director Paolo Sorrentino, Sean Penn plays Cheyenne, a onetime goth-rock idol who now spends his empty days—still in heavy makeup—on Dublin's south side, moving between his clinical mansion, drab shopping centers, and visits to a nameless woman in a suburban terraced house. His retirement from public life followed the suicide of two of his fans, but another aspect of his past weighs even more heavily: his father's incarceration and death at Auschwitz, where he was persecuted by SS officer Alois Lange.

Prompted by the discovery of his father's diary, Cheyenne begins a journey across the United States to track down Lange, first finding his wife and eventually discovering the former Nazi, now very old and blind. After an extended confrontation and meditation on evil and retribution, Cheyenne leaves the old man and returns to Ireland.

Besides its function as a coproduction partner, there seems little to justify the inclusion of Ireland in the narrative. There are small roles for Eve Hewson (daughter of U2 leader Bono) and the striking Olwen Fouéré. Nevertheless, we might also read the film as another in a long line of cinematic texts that position Ireland as home—a space of masculine return and psychic restoration. The title is taken from a Talking Heads song (performed by David Byrne in the film): "Home is where I want to be / Pick me up and turn me round I feel numb." Despite its plot and general indifference to any sense of context, *This Must Be the Place* bears a distant but recognizable kinship with texts as distant and varied as *The Quiet Man* and *Parked*.

THIS OTHER EDEN **(1959).** Directed by Muriel Box, the film is critically considered an acerbic response to the "paddywhackery" of ***The Quiet Man***. The director presents an interesting take on the national mores and presents an engaging historical evaluation of the period. As affirmed through critical work on this radical film, the narrator subverts everything from the romanticism and hero worship of the national struggle to the absolute power of the Catholic Church and other sacred cows of the period. It was also arguably the most interesting film produced by **Ardmore Studios** cofounder **Emmet Dalton**.

THE TIGER'S TAIL **(2006).** Long resident in Ireland and a key figure in supporting an indigenous industry, **John Boorman** is best known for his American and British subjects and has made few efforts to represent his adopted homeland. An exception was *The General* (1998), in **which Brendan Gleeson**—relatively unknown outside Ireland at the time—played infamous Dublin criminal Martin Cahill in a true-crime biopic rendered as farce. It made an international star of Gleeson, and it was therefore unsurprising that Boorman should call on him to play the lead in his very different meditation on contemporary Ireland, the punningly titled *The Tiger's Tail*.

Made at the height of Celtic Tiger hubris, the film centers on property developer Liam O'Leary (Gleeson) as he sets about bringing his fortune and career to new heights by building a sports stadium. However, no sooner has he been awarded Developer of the Year than his seemingly implacable self-belief is shaken by the sudden appearance of a doppelgänger. The intruder soon penetrates his previously inviolable life: buying cars and clothes with his credit and even sleeping with his unsuspecting wife (Kim Catrell). Unnerved, O'Leary returns to the humble rural home of his aging mother in the hope of an explanation.

While topical and well executed by Gleeson, the narrative's all-too-obvious allegorical ambitions ultimately overshadow its dramatic purpose, leading to a film that is unquestionably sincere but self-defeating. Still, it stands as a document of its time and one of a number of film and TV texts from the period that attempted to make sense of the dramatic social and cultural changes wrought by the credit-fueled economic boom.

TIMBUKTU (2004). The second feature release from **Alan Gilsenan** shares much of the fatalism that characterized the narrative of his earlier **All Souls' Day**. When Isobel's (**Eve Birthistle**) brother, a Christian monk (played by Irish singer Liam O'Maonlai), is kidnapped by Algerian rebels, she reunites with their childhood friend Deecy (Karl Geary), and together they set off across the Sahara to find her brother. On arrival, they are assisted by a local hustler whose presence ultimately proves to be a double-edged sword. Again like *All Souls' Day*, the film is characterized by avant-garde camera techniques and the use of multiple shooting formats. The result is less a straight narrative film than a collage of textures and colors that effectively captures the otherness of the Algerian setting. The downside of this technique is underdevelopment of some of the characters: the monk whose disappearance nominally drives the narrative is a chimera, represented mainly by his voice reading letters that he has written to his sister. Meanwhile, the film hints at some childhood trauma as an "explanation" for Deecy's sexuality but never clarifies what this might be. Nonetheless, the sheer strangeness of the context draws the viewer on, and the film is rarely less than absorbing.

***TITANIC TOWN* (1997).** Set during the 1970s, Roger Michell's "postconflict" film foregrounds the impact of the Troubles on the lives of the ordinary inhabitants of Belfast—the town where the ill-fated cruise liner of the title was built. Drawn from Mary Costello's autobiographical novel of her upbringing in 1970s Andersontown, the narrative focuses on Bernie McPhelimy (Julie Walters), whose family has become inured to the presence of helicopters hovering overhead, armored cars patrolling their street, soldiers lying on their lawn, and gunmen crouching in their doorways. But she draws the line when one of her friends is caught in crossfire and killed in front of her young son's eyes. Despite friendly warnings not to get involved in politics, she speaks out in public and becomes involved in the peace process. Despite the opposition of her family, her husband (**Ciarán Hinds**), and a pro-British press, she works to mediate between the British government and the Irish Republican Army, collecting 25,000 petition signatures to limit residential neighborhood fighting. Shot in a realist mode and featuring a compelling central performance from Walters, the film offers an inspirational portrait of one woman's fight to resist the status quo made at a moment when the contemporary peace process was paying dividends.

TOIBIN, NIALL (1929–). In his autobiography, Toibin refers to his screen roles as "the compulsory series of priests, IRA men and drunkards that were the lot of your middle-grade Irish Thespian before it started showering Oscars from Heaven" (Toibin 1995). However, this is an all-too-modest assessment of his career. Toibin's wily and adaptable persona made him a highly visible incarnation of a certain brand of stage/screen Irishness for many years.

Born in Cork, he made his first stage appearance in primary school. On leaving secondary school, he took the civil service entrance exam and in January 1947 moved to Dublin to join the Department of Supplies. He would later move to the Department of External Affairs, where he was assigned to work to the **Cultural Relations Committee**. On arriving in Dublin, he also joined the Gaelic League, where he renewed his interest in drama. Between 1947 and 1953, he also worked with the Compántas Amharclainne na Gaeilge theater group and did some semiprofessional work at the **Abbey Theatre**.

In 1953, he left the civil service to take up a position with the **Radio Telefís Éireann** (RTÉ) Repertory Company, where he remained until 1967. In addition to his radio and (from 1962) television work, he was also a constant presence on Dublin stages and became involved in film, acting as narrator on three **Louis Marcus** shorts—*Capallology, Golf,* and *Fleadh.* In 1964, he appeared in Brendan Behan's *The Hostage* at the Gaiety Theatre, commencing an association with the playwright that would establish Toibin as the definitive interpreter of Behan's works. (Toibin had known Behan since 1952, before any of his plays were staged, and bore a remarkable resemblance to the writer.) Despite this, Toibin did not appear in either of the two English-language features based on Behan's works: *The Quare Fellow* (1962) and **Borstal Boy** (2000).

Having played every conceivable type of role in his stint with RTÉ, Toibin went freelance in 1967, attracted by the prospect of appearing in Brian Friel's *Lovers* at the Gaiety. It proved a safe move, for he was rarely been out of work thereafter. In 1968, he appeared in a Disney film shot in Ireland, *Guns in the Heather*, then spent several months in 1969 in Dingle for his role as O'Keefe, a political Irish Republican Army member, in **Ryan's Daughter**. From Dingle, he went straight to Broadway to appear in a Tony Award–winning production of *Borstal Boy*. In the early 1970s, he also developed a comedy sideline, devising a one-man show that he continued to perform for decades after. (Two comedies produced for RTÉ—*If the Cap Fits* [1973] and *Time Now, Mr T* [1977]—were considered too risqué to receive extended runs.)

His key film role of the 1970s was in **Bob Quinn**'s **Poitín**, where he played Labhcas opposite **Cyril Cusack** and **Donal McCann**. Gone was the comic persona that Irish audiences had become familiar with, replaced by a sly and ruthless "cute hoor," concerned only with his own advancement. It is his least garrulous screen role and arguably his best.

In 1977, RTÉ television commissioned Toibin to create a satirical weekly comedy, *Time Now, Mr T*. Although critically well received, the show's merciless skewering of Irish society generated some enmity, and RTÉ declined to renew it after one series. At a loose end, he decamped to London to join the National Theatre, and a slew of roles on British television followed. These included his turn as Slipper—another cute hoor—in the **Channel 4** comedy *The Irish R.M.* He has remained a staple of such series ever since, becoming a recurring character in *Stay Lucky* (1990–1993) opposite Dennis Waterman, as Father MacAnally in the BBC's *Ballykissangel* in the 1990s, and from 2003 to 2005 as the father of **Amy Huberman**'s character in in RTÉ's *The Clinic*. This work was interspersed with the occasional feature film: he played a comic show band promoter in **Eat the Peach** (1986), appeared down the cast in **Pat O'Connor**'s *Fools of Fortune* (1990) (having earlier appeared in that director's *Ballroom of Romance* [1982]), and then played Tom Cruise's father in **Far and Away** (1992). Toward the end of the 2000s, he effectively withdrew from public performing. *The Clinic* proved his last major screen role, and the curtain fell on his renowned stage comedy for the last time in 2008. Awarded a Lifetime Achievement Award by the **Irish Film and Television Academy** in 2011, he still makes very occasional forays onto the big screen in locally produced work, including the Ian Campnell–directed *Remains* (2018).

TOWNSEND, STUART (1972–). Townsend grew up in Howth, County Dublin, son of international golfer Peter Townsend and international model Lorna Townsend. He made his stage debut at school before appearing in two productions of *Borstal Boy* at the Gaiety Theatre. His first major theater role was in *Intermission* director John Crowley's critically acclaimed *True Lines* after appearing in a number of student films (including Eve Morrison's acclaimed *Summertime*). Townsend made an eye-catching feature film debut in Gilles Mackinnon's film of Billy Roche's *Trojan Eddie* (1996) as a young Traveller who runs off with **Richard Harris**'s new bride. He immediately followed this with low-budget British indie hit *Shooting Fish* (1997) opposite Kate Beckinsale, bringing him to the attention of a much wider audience.

In 1998, he played the title role in the adaptation of Eoin McNamee's novel *Resurrection Man*, playing an almost seductively psychotic Loyalist paramilitary with a perverse sexuality. More roles in British films followed before what is arguably his best role to date: the eponymous lead in **Gerry Stembridge**'s *About Adam* (2000). The film again played on Townsend's seductive appeal, but this time, it was wrapped up in a much more palatable package: a character whose background alters to suit whatever the listener wants to hear. Adam is quickly established as someone for whom constancy is impossible, but Townsend successfully pulls off the task of retaining audience sympathy for his mysterious Lothario.

Since then, he has worked largely in American cinema, first in *Queen of the Damned* opposite pop singer Aaliyah and then in a series of films that despite A-list stars and directors somehow failed to make an impact. These include *Trapped* (2002) opposite Charlize Theron, who subsequently became his partner—inexplicably, as her star ascended his began to fade. Even those films that succeeded in achieving global releases, such as *The League of Extraordinary Gentlemen* (2004), in which he played Dorian Gray, were considered to have underperformed. He was notoriously cast in the key role of Aragorn in Peter Jackson's take on *The Lord of the Rings* trilogy but was replaced by Viggo Mortensen after a few weeks of shooting as "creative differences" emerged between himself and Jackson.

Thereafter, Townsend has been seen mainly as a lead in often short-lived North American television series: as newspaper reporter Cal Kolchak investigating supernatural disturbances in *Night Stalker* (2005–2006), the reboot of the 1970s chiller *Kolchak*; as the titular XIII (Thirteen), an amnesiac secret agent in *XIII* (2011); as a lawyer engaged in a torrid affair with a married woman in ABC's *Betrayal* (2013–2014); and as the inquisitive Dr. Samuel Wainright in 17th-century America in *Salem* (2014–2017).

TRAVELLER (1981). Adapted from **Neil Jordan**'s first screenplay (though he has since disowned the film, saying it did not reflect his vision), this pioneering and infrequently seen story by **Joe Comerford** (his first feature film) concerns a newlywed couple of **Travellers** (Irish Gypsies)—Angela Devine (Jody Donovan) and Michael Connors (Davy Spillane)—as they embark on a road journey through 1980s Ireland.

Michael's father has demanded a dowry for the marriage, so the newlyweds are sent up north to smuggle radios and televisions back to the south. They pick up a hitchhiker, a renegade Irish Republican Army member, Clicky (Alan Devlin), whose presence complicates their attempts to negotiate unapproved roads around the border and encounters with the British army. The elliptical narrative is effectively directed with an almost anthropological attention to the music and outlook of the Traveller community, with music and singing performed by Spillane. Critics singled the film out for its raw realism and the refusal to apply Hollywood sentimentality or romanticization to its depiction of landscape and outcasts. This is most reflected in the ending, which, as is the case in many films of the Irish "first wave" (as well as 1970s films more generally), is open and inconclusive. Recasting a narrative trope of emigration for the 1980s, the film's protagonists leave their hopeless and inhospitable native land for an uncertain future overseas.

TRAVELLERS. Travellers are an indigenous minority of about 30,000 people living in Ireland. The most widely held belief about their origins holds that they were peasant farmers who had been thrown off the land in the wake of the Famine of the 1840s, although other accounts suggest earlier origins. Many still continue to be involved in scrap collection work as well as horse dealing and other short-term occupations. Their community is typically associated with strong Catholic beliefs and tight communal and family values. Furthermore, many speak their own dialect—Cant—which is rarely included in Irish film (although, ironically, Hollywood star Brad Pitt delivered a version of it in the comic British gangster film *Snatch* [2000]). Described as a nomadic group, many travel throughout the islands of England and Ireland while living temporarily in designated halting sites or, more controversially, camping illegally on the side of the road. Over the years, many Travellers have become "settled," living in various designated sites, but continue to encounter prejudicial and even racial resentment from the majority settled community.

Irish cinema has a long history of using Travellers as shorthand for ethnic "otherness," thereby reinforcing a sense of difference between them and the settled Irish community. Such conflicts are evident in films like *The Field* (1990), in which the Traveller's horse is disposed of at the start of the film and whose owners later demand compensation; *Country* (2000), in which Travellers are scapegoated for a crime; or *Man About Dog* (2004), in which they are portrayed as comic characters who buy a dog and prove the animal's worth in a subsequent race.

However, in a number of Irish films, Travellers are romanticized, seen as a group free to roam the country, unfettered by the socially imposed obligations faced by the settled community. This is most evident in *Into the West* (1992), which nostalgically re-creates a close-knit Traveller family and follows two young boys as they ride their mythic white horse west to discover their mother.

Alternative examples tend to look more critically and adapt a less nostalgic lens as the Travellers strive to survive and change with the times, as they do in films like **Joe Comerford**'s *Traveller* and *Trojan Eddie*. *Traveller* tells the often violent story of interfamily rivalry and uses an avant-garde style that often draws attention to its study of the otherness of the Travellers. Nevertheless, the strength of the film comes from its ability to get beyond the violence and shine a light on the pleasures of the Traveller community. Similarly, *Trojan Eddie*, although operating on a more conventional and prosaic level, also foregrounds a very strong and self-contained Traveller community and tries to frame the story from the inside out rather than voyeuristically objectifying this alien community.

In *Travellers* (2001), photographer Alen Weeney (together with director **John T. Davis**) effectively applies a tradition of the ethnographic study of the romantic exoticism of the Travellers, revisiting the Traveller subjects of photographs he took in the 1960s. Similarly, Perry Ogden, who spent a lot of time photographing the Travellers for his 1999 study *Pony Kids* (romanticized in *Crushproof* [1998]), subsequently made the sensitive and well-regarded art house film *Pavee Lackeen* (Traveller Girl) (2005), which was a domestic art house success and won several awards for its sense of authenticity and respect for its subjects. The film treads the line between **documentary** realism and fiction, with the audience invited into the life of 10-year-old Winnie (Maughan) as her family confront various authority figures. All the actors were nonprofessionals from the Traveller community.

More recently, actor/screenwriter/activist (and former Irish boxing champion) John Connors has broken new ground for the Traveller community through his profile and performances in **Mark O'Connor**'s *Stalker*, *King of the Travellers* (2012), *Cardboard Gangsters* (2017) (which he coscripted), and **Radio Telefís Éireann**'s *Love/Hate*. While *Cardboard Gangsters* was the largest-grossing Irish film of 2017 and won Connors the 2018 IFTA Best Actor award for his performance, his acceptance speech observation that it remains difficult for him to find an agent or be cast outside of his background points to the ongoing prevalence of ethnic divides in Irish society.

TREASURE FILMS/TREASURE ENTERTAINMENT. Treasure Films was jointly founded by producer Robert Walpole and director **Paddy Breathnach** in 1992 in the wake of their critically successful 1991 **short film** *A Stone of the Heart*, which won the Special Jury Prize at the 1991 Cork

Film Festival. Since then, Treasure has produced a wide range of material for broadcast and cinema release. Treasure Entertainment, a related but distinct entity, was set up by Walpole and fellow producer Rebecca O'Flanagan in 2001.

Walpole studied economics and political philosophy at the university before embarking on a film career as a location scout on *The Commitments* (1991) and then as an assistant director on *The Snapper* (1993). Breathnach and Walpole's first production as Treasure Films came the following year with *The Road to America*, a **documentary** on Ireland's 1994 World Cup campaign. It was a major hit and provided a sound financial basis for the company.

The company initially concentrated on television production work, including the Breathnach-directed *W.R.H.*, a documentary series focusing on a regional hospital in Waterford. Although Breathnach's first feature, *Ailsa* (1994), was produced by **Ed Guiney** for **Temple Films**, its success at the San Sebastian Film Festival, where it won the Euskal Media prize, directly benefited Treasure. Treasure used part of the prize funds to finance the company's first feature, *I Went Down* (1997), which Breathnach directed from a **Conor McPherson** script.

The film was a major commercial and critical success in Ireland and was widely distributed across Europe, where it recorded 240,000 admissions. In 1998, Artisan Entertainment picked up the U.S. rights and released the film in 69 cinemas. Although it performed relatively poorly—peaking at 100,000 admissions—it was nonetheless sufficient to secure Treasure a two-year first-look deal with Fine Line Features, the art house subsidiary of mini-major New Line. The deal was brokered by Justin Moore-Lewy, a Dublin-based agent for the International Creative Management talent agency, who would subsequently become a director of the company that grew out of Treasure Films: Treasure Entertainment.

Treasure's first project under the Fine Line deal was to have been an adaptation by Dublin author Joe O'Connor of his own novel *Cowboys and Indians*. However, the deal fell through, and although Treasure's next feature release—*Southpaw*, a 1999 documentary on boxer Francis Barrett—was released in the United States, it was distributed by an independent company: The Shooting Gallery.

Treasure produced three more features before reestablishing as Treasure Entertainment. *I Went Down* screenwriter McPherson turned director in 2001, adapting his play *This Lime Tree Bower* as the Walpole-produced *Saltwater*, which premiered at the 2001 Berlin Film Festival.

In 2004, founding partner Breathnach made his second feature for the company, *Man About Dog*, which, despite a lukewarm critical response, was one of the most successful indigenous films of recent years at the Irish box office, becoming the 10th most successful release of 2004. And in 2005, Treasure produced *The Mighty Celt*, directed by *Man About Dog*'s screenwriter Pearse Elliott and starring Robert Carlyle and Gillian Anderson.

Treasure Entertainment consists of Walpole and **Rebecca O'Flanagan**, former development manager of the **Irish Film Board**, and together they have assembled a busy, commercially minded slate of projects with a strong international focus. Along with Breathnach—with whom they produced *Viva* (2016)—Treasure formed an ongoing creative relationship with John Butler, with whom they have made *The Stag* (2013), *Handsome Devil* (2016), and *Papi Chulo* (2018). Other credits include BAFTA-nominated *Good Vibrations* (2012) and the multitalented **Hugh O'Conor**'s directorial debut, *Metal Heart* (2018).

***TROJAN EDDIE* (1996).** This British–Irish crime drama film is directed by Glasgow-based Gillies MacKinnon from a screenplay by acclaimed Wexford playwright Billy Roche. While it notably shares themes with several other Irish films of the 1990s (**Travellers**, masculinity, and a longing for the past), its central drama is realized with great sensitivity and offered audiences another highlight in **Richard Harris**'s later career revival.

Trojan Eddie (**Stephen Rea**) is a market hawker with a gift of gab who sells a variety of wares from the back of his van on behalf of the tyrannical John Power (Harris), the self-styled "King of the Travellers." Eddie is a likable but hapless ex-convict whose wife has left him, and he is bringing up their two children alone. However, his relationship with Power sours when his nephew Dermot (**Stuart Townsend**) runs away with Power's new young bride, Kathleen (Alison McGuckian). It is left to Eddie to try to pursue them in order to defend himself against criminal masculinities more brutal than himself.

Told from the point of view of Eddie, the film is unusual in that it positions a member of the settled community as the outsider in a world where the norms and customs of the Traveller community are hegemonic. Furthermore, the Travellers' lifestyle is not romanticized but rather is offered as a peculiar blend of old traditions and often unpleasant contemporary practices. McKinnon's direction was widely praised for both the performances he elicits from a talented cast and the atmospheric quality of the cinematography that simultaneously reveals and romanticizes contemporary rural Ireland.

***TROUBLE WITH SEX* (2005).** After his feature debut with *Flick* (2000) and numerous documentaries on television, Fintan Connolly went on to make this Celtic Tiger–set romantic drama. A relatively conventional story line is imbued with strong sexual tension and emotional conflict intended to reflect a changed Ireland.

The story concerns Michelle (Renée Weldon), a hardworking lawyer who, dissatisfied with her relationship with Ivan (Declan Conlon) and over-wrought by her mother's illness, walks into a pub run by Conor (**Aidan Gillen**). Conor, lonely and single, becomes Michelle's new romantic focus, although she fails to mention her disintegrating relationship with Ivan. By the time he discovers the truth, an intense sexual bond has been established with Conor, and, hurt, he abruptly leaves, never to return. In a late scene, they pass each other on the street, at first ignoring each other before embracing.

Notwithstanding its rather juvenile plot and an emotional simplicity, *Trouble with Sex* can be seen as a sincere effort to create a new palate of concerns for Irish cinema, locating it in the tradition of the kind of cosmopolitan romance revisited time and again in French cinema. That it fails to achieve this is largely due to a lack of emotional depth and the characters being drawn too broadly: nothing here feels entirely convincing. Its enticing tagline conveys its aspirations toward a newly liberated Ireland as well as its inad-vertent, lingering conservatism: "The trouble with sex is that you can fall in love."

TV3. TV3 is a commercial television broadcaster that was first licensed in 1989 but did not commence operations in Ireland until 1998 due to difficulty securing adequate financial backing. These were largely addressed in 1997 when Canadian media conglomerate CanWest took a 45 percent stake in the station, endowing it with the financial and programming muscle to go on air. British independent broadcaster GranadaCarlton subsequently also acquired a 45 percent stake in the station, leaving the remaining 10 percent in Irish hands.

Although in its early years TV3 came under consistent criticism for its reliance on imported material and its failure to commission local producers, between 2000 and 2004, it was arguably more supportive of Irish film than **Radio Telefís Éireann** (RTÉ), investing in seven television dramas or films, including *The Mapmaker* (2001), *The Honeymooners* (2003), and *The Halo Effect* (2004). In contrast to RTÉ, which in the mid-1990s, for example, partially funded a series of films as a means of fulfilling public service obligations, TV3's strategy has been to invest small amounts (around €50,000) in low-budget films for commercial purposes with a view to devel-oping long-term business relationships with filmmakers. TV3 also supported the theatrical release of films it invests in with on-air advertising promotion. Responsibility for deciding which films to invest in initially lay with then commissioning editor Jane Gogan, a founding member of **Film Base** and an independent film producer in her own right who subsequently became head of drama at RTÉ.

In 2006, TV3 was acquired by Doughty Hanson, a U.K. venture capital fund, for €260 million. Confounding standard venture capital practice, Doughty Hanson invested heavily in local programming led by former Channel 4 commissioning editor Ben Frow. Although such programming was dominated by nonfiction formats, the channel did make a tentative move into serial drama production with *The Guards* (2007) and *Deception* (2011). Faced with the loss of key dramas imported from the United Kingdom (e.g., *Coronation Street* and *Emmerdale*) after they were acquired by new market entrant UTV Ireland in 2015, TV3 significantly upped its drama investment, launching *Red Rock*, a soap serial set around an Irish police station. However, between 2015 and 2016, both TV3 and UTV Ireland were acquired by U.S. cable giant Liberty Global, which folded both into the TV3 stable. Such backing has allowed TV3 to continue funding both local television drama and indigenous film production, including small investments in recent hits *A Date for Mad Mary* (2016) and *Cardboard Gangsters* (2017).

TWICE SHY (2017). While unplanned pregnancies are a recurring theme in Irish cinema (e.g., **Hush-a-Bye Baby** [1989], *The Snapper* [1993], and *Felicia's Journey* [1999]), extensive explorations of abortion as a possible response to that scenario are much rarer, not least due to the constitutional prohibition on terminations upheld by the eighth amendment to the Irish Constitution in 1983. *Twice Shy*, then, joined a select body of Irish fiction works and arrived at a time when there was growing pressure on Irish politicians to liberalize laws relating to fertility and female bodily autonomy. (This would ultimately result in a May 2018 referendum that saw the constitutional ban on abortion removed.)

Structured as a series of flashbacks over the course of a car journey, the film follows the burgeoning romance between Maggie (Iseult Casey) and Andy (Shane Murray-Corcoran) as they prepare to leave secondary school. The triptych narrative moves from Tipperary to—as their relationship develops—Dublin and then, after Maggie becomes pregnant with a child neither are prepared for, on to London to secure a termination. Both are counseled by their respective fathers—**Pat Shortt** and Ardal O'Hanlon in extended cameos—as they contemplate what impact the termination will have on their relationship.

Given the febrile atmosphere around the abortion debate in Ireland out of which *Twice Shy* emerged, one might have expected an "issues" movie where the respective positions of pro-choice and antiabortion groups were dutifully outlined and worked through. However, while these perspectives are acknowledged in passing, *Twice Shy* pulls off the neat trick of avoiding polemic and treating abortion—and the associated trip to London that Irish legal restrictions necessitated—as a simple reality (albeit one rarely publicly discussed) of Irish life. (In this regard, official figures in Ireland estimate that between 1980 and 2016, an average of 17 women left Ireland every day to travel overseas to secure abortion services.)

Having completed his debut feature, *Trampoline* (2014), for less than €1,000, Nenagh native Tom Ryan had a bigger budget (secured from private sources) for his follow-up, but the film remained a low-budget undertaking limited to a three-week shoot. Nonetheless, sympathetic casting (Casey and Murray-Corcoran have real chemistry, while Shortt and O'Hanlon, as psychologically frail paternal figures, turn in sensitive performances), a straightforward visual look, and, in particular, a remarkably mature script facilitate an evenhanded treatment of a subject the discussions of which in Ireland are more often characterized by heat than light.

2BY4 (1997). The central character, Johnny (Jimmy Smallhorne, who also directs the film), has moments of severe trauma due to well-sublimated memories. He works for his uncle, Trump (Chris O'Neill), who embezzles wages to pay for illicit sex with black male prostitutes. Finally, Johnny uncovers the root of his trauma, which occurred when he was a child back in Ireland and involved his uncle. Issues of gay and bisexual identity, which some critics regard as somewhat problematic in its apparent linkage of pedophilia and homosexuality, are transferred to the Irish American diaspora.

U

***ULYSSES* (1967).** Given cinema's historical tendency to borrow from other media, it was inevitable that someone would attempt to adapt what was arguably the 20th century's most famous novel. However, the very characteristics that won the book renown—stream-of-consciousness narrative, constantly shifting style, and so on—arguably rendered it unfilmable. It is also very long, hardly surprising given that **James Joyce** described his intent in writing it as being to create a picture of Dublin so complete that if the city suddenly disappeared from the earth, it could be reconstructed from the book.

Although Joyce suggested in correspondence with Sergei Eisenstein that the great Soviet master himself should film it, it was left to American independent director **Joseph Strick** to make the first stab at portraying the fictional events of 16 June 1904, the day in the life of his beloved city, Dublin, that the emigrant writer Joyce re-creates. Nothing if not ambitious, Strick attempted to include each of the book's original "episodes" but adapted an accessible, humorous approach in doing so, one that arguably has more in common with the writing of Flann O'Brien than that of Joyce. The most attractive part of the film is its cast; it is a who's who of Irish actors and actresses, including **Milo O'Shea** (as Bloom), **T. P. McKenna**, Anna Manahan, Maureen Potter, Martin Dempsey, Joe Lynch, **Fionnuala Flanagan**, **David Kelly**, **Rosaleen Linehan**, Brendan Cauldwell, **Tony Doyle**, Des Keogh, Eugene Lambert, O. Z. Whitehead, Biddy White-Lennon, Tomas Mac-Anna, and a host of others.

Ironically, despite being shot in Ireland, it was banned by the **censor** when presented for certification because of Molly's famous sexually explicit soliloquy and other explicit content in the novel that was faithfully adapted. In a double irony, Strick's script (written with Fred Haines) subsequently received an **Oscar** nomination for Best Screenplay.

V

***THE VAN* (1996).** This film is part of **Roddy Doyle**'s Barrytown novel trilogy, alongside **Alan Parker**'s *The Commitments* (1991) and *The Snapper* (1993), directed by Stephen Frears. **Colm Meaney** reprises his *Commitments* role of Jimmy Curley, whose best friend, Bimbo (Donal O'Kelly), loses his job in a bakery, reducing him to the status long endured by Jimmy and the rest of his mates. Out on the town to drown Bimbo's sorrows, the pair curse the lack of a fish-and-chips van in the locality and decide to invest Bimbo's redundancy money in providing one. As in the rest of the trilogy, Dublin argot and the working-class vernacular are used for humorous effect, but the film as a whole feels less fully realized than previous adaptations of Doyle's novels.

***VERONICA GUERIN* (2003).** Both *Veronica Guerin* (2003), directed by Joel Schumacker, and *When the Sky Falls* (1999), directed by John McKenzie, are based on the true story of a *Sunday Independent* journalist who was assassinated by a criminal gang in 1996 and whose death indirectly sparked a radical overhaul of the criminal justice system in Ireland. At the outset, one could suggest that this heroic story of human sacrifice is reminiscent of the Irish mythos of self-sacrifice and that it plays into stereotypical clichés that a Hollywood director can draw on while making it easier for universal audiences to identify with.

Veronica Guerin in particular conforms to a feel-good Hollywood convention of heroes fighting for justice. Only when individuals take a stand for what is transparently good and right does change for the better take place. Such broad Hollywood narrative trajectories usually privilege personal agency while negating the effectiveness of reorganizing the system in the fight against political and other societal problems. This approach has come under extensive academic criticism under the rubric of what has come to be called "screen theory." Nevertheless, one might argue that such a simplistic structural reading belies a more complex engagement with the representation of the heroine's performance as a journalist.

When the Sky Falls was the first cinematic take on the Veronica Guerin story, although the names of the characters were fictionalized. American actress Joan Allen plays the Guerin character, with **Patrick Bergin** as Detective Mackie and Pete Postlethwaite as a criminal modeled on "The General" (a criminal overlord also at the center of **John Boorman**'s film *The General* [1998]). This more authentic yet strangely dispassionate version fails to connect with audiences as effective fictional narrative. Nevertheless, it provides sharper dialogue that allows for an appreciation of the function of the journalist and a more explicit critique of the role of the *Sunday Globe* (*Sunday Independent*), where Guerin worked when she was killed. But much of the discursive analysis of the circumstances of Veronica's death is frequently delivered in a nondramatic and somewhat uninteresting fashion. Consequently, this version received poor reviews and fared badly at the box office, while the later, less discursive big-budget version, *Veronica Guerin*, was much more successful.

Comparing the two versions of the story, the latter Hollywood cinematic treatment wins hands down. While certainly compromised, at least *Veronica Guerin* provides a stronger sense of drama, empathy, and enjoyment. The film passed the €4.1 million box office mark by the end of 2003 in Ireland, thus eclipsing any other "Irish" film. The casting of Cate Blanchett in the title role, with her proficient Irish accent, is regarded by many as a major reason for its success in Ireland compared with Joan Allen's more staid and less celebrity-driven performance.

Generically, *When the Sky Falls* fits more neatly into the crime genre, with highly conventional and stereotypical evocations of criminals and the police. This doubtless explains the choice of director John McKenzie, who two decades earlier directed the seminal gangster film *The Long Good Friday* (1979). In particular, Detective Mackie (Patrick Bergin) is presented as totally frustrated in his attempts to capture the criminals and blames the switching of resources to protect the border in the north. Like many Hollywood crime busters, he becomes as devious and ruthless as the criminals, supporting the proposition that the end justifies the means. Like similar characters in films like *The Untouchables* (1987) but lacking their ethical values, he calls on his fellow officers to follow him in an attempt to capture the enemy while citing the slogan over the police station that translates as "Let justice be done or the sky falls."

The forces of law and order are less compromised in *Veronica Guerin*, and in a more heroic dénouement, the emotional effect of her murder is reinforced by an unseen boy singing the classic Irish ballad "The Fields of Athenry" alongside the hypnotic voice of **Sinead O'Connor**, while the audience is visually treated to a bird's-eye view of her body as it lies in a painterly repose with her eyes wide open. Her martyred body is symmetrically positioned within her sporty red car, seen through an open sunroof, whereas in *When the Sky Falls*, the re-creation of her death is less dramatic both aurally and visually: we see her car sans sunroof, and the scene lacks cinematic potency.

VOLTA.IE. Deriving its name from one of the earliest dedicated picture houses in Ireland, Volta is an online direct download platform offering access to Irish (and international) films developed by **Element Pictures** with financial support from the **Irish Film Board** and the European Union's MEDIA program. The site was developed in conjunction with Universcine, a platform owned by a consortium of French film producers and distributors that had been offering access to French content since 2007. As of 2019, the heavily curated site offers access to just under 1,000 titles, of which about 10 percent are Irish. However, Irish titles account for a substantially higher proportion of revenues: 40 percent of all rentals (i.e., short-term downloads) and 70 percent of sell-through downloads (which permanently reside on customer hard disks). Although offering access to more Irish titles than any other site, the nature of international distribution deals means that Volta's offering is geo-blocked and thus exclusively available to customers with Irish IP addresses. Volta's status as part of the Element Pictures stable, which also includes two cinemas—the **Light House** in Dublin and Pálás in Galway—allows the parent company an unusual copresence in both traditional and new media routes to content distribution. Films that are acquired for screening in the Light House thus often appear simultaneously on the online platform.

WAKE WOOD (2009). Producer Brendan McCarthy of **Fantastic Films** (noted for its slate of horror-themed work) took a draft script he had produced for a screenwriting master's program at the Dún Laoghaire Institute of Art, Design, and Technology and turned it into a finished piece. Support from the newly re-formed Hammer Films label in the United Kingdom raised a €2.5 million budget and secured the services of David Keating (*Last of the High Kings*) as director, with **Aiden Gillen**, **Eva Birthwhistle**, and, in a twinkle-eyed turn, British actor Timothy Spall in the lead roles.

Shot in Pettigo, Donegal, the film follows Patrick, a veterinarian, and his pharmacist wife, Louise, as they flee to Wake Wood, a small Irish village, after their daughter, Alice, is savaged to death by an attack dog. There, they encounter Arthur (Spall), the local embodiment of the landed gentry but also, it emerges, the principal figure of Wake Wood's coven of witches who have harnessed the power to—temporarily at least—restore the dead to life. Still distraught with grief, the couple accede to Arthur's suggestion that they bring Alice back to enjoy three final days with her. However, unwilling to let Alice "return to the ground," the couple embark on a course that unleashes a savage, dark force.

On one level, *Wake Wood* is an exploration of the struggle between a civilized humanity and a not-entirely-tamed nature. The reanimated Alice opines to her father (as he stitches an injured dog) that humans shouldn't hurt animals but, equally, that animals shouldn't hurt humans. He agrees with the first premise but suggests that the second is something different: animals—and, by extension, nature—are posited as something we cannot fully understand and therefore beyond human agency. Wake Wood village embodies this divide, its boundaries demarcated by constantly turning wind turbines, a modern manifestation of an ancient attempt to harness of nature.

As a genre piece, the film is inevitably derivative, echoing the work of Stephen King (notably *Carrie* and *Pet Sematary*), Robin Hardy's *The Wicker Man* (in its depiction of an apparently contemporary community versed in something like witchcraft), and even Nicholas Roeg's *Don't Look Now*. For the most part, however, director Keating eschews the heart-stopping-horror-edit-every-five-minutes characteristic of modern horror: though there's gore aplenty, it's well signaled in advance. What emerges instead is a potentially more interesting drama of the impossibility of coping with loss as a parent. The couple clearly know that their pact with the beyond (mediated by Arthur) can come to no good but (such is their grief) blindly enter into it regardless. Although that experience turns sour, a truly macabre coda suggests that the desire to conquer death will trump any rational attempt to come to terms with it.

***WAKING NED (WAKING NED DEVINE)* (1998).** This Kirk Jones–directed film stars Ian Bannen and **David Kelly** as Jackie and Michael, two senior citizens living in the fictional coastal village of Tullymore. When the National Lottery announces that a local has won the top prize, the whole village goes to great lengths to find out who it is. However, when it emerges that the winner—Ned Devine—has died of shock on discovering his win, the village engages in an elaborate plot to pretend he is still alive to allow them all to collect the money. Shot on the Isle of Man to avail itself of local tax incentives, the film became an international hit (taking in $24 million in the United States), apparently confirming the view that only films representing Ireland as prelapsarian, pastoral, and populated by lovable rogues and amiable drunks can find favor in the international market.

WALSH, AISLING (1958–). After studying fine art at the Dún Laoghaire Institute of Art, Design, and Technology, writer and director Walsh graduated from the National Film School, Beaconsfield. After an early short film, *Hostage* (1984), her first feature, *Joyriders* (1998), told the story of a widow, Mary (Patricia Kerrigan), who is forced to leave her home with her two children and face life on the streets, where she is vulnerable but defiant. Over the next few years, she honed her skills in British TV. She returned to Irish topics with *Sinners* (2002), a pioneering feature-length TV drama on the Magdalen laundries. (*The Magdalene Sisters* was made the same year but received wider attention.) Her many prestigious TV credits include the Victorian-set miniseries *Fingersmith* (2005), adapted from Sarah Waters's Man Booker Prize–nominated novel; *A Poet in New York* (2014), dealing with Dylan Thomas's last day at the Chelsea Hotel; and *An Inspector Calls* (2015), an adaptation of the J. B. Priestly novel. Her TV career has been interspersed with notable forays into theatrical feature films. *Song for a Raggy Boy* (2003)—arguably her most effective film to date—continued her interest in Irish-set narratives dealing with themes of gender and power. *The Daisy Chain* (2007) was an uncharacteristic—and largely unsuccessful—genre piece starring Samantha Morton. A psychological horror/changeling narrative set in the Irish countryside, it dealt with a young couple grieving for their deceased baby who adopt an orphaned autistic girl called Daisy with unexpected consequences. The well-received *Maudie* (2016) was set in 1930s rural Nova Scotia and based on the real life and times of a folk artist, Maudie, who suffers from severe arthritis. A touching and delicately told love story starring Ethan Hawke and Sally Hawkins, the film can be seen as continuing Walsh's interest in female characters in marginal settings.

WALSH, ENDA (1970–). Best known as a writer for the stage, Dublin-born Walsh has had a tangential relationship with film to date, mostly through adaptations. At the forefront of a hugely talented generation of "new" Irish dramatists (including **Conor McPherson**, Mark O'Rowe, Martin McDonagh, and Marina Carr), Walsh came to widespread attention with his remarkable play/screenplay *Disco Pigs*, the filmic adaptation of which, directed by Kirsten Sheridan in 2001, gave **Cillian Murphy** his screen debut. (Murphy had played the role in the original 2006 stage production.) In the intense and highly verbal play, two friends, "Pig" and "Runt," set out to celebrate their 17th birthdays in the nightclubs of Cork. Inseparable and violent creatures, they have developed their own language from birth, and the play captures their intense energy with equal feeling for the monstrous amid the mundane—elements also present in Walsh's later plays, which include *The Walworth Farce* and *Ballyturk*.

In 2008, Walsh wrote the screenplay for Steve McQueen's award-winning debut, ***Hunger***, based on the incarceration and death of Irish Republican Army hunger striker Bobby Sands, played with physical and psychological intensity by **Michael Fassbender** in his breakthrough role. Psychologically austere and punishing, the film is especially remembered for Walsh's brilliant 23-minute dialogue sequence between Sands and moderate Belfast priest Father Moran (**Liam Cunningham**), which brings their conflicting ideological positions to the fore. While he also scored commercial and critical success with the stage adaptation of **John Carney**'s *Once* (2007) and David Bowie's *Lazarus*, Walsh has tended to avoid the lure of film, preferring the intensely interpersonal dynamics of the theater.

WARD ANDERSON. Although long synonymous with a position of prominence in the Irish **exhibition** sector, there has never been a single company called Ward Anderson. Instead, there was a group of (at one point at least 50) companies, including Provincial Cinemas Ltd, the Dublin Cinema Group, the Green Group, and others, that were jointly owned by Leo Ward (1919–2013) and Kevin Anderson (1915–2016). The two men were half brothers—Anderson's father, Thomas, died when he was two, and his mother, Martha, remarried to John Ward. When Anderson left school, he joined the civil service and subsequently worked in a builder's company. Meanwhile, Leo Ward was working with the Irish International Film Agency, which distributed German films in Ireland. However, when Ward, who also played soccer for Drumcondra, was offered a professional contract in England with Manchester City, Anderson took over his place at the agency.

When World War II began, Ward returned to Ireland, and though he continued playing soccer for Drumcondra (winning two FAI Cups in the process), he became increasingly involved in the film business. Having raised some capital via a 1946 benefit soccer match, Ward and Anderson started their own distribution company—Abbey Films—acquiring Irish rights for Irish-themed British and American films like *The Hills of Donegal* (1947) and the Lucan and McShane *Mother Riley* series (1937–1952). A later deal with Anglo Amalgamated Film saw Ward Anderson distribute the highly successful British comedy *Carry On* series and some of the James Bond sequence in Ireland.

Anderson was responsible mainly for looking after the day-to-day finances of the company, and Ward spent the 1940s and 1950s touring the country with prints, building contacts with smaller cinema owners in the provinces. As the industry entered a period of decline in the 1950s, Ward gradually became a partner in many of the cinemas he had been supplying, and eventually the exhibition side of the business became more financially significant than distribution. The acquisition of the cinemas was facilitated by Anderson's success on the stock market, earning him some of the capital used to acquire the cinemas.

Anderson also used this money to dabble in film production. In the early 1950s, he used Abbey Films as a vehicle to produce a short film on the United Irishmen, *Who Dares to Speak of '98*, with **Peter Hunt**, **George Fleischmann**, **Liam O'Leary**, and **Cyril Cusack**. He also approached the Department of Foreign Affairs in 1955 seeking support for a documentary project on the Irish in London.

By the 1960s, Ward Anderson was the dominant player in the provincial market (i.e., outside Dublin). The first move into the capital came in 1968 when the company purchased the Green Cinema on Saint Stephen's Green. By the mid-1970s, the company had added three more city-center cinemas—the Ambassador, the Regent, and the Academy. The company's position in the capital was cemented in 1983 when the Rank Organization sold its Dublin cinemas—the Savoy, the Metropole, and the Odeon.

This dominance enjoyed by the company (at least until the 1990s) was not unchallenged. In the early 1970s, the Irish Cinemas Association (which represented independent provincial cinema owners) leveled a series of accusations to the effect that the group was being favored by the major distributors. Although an initial report from the examiner of the Restrictive Practices Commission found that there was some evidence of such collusion, a subsequent full-scale enquiry dismissed the accusation, arguing that purely commercial considerations had contributed to the group's dominance. Indeed, Ward Anderson emerged from the process in a stronger position than it had before it started. Not only did the enquiry find that it was in the interests of consumers to have a strong chain like Ward Anderson, but it also recommended some modification of practices in the Dublin city-center market, which had arguably disadvantaged Ward Anderson cinemas relative to the Adelphi-Carlton and Rank Odeon circuits.

Throughout this period, Abbey Films continued to act as a distributor, although for the most part, it acted as agent for U.K.-based companies like EMI, Hemdale, and Gala rather than acquiring Irish rights outright.

Ward Anderson rode out the exhibition recession of the 1980s, in part by simply closing cinemas when they were no longer viable as ongoing operations but retaining the buildings as potentially valuable properties. With the arrival of multiplexes in 1990, however, the company was forced to consider new strategies. Initially, the company toyed with a direct confrontation with internationally backed players like UCI. When the latter opened a 10-screen cinema in Coolock, Ward Anderson countered with a 10-screen in Santry, another North Dublin suburb. For the most part, however, subsequent developments concentrated on the provincial market, where the company had long enjoyed a dominant position. As a result, the 1990s witnessed the closure of a plethora of older Ward Anderson cinemas in provincial towns and the building of new mini-multiplexes (anything from three- to seven-screen theaters) under the Cineplex and Omniplex brands. They also opened 12-screen cinemas in Limerick and—under the IMC Cinemas logo—in Dun Laoire, and as of the mid-2000s, the Ward Anderson cinemas still cumulatively accounted for approximately 40 percent of all screens in the Republic of Ireland. Abbey Films also continued to play a small but significant role, agenting for smaller U.S. distributors, such as New Line, and distributing some domestically produced films, such as *Song for a Raggy Boy* (2003) and *Adam and Paul* (2004). And, half a century after Kevin Anderson's experience with filmmaking, the group even tentatively returned to production through an alliance with Stone Ridge Productions. *Peaches* (2000)—the first feature from that company—was partially funded by Abbey Films, which also distributed it.

However, the 21st century saw a schism emerge between the Wards and the Andersons. Kevin Anderson semiretired in the 1980s, although he continued to be a significant player on the Irish stock market across a range of companies. Leo Ward, by contrast, continued playing a management role until around 2010. Yet by 2000, the dominant roles were played by two sons of the founders: Paul Ward and Paul Anderson. In 1997, tension emerged over the development of a new multiplex cinema in Dún Laoghaire on Dublin's south side: in a later court case, it was asserted that the Ward family had refused to include the Andersons in the establishment of the cinema. Relations were not improved when, in 2003, the Wards moved their offices out of the long-established Abbey Films premises in the city center, relocating to Dún Laoghaire. However, matters finally came to a head over a move in 2011 by Paul Anderson's Omniplex Cinemas (rather than the jointly Ward Anderson–owned Dublin Cinema Group) to develop a multiplex on Dublin's St. Stephen's Green. Arguing that this would cannibalize the audiences of the Dublin Cinema Group's existing cinemas (the Savoy and the Screen), in 2012, Paul Ward brought a legal action against Paul Anderson in a bid to prevent the project from proceeding. The court case effectively marked the demise of the Ward Anderson relationship, and in 2013 the empire was effectively divided into two competing halves. The directors of the Dublin Cinema Group are now exclusively drawn from the Ward family, whose cinemas operate mainly under the IMC banner: as of 2017, the family operates 15 cinemas across the Republic of Ireland, including the flagship Savoy in Dublin's city center. For their part, the Andersons operate under the "Omniplex" umbrella, owning 26 cinemas on the island of Ireland, of which 13 are in the Republic. There remains tension between the groups: when the Andersons opened a new cinema in Dundalk in County Louth, a location where IMC were already present, the latter appealed (unsuccessfully) against the planning permission granted to Omniplex on the grounds that the cinema officially opened three days before the planning permission had been formally approved.

WHAT RICHARD DID (2012). **Lenny Abrahamson**'s third film was his first without Mark O'Halloran as writer but can nevertheless be read as the third part of a loose trilogy of works dealing with contemporary Irish masculinities. *What Richard Did* is loosely based on Kevin Power's *Bad Day in Blackrock*, a quasi-fictionalized account of the violent assault and death of an Irish teenager outside a Dublin nightclub in 2000 at the hands of a group of middle-class schoolboys. Young, confident, handsome, and popular, Richard is unlike the male protagonists of Abrahamson's preceding films—Adam, Paul or Josie—in almost every respect. Here, the director's concern is less with the rejection than with the acceptance of his central character and the social mechanisms that permit and perpetuate such privileged belonging.

The narrative follows Richard Karlsen (**Jack Reynor**), golden-boy athlete and undisputed alpha male of his privileged set of South Dublin teenagers, through the summer between the end of secondary school and the beginning of college. He is an unsurprising magnet for the attentions of Lara (Roisin Murphy), even though she is attached to a lanky introvert named Conor (Sam Keeley). This competition comes to a head midway through the film at a house party when, sensing that Conor is making a move, a drunken fight erupts. Richard is not a fighter by nature, but as passions and egos rise, Conor punches him. As Richard attempts to find his bearings, mayhem briefly ensues, during which Conor is hit and falls to the ground, taking a blow to the head that will eventually lead to his death. Richard confesses his role to his father, but the latter suggests that he stay at the family's summer home until the investigation blows over. Given the confusion on the night, neither Richard nor his friends are identified and are later seen at Conor's funeral. As the film ends, Richard begins a new life in college.

What Richard Did ponders big philosophical questions of privilege, culpability, and guilt, themes explored elsewhere in the cinema of Bergman (*Persona*) and Woody Allen (*Crimes and Misdemeanors*) and given freshness and topicality through strong performances and a keen feeling for a social milieu. However, while highly accomplished and offering an unprecedented portrait of an overlooked section of contemporary Irish society, it is harder to like than Abrahamson's preceding films and offers limited opportunity for an audience to engage with its protagonist's plight. Like those works, it concludes with its central male figure seen alone, only here he not only survives (in contrast to *Garage* and *Adam and Paul*) but also seems likely to prosper while his friend's family forever grieves.

WHELAN, DES. One of a handful of Irish technical crew members with an international reputation, Des Whelan began his career as rostrum camera trainee at the Gunther Wulf animation studio at Ardmore in the late 1970s. After four years there, he retrained as a clapper loader, traditionally the first step to becoming a cinematographer. After four more years, he graduated to focus puller, and in 1987, he was given his first opportunity to work as a camera operator on the **Radio Telefís Éireann** drama series *Troubles*. From that point on, Whelan has secured work on virtually every major production shot in Ireland, including *My Left Foot*, *The Field*, *The Playboys*, and *Into the West*. More recently, he has worked as camera operator on **John Boorman**'s *Tailor of Panama* (2001), **John Moore**'s *Flight of the Phoenix* (2004), and Tim Burton's *Charlie and the Chocolate Factory* (2005), among other films. He is also much sought after for commercial shoots, and he has taught at the National Film School.

WHEN BRENDAN MET TRUDY (2000). Directed by Kieran J. Walsh and written by **Roddy Doyle**, *When Brendan Met Trudy* is a film buff's film (and a tacit acknowledgment of the particular popularity of the medium in 20th-century Ireland). The titular Brendan (**Peter McDonald**) is a quiet, shy schoolteacher obsessed with cinema. He is rescued from his lonely existence by the arrival of Trudy, a vivacious but unpredictable woman whose day job remains mysterious to Brendan. Is she a Montessori teacher, as she claims? Or is she the militant radical feminist who has been castrating men around Dublin (as reported in the press)? Or (as is actually the case) is she a cat burglar who inveigles Brendan into becoming her accomplice (and lover).

The film frames the pair's nighttime excursions as reworkings of famous film sequences, and Brendan's acquiescence in criminal activity is clearly motivated by the opportunity to replay these sequences in real life. In the opening scene, Brendan lies facedown in the gutter as it rains, remaining there as much because it evokes one of his favorite films, *Sunset Boulevard* (1950), as because he is injured. Posters from Jean-Luc Godard's *A Bout de Souffle* (1959) decorate both his home and school, and as the narrative progresses, Brendan slowly acquires Jean-Paul Belmondo's mannerisms and clothes from Godard's text. Even the conclusion pays homage to the close of *The Searchers* (1956) when John Wayne holds his hand in a certain pose (itself an homage to an older western actor, Harry Carey Sr.), framed against the homestead entrance.

Although the film plays with gender and race stereotypes, its core lies in tracing Brendan's liberation from his buttoned-down upbringing toward self-realization. His encyclopedic knowledge of film (and music) hints at a persona the more outrageous elements of which have long been suppressed though expressed vicariously through his consumption of popular culture. Trudy is the spark emancipating him from his largely self-applied repression. In that regard, Brendan operates (intentionally?) as an analogue of the manner in which Irish society used officially disapproved-of expressions of American popular culture to counter the Catholic social conservativism that dominated Ireland for much of the 20th century.

WHEN THE SKY FALLS (1999). *See VERONICA GUERIN* (2003).

WIDOWS' PEAK (1993). Directed by English director John Irvin from an original story and screenplay by playwright Hugh Leonard, *Widows' Peak*'s initial primary significance seemed to lie in the fact that it represented Mia Farrow's first major film role after her highly public breakup with director Woody Allen. Set in the 1920s on a hill overlooking the picturesque village of Kilshannon, the Widows' Peak community is, appropriately, made up mostly of widows, including the rich and well-heeled Mrs. Doyle Counihan (Joan Plowright), who excels in knowing everyone's business and who seeks in particular to influence the life of the poverty-stricken and profoundly shy spinster Miss O'Hare (Farrow). Into the mix comes another widow, the highly sexed American interloper Edwina Broome (Natasha Richardson), who immediately locks horns with Ms. O'Hare, who views her as a potential rival for the affections of the few men left in town (including **Adrian Dunbar** and Jim Broadbent). Although the narrative is somewhat complicated by a murder mystery subplot (with Miss O'Hare squarely pointing the finger at Broome), the film operates mainly as a gentle, heritage-inflected comedy of manners, its pleasures lying less in the unraveling of events and more in its

Quiet Man–esque exploitation of landscape and the charm of the Irish natives even if the actors playing the lead Irish roles are, for the most part (Farrow, Plowright, and Broadbent), actually from the United States and the United Kingdom.

WILLY REILLY AND HIS COLLEEN BAWN (1920). Derived from an 1855 novel of the same name by William Carleton (rather than Dion Boucicault's 1860 play *The Colleen Bawn*), *Willy Reilly* was the last of the **Film Company of Ireland**'s major features. Directed by John McDonagh, the film is set in the 18th century in the context of the operation of the Penal Laws, a legal code designed to place Irish Catholics in a subordinate position relative to their Protestant counterparts. The eponymous Willy Reilly plays a disenfranchised Catholic who falls in love with Helen (the Colleen Bawn), daughter of Squire Folliard, a local Protestant landowner whom Reilly rescues from a local bandit. Helen, however, is engaged to notorious Catholic hunter Sir Robert Whitecraft. But when Whitecraft's sectarianism becomes violent, leading to the destruction of O'Reilly's home, he is arrested, and the major obstacle to O'Reilly and Helen's relationship is removed.

Although the film nominally suggests that the distinction between Catholic and Protestant is largely illusory, *Willy O'Reilly and His Colleen Bawn* isn't an entirely ecumenical film. The Catholic O'Reilly is clearly constructed as a thrusting agent of change, in stark contrast to the Folliards, who are portrayed largely as passive victims of circumstance. In this respect, director McDonagh's own overt nationalist politics (his brother Thomas was executed for his part in the 1916 Easter Rising) clearly show through. Indeed, one could argue that rather than preaching ecumenism, the film demonstrates the inevitability of the decline of the Protestant order associated with unionism and its replacement with a Catholic nationalism.

WILSON, JUANITA. Writer/director/producer Wilson's career in Irish film has been atypical in scope and trajectory. Cofounder with James Flynn of **Octagon Films** (they have been married since 1998), she commenced her career as a producer (*H3* and *Inside I'm Dancing*) after studying fine art at the National College of Art and Design (NCAD) and Arts Management at University College Dublin. Although her filmography as director is relatively small, each of her films to date has been distinguished by a keen eye for adaptation, a deeply personal commitment to story and character, and the fact that none has been set in Ireland. Set in Belarus and detailing a father's attempt to come to terms with the Chernobyl tragedy, her powerful short film *The Door* (2010) (based on the "Monologue About a Whole Life Written Down on Doors, the testimony of Nikolai Fomich Kalugin" by Nobel laureate Svetlana Alexievich) secured an **Academy Award** nomination (Best

Short Film). A year later, her feature debut, *As If I Am Not There*, was the Irish selection for Best Foreign Language Film. This was also based on a book by a female journalist concerning the fringes of contemporary Europe, this time Slavenka Drakulic's testimony about the horrific sexual abuse of women in the Bosnian War.

Her second feature, *Tomato Red* (2016), was another adaptation, this time set in the rural United States and produced by **Element Pictures**. A neo-noir based on a novel by Daniel Woodrell (*Winter's Bone*), *Tomato Red* tells the story of a drifter, Sammy Barlach, who falls in with a highly dysfunctional white-trash family in Venus Holler. *Unremarried Widow* (2018) is her planned third feature and is again adapted from a work of female-centered nonfiction: Artis Henderson's memoir details the author's experiences after her husband's death in the Iraq War.

***THE WIND THAT SHAKES THE BARLEY* (2006).** British director Ken Loach's second foray into Irish matters offers a politically inflected take on the Irish War of Independence and the Irish Civil War, rehabilitating the era's socialist politics, which were subsequently obscured by the postinde-pendence dominance of two centrist political parties: Fine Gael and Fianna Fáil.

Commencing in 1920, the film follows neophyte doctor Damien O'Donovan (**Cillian Murphy**) as he prepares to enter practice. His brother Teddy (Paraic Delaney), already involved in the armed struggle against Brit-ain, pleads with Damien to join the Irish volunteer guerrilla army. Initially reluctant, Damien changes his mind when he witnesses instances of British army violence in Ireland. Betrayed by a fellow volunteer, Damien and Teddy are arrested and sent to prison, where they meet Dan (**Liam Cunningham**), a leftist Irish Republican Army member. Escaping prison, Damien executes the informer and takes up the struggle for independence. As the fighting esca-lates, Britain sues for peace, and a treaty, creating an Irish Free State, is signed. Although falling short of an Irish Republic, Teddy accepts the treaty, but Damien cannot, and they find themselves on opposite sides in the ensuing Civil War. Captured by the Irish Free State army while stealing weapons, Damien is sentenced to death. Teddy offers him amnesty but only if Damien agrees to betray the antitreaty side.

Loach's film, based on a script by longtime collaborator Paul Lavery, is a powerful demonstration of just why it was so hard to contemplate bringing the story of the Irish Civil War to the big screen and why it took so long. Early works like *Irish Destiny* (1926) and *The Dawn* (1936) are exclusively focused on the War of Independence, where the identity of the enemy is unproblematic. Although the wave of films following the reestablishment of the **Irish Film Board** in 1993 included several harking back to the Civil War (***Broken Harvest*** [1994] and ***Korea*** [1995]), their setting in the 1950s cushioned the pain of recalling the internecine conflict, where families with divided loyalties literally fought against one another and atrocities on both sides created decades of bitterness.

Neil Jordan's *Michael Collins* (1996) addressed the conflict head-on but arguably reduced it to a battle of wills between Collins and Eamon de Valera, with the latter depicted as a calculating politician willing to sacrifice lives in the short term for a longer-term strategic political advantage. Loach's achievement is to combine the personal narratives of Damien and Teddy with a sense of the much wider political engagement. **Liam Cunningham**'s Dan plays a critical role in this regard, outlining a vision for an alternative Ireland that he fears the treaty will prevent. In *Michael Collins*, the distinction between free state and republic is somewhat abstract. Dan's argument in *The Wind That Shakes the Barley*, that the Republic is a precondition for achieving the goals of an inclusive and progressive society (e.g., the film is careful to emphasize the role played by women in the War of Independence) outlined in the 1916 Proclamation of Independence, transforms the representation of the antitreaty side from bloodthirsty savages to committed idealists.

But the film also operates as a broader critique of imperialism: his own nationality notwithstanding, Loach is unstinting in his depiction of the violence meted out on the native population by the occupying British army. There are hints of the brutalizing nature of imperialism and its need to construct subjugated peoples as somehow less than fully human in order to justify itself. (Teddy's decision in the film's last act to side with the Free State, which the film at least partially construes as an imperial proxy, perhaps illuminates his own brutalization and his willingness to contemplate fratricide.) That the film's release coincided with the presence of the British army in various Middle Eastern hot spots suggests that its sights were trained both within and beyond the island of Ireland.

***WINGS OF THE MORNING* (1937).** This was the first Technicolor film made in the British Isles (and indeed Europe) and was filmed partly in **Killarney**, County Kerry; it was also the setting for the very first films produced in Ireland by the **Kalem Company** and for *The Dawn* (1926), Ireland's first indigenous feature film. Directed by first-time director Harold Schuster and financed by the British subsidiary of 20th Century Fox, the film tells the story of a Spanish gypsy girl, Maria (French star "Annabella"), who escapes to Ireland (dressed as a boy) during the Spanish Civil War and meets Kerry Gilfallen (an early star role for Henry Fonda). It was based on the short story *A Tale of a Gypsy Horse* by Irish-born writer **Donn Byrne** (who also wrote **John Ford**'s *Hangman's House* [1928]) and adapted by famed Irish American screenwriters Meehan and Thomas J. Geraghty. While its horse-racing scenes, romance, and cross-dressing escapades are generally amusing, the film is interesting primarily for its evocative photography of the Kerry landscape by Ray Rennahan (who would later photograph *Gone with the Wind* [1939]), assisted by Jack Cardiff (Powell and Pressburger films), as well as the singing of John McCormack. *Newsweek* reported that a preview audience burst into spontaneous applause when the beautiful couple are caught in a rainstorm and forced to take shelter in a hayloft. Count McCormack was apparently added into the film as an afterthought, aimed at attracting as wide an American audience as possible. In its Technicolor rendering of romance and Ireland as pastoral landscape, the film can be seen as something of a precursor to **John Ford**'s *The Quiet Man* (1952) while also looking back to his silent romance *The Shamrock Handicap* (1926).

WOMEN IN IRISH FILM. Among the earliest explorations of this topic is Barbara O'Connor's 1984 article "Aspects of Representation of Women in Irish Film" (*The Crane Bag* 8, no. 2, Media and Popular Culture [1984]), which begins, "Cinema, as one of the mainstream media, has been instrumental in the repression of a women's discourse." O'Connor was writing at a precipitous moment—in the midst of the "first wave" of an indigenous Irish film—with a clear and edgy interest in questions of representation and groundbreaking feminist film theory by Christine Gledhill, Claire Johnson, Laura Mulvey, and others. This intersection of forces supplied not only a range of texts to study—**Kieran Hickey**'s *Exposure* (1978) and *Criminal Conversation*, and **Tommy McArdle**'s *The Kinkisha*—but also a radical theoretical framework in which to consider them. In questioning "the direction which a feminist film project should take; what kind of films should be made, who should produce them and for whom," O'Connor invokes (but here avoids) extended discussion of **Pat Murphy**, arguably the most important feminist filmmaker of this (or any) period whose oeuvre traces the evolution of the concept in Irish film from the radical avant-garde polemic of *Maeve* (1981), to the linking of Republican and feminist melodramatic discourses in *Anne Devlin* (1984) (which can can be linked to Northern Ireland–set films from this period, such as Ann Crilly's *Mother Ireland* and Margo Harkin's *Hush-a-Bye Baby* [1990]) to what some describe as the postfeminist aesthetic in her period drama *Nora* (1990).

Outside of these, a feminist cinema (or even what one might describe as more complex or progressive narratives of women) has been frustratingly slow to emerge, and an overwhelming majority of Irish films have been naturalist and told from a male perspective. One reason for this (though not the only one) is that, as in many other film industries, men tend to dominate Irish production. A 2016 study of Irish films produced during the first 20 years of the **Irish Film Board** (IFB) (1993–2013) revealed that 19 percent of directors were women and that 17 percent of feature titles were written by women, while just 16 films—6.6 percent of the total—identified female lead producers (Flynn and Tracy 2016).

Among the growing number of female directors of contemporary Irish feature film production, we can include (in no particular order) **Juanita Wilson**, **Rebecca Daly**, **Mary McGuckian**, Liz Gill (*Gold in the Streets* [1995] and *Goldfish Memory* [2003]), Kirsten Sheridan (*Disco Pigs* [2001] and *Dollhouse* [2012]), Trish McAdam (*Snakes and Ladders* [1996]), **Aisling Walsh** (*Song for a Raggy Boy* [2003] and *Maudie*), and Sue Clayton (*The Disappearance of Finbar* [1996]). Outside of live-action narrative features, Nora Twomey has secured international recognition for her direction of the **Cartoon Saloon** animated feature *The Breadwinner* (2017) and *The Secret of Kells* (2009) (which she codirected), while Neasa Ní Chianáin (*School Life* [2017]), Aoife Kelleher (*One Million Dubliners* [2014]), and Ciarin Scott (*Christine Noble: In a House That Ceased to Be* [2014]) have made well-received documentaries. However, we need also to note that in more recent years, several Irish female directors have established international reputations within TV drama production, notably, Dearbhla Walsh (*Shameless* [**Channel 4**]; *Little Dorrit* [BBC], which won seven Emmy Awards]; and the Netflix series *Fargo*), Neasa Hardiman (*Happy Valley* [BBC], *Tracy Beaker Survival Files* [BBC], and *Z: The Beginning of Everything* [Amazon]), and **Aisling Walsh**, among others. That such directors are forging careers outside of feature films prompts questions around access within these media as well as gender issues linking the feature form and modes of address and reception.

As noted, gender imbalance is even more pronounced among Irish producers, although there have been significant inroads made in recent years by the likes of Katie Holly (**Blinder Films**), Rachel Lysaght (Underground Films), Rebecca O'Flanagan (**Treasure Entertainment**), Julie Ryan (MK 1 Productions), and **Juanita Wilson** (**Octagon Films**), among others, building on the work of Katy McGuinness, Martha O'Neill, and **Lelia Doolan**.

Irish female actors have, of course, made enormous contributions to films set in and about Ireland. It is invidious to attempt to quantify this group, but we note nevertheless the representative contributions of **Maureen O'Hara**, **Brenda Fricker**, **Fionnula Flanagan**, **Brid Brennan**, **Orla Brady**, **Susan Lynch**, **Fiona Shaw**, **Ruth Negga**, **Eva Birthistle**, Eileen Walsh, and **Saoirse Ronan** (the last the most commercially and critically successful actor of her generation), among others. Behind the camera, Irish women have long made distinguished and widely recognized contributions in a range of other roles, including production manager (Mary Alleguen), editing (**Emer Reynolds** and Una Ní Dhonghaile), costume (**Josie MacAvin**, Eimer Ni Mhaoldomhnaigh, Consolata Boyle, and Joan Bergin), and, more recently, cinematography (Kate McCullough and Suzie Lavelle).

In the aftermath of the 2015 "Waking the Feminists" intervention at the **Abbey Theatre**, the IFB significantly stepped up initiatives to address gender imbalance in the industry. To a large extent, this can be traced to the influence of chairperson Annie Doona, under whom the IFB introduced a six-point plan in the summer of 2015 to address inequality under the headings of education, training, awareness, and unconscious bias and aimed for 50/50 gender parity in future funding. In the summer of 2018, the IFB launched an unprecedented series of targeted initiatives based on these aspirations. These included a new low-budget production program (up to €400,000) for emerging female writers and directors, increased support of up to €100,000 for feature films that are creatively led by Irish female writers and directors, one round of funding applications on the Screenplay Development scheme each year now being open only to female applicants, and a gender equality and diversity subcommittee for the IFB to be responsible for implementing these measures to attain gender parity. Such initiatives seem likely to radically transform rates of participation in the future and the kinds of stories that come under the banner of Irish film.

WOODS, MARK. Woods became chief executive of the **Irish Film Board** (IFB) in 2003 after the 10-year tenure of **Rod Stoneman**. Raised in Ireland, Woods studied law before moving to Los Angeles, where he worked for *Variety* before relocating to Australia, where he subsequently took over as head of international acquisitions and local content organization for Showtime, an Australian film and television network. During his time there, the company invested in 29 local films, including *Rabbit-Proof Fence* (2002) and *Innocence* (2000). In total, Woods spent 12 years abroad before returning to Ireland to head the IFB. Despite this background, Woods came under increasing criticism from elements of the Irish filmmaking community who argued that he stressed supporting safer projects to the detriment of developing smaller or more personal work. The decision to award €1.5 million to **Neil Jordan**'s *Breakfast on Pluto* (a disproportionately large amount of production funding) was cited as an example of this approach. In any case, Woods's tenure at the IFB turned out to be the shortest of all its chief executive officers, as he announced in April 2005 that he was resigning after 18 months in his post to take up a post in AusFilm, the agency that promotes Australia as a location.

***WORDS UPON THE WINDOW PANE* (1994). Mary McGuckian**'s debut feature is based on a play by Irish poet and playwright William Butler Yeats first performed in 1930. The play demonstrates Yeats's interest in the occult—he was a founder of the Dublin Hermetic Society and later a member of the London Lodge of Theosophists—and his use of symbolism, which shows the strong influence of the Japanese Noh tradition. The story tells of a London medium invited by the Dublin Spiritualist Society to conduct a series of séances that unexpectedly result in contact with the spirit of Jonathan

Swift (played here by director **Jim Sheridan**). The medium and her hostess become possessed by the jealous ghost, reenacting scenes of violent confrontation that occurred in the very same house centuries before. Unfortunately, most critics find the film adaptation overly confusing at times in spite of a very provocative backstory. The film stars Geraldine Chaplin, Geraldine James, **Brid Brennan**, **Orla Brady**, and **John Lynch**.

WORLD 2000 ENTERTAINMENT. Under the direction of Dubliner **Morgan O'Sullivan**, World 2000 has been one of the most important and influential production companies in the transformation of the Irish audiovisual sector from national cinema to a transnational industry. Born in 1945, as a teenager, O'Sullivan attended Presentation College, Bray (near **Ardmore Studios**), where he ran film shows on Saturday nights. He was simultaneously employed as a child actor on radio by **Radio Telefís Éireann** (RTÉ). On leaving school, he joined the **Peter Hunt** Studio, which, in addition to recording music, serviced the sound needs of non-RTÉ film productions in Ireland. Consequently, O'Sullivan worked with **Louis Marcus** on the **Gael Linn** newsreel before moving to Australia in 1966 to take up a position as a host with the local radio and television station. This was followed by work with the Australian Broadcasting Commission in Sydney and then for commercial television. In 1969, he returned to Ireland and RTÉ, where he remained until 1984, presenting a series of radio shows. In 1970, he traveled to Los Angeles to make a documentary on the making of *Hawaii 5-0* and met Irish-born Los Angeles–based TV director Michael O'Herlihy (brother of **Dan O'Herlihy**).

Eight years later, O'Herlihy came to Ardmore to direct O'Sullivan's first film as a producer, the Frederick Forsyth–scripted *Cry of the Innocent* (1980). With this film, O'Sullivan's Tara Productions became the first non-U.S. company to presell a film to any American television network, in this case NBC for its *Movie of the Week*. This led to a relationship with Mary Tyler Moore Enterprises. Two years after leaving RTÉ to run Tara Productions full-time, he put together a package with Mary Tyler Moore Enterprises and NADCorp to buy Ardmore Studios out of liquidation, and for a period, O'Sullivan was the managing director of the studio.

From 1990 to 1992, O'Sullivan lived in Los Angeles, developing relationships with Hollywood studios and production companies, before again returning to Ireland and forming World 2000 Entertainment Ltd with a view to developing, producing, and distributing feature and television entertainment for the global market. O'Sullivan quickly pulled off the remarkable coup of "stealing" Mel Gibson's ***Braveheart*** from its Scottish production base and bringing the $70 million movie to Ireland.

World 2000 has for the most part continued to operate as a local production partner for foreign (mainly U.S.) productions that use Ireland as a double for other locations. These included the largest productions shot in Ireland during the 1990s, such as *King Arthur* and ***Veronica Guerin*** (both Disney/ Jerry Bruckheimer productions) and *Reign of Fire* and *The Count of Monte Cristo* (both Spyglass Entertainment productions). An ongoing relationship with Hallmark Entertainment also led World 2000 to bring productions of *Animal Farm* and *David Copperfield* and adaptations of two Irish novels— *Durango* and *The Blackwater Lightship*—to Ireland.

The commencement of *The Tudors* in late 2006 can be seen as a landmark development not only in Sullivan's business model but also in Irish film and TV production history. Coinciding with shifts in the Irish tax regime, currency fluctuations, and production trends driven by American cable TV channels such as HBO and Showtime, *The Tudors* was initially commissioned as a two-part drama created and written by Michael Hirst. Drawing on his experience with big-budget Hollywood drama, Sullivan proposed bringing the high production values developed on films such as *King Arthur* to the project. So impressed was Showtime with this vision that it quickly developed the initial proposal as a single miniseries. Strong media attention and audience numbers led to five seasons in total being commissioned between 2006 and 2010, bringing an unprecedented run of production and stability to Irish cast, crew, and studio facilities and positioning Sullivan at the forefront of international quality TV production. The success of *The Tudors* led to *Camelot*—which was canceled after just one season—and *The Vikings*.

WYCHERLEY, DON (1967–). Since the mid-1990s, Don Wycherley has been seen by Irish and United Kingdom audiences primarily as a television actor. However, he routinely appears midway down the casts of domestically produced films, frequently playing rural or Dublin working-class grotesques. (His first screen credit, in ***Widows' Peak*** [1994], was as "Rural Lout.")

Born in Skibbereen in West Cork, Wycherley began to explore acting while attending the local secondary school. In a move indicative of the economic opportunities and mind-set of the 1980s, he then trained as a primary teacher at St. Patricks, Drumcondra, and it was not until his mid-20s that he began to regularly appear onstage and on-screen. His *Widows' Peak* debut was quickly followed by small roles in *Scarlett* (1994), ***Michael Collins*** (1996), and ***The Last of the High Kings*** (1996).

By the end of the 1990s, in no small part due to the attention garnered by his recurrent cameos as the imbecilic Father Cyril MacDuff in the cult comedy *Father Ted*, he was increasingly prominent in leading roles. In danger of being typecast, his lilting tones and blue eyes led to the leading role of Father

Aidan O'Connell in the BBC's *Ballykissangel*, and between 2001 and 2003, he played the melancholic romantic Raymond in the popular **John Carney/ Tom Hall Radio Telefís Éireann** series *Bachelor's Walk*.

Wycherley's run as a poetic heartthrob proved relatively short lived, and as he moved into his 30s, he found himself increasingly cast in less sympathetic roles. The discreetly racist Eugene in *Bad Day in Blackrock* (2001) was then casting against type, but by 2007, he was the local bully Breffni, who torments **Pat Shortt**'s Josie in **Lenny Abrahamson**'s *Garage* (2007); the *Deliverance*-esque rural hillbilly tormenting drug-addled teens in *Shrooms* (2007); and the alcoholic political campaign manager in TG4's underrated *The Running Mate* (2007). Frequently cast playing caricatures of establishment figures—policemen in *Speed Dating* (2007) and *Zonad* (2009), clerics in *Pentecost* (2011), and *Sing Street* (2015)—on the big screen, he has also enjoyed strong reviews for his theater work, notably *The Shaughran* and (opposite **Eileen Walsh**) *Eden*, Eugene O'Brien's searing portrait of small-town Ireland (subsequently adapted for the screen in 2008).

Indeed, since 2007, Wycherley's fluency in the Irish language has meant that he has become a staple of TG4 comedies and dramas. *The Running Mate* was followed by lead roles in *Rasai na Gailimhe* (2009–2012), *An Crisis* (2010), *Scup* (2013–2014), and *Fir Bolg* (2016). Unfortunately, the limited audience for Irish-language material means that his considerable gifts for both comedy and drama have not received the attention they might. In any other context, that much television work would make him a national star.

Y

***THE YOUNG OFFENDERS* (2016).** Having cofounded Vico Films in 2004 and enjoyed some international festival success with the macabre comedy short *The Carpenter and His Clumsy Wife* (2006), Cork director Peter Foott concentrated largely on television comedy work in the following decade, often working with Limerick-based comedy duo The Rubberbandits. However, shot for just €50,000, his genial, sweet-natured feature debut, *The Young Offenders*, became an instant comic sensation on release, taking in a remarkable €1.2 million at the Irish box office, securing distribution as far away as New Zealand, and spawning a BBC television sequel series.

Loosely tied to real-life events in 2007 when Irish police seized €440 million worth cocaine off the Irish coast as the vessel smuggling it sank, the narrative follows two 15-year-old Cork City wasters, Jock (Chris Walley) and Conor (Alex Murphy), as they determine to track down one of the errant bales of cocaine, thus setting them up financially for life. Both come from difficult backgrounds: recidivist bike thief Jock lives with his alcoholic father, while Conor has a tense though loving relationship with his lone parent mother (Hilary Rose). Stealing bikes to make the journey of more than 100 miles out to the site of the wreck, the pair cycle through the western Cork countryside, pursued by a local guard (Dominic MacHale) determined to end Jock's criminal career. Along the way, they encounter a motley crew of local color before encountering smugglers equally determined to retrieve the cocaine.

In truth, the cocaine is a MacGuffin that legitimates the film's road movie narrative and the pair's navigation of a series of absurd but hilarious episodes. A modern-day Laurel and Hardy (or, indeed, a more southerly take on ***Adam and Paul*** [2004]), the core of the film is the central relationship between the two leads. Not too bright and generally identified by officialdom—school, police, and even parents—as destined for failure, Jock and Conor are nonetheless portrayed as a fundamentally decent pair, their sallies into criminality a function of their social circumstances rather than innate malevolence. Essentially innocent (the offer of a live chicken as food threatens to traumatize Conor), their quest for the cocaine is driven by a vision of living "like Batman" in a mansion surrounded by butlers and topless girls.

The relationship between the two leads lies at the core of the film's appeal. Not afraid to acknowledge the darker aspects of their existence—poverty, depression, and alcoholism—the film depicts the pair as recognizing that their mutual loyalty offers the best hope of surviving their circumstances. Driven by an irrepressible energy and judiciously selected contemporary sound track, *The Young Offenders* does for Cork youth what prior teenage comedy classics (*Ferris Bueller's Day Off* and Judd Apatow's *Superbad* are almost certainly influences) did for their U.S. counterparts: retrieve them from the opprobrium of judgmental adults.

***YOU'RE UGLY TOO* (2015).** This highly assured debut from writer/director Mark Noonan adopts a restrained approach in recounting an open-ended and melancholic narrative about identities and relationships at the margins of mainstream Ireland. Will (**Aiden Gillen**) is offered temporary compassionate release from prison to take care of his 11-year-old niece Stacey (played with considerable composure by Lauren Kinsella). They depart Dublin for the unnamed Midlands town where the family owns a mobile home and encounter Emilie (Erika Sainte), a Belgian-born primary school teacher who lives there with her husband and their son. A cautious relationship develops between the two family units: not quite a friendship but at least an accommodation, complicated by the mutual sexual attraction of Will and Emilie.

The film concentrates on the connection between Will and Stacey: both have secrets, and both must earn the trust of the other before these can be revealed. Will and Stacey have found themselves in various states of incarceration (he in prison, she in foster homes) as a consequence of forces beyond their control. The film's nuanced and well-rounded characterizations present the protagonists as flawed but essentially well intentioned. While avoiding crude social commentary, the film also quietly demonstrates how social structures (Will and Stacey are coded as working class) can place individuals in situations of inescapable necessity. Emilie faces similar strictures: her teaching qualification being unrecognized in Ireland, she is restricted to home tutoring Stacey. Her (unhappy?) marriage also sets bounds to her agency. While Emilie and Will contemplate escape, he is ultimately unwilling to become a fugitive.

Avoiding pat answers to these difficulties, the film's conclusion leaves the characters in similar situations to where they began. Stacey returns to a Dublin foster home, and Will begins a new job based in Cork. The foundations of mutual trust have been laid but are not yet sufficient to convince either that their best interests lie in setting out together.

Although shot on a low budget (consisting mainly of €100,000 in production funding from the **Irish Film Board**), *You're Ugly Too* feels like a much-better-resourced undertaking. Much of the credit for this lies with cinematographer Tom Comerford, whose camera works with muted tones to display the rural setting to arresting effect. (Sound mixing is also unusually and, in a narratively crucial way, particularly deft.) But it is Gillen's star power that arguably lends the production the greatest heft. Once again, his work in a low-budget indigenous Irish film produces a quietly compelling and ultimately sympathetic performance that contrasts with the smirking screen villains he is more commonly associated with in more mainstream film and TV drama (*The Wire* and *Game of Thrones*).

Z

***ZONAD* (2009).** Originally conceived as TV pilot by brothers John and Kieran Carney, *Zonad* first saw the light of day as a short in 2003. In the wake of the success of John Carney's *Once* (2007), the brothers revisited the script, amping it up to a feature-length comedy. Small-time criminal Liam Murphy (Simon Delaney) flees a rehab facility during a fancy dress party. He escapes to the small town of Ballymoney still costumed as a spaceman. There, he presents himself as "Zonad," an alien seeking a new home after the destruction of his home planet. The town accepts this at face value, and he is taken in by the Cassidy family, who happily tolerate Zonad's exploitation of their hospitality. However, Liam/Zonad's ruse becomes increasingly difficult to maintain when another rehab escapee, Francis (David Pearse), turns up in the same town.

The absence of science fiction in Irish cinema is hardly surprising: unless one has Ruairi Robinson–type skills, few local production companies have access to the kind of financial resources required to pull off the special effects demanded by the genre. In *Zonad*, the Carney brothers' solution to this is simply to play science fiction as farce: Liam's attempt to convince the locals of his alienness depends on his less-than-perfect recall of pulp science fiction texts from the 1950s. Like a child playing dress-up, he literally verbalizes his own futuristic swoosh-and-beep sound effects. *Zonad* is an unabashed about its status: a film where the main joke is the fact of its rotund leading man striding around an Irish town in a skintight red PVC jumpsuit eating junk food is not seeking to offer a profound statement about contemporary Irish society. Happy to resort to penis jokes if they get a laugh, *Zonad* is best appreciated as a brief (80-minute) showcase for Irish screen comedy talent (Delaney, Pearse, and even **Don Wycherly**).

Bibliography

CONTENTS

INTRODUCTION

Like the Irish film industry itself, writing on the field has really come into its own only in the past two decades. Prior to 1987, with the exception of Liam O'Leary's broad-ranging 1945 publication *Invitation to the Film*, there was virtually nothing in book form on Irish cinema, although a number of journal articles and pamphlets, with varying degrees of comprehensiveness, had been published.

However, in 1987, three authors—Kevin Rockett, Luke Gibbons, and John Hill—almost single-handedly created the field of Irish film studies with the publication of *Cinema and Ireland*. Divided into three nearly self-contained sections relating to the interests of the different authors, the book addressed the political economy of Irish cinema, the representation of Northern Irish political violence, and the romanticization of Ireland through Hollywood cinema. Arguably, many of the books that followed were effectively footnotes—albeit often very useful footnotes—to this founding text.

The effect of *Cinema and Ireland*, however, was to valorize the work of what would later become known as the "first wave" of Irish filmmakers—those who, in difficult financial conditions, managed to produce culturally specific filmic texts, exploring aspects of Irish society and culture rarely touched by overseas films shot in Ireland.

As the number of academics working in the area increased over the years, more contemporary general studies emerged that dealt with the growing number of "second-wave" films. These include Lance Pettitt's broad review of film and television in *Screening Ireland*; Martin McLoone's well-honed *Irish Film: The Emergence of a Contemporary Cinema* with its definitive reading of *Butcher Boy*, for example; and Ruth Barton's student-accessible *Irish National Cinema* with its extensive overview of a large number of new Irish films.

While the academic output continued to grow over recent decades, important links and comparisons were made with British film and television in particular by well-established writers, including Rockett, Hill, Gibbons, and McLoone, who ensured that Irish film analysis would be placed in the context of a broader international framework. Furthermore, international conferences, in the United States especially, ensured that that diasporic dimension of the study of Irish film continued to grow, as evidenced in readers such as MacKillop's. In Ireland as elsewhere, strong connections have been forged particularly with literary studies; many ostensibly literary readers frequently include original work on film adaptations.

In Ireland recently, research links between various universities have led to a number of graduate seminars and publications of edited books. Young film academics have entered new avenues of investigation and extended the range of study, which is always a healthy sign. In particular, new genre, narrative, and gender studies have enabled Irish film study to move beyond what some perceive as a self-enclosed ghetto of national film study into more mainstream and universal aesthetic concerns.

The broad disciplinary areas of cultural studies and identity politics have also been very active in Ireland, as elsewhere, with a growth in studies of race, class, and, of course, gender issues feeding off graduate research in women's studies.

The "troubles" and the forming of a historical identity have remained a major category of film and cultural analysis, as evidenced by the large number of studies in this area, while more recently, the contested notion of definable Irish identity continues to attract academic interest. Coupled with this is the less developed area of political economic study, which is concerned with how the often-volatile public sphere directly affects which films get made as well as their reception.

The evolution of the Irish film industry can be seen through the history of censorship and the changing responsibility of the state, which act as a barometer of national identity. Studies such as those of Rockett, O'Brien, and Flynn effectively flesh out these complex and historical contextual issues within Irish film.

At the level of textual analysis, a growing number of studies of directors such as Sheridan, Jordan, and others; a number of fascinating book-length studies of individual films; and biographies ensure that researchers have lots of material to help them uncover the mosaics of creative production in Ireland. But there is always room for more studies, particularly about audiences and how films are received.

For researchers looking to go beyond secondary sources, the key center for Irish films and film-related documents is unquestionably the Irish Film Archive, which is currently located in the Irish Film Institute in Dublin's Temple Bar. The archive holds some 20,000 pieces of film, and the attached library keeps extensive material on Irish directors, actors, cinemas, and production companies. It also holds a fairly comprehensive stock of "gray literature," official reports on various aspects of Irish film policy since the 1960s. It is not entirely comprehensive, however, and it is worth contacting the archive in advance of a visit to ensure that they have the material you're looking for. It should also be acknowledged that much film and document material from the earlier period of Irish film is still unavailable. The 1942 *Report of the Intern-Departmental Committee on the Film Industry*, a key text discussed in this volume, was, until 2005, considered lost before it turned up in the National Archive. Researchers interested in aspects of Irish film policy should consider looking at files from the Department of the Taoiseach and from the Department of Industry and Commerce, which are held in the National Archive.

Ironically, researchers may have to travel outside Ireland to explore some aspects of Irish film. The U.S. Library of Congress has been the source of more than one "lost" film from the silent period of Irish cinema, while the British Library Periodicals section at Collinswood in the United Kingdom is a useful source of early (pre-1930) journals and magazines related to Irish cinema.

One final source for researchers interested in the political economy of modern Irish cinema is the Irish Film and Television Network, whose website was originally established as an offshoot of Paradox Films, a local feature film production company accessible at www.iftn.ie. Although oriented largely toward the industry itself, the site offers general information on production, distribution, and exhibition in Ireland. It also offers a searchable news archive and a filmography. The content of the latter is somewhat patchy—some of the films are discussed in detail, while others have information only on the key production personnel attached. Nonetheless, it is much more comprehensive on Irish audiovisual production than international sources, such as the Internet Movie Database.

For a wide variety of Irish-themed television and cinema, visit the Irish Film and TV Research Online website at www.tcd.ie/Irishfilm.

IRISH FILM STUDIES

Books

Barton, Ruth. *Irish National Cinema*. London: Routledge, 2004.

Byrne, T. *Power in the Eye: An Introduction to Contemporary Irish Film*. Lanham, MD: Scarecrow Press, 1997.

Caughie, John, with Kevin Rockett. *The Companion to British and Irish Cinema*. London: Cassell, 1996.

Crosson, Seán. *Sport, Cinema and National Culture: Gaelic Games on Film*. Cork: Cork University Press, 2018.

Curran, J. M. *Hibernian Green on the Silver Screen: The Irish and American Movies*. Westport, CT: Greenwood Press, 1989

Flynn, Arthur. *The Story of Irish Film*. Dublin: Currach Press, 2005.

Gillespie, Michael Patrick. *The Myth of an Irish Cinema: Approaching Irish-Themed Films*. Syracuse, NY: Syracuse University Press, 2008.

Hill, John. *Cinema and Northern Ireland: Film Culture and Politics*. London: British Film Institute, 2006.

Hill, John, and Martin McLoone. *Big Picture, Small Screen: The Relations between Film and Television*. Luton: John Libby Press, 1996.

Holohan, Conn. *Cinema on the Periphery: Contemporary Irish and Spanish Cinema*. Dublin: Irish Academic Press, 2010.

McCourt, John. *Roll Away the Reel World: James Joyce and Cinema*. Cork: Cork University Press, 2010.

McIlroy, Brian. *Irish Cinema: An Illustrated History*. Dublin: Anna Livia Press, 1988.

McLoone, Martin. *Irish Film: The Emergence of a Contemporary Cinema*. London: British Film Institute, 2000.

———. *Film, Media and Popular Culture in Ireland: Cityscapes, Landscapes, Soundscapes*. Dublin: Irish Academic Press, 2007.

Monahan, Barry. *Ireland's Theatre on Film: Style, Stars and the National Stage on Screen*. Dublin: Irish Academic Press, 2009.

O'Connell, Diog. *New Irish Storytellers: Narrative Strategies in Contemporary Film*. Bristol: Intellect, 2010.

O'Leary, Liam. *Invitation to the Film*. Tralee: The Kerryman, 1945.

Pettitt, Lance. *Screening Ireland: Film and Television Representation*. Manchester: Manchester University Press, 2000.

Pramaggiore, Maria. *Irish and African American Cinema since 1980: Identifying Others and Performing Identities*. New York: State University of New York Press, 2007.

Rockett, Kevin. *Film and Ireland: A Chronicle*. London: A Sense of Ireland [Booklet], 1980.

———. *Still Irish: A Century of the Irish in Film*. Dun Laoghaire: Red Mountain Press, 1995.

———. *The Irish Filmography*. Dublin: Red Mountain Press, 1996.

———. *Ten Years After: The Irish Film Board 1993–2003*. Dublin: Irish Film Board, 2003.

Rockett, Kevin, Luke Gibbons, and John Hill. *Cinema and Ireland*. London: Routledge, 1988.

Slide, Anthony. *The Cinema and Ireland*. Jefferson, NC: McFarland, 1988.

Edited Collections

Barton, Ruth, and Harvey O'Brien, eds. *Keeping It Real: Irish Film and Television*. London: Wallflower Press, 2004.

Caughie, John, with Kevin Rockett, eds. *The Companion to British and Irish Cinema*. London: Cassell, 1996.

Flannery, Eoin, and Michael Griffin, eds. *Ireland in Focus: Film, Photography, and Popular Culture*. Syracuse, NY: Syracuse University Press, 2009.

Hill, John, ed. *The Blackwell Companion to British and Irish Cinema*. Oxford: Blackwell, 2019.

Hill, John, Martin McLoone, and Paul Hainsworth, eds. *Border Crossing: Film in Ireland, Britain and Europe*. London: British Film Institute, 1994.

Huber, Werner, and Seán Crosson, eds. *Contemporary Irish Film: New Perspectives on a National Cinema*. Vienna: Braumuller, 2011.

Le Corff, Isabelle, and Estelle Epinoux, eds. *Cinemas of Ireland*. Newcastle: Cambridge Scholars Publishing, 2009.

MacFarlane, Brian, ed. *The Cinema of Britain and Ireland*. London: Wallflower Press, 2005.

MacKillop, James, ed. *Contemporary Irish Film*. Syracuse, NY: Syracuse University Press, 1999.

McLoone, Martin, and Kevin Rockett, eds. *Irish Films, Global Cinema*. Dublin: Irish Academic Press, 2007.

Monahan, Barry, ed. *Irish Cinema: Culture and Contexts*. Basingstoke: Palgrave Macmillan, 2015.

Rockett, Kevin, and John Hill, eds. *National Cinema and Beyond*. Dublin: Four Courts Press, 2004.

General Articles and Chapters

Barton, Ruth. "The Ballykissangelisation of Ireland." *Historical Journal of Film, Radio and Television* 20, no. 3 (2000): 413–42.

———. "Kitsch as Authenticity." *Irish Studies Review* 9, no. 2 (2001): 193–202.

———. "Changing Direction: Irish Cinema Revisits Its Borders." In *Zoom In, Zoom Out: Crossing Borders in Contemporary European Cinema*, edited by Marjorie Salvodon and Sandra Barriales. Cambridge: Cambridge Scholars Publishing, 2007.

———. "Between Modernity and Marginality: Celtic Tiger Cinema." In *From Prosperity to Austerity*, edited by Eamon Maher and Eugene O'Brien. Manchester: Manchester University Press, 2014.

Brereton, Pat. "Characteristics of Contemporary Irish Film." In *Mapping Irish Media: Critical Explorations*, edited by John Horgan, Barbara O'Connor, and Helena Shenhan. Dublin: University College Dublin Press, 2007.

Brodie, Patrick. "Deterritorialising Irish Cinema." *Nordic Irish Studies* 15, no. 2 (2016): 79–96.

Gibbons, Luke. "Romanticism in Ruins: Developments in Recent Irish Cinema." *Irish Review* 2, no. 1 (1987): 59–63.

Gillespie, Michael Patrick. "The Direction of Irish Film: Or, a Certain Tendency of the Irish Cinema." *Canadian Journal of Irish Studies* 35, no. 1 (2009): 32–38.

Ging, Debbie. "Screening the Green: Irish Cinema under the Celtic Tiger." In *Reinventing Ireland: Culture and the Celtic Tiger*, edited by Peadar Kirby, Luke Gibbons, and Michael Cronin. London: Pluto, 2002.

Hill, John. "Irish Cinema." In *The Cinema Book*, ed., Pam Cook. London: British Film Institute, 2007.

Kearney, Richard. "Modern Irish Cinemas: Re:Viewing Traditions." In *Irish Literature and Culture*, edited by Michael Kenneally. Lanham, MD: Rowman & Littlefield, 1992.

McLoone, Martin. "National Cinema and Global Culture: The Case of Irish Cinema." In *Cinemas of Ireland*, edited by Isabelle le Corff and Estelle Epinoux. Newcastle: Cambridge Scholars Publishing, 2009.

McLoone, Martin. "Cinema Irish Style." *Studies* 74, no. 294 (1985): 220–24.

———. "Reimagining the Nation: Themes and Issues in Irish Cinema." *Cineaste* 24, no. 2–3 (1999): 28–35.

———. "National Cinema in Ireland." In *Theorising National Cinema*, eds., Valentina Vitali and Paul Willemen. London: British Film Institute, 2006.

Pettitt, Lance. "Irish Exilic Cinema in England." *Irish Studies Review* 19, no. 1 (2011): 41–54.

Pine, Emilie. "Remembering and Forgetting: Memory and Legacy in Irish Theatre and Film." *Éire-Ireland* 43, no. 1–2 (2008): 222–36.

Rains, Stephanie. "Home from Home: Diasporic Images of Ireland in Film and Tourism." In *Irish Tourism: Image, Culture and Identity*, edited by Michael Conin and Barbara O'Connor. Clevedon: Channel View Publications, 2003.

Rockett, Kevin. "Constructing a Film Culture: Ireland." *Screen Education* 27 (1978): 23–33.

———. "Irish Cinema-Notes on Some Nationalist Fictions." *Screen* 20, no. 3/4 (1980): 115–23.

———. "Aspects of the Los Angelesation of Ireland." *Irish Communications Review* 1, no. 1 (1991): 18–23.

———. "Irish Cinema: The National in the International." *Cineaste* 24, no. 2–3 (1999): 23–25.

———. "(Mis)Representing the Irish Urban Landscape." In *Cinema and the City*, edited by Mark Shiel and Tony Fitzmaurice. Oxford: Blackwell, 2001.

EARLY IRISH CINEMA

Barton, Ruth. "The O'Kalem Collection on DVD: Implications for Future Research." *New Hibernia Review* 16, no. 2 (2012): 137–42

Condon, Denis. "Touristic Work and Pleasure: The Kalem Company of Killarney". *Film and Film Culture* 2, no. 1 (2003): 7–16.

———. *Early Irish Cinema, 1895–1921.* Dublin: Irish Academic Press, 2008.

———. "Politics and the Cinematograph: The Boer War and Thomas Ashe. *Field Day Review* 4 (2008): 133–45.

———. "Pointing a Topical Moral at the Present: Watching Knocknagow in 1918." *Screening the Past* 33 (2012): 1–13.

———. "'Brightening the Dreary Existence of the Irish Peasant': Cinema Transforms Leisure in Provincial Ireland." *Early Popular Visual Culture* 11, no. 2 (2013): 126–39.

————. "Temples to the Art of Cinematography: The Cinema on the Dublin Streetscape 1910–1920." In *Visualizing Dublin: Visual Culture, Modernity and the Representation of Urban Space*, edited by Justin Carville. Bern: Peter Lang, 2013.

————. "'Offensive and Riotous Behaviour'? Performing the Role of an Audience in Irish Cinema of the Mid-1910s." In *Performing New Media, 1890–1915, Early Cinema in Review*. Proceedings of Domitor. Bloomington: John Libbey Publishing, Indiana University Press, 2015.

————. "'Pictures in Abeyance': Irish Cinema and the Aftermath of the 1916 Easter Rising." *Moving Worlds: A Journal of Transcultural Writings* 16, no. 1 (2016): 30–43.

Felter, Mary Anne. "James Mark Sullivan and the Film Company of Ireland." *New Hibernian Review* 8, no. 2 (2004): 24–40.

Gilligan, Paula. "A Monotonous Hell: Space, Violence and the City in the 1930s Films of Liam O'Flaherty." *Early Popular Visual Culture* 5, no. 3 (2007): 301–16.

Hill, John. "'Purely Sinn Fein Propaganda': The Banning of Ourselves Alone (1936)." *Historical Journal of Film, Radio and Television* 20, no. 3 (2000): 317–33.

McCole, Niamh. "The Magic Lantern in Provincial Ireland 1896–1906." *Early Popular Visual Culture* 5, no. 3 (2007): 247–62.

Screening the Past 33 (2012). Special issue: "Knocknagow (1918)."

Tracy, Tony. "Outside the System: Gene Gauntier and the Consolidation of Early American Cinema." *Film History* 28, no. 1 (2016): 71–106.

DOCUMENTARY AND NONFICTION FILM

Barton, Ruth, "A Female Voice in Irish Cinema: Women Filmmakers and the Creative Documentary." *New Hibernia Review* 21, no. 2 (2017): 17–32.

Brereton, Pat. "Digital Impacts on Documentary in Ireland." In *Documentary in a Changing State: Ireland since the 1990s*, edited by Diog O'Connell. Cork: Cork University Press, 2012.

Chambers, Ciara. "Partitionist Viewing: The Split in Newsreel Coverage of Ireland during the Second World War." In *National Cinemas and World Cinema*, edited by Kevin Rockett and John Hill. Dublin: Four Courts Press, 2006.

————. "Time Marches On: Representations of 1930s Ireland in March of Time Newsreels." In *Irish Films: Global Cinema*, eds., Martin McLoone and Kevin Rockett. Dublin: Four Courts Press, 2007.

————. "Capturing the Nation: Irish Home Movies 1930–1970." *Journal of Film Preservation* 82 (2010): 60–63.

———. *Ireland in the Newsreels*. Dublin: Irish Academic Press, 2012.

———. "'British for the British—Irish Events for the Irish': Indigenous Newsreel Production in Ireland." *Historical Journal of Film, Radio and Television* 32, no. 3 (2012): 361–77.

———. "The 'Aftermath' of the Rising in Cinema Newsreels." In *Object Matters: Making 1916*, edited by Joanna Brück and Lisa Godson. Liverpool: Liverpool University Press, 2015.

Chambers, Ciara, Mats Jönsson, and Roel Vande Winkel, eds. *Researching Newsreels: Local, National and Transnational Case Studies*. New York: Palgrave Macmillan, 2018.

Crosson, Seán. "Ar son an Naisiuin: The National Film Institute of Ireland's All-Ireland Films." *Éire-Ireland* 48, no. 1–2 (2013): 191–210.

———. "Configuring Irishness through Coaching Films: Peil (1962) and Christy Ring (1964)." In *Representations of Sports Coaches in Film: Looking to Win*, edited by Katharina Bonzel and Nicholas Chare. London: Routledge, 2017.

Crosson, Seán, and Dónal McAnallen. "'Croke Park Goes Plumb Crazy': Pathé Newsreels and Gaelic Games." *Media History* 17, no. 2 (2011): 161–76.

Le Corff, Isabelle. "Rocky Road to Dublin: The Influence of the French Nouvelle Vague on Irish Documentary Film." *Irish Communications Review* 13 (2012): 133–44.

McLaughlin, Cahal. *Recording Memories from Political Violence: A Filmmaker's Journey*. Bristol: Intellect Books, 2010.

O'Brien, Harvey. *The Real Ireland: The Evolution of Ireland in Documentary Film*. Manchester: Manchester University Press, 2004.

O'Connell, Diog, ed. *Documentary in a Changing State: Ireland since the 1990s*. Cork: Cork University Press, 2012.

Pettitt, Lance, and Beatriz Kopschitz Bastos, eds. *The Road to God Knows Where*. São Paulo: Humanitas, 2013.

———, eds. *The Uncle Jack/John T. Davis*. São Paulo: Humanitas, 2013.

Pratschke, Mairead B. "The Amharc Éireann Early Documentary Film Series: Milled Peat, Music, and Mná Spéire." In *Ireland in Focus: Film, Photography, and Popular Culture*, edited by Eoin Flannery and Michael Griffin. Syracuse, NY: Syracuse University Press, 2009.

———. *Visions of Ireland: Gael Linn's Amharc Eireann Film Series 1956–1964*. Oxford: Peter Lang, 2015.

Young, Gwenda. "'Glimpses of a Hidden History: Exploring Irish Amateur Collections, 1930–1970." In *Amateur Filmmaking: The Home Movie, the Archive, the Web*, edited by Laura Rascoli, Gwenda Young, and Barry Monahan. New York: Bloomsbury, 2014.

GENRE

Barton, Ruth. "Irish Cinema—From History to Heritage." *The Irish Review* 21 (1997): 41–56.

Connolly, Maeve. "Sighting an Irish Avant-Garde in the Intersection of Local and International Film Cultures." *Boundary 2: International Journal of Literature and Culture* 31, no. 1 (2004): 244–65.

Crosson, Seán. "Horror, Hurling, and Bertie: Aspects of Contemporary Irish Horror Cinema." *Kinema* 37, no. 1 (2012): 65–83.

McIlroy, Brian, ed. *Genre and Cinema: Ireland and Transnationalism*. London: Routledge, 2007.

Radley, Emma. "Violent Transpositions: The Disturbing 'Appearance' of the Irish Horror Film." In *Viewpoints: Theoretical Perspectives on Irish Visual Texts*, edited by Claire Bracken and Emma Radley. Cork: Cork University Press, 2013.

THEMES OF RACE

Asava, Zélie. "The Nephew (Brady, Ireland, 1998) and The Front Line (Gleeson, Ireland, 2006): Black and Mixed Masculinities in Irish Cinema." In *Contemporary Irish Cinema: New Perspectives on a National Cinema*, edited by Werner Huber and Seán Crosson. Vienna: Braumüller and New Academic Press, 2011.

———. *The Black Irish Onscreen: Representing Black and Mixed Race Identities on Irish Film and Television.* Bern: Peter Lang, 2013.

———. "New Identities in the Irish Horror Film: Isolation (O'Brien, Ireland, 2005) and Boy Eats Girl (Bradley, Ireland, 2005)." In *Viewpoints: Theoretical Perspectives on Irish Visual Texts*, edited by Claire Bracken and Emma Radley. Cork: Cork University Press, 2013.

———. "Thrill Me, Kiss Me, Kill Me: Trafficked and the Multicultural Irish Thriller." In *Masculinity and Irish Popular Culture: Tiger's Tales*, edited by Tony Tracy and Conn Holohan. London: Palgrave Macmillan, 2014.

Connolly, Maeve. "A Bit of a Traveller in Everybody: Traveller Identities in Irish and American Culture." In *The Irish in Us: Irishness, Performativity and Popular Culture*, edited by Diane Negra. Durham, NC: Duke University Press, 2006.

Goff, Loretta. "'Racism's Part of My Culture': Nation, Race and Humour in *Irish Jam* (2006) and *The Guard* (2011)." *Alphaville: Journal of Film and Screen Media* 13 (2017): 33–53.

HISTORICAL THEMES

Barton, Ruth. "Jimmy's Hall, Irish Cinema and the Telling of History." *Review of Irish Studies in Europe* 1, no. 1 (2016): 93–106

Crawdus, Gary. "The Screenwriting of Irish History: Neil Jordan's *Michael Collins*." *Cineaste* 22, no. 4 (1997): 14–19.

Cullingford, Elizabeth Butler. "Re-reading the Past: *Michael Collins* and Contemporary Popular Culture." In *Ireland in the New Century*, edited by Robert J. Savage Jr. Dublin: Four Courts Press. 2003.

Gibbons, Luke. "Lies That Tell the Truth: *Maeve*, History and Irish Cinema." *The Crane Bag* 7, no. 2 (1983): 148–55.

———. "Engendering the State: Narrative, Allegory and Michael Collins." *Éire-Ireland* 31, no. 3–4 (1996): 261–69.

———. "Framing History. Neil Jordan's Michael Collins." *History Ireland* 5, no. 1 (1997): 47–51.

Rockett, Kevin. "Representations of Irish History in Fiction Films Made prior to the 1916 Rising." In *Rebellion and Remembrance in Modern Ireland*, edited by Lawrence Geary. Dublin: Four Courts Press, 2000.

———. "Emmet on Film." *History Ireland* 11, no. 3 (2003): 46–49.

THEMES OF GENDER/SEXUALITY

Barton, Ruth. "Feisty Colleens and Faithful Sons: Gender in Irish Cinema." *Cineaste* 24, no. 2–3 (1999): 40–45.

———. "From Symbol to Symptom—Changing Representations of Fatherhood in Recent Irish Cinema." In *Masculinity and Irish Popular Culture*, edited by Conn Holohan and Tony Tracy. Basingstoke: Palgrave Macmillan, 2014.

Bracken, Claire. *Irish Feminist Futures*. London: Routledge, 2016.

Bradley, A., and M. G. Valiulis, eds. *Gender and Sexuality in Modern Ireland*. Amherst: University of Massachusetts Press, 1997.

Brewster, Scott, Virginia Crossman, Fiona Becket, and David Alderson, eds. *Ireland in Proximity: History, Gender, Space*. London: Routledge, 1999.

Cullingford, Elizabeth Butler. "Gender, Sexuality, and Englishness in Modern Irish Drama and Film." *ACIS Journal* 1, no. 1 (1997): 159–86.

———. *Ireland's Others: Ethnicity and Gender in Irish Literature and Popular Culture*. Cork: Cork University Press, in association with Field Day, 2001.

———. "Virgins and Mothers: Sinead O'Connor, Neil Jordan, and The Butcher Boy." *Yale Journal of Criticism* 15, no. 1 (2002): 185–210.

————. "The Prisoner's Wife and the Soldier's Whore: Female Punishment in Irish Popular Culture." In *Keeping It Real: Irish Film and Television*, edited by Ruth Barton and Harvey O'Brien. London: Wallflower Press, 2004.

Farley, Fidelma. "Interrogating Myths of Maternity in Irish Cinema: Margo Harkin's Hush-a-Bye Baby." *Irish University Review* 29, no. 2 (1999): 219–37.

Ging, Debbie. "The Lad from New Ireland: Marginalised, Disaffected and Criminal Masculinities in Contemporary Irish Cinema." *Film and Film Culture* 3 (2004).

————. "New Lads or Protest Masculinities? Investigating Marginalised Masculinities in Contemporary Irish Film." In *Mapping Irish Media: Critical Explorations*, edited by John Horgan, Barbara O'Connor, and Helena Sheehan. Dublin: University College Dublin Press, 2007.

————. "Goldfish Memories? On Seeing and Hearing Marginalised Identities in Contemporary Irish Cinema." In *Facing the Other: Interdisciplinary Studies on Race, Gender and Social Justice in Ireland*, edited by Borbala Farago and Moynagh Sullivan. Newcastle: Cambridge Scholars Publishing, 2008.

————. *Men and Masculinities in Irish Cinema*. Basingstoke: Palgrave Macmillan, 2013.

Holohan, Conn. "Queering the Green? The Limitations of Sexuality as Metaphor in Contemporary Irish Cinema." In *Cinemas of Ireland*, edited by Isabelle le Corff and Estelle Epinoux. Newcastle: Cambridge Scholars Publishing, 2009.

Kirkland, Richard. "Gender, Nation, Excess: Reading Hush-a-bye Baby." In *Ireland in Proximity: History, Gender, Space*, edited by Scott Brewster, Virginia Crossman, Fiona Becket, and David Alderson. London: Routledge, 1999.

McIlroy, Brian. "Irishness, Anger and Masculinity in Recent Film and Television." In *Screening-Irish America*, edited by Ruth Barton. Dublin: Irish Academic Press, 2009.

O'Leary, Alan. "The Gendered Space of Cinema and Nation in *Elizabeth* and *Michael Collins*." *Studies in European Cinema* 1, no. 2 (2004): 117–28.

Pettitt, Lance. "Pigs and Provos, Prostitutes and Prejudice: Gay Representation in Irish Film: 1984–1955." In *Sex, Nation and Dissent in Irish Writing*, edited by Eibhear Walsh. Cork: Cork University Press, 1997.

Pramaggiore, Maria. "'Papa Don't Preach': Pregnancy and Performance in Contemporary Irish Film." In *The Irish in Us*, edited by Diane Negra. Durham, NC: Duke University Press, 2006.

Scarlata, Jessica. *Rethinking Occupied Ireland: Gender and Incarceration in Contemporary Irish Film*. Syracuse, NY: Syracuse University Press, 2014

Tracy, Tony, and Conn Holohan, eds. *Masculinity and Irish Popular Culture.* Basingstoke: Palgrave Macmillan, 2014.

IRISH AMERICA AND CINEMA

Barton, Ruth, ed. *Screening Irish-America: Representing Irish-America in Film and Television.* Dublin: Irish Academic Press, 2009.

Brereton, Pat. "Ireland's America: A Case Study of Sheridan's In America (2002) and Get Rich or Die Tryin' (2005)." In *Screening Irish-America: Representing Irish-America in Film and Television*, edited by Ruth Barton. Dublin: Irish Academic Press, 2009.

Crosson, Sean, and Rod Stoneman, eds. *The Quiet Man . . . and Beyond: Reflections on a Classic Film, John Ford and Ireland.* Dublin: Liffey Press, 2009.

Goff, Loretta. "The Hyphenated Persona: Aidan Quinn's Irish-American Performances." *Persona Studies* 3, no. 1 (2017): 60–73.

McIlroy, Brian. "Searching for the (Sub) Genre: Irish-American Film Comedy." In *Screening Irish-America: Representing Irish-America in Film and Television*, edited by Ruth Barton. Dublin: Irish Academic Press, 2009.

Radley, Emma, and Claire Bracken. "A Mirror Up to Irishness: Hollywood Hardmen and Witty Women." In *Irish Postmodernisms and Popular Culture*, edited by Wanda Balzano, Anne Mulhall, and Moynagh Sullivan. Basingstoke: Palgrave Macmillan, 2007.

Rains, Stephanie. *The Irish American in Popular Culture, 1945–2000.* Dublin: Irish Academic Press, 2007.

Tracy, Tony. "The Musical Melting Pot: Edgar G. Ulmer's Carnegie Hall as Immigrant Text." In *Edgar G. Ulmer: Detour on Poverty Row*, edited by Gary Rhodes. Lanham, MD: Lexington Books, 2009.

———. "This Tempting Indulgence: William McGivern's Rogue Cops." In *After the Flood: Irish America 1945–1960*, edited by Matthew O'Brien and James Rodgers. Dublin: Irish Academic Press, 2009.

"THE TROUBLES" IN FILM

Crosson, Seán. "The Shore (2011): Examining the Reconciliation Narrative in Post-Troubles Cinema." In *The Legacy of 1998: Northern Irish Politics, Culture and Art after the Good Friday Agreement*, edited by Charles I. Armstrong, David Herbert, and Jan Erik Mustad. London: Palgrave, 2018.

Greene, Liz. "Music and Montage: Punk, Speed and Histories of the Troubles." In *Film, History and Memory*, edited by Jennie Carlsten and Fearghal McGarry. Basingstoke: Palgrave Macmillan, 2015.

Haslam, Richard. "Irish Film: Screening the Republic." In *Writing in the Irish Republic: Literature, Culture, Politics 1949–1999*, edited by Ray Ryan. London: Macmillan, 2000.

Herron, Tom, and John Lynch. *After Bloody Sunday: Representation, Ethics, Justice*. Cork: Cork University Press, 2007.

Hill, John. "Representing Violence: The British Cinema and Ireland." In *Ireland's Terrorist Dilemma*, edited by Yonah Alexander and Alan O'Day. Dordrecht: Martinus Nijhoff, 1986.

McIlroy, Brian. *Shooting to Kill: Filmmaking and the Troubles in Northern Ireland*. London: Steveston Press, 1998.

———. "Symbolic and Hyperreal Violence in the Irish Troubles Movie." In *Shadows of the Gunmen: Violence and Culture in Modern Ireland*, edited by Sean Farrell and Danine Farquharson. Cork: Cork University Press, 2008.

McLaughlin, Cahal. "Cold, Hungry, and Scared: Prison Films about the 'Troubles.'" In *Ireland in Focus: Film, Photography, and Popular Culture*, edited by Eoin Flannery and Michael Griffin. Syracuse, NY: Syracuse University Press, 2009.

McLoone, Martin. "Traditions of Representation: Political Violence and the Myth of Atavism." In *Terrorism, Media, Liberation*, edited by J. David Slocum. New Brunswick, NJ: Rutgers University Press, 2005.

Rockett, Kevin. "Irish Cinema: Notes on Some Nationalist Fictions." *Screen* 20, no. 3–4 (1978–1979): 115–23.

———. "Irish Cinema: The National in the International" *Cineaste* 24, no. 2–3 (1999): 23–25.

Rolston, B., and D. Miller, eds. *War and Words: A Northern Ireland Media Reader*. Belfast: Beyond the Pale, 1996.

CATHOLICISM

Brereton, Pat. "Religion and Irish Cinema." *Studies* 97 (2008): 321–32.

Cullingford, Elizabeth Butler. "'Our Nuns Are Not a Nation': Politicizing the Convent in Irish Literature and Film." *Éire-Ireland* 41, no. 1–2 (2006): 9–39.

McLoone, Martin. "Settling Old Scores? Religion, Secularisation and Recent Irish Cinema." In *Multiculturalism at the Start of the 21st Century*, edited by Krystyna Kujawinska Courtney and Maria A. Kukowska. Lodz: Lodz University Press, 2008.

Rockett, Kevin. "Catholic Film Policy in Twentieth Century Ireland." In *Moralizing Cinema: Film, Catholicism, and Power*, edited by Daniel Biltereyst and Daniela Treveri Gennari. New York: Routledge, 2014.

INDUSTRY STUDIES AND POLITICAL ECONOMY

Barton, Ruth. "The Bums on the Seats: Irish Films and the Overseas Market." In *Cinemas of Ireland*, edited by Isabelle le Corff and Estelle Epinoux. Newcastle upon Tyne: Cambridge Scholars Publishing, 2009.

Brereton, Pat. "Branding Irish Cinema: Reflections upon Celtic Consumer Society and Social Change in Dublin." *Irish Marketing Review* 20 (2009): 27–39.

Connolly, Maeve. "Theorising Irish Animation: Heritage, Enterprise and Critical Practice." In *National Cinema and Beyond*, edited by John Hill and Kevin Rockett. Dublin: Four Courts Press, 2005.

Flynn, Roderick. "The Last Semi-State? Lemass and Film Policy." In *The Lemass Era*, edited by Gary Murphy and Brian Girvin. Dublin: University College Dublin Press, 2005.

———. "About Adam and Paul." In *Mapping Irish Media: Critical Explorations*, edited by John Horgan, Barbara O'Conor, and Helena Sheehan. Dublin: University College Dublin Press, 2007a.

———. "Raiders of the Lost Archives: The Report of the Inter-Departmental Committee on the Film Industry 1942." *Irish Communications Review* 10, no. 1 (2007b): 30–41.

———. "Projecting or Protecting Ireland? The Department of External Affairs and Hollywood 1946–1960." In *Screening Irish-America: Representing Irish-America in Film and Television*, edited by Ruth Barton. Dublin: Irish Academic Press, 2009.

———. "Talking a Little Treason: The Quiet Man and the Irish State." In *The Quiet Man and Beyond*, edited by Rod Stoneman and Seán Crosson. Dublin: Liffey Press, 2009.

———. "John Huston and an Irish Film Industry." In *John Huston: Essays on a Restless Director*, edited by Tony Tracy and Roddy Flynn. Jefferson, NC: McFarland, 2010.

———. "An Irish Film Industry or a Film Industry in Ireland? The Paradoxes of State Aid." In *The Handbook of State Aid for Film*, edited by Paul Clemens Murschetz, Roland Teichmann, and Matthias Karmasin. Cham: Springer International, 2018.

———. "The Film Industry and Film Policy." In *A Companion to British and Irish Cinema*, edited by John Hill. London: Wiley-Blackwell, 2019.

Flynn, Roderick, and Tony Tracy. "Quantifying National Cinema: A Case Study of the Irish Film Board 1993–2013," *Film Studies* 15 (2016): 32–53.

———. "Contemporary Irish Film: From the National to the Transnational." *Éire-Ireland* 52, no. 1–2 (2017): 169–97.

Monahan, Barry. "A Frayed Collaboration: Emmet Dalton and the Abbey Theatre Adaptations at Ardmore Studios, 1957–60." In *National Cinema and Beyond*, edited by John Hill and Kevin Rockett. Dublin: Four Courts Press, 2004.

———. "The Pedagogical Culture of Irish Film Production: A Short History." In *Cinemas of Ireland*, edited by Isabelle le Corff and Estelle Epinoux. Newcastle: Cambridge Scholars Publishing, 2009.

O'Connell, Diog. "Irish Film Board—Gatekeeper or Facilitator: The Experience of the Irish Screenwriter." In *Screenwriters and Screenwriting*, edited by Craig Batty. Basingstoke: Palgrave Macmillan, 2013.

———. "Small Nation/Big Neighbours—Co-Producing Stories in a European Context." In *European Cinema and Television: Cultural Policy and Everyday Life*, edited by Ib Bondebjerg, Andrew Higson, and Caroline Pauwels. Basingstoke: Palgrave Macmillan, 2014.

Rockett, Kevin. "From Radicalism to Conservatism: Contradictions within Fianna Fail Film Policies in the 1930s." *Irish Studies Review* 9, no. 2 (2001): 155–65.

Stoneman, Rod. "Sins of Commission." *Screen* 33, no. 2 (1992): 127–44.

———. "Under the Shadow of Hollywood: The Industrial versus the Artisanal." *The Irish Review* 24 (1999): 96–103.

———. "Sins of Commission II." *Screen* 46, no. 2 (2005): 247–64.

EXHIBITION AND AUDIENCES

Beere, Thecla J. "Cinema Statistics in Saorstat Eireann." *Journal of the Statistical and Social Inquiry Society of Ireland* 15, no. 6 (1935–1936): 83–100.

Condon, Denis. "Limelight on the Colleen Bawn: Resisting Autoexoticism in Provincial Irish Picture Houses in the Early 1910s." In *Les cinémas périphériques dans la période des premiers temps/Peripheral Early Cinema*. Proceedings of Domitor. Perpignan: Presses Universitaires de Perpignan, 2008.

———. "Irish Audiences Watch Their First US Feature: The Corbett-Fitzsimmons Fight (1897)." In *Screening Irish-America: A Reader*, edited by Ruth Barton. Dublin: Irish Academic Press, 2009.

———. "Receiving News from the Seat of War: Dublin Audiences Respond to Boer War Entertainments." *Early Popular Visual Culture* 9, no. 2 (2011): 93–106.

———. "'Baits to Entrap the Pleasure-Seeker and the Worldling': Charity Bazaars Introduce Moving Pictures to Ireland." In *Beyond the Screen: Institutions, Networks and Publics of Early Cinema*, edited by Marta Braun, Charles Keil, Rob King, Paul Moore, and Louis Pelletier. Bloomington: Indiana University Press, 2012.

———. "A Taste in Pictures: The Second Birth of Cinema in Cork." *Alphaville Journal of Film and Screen Media* 6 (2013): 1–18.

Keenan, Jim. *Dublin Cinemas: A Pictorial Selection*. Dublin: Picture House Publications, 2005.

McBride, Stephanie, and Roddy Flynn. *Here's Looking At You, Kid!* Dublin: Wolfhound Press, 1996.

Rockett, Kevin, with Emer Rockett. *Film Exhibition and Distribution in Ireland, 1909–2010*. Dublin: Four Courts Press, 2011.

———. *Magic Lantern, Panorama and Moving Picture Shows in Ireland, 1786–1909*. Dublin: Four Courts Press, 2011.

CENSORSHIP

Adams, Michael. *Censorship: The Irish Experience*. Tuscaloosa: University of Alabama Press, 1968.

Carty, Ciaran. *Confessions of a Sewer Rat: A Personal History of Censorship and the Irish Cinema*. Dublin: New Island Books, 1995.

Martin, Peter. *Censorship in the Two Irelands 1922–1939*. Dublin: Irish Academic Press, 2006.

O'Drisceoil, Donal. *Censorship in Ireland 1939–1945*. Cork: Cork University Press, 1996.

Rockett, Kevin. "Film Censorship and the State." *Film Directions* 3, no. 9 (1979): 11–15.

———. *Irish Film Censorship*. Dublin: Four Courts Press, 2004.

———. "Irish Film Censorship: Refusing the Fractured Family of Foreign Films." In *Silencing Cinema: Film Censorship around the World*, edited by Daniel Biltereyst and Roel Vande Winkel. New York: Palgrave Macmillan, 2013.

INDIVIDUAL FILMS

Barry, Kevin. *The Dead*. Cork: Cork University Press, 2001.

Brereton, Pat. "'Hollywood Representations of Irish Journalism: A Case Study of Veronica Guerin." *Irish Communications Review* 11, no. 1 (2009): 104–14.

Cronin, Michael. *The Barrytown Trilogy*. Cork: Cork University Press, 2007.

Crosson, Seán. "'Is It Another of Their Rebellions?': Gaelic Games and the Films of John Ford." In *Beyond Ireland: Boundaries, Passages, Transitions: Essays in Honour of Prof. Dr. Werner Huber*, edited by Hdway Schwall. Trier: Wissenschaftlicher Verlag Trier, 2018.

Crosson, Seán, and Rod Stoneman, eds. *The Quiet Man . . . and Beyond: Reflections on a Classic Film, John Ford and Ireland*. Dublin: Liffey Press, 2009.

Devlin, Ann. *Ourselves Alone*. London: Faber, 1986.

Farley, Fidelma. *Anne Devlin*. Throwbridge: Flicks Books, 2000.

———. *This Other Eden*. Cork: Cork University Press, 2001.

FitzPatrick Dean, Joan. *Dancing at Lughnasa*. Cork: Cork University Press, 2003.

Gibbons, Luke. "The Politics of Silence: Anne Devlin, Women and Irish Cinema." In *Transformations in Irish Culture*. Cork: Cork University Press, 1996.

———. "'The Cracked Looking Glass' of Cinema: James Joyce, John Huston, and the Memory of 'The Dead.'" *Yale Journal of Criticism* 15, no. 1 (2002): 127–48.

———. *The Quiet Man*. Cork: Cork University Press, 2002.

———. "Ghostly Light: Spectres of Modernity in James Joyce's and John Huston's 'The Dead.'" In *A Companion to James Joyce*, edited by Richard Brown. Oxford: Blackwell, 2007.

Gillespie, Michael Patrick. "The Myth of Hidden Ireland: The Corrosive Effect of Place in 'The Quiet Man.'" *New Hibernia Review/Iris Éireannach Nua* 6, no. 1 (2002): 18–32.

———. "The Odyssey of Adam and Paul: A Twenty-First-Century Irish Film." *New Hibernia Review / Iris Éireannach Nua* 12, no. 1 (2008): 41–53.

Herr, Cheryl. *The Field*. Cork: Cork University Press, 2002.

Holohan, Conn. "Trauma, Subjectivity and Narrative in Breakfast on Pluto." In *Irish Films, Global Cinema*, edited by Martin McLoone and Kevin Rockett. Dublin: Four Courts Press, 2007.

———. "Dreams of Home: Migrant Spaces and Narrative Desire in Felicia's Journey." *Irish Studies Review* 19, no. 1 (2011): 87–97.

Le Corff, Isabelle. "Extimacy and Embodiment in Hunger and Shame." In *Intimacy in Cinema*, edited by David Roche and Isabelle Schmitt-Pitiot. Jefferson, NC: McFarland, 2014.

McCabe, Colin. *The Butcher Boy*. Cork: Cork University Press, 2007.

McGuinness, Frank. *Dancing at Lughnasa*. London: Faber, 1998.

McHale, Des. *A Quiet Man Miscellany*. Cork: Cork University Press, 2009.

McLoone, Martin. "December Bride: A Landscape Peopled Differently." In *Contemporary Irish Cinema*, edited by James MacKillop. Syracuse, NY: Syracuse University Press, 1999.

———. "Man of Aran." In *The Cinema of Britain and Ireland*, edited by Brian McFarlane. London: Wallflower Press, 2005.

Meaney, Geraldine. *Nora*. Cork: Cork University Press, 2004.

Monahan, Barry. "Defining Ourselves through the Irishness That We Sell: The Comedy of Cultural Commodification in Mark Joffe's The Matchmaker (1997)." In *Screening Irish-America: Representing Irish Film and Television*, edited by Ruth Barton. Dublin: Irish Academic Press, 2009.

Mooney, T., and S. Eustace. *BattleGround: The Making of Saving Private Ryan*. Wexford: Milestone L. Press, 1998.

Mullen, Pat. *Man of Aran*. London: Faber and Faber, 1934.

Norris, Margot. *Ulysses*. Cork: Cork University Press, 2004.

Pettitt, Lance. *December Bride*. Cork: Cork University Press, 2001.

Pettitt, Lance, and Beatriz Kopschitz Bastos, eds. *The Woman Who Married Clark Gable*. São Paulo: Humanitas, 2013.

Pine, Emilie. "The Great Escape? The Islandman (1938)." In *National Cinema and Beyond: Studies in Irish Film 1*, edited by Kevin Rockett and John Hill. Dublin: Four Courts Press, 2009.

———. "The Whole Picture: *The Dawn* (1936)—Tom Cooper." In *Ireland in Focus: Film, Photography, and Popular Culture* , edited by Eoin Flannery and Michael Griffin. Syracuse, NY: Syracuse University Press, 2009.

———. "'This Is What I Need You to Do to Make It Right': Conor McPherson's I Went Down." In *The Theatre of Conor McPherson: "Right Beside the Beyond,"* edited by Lillian Chambers and Eamonn Jordan. Dublin: Carysfort Press, 2012.

Pramaggiore, Maria. "Unmastered Subjects: Fabricating Identity in Joseph Strick's Ulysses and Portrait of the Artist as a Young Man." In *James Joyce and the Fabrication of an Irish Identity*, edited by Michael Patrick Gillespie. Amsterdam: Rodopi, 2001.

Roche, B. *Trojan Eddie: A Screenplay*. London: Methuen, 1997.

Scarlata, Jessica. "Reading of *The Butcher Boy*." In *Literature and Film: A Guide to the Theory and Practice of Film Adaptation*, edited by Robert Stam and A. Raengo. Oxford: Blackwell, 2005.

Sheeran, P. F. *The Informer*. Cork: Cork University Press, 2002.

Tracy, Tony. "Adapting McGahern: Cathal Black's Wheels (1977)." In *The John McGahern Yearbook*, vol. 2, edited by John Kenny. Galway: NUI Galway, 2009.

———. "When Disney Met Delargy: Darby O'Gill and the Irish Folklore Commission." *Béaloideas: Journal of the Irish Folklore Society* 78 (2010): 50–59.

————. "Inventing the Past: Perspectives on How Harry Became a Tree." In *Contemporary Irish Film: New Perspectives on a National Cinema*, edited by Werner Huber and Seán Crosson. Vienna: Braumuller, 2011.

————. "Parnell." In *The Call of the Heart: John M. Stahl and Hollywood Melodrama*, edited by Bruce Babington and Charles Barr. Bloomington: John Libbey/Indiana University Press, 2018.

————. "'A Wandering to Find Home': Space and Place in Adam and Paul (2004)." In *The Vibrant House: Irish Writing and Domestic Space*, edited by Lucy MacDiarmid and Rhona Richman Kenneally. Dublin: Four Courts Press, 2018.

Vaughan, D. *Odd Man Out*. London: British Film Institute, 1995.

DIRECTORS AND WRITERS

Allon, Yoram, Del Cullen, and Hannah Patterson, eds. *Contemporary British and Irish Film Directors: A Wallflower Critical Guide*. London: Wallflower Press, 2001.

Barsam, Richard. *The Vision of Robert Flaherty: The Artist as Myth and Filmmaker*. Bloomington: Indiana University Press, 1988.

Barton, Ruth. *Jim Sheridan: Framing the Nation*. Dublin: Liffey Press, 2002.

————. "Jim Sheridan." In *The UCD Aesthetic*, edited by Anthony Roche. Dublin: New Island, 2005.

————. "Neil Jordan: Superstition and Religion." In *Contemporary Irish Film*, edited by Werner Huber and Seán Crosson. Vienna: Braumuller, 2011.

————. *Rex Ingram: Visionary Director of the Silent Screen*. Lexington: University Press of Kentucky, 2014

Boorman, John. *Adventures of a Suburban Boy*. London: Faber and Faber, 2003.

Brownlow, Kevin. *David Lean: A Biography*. London: Faber and Faber, 1998.

Connolly, Maeve. "From No Wave to National Cinema: The Cultural Landscape of Vivienne Dick's Early Films (1978–1985)." In *National Cinema and Beyond*, edited by Kevin Rockett and John Hill. Dublin: Four Courts Press, 2004.

Cullingford, Elizabeth Butler. "Debunking de Valera: Neil Jordan and the Revision of Irish Identity." In *Ireland, Culture, Politics and Identity*, edited by Rob Savage. Dublin: Four Courts Press, 2003.

Hill, John. "Routes Irish: 'Irishness,' 'Authenticity' and the Working Class in the Films of Ken Loach." *Irish Studies Review* 19, no. 1 (2011): 99–109.

Huston, John. *An Open Book*. London: Macmillan, 1981.

McBride, Joseph. *Searching for John Ford*. New York: Faber and Faber, 2001.

McCarthy, Dermot. *Roddy Doyle: Raining on the Parade*. Dublin: Liffey Press, 2003.

McIlroy, Brian. "Between History and Fantasy: The Irish Films of Neil Jordan." In *The Blackwell Companion to Irish Literature*, vol. 2, edited by Julia White. Oxford: Blackwell, 2010.

Monahan, Barry. *The Films of Lenny Abrahamson: A Filmmaking of Philosophy*. London: Bloomsbury, 2018.

O'Brien, Harvey. "Violated Sanctuaries: The Screenplays of Mark O'Rowe." In *Sullied Magnificence: The Theatre of Mark O'Rowe*, edited by Sara Keating and Emma Creedon. Dublin: Carysfort Press, 2016.

O'Leary, Liam. *Rex Ingram: Master of the Silent Cinema*. Dublin: Academy Press, 1980.

Pettitt, Lance, ed. *Thaddeus O'Sullivan: Early Films, 1973–1986*. Dublin: Irish Film Institute, 2014.

Pramaggiore, Maria. "The Celtic Blue Note: Jazz in Neil Jordan's Angel, The Miracle, and 'Night in Tunisia.'" *Screen* 39 (1998): 272–88.

———. "Neil Jordan's Postmodern Gothic: or, Why The Good Thief Was Originally Called Double Down." In *Genre and Cinema: Ireland and Transnationalism*, edited by Brian McIlroy. London: Routledge, 2007.

———. *Neil Jordan*. Champaign: University of Illinois Press, 2008.

———. "Neil Jordan." In *50 Contemporary Film Directors*, edited by Yvonne Tasker. London: Routledge, 2010.

Robbins, Christopher. *The Empress of Ireland: A Biography of Brian Desmond Hurst*. London: Scribner, 2004.

Rockett, Emer, and Kevin Rockett. *Neil Jordan: Exploring Boundaries*. Dublin: Liffey Press, 2003

Woods, Gerald C. *Conor MacPherson: Imagining Mischief*. Dublin: Liffey Press, 2003.

ACTORS

Barton, Ruth. *Acting Irish in Hollywood: From Fitzgerald to Farrell*. Dublin: Irish Academic Press, 2006.

———. "Maureen O'Hara: Pirate Queen, Feminist Icon?" *Éire-Ireland* 41, no. 1–2 (2006): 142–68.

Barton, Ruth. "The Voice of Pierce Brosnan." In *Affecting Irishness: Negotiating Cultural Identity within and beyond the Nation*, edited by James P. Byrne, Padraig Kirwan, and Michael O'Sullivan. Oxford: Peter Lang, 2009.

Bryan, Phillip. *Noel Purcell: A Biography*. Dublin: Poolbeg Press, 1992.

Byrne, Gabriel. *Pictures in My Head*. Dublin: Wolfhound Press, 1994.

Carrick, Peter. *Pierce Brosnan*. London: Robert Hale, 2000.

Freedland, Michael. *Peter O'Toole: A Biography*. London: W. H. Allen, 1983.

Miller, Ingrid. *Liam Neeson: The First Biography*. London: Hodder and Stoughton, 1995

O'Connor, Aine. *Leading Hollywood*. Dublin: Wolfhound Press, 1996.

O'Hara, Maureen, with John Nicoletti. *'Tis Herself: An Autobiography*. New York: Simon and Schuster, 2004.

Ryan, Philip B. *Jimmy O'Dea: The Pride of the Coombe*. Dublin: Poolbeg, 1990.

———. *Noel Purcell: A Biography*. Dublin: Poolbeg, 1992.

Smith, Gus. *Richard Harris: Actor by Accident*. London: Robert Hale, 1990.

Toibin, Niall. *Smile and Be a Villain*. Dublin: Town House, 1995.

Wapshott, Nicholas. *Peter O'Toole: A Biography*. London: New English Library, 1984.

About the Authors

Roddy Flynn was born in Ireland and received his secondary and third-level education in Dublin. He has a bachelor's degree in history and politics from University College Dublin and a master's in film and television studies from Dublin City University (DCU). In 1998, he completed a doctorate on Irish telecommunications history and policy, also at DCU. He began lecturing in 1995 and became a permanent member of the faculty at the School of Communications, DCU, in 1999. Since then, he has coauthored and coedited four books and nearly 30 book chapters and peer-reviewed journal articles relating to the screen industries. He is an associate professor and chair of the Contemporary Screen Industries Department at the School of Communications, DCU.

Tony Tracy is director of the Huston School of Film & Digital Media at NUI Galway, where he teaches classes on film history and theory. He has a bachelor's in theology and English from the University of Maynooth, a master's in film studies from UCD, and a PhD from Trinity College Dublin. He is the author of many articles on Irish and American film and, with Roddy Flynn, is coeditor of the annual review of Irish cinema for the online journal *Estudios Irlandeses*. He is coeditor of *Masculinity and Irish Popular Culture: Tiger's Tales* (2014) and *John Huston: Essays on a Restless Director* (with Roddy Flynn, 2010). He produced the educational docudrama *The Hunger Times* (2018) for Ireland's Great Hunger Museum (Quinnipiac University) and the feature documentary *Blazing the Trail: The O'Kalems in Ireland* (2011) and coproduced the DVD compilation *The O'Kalem Collection 1910–1915* (2012) with the Irish Film Institute.